D1488541

Health Economics

Peter Zweifel · Friedrich Breyer · Mathias Kifmann

Health Economics

Second Edition

 Springer

Professor Peter Zweifel
Socioeconomic Institute
University of Zurich
Hottingerstr. 10
8032 Zurich
Switzerland
pzweifel@soi.uzh.ch

Professor Friedrich Breyer
Department of Economics
University of Konstanz
Fach 135
78457 Konstanz
Germany
friedrich.breyer@uni-konstanz.de

Professor Mathias Kifmann
Department of Economics
University of Augsburg
Universitätsstr. 16
86159 Augsburg
Germany
mathias.kifmann@wiwi.uni-augsburg.de

Original English edition published by Oxford University Press, 1997

ISBN 978-3-540-27804-7   e-ISBN 978-3-540-68540-1
DOI 10.1007/978-3-540-68540-1
Springer Dordrecht Heidelberg London New York

Library of Congress Control Number: 2009931221

Cover design: WMX Design GmbH, Heidelberg

Printed on acid-free paper

Springer is part of Springer Science+Business Media (www.springer.com)

Preface

Health Economics is a fascinating subject. This book provides a systematic treatment of this field of study. It is based on a German version which has been well received since 1992, resulting in five editions so far. It serves both as a textbook in university courses at the Master level and as a reference book.

The book's distinguishing feature is that it consistently builds on formal economic models that have been used in academic Health Economics journals for several decades but have not been integrated in the leading undergraduate textbooks of the field. As we are convinced that many problems in Health Economics are too complicated to be analyzed only graphically, we are now offering this text for Master level courses at universities worldwide. Our premise is that readers are familiar with basic calculus. Some knowledge of econometrics is also useful. At the same time, we have taken care to explain the reasoning in the more technical sections. In addition, we state our main results in non-technical Conclusions and in Summaries at the end of each chapter.

We are grateful to those who have provided their generous assistance to the completion of this book. Ana Ania, Han Bleichrodt, Laszlo Goerke, Normann Lorenz, Thomas McGuire, Robert Nuscheler and Luigi Siciliani have read parts of the manuscript and made valuable suggestions for improvement. We also would like to thank Stefan Felder, Kristin Grabe, Andreas Haufler, Tobias Laun, Hansjörg Lehmann, Maximilian Rüger, Florian Scheuer, Carlo Schultheiss, Lukas Steinmann, Harry Telser, Silke Uebelmesser and Matthias Wrede for their comments on versions of the German manuscript. Finally, we are grateful to Patrick Eugster, Ilja Neustadt, Maurus Rischatsch, Kerstin Roeder, Maximilian Rüger, Clarissa Schnekenburger, Johannes Schoder, Susanna Sedlmeier, Michèle Sennhauser, Sandra Strametz and Philippe Widmer for their assistance in preparing the manuscript.

Zürich, Konstanz and Augsburg
April 2009

Peter Zweifel
Friedrich Breyer
Mathias Kifmann

Contents Overview

Detailed Table of Contents

1

Introduction

1.1 Health – a Priceless Commodity?

When trying to connect 'health' and 'economics', one usually thinks of

(1) health being the most precious good. In order to remain in good health just about anything should be done;

(2) health care being in a crisis. If the costs of health care were to continue to increase at the current rate, then health might become unaffordable to most people.

Although the two statements seem to be contradictory, they agree that both of them assume that health is 'priceless' either in an ethical sense ('invaluable') or in a more economic sense ('very expensive').

So why should economists, presumably emphasizing the latter, deal with health-related subjects? In the eyes of most people, the answer lies in the development of health care expenditure (HCE): in all western industrialized countries, public HCE have strongly increased, during the past decades (that is from the 1960s until 2005, see Table 1.1) not only in absolute figures but also as a share of GDP (Gross Domestic Product). Given continued growth, the entire GDP of many industrialized could be consumed by HCE before the end of the twenty-first century. This so-called 'cost explosion' has led to a number of legislative measures in many industrialized countries. They all had the objective of reducing the rate of increase in public HCE.[1]

Obviously, HCE are not the only outlay that has increased strongly in the past. So have the expenditures on private transportation and on haircuts. Nonetheless no one has ever heard of a 'crisis in hair care' and the media have not drawn our attention as

---

[1] In countries with public health insurance such as Germany, policymakers seek to stabilize the contribution rate which is the part of labor income that workers have to pay to their sickness funds. In other countries, such as the United States, the federal government tries to limit its ever-rising subsidies paid to Medicaid (a program for the poor) and Medicare (for the elderly).

P. Zweifel et al., *Health Economics*, 2nd ed., DOI 10.1007/978-3-540-68540-1_1,
© Springer-Verlag Berlin Heidelberg 2009

Table 1.1. Health Care Expenditure as a Share of Gross Domestic Product (in Percent)

Year	1960	1970	1980	1990	2000	2005
Austria	4.3	5.2	7.5	8.4[a]	9.9	10.3
Canada	5.4	6.9	7.0	8.9	8.8	9.9
Federal Republic of Germany	–	6.0	8.4	8.3	10.3	10.7
France	3.8	5.4	7.0	8.4	9.6	11.2
Italy	–	–	–	7.7	8.1	8.9
Japan	3.0	4.6	6.5	6.0	7.7	8.2
Sweden	–	6.8	8.9	8.2	8.2	9.2
Switzerland	4.9	5.4	7.3	8.2	10.3	11.4
United Kingdom	3.9	4.5	5.6	6.0	7.2	8.2[b]
United States	5.1	7.0	8.7	11.9	13.2	15.2

a: break in series; b: differences in methodology.

Source: OECD (2008)

much to the risk of walking around long-haired one day, contrary to the nightmare of not being able to afford medical treatment. In looking for peculiarities of health care that have prevented such a comparison (so far), one comes mainly across the following three characteristics:

(1) *The size of the health care sector.* Health care services constitute an industry of considerable economic importance. Its share in GDP today is close to or even above ten percent in most western industrialized countries (depending on the method of measurement and the delimitation of the industry, see Table 1.1). This means that a great number of people owe their income to this industry. For economists, this is a good reason to acquire knowledge of the subject and to analyze the industry, following the example of agricultural, energy, transportation, and recently tourism and cultural economics.

(2) *Public regulation of health services.* Even more important than their sheer size is the fact that health care services are regulated by the state to a considerable extent. Just consider compulsory health insurance in many countries, the fixing of fee schedules for medical services, or even the National Health Service of the UK and similar institutions in other countries, where almost all care is provided by public employees. These departures from market forces raise the question whether an optimal allocation of scarce resources can be achieved.

(3) *Ethical significance.* Finally, health and everything related to it is an extremely emotional issue. This fact poses a particular challenge to economists, who are called upon to devise rules of allocation doing justice to the specific character of health wants. Often there is a conflict between the economic and the ethical way of looking at the allocation of scarce resources, both within health care and between health and other goods.

Nevertheless, the health care 'cost explosion' should not become an obsession. First, we are dealing with a changing group of goods over time, so that the term 'cost explosion' is not appropriate anyway and we should rather speak of a growth in expenditure instead. Second, from a welfare point of view, the problem is not so much the development of expenditures of health care, but rather their structure: the economic principle generally requires that a given degree of satisfaction of one's needs be achieved with the minimum amount of scarce resources. Thus, the demand for some particular type of goods or services may have grown – as has been the case in the services sector during recent decades – causing expenditure devoted to it to strongly increase in spite of perfect efficiency in the use of resources. Conversely, the shrinking of an industry does not imply an increase in efficiency.

Conclusion 1.1. *From an economic perspective, the rules that determine the allocation of resources rather than the amount of expenditure on health are of interest. They indicate if the participants involved – both those supplying and those demanding health care services – have incentives to use scarce resources efficiently.*

1.2 The Micro- and Macroeconomic Views of Health

From the microeconomic point of view, the behavior of an insured individual, a physician, the management of a hospital or the decisions made by a pharmaceutical company are in the focus of interest. In public debate, by contrast, the macroeconomic approach dominates, with the share of health expenditure in GDP usually serving as the point of reference. Therefore it seems appropriate to connect these two approaches and to clarify why the objective of keeping the health share in GDP constant, commonly pursued by governments, is misguided.

1.2.1 A Simplified Microeconomic View of Health

For an individual, health has two functions. On the one hand, perfect health represents a value of its own, a target that is to be attained as closely as possible. On the other hand, there are other aims in life. The gourmet who prefers a foie gras to a wholesome salad justifies the presumption that health is traded off for other objectives. And who has never crossed a busy street instead of using the underground crossing, only to save a little time? These modes of behavior contradict the claim that health is a priceless commodity (see statement (1) at the beginning of Section 1.1). This contradiction rarely becomes obvious because no one sacrifices his health in an immediate sense. People only allow the probability of living healthy in the future to be a little smaller than it could be.

In Chapter 3, we analyze individual health behavior in detail. For a beginning, we present a model by WAGSTAFF (1986a) which is a simplified version of the model by GROSSMAN (1972b) (see Section 3.3). It is based on the fact that individuals implicitly trade off 'health' (H) against all other aims, which for simplicity will be aggregated into 'consumption' (C). This weighing-up of objectives is, as usual in microeconomics, symbolized by a set of indifference curves (see quadrant I of Figure 1.1).

There are two characteristics, however, which make health particularly important to most people:

(1) The consumptive benefit that one can derive from one's income depends on one's state of health. Depression for instance, the most widespread mental illness, makes it just about impossible for the person affected to enjoy the nice things in life. Similarly, in the event of a disease of the digestive tract, a foie gras is not a pleasure even to the gourmet.

This characteristic can be reproduced in quadrant I of Figure 1.1 by the shape of the indifference curves. As soon as the ratio of health to consumption becomes small, additional consumption does not have positive marginal utility any longer, causing the indifference curve in the northwest area of quadrant I to run vertical rather than negatively sloped.

(2) Only someone who is in good health can earn an income on the labor market. This feature is represented in quadrant III of Figure 1.1 showing how individuals can divide their budget (disposable income, Y) between medical care (M) and consumer goods (X). The prices for medical care (net price q after deduction of insurance benefits) and consumer goods (p) are exogenous. The peculiarity of the budget constraint,

$$Y(H) = pX + qM \qquad (1.1)$$

lies in the fact that disposable income Y depends on the state of health H. If income did not depend on the state of health, i.e., if H were fixed to $\overline{H}$, the budget constraint would be linear, as shown by the dashed line $A'B$. Point B indicates where the entire income is spent on medical care.

If, starting at point B, the expenditure on medical care is reduced, the state of health H deteriorates according to the function $H(M)$ shown in quadrant IV. This decrease results in a reduction of income $Y(H)$ in the third quadrant.[2] Consequently, the quantity of consumer goods rises at a decreasing rate up to point A. At this turning point, a further reduction of medical care lets health deteriorate so much that the associated drop in income neutralizes the savings in health expenditure. Beyond point A, a further reduction of M would result in a loss of income to such an extent as to require a reduction of consumption. And finally, at $M = 0$, income would drop to $Y = 0$ and with it purchases of consumer goods ($X = 0$).

---

[2] We assume that the functions $H(M)$ and $Y(H)$ are both strictly concave.

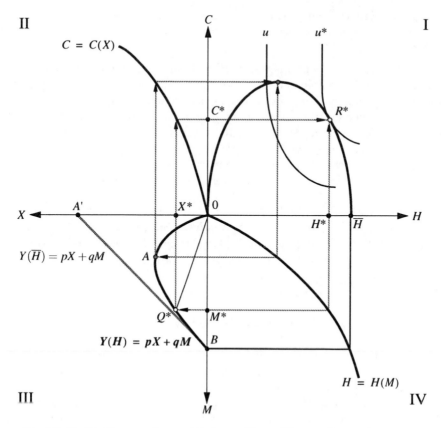

Fig. 1.1. Health, Consumption, and Optimum Share of Income Devoted to Health

Quadrant IV shows the amount of medical care M required to guarantee a given state of health. The more medical care (of curative nature), the better the state of health. The individual's own efforts at preserving his good health (prevention) are not taken into consideration here (in Chapter 3 the model will be extended to preventive efforts).

Finally, quadrant II shows the positive relationship between consumer goods (X) and consumable services ('consumption', C) according to the equation $C = C(X)$. This relationship is assumed to depend on household characteristics, e.g., the ability to use technology. Combined with the equation $H = H(M)$ pictured in the fourth quadrant, we can assign to each point on the budget curve in quadrant III a point in the (C,H)-space of quadrant I (see the dashed arrows in Figure 1.1). The set of all these points indicates the individual's production frontier. It differs from the usual production frontiers known in microeconomics by running through the origin. That is because, as explained above, a very poor physical constitution ($H = 0$) is associated with an income of zero and consequently also with a consumption of $C = 0$. At first, it slopes upward with an increasing value of H. This means that, initially, better health enables one to consume more, not less (detailed reasons for this will be given in Chapter 3).

The tangency point of the highest attainable indifference curve and the production frontier defines the combination of consumption and health (C^*, H^*) yielding maximum utility. Quadrant IV shows the corresponding optimal expenditure on medical care M^* and quadrant II the optimal purchase of consumption goods X^*. Point Q^* on the budget curve in quadrant III finally indicates the individual's optimal budget allocation. Connecting Q^* with the origin, one can interpret the slope of this line as the 'optimal health share': the steeper the line the bigger the optimal share of income spent on medical care. These reflections can be summed up in

Conclusion 1.2. *The trade-off between the objectives 'consumption' and 'health' can be illustrated as a conventional microeconomic optimization problem. When solving this, one has to consider that health serves as an input into the generation of income, which in turn is necessary to buy consumer goods.*

1.2.2 Health Care at the Macroeconomic Level

In principle, the functions shown in Figure 1.1 can be aggregated over all individuals. They are therefore valid at a macroeconomic level as well. The problem is their limited observability. Precisely the two quantities of utmost importance to the individual, state of health H and consumption C, are captured only rudimentarily by official statistics. However, the quantity of medical treatment (M^* or its monetary value qM^*) and purchases of consumer goods (X^* and pX^*, respectively) are well known. As a consequence, attempts at controlling health care usually focus on these quantities.

Why should there be a need for controlling HCE? Chapter 5 deals with this question. It will be shown that subsidies for health insurance, possibly even compulsory insurance for individuals combined with open enrollment by insurers can be justified. But more far-reaching interventions such as stabilizing the share of health expenditure in the Gross Domestic Product (GDP), limiting the increase in costs to a specified percentage, or stabilizing contributions as a share of wage income are difficult to justify.[3] In the following, we will show that fixing the share of HCE in GDP or in wage income easily results in efficiency losses which accumulate over time.

As soon as the government is involved in the financing of health care, its budget is affected by individual decisions with regard to health care. The more people rely on medical treatment, the larger is public HCE (at least in the long run) due to

---

[3] In Germany, the premiums for public health insurance are tied to income from salaried employment, in contrast to, e.g., Dutch and Swiss public health insurance where premiums are quoted in absolute terms. An important objective of a series of reform laws in the German health care system is to stabilize the contribution rate.

additional subsidies for medical students and for investments of hospitals. Further-more, the operating deficits of hospitals are covered by the state in many countries and higher payments for the medical treatment of senior citizens arise in countries such as the United States and Germany (to name just a few of the lagged influences on the budget).

On the other hand, public expenditure secures votes, helping to secure re-election to politicians. Chapter 13 will focus on this issue; here we would simply like to point out that politicians prefer a specific division of the budget to any other division, just as the individual of Figure 1.1 prefers the division of his budget according to Q^* to other solutions. But by pushing through its preferences regarding the budget, the government more or less fixes the share of health in GDP. The consequences of this policy will be highlighted in the following section.

1.2.3 A Critique of Global Budgeting

In their struggle against the 'cost explosion' in health care, governments refer to the figures of Table 1.1 arguing that the share of health in the Gross National Product is rising too fast. Assuming that one could succeed in stabilizing this share at a certain percentage of GDP, what could be gained?

To answer this question, the transition from the micro- to the macroeconomic level is made in the simplest possible way by applying the features of Figure 1.1 to all individuals of a society, who are assumed to be identical. Accordingly H becomes the number of person-years spent in good health, qM the national health expenditure, and pX the aggregate consumption expenditure. The allocation of GDP between these two categories is given by point Q^* in the third quadrant, symbolizing the aggregate outcome of individual decisions. For the sake of simplicity, the health share set by the government is assumed to coincide with the optimal Q^* in the initial situation.

This equality may now be disturbed by an exogenous shock, e.g., an improvement in medical technology. This causes the function $H(M)$ to shift to $H'(M)$ in the fourth quadrant of Figure 1.2, implying that a given supply of medical services now guar-antees a better health status than before. This leads to an outward shift of the budget curve in quadrant III. Consequently, the production possibility frontier shown in the first quadrant shifts outward. Society evidently can reach new (C, H)-combinations, lying to the right and above the old optimum R^* in quadrant I.

Let us now assume that the government learns about the improved medical tech-nology but wants the share of GDP devoted to health to remain unchanged. This means that it is trying to keep the global allocation between consumption and health expenditure the same, which requires the new point Q' to lie on the same ray through the origin as Q^*. Thereby a new (C, H)-combination would be reached, symbolized by R' in the first quadrant (see the solid arrows in Figure 1.2).

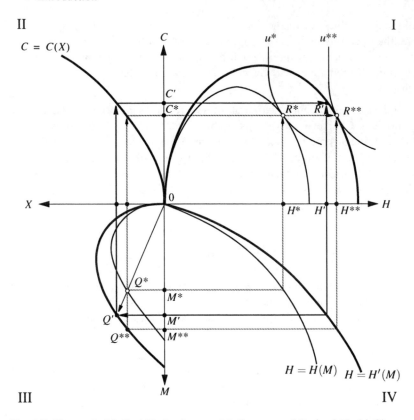

Fig. 1.2. Change in Medical Technology and Adjustment of Optimal Health Share

If the (identical) members of this society value their health as highly as the relative steepness of their indifference curves in the first quadrant indicates, they would opt for R^{**} rather than R', implying the following outcome:

(1) By assumption, the extension of the choice set will be used exclusively for an improvement of the health status (see the transition from R^* to R^{**}).[4]

(2) This is achieved by an increasing use of medical care (new value: M^{**}) not only in comparison to the initial optimum M^* but also in comparison to M' as fixed by the government.

(3) Due to the improved state of health, there is a rise in labor income and therefore in financial means available, so that this increase of M is possible without changing consumption expenditure $X^{**} = X^*$.

(4) The new optimal budget allocation Q^{**} (in quadrant III) of society calls for an increase of the optimal health share. This is shown by the rotation of the ray from the origin to $0Q^{**}$, which is steeper than the original ray $0Q'$.

---

[4] This is assumed for simplicity. The same conclusions can be drawn from a predominant tendency toward improved health.

Now if politicians hold on to the existing allocation of the public budget, they force individuals as a group to settle with Q' and R', respectively. This means, e.g., that medical services are not available because of restricted access to medical schools or that hospital treatments cannot be performed due to a lack of investment in equipment. Thus, individuals reach a lower level of utility in quadrant I than the highest possible value at point R^{**}.

The example of technological change in medicine stands for just one of many possible changes which can lead to discrepancies between the optimal health share in income from the perspective of the individual and a politically established health share in the GDP. Going through the four quadrants of Figure 1.2, one comes across the following changes:

(a) The preferences between health and consumption may change, e.g., in the course of a fitness wave.

(b) The relationship between consumer goods and consumption services may be modified by innovations in household technology (e.g., time-saving devices) or improved education (e.g., permitting more informed choices of consumer goods). In both instances, this enables individuals to extract more consumption services from a given quantity of consumer goods, resulting in an upward shift of the $C(X)$ function in quadrant II.

(c) The budget constraint is subject to continuous change. Increasing incomes shift it away from the origin whereas its slope becomes steeper if the relative price of consumer goods increases.

(d) The connection between the use of medical care and the state of health is not only modified by technological change in medicine but also by environmental factors or an increase or decrease of health-enhancing efforts on the individuals' part, the latter especially as a result of insurance coverage (see Chapter 6 for a detailed discussion). Besides, the performance of physicians and hospitals generally falls short of their efficient levels as a consequence of the remuneration system. Therefore, the location of the function $H = H(M)$ also reflects the system of remuneration (see Chapter 10).

This clearly shows that there are a number of reasons for the politically determined health share to differ from its optimal value.

Conclusion 1.3. *There are several arguments against fixing the share of health expenditure in the GDP at a certain level. This policy is likely to cause losses in efficiency which tend to accumulate over time.*

This insight is reflected in the general approach of this book. We will emphasize the microeconomic view of health and concentrate on how patients, physicians, the management of a hospital or of a pharmaceutical company behave and how they interact.

1.3 'Economics of Health' vs. 'Economics of Health Care'

Up to this point, reasons for the existence of health economics as a discipline were given and the relationship between macroeconomic and microeconomic ways of looking at health and health care was examined. To classify issues, we propose a distinction between 'economics of health' and 'economics of health care'.

1.3.1 Economics of Health

In their titles, some publications in the field (textbooks and edited volumes) talk of 'economics of health', while others refer to 'economics of health care' or 'economics of medical care'.[5] This suggests that health itself is an interesting economic issue. Indeed, there are many questions connected with health, which have nothing to do with 'health care', i.e., the provision of medical services by physicians and other professional suppliers. These deal with both positive and normative aspects of health.

One of the most important questions raised by the economics of health concerns the valuation of health in monetary terms, i.e., the weighing of good health against other objectives, in particular consumption of other goods. This normative issue ('How much consumption should society sacrifice to increase its average life expectancy by one year? How much should an improvement of the state of health measured by suitable indicators be worth?') arises primarily in connection with public projects, financed by levies, such as taxes or social security contributions, whenever they have an effect on the life expectancy or health of citizens. The typical feature is that the individual does not weigh himself health against consumption. Rather, government or parliament decide on behalf of the citizens, and it is the task of health economics to provide these authorities with decision-making rules which are well-founded in welfare economics. This will be the subject of Chapter 2.

The positive branch of health economics, by contrast, deals with individual health behavior, using the instruments of modern microeconomic theory. The basic paradigm of rational choice is applied to health, i.e., the individual is considered to maximize utility, which depends, among other things, on material consumption as well as on health. With the help of such a model (see Chapter 3), one can examine the effect on the individual's 'demand' for health (i.e., his health behavior) of changes in his budget constraint, i.e., in his income, or of changes in relative prices, caused, e.g., by changes in health insurance coverage.

---

[5] Examples are FELDSTEIN (2005), FOLLAND ET AL. (2006), FUCHS (1986), MCGUIRE ET AL. (1988), MOONEY (2003), NEWHOUSE (1978), and PHELPS (2003).

1.3.2 Health and the Use of Health Care Services

The connection between the health status of the individual (or the population on the whole) and the use of medical services builds the link between 'economics of health' and 'economics of health care'. There are two relationships to be distinguished. They are represented by the headings, 'production function of health' and 'demand function for medical services'.

In the first case, the point at issue is the question, how much do medical services contribute to the preservation or improvement of health status? Economists, statisticians, and econometricians have applied empirical methods to answer this question (see Chapter 4). In general, the influence of health care on health

(1) can be assumed to be positive: higher consumption of medical services results in better health.

For logical reasons, this effect

(2) is supposed to set in with a time-lag: it is to be expected in empirical investigations that consumption of medical services in period t does not give rise to better health immediately but in some later period (say $t + 1$).

The second relationship runs from the state of health to the consumption of medical services, the so-called demand function for medical services. In this function, the state of health represents the explanatory variable. Here, the plausible assumptions are that

(a) the theoretically expected effect is negative (worse health goes along with increased consumption of medical services) and

(b) this relationship applies to simultaneously measured values of the two quantities.

1.3.3 Economics of Health Care

The demand function for medical services already belongs to the domain of the economies of health care. Taking the positive contribution of medical services to health as a given fact, the economics of health care – in its positive form – raises the issues of what determines the quantity and quality of medical services produced in a society. In its normative form, it sets out to investigate the conditions of production of these services and their distribution among individuals, identifying those mechanisms that are particularly appropriate for efficiency, taking the scarcity of resources used in their production into due account.

This leads us to the issues of organizing and financing medical services. Microeconomic analysis, with its concept of 'incentives', is well suited to investigate the effects of alternative regulations. The terms 'financing' and 'incentives' in fact amount to two sides of a coin.

(1) On the one hand, they describe how the recipients of medical services (the patients) pay for these services. Here, the point at issue is health insurance with its incentive effects on the insured dealt with in Chapters 5 and 6.

(2) On the other hand, they describe the way the money is channeled to the providers of services. Here, the analysis deals with the incentive effects of alternative payment systems for physicians and hospitals (Chapter 10) and suppliers of drugs (Chapter 12).

1.4 A System Analysis of the Economics of Health and Health Care

To conclude this introduction, an overview of the issues dealt within this book is given in Figure 1.3. This simplified system analysis begins with individuals and their objectives, among them to live as long and healthy as possible while consuming as much as possible. In their health-related behavior, they are guided by a variety of incentives, which are shaped especially by the form of their health insurance (see Chapters 5, 6, and 7).

Admittedly, the state of health is not fully under the individual's control. While chance has an important impact, individuals can still opt for more or less health through their behavior that exerts a systematic influence (see Chapter 3). This also means that an additional day spent in good health has its 'price' even if there is no market where it can be traded. This price consists in the additional consumption the individual could have enjoyed, had he not used his time and money to improve his health.

Opting for a probability with which a certain state of health is attained also calls for a decision on how to influence this probability. Very often people are willing to go through a phase of illness with minimal use of pharmaceuticals and no medical treatment. Instead they use their time as an input. Presumably, material incentives influence this choice between one's own and other inputs (see Chapter 3; for empirical evidence, see Chapter 4). If this choice increasingly tends towards inputs provided by a third party, i.e., health care services, then the result can be a cost explosion in health care.

The extent to which changes in individual health-related behavior affects HCE is very much dependent on the physician. She or he, positioned just below the patient in Figure 1.3, acts as a 'gatekeeper' to health care. In particular, the choice between outpatient and inpatient treatment has important consequences in terms of cost incurred. This is due to the fact that a hospital stay typically involves the use of a great deal

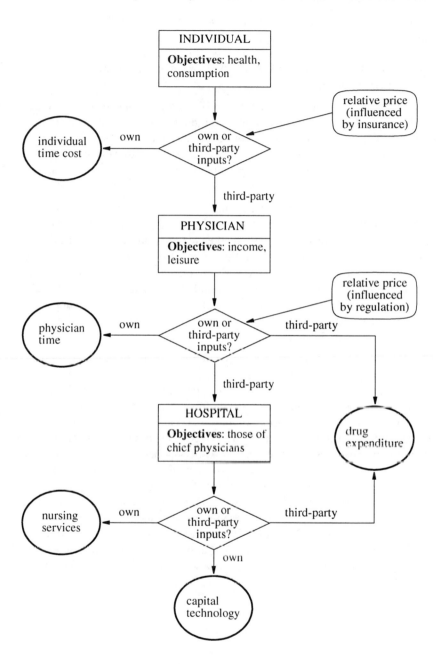

Fig. 1.3. A Systems Analysis of Health Care

of nursing services as well as expensive technology. Again we will look for material incentives which may govern a physician's decision to rely on services by others versus her or his own input (Chapters 8 and 10). This approach, of course, is totally contrary to the traditional medical view which claims that the treatment decision is only based on medical need.

By referring a patient to the hospital, the physician passes on part of the demand for medical treatment. Closer inspection reveals material incentives at work in hospitals as well, which can influence the conduct of chief physicians (see Chapters 9 and 10). Economic theory has a lot to say about the way profit-oriented enterprises respond to and manage changes in the environment. We will see to what extent this body of knowledge is applicable to non-profit-organizations such as hospitals.

Finally, doctors as well as hospitals determine the derived demand for secondary inputs such as pharmaceuticals. In this context, we will be interested to see (in Chapter 12) how prices are determined in the market for pharmaceuticals and how attempts to promote price competition may affect advances in medical technology, resulting in an extension of therapeutical choices. Besides the market for pharmaceuticals, other derived markets could be examined, as for example those for health aids, mental treatment, and medical appliances but also the market for nurses and other categories of health care workers. In order to keep this book manageable, we will not deal with these derived markets.

The circles of Figure 1.3 stand for resource inputs, which are triggered by decisions made along this stylized sickness episode. If incentives are such as to induce individuals to increasingly substitute physician time, pharmaceuticals, and hospital services for their own time input in favor of health, this cannot happen at constant cost. As in any other industry an increasing volume of services entails increasing costs. Indeed, a single medical treatment and a single day in hospital have become much more expensive over time. It is this increase of HCE that has become what is called the 'cost explosion'. These incentives, however, are very much related to the way health care is organized. Therefore, organizational issues connected to health care systems are described in Chapter 11. But then, an observed organizational structure is the result of decisions usually taken by members of parliament (or the voters themselves in direct democracies). These decisions are analyzed in Chapter 13 which is devoted to the political economy of health care. Future challenges confronting health policy, such as ageing of the population and technological change in medicine, are the topic of Chapter 14.

1.5 Summary

(1) From an economic perspective, the rules that determine the allocation of resources rather than the amount of expenditure on health are of interest. The issue
is whether the participants involved – both those supplying and those demanding
health services – have incentives to use scarce resources economically.

(2) Both the role of 'consumption' and 'health' as objectives and the trade-off in
their production, with 'health' also serving as an input, can be represented as
parts of a conventional microeconomic optimization problem.

(3) Many governments seek to keep the share of health care in the GDP constant.
This endeavor is likely to cause losses in efficiency which tend to accumulate
over time.

(4) 'Health economics' consists of the 'economics of health' and the 'economics of
health care'. These subdisciplines are connected by the relationship between the
state of health and the use of medical services.

(5) The positive branch of the 'economics of health' tries to explain individual
health-related behavior on the basis of modern microeconomic theory. By contrast, the normative branch of the 'economics of health' seeks to determine
whether there are health policies that are welfare improving. Ultimately, it is
based on the valuation of health compared to other goods.

(6) The 'economics of health care' can also be divided in a positive and a normative branch. From a positive perspective, the main issue is to explain the factors
which determine the quantity and quality of medical services produced in the
economy. The normative branch deals with the question of designing incentives
for both suppliers and users of medical services.

2

Economic Valuation of Life and Health

2.1 Introduction

'Life is priceless.' Most people would probably agree with this statement. However, decisions affecting lives are not only made by individuals but (necessarily) also by parliaments and public authorities on a regular basis. This implies weighing up the preservation and lengthening of human life against the input of scarce resources (i.e., money). Examples for such decisions in the public sector can be found not only in health care but also in many other sectors, especially those related to transportation and the environment.

Countries with a national health service or national health insurance usually let political authorities decide on new pharmaceuticals, new therapies, and new medical devices to be covered by the plan. As a rule, cost-increasing product innovations prevail that bring about therapeutic advantages, often by reducing the risk of early death in a certain population at risk. Such new products involve additional expenditure. Cost-reducing process innovations, by contrast, are rare and shall not be dealt with here.

For instance, the provision of a mobile coronary unit with total costs of several million dollars may help to treat heart attack patients on the spot, serving to significantly reduce the number of those dying prior to arriving at the hospital. Long-term drug therapy of hypertonic patients using anti-hypertensives may prevent a heart attack as well, at a considerable cost to the economy for research and development of pharmaceuticals. Another well-known example is the installation of dialysis equipment for patients with chronic kidney failure.

Outside health care, there are numerous other examples where 'life' and 'costs' have to be pitted against each other. Communities and countries have to decide whether notorious sites of accidents, for example narrow blind curves, should be eliminated by widening and straightening the road. In residential areas, the opposite can be appropriate, i.e., planting trees and installing bumps may reduce risks for playing children by lowering driving speed. All those measures of course involve additional expenditure from the public purse.

P. Zweifel et al., *Health Economics*, 2nd ed., DOI 10.1007/978-3-540-68540-1_2,
© Springer-Verlag Berlin Heidelberg 2009

Environmental policy provides additional cases in point. Costly 'redundant' safety systems in nuclear power plants do not only diminish the likelihood of catastrophes with thousands of deaths but also the emission of radiation exposing the population to an increased risk of suffering from leukemia (as in the case of Chernobyl in 1986). Costly filters retaining sulphur dioxide and other harmful substances from the combustion of coal serve to improve the quality of air and reduce the incidence of respiratory disease.

In all the areas of application mentioned so far, rational decisions cannot be made by authorities unless there is a comprehensive and precise valuation of future advantages (and possibly disadvantages) resulting from a specific measure taken, permitting comparison with the present value of the cost stream associated with the project. To be helpful to decision makers, costs and benefits should ideally be commensurable, i.e., have a common unit of measurement. As the cost of the project is usually measured in monetary units, it makes sense to measure all benefits in the same way. Of course, this implies that the prolongation of human life or the improvement of the state of health due to the realization of a project must be valued in money units as well. A valuation of health and, a fortiori, human life in terms of money, however, meets with considerable objections. For this reason, economists have developed alternative methods of evaluation which are not based on monetization. These approaches, their potentials and their limitations will be the subject of this chapter as well.

This chapter is organized as follows. Section 2.2 gives a general overview of the different approaches to the economic evaluation of health. Section 2.3 is devoted to the method of Cost-Utility Analysis, Section 2.4 to Cost-Benefit Analysis. Section 2.5 compares these two approaches and considers Social Welfare Analysis as an alternative.

2.2 Approaches to the Economic Evaluation of Health

The various approaches to economic evaluation of health compare the benefits of a health intervention to its cost. With regard to the benefits of the intervention, three alternative units of measurement can be distinguished,

(1) natural units on a one-dimensional scale;

(2) units of a cardinal utility function which maps the multi-dimensional concept of health into a scalar index;

(3) units of money.

Measuring benefits in natural units. The 'natural' scale can either be a clinical parameter such as the lowering of blood pressure by x mmHg, or the length of life in years. Measurements of this type are meaningful only in cases where the alternatives (e.g., performing an intervention or not) differ in only one specific effect and have no side effects. In the first example given above, the comparison could be between different anti-hypertonic drugs without side effects, and in the second example, traffic interventions which can prevent fatal road accidents.

The corresponding method of evaluation is called *Cost-Effectiveness Analysis* (CEA). Consider first independent interventions, i.e., interventions whose costs and benefits are not affected by other interventions. Examples are hip replacements and heart transplants. The index of comparison is the 'average cost-effectiveness ratio' (ACER). If effectiveness is measured by length of life, it is defined as

$$\text{ACER} = \frac{\text{costs in units of money}}{\text{benefits in life years gained}}.$$

If interventions are mutually exclusive (e.g., two incompatible medications for the same condition), one needs to consider the rate at which higher expenses can purchase additional benefits. For this reason, 'incremental cost-effectiveness ratios' (ICERs) are used [see WEINSTEIN (2006)]. The ICER of an intervention is defined as the ratio of incremental costs and incremental benefits compared to the next most effective intervention,

$$\text{ICER} = \frac{\text{additional costs}}{\text{additional benefits in natural units}}.$$

The example in Box 2.1 illustrates how ICERs are calculated.

Note that the average cost-effectiveness ratios for independent interventions can also be regarded as incremental because they are compared with the alternative of 'doing nothing'. All interventions can therefore be ranked according to their incremental cost-effectiveness ratios. Interdependencies between the benefits and costs of interventions can be taken into account by defining combinations of interventions as the unit of comparison [see WEINSTEIN (2006, p. 476)].

Prior to a ranking, it is important to exclude dominated alternatives in the case of mutually exclusive interventions and to recalculate the ICERs. An obvious case is an intervention that is more costly and less effective than an alternative. Furthermore, if the ICER of an intervention is larger than the ICER of a more expensive intervention, it is ruled out by 'extended dominance', provided that it is possible to scale down interventions proportionally [WEINSTEIN (1990)]. The example in Box 2.1 illustrates the argument.

The limitations of cost-effectiveness analysis are obvious.

(a) CEA implicitly assumes that it is ethically irrelevant how the life years gained are distributed among the members of society. This criticism, however, applies to all methods of economic evaluation discussed in this section.

(b) CEA is not suitable for comparing interventions that differ in more than one effect. If, e.g., a traffic regulation does not only reduce the number of deaths but also the number of injuries, CEA cannot be applied because it has no way to aggregate multi-dimensional effects.

(c) While CEA yields a rank order of measures, it does not answer the question of whether or not the highest-ranked measure should be performed at all. The only practical case for which CEA provides a meaningful answer to this type of

Box 2.1. Calculating Incremental Cost-Effectiveness Ratios

Consider a condition affecting 100 patients that can be treated by three mutually exclusive health care interventions A, B and C. Intervention A costs €300,000 and increases life duration per patient by 0.3 years, implying a total of 30 life years gained. Intervention B yields 40 additional life years at a cost of €500,000 while intervention C costs €600,000 and yields 50 additional life years. All interventions can be scaled down proportionally. For example, it costs €6,000 to treat one patient with intervention C. The life duration of this patient increases by 0.5 years.

Intervention	Cost in €000	Gain in Life Years	ICER in €000 with B	without B
A	300	30	10	10
B	500	40	20	–
C	600	50	10	15

For intervention A, the next most effective intervention is to do nothing. The ACER and the ICER of A therefore coincide and are equal to €10,000 per life year gained. The ICER of B is obtained by calculating the ratio of incremental costs and incremental benefits compared to the next most effective intervention, i.e., intervention A. We obtain $(€500,000 - €300,000)/(40\text{yrs.} - 30\text{yrs.}) = €20,000$ per life year gained. Intervention B is thus able to save an additional life year at a cost of €20,000 compared to intervention A. By contrast, using the ACER for intervention B of €12,500 per life year gained would lead to an overestimate of cost effectiveness because one does not consider that intervention A can generate 75 percent of the health gain of B at only 60 percent of the cost.

To obtain the ICER of C, costs and benefits need to be compared with intervention B. This yields an ICER of $(€600,000 - €500,000)/(50\text{yrs.} - 40\text{yrs.}) = €10,000$ per life year gained which is below the ICER of B. Intervention B can therefore be ruled out by extended dominance and should be removed from the choice set because an upgrade from intervention A to C requires less additional expenditure per life year than an upgrade from A to B. The ICER of intervention C must therefore be recalculated. Comparing intervention C with A yields an ICER of €15,000.

To see why intervention B is not cost effective, assume that the budget for the treatment of the 100 patients is €330,000. This allows to treat some patients with the more effective interventions B and C. If B where chosen, 15 patients could be treated with B while 85 patients receive treatment A. This yields a gain of $15 \times 0.4 + 85 \times 0.3 = 31.5$ life years since all interventions can be scaled down proportionally. Combining treatments A and C, by contrast, allows to treat 10 patients with C, implying $10 \times 0.5 + 90 \times 0.3 = 32$ additional life years.

question is when a fixed budget is to be allocated among a fixed set of possible measures. In this case, the recommendation to be derived from the result of CEA is to start with the measure with the lowest incremental cost-effectiveness ratio and to continue until the budget is exhausted. Of course, this fails to address the question of how the size of the budget is to be determined in a rational way.

Measuring benefits in units of cardinal utility. Here the multi-dimensionality of the concept of health is taken care of by including all effects of an intervention – in particular, lengthening of life and changes in health status but also side effects – in the evaluation by assigning them appropriate weights. To this purpose, several methods have been developed, which will be presented in detail in Section 2.3. The best-known and most frequently used utility index is called 'quality-adjusted life years' (QALYs).

To derive QALYs, all conceivable health states are evaluated on a 0 to 1 scale, where the state of death is assigned the value 0 and perfect health, the value 1. The other values are defined in such a way that for any number x between 0 and 1, a representative individual is indifferent between the following alternatives, "survive one year in a health state with a utility index of x" and "survive the fraction x of a year in a state of perfect health". In this way, all health effects of an intervention are made comparable, permitting them to be aggregated into a single number which can be interpreted as the 'gain in QALYs'.

Evaluation based on utility units is known as *Cost-Utility Analysis* (CUA). The index of comparison is defined in analogy to CEA. For independent interventions, 'average cost-utility ratios' (ACURs) are appropriate,

$$\text{ACUR} = \frac{\text{costs in units of money}}{\text{benefits in utility units}}.$$

For mutually exclusive intervention, 'incremental cost-utility ratios' (ICURs) are used. They are defined in analogy to ICERs in Cost-Effectiveness Analysis, i.e., the ICUR of an intervention is given by the ratio of incremental costs and incremental benefits compared to the next most effective intervention,

$$\text{ICUR} = \frac{\text{additional costs}}{\text{additional benefits in utility units}}.$$

From this ratio, it can be seen that utility must be cardinally measurable. Otherwise, differences in utility units would have no meaning.[1]

---

[1] Cardinal utility functions are unique up to a positive affine transformation. Ratios of utility differences are therefore specified. This implies, for example, that it must be possible to say that the utility difference between measures A and B is twice as high as the utility difference between measures C and D. Ordinal utility functions, by contrast, are unique up to a positive monotonic transformation. In this case, only the utility ordering of the interventions is determined.

Compared to CEA, CUA has the advantage of being applicable both to medical interventions of different types as well as non-medical interventions because it makes effects measured on different (e.g., clinical) dimensions comparable by mapping them into a single utility index. Apart from this difference, however, CEA and CUA are very similar. For this reason, CEA and CUA are sometimes not distinguished from each other in the literature. For example, WEINSTEIN (2006) uses the term ICER to denote incremental cost-utility ratios.

Cost-Utility Analyses can be employed to construct 'league tables' of medical interventions which can be used to demonstrate that a similar increase in QALYs can be achieved at very different costs. An example is shown in Table 2.1. This type of information is useful to political decision makers who are responsible for allocating resources within the health care sector.

Cost-Utility Analysis has its limitations, too. Apart from the fact that it might be ethically relevant how the additional QALYs are distributed among the members of society, these are the following.

(a) It must be decided *whose* utility function is used to evaluate the various health states;

(b) Like CEA, CUA provides only a rank order of measures but does not help to decide up to which cost-utility ratio an intervention should be performed. While this question can be answered in the presence of a fixed budget, the determination of the optimal size of the budget is left as an open issue.

Even if there is agreement about the optimal size of the budget, it is far from trivial to determine the optimal set of health care interventions. Indivisibilities of interventions and size effects limit the use of the league-table approach, calling for mathematical programming techniques [see DRUMMOND ET AL. (2005, p. 129)]. Furthermore, information on the costs and health gains of all current and potential interventions is necessary to allocate the budget efficiently. In practice, however, this information is not available and league tables can only be constructed based on the existing evaluations, providing only limited guidance for decision-makers.[2]

As an alternative, threshold values for cost-utility ratios have been employed. For example, the National Institute for Health and Clinical Excellence (NICE) in the United Kingdom uses two different thresholds [see NATIONAL INSTITUTE FOR HEALTH AND CLINICAL EXCELLENCE (2008, p. 58–59)]. ICUR values below £20,000 per QALY usually warrant that an intervention is adopted. For ICUR values between £20,000 and £30,000, further considerations must support the intervention, e.g., whether it adds additional benefits not captured by the change in QALYs. Finally, an intervention with an ICUR above £30,000 requires "an increasingly stronger case" with regard to additional factors supporting the intervention.

---

[2] BIRCH AND GAFNI (1992) propose a method to compare the increase of health caused by a new intervention to the combinations of interventions which are given up to fund the new intervention. This approach ensures that the new intervention leads to a net health improvement.

Table 2.1. League Table of Medical Interventions in Terms of Cost per QALY Gained (United Kingdom, £ in 1990 prices)

Medical Intervention	Cost per QALY
Cholesterol testing and diet therapy only	
(all adults, aged 40-69)	220
Neurosurgical intervention for head injury	240
GP advice to stop smoking	270
Neurosurgical intervention for subarachnoid haemorrhage	490
Anti-hyperintensive therapy to prevent stroke (ages 45-64)	940
Pacemaker implantation	1,100
Valve replacement for aortic stenosis	1,140
Hip replacement	1,180
Cholesterol testing and treatment	1,480
Coronary artery bypass graft	
(left main vessel disease, severe angina)	2,090
Kidney transplant	4,710
Breast cancer screen	5,780
Heart transplantation	7,840
Cholesterol testing and treatment (ages 25-39)	14,150
Home haemodialysis	17,260
Coronary artery bypass graft	
(one vessel affected, moderate angina)	18,830
Continuous ambulatory peritoneal dialysis	19,870
Hospital haemodialysis	21,970
Erythropoietin treatment for anaemia in dialysis	
patients (assuming a 10 percent reduction in mortality)	54,380
Neurosurgical intervention for malignant intracranial tumors	107,780
Erythropoietin treatment for anaemia in dialysis	
patients (assuming no reduction in mortality)	126,290

Source. MAYNARD (1991)

The threshold rule is simple but it is not evident that following this approach will guarantee that the budget is used in a way that maximizes health benefits [see BIRCH AND GAFNI (2006a, 2006b)]. This would call for a threshold which measures the marginal opportunity cost of resources of the budget, a variable which can only be determined if all current and potential interventions are taken into account. Furthermore, the threshold would need to be recalculated whenever the budget changes and if new interventions are adopted. So far, however, thresholds have not been derived along these lines and it remains unclear to what extent following a threshold rule serves to increase health benefits given the available resources.[3]

---

[3] An alternative is to define a threshold based on willingness to pay for a QALY (see Section 2.5.1). In effect, the method of evaluation becomes Cost-Benefit-Analysis, implying an endogenous budget for health care. It is also possible to calculate benefits in units of money by multiplying the gain in QALYs with willingness to pay for a QALY. The net benefit criterion of Cost-Benefit-Analysis can then be applied [see DRUMMOND ET AL. (2005, p. 130–132)].

Measuring benefits in units of money. Using money to measure outcomes means that extension of human life and changes in the quality of life are assigned a money equivalent. After expressing both positive and negative effects of an intervention in money terms, *Cost-Benefit Analysis* (CBA) can be applied. Of the three evaluation methods presented here, it is the only one which is suitable to evaluate each intervention separately. An intervention is worthwhile if the 'average cost-benefit ratio' (ACBR) is below one, i.e., if

$$\text{ACBR} = \frac{\text{costs in units of money}}{\text{benefits in units of money}} < 1.$$

An equivalent decision rule is

$$\text{net benefit} \equiv \text{benefits in units of money} - \text{costs in units of money} > 0.$$

If there is a stream of net benefits over time, future net benefits need to be converted into present values by using an appropriate discount rate. The sum of discounted net benefits yields the 'net present value' as a generalized decision criterion [see BOADWAY AND BRUCE (1984, p. 294–295)].

In the case of several mutually exclusive interventions with a positive net benefit, the one with the highest net benefit should be adopted. An equivalent approach is to calculate 'incremental cost-benefit ratios' (ICBRs) and to apply a threshold value of one. The ICBR of an intervention is defined by the ratio of incremental costs and incremental benefits compared to the next most effective intervention,

$$\text{ICBR} = \frac{\text{additional costs}}{\text{additional benefits in units of money}}.$$

Dominated alternatives need to be excluded. Of the remaining interventions with an ICBR below one, the intervention yielding the highest benefits is also the one with the highest net benefit. ICBRs are usually dispensable, however, because it is much easier to calculate net benefits directly.

In contrast to both CEA and CUA, the method of CBA does answer the question how much money should be spent on interventions that prolong life and enhance quality of life. It is usually justified by the welfare economic criterion of 'potential Pareto-improvement' ('Kaldor-Hicks criterion'), which we will discuss in greater detail in Section 2.4.4.

Conclusion 2.1. *Cost-Effectiveness Analysis (CEA) only serves for a comparison of measures with uni-dimensional effects. Cost-Utility Analysis (CUA) also allows comparisons among measures with several heterogeneous effects. To indicate whether a measure is desirable, both methods require a fixed budget for health care. By contrast, Cost-Benefit Analysis (CBA) provides an evaluation of life and health in terms of money and thus permits to assess every project separately.*

The prevailing method to evaluate benefits in CBA relies on subjective utility theory and uses aggregate willingness to pay of the persons involved as a money measure of utility. By contrast, both CEA and CUA focus on the effects on health status. Thus, these are fundamentally different approaches to the evaluation of health care interventions. In the remainder of this chapter, we therefore focus on the basic differences between the two most commonly applied methods, CUA and CBA, without further discussing CEA because of its limited applicability.

2.3 Cost-Utility Analysis

2.3.1 Concepts of Utility Measurement

Several utility concepts have been developed to summarize the multi-dimensional effects of an intervention in a scalar index. Among the best-known are the following.

(1) Disability-Adjusted Life Years (DALYs)

This concept was first developed in 1993 in the World Development Report of the World Bank [see WORLD BANK (1993), for a detailed exposition MURRAY (1994)]. DALYs measure the loss of life years in full health starting from a standardized life expectancy of 80 years for men and 82.5 years for women. Morbidity weights determined by experts are then used to assess states with less than full health. Moreover, different weights apply to years lived in different ages. The top weight is assigned a year spent at the age of 25 years. The utility of an intervention is measured by the number of DALYs prevented. DALYs are used, e.g., by the WHO to compare population health in different countries.

(2) Quality-Adjusted Life Years (QALYs)

The concept of a QALY is based on the work by KLARMAN ET AL. (1968), who first captured explicitly the number of life years gained and changes in the quality of life in a single index. As with DALYs, each health state is assigned a morbidity weight. However, these weights are regularly determined by surveying the people concerned by the intervention. The number of QALYs of a person is found by multiplying the expected duration of a health state with its morbidity index and summing up these numbers. The utility of an intervention is given by the number of QALYs gained.

(3) Healthy-Years Equivalents (HYEs)

This concept by MEHREZ AND GAFNI (1989) is based on 'health profiles'. Individuals are asked how they evaluate the likely sequence of health states caused by an intervention. In particular, they are asked how many years in perfect health they would find equally attractive as the profile in question.

DALYs, QALYs and HYEs differ in the two following aspects.

(a) Who evaluates the quality of life

In the DALY concept, the quality of life is assessed by experts, whereas in the case of the other two concepts, evaluation is by potential or actual patients. The latter approach is more appropriate because (potentially) affected individuals are best able to value their own health; moreover, they are the ones who ultimately finance public health care expenditures. By way of contrast, experts have a special competence only with respect to technical aspects of medicine. Therefore, the DALY concept seems to be hardly adequate as a basis for decision-making. Accordingly, it is mainly used for international comparisons.

(b) Whether or not the temporal sequence of health states is taken into account

In DALYs and QALYs, the order in which health states occur plays no role. By contrast, the HYE concept evaluates the profile of health states, which results from an intervention, as a whole. Therefore, HYEs are in principle to be preferred, but at the same time they are considerably more costly to measure because a whole health profile requires a lengthy description. For this reason, HYEs have rarely been applied so far.

In the following, we concentrate on QALYs, which are by far the most popular measure of health states. For instance, the National Institute for Health and Clinical Excellence (NICE) in the United Kingdom uses QALYs to compare different drugs and measure their clinical effectiveness.[4] In particular, we focus on the implicit assumptions concerning the preferences with respect to health.

2.3.2 The QALY Concept

2.3.2.1 Calculating QALYs

Using interviews (typically with health workers), utility weights for the various health states are determined (see Section 2.3.3). For this purpose, the weight for the state of perfect health is calibrated to the value 1, while the state of death is assigned the value 0. Using these values, a year spent in the respective health state is weighted to obtain quality-adjusted life years (QALYs). Quality adjustments can then be performed, in which the expected duration of a health state is multiplied by the respective utility weight and the resulting products are added together.

Figure 2.1 illustrates the logic of QALYs in two cases,

(a) an increase of the length of life by x years, which have to be spent in a worse health state, e.g., H_1;

(b) a change in the health state from, let us say, H_2 to H_3, which lasts for x years.

---

[4] See SCHLANDER (2007) for a study of economic evaluations by NICE.

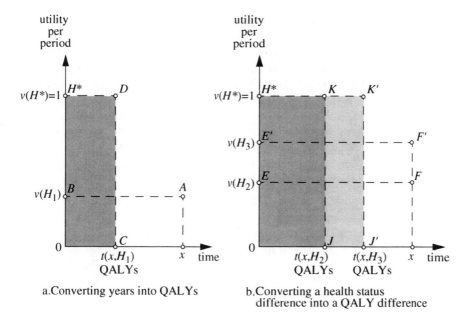

a. Converting years into QALYs

b. Converting a health status difference into a QALY difference

Fig. 2.1. QALYs as the Link between Length of Life and Health Status

Case (a) is depicted in Figure 2.1a. The utility of spending x years in state H_1 is given by the area of the rectangle $0xAB$. The same utility can be achieved by spending $t(x, H_1)$ years in perfect health ($0CDH^* = 0xAB$). The number of QALYs which correspond to x years in the state H_1 is therefore given by $t(x, H_1) < x$.

Now it is only a short step to the solution of a problem of type (b): let $t(x, H_2)$ be the number of QALYs corresponding to x years in state H_2, while $t(x, H_3)$ denotes the number of QALYs corresponding to x years in a better state H_3. The difference $t(x, H_3) - t(x, H_2)$ thus represents the number of life years gained in perfect health, which is equal in value to the underlying change of health status from H_2 to H_3 for x years. Figure 2.1b illustrates. First, x years lived in state H_2 are converted into $t(x, H_2)$ QALYs using the equality of areas $0xFE$ and $0JKH^*$. Next, x years lived in state H_3 are turned into $t(x, H_3)$ QALYs because of the equality of areas $0xF'E'$ and $0J'K'H^*$. The QALY difference, measured by the area $JJ'K'K$, then reflects the health status difference (area $EFF'E'$) as evaluated by the affected individual. Therefore, the instruments available for valuing prolongations of life can also be applied to evaluating changes of health status, provided that the utility of different states of health was determined and converted to 'years in perfect health' using the function $t(\cdot)$.

Conclusion 2.2. *The concept of 'quality-adjusted life years' (QALYs) allows to make changes in the quality of life and changes of the length of life comparable.*

2.3.2.2 Decision-Theoretic Foundation

The QALY concept is easy to apply. Once utility weights have been determined, the evaluation of a specific intervention is straightforward. However, since QALYs are used to support decisions regarding the allocation of resources in health care, they should have a sound decision-theoretic foundation. Therefore, we analyze in the following how QALYs can be justified in the light of expected utility, the most common theory of decisions under uncertainty.[5] While expected utility is not without problems as a descriptive theory of behavior under uncertainty,[6] it can serve as a normative guide to rational decision making, provided one accepts that choices should satisfy the axioms on which the theory is founded.

We start from a simple version of the QALY model, where there is no discounting of the future and no risk aversion with respect to the length of life. Ways to take these factors into account will be discussed later. For simplicity, let all health states $H_h, h = 1, ..., m$ be *chronic*, i.e., the health state does not change up to T_h. This assumption is used only to simplify the exposition and is no inherent characteristic of the QALY model. The combination (H_h, T_h) occurs with probability π_h. Thus, an individual is confronted with a lottery of chronic conditions $(\pi_h, H_h, T_h), h = 1, ..., m$. Assume that preferences satisfy the von-Neumann-Morgenstern axioms. If the utility of spending T_h years in the chronic condition H_h is denoted by $u(H_h, T_h)$, the preferences of the individual are therefore represented by expected utility[7]

$$EU = \sum_{h=1}^{m} \pi_h u (H_h, T_h).$$ (2.1)

To reduce expected utility to the number of QALYs, the utility function must take the form

$$u(H_h, T_h) = v(H_h)T_h.$$ (2.2)

Using (2.2), equation (2.1) simplifies to

$$EU = \text{QALYs} = \sum_{h=1}^{m} \pi_h T_h v(H_h),$$ (2.3)

i.e., expected utility equals the sum of the utilities of the various health states, weighted by their duration and the probability with which they occur.

---

[5] BLEICHRODT AND QUIGGIN (1997) also examine QALYs using the general rank-dependent utility model. MIYAMOTO (1999) provides a general treatment of QALY models under expected utility and rank-dependent utility assumptions.

[6] In particular, the independence axiom has been criticized on the basis of experimental results. It states that if two lotteries L_1 and L_2 are mixed to the same extent with a third lottery L_3, then the preference ordering of the resulting lotteries is the same as the ordering of L_1 and L_2 and therefore independent of the third lottery. The most famous challenge to the independence axiom has been posed by ALLAIS (1953) and is known as the Allais paradox [see, e.g., LAFFONT (1989, p. 14)].

[7] See, e.g., LAFFONT (1989, Chapter 1) and MAS-COLELL ET AL. (1995, Chapter 6) for a proof of the expected utility theorem.

Since in expected utility theory, the utility function $v(\cdot)$ is cardinal and therefore determined only up to positive affine transformations, $v(\cdot)$ can be chosen without loss of generality in such a way that the utility of perfect health $v(H^*)$ is arbitrarily set at 1 and utility of death is set at 0. Consequently, the expected utility of an individual can be interpreted as the number of quality-adjusted life years.

From a decision-theoretic perspective, the simplicity of the calculation of QALYs is based on the particular form of the utility function in equation (2.2). This form requires that *preferences for health states are stable over one's entire life*, i.e., $v(H_h)$ does not depend upon the age of the individual.

Furthermore, the utility function $u(H_h, T_h)$ needs to satisfy certain fundamental assumptions. To begin with, equation (2.2) implies that individuals are *risk neutral with respect to length of life*, i.e., for a given health state, they are indifferent between a certain life length T and a lottery with uncertain length of life and life expectancy T. But risk neutrality with respect to length of life does not completely characterize the form of the utility function (2.2). In general, it only implies that in the absence of discounting the utility function has the following form,

$$\forall H \quad u(H,T) = g(H) + v(H)T \quad \text{with} \quad v(H) > 0. \tag{2.4}$$

Equation (2.2) requires in addition that $g(H)$ is zero for all health states H.

One solution is to impose the *zero-condition*, which says that all health states with a duration of zero are equivalent [BLEICHRODT ET AL. (1997), MIYAMOTO AND ERAKER (1988)]. Put formally,

$$\forall H \quad u(H,0) = \text{const.} \tag{2.5}$$

MIYAMOTO ET AL. (1998) argue that the zero-condition is completely evident since all combinations of health states with zero duration are identical physical objects.[8] An immediate consequence of the zero-condition is that $g(H)$ must be a constant in (2.4). Since the utility function must be cardinal, an arbitrary constant can be added without loss of generality. Hence, one can set $g(H) = 0$ in equation (2.4) to obtain equation (2.2). Risk neutrality with respect to length of life and the zero-condition are therefore sufficient to characterize QALYs.

In addition to risk neutrality with respect to length of life, mutual utility independence and constant proportional trade-off are stated as the assumptions underlying the QALY model [PLISKIN ET AL. (1980)]. Mutual utility independence holds if conditional preferences for lotteries over length of life given a health state are independent of the particular health status and vice versa.[9] Constant proportional trade-off means that the share of life-years which the individual is prepared to sacrifice for a given improvement in quality of life is independent of the remaining life expectancy.

---

[8] See MIYAMOTO (1999, p. 208) for a heuristic argument supporting the zero-condition.

[9] See KEENEY AND RAIFFA (1976, Section 5.2) for the concept of utility independence.

BLEICHRODT ET AL. (1997) demonstrate that constant proportional trade-off and mutual utility independence are stronger assumptions than the zero-condition. Consider the constant proportional trade-off property,

$$\forall H, H' \text{ with } H' > H: \ \exists q \in (0,1) \text{ such that } u(H,T) = u(H',qT) \ \forall T. \qquad (2.6)$$

PLISKIN ET AL. (1980) show that this property is satisfied if (i) there is mutual utility independence and (ii) constant proportional trade-off holds for the best and the worst health state. For $T = 0$ in (2.6), one obtains that $u(H,0)$ is equal for all health states, i.e., the zero-condition. Thus, it is not necessary to impose constant proportional trade-off and mutual utility independence to characterize QALYs. The weaker zero-condition is sufficient.

A further result by BLEICHRODT ET AL. (1997) is that risk neutrality with respect to length of life for all health states as in (2.4) holds if and only if (a) length of life is utility independent of health states, i.e., if preferences over lotteries over length of life for a fixed state of health do not depend on the particular health state, and (b) risk neutrality holds for perfect health only. Therefore, QALYs can alternatively be characterized by the assumptions (a) and (b) in addition to the zero-condition.

In Figure 2.2, the block arrows illustrate the sets of sufficient conditions for QALY preferences. In addition, the conditions implied by the QALY model are of interest. The thin arrows in Figure 2.2 show these necessary conditions for QALY preferences. First, it is easy to see that the zero-condition and risk neutrality are not only sufficient but also necessary conditions for the QALY model [BLEICHRODT ET AL. (1997, Theorem 1)]. Furthermore, QALYs imply constant proportional trade-offs with q in equation (2.6) corresponding to $v(H)/v(H')$. Finally, mutual utility independence is a necessary condition for QALY preferences. Length of life is utility independent of health status because of risk neutrality with respect to length of life. Irrespective of any fixed health state considered, lotteries with a longer life expectancy are preferred. Likewise, the conditional preferences for lotteries over health states do not depend on length of life. To see this, assume a fixed length of life T. Equation (2.3) then simplifies to

$$\text{QALYs} = T \sum_{h=1}^{m} \pi_h v(H_h). \qquad (2.7)$$

Thus, if lottery (π_h, H_h, T) is preferred to lottery $(\hat{\pi}_h, \hat{H}_h, T)$, then it must also be the case that lottery (π_h, H_h, T') is preferred to lottery $(\hat{\pi}_h, \hat{H}_h, T')$ for any length of life T' different from T.[10]

---

[10] A further result not displayed in Figure 2.2 is that risk neutrality and constant proportional trade-offs imply mutual utility independence.

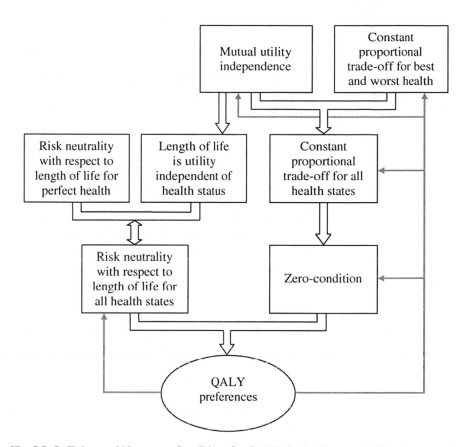

Fig. 2.2. Sufficient and Necessary Conditions for QALYs in the Expected Utility Framework

There are two generalizations in which the assumptions of the QALY model are somewhat relaxed. First, discounting of future utility can be taken into account by replacing (2.2) by the following form of the utility function,

$$u_D(H_h, T_h) = \sum_{t=1}^{T_h} \beta_t^{t-1} v(H_h), \quad 0 \le \beta_t \le 1. \tag{2.8}$$

Here, β_t denotes the discount factor in period t. The number of QALYs is then given by

$$\text{QALYs}_D = \sum_{h=1}^{m} \pi_h \sum_{t=1}^{T_h} \beta_t^{t-1} v(H_h). \tag{2.9}$$

In contrast to the model without discounting, this approach assumes that the individual is risk neutral with respect to the discounted remaining length of life [see JOHANNESSON ET AL. (1994)].

Secondly, risk aversion with respect to length of life can be taken into account by replacing (2.2) by

$$u(H_h, T_h) = v(H_h)w(T_h),$$ (2.10)

where $w(\cdot)$ is increasing and strictly concave. Holding life expectancy constant, a certain length of life is always preferred to an uncertain one.[11] With the utility function (2.10), the number of QALYs is given by

$$QALYs_R = \sum_{h=1}^{m} \pi_h w(T_h) v(H_h).$$ (2.11)

Conclusion 2.3. *A decision-theoretic analysis based on expected utility theory shows that the concept of QALYs requires several assumptions, viz. preferences for health states must be stable over the whole life cycle, there must be risk neutrality with respect to length of life, and preferences must obey the 'zero-condition'. To some extent, it is possible to relax these assumptions. For example, risk aversion with respect to length of life can be dealt with in a generalized QALY model.*

Empirical studies suggest that the requirements of the QALY model are violated to some extent [see DOLAN (2000) for a survey]. Therefore it has to be asked whether its main alternative, the HYEs, is preferable. This method places far weaker restrictions on the utility function. For example, preferences for health states do not have to be stable over the life cycle. But HYEs are extremely difficult to measure since all possible health profiles must be presented to respondents. In the attempt to determine the utility of an intervention, there is thus a conflict between accurate preference measurement and the costs of the interview study. The QALY method seems to be a pragmatic solution of this conflict. Whether other methods such as HYEs indeed serve to measure preferences better, therefore constitutes an important topic for further research.

2.3.2.3 QALYs and Consumption

So far it has been assumed that the utility of the individual depends on health-related variables only. In reality, it is also affected by other factors such as consumption, which plays an important role in utility theory in general. Ceteris paribus, for expected utility to be measured correctly by QALYs, the utility function for health and disposable income y as an indicator of consumption must be separable,

$$U_t(y_t, H_{h,t}) = a_t(y_t) + b_t(y_t)v(H_{h,t}), \quad b_t(y_t) > 0, \forall y_t$$ (2.12)

with $H_{h,t}$ denoting the health state in period t.

---

[11] This model is further analyzed by BLEICHRODT AND PINTO (2005).

A sufficient condition for (2.12) to be satisfied therefore is that the valuation of health is independent of disposable income.[12]

If we assume as BLEICHRODT AND QUIGGIN (1999) that utility in the state of death must be zero regardless of disposable income y, we get $a_t(y_t) = 0$, and (2.12) simplifies to

$$U_t(y_t, H_{h,t}) = b_t(y_t)v(H_{h,t}), \quad b_t(y_t) > 0, \forall y_t. \tag{2.13}$$

Let $\pi_{h,t}$ be the probability of spending period t in health state h, and $\hat{T}$ the maximum length of life. Furthermore, assume that life-cycle utility is the sum of per-period utilities and there is no discounting. Then expected utility of an individual is

$$EU = \sum_{t=1}^{\hat{T}} \left(\sum_{h=1}^{m} \pi_{h,t} U_t(y_t, H_{h,t}) \right) = \sum_{t=1}^{\hat{T}} \left(\sum_{h=1}^{m} \pi_{h,t} b_t(y_t)v(H_{h,t}) \right). \tag{2.14}$$

If $b_t(y_t) = b(y_t)$, i.e., the per-period utility function $b_t(y_t)v(H_{h,t})$ does not depend on t, and if disposable income is constant over time, i.e., $y_t = y \; \forall t$, equation (2.14) simplifies to

$$EU = b(y) \sum_{h=1}^{m} \sum_{t=1}^{\hat{T}} \pi_{h,t} v(H_{h,t}). \tag{2.15}$$

The expected time span which the individual spends in health state h is measured by the term $\sum_{t=1}^{\hat{T}} \pi_{h,t}$. Accordingly, $\sum_{h=1}^{H} \sum_{t=1}^{\hat{T}} \pi_{h,t} v(H_{h,t})$ can be interpreted as the number of QALYs and we obtain

$$EU = b(y)\text{QALYs}. \tag{2.16}$$

It becomes clear that QALYs can in principle be an independent argument of a standard utility function. But this result requires a number of restrictive assumptions. Specifically, if condition (2.12) is violated, if the per-period utility function changes over time, or if consumption is not constant, then the utility of changes in health-related variables cannot in general be captured by QALYs. In this case, an increase or a decrease in the QALYs of a person fails to indicate an improvement or deterioration of utility because changes in health cannot be evaluated independently of consumption behavior (see also Exercise 2.9).

Conclusion 2.4. *Taking into account that utility depends not only on health but also on consumption, restrictive assumptions are necessary to ascertain that QALYs capture all health-related benefits in a scalar index.*

---

[12] See KEENEY AND RAIFFA (1976, p. 226) on the definition of utility independence. A detailed derivation of the relationships described in this section can be found in BLEICHRODT AND QUIGGIN (1999).

2.3.2.4 Aggregation of QALYs and Collective Decision-Making

Cost-Utility Analysis serves to support collective decision-making. If QALYs are used, the rule of choice among a set of possible measures is to pick the one which maximizes *the number of* QALYs for a given budget. This rule is based on two fundamental value judgments.

(1) The welfare of the affected person enters the collective decision rule exclusively through its QALYs gained.

(2) It is irrelevant who experiences the increase in QALYs.

What are the arguments for and against these value judgments? With regard to (1) it was argued in Chapter 1 that the welfare of a person depends not only on health but also on other goods. This fact is taken into account by letting welfare (and not health) of the person enter the collective decision rule as an argument. In welfare economics, this corresponds to the principle of *welfarism*, which says that each person's individual utility is to be considered in a collective decision.[13] From this point of view, the concept of QALYs is unsatisfactory because welfarism requires using the whole utility of a person as a basis for collective decisions. As was shown above, QALYs are only one argument in the utility function and even this is true only if the utility function has a certain structure.

Taking total utility into consideration is disputed by *extra-welfarists*.[14] They argue that individual utility is not an adequate basis of collective decision-making but the purpose of these decisions is to provide the conditions for a good life, with health constituting a crucial prerequisite. Therefore, only QALYs should be used as preference-based health measure, neglecting other factors.

The second welfare judgment can be disputed on the grounds that the distribution of QALYs should play a role in the evaluation. The extreme opposite to the maximization of the sum of QALYs would be the maximin principle, which seeks to maximize the QALYs of those characterized by the lowest number of QALYs.

These and other positions can be expressed using a health-related social welfare function

$$HRSW = HRSW\{QALYs_1, ..., QALYs_n\} \tag{2.17}$$

which depends on the QALYs of the affected persons $i = 1, ..., n$ at birth.[15] In Figure 2.3 this is illustrated for the two-person case. In the initial situation the QALYs at birth are given by $\overline{QALYs_i}, i = 1, 2$. The QALY possibility curve QPC depicts the efficient distributions of QALYs between the two persons which can be achieved by

---

[13] See BOADWAY AND BRUCE (1984, p. 5)

[14] See CULYER (1989,1990).

[15] This approach was first proposed by WAGSTAFF (1991) [See also WILLIAMS AND COOKSON (2000)]. An alternative way to value health outcomes from a societal perspective has been developed by NORD (1999). It is based on questions in which members of a society are asked to compare health care interventions in terms of person trade-offs.

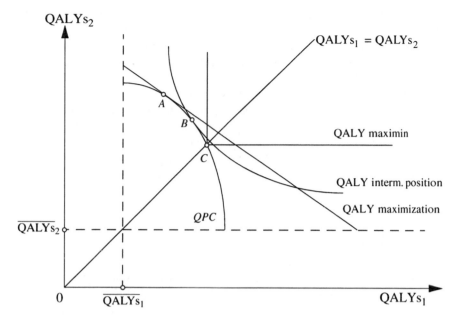

Fig. 2.3. The Conflict between Equality and Maximization of Total QALYs

health-improving interventions out of a given budget. The maximization of QALYs corresponds to a social welfare function with straight indifference curves of slope -1, resulting in point A as the optimum. In this example, QALY maximization leads to an unequal distribution of QALYs. Person 2 would receive more QALYs than person 1 because the resources spent on her have the greater effect. By contrast, the maximin principle corresponds to a social welfare function with L-shaped indifference curves. The optimal allocation is given by point C in this case, with both persons getting the same number of QALYs.[16] A social welfare function between these extremes has convex indifference curves that render a point like B optimal, which lies between A and C.

Figure 2.3 shows that it is possible in principle to account for the distribution of QALYs in a generalized Cost-Utility Analysis. However, this requires considerably more information than basic CUA. First, the exact location and shape of the

---

[16] If it is not possible to increase the QALYs of a person above a certain level, the maximin principle may not yield a clear recommendation. Consider, e.g, that person 1 can only reach the level of QALYs corresponding to point B in Figure 2.3. In this case, the QALY possibility curve would drop vertically at B. The maximin principle would be indifferent between point B and all other distributions on the vertical line between B and the 45-degree line. This problem can be solved by applying the leximin rule which calls for the maximization of QALYs of the person who is second worst off in terms of QALYs after QALYs for the worst off have been maximized. This would render point B optimal. Unequal distributions of QALYs can therefore be justified by this extension of the maximin principle.

QALY possibility curve must be known. This is not necessary in the traditional CUA which only uses the gain in QALYs, not their distribution, as the decision criterion. Second, the health-related social welfare function expressing the preferences of the population with respect to the distribution of QALYs must be determined.

> **Conclusion 2.5.** *Cost-Utility Analysis is not compatible with a welfarist position, which claims that collective decisions should be based on total utility of the affected persons. The use of QALYs can, however, be justified with an extra-welfarist position, according to which only health – as measured by QALYs – is relevant for particular collective decisions. The principle of maximization of QALYs can be criticized on the grounds that the distribution of QALYs should also play a role.*

2.3.3 Evaluating Health States

To determine the number of QALYs in a specific situation, it is necessary to measure the preferences of the individuals with respect to all possible health states. Several methods to accomplish this have been developed. The most frequently used are the the Rating Scale, the Time Trade-off, and the Standard Gamble methods.[17]

2.3.3.1 Rating Scale

A rating scale consists of a line with clearly defined end points describing the worst health state (usually taken to be death) and the best health state. In a survey, the respondents are asked to evaluate a certain health state by assigning a point on the line to it. After normalizing the line to a [0,1] scale, the QALY weight for each health state can be read off as the corresponding value on the [0,1] interval.

The advantage of the rating scale method is its easy application. However, it suffers from several sources of bias. Specifically, respondents refrain from placing health states near the end-points of the scale (end-of-scale bias), and they tend to space them equally across the scale (spacing-out bias) [see BLEICHRODT AND JO-HANNESSON (1997)]. Its major disadvantage, however, is that it is hard to interpret, not being based on a choice among two or more alternatives. The next two methods do not share this drawback.

2.3.3.2 Time Trade-Off

In this procedure, the test persons are asked the following question, "Suppose you had a disease which would leave you in a state of H_h for T years if not treated. The only possible treatment is free and would cure you perfectly; however, it shortens the

---

[17] For further methods see DRUMMOND ET AL. (2005, Chapter 6).

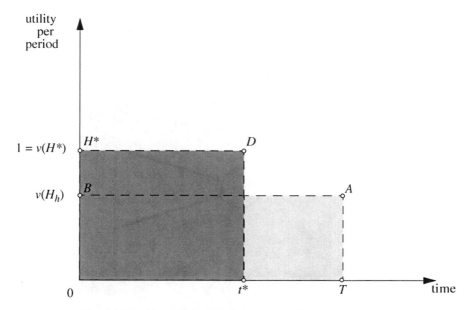

Fig. 2.4. The Time Trade-Off Method to Evaluate Health States

rest of your life span to t years." In the following, life span t is varied until the person interviewed is indifferent between the alternatives 'treatment' and 'no treatment'.

In the simple version of the QALY model with no discounting and no risk aversion, the point of indifference, $t^*(T, H_h)$, can be interpreted as follows. Without treatment, expected utility is $Tv(H_h)$, while with treatment, it is $t^*(T, H_h)v(H^*) = t^*(T, H_h)$, since the utility of perfect health, $v(H^*)$, was normalized to 1. Hence we obtain from indifference,

$$v_{\text{TTO}}(H_h) = \frac{t^*(T, H_h)}{T}, \qquad (2.18)$$

i.e., the utility weight of health state H_h is equal to the ratio t^*/T. This ratio must be independent of T according to the QALY model. This follows from the constant proportional trade-off property (2.6) with $H' = H^*$ and $H = H_h$. As Figure 2.2 shows, constant proportional trade-offs are implied by the QALY model.

Figure 2.4 illustrates the method graphically. The procedure is analogous to the conversion of years in a less than perfect health state into QALYs, as in Figure 2.1a. The only modification is that the reference time span x is replaced by the remaining lifetime T. The value $t^*(T, H_h)$ in Figure 2.4 follows from the equality of the areas $0TAB$ and $0t^*DH^*$. The ratio $t^*(T, H_h)/T$ is then interpreted as the utility weight $v_{\text{TTO}}(H_h)$ for health state H_h.

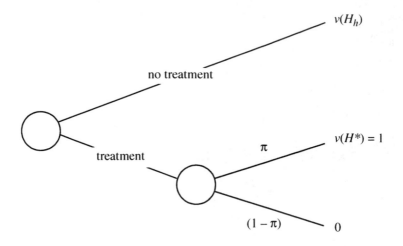

Fig. 2.5. The Standard Gamble Method to Evaluate Health States

Unlike the rating-scale alternative, the time trade-off method is rooted in expected utility theory. However, it yields unbiased measures of the utility weights only if respondents are risk neutral with respect to their remaining length of life. If they are risk averse, then indifference between the alternatives (H_h, T) and (H^*, t^*) implies in view of equation (2.10)

$$v(H_h)w(T) = v(H^*)w(t^*) = w(t^*),\qquad(2.19)$$

and thus

$$v(H_h) = \frac{w(t^*)}{w(T)} > \frac{t^*}{T}\qquad(2.20)$$

because of the concavity of w and $t^* < T$. In other words, risk aversion causes the fraction t^*/T to be a downward biased estimator of the 'true' utility weight $v(H_h)$.

2.3.3.3 Standard Gamble

Here, the following scenario is used, "Suppose you had a disease which would leave you permanently in state H_h without treatment. The only possible treatment is free and would cure you perfectly with probability π but lead to your immediate death with probability $1 - \pi$." The probability π is now varied until the respondent is indifferent between the alternatives 'treatment' and 'no treatment' (see Figure 2.5).

The value of indifference, $\pi^*(H_h)$, can be easily interpreted within the simple version of the QALY model without discounting and risk aversion.[18] With a remaining life span of $\bar{T}$, expected utility without treatment amounts to $v(H_h)\bar{T}$. With treatment, expected utility is given by $(1-\pi^*) \times 0 \times 0 + \pi^* \times 1 \times \bar{T} = \pi^* \times \bar{T}$, as the utility of death is normalized to 0 and the utility of perfect health to 1. Hence the utility of health state H_h is equal to

$$v_{SG}(H_h) = \frac{\pi^* \times \bar{T}}{\bar{T}} = \pi^*, \tag{2.21}$$

i.e., the value π^* at which the respondent is indifferent can be interpreted as the utility weight of health status H_h. Note that π^* is independent of the remaining life span $\bar{T}$ since conditional preferences for lotteries over health states are independent of length of life in the QALY model. This is a consequence of mutual utility independence which is a necessary condition for the QALY model (see Figure 2.2).

Like the time trade-off alternative, the standard gamble method is choice-based and firmly rooted in expected utility theory. Moreover, it is fully compatible with risk aversion with respect to length of life because the utility weight $w(\bar{T})$ would appear both in the numerator and the denominator of (2.21) and would thus cancel.

Conclusion 2.6. *If preferences of respondents satisfy the assumptions of the QALY model, with utility linear in length of life, the time trade-off and the standard-gamble methods lead to an analogous result in that they measure the utility weights of respective health states on a scale ranging from 0 (death) to 1 (perfect health). The standard-gamble method, however, is more general because it does not require utility to be linear in remaining length of life. By contrast, the rating scale method is less suitable since it lacks a utility-theoretic basis.*

In empirical applications, the time trade-off method and the standard-gamble method frequently lead to different results. On the one hand, individuals may not be risk neutral with respect to length of life. On the other hand, there is a good deal of experimental evidence questioning the validity of expected utility theory [KAHNEMAN AND TVERSKY (1979), POMMEREHNE ET AL. (1982)]. The difficulties associated with applying the two methods should therefore not be underestimated.[19]

---

[18] This way of putting the trade-off presupposes that the respondent prefers health state H_h to immediate death. For situations in which the individual would opt for death, a slightly modified lottery can be constructed [see TORRANCE (1986, p. 21)].

[19] BLEICHRODT (2002) shows that if respondents violate the assumptions of the expected utility model in a plausible way, the time trade-off method is likely to lead to a smaller bias than the standard-gamble method.

2.4 Cost-Benefit Analysis

In Cost-Benefit Analysis (CBA), a money value is assigned to an improvement in length or quality of life. To achieve this, two entirely different concepts have been developed, the human-capital approach and the willingness-to-pay approach. In Section 2.4.2 we shall briefly discuss the human-capital approach, which we do not deem appropriate because of its economic and ethical flaws. Our main focus is then on the willingness-to-pay approach in Section 2.4.3. However, there are very fundamental objections against valuing human life in terms of money which need to be addressed first. These are discussed in Section 2.4.1.

2.4.1 Ethical Objections and Counterarguments

Adapting freely Oscar Wilde's definition of a cynic, economists are sometimes said to 'know the price of everything but the value of nothing'. The idea of assigning a money value to human life may therefore meet with widespread disapproval. The objections raised are of two different kinds. One is at a most basic level stating that any attempt to pit life against money is unethical. The other is less fundamental. While accepting the notion that life has a price, it calls into question any other result than that of an infinite value of life. These two arguments will be discussed in turn.

2.4.1.1 Objections Against Weighing Life Against Money

The weighing up of life and freedom of disease on one side and money on the other is considered profane by moral rigorists who are inspired by Christian belief, the Hippocratic oath, or humanistic philosophy of life. Sometimes economic approaches to these valuations are even put on a par with the euthanasia programs of the Third Reich. Does such a valuation not imply that it is acceptable to kill those human beings whose 'value' does not cover their cost of living, such as food and medical treatment?

First, this argument fails to take into consideration the morally relevant difference between actively intervening and letting nature run its course, i.e., between the act of killing people who suffer from an incurable disease and refraining from efforts at prolonging their lives. This distinction plays a major role in the debate about 'dying in dignity'. Of course it can be said that refusing to provide a person with essential medical care or food for free is morally equivalent to killing that person. The greater the efforts required to save a human life, however, the less convincing is this argument. For example, assume that rescuing a group of miners buried in a pit would cost thousands of billions of dollars, causing the rest of the country to survive in misery. Can a refusal to rescue these miners be considered equivalent to killing them in this case?

Second, it is important to keep in mind that most public decisions do not affect 'identified' but 'statistical' lives. If personally identified individuals are at risk, politicians usually are expected to do everything which is possible to save their lives, probably because the public is aware that even a maximum effort would only consume a very small percentage of the Gross National Product. To see this point, assume it would take € 10 million for every miner buried in the pit to be rescued. This does not imply that the public would consent to the government spending the same amount on averting a risk of one in a thousand for one thousand miners of being buried in the pit. 'Statistical' lives tend to cause less emotion than 'identified' lives.

Third, the issue is not so much weighing life against money but rather remaining life expectancy. When thinking of medical treatment or public safety measures, we usually think of lives actually saved. In reality however, life is prolonged at best (often with some heroic performances of high-tech medicine resulting in a gain of a few months), for in the long run everybody has to die. As long as the time of death is beyond human control, it is even only remaining life expectancy that is increased. Therefore, life expectancy must be weighed against quality of life since 'more money' means more consumption possibilities, permitting a higher quality of life. Therefore the moral argument of an inadmissible valuation of life in terms of money is not as convincing as it appears at first sight.

However, the main justification for elaborating and applying an economic approach is based on the simple observation, mentioned in Section 2.1, that political decisions involving such valuations have to be made regularly. The mere fact that some action is undertaken (or refrained from) implicitly means that a weighing up of (prolonged statistical) lives against money has occurred. The economic calculus facilitates awareness of this fact, helping to make policies more consistent.

Conversely, doing without an economic valuation of 'life' entails risks of its own. A country may take a measure (such as introducing new medical technology) resulting in costs of € 1 million for avoiding premature deaths, failing to take into account alternative measures (for example road works) which could achieve the same for only €50,000. Society as a whole will then be deprived of both a longer life expectancy and consumption.[20]

Parliaments in many countries decide about public projects only after a thorough valuation of all of their costs and benefits. But when it comes to human lives, there has been a lack of an approved procedure to evaluate them in terms of money. As a substitute, it has become customary to mention such costs and benefits known as 'intangibles', which amounts to neglecting them as net benefits in the actual evaluation process. As a consequence, projects with a high risk in terms of human lives are too easily approved, while those with a lower risk tend to be rejected. Ironically, those who are against a valuation of life in terms of money thus jeopardize lives, the exact opposite of what they intend.

---

[20] This reference to society as a whole presupposes that life years won or premature deaths avoided do not depend on who is obtaining them (see Subsection 2.3.2.4).

Finally, public policies in a democracy should not only be consistent in the above-mentioned sense but also reflect the preferences of the citizenry. Since permitting citizens to express their preferences is a prerequisite of democracy, moral condemnation of weighing money against life is at odds with the democratic principle.[21] By taking the preferences of citizens regarding length and quality of life into account, economic analysis thus also serves to enhance the process of democratic decision-making.

Conclusion 2.7. *Since many public decisions inevitably imply a weighing of prolonging statistical lives against other goods, it is beneficial for society to undertake such a valuation explicitly. Citizens' preferences should be reflected in this valuation.*

2.4.1.2 Arguments Against a Finite Value of Life

The reliance on individual preferences stated at the end of the previous section relates to the second objection against CBA. While not questioning the idea of an economic valuation of life as such, it claims that any resulting value less than infinity is unacceptable. It is argued that there are in principle only two possible approaches to determining the value individuals place on their lives.[22] One either has to find

(a) the amount someone would be willing to pay to avoid certain (and immediate) death, or

(b) the compensation that would have to be paid to someone as to make him or her accept (immediate) death.

The amount determined according to formulation (a) is not very useful as most people would be willing to give up their entire wealth including most of their future income stream (except a small reserve for subsistence) when facing immediate death. Therefore (a) tells us more about an individual's wealth and ability to obtain credit than about his or her preferences.

On the other hand, question (b) will fail to call forth a limited amount – abstracting from a bequest motive – for the simple reason that money is of no use for the dead. This seems to result in an indeterminate value of life. This indeterminacy, however, can be resolved by noting that formulation (a) implicitly assigns the 'property right' to life to someone else than the individual concerned. Only alternative (b) says that the individual has the right to live and to give it up voluntarily. Given such a right to live, the correct 'value of an identified life' should indeed be infinite.

---

[21] The persons affected are not only those having a certain disease, but all people with a positive probability of contracting the disease in the future. For those who cannot be held accountable (young or mentally ill persons), the preferences of suitable agents should be considered.

[22] Both formulations can be accommodated within the framework of the expected utility rule. See Subsection 2.3.2 for further details.

This train of thought goes back to JOHN BROOME (1982a,b) who turns against a distinction of identified and statistical lives, as in his view the latter concept is based on incomplete information about who is going to lose his or her life. If statistics were able to tell us that in the course of a construction project one worker, who is not identified yet, is going to be killed, this statistical life is in fact infinitely precious. For as soon as the veil of ignorance is lifted and the name of the victim known, approach (b) would call for an infinite compensation for the loss of this identified life.

The flaw in BROOME's argument is revealed when one takes a closer look at the way he constructs his case. It is very hard to imagine a risk where the number of victims is known in advance with certainty. In most cases, it cannot even be said with certainty that there will be any victims at all. For example, a road bend may have taken an average toll of one human life per year in the past. But this does not mean that exactly one person will die during the next year. To the contrary, observing exactly one death during a given year is a rather unlikely event. To see this, let there be 100,000 users of the road per year, each of whom facing the risk of 1 in 100,000 of being killed in an accident. The statement 'individual i will die but not individuals $j,k,\ldots$' actually is a very strong one, implying perfect negative correlation across individual risks. Assuming stochastic independence or even a positive correlation – which is far more plausible when speaking of accidents - there is a strictly positive probability that no one will be killed while with a positive albeit very small probability all 100,000 persons will be killed. The total number of casualties thus is unknown, causing the 'statistical life' to be the relevant concept for an economic valuation of safety measures.

In sum, most relevant decisions with regard to life and death seem to involve small risks that can be avoided (or must be accepted). In these situations, we can expect limited amounts of money to be sufficient to compensate an individual for taking a risk. There are numerous examples showing that people are willing to risk their lives for the sake of pleasure, comfort or thrill. Activities such as smoking, driving without seat belts, traveling by car or plane rather than by train, and riding on a roller-coaster demonstrate that avoiding small risks is not infinitely valuable to people.

Since individuals clearly act as if their lives have only a finite value to them, the government should not (implicitly nor explicitly) attribute an infinite value to life when taking decisions in the public domain. Otherwise, inefficiencies due to the discrepancy between the costs of lives saved in the private and public domains would be the result. Such a discrepancy could be justified only if external effects were present.

2.4.2 The Human-Capital Approach

The value of an asset can be determined by measuring the owner's financial loss from losing it. This loss, in turn, is measured by the revenue stream that could have been obtained through careful management of the asset. The application of this simple accounting rule ('productive value principle') to human beings leads to a definition of the value of life based on the loss of human capital resulting from the death of that human being. The value of life is therefore equal to the discounted sum of the individual's future (marginal) contributions to the social product, which corresponds to future labor income, provided the wage is equal to the value marginal product.

When applied to the situation of a human being that falls victim to an accident at work, this definition seems a reasonable way to ascertain the claims for compensation of surviving relatives. The summation of foregone earnings is called 'gross human capital'. By deducting the deceased's future consumption from his earnings, 'net human capital' can be estimated. This quantity corresponds to the material loss that others suffer because of an individual's death.

The human-capital approach is based on two implicit postulates.

(1) An individual's value depends on the contribution that he or she makes to the welfare of fellow citizens.

(2) The appropriate measure of society's welfare is the Gross National Product (GNP).

Postulate (1) is more appropriate to a slave holder society than to a liberal democracy of the 21st century. It makes no essential difference between a person and a machine. Moreover, reliance on the 'net human-capital' approach implies that the individuals themselves do not even count as members of society, because their own loss (of future consumption) is not included in the calculation of the value of their lives.

The main advantage of the human-capital approach is that it can be made operational rather easily.[23] For this reason, it has often been applied in cost-benefit analyses in the past. However, it is completely foreign to microeconomic theory, which focuses on individual valuation. In addition, its ethical underpinnings are very much open to attack. For one, the result of such a human-capital calculation is considered unacceptable by many. Indeed, the value of the life of pensioners and others who are unable to work is always zero (even negative according to the net human-capital approach)! Second, and even more fundamentally, the GNP measure entirely ignores the pleasure of living as such. According to the opinion of most students of the field, this objection has served to discredit the human-capital approach despite its advantages of application.

Conclusion 2.8. *According to the human-capital approach, the value of life is determined by the contribution the individual could make to the social product. Its relatively easy application is outweighed by serious economic and ethical shortcomings.*

---

[23] However, there remain the well-known problems of estimating the contribution of housewives (and housemen) to the national product and possible discrepancies between wage and marginal productivity of labor owing to imperfect labor markets.

2.4.3 The Willingness-To-Pay Approach

The standard approach to measure the benefits in CBA is willingness to pay (WTP). This method is based on the concept of subjective utility which is assumed to depend both on disposable income and on length and quality of life. As a more detailed specification of the factors influencing length and quality of life is not needed, we can summarize these variables in the vector θ_i, while y_i denotes disposable income. Thus, the utility of person i is given by

$$U_i = U_i(\theta_i, y_i). \tag{2.22}$$

In the reference situation, length and quality of life are denoted by the vector θ_i^1. Suppose that an intervention which costs K Euros can cause situation θ_i^2. The willingness to pay WTP_i of person i for this measure can then be defined by the following equation

$$U_i[\theta_i^1, y_i] = U_i[\theta_i^2, y_i - WTP_i]. \tag{2.23}$$

Thus WTP_i measures the maximum amount of money which the person i would be prepared to pay in order to obtain the intervention.[24] The decision-making rule in Cost-Benefit Analysis states that an intervention is worthwhile if and only if

$$\sum_i WTP_i > K, \tag{2.24}$$

i.e., if total WTP exceeds the cost of the intervention, denoted by K.

Conclusion 2.9. *In contrast to the human-capital approach, the willingness-to-pay approach is based on the concept of subjective utility.*

If the health effects of an intervention can be measured in a continuous variable, the *marginal willingness to pay* of person i ($MWTP_i$) can be determined. In this case, θ_i is a scalar and we obtain

$$MWTP_i = -\left.\frac{dy_i}{d\theta_i}\right|_{dU_i=0} = \frac{\dfrac{\partial U_i}{\partial \theta_i}}{\dfrac{\partial U_i}{\partial y_i}}. \tag{2.25}$$

Of particular interest is the MWTP for an increased chance of survival which corresponds to the *value of a statistical life* (VSL) [see, e.g., ROSEN (1988) and HAMMITT AND TREICH (2007)]. For preferences that satisfy the axioms of expected

---

[24] This definition of willingness to pay is also called 'compensating variation'. An alternative concept is the 'equivalent variation' EV_i. It is defined by $U_i[\theta_i^1, y_i + EV_i] = U_i[\theta_i^2, y_i]$ and measures the minimum amount of money which the individual would be willing to accept in order to forgo the intervention [see BOADWAY AND BRUCE (1984, Chapter 7)].

utility theory, this MWTP can be determined more accurately. Consider a one-period model and let σ_i denote the probability of survival.[25] Following DRÈZE (1962) and JONES-LEE (1974) suppose that the utility function is state dependent and given by $u(L, y_i)$ in the case of survival and by $u(D, y_i)$ in the case of death, both functions being concave in y_i. Assuming, for simplicity, that disposable income is the same in both states, the expected utility of person i is

$$U_i = E[u(y_i)] = \sigma_i u(L, y_i) + (1 - \sigma_i) u(D, y_i). \tag{2.26}$$

As a reduction of the mortality risk is equivalent to an increase in the probability of survival σ_i, we get for the marginal willingness to pay for the reduction of the mortality risk and therefore for the value of a statistical life

$$\text{VSL} = \text{MWTP}_i = -\left.\frac{dy_i}{d\sigma_i}\right|_{dU_i=0} = \frac{\dfrac{\partial U_i}{\partial \sigma_i}}{\dfrac{\partial U_i}{\partial y_i}} = \frac{u(L, y_i) - u(D, y_i)}{E[u'(y_i)]}. \tag{2.27}$$

It is therefore higher, the more strongly the individual prefers life over death and the smaller is the expected marginal utility of money $E[u'(y_i)]$. Note that equation (2.27) implies that the VSL depends on the initial level of σ_i, on the individual's wealth, as well as other factors which affect the shape of the utility function. Furthermore, the access to markets for annuities and life insurance has an impact on the VSL [see BREYER AND FELDER (2005)].

To see why the marginal willingness to pay for the reduction of the mortality risk measures the value of a statistical life, consider a small change in population risk. For example, a health care intervention may increase the survival probability σ by $\Delta \sigma = 0.1$ percent for each member of a population of 20,000 individuals. Assume the VSL for a representative individual to be given by €300,000. If the intervention is undertaken, it can be expected that $20,000 \times \Delta \sigma = 20$ lives are saved. On average, individual willingness to pay is approximated by $\text{VSL} \times \Delta \sigma = €300$. Total willingness to pay is therefore given by $20,000 \times €300$. Thus, for each of the 20 statistical lives saved, the population is willing to pay

$$\frac{\text{WTP}}{\text{Statistical lives}} = \frac{20,000 \times \text{VSL} \times \Delta \sigma}{20,000 \times \Delta \sigma} = \text{VSL} = €300,000.$$

For small risk changes in a population, the VSL therefore provides an approximation to the total willingness to pay for a statistical life.

---

[25] See SHEPARD AND ZECKHAUSER (1982, 1984) and ROSEN (1988) for models which determine the VSL in life-cycle models.

2.4.4 Aggregating Willingness To Pay and Principles of Collective Decision-Making

Cost Benefit Analysis (CBA) supports a measure if total WTP exceeds the cost of this measure. This rule is based on two value judgments.

1. Subjective WTP is the only criterion to be used in assessing the benefits of a measure.
2. The distribution of benefits among individuals is irrelevant (in inequality (2.24), only the sum of individual WTP values enters).

The first value judgment reflects the fundamental difference between CBA and Cost-Utility Analysis (CUA). It states that WTP, derived from subjective utility theory, measures the benefits of health-improving interventions. By relying on WTP as the only source of information, CBA represents a welfarist approach. Extra-welfarists would argue that the improvement of health by itself must be taken into account, replacing (or at least complementing) WTP.

As to the second value judgment, it seems attractive at first sight because WTP values have the same weight across individuals. Whether a person benefits from the measure, however, depends also on his or her *contribution to its financing*. A person's *net benefit*, is defined as follows,

$$NB_i = \text{WTP}_i - \alpha_i K \tag{2.28}$$

where α_i denotes person i's share in financing and $\sum_i \alpha_i = 1$.

From the CBA condition,

$$\sum_i \text{WTP}_i > K \quad \Leftrightarrow \quad \sum_i NB_i > 0, \tag{2.29}$$

one cannot conclude that all affected individuals will have a positive net benefit. Therefore CBA cannot be justified by the Pareto criterion. Figure 2.6 illustrates this result for the case two individuals A and B. The shaded area contains all combinations of net advantages for which CBA supports a measure. However, only area II represents a Pareto improvement. In area I, person A is better off at the expense of person B, while in area III it is the other way around.

How can we still justify CBA? In the following, we discuss two arguments in its favor. On the one hand, the potential Pareto criterion can be invoked. On the other hand, it is claimed that applying CBA to a whole set of interventions leads to a Pareto improvement. Finally, the consistency of CBA with Social Welfare Analysis is examined.

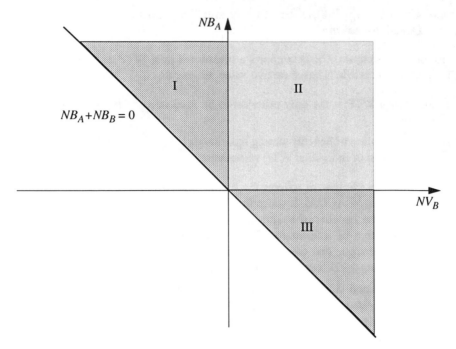

Fig. 2.6. Cost-Benefit Analysis and Net Benefits

2.4.4.1 Cost-Benefit Analysis and the Potential Pareto Criterion

The potential Pareto criterion, also known as Kaldor-Hicks criterion, is frequently used in welfare economics. According to it, an action should be undertaken if it either causes a Pareto improvement or if potential losers could be compensated by the beneficiaries of the action so that there would be a Pareto improvement. It is irrelevant whether the compensation actually takes place. CBA can be justified using this criterion. Suppose $NB_A < 0$, while $NB_A + NB_B > 0$. Then individual B could transfer $T = -NB_A$ to individual A, whose welfare would thus be unaffected by the project. Individual B would still be better off because $NB_B - T = NB_B + NB_A > 0$ by assumption.

A famous proverb says 'Actions speak louder than words'. It implies a rather strong criticism of the potential Pareto criterion, which suggests that the mere possibility of doing something good already counts, no matter whether it materializes or not. Indeed, in a situation in which some people are made better off at the expense of others, it is not a comforting argument to state that basically everybody could be made better off. A more persuasive justification is necessary.[26]

---

[26] If equilibrium effects are taken into account, the relationship between CBA and the potential Pareto criterion becomes ambiguous. CBA may support a project although a potential Pareto improvement is not possible [see BLACKORBY AND DONALDSON (1990)].

2.4.4.2 Cost-Benefit Analysis with Many Interventions

In the presence of a whole set of interventions, the cases in which a person is made better off at the expense of others and the cases, in which he or she suffers a loss may neutralize each other. Overall, this would make CBA satisfy the Pareto criterion. In Figure 2.6, this means that person A's utility lies in area I at least as often as in area III, leaving those cases of area II only, where both individuals are better off.

To be valid, this justification requires that the amount of net benefits does not *systematically* vary among affected individuals. If, e.g., WTP for health-improving interventions does not depend on income whereas the financial contribution does, net benefits are negatively correlated with income. As a result, CBA would systematically support interventions improving the situation of people with low income at the expense of people with high income. Suppose person A of Figure 2.6 has low income, then more outcomes would fall in area I than in area III. This may be judged desirable by some but undesirable by others. At any rate, the Pareto criterion cannot be invoked anymore to justify CBA in this case.

2.4.4.3 Cost-Benefit Analysis and Social Welfare Analysis

The difficulties encountered in the preceding two subsections motivate a more general investigation into the nature of the relationship between CBA and social welfare. For this endeavor, welfare economics provides the useful concept of a social welfare function. Its aim is to express value judgments of an observer on the 'welfare of society' by using a real-valued function W. Assume that W satisfies the following two requirements.

(1) *Welfarism:* W does not depend on the process of allocation but only on the utilities reached by an allocation;

(2) *Individualism:* the only benchmark for welfare is the utility U_i of the individual.

A function W satisfying these conditions permits social welfare to be expressed in a *Bergson-Samuelson welfare function*,

$$W = W(U_1, ..., U_n) \quad \text{with} \quad \frac{\partial W}{\partial U_i} \geq 0. \tag{2.30}$$

This function can have different functional forms, depending on the degree of inequality aversion prevalent in society. A well-known example is the utilitarian social welfare function

$$W = \sum_{i=1}^{n} U_i \tag{2.31}$$

which attributes the same weight to all members of society. The utilitarian welfare function satisfies the *strong Pareto principle* which states that welfare W must rise, if utility U_i of any individual i increases, with the utilities of all other individuals held constant.

By way of contrast, the maximin social welfare function

$$W = \min\{U_1, ..., U_n\} \tag{2.32}$$

makes social welfare equal the utility of the worst-off person. Thus, increasing a person's utility raises social welfare only if this person is worst-off. Therefore the maximin welfare function violates the strong Pareto principle. However, it satisfies the *weak Pareto principle* according to which welfare rises if the utility of each person increases [see BOADWAY AND BRUCE (1984, p. 146)].

These are just two out of a great many formulations, which differ not only with regard to their equity concept but also to their information demands.[27] Here, we only assume that a function as in (2.30) exists. To keep things simple, we limit our analysis to the case of two individuals $i = A, B$. Vector θ_i^1 describes a person's health-related characteristics in the initial situation. Social welfare is then given by

$$W^1 = W(U_A(\theta_A^1, y_A), U_B(\theta_B^1, y_B)). \tag{2.33}$$

Let there be an intervention costing K that results in the characteristics θ_i^2. Individuals' WTP for it, denoted by WTP_i, is defined by

$$U_i(\theta_i^2, y_i - \mathrm{WTP}_i) = U_i(\theta_i^1, y_i). \tag{2.34}$$

Individuals contribute α_i to the cost, where $\alpha_A + \alpha_B = 1$. Then, social welfare after the intervention can be written as

$$W^2 = W(U_A(\theta_A^2, y_A - \alpha_A K), U_B(\theta_B^2, y_B - \alpha_B K)). \tag{2.35}$$

The change in social welfare is defined as

$$W^2 - W^1 = \Delta W \approx \frac{\partial W}{\partial U_A} \Delta U_A + \frac{\partial W}{\partial U_B} \Delta U_B. \tag{2.36}$$

Using equation (2.34), one obtains for a change in utility

$$\begin{aligned} \Delta U_i &= U_i(\theta_i^2, y_i - \alpha_i K) - U_i(\theta_i^1, y_i) \\ &= U_i(\theta_i^2, y_i - \alpha_i K) - U_i(\theta_i^2, y_i - \mathrm{WTP}_i). \end{aligned} \tag{2.37}$$

Define $\hat{y}_i^2 \equiv y_i - \alpha_i K$ and $\hat{y}_i^1 \equiv y_i - \mathrm{WTP}_i$. Then, it is approximately true that

$$U_i\left(\theta_i^2, \hat{y}_i^2\right) - U_i\left(\theta_i^2, \hat{y}_i^1\right) \approx \frac{\partial U_i}{\partial y_i}\left(\hat{y}_i^2 - \hat{y}_i^1\right). \tag{2.38}$$

Note that in view of (2.28), the difference $\left(\hat{y}_i^2 - \hat{y}_i^1\right)$ is nothing but the individual net benefit NB_i. Therefore (2.37) can be rewritten to become

$$\Delta U_i \approx \frac{\partial U_i}{\partial y_i} NB_i. \tag{2.39}$$

---

[27] See, e.g., ROEMER (1996).

Inserting this into (2.36) finally yields

$$\Delta W \approx MU_A NB_A + MU_B NB_B, \quad \text{with} \quad MU_i \equiv \frac{\partial W}{\partial U_i} \frac{\partial U_i}{\partial y_i}. \tag{2.40}$$

That is, the change in welfare approximately corresponds to the sum of net benefits of the measure, weighted by the social marginal utility of income MU_i. Now this expression can be compared with the CBA criterion defined in (2.29), which calls for summing up the individual net benefits NB_i. Therefore, an intervention satisfying the CBA criterion improves social welfare *with certainty* if – as judged by the observer – both individuals have the same social marginal utility of income. Assuming this equality, one indeed obtains

$$\Delta W \approx MU_i(NB_A + NB_B), \quad i = A, B \tag{2.41}$$

and consequently

$$\Delta W > 0 \Leftrightarrow NB_A + NB_B > 0 \quad \Leftrightarrow \quad \text{WTP}_A + \text{WTP}_B > K. \tag{2.42}$$

Of course, this development gives rise to the question as to the conditions under which equality of social marginal utility holds. Maximizing social welfare subject to an aggregate income constraint,

$$\max_{y_A, y_B} W = W(U_A(\theta_A, y_A), U_B(\theta_B, y_B)) \quad \text{s.t.} \quad y_A + y_B = \bar{y}, \tag{2.43}$$

and assuming the social welfare function to be concave in utilities and the utility functions to be strictly concave in income, the optimal income distribution is characterized by

$$MU_A = \frac{\partial W}{\partial U_A} \frac{\partial U_A}{\partial y_A} = \frac{\partial W}{\partial U_B} \frac{\partial U_B}{\partial y_B} = MU_B. \tag{2.44}$$

Thus, when the observer judges the income distribution to be optimal, social marginal utilities of income are equal. This guarantees that a decision based on CBA always causes an increase in social welfare.

If income is not optimally distributed, however, an intervention supported by CBA may diminish social welfare as soon as for some individual i, WTP$_i$ falls short of the cost share $\alpha_i K$ and therefore $NB_i < 0$. According to equation (2.40), this is the case if a net loss accrues to individuals who have a particularly high social marginal utility of income. Analogously, CBA may reject an intervention even though it increases social welfare, provided that positive net benefits are received by individuals with a high social marginal utility of income.

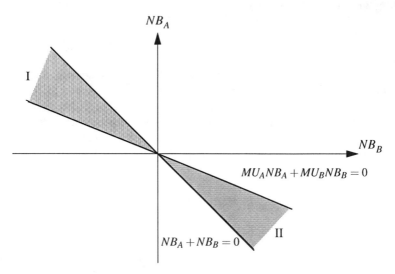

Fig. 2.7. Cost-Benefit Analysis and Social Welfare Analysis

Figure 2.7 illustrates. In addition to $NB_A + NB_B = 0$, it also contains the locus $\Delta W = 0$ from equation (2.40) assuming $MU_A > MU_B$, i.e., person A's social marginal utility exceeds the one of person B. Thus,

$$-\frac{dNB_A}{dNB_B}\bigg|_{\Delta W=0} = \frac{MU_B}{MU_A} < 1, \tag{2.45}$$

causing the graph of the CBA condition to be (absolutely) steeper than that of social welfare improvement.

In Figure 2.7, the shaded areas represent cases in which CBA and Social Welfare Analysis differ in their recommendations. In area I, Social Welfare Analysis supports a measure while CBA does not because A's net benefit is more strongly weighted than person B's net loss. In area II, Social Welfare Analysis rejects a measure that is supported by CBA because it weighs the net loss suffered by A more strongly than the net benefit accruing to B.

In the light of Social Welfare Analysis, the crucial issue for applying CBA is whether – from the point of view of the observer – income is optimally distributed. If this is not the case, Social Welfare Analysis requires

$$\Delta W \approx MU_A NB_A + MU_B NB_B > 0 \tag{2.46}$$

for an intervention to be recommended, i.e., the sum of individual net benefits weighted by their social marginal utility of income must be positive.[28] This decision criterion was first proposed by WEISBROD (1968). Using the definition of net

---

[28] Alternatively, one may use the weights $w_i = \dfrac{MU_i}{\Sigma_i MU_i}$ which add up to one.

benefits $NB_i \equiv \mathrm{WTP}_i - \alpha_i K$, the social welfare rule can alternatively be expressed as

$$SB \equiv \underbrace{MU_A \mathrm{WTP}_A + MU_A \mathrm{WTP}_B}_{\text{social benefit}} > \underbrace{MU_A \alpha_A K + MU_B \alpha_B K}_{\text{social cost}} \equiv SC, \qquad (2.47)$$

where the social benefit corresponds to the sum of individual WTP weighted by the social marginal utility of income. Likewise, social cost is the weighted sum of individual contributions.[29]

Notice that the information requirements of Social Welfare Analysis exceed those of CBA. First, not only willingness to pay, but also the financial contributions $\alpha_i K$ need to be determined. Secondly, society must agree on a social welfare function from which to derive social marginal utilities MU_i. Opinions about the relative merits of members of a society will differ, and it is not clear whether a consensus can be achieved. However, this is not a problem of Social Welfare Analysis but arises from the fact that evaluation typically involves value judgments. CBA only appears to circumvent this problem by implicitly assuming an optimal income distribution.

Conclusion 2.10. *Cost-Benefit Analysis can be justified by the potential Pareto criterion. However, the problem with this standard is that Pareto improvements may only be hypothetical. When a whole set of interventions is to be evaluated, overall Pareto improvement can be achieved, provided that the net benefits do not differ systematically among the affected persons. From the point of view of Social Welfare Analysis, CBA can only be applied if the income distribution is deemed optimal. Otherwise, net benefits must be weighted by social marginal utility of income.*

The difference between Cost-Benefit and Social Welfare Analysis may suggest a division of labor between income taxation and economic evaluation, the former being concerned with an optimal income distribution, the latter applying the cost-benefit rule to health-improving interventions. In the light of our model which assumed exogenous incomes this seems to be the adequate response. However, this assumption was only made for ease of exposition. In practice, income is determined to a great extent by labor supply. This puts a limit on the ability of income taxation to redistribute, a problem analyzed by the theory of optimal income taxation which studies the trade-off between distortions in labor supply and redistribution from high to low-ability individuals.[30] A solution which equalizes the social marginal utilities of income is usually not optimal as it would imply excessively high marginal tax rates.

---

[29] Defining the 'net social benefit' as the difference between social benefit and social cost, social welfare analysis can be used to evaluate mutually exclusive interventions. If there are a number of mutually exclusive interventions with a positive net social benefit, the one with the highest net social benefit should be adopted.

[30] At the heart of this problems is the fact that individuals have private information about their ability. The classic contribution is MIRRLEES (1971); an introduction to the theory of optimal income taxation can be found in MYLES (1995, Chapter 5) and SALANIÉ (2003, Chapter 4).

2.4.5 Measuring Willingness To Pay: Using Surveys

Both Social Welfare Analysis and CBA have WTP – as defined by equation (2.23) – as their point of departure. Therefore, it is crucial to be able to measure WTP. In general, economists prefer to infer WTP from actual behavior. The market price provides a lower bound for WTP because consumers buy a product only if their WTP exceeds or equals the price paid. Markets for medical care are both influenced by health insurance and heavily regulated, however, causing observed price to be too low and estimated WTP too high as a rule. Still, there is the possibility of indirectly inferring WTP from other, less regulated markets in the spirit of revealed preferences. Recently, health economists have increasingly resorted to the direct alternative of interviewing people, thus relying on stated preferences. Both methods have their specific pros and cons which will be discussed in the following. The current subsection is devoted to stated preferences whereas subsection 2.4.6 will deal with revealed preferences.

There are two approaches to measuring WTP directly. The *Contingent Valuation Method* confronts participants with one hypothetical scenario which involves the health care measure to be evaluated. The only attribute that varies is price. By way of contrast *Discrete Choice Experiments* present participants with a series of yes/no choices between the status quo and an alternative that differs with regard to several attributes, not only price. Before describing the two methods in detail, however, a few general problems associated with the use of interviews for WTP measurement need to be discussed.

2.4.5.1 General Problems of Surveys

The interview is not only the most direct but also the most transparent method to find out preferences. However, participants may not understand the questions, fail to take them seriously enough – as the situations are only hypothetical – or even hide their real preferences. Specifically, the following problems occur in the context of health.

(1) *Dealing with small probabilities.* If the scenarios described in the questionnaire are to roughly reflect reality, it is essential to consider very small probabilities and probability differences as soon as the intervention considered changes the chances of survival. Small probabilities, however, have little meaning to most people, who often fail to distinguish between probabilities that differ by powers of ten.[31] Answers therefore will not be very reliable, and by asking similar questions involving different probabilities, it is easy to obtain results which contradict the transitivity of preferences or the axioms of expected utility maximization. In this case, the theoretical framework of Subsection 2.4.3 is no longer applicable.

---

[31] In another context this was already observed by KAHNEMAN AND TVERSKY (1979).

(2) *Emotional rejection of questions.* Another problem is getting participants to answer delicate questions involving the trade-off between life and wealth. Refusal to answer such questions is likely to bias results if it occurs predominantly among people who place a very high value on their own life. Emotional rejection of questions could also result in a conscious or unconscious distortion of revealed preferences.

(3) *Insufficient motivation of the interviewed.* Even if there is a basic willingness to answer the questions, there is no motivation to seriously think about one's preferences in a real rather than hypothetical situation. Respondents could be tempted to express what they think the interviewer wants to hear or what will help their personal image.

(4) *Strategic behavior.* If the interviewed know that the decision for a specific project will be based on their responses, they have an incentive to behave strategically. Persons anticipating benefits from the project will overstate their WTP in order to increase the probability of the project being accepted. In the opposite case, they will understate their WTP to help prevent the project.

2.4.5.2 The Contingent Valuation Method

The predominant approach to WTP measurement has been the Contingent Valuation (CV) Method, developed in environmental economics for evaluating public goods.[32] Since the mid-1970s, CV has also been applied to health care.[33]

In CV studies, two procedures can be distinguished.

(1) When applying the *open-ended technique*, individuals are directly asked for the maximum amount they would pay for the hypothetical project. As this may be too demanding, tools such as the *bidding game* have been developed. Respondents are asked whether they would pay a certain price and in case they agree, the price is raised until they finally reject. If the initial price is rejected, it is reduced until the respondent accepts the project. The resulting price represents the maximum willingness to pay.

(2) The *closed-ended technique* attempts to create a situation familiar to respondents by asking just yes-or-no questions. Therefore, participants merely have to decide whether or not they are willing to pay the suggested price, which varies between them. This technique can be used to calculate the share of yes-votes as a function of the price. Multiplying this share with the total number of participants yields a function which can be interpreted as the aggregate demand function for the

---

[32] For an overview of more than one hundred CV studies, see CUMMINGS ET AL. (1986) and MITCHELL AND CARSON (1989).

[33] KLOSE (1999) presents an overview of the Contingent Valuation reports with respect to health economics.

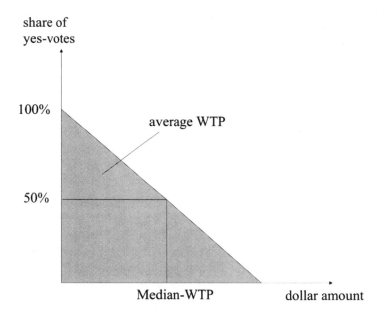

Fig. 2.8. Calculating the Willingness to Pay Using the Survival Function

good. Figure 2.8 shows aggregate WTP as the area of this demand function, which is specified as a survival function.[34] Median WTP can be read off the price fifty percent of the respondents are just about to accept. Average WTP can be higher or lower than the median value, depending on the distribution of WTP. If this distribution is skewed towards low WTP values, it falls short of the median. In the case of a linear survival function (which is nothing but a cumulative distribution function), the two values coincide.

It is still an open question whether the open-ended or the closed-ended technique should be preferred in CV studies. The main advantage of the latter is that the decision resembles a familiar market situation. A general disadvantage of CV, however, is its liability to bias, in particular of the following types.[35]

(a) *Bias caused by reference values and the order of questions.* CV is prone to so-called 'anchoring' effects. Respondents indicate their WTP relative to a reference value rather than their value. For example, in bidding games, stated WTP frequently depends on the starting point (starting-point bias). When several projects are presented at a time, the answer to the first question can influence all the following ones (question-order bias).

---

[34] For an overview of the different methods to estimate a survival function, see NOCERA ET AL. (2003).

[35] See MITCHELL AND CARSON (1989, Chapter 11) for a detailed description of possible sources of bias when using CV.

(b) *Sensitivity to wording of questions.* The results of CV studies are very sensitive to the wording of the questions. For instance, the definition of property rights or the means of payment used can bias WTP values. At an even more basic level, there is the risk that respondents perceive the presented good or program quite differently from what the investigator intended.

(c) *Attitude towards the object of investigation.* When applying the closed-ended technique, there is the danger of 'yea-saying'. To express their general agreement with the object of investigation, respondents accept prices in excess of their true WTP [see BLAMEY ET AL. (1999)].

Considering in addition the general problems associated with interview studies mentioned in the preceding subsection, it seems doubtful that reliable WTP measurement can be obtained from a CV study. Nevertheless, this method has yielded theoretically plausible results, when applied to health care [see KLOSE (1999)]. Specifically, individuals with high incomes have been found to have a higher WTP than others. Moreover, measured WTP increases with the quantity of health services offered by a program. It could not yet be established, however, that stated WTP is consistent with actual buying decisions (constituting so-called criterion validity). Also, with regard to the reliability of the method, there is evidence of only a limited degree of reproducibility of results obtained using the CV method.

> **Conclusion 2.11.** *Contingent Valuation calls on respondents to evaluate a hypothetical program or good whose attributes are held constant across scenarios except for price. While theoretically plausible results can be obtained with this method, it is very sensitive to several types of bias. Furthermore, there is still no firm evidence that the stated willingness to pay matches actual decisions.*

Frequently, surveys are used to determine the *value of a statistical life* (VSL) (see Section 2.4.3). VISCUSI (1993) and more recently HAMMITT AND GRAHAM (1999) report on nearly two dozen survey studies investigating the value of a statistical life. These studies were mainly performed in the United States and in Great Britain. Sample sizes differ considerably (from 30 up to more than 1,000). In some cases, respondents were students attending classes taught by the authors; in other cases, they constituted representative samples of the country's population. All questionnaires defined realistic scenarios stating plausible reasons for changes in the risk of dying such as additional safety measures in road traffic, nuclear power plants, or the removal of toxic waste. The intent was to make respondents take the questions seriously.

The results show considerable *variation* in the calculated value of life. This is because of the fact that average stated WTP values for large risk reductions of about $1:10^3$ are not substantially larger than for risk reductions in the order of $1:10^5$ to $1:10^6$. Studies using large risk reductions thus lead to estimates of the VSL that are lower by several orders of magnitude. For example, FRANKEL (1979) found values of a statistical life ranging from US$57,000 to US$3.37 million in the *same study*, depending on the size of the assumed risk reduction.

These results confirm the presumption mentioned above that most respondents have difficulties in dealing with very small probabilities. Indeed, hypothetical probabilities below a certain level (which could be around 1:1,000) are 'mentally adjusted' to a higher value.

However, JONES-LEE ET AL. (1985) report that their (arithmetic) mean was strongly influenced by some outliers on the high side. Using the median instead of the mean yielded a value of a statistical life of only £800,000 rather than £1.5 million. While the potential Pareto criterion has to be based on the arithmetic mean, using the median can be justified by the principle of majority rule, which applies when risk-reducing measures proposed by the government are voted upon in a poll. There are some further considerations which suggest that the results presented may fail to mirror 'true' willingness to pay.

- A considerable percentage of respondents indicate *the same* WTP for risk reductions of *different* sizes, starting from the same initial risk level.

- Some respondents even indicate *smaller* amounts for *higher* risk reductions [see JONES-LEE ET AL. (1985), SMITH AND DESVOUSGES (1987)].

- Considerable differences between WTP for a small decrease in risk and compensation demanded for small increases in risk are found in the same study.

Finally, the type of death described in the scenarios (for example dying of cancer vs. dying in a car accident) affects the stated WTP as well. This is relevant because, e.g., in the case of cancer, being able to avoid a long period of suffering may call forth substantial WTP.

Conclusion 2.12. *Considerable variation and widespread inconsistencies in results suggest that 'stated preferences' – at least in the guise of Contingent Valuation – lack reliability when applied to WTP for risk reduction.*

2.4.5.3 Discrete Choice Experiments

Discrete Choice Experiments (DCE) are a variant of *conjoint analysis*, which was developed in psychology in the late 1960s [see LUCE AND TUKEY (1964)]. This method attempts to explain and predict consumers' behavior on the basis of their preferences for the attributes of a good. It is based on the New Demand Theory [see LANCASTER (1966)] which defines preferences in terms of attributes rather than quantities of goods. Since decisions typically are to buy or not to buy one unit of the good, they are of the discrete type. In contradistinction to the CV approach, the status quo and the hypothetical alternative differ with regard to several or all attributes rather than price only.

Since the beginning of the 1980s, DCEs have been applied in transport economics and more recently to environmental economics [see for example HENSHER (1997), BENNETT AND BLAMEY (2001)]. In the mid-1990s, the method was implemented in health economics as well [RYAN (1995), RYAN AND HUGHES (1997)], and in the meantime quite a few DCE studies have been conducted.[36]

Before starting a DCE, the attributes characterizing both the status quo and the alternative need to be defined. In the case of knee surgery, e.g., this could be the following:

- desired effects;
- possible complications;
- length of wait for surgery;
- length of hospital stay;
- out-of-pocket cost as the price attribute.

These attributes can be combined to form various (hypothetical) products. Every product or program is therefore characterized by a vector of parameter values. These hypothetical alternatives are usually juxtaposed against a fixed status quo, and respondents are asked sequentially whether they prefer the status quo or the current alternative. A DCE therefore amounts to tracing out an indifference curve in attribute space, with the status quo defining a reference point. A preferred combination of attributes must lie above the indifference curve (or surface, respectively in the case of more than two attributes), a rejected one, below. Through repeated choices, the indifference locus can be interpolated.

DCEs make the following assumptions on preferences:

(1) *Existence of a representative consumer.* The aggregated preferences of the study population can be represented by a single utility function. However, group-specific differences in preferences are taken into account by a vector of socio-economic control variables in the utility function.

(2) *Restrictions imposed on the form of the utility function.* Almost all applications assume linearity, which implies constant marginal utilities of attributes. Since this assumption is too restrictive, especially when price (and with it disposable income) varies over a wide range in the experiment, a quadratic utility function is used alternatively. However, this still implies rather restrictive assumptions.[37]

---

[36] See, e.g., BRYAN ET AL. (1998), JOHNSON ET AL. (2000), RATCLIFFE AND BUXTON (1999), TELSER AND ZWEIFEL (2002) and VICK AND SCOTT (1998). A preliminary survey of the applications in health care is given by RYAN AND GERARD (2004).

[37] A quadratic utility function is used, e.g., by GEGAX AND STANLEY (1997) and PECKEL-MAN AND SEN (1979).

The decision-theoretic model can be presented as follows.[38] Each alternative j is characterized by its price p_j and a vector of characteristics $b_j = (b_j^1, ..., b_j^z)$, while y_i denotes the income of individual i. The indirect utility of alternative j for individual i can thus be written as

$$V_{ij} = v(p_j, b_j, y_i, \varepsilon_{ij}),\tag{2.48}$$

where ε_{ij} denotes a random variable. This is the random utility model developed by MCFADDEN (1974). Note that this model does not imply that individuals choose at random. Rather, ε_{ij} stands for those determinants of choice that are not captured by equation (2.48) but cannot be observed by the experimenter. The individual will choose the alternative j if its utility exceeds the utility of the status quo (more generally, of all alternatives l available), i.e.,

$$v(p_j, b_j, y_i, \varepsilon_{ij}) \geq v(p_l, b_l, y_i, \varepsilon_{il}), \quad \forall l \neq j.\tag{2.49}$$

Since individuals' decisions are random variables, one can only define the probability for choosing alternative j,

$$P_j = \text{Prob}[v(p_j, b_j, y_i, \varepsilon_{ij}) \geq v(p_l, b_l, y_i, \varepsilon_{il})], \quad \forall l \neq j.\tag{2.50}$$

In order to estimate (2.50), an assumption not only regarding the functional form of $v(\cdot)$ but also the distribution of the error terms ε must be made. For the latter, Probit and Logit models constitute the dominant alternatives.

Using the results of this estimation, one can calculate the marginal rate of substitution (MRS) between any two attributes. The MRS states how much of one attribute someone is willing to give up in order to obtain one more unit of the other attribute. The MRS is defined by the ratio of the two partial derivatives of the indirect utility function with respect to attributes k and m:

$$\text{MRS}_{k,m} = \frac{\dfrac{\partial v(p_j, b_j, y_i, \varepsilon_{ij})}{\partial b_j^k}}{\dfrac{\partial v(p_j, b_j, y_i, \varepsilon_{ij})}{\partial b_j^m}}.\tag{2.51}$$

Specifically the MRS between attribute b_j^k and price p_j captures the amount of disposable income (i.e., the negative of price) a person is willing to pay in order to receive one more unit of attribute k. But this is nothing else than WTP for attribute k,

$$\text{WTP}_k = -\frac{\dfrac{\partial v(p_j, b_j, y_i, \varepsilon_{ij})}{\partial b_j^k}}{\dfrac{\partial v(p_j, b_j, y_i, \varepsilon_{ij})}{\partial p_j}}.\tag{2.52}$$

---

[38] A detailed description of the method and the underlying theoretical model can be found in LOUVIERE ET AL. (2000).

Given a linear utility function, WTP values are constant. Therefore, WTP for non-marginal changes is obtained by multiplying (2.52) by the respective changes in the attributes between the status quo and the alternative. In this simple case, WTP for the program as a whole can be estimated by simply adding the WTP values of its attributes.

An important advantage of DCE over CV follows from the fact that respondents tend to evaluate all attributes of a program rather than focusing on price only. This makes DCE less susceptible to strategic behavior. Moreover, being based on an esti-mated utility function, the results of a DCE can be used to determine WTP for any program that has the same set of attributes. On the other hand, as in the QALY model of Cost-Utility Analysis, rather restrictive assumptions concerning individuals' pref-erences have to be made. Therefore, their validity needs to be checked. To this day, few studies have investigated the validity and reliability of DCE. However, first re-sults obtained by BRYAN ET AL. (2000), RYAN ET AL. (1998), TELSER (2002), TELSER AND ZWEIFEL (2002) and ZWEIFEL ET AL. (2006) indicate that DCE may be a valid and reliable approach to WTP measurement in the case of health as well.

Conclusion 2.13. *Discrete Choice Experiments attempt to determine and forecast individuals' preferences for the attributes of a product from their accept/reject decisions. The significant advantages of this method are lim-ited susceptibility to strategic behavior and applicability of its results to projects having the same attributes. However, its restrictive assumptions re-garding preferences still need to be tested.*

2.4.6 Measuring Willingness to Pay: Using Market Data

The major advantage of inferring WTP indirectly from market data is that market observations reflect real rather than hypothetical decisions. This holds true also of situations involving risk. Risk preferences can be inferred from actions designed to avoid risks. A well-known example is the choice (or avoidance) of a job that is known for its risks to life and health (examples are race car drivers, truck drivers, stuntmen, miners, or electricians). But everyday decisions like putting on the safety belt also provide information about risk preferences.

Using 'revealed preference' for measuring WTP, however, has its problems as well. Take the example of occupational choice. Here, the basic idea is to estimate the compensation required for accepting a higher risk of death from the difference in wage rates for occupations with and without an increased threat to life. The problems with this approach are the following.

(1) *Separating risk from other influences.* In contrast to the hypothetical situations described in questionnaires, real life situations have many aspects, making it dif-ficult to isolate a single determining factor. One hardly finds two occupations that are identical except for their risk to life and health. Differences in wage rates also

reflect differences in educational requirements, mental and physical demands, and many other characteristics of occupations. As long as these characteristics cannot be held constant, it is quite daring to identify a wage differential with a risk premium.

(2) *Discrepancy between subjective probability and relative frequency.* Even if the wage differential were a pure risk premium, the marginal rate of substitution between risk and wealth can only be determined with the help of subjective estimates of relevant probabilities. According to expected utility theory, decisions are based on subjective probabilities. By way of contrast, in the case of occupational hazards (e.g., fatal industrial accidents), only relative frequencies can be observed. As these fatal accidents are relatively rare, it is questionable whether those affected know the frequencies, let alone use them as a basis for their subjective probability estimates. Surveys among drivers indicate that most underestimate their personal risk of causing an accident relative to the frequency observed in the total population. Another question is whether observed behavior actually can be interpreted as the outcome of expected utility maximization as required by theory. Empirical evidence [already by EISNER AND STROTZ (1961)] indicates that when dealing with relatively small risks, individuals systematically violate this rule – as was already noted in Subsection 2.4.5.2 in the context of hypothetical questions.

(3) *Representativeness of persons in risky occupations.* Finally, it can be called into question whether persons in risky occupations are representative of the total population. The fact that such an occupation and no other was chosen by them implies that – even ignoring objections (1) and (2) for the moment – the wage differential constitutes the *upper limit* of their compensation asked for bearing the increased risk (conversely their WTP for a risk reduction). Simultaneously, it marks the *lower limit* for the rest of the population (assuming that these individuals are in principle suited for the job as well). This consideration, however, is not very helpful in cases in which the measured 'compensating wage differential' is extremely small or even negative. In this case, we have to conclude that members of such a profession may have a special preference for risky situations (perhaps for the thrill that comes with them) that is not shared by the rest of the population.[39]

Conclusion 2.14. *Measuring willingness to pay on the basis of market data has the advantage of relying on real rather than hypothetical decisions. This method, however, has its problems as well. In particular, one needs to make sure that individuals know the relevant risks and that preferences are singled out as a determinant of observed behavior.*

---

[39] It is doubtful, however, that people who take high risks professionally or privately for the sake of 'thrill' (stuntmen, hang gliders) feel the same way about a less spectacular risk of equal magnitude (e.g., poisoning due to harmful substances).

The first extensive empirical survey of wage differentials among occupations entailing differing threats to life was conducted by THALER AND ROSEN (1975). Their data refer to 900 workers in 37 *risky occupations*. The authors relate workers' wage incomes to various causes, using multiple regression analysis to isolate occupational risk. Probabilities of death are taken from life insurance statistics. Depending on the specification of the estimated equation, estimated regression coefficients yield values of statistical life between US$136,000 and 260,000 (referring to 1967).

More recent surveys using data from the United States and Great Britain indicate larger wage differentials in response to comparable risk increments. The value of a statistical life often exceeds US$1 million while continuing to exhibit variations of up to two powers of ten.

Another approach is to derive the 'value of life' from the observed *behavior of consumers*, using data such as

- the higher price of houses in neighborhoods with better air quality;
- the purchase and installation of smoke detectors in wooden houses;
- the use of safety belts and the choice of speed when driving a car;
- the use of subways to cross streets with heavy traffic.

Surprisingly, the results of these completely different studies bunch more closely than those comparing wage rates. They imply a value of life between US$200,000 and US$600,000 in 1983 prices [see JONES-LEE ET AL. (1985)]. In view of the reservations, both against the direct and the indirect method of measuring WTP for changes in the risk of death (see Subsection 2.4.5.1 again), however, it cannot be concluded with certainty that the value of a statistical life lies within this interval.

2.5 Cost-Utility, Cost-Benefit and Social Welfare Analysis

2.5.1 Comparing Cost-Utility and Cost-Benefit Analysis

When comparing Cost-Utility Analysis (CUA) with Cost-Benefit Analysis (CBA), one similarity and two major differences stand out. Neither method considers how the net benefits from an intervention are distributed. This is a weakness for policy makers (and indeed, citizenries) who prefer the net benefits of a measure not to be distributed too unequally among those affected. As demonstrated above, this aspect can be taken into account by using a health-related or social welfare function.

The first principal difference is that CUA as such fails to provide a recommendation whether or not a project should be carried out unless there is a predetermined health care budget. It leaves open the question of how that budget should be set. Second, the two methods differ in how the benefits accruing to the affected persons should be taken into account in the decision-making process. CUA draws upon the extra-welfarist concept of health while CBA relies on the conventional utility concept of welfare economics. The two methods are therefore based on different value judgments and not just on different technical procedures. By opting for a specific method, a decision is made as to the factors that are taken to be relevant for individual welfare. The analyst can only try to clarify the welfare-economic relationships. Ultimately, the decision for or against an evaluation method can only be made by society.

> **Conclusion 2.15.** *Cost-Utility Analysis and Cost-Benefit Analysis differ not only technically but, above all, in how they incorporate the welfare of those affected. CUA focuses on health, CBA on utility. They are thus based on different value judgments.*

An advocate of CBA may ask an interesting question regarding the compatibility of the two methods, viz. can one use the results of CUA for CBA? In particular, we pose the question whether a unique 'willingness to pay for a QALY' exists, which can be compared to the cost per QALY of specific interventions to assess whether the intervention is worth doing. This would be particularly helpful for health care systems that do not use fixed budgets.[40]

For an answer to this question, note first that the assumptions of the QALY model have to be satisfied (see Section 2.3.2.2). As shown in Section 2.3.2.3, QALYs are an argument of an expected utility function which also depends on disposable income y only if a number of assumptions are satisfied. Specifically, expected utility must take the form presented in equation (2.16). Then expected utility of an individual i with income y_i and an initial QALY endowment $QALYs_i$ is given by

$$EU_i = b(y_i)QALYs_i. \tag{2.53}$$

From this, the marginal WTP for a QALY can be derived,

$$MWTPQ_i = -\left.\frac{dy_i}{dQALYs_i}\right|_{dEU_i=0} = \frac{\frac{\partial EU_i}{\partial QALYs_i}}{\frac{\partial EU_i}{\partial y_i}} = \frac{b(y_i)}{b'(y_i)QALYs_i}. \tag{2.54}$$

Given a positive marginal utility of income, this quantity is positive.

Based on (2.54), one can estimate an individual's WTP for a health care intervention by multiplying the marginal WTP for a QALY by the number of additional QALYs achieved,

$$WTP_i \approx MWTPQ_i \times \Delta QALYs_i = \frac{b(y_i)}{b'(y_i)QALYs_i}\Delta QALYs_i. \tag{2.55}$$

Based on the resulting values, a CBA (or a Social Welfare Analysis, see below) can be performed. This would be easy because evaluation of health states from surveys serve as input to CUA. However, the following aspects have to be considered.

---

[40] See also BLEICHRODT AND QUIGGIN (1999).

(a) Equation (2.16) requires restrictive assumptions which are only partially satisfied in practice (see Section 2.3.2.3).

(b) Equation (2.54) shows that individuals' marginal WTP for a QALY depends on their disposable income and their initial QALY endowment. This likely causes WTP for a QALY to vary between them. In particular, equation (2.54) implies that marginal WTP for a QALY should increase with disposable income if $b''(y) < 0$, i.e., if the standard assumption holds that marginal utility of income is decreasing ceteris paribus. This hypothesis is supported by empirical studies which find evidence for a positive income effect on WTP per QALY [see BYRNE ET AL. (2005) and KING ET AL. (2005)].

A pragmatic approach would be to use average MWTPQ in a population. If the measure to be evaluated affects groups with different incomes or initial QALYs in different ways, however, this way may result in the wrong choice. Suppose, for example, that mainly people with low incomes benefit while MWTPQ increases with income. In this case, using average MWTPQ would lead to an overestimation of total WTP. This approach can only be justified if there is no systematic relationship between MWTPQ and the additional number of QALYs gained.

In general, it is necessary to differentiate MWTPQ according to income and initial health (and possibly further factors). For this reason, there exists no unique marginal willingness to pay for a QALY which can be used in CBA. Furthermore, group-specific estimates of the numbers of QALYs gained are needed. However, these are frequently not available from Cost-Utility Studies.

These considerations also show that it is highly unlikely for CUA and CBA to yield the same result. This would require not only that the assumptions of the QALY model are satisfied and preferences are given by equation (2.53) but also that WTP for a QALY must be the same for everyone so that CBA weights the changes in QALYs equally. In addition, the budget defining the scope of CUA would have to correspond to the optimum expenditure resulting from CBA. Nevertheless, the analysis shows that QALYs can in principle be used in CBA, provided that differences in MWTPQ and the numbers of QALYs gained are adequately captured.

Conclusion 2.16. *Individuals' marginal willingness to pay for a QALY depends on their disposable income and their initial QALY endowment. The use of QALYs in CBA therefore requires group-specific values of marginal willingness to pay for a QALY and of the numbers of QALYs gained. In general, Cost-Benefit Analysis leads to a different result than Cost-Utility Analysis.*

Thus, not only do the two methods differ in their value judgments, but it is also difficult to use the results of CUA for CBA. We can conclude that these two are basically different concepts for evaluating health-related measures. The major practical advantage of CBA is that it answers the question of whether or not an intervention should be carried out at all. By contrast, CUA takes the budget devoted to health care as given, failing to provide guidance as to how this budget should be set.

2.5.2 Social Welfare and QALYs

In Section 2.4.4.3, we discussed how Social Welfare Analysis can be used to evaluate health care interventions. This method is based on the concept of a *Bergson-Samuelson welfare function*,

$$W = W(U_1, ..., U_n).$$

It was shown that Social Welfare Analysis generally differs from Cost-Benefit Analysis.[41] Whereas CBA simply sums up WTP, Social Welfare Analysis requires to consider separately each person's WTP and her or his contribution to financing a health-improving measure. To obtain the change in social welfare, these have to be weighted by social marginal utility of income, MU_i. Generalizing equation (2.47) to a population with n individuals, the social welfare rule for the adoption of a medical intervention is

$$SB \equiv \underbrace{\sum_{i=1}^{n} MU_i \text{WTP}_i}_{\text{social benefit}} > \underbrace{\sum_{i=1}^{n} MU_i \alpha_i K}_{\text{social cost}} \equiv SC, \tag{2.56}$$

where α_i denotes person i's share in financing the cost K of the intervention. In the following, we analyze how Social Welfare Analysis can be performed using QALYs. In particular, we examine how changes in QALYs and contributions to financing should be weighted.

Assume that QALYs are an argument of an expected utility function independent of consumption. Preferences are therefore given by equation (2.53). Then social marginal utility of income reads as

$$MU_i \equiv \frac{\partial W}{\partial U_i} \frac{\partial U_i}{\partial y_i} = \frac{\partial W}{\partial U_i} b'(y_i) \text{QALYs}_i, \tag{2.57}$$

with U_i being equal to EU_i in the present context. Using the individual's WTP for a health care intervention derived in (2.55), one therefore obtains the following approximation for social benefit

$$SB = \sum_{i=1}^{n} \frac{\partial W}{\partial U_i} b'(y_i) \text{QALYs}_i \times \text{WTP}_i \approx \sum_{i=1}^{n} \frac{\partial W}{\partial U_i} b(y_i) \Delta \text{QALYs}_i.$$

Likewise, (2.57) implies that social cost is given by

$$SC = \sum_{i=1}^{n} \frac{\partial W}{\partial U_i} b'(y_i) \text{QALYs}_i \alpha_i K.$$

---

[41] An exception was the unlikely case that income is optimally distributed according to chosen social welfare function.

Thus, the social welfare rule becomes

$$\sum_{i=1}^{n} \frac{\partial W}{\partial U_i} b(y_i) \Delta QALYs_i > \sum_{i=1}^{n} \frac{\partial W}{\partial U_i} b'(y_i) QALYs_i \alpha_i K. \tag{2.58}$$

To obtain further results, it is necessary to specify the social welfare function. Let us first consider the utilitarian social welfare function $W = \sum_i U_i$ which implies $\partial W / \partial U_i = 1$. The rule for financing a health-care measure is then given by

$$\sum_{i=1}^{n} b(y_i) \Delta QALYs_i > \sum_{i=1}^{n} b'(y_i) QALYs_i \alpha_i K. \tag{2.59}$$

Imposing the standard assumption of diminishing marginal utility of income, $b''(y) < 0$, one finds that

(a) health improvements should be valued more highly for high-income individuals (because of $b'(y) > 0$). This follows from the utility function (2.53) which implies that health and consumption are complements. Furthermore, it does not matter whether a person is initially healthy or not as measured by the initial QALY endowment. This follows from the linearity of the utility function (2.53) in QALYs.

(b) the financial contribution $\alpha_i K$ has a higher impact on social cost if individuals have low income. Due to diminishing marginal utility, the loss of utility for these individuals is larger. The contributions of those with a high QALY endowment, i.e., high initial health, also receive more weight in social cost. Again, this is a consequence of the complementarity of health and consumption.

The judgment that health improvements are more valuable for those with high income while those with better health should be given more weight in social cost will not be shared by most people. This can mean that utilitarianism, which is more widely accepted in matters of pure income distribution, does not express people's value judgments in a wider context. Alternatively, the problem may lie in the particular shape of the utility function (2.53), which expresses linearity in QALYs and complementarity of QALYs and consumption.

Instead of giving up the utility function (2.53), we now look at different aggregation rules which express aversion to inequalities not only in income but also in utility. Consider the social welfare function

$$W = \frac{1}{1-\rho} \sum_{i=1}^{n} U_i^{1-\rho}, \quad \rho \geq 0, \rho \neq 1.^{42} \tag{2.60}$$

The parameter ρ can be interpreted as a measure for the aversion to inequality in utilities. For $\rho = 0$, inequalities in utilities do not matter and one obtains the utilitarian social welfare function. With positive values of ρ, social welfare becomes averse to utility inequalities.[43] As ρ goes to infinity, the social welfare function approaches the maximin case $W = \min\{U_1, ..., U_n\}$.

---

[42] For $\rho = 1$, social welfare can be defined as $W = \sum_i \ln U_i$.
[43] In the two-person case, welfare indifference curves in the utility space become convex.

From the social welfare function (2.60), one obtains that marginal social utility $\partial W/\partial U_i = U_i^{-\rho}$ is isoelastic in U_i: a one percent increase in U_i leads to ρ percent decrease in marginal social utility. Thus, individuals with low total utility are given more weight. This increases the weight of individuals with low income and a low QALY endowment in social benefit and cost. Using (2.53) yields

$$\frac{\partial W}{\partial U_i} = U_i^{-\rho} = b(y_i)^{-\rho} \text{QALYs}_i^{-\rho}.$$

Inserting in (2.58) leads to the social welfare rule

$$\sum_{i=1}^{n} b(y_i)^{1-\rho} \text{QALYs}_i^{-\rho} \Delta \text{QALYs}_i > \sum_{i=1}^{n} b'(y_i) b(y_i)^{-\rho} \text{QALYs}_i^{1-\rho} \alpha_i K. \qquad (2.61)$$

With the utilitarian rule as a reference case ($\rho = 0$), we find with regard to social benefit (left-hand side)

- for $\rho > 0$, individuals with low health are given more weight.
- for $\rho > 1$, health improvements for those with low income are valued higher.

Concerning social cost (right-hand side), we observe

- a reinforced emphasis on low-income individuals if $\rho > 0$. The factor $b(y_i)^{-\rho}$ gives their contribution a higher weight apart from diminishing marginal utility.
- for $\rho > 1$, a higher weight for individuals with low initial health.

With aversion to inequalities in utility, the results therefore seem to conform much better to widely held value judgments. If this aversion is high ($\rho > 1$), then low-income and low-health individuals receive more weight in social benefit as well as social cost.

From a practical point of view, Social Welfare Analysis calls for considering the distribution of income and health in economic evaluation. This makes the analysis more difficult. A pragmatic approach would be to identify particular groups who show significant differences with respect to health and income. Furthermore, note that social cost is also influenced by the way health care is financed, here the share of cost α_i which is financed by individual i. These shares are also policy variables which can be optimized.

Conclusion 2.17. *Social Welfare Analysis based on QALYs can be employed if these are an argument of an expected utility function independent of consumption. How changes in QALYs and contributions to financing should be weighted according to income and initial health depends on the particular social welfare function assumed. If aversion to inequality in utilities is sufficiently high, low-income and low-health individuals should be given more weight in both respects.*

2.6 Summary

(1) Cost-Effectiveness Analysis (CEA) only serves for a comparison of measures with uni-dimensional effects. Cost-Utility Analysis (CUA) also allows comparisons among measures with several heterogeneous effects. To indicate whether a measure is desirable, both methods require a fixed budget for health care. By contrast, Cost-Benefit Analysis (CBA) provides an evaluation of life and health in terms of money and thus permits to assess every project separately.

(2) The concept of 'quality-adjusted life years' (QALYs) allows to make changes in the quality of life and changes of the length of life comparable. A decision-theoretic analysis based on expected utility theory shows that the concept of QALYs requires several assumptions, viz. preferences for health states must be stable over the whole life cycle, there must be risk neutrality with respect to length of life, and preferences must obey the 'zero-condition'. To some extent, it is possible to relax these assumptions. Taking into account that utility depends not only on health but also on consumption, further assumptions are necessary to ascertain that QALYs capture all health-related benefits in a scalar index.

(3) Cost-Utility Analysis is not compatible with a welfarist position, which claims that collective decisions should be based on total utility of the affected persons. The use of QALYs can, however, be justified with an extra-welfarist position, according to which only health – as measured by QALYs – is relevant for particular collective decisions. The principle of maximization of QALYs can be criticized on the grounds that the distribution of QALYs should also play a role.

(4) If preferences of respondents satisfy the assumptions of the QALY model, with utility linear in length of life, the time trade-off and the standard-gamble methods lead to an analogous result in that they measure the utility weights of respective health states on a scale ranging from 0 (death) to 1 (perfect health). The standard-gamble method, however, is more general because it does not require utility to be linear in remaining length of life. By contrast, the rating scale method is less suitable since it lacks a utility-theoretic basis.

(5) In Cost-Benefit Analysis (CBA), a money value is assigned to an improvement in length or quality of life. To achieve this, two entirely different concepts have been developed, the human-capital approach and the willingness-to-pay approach. According to the human-capital approach, the value of life is determined by the contribution the individual could make to the social product. Its relatively easy application is outweighed by serious economic and ethical shortcomings. In contrast to the human-capital approach, the willingness-to-pay approach is based on the concept of subjective utility.

(6) Cost-Benefit Analysis can be justified by the potential Pareto criterion. However, the problem with this standard is that Pareto improvements may only be hypothetical. When a whole set of measures is to be evaluated, overall Pareto improvement can be achieved, provided that the net benefits do not differ systematically among the affected persons. From the point of view of Social Welfare

Analysis, CBA can only be applied if the income distribution is deemed optimal. Otherwise, net benefits must be weighted by social marginal utility of income.

(7) There are two alternative approaches to WTP measurement. According to the stated-preference method, surveys are used to determine respondents' WTP. The method of 'revealed preference' infers willingness to pay from the individuals' market behavior.

(8) To determine WTP using stated preferences, there are again two alternatives. The Contingent Valuation Method uses questionnaires or personal interviews to ask participants directly for their WTP for a good or program. Discrete Choice Experiments, by contrast, attempts to interpolate an indifference curve by confronting respondents with a series of choices between the status quo and an alternative with changed attributes. Considerable variation and widespread inconsistencies in results suggest that the Contingent Valuation Method lacks reliability when applied to WTP for risk reduction. Discrete Choice Experiments impose restrictive assumptions regarding preferences which still need to be tested.

(9) Measuring WTP on the basis of market data has the advantage of relying on real rather than hypothetical decisions. This method, however, has its problems as well. In particular, one needs to make sure that individuals know the relevant risks and to single out preferences as a determinant of observed behavior.

(10) Cost-Utility Analysis and Cost-Benefit Analysis differ not only technically but, above all, in how they incorporate the welfare of those affected. CUA focuses on health, CBA on utility. They are therefore based on different value judgments.

(11) Individuals' marginal willingness to pay for a QALY depends on their disposable income and their initial QALY endowment. Unless there is no systematic relationship between the marginal willingness to pay for a QALY and the additional number of QALYs gained, group-specific values of willingness to pay for a QALY and of the numbers of QALYs gained must be determined. In general, Cost-Benefit Analysis leads to different recommendations than Cost-Utility Analysis.

(12) Social Welfare Analysis based on QALYs can be employed if these are an argument of an expected utility function independent of consumption. How changes in QALYs and contributions to financing should be weighted according to income and initial health depends on the particular social welfare function. If aversion to inequality in utilities is sufficiently high, low-income and low-health individuals should be given more weight in both respects.

2.7 Further Reading

For a detailed description of evaluation methods in health economics, we recommend DRUMMOND ET AL. (2005) and JOHANNESSON (1996). In the HANDBOOK OF HEALTH ECONOMICS, articles by HURLEY (2000), GARBER (2000), DOLAN (2000) and WILLIAMS AND COOKSON (2000) deal with the issues of this chapter.

2.E Exercises

2.1. What do the approaches to economic evaluation presented in Section 2.2 have in common? What are the differences?

2.2. Discuss possible equity concerns in economic evaluation. How can they be addressed?

2.3. What are the strengths and weaknesses of the QALY concept?

2.4. Discuss the pros and cons of the different approaches to measure willingness to pay.

2.5. Consider the following independent health care interventions A to E:

Intervention	Cost in €000	Gain in QALYs
A	300	10
B	380	20
C	600	25
D	720	40
E	500	10

(a) Assume that the budget for health care interventions is €2 million.

 (i) Rank the interventions according to the ACURs.

 (ii) Use your result from (i) to determine which interventions should be implemented to maximize the total gain in QALYs.

 (iii) Consider a new intervention F which is mutually exclusive with intervention B. It generates 28 QALYs at a cost of €700,000. Calculate the ACUR and the ICUR of intervention F. Show that it is optimal not to adopt F even though its ACUR is lower than the ACUR of another intervention which should be used. Explain your result.

(b) Consider again interventions A to E and suppose that the budget is €1.4 million.

 (i) Assume that all interventions can be scaled down proportionally without any restrictions. Use the ACUR-ranking to determine which interventions should be implemented to maximize the total gain in QALYs.

 (ii) Which interventions should be implemented if C is indivisible? Explain your result and comment on the limitation of using a ranking according to cost-utility ratios.

2.6. Consider the following mutually exclusive health care interventions A to E:

Intervention	Cost in €000	Gain in QALYs
A	300	20
B	460	22
C	600	30
D	780	32
E	1,000	40

All interventions can be scaled down proportionally without any restrictions. Show that a combination of other interventions always dominates interventions B and D. Relate your result to the ICURs of interventions B and D.

2.7. Consider again the mutually exclusive health care interventions A to E given in Exercise 2.6 and assume a unique willingness to pay for a QALY. Determine the optimal intervention according to Cost-Benefit Analysis for a willingness to pay of (i) €20,000, (ii) €37,500 and (iii) €50,000 per QALY using

(a) the net benefit method;

(b) incremental cost-benefit ratios.

Comment on your result.

2.8. Suppose an individual has an expected utility function compatible with the QALY model. There are three possible health states $H_h; h = 1,2,3$ with probabilities π_h. Health state h yields constant utility $u(H_h)$ until death, which occurs after T_h periods. The following table describes the initial situation,

h	$u(H_h)$	π_h	T_h
1	0.2	0.1	3
2	0.5	0.2	5
3	0.8	0.7	7

(a) Determine the number of QALYs and life expectancy in the initial situation.

(b) Determine the change in QALYs due to measures A, B und C with the following effects.

   A: a reduction of life expectancy in state 1 by 2 periods and in state 2 by 1 period, respectively, combined with an increase in life expectancy in state 3 by 2 periods.

B: a reduction in the probabilities of states 1 and 3 by 0.05 each, combined with an increase by 0.1, for state 2.

C: a reduction in life expectancy in state 1 by 2 periods, an increase in life expectancy in state 3 by 1 period, reductions in the probability of state 1 by 0.05 and of state 3 by 0.15 respectively, and an increase in the probability of state 2 by 0.2.

2.9. Suppose expected utility of an individual can be expressed by the function

$$\sum_{t=1}^{2} \sum_{h=1}^{2} \pi_{h,t} y_t^{0.5} u(H_h)$$

and assume that $y_1 = 25$, $y_2 = 4$, $u(H_1) = 0.4$ and $u(H_2) = 0.6$.

(a) For the values $\pi_{1,1} = \pi_{1,2} = \pi_{2,1} = \pi_{2,2} = 0.5$, determine expected utility and number QALYs of the individual.

(b) Now assume $\pi_{1,1} = 0.6$, $\pi_{2,1} = 0.4$, $\pi_{1,2} = 0.3$ and $\pi_{2,2} = 0.7$. Again determine expected utility and QALYs of the individual. Compare your result with part (a) and explain the difference.

2.10. Suppose expected utility of individual i with survival probability σ_i and income y_i is given by

$$EU_i = \sigma_i (y_i)^{0.5},$$

i.e., utility in case of death is zero. There are two individuals A and B, who differ only in their incomes, with $y_A = 1000$, and $y_B = 500$. In the initial situation, probability of survival is 90 percent for both. An intervention which costs $K = 64$ raises survival probability to 92 percent.

(a) Is this intervention supported by an unweighted CUA?

(b) How must the intervention be financed in order to achieve a Pareto improvement?

(c) Suppose social welfare is defined by $W = EU_A + EU_B$. Each individual has to bear one-half of the cost.

(i) Determine social welfare with and without the intervention.

(ii) Determine the approximate weights for a CBA that correctly indicate an increase in social welfare.

2.11. Suppose there are two individuals $i = A, B$ with income y_i and initial QALY endowment $QALYs_i$. Expected utility of individual i is given by

$$EU_i = \ln(y_i)QALYs_i.$$

A health care intervention with cost $K = 50$ leads to an increase in $QALYs_i$ by $\Delta QALYs_i$. Individual A has income $y_A = 200$, a QALY endowment $QALYs_A = 100$ and benefits by $\Delta QALYs_A = 1$. For individual B consider the following three scenarios (i) to (iii):

	(i)	(ii)	(iii)
y_B	200	200	100
$QALYs_B$	50	50	100
$\Delta QALYs_B$	2	1	6

For each scenario, determine the result of CBA

(a) based on individual willingness to pay as given by equation (2.55).

(b) based on average marginal willingness to pay, i.e., calculate total willingness to pay using the formula

$$(MWTPQ_A + MWTPQ_B)/2 \times (\Delta QALYs_A + \Delta QALYs_B).$$

Discuss your results.

2.12. Suppose there are two individuals $i = A, B$ with income y_i and initial QALY endowment $QALYs_i$. Expected utility of individual i is given by

$$EU_i = \ln(y_i)QALYs_i.$$

A health care intervention increases $QALYs_i$ by $\Delta QALYs_i$. Each person finances half of the cost K of the intervention. Consider the following four scenarios (i) to (iv):

	(i)	(ii)	(iii)	(iv)
y_A	100	100	50	100
$QALYs_A$	50	50	100	120
$\Delta QALYs_A$	1	1	5	1
y_B	100	200	200	200
$QALYs_B$	100	100	100	100
$\Delta QALYs_B$	1	2	1	1
K	13	30	20	12

For each scenario, determine the result of CBA, a Social Welfare Analysis based on a utilitarian welfare function, and a Social Welfare Analysis using the function (2.60) with $\rho = 0.5$. Discuss your results.

3

Individuals as Producers of Their Health

3.1 Introduction

"Health is not everything in life, but without health, life is nothing". This proverb points to the dual property of health.

(1) *Health is a highly valued asset.* Sometimes it is even claimed that health is the only thing which counts in life. The first part of the proverb reminds us that other values and goals do exist in life, yet, compared with health, they rank lower on the *preference scale* of most people. While this priority of health is accepted as a fact in the following section, it does not rule out that health risks (i.e., an increased probability of poor health) are taken in order to achieve other goals.

(2) *Health is a prerequisite for other activities.* The second part of the proverb points to health as a precondition for success in other activities. Poor health limits the *production capabilities* of the affected person, including his or her ability to enjoy the good things of life (apart from health). In particular, consumption services do not flow automatically from consumer goods but require a great deal of time, knowledge and skills, all of which can be impaired by a poor state of health.

An aspect not included in the proverb cited above is that health can be 'produced'. Health economists, however, have adopted this idea, which is mirrored in the title of this chapter. Not so long ago, good health was considered to be a gift of God and poor health to be simply bad luck. The successes of modern medicine have fostered the conviction that almost everyone can reach a good state of health, provided one uses the appropriate means. However, if health is perceived as being produced, the question of the *producer* arises immediately. Even though much of healing continues to be attributed to physicians, it cannot be denied that every healing process ultimately begins in the psyche and body of the individual concerned. The fact that many illnesses heal spontaneously also lends support to the view that individuals are the ultimate producers of their health.

P. Zweifel et al., *Health Economics*, 2nd ed., DOI 10.1007/978-3-540-68540-1_3,
© Springer-Verlag Berlin Heidelberg 2009

The expression 'producer of health'or even 'health production' must not mask the fact that individuals (with or without the help of a physician) can only influence their state of health but not effectively determine it. Apart from hereditary and environmental factors, chance may always annihilate one's efforts to preserve or improve health. Thus, large, unexpected changes in health can occur at any time.

The latter part of the proverb, "Without health, life is nothing", refers to the second property of health. Good health is a precondition for success in other activities. Evidently, good health contributes to the production of consumable services because the better the state of health, the more time available for income-generating or health-enhancing activities.

The aim of this chapter is to analyze the production of health (or more generally, health behavior) as an optimizing problem, taking account of the peculiarities just mentioned. The focus will be on answering the following questions:

(a) From the individual's point of view, what are the conditions which determine the *optimal resource allocation* between health and other goods?

(b) Can the often volatile pattern of behavior ("Sinning against health as long as health is good, sacrificing everything for health when health is bad") be brought into line with *rationality*? Or are individual preferences indeed inconsistent, implying that medical experts should perhaps determine the appropriate amount of preventive measures?

(c) Can the economic concept of *substitution* be applied to health production, even though situations can easily be envisaged in which only medical services (rather than one's own health-enhancing efforts) offer the prospect of improvement?

With these questions in the background, we will present models of health production. This will then serve as a basis for interpreting empirical studies in Chapter 4. Section 3.2 is devoted to critical objections to the application of the economic production concept to health. In Section 3.3 we deal with the case of a deterministic influence on health, which is viewed as a capital stock. In an attempt to alleviate these concerns, a stochastic formulation is proposed in Section 3.4 which assumes that individuals (and their physician) can do no more than marginally influence the probability of transition from one health state to another. Willingness to pay for improved chances of health is derived in this short-run context. Subsequently a model of state-dependent production is presented. If healthy in the current period, individuals may themselves enhance health through activities; once they are ill however, their only chance for recovery is to rely on medical care. From this it can be seen that the opportunity costs of 'better health' are state-dependent, which could also explain the volatile nature of health behavior mentioned above.

3.2 The Concept of Health Production

For economic laymen it is strange, perhaps even offensive, to talk of health production. Associating the concept of production with methods of cultivation in agriculture and in particular with production processes in industry, they may immediately point to at least two peculiarities that seem to set health and health care apart from production as commonly understood.

- *Lack of control.* Production processes in agriculture and industry can be controlled to a large extent. If farmers expect a future increase in demand, they usually produce on inventory; if they expect a drop in demand, they will limit production or reduce stock. The process of producing health seems to lack this type of control.
- *Lack of tradability.* The output of production is usually sold to a third party. In the case of health, such a sale would be conceivable only in a slave economy, in that a higher price would be obtained for a healthy slave than for a sick one. In today's societies, a higher wage can be obtained by a healthy worker. However, the wage rate depends on other factors as well, not least the skills of the individual. These skills are not transferable either, posing an additional challenge to non-economists who are reluctant to view education as the 'production of skills'.

While these objections are not without merit, they are not as strong as they may appear. In the first place, lack of complete control over the production process does not preclude the existence of a systematic relationship between inputs and outputs. The fact that harvest yield in agriculture in a given year crucially depends on the weather does not rule out that increased use of fertilizer generally increases the yield, and farmers behave in accordance with this. In the same way, efforts taken to maintain health can be considered as inputs in a production process. While they do not always help to avoid illness, on the whole they do contribute to better health.

Part of the lack of control is the apparent perishability of the finished product 'health'. However, both health and education may be viewed as *invisible capital stocks*, which are augmented by investment, provide services, and are subject to depreciation [see Section 3.3]. In the case of health, for instance the QALYs of Section 2.3.2 can be considered as the service flowing from health capital. For education capital, the service would be an increase in wage income. The annual holiday, and more generally a lifestyle that avoids excessive demands on one's health, corresponds to an investment in health. If a loss in health capital ('depreciation') occurs in the wake of illness, then the health stock of an individual who has previously invested in his or her health is still higher than those of another. It is a known fact that rested people withstand most illnesses better than over-tired people, non-smokers better than smokers, those of normal weight better than those of overweight. Thus, while 'producing on inventory' cannot be directly observed, the concept of production need not be dismissed out of hand.

Lack of tradability of the produced good seems to present another obstacle for adopting the concept of a production process or a production function. However, individuals trade with themselves as it were. Indeed, they trade off better health against something else of value. They hardly have to give up money as a rule because medical services in most industrialized countries are almost free, thanks to comprehensive health insurance. However, they must still sacrifice something, such as consumption of alcohol, tobacco or food and in particular time that could be used for other purposes. On the other hand, applying the concept of production, or more precisely, of a production function, to health has considerable advantages.

(1) *Optimality conditions as a point of reference.* Production has a cost, and the cost resulting from securing better health can be compared to the marginal cost of other goods produced by individuals, in particular consumption services. In an optimal state, the marginal cost of health relative to the marginal cost of consumption should be equal to the individual's marginal willingness to pay for health relative to consumption. The relative (marginal) willingness to pay for health can be determined in principle using the model of Section 2.4.3, and it can be compared to the relative marginal cost. There is reason to expect a discrepancy between the two ratios, since the marginal willingness to pay in the health care sector may be distorted both by health insurance (*moral hazard*) and the physician (*supplier-induced demand*) (see Chapters 6 and 8), while negotiated fees for medical services do not have much in common with their true marginal costs.

(2) *Relative marginal productivity of inputs.* The concept of the production function comprises the notion that different inputs make different contributions to the resulting output. One such input are medical services, whose true marginal cost can be extremely high in today's health care systems. The huge expenditure on medical care can only be justified, from the economist's viewpoint, if it is characterized by a very high marginal productivity compared to other inputs in the production of health. In this context, it should be noted that, for example, an improvement of environmental quality could perhaps have a greater marginal productivity in terms of health (measured, e.g., in QALYs, see Section 2.3.2), than a continued increase in health care expenditure.

These advantages may on the whole justify applying the economic concept of the production function to health.

Conclusion 3.1. *The fact that the health status of a person importantly depends on chance and that health is perishable and lacks tradability does not rule out considering health as being the result of a production process. Moreover, using the concept of a production function one is able to assess the optimality of individual behavior and the efficient use of scarce resources.*

3.3 Health as Part of Human Capital

If one is to accept the economist's view of health as an asset capable of being produced, then health production can be viewed as an investment which makes up for the capital consumption owing to aging and lifestyle, possibly even resulting in a net increase of the capital stock 'health'. Investment is achieved by the input of (curative) medical services and of one's own effort, in particular on prevention. The return on the stock of health capital is spending less time in bad health. Healthy time gained can increase utility directly or indirectly due to higher labor income and thus higher consumption. Rational individuals will maximize utility by the optimal management of their stock of health over lifetime. GROSSMAN (1972b) investigated this dynamic optimization problem using optimal control theory. In the following, a simplified version of his model is presented. The planning period comprises just two rather than T periods. The main implications of the model still follow, and they can be pitted against empirical evidence. An alternative formulation that emphasizes the limited control individuals have over their health will be laid out in Section 3.4.

3.3.1 A Simplified Grossman Model

Consider an individual with a planning horizon of two time periods. During each period he or she experiences a nonnegative amount of sick time t^s, which is the lower the larger health stock H. In other words, healthy time constitutes the nontradable return of the unobserved stock of health. The individual derives positive utility from consumption goods X while deriving disutility from sick time $t^s(H)$. The utility function defined over these arguments is assumed to be time independent, i.e., the marginal rate of substitution between sick time and consumption does not change with aging. Future utility is discounted by a subjective factor $\beta \leq 1$. Thus, the individual maximizes discounted utility u (see also Box 3.1),

$$u = U\left(t^s(H_0), X_0\right) + \beta U\left(t^s(H_1), X_1\right), \tag{3.1}$$

$$\frac{\partial U}{\partial t^s} < 0, \frac{\partial^2 U}{\partial (t^s)^2} > 0, \frac{\partial U}{\partial X} > 0, \frac{\partial^2 U}{\partial X^2} < 0, \frac{\partial t^s}{\partial H} < 0.$$

The crucial component of the Grossman model is the equation that defines the change in the health stock over time. On the one hand, health capital depreciates at a rate δ, causing health to worsen over time. Although the notation does not tell for simplicity, the rate of depreciation δ is not constant.[1] On the other hand, the individual can increase health capital by investing I. This involves the purchase of medical services M or spending t^I units of time on preventive effort. In all, one has

$$H_1 = H_0(1 - \delta) + I(M_0, t^I), \tag{3.2}$$

$$\frac{\partial I}{\partial M} > 0, \frac{\partial^2 I}{\partial M^2} < 0, \frac{\partial I}{\partial t^I} > 0, \frac{\partial^2 I}{\partial (t^I)^2} < 0.$$

---

[1] At a minimum, δ increases with age. It can also depend positively or negatively on consumption X, representing the influence of lifestyle on health.

Equation (3.2) constitutes a constraint that will enter the individual's maximization problem. However, there is not only a change in health over time but also in wealth and wisdom (i.e., skills). In particular, savings S_0 achieved in the first period are available for consumption in the second period. Savings yield interest r to become RS_0, with $R \equiv 1 + r$. By equation (3.2), investment in health occurs during the initial period only.[2]

Abstracting from health insurance, this means that health care expenditure amounting to pM to be financed out of labor income or initial wealth A_0, with w_0 denoting the wage rate of the initial period and p denoting the price of medical care. By way of contrast, consumption (at price c) must be positive in both periods. Total time available is normalized at 1 in both periods. Altogether, the following budget constraint holds after discounting to present value,

$$A_0 + w_0 \left(1 - t^s(H_0) - t^I\right) + \frac{w_1(1 - t_1^s(H_1))}{R} = pM + cX_0 + \frac{cX_1}{R}. \tag{3.3}$$

To solve this maximization problem, consider the Lagrangian function,

$$\begin{aligned}
\mathcal{L}(H_1, t^I, M, X_0, X_1) &= U[t^s(H_0), X_0] + \beta U[t^s(H_1), X_1] \\
&\quad + \mu[H_0(1 - \delta) + I(M, t^I) - H_1] \\
&\quad + \lambda \Bigg[A_0 + w_0 \left(1 - t^s(H_0) - t^I\right) + \frac{w_1(1 - t_1^s(H_1))}{R} \\
&\quad - pM - cX_0 - \frac{cX_1}{R} \Bigg].
\end{aligned}$$

The Lagrangian multipliers $\mu, \lambda > 0$ indicate the extent to which a relaxation of the pertinent constraints would improve the achievement of the overall objective as measured by discounted utility.[3] First-order conditions for an interior optimum are obtained by setting the derivatives with respect to all decision variables equal to zero. The derivatives with respect to μ and λ simply ensure that the constraints (3.2) and (3.3) are satisfied; they will not be reported. Treating H_0 as predetermined, one obtains

$$\frac{\partial \mathcal{L}}{\partial H_1} = \beta \frac{\partial U}{\partial t^s} \frac{\partial t^s}{\partial H_1} - \frac{\lambda}{R} w_1 \frac{\partial t^s}{\partial H_1} - \mu = 0 \tag{3.4}$$

$$\frac{\partial \mathcal{L}}{\partial t^I} = \mu \frac{\partial I}{\partial t^I} - \lambda w_0 = 0 \tag{3.5}$$

$$\frac{\partial \mathcal{L}}{\partial M} = \mu \frac{\partial I}{\partial M} - \lambda p = 0 \tag{3.6}$$

$$\frac{\partial \mathcal{L}}{\partial X_0} = \frac{\partial U}{\partial X_0} - \lambda c = 0 \tag{3.7}$$

$$\frac{\partial \mathcal{L}}{\partial X_1} = \beta \frac{\partial U}{\partial X_1} - \frac{\lambda}{R} c = 0. \tag{3.8}$$

---

[2] In a formulation comprising more than one period, one would have periods where net investment in health is zero or negative ($M_t \leq 0, t_t^I \leq 0$ but $\delta_t > 0$).

[3] In the multi-period optimal control formulation, the Lagrangian multipliers change over time. For example, if the individual failed to invest in health during period t, the value of μ_{t+1} is increased because the health capital constraint has become more binding.

Box 3.1. A Simplified Grossman Model

$$u = U\left(t^s(H_0), X_0\right) + \beta U\left(t^s(H_1), X_1\right), \tag{3.1}$$

$$\frac{\partial U}{\partial t^s} < 0, \frac{\partial^2 U}{\partial (t^s)^2} > 0, \frac{\partial U}{\partial X} > 0, \frac{\partial^2 U}{\partial X^2} < 0, \frac{\partial t^s}{\partial H} < 0$$

$$H_1 = H_0(1-\delta) + I(M, t^I) \tag{3.2}$$

$$\frac{\partial I}{\partial M} > 0, \frac{\partial^2 I}{\partial M^2} < 0, \frac{\partial I}{\partial t^I} > 0, \frac{\partial^2 I}{\partial (t^I)^2} < 0$$

$$-\beta \frac{\partial t^s}{\partial H_1}\left[\frac{w_1}{c}\frac{\partial U}{\partial X_1} - \frac{\partial U}{\partial t^s}\right] = \frac{\partial U/\partial X_0}{\partial I/\partial M}\frac{p}{c} \tag{3.13}$$

U:	utility
H:	stock of health capital
δ:	rate of the depreciation of the health stock
w:	wage rate
X:	consumption goods
c:	unit price of consumption goods
M:	medical services
p:	unit price of medical services
I:	investment in health (in units of quantity)
t^s:	sick time
t^I:	time invested in favor of health
λ, μ:	Lagrangian multipliers

These conditions can be made easier to interpret. First, dividing equation (3.5) by equation (3.6) yields

$$\frac{\partial I/\partial t^I}{\partial I/\partial M} = \frac{w_0}{p}. \tag{3.9}$$

Second, dividing equation (3.7) by equation (3.8) yields

$$\frac{\partial U/\partial X_0}{\partial U/\partial X_1} = \beta R. \tag{3.10}$$

Equation (3.4) may be rewritten by solving (3.8) for λ/R,

$$-\beta \frac{\partial t^s}{\partial H_1}\left[\frac{w_1}{c}\frac{\partial U}{\partial X_1} - \frac{\partial U}{\partial t^s}\right] = \mu. \tag{3.11}$$

Using (3.6) and (3.7), one obtains

$$\mu = \frac{\partial U/\partial X_0}{\partial I/\partial M}\frac{p}{c}. \tag{3.12}$$

Substituting (3.12) in (3.11) yields

$$-\beta \frac{\partial t^s}{\partial H_1} \left[\frac{w_1}{c} \frac{\partial U}{\partial X_1} - \frac{\partial U}{\partial t^s} \right] = \frac{\partial U/\partial X_0}{\partial I/\partial M} \frac{p}{c}. \tag{3.13}$$

This condition requires the marginal utility of an investment in health to be equal to its marginal cost. Its left-hand side may be interpreted as follows.

- *Effectiveness as a precondition.* For the investment in health to have a positive payoff, it must reduce sick time. A negative value of $\partial t^s/\partial H_1$, in combination with the positive values of the terms in the large parentheses, results in a positive value of the left-hand side of condition (3.13), indicating positive marginal utility.

- *Valuation of health as a consumption good.* The reduction of lost sick time (and hence gain of healthy time) increases utility directly since $\partial U/\partial t^s < 0$. Subjectively discounted, this benefit from utility amounts to $\beta \partial U/\partial t^s$. Versions of condition (3.13) which only involve the first component of the marginal utility of an investment in health are called *pure consumption models*.

- *Valuation of health as an investment good.* The reduction of sick time has an immediate impact on wealth through $-\beta(\partial t^s/\partial H_1)$ and the real wage rate (w_1/c). This is valued according to $\partial U/\partial X_1$, the marginal utility of the extra consumption goods that can be purchased. Thus, even if sick time is not disliked for its own sake, investment in health has a return in terms of added labor income and wealth. Since health then becomes a commodity that is not valued per se but only for its impact on wealth, versions of condition (3.13) retaining only this second component are known as *pure investment models*.

The right-hand side of condition (3.13) reflects the marginal cost of holding an additional unit of health stock. It may be interpreted as follows.

- The marginal utility $(\partial U/\partial X_0)$ indicates the subjective loss suffered from foregoing consumption in favor of health.

- However, this loss is mitigated to the extent that the medical services purchased are highly effective $(\partial I/\partial M$ large).

- Finally, this productivity must be deflated by the price of medical care p because the investment in health brings but few units of M if p is high. Likewise, the actual utility loss from sacrificed consumption must be deflated by the price c of consumer goods, since with a high c, only few units of X_0 are actually given up.

Conclusion 3.2. *In the Grossman model, health and wealth constitute two interrelated assets. Their values are optimally managed over time by the individual. In the case of health, the marginal utility of holding an extra unit of the stock has a consumption and an investment component. Their sum has to be equal to marginal cost associated with holding an additional unit of health stock.*

3.3.2 The Demand for Health and Medical Services

Based on the Grossman model, one can derive demand functions with respect to health and medical services. However, this requires specific functional forms to be imposed both on the utility function and the functions $t^s(H_1)$ and $I(M,t^l)$. In spite of its limitations, a Cobb-Douglas function is usually assumed for $t^s(H_1)$ and $I(M,t^l)$. According to the Cobb-Douglas technology, health investments I are generated by medical services M and the individual's own input of time t^l. In addition, a higher level of education E is assumed to increase the efficiency of the investment. Furthermore, a number of specific assumptions with respect to the parameters of the model need to be made. In the following, we assume $\beta = R = \delta = 1$, i.e., no discounting, a zero interest rate, and full depreciation of health capital. These assumptions allow us to derive demand functions which are in line with the multi-period Grossman model. In the extended model, weaker but nevertheless still questionable assumptions need to be imposed. In the following, we use the specification by WAGSTAFF (1986b) as a point of reference.

3.3.2.1 The Structural Demand Function for Medical Services

The structural demand function for medical services gives the cost-minimizing demand for medical services for given (not necessarily optimal) health capital H_1. To derive an explicit form, one needs to specify the investment function $I(M,t^l)$. It is assumed to be of the Cobb-Douglas type,

$$I = M^{\alpha_M}(t^l)^{1-\alpha_M}e^{\alpha_E E}, \quad 0 < \alpha_M < 1, \ \alpha_F > 0. \tag{3.14}$$

Note that education E serves to magnify the effects of medical services M and time spent in favor of health t^l. Its effectiveness is measured by $\alpha_E > 0$. α_M and $(1 - \alpha_M)$ are the production elasticities of M and t^l. In Appendix 3.A.1, it is shown that given the investment function (3.14) cost-minimization gives rise to the *structural demand function for medical services*

$$\ln M = const. + \ln H_1 - (1 - \alpha_M)\ln p + (1 - \alpha_M)\ln w_0 - \alpha_E E \tag{3.15}$$

specified in logarithmic form (like all following demand functions). This equation indicates that a higher health capital is predicted to result in an increasing demand for medical services M, in the guise of a derived demand for a factor of production. The impacts of the exogenous variables p and w_0 can be interpreted as follows (the endogenous variable H_1 is kept constant).

- The higher the price p of medical services, the smaller the quantity demanded. Given only two factors of production, M is substituted by more individual time t^l spent on health.

- The higher the initial wage rate w_0, the higher the demand for medical services (given education E). In view of the increased opportunity cost of time, t^l is substituted by M.

A higher level of education has a negative effect on the demand for medical services in (3.15). Since education increases the productivity of medical services, less medical services are necessary to maintain a given stock of health capital. In the multi-period model, one furthermore finds that the demand for medical services goes up over the life span to the extent that the rate of depreciation δ increases with age [see WAGSTAFF (1986b)].

3.3.2.2 The Demand Functions in the Investment Model

The structural demand function for medical services (3.15) depends on the health capital H_1 which is chosen optimally by the individual. To solve this problem, one first needs to specify how sick time t^s depends on health capital. The following functional form is assumed[4]

$$t^s(H_1) = \theta_1 H_1^{-\theta_2}, \quad \theta_1 > 0, \theta_2 > 0. \tag{3.16}$$

In the pure investment model, health is only valued for its impact on wealth. In Appendix 3.A.1, it is shown that in this case one obtains the *demand function for health*,

$$\ln H_1 = const. - \varepsilon \alpha_M \ln p + \varepsilon \alpha_M \ln w + \varepsilon \alpha_E E, \tag{3.17}$$

with $w \equiv w_0 = w_1$ and $\varepsilon \equiv 1/(\theta_2 + 1) < 1$. The elasticity ε reflects the marginal efficiency of health capital H_1. The predicted partial correlations are the following.

- An increase in the price p of medical services raises the costs of investment in H_1 and thus reduces the optimum quantity of H_1.

- A higher attainable wage level w increases demand for health as a capital good. This effect dominates the increased cost of time, since medical services consume less time than the working time gained. Therefore a rise in the wage rate causes the optimum quantity of H_1 to increase.

- A higher level of education E raises the productivity of investment in health I. Consequently, the optimum quantity of H_1 increases.

In the multi-period model, there is an additional negative age effect if the rate of depreciation δ increases with age, serving to reduce the return of investment in health.

---

[4] Taking logs and differentiating (3.16), one obtains $\partial \ln t^s / \partial \ln H_1 = -\theta_2$. Multiplying both sides by (-1), adding 1 on both sides, and inverting, one has $1/[1 - \partial \ln t^s / \partial \ln H_1] = 1/(\theta_2 + 1) < 1$ which is positive and increasing in $|\partial \ln t^s / \partial \ln H_1|$ as long as $|\partial \ln t^s / \partial \ln H_1| < 1$.

Inserting (3.17) in (3.15) yields the *reduced demand function for medical services*

$$\ln M = const. - (1 + \alpha_M(\varepsilon - 1)) \ln p + (1 + \alpha_M(\varepsilon - 1)) \ln w - (1 - \varepsilon)\alpha_E E. \quad (3.18)$$

In contrast to the structural demand function for health in (3.15), this function depends only on exogenous variables. The predicted partial correlations are identical with those of (3.15). However, $\varepsilon < 1$ implies that the effects of w and p are larger while E has a smaller impact than in (3.15). This is due to the identical signs of p and w and the opposite sign of E in equations (3.15) and (3.17). Likewise, the effect of ageing in the multi-period model is less pronounced.

3.3.2.3 The Demand Functions in the Consumption Model

In order to derive the demand function, assume the following utility function, separable in sick time and consumption goods [see WAGSTAFF (1986b)],

$$U = \alpha_1 (t^s)^{\alpha_2} + g(X), \quad \alpha_1 > 0, 0 < \alpha_2 < 1, g'(X) > 0, g''(X) < 0. \quad (3.19)$$

In Appendix 3.A.1, the following *demand function for health* is derived,

$$\ln H_1 = const. - \kappa \alpha_M \ln p - \kappa (1 - \alpha_M) \ln w + \kappa \alpha_E E - \kappa \ln \lambda \quad (3.20)$$

with $\kappa \equiv 1/(1 + \alpha_2 \theta_2) < 1$ measuring the elasticity of marginal utility of less sick time with respect to health stock H_1. The predicted partial correlations are as follows.

- Contrary to the investment model, a higher wage rate w affects the production of health merely as an expense factor; its sign is therefore negative.

- A higher price p of medical care increases the cost of holding a unit of health stock, resulting in less demand.

- More education lowers the marginal cost of health through its productivity-increasing effect on investment in health, resulting in more demand.

- A high value of the Lagrangian multiplier λ indicates that the wealth constraint is strongly binding, causing the opportunity cost of holding an additional unit of health stock to be high. With more initial wealth A_0, this constraint would be less binding, and the value of the multiplier would be lower. Accordingly, demand for health is higher, indicating that health is a normal rather than an inferior good.

The *reduced demand function for medical services* in the consumption model is obtained by inserting (3.20) into (3.15). This yields

$$\ln M = const. - [1 + \alpha_M(\kappa - 1)] \ln p + (1 - \kappa)(1 - \alpha_M) \ln w \quad (3.21)$$
$$- (1 - \kappa)\alpha_E E - \kappa \ln \lambda.$$

Again, the predicted partial correlations of p, w and E are identical to the structural demand curve (3.15). $\kappa < 1$ implies that the effects are less pronounced for w and E

Table 3.1. Predicted Partial Correlations

	DEMAND FOR MEDICAL SERVICES			DEMAND FOR HEALTH	
	Struct. demand (3.15)	Invest. model (3.18)	Cons. model (3.21)	Invest. model (3.17)	Cons. model (3.20)
Price p	−	−	−	−	−
Wage rate w	+	+	+	+	−
Education E	−	−	−	+	+
Wealth A_0	0	0	+	0	+
Health stock H_1	+	n.a.	n.a.	n.a.	n.a.
Age	+	+	+	−	−

n.a.: not applicable

since the signs differ in (3.15) and (3.20). By contrast, p has a larger impact compared to the structural demand function. In addition, an increase in initial wealth (decrease in λ) increases the demand for medical care as health is a normal good.

Like in the investment model, the multi-period model entails an age effect in both demand functions. The demand for health falls with higher age due to an increasing rate of depreciation. Nevertheless, the demand for medical services increases with age to compensate partially for this effect [see WAGSTAFF (1986b)].

> **Conclusion 3.3.** *From the Grossman model, demand functions for health and for medical services can be derived. However, this requires the specification of functional forms, entailing a certain loss of generality. The demand for health and medical care are both predicted to depend on the real wage rate, the real price of medical care, education, and wealth. In the multiperiod model, both demand functions also depend on age if the rate of depreciation increases with age.*

Table 3.1 provides an overview of the predicted partial correlations.

3.3.3 Preliminary Assessment of the Grossman Model

The basic optimality condition (3.13) contains very important insights into the conditions governing the behavior of individuals who consider to marginally modify their stock of health. In particular, the distinction between marginal returns to health in terms of consumption and investment is a crucial one. This does not imply, however, that individual behavior can be sufficiently described by either set of motives. Yet in order to arrive at empirically testable predictions, it has proven necessary to choose between a 'consumption' and an 'investment' variant of the model. Even then, a very specific production function must be introduced to link health stock H_1 to sick time t^s, while a Cobb-Douglas production function links investment I to inputs medical care M, own effort t^I, and education E. In applied economic research, this function has long been replaced by more flexible alternatives (e.g., the Translog) because its implication of unitary elasticity of substitution is contradicted by empirical evidence. Similar problems beset the (additive) utility function of the consumption variant. However, more flexible functional forms would introduce additional parameters, resulting in predictions that become so malleable as to be almost without empirical content.

This problem has surfaced in empirical estimations of the Grossman model that have been performed (among many others) by GROSSMAN (1972a). Depending on their choice of functional form, they result in different predictions. Three partial relationships are of particular concern.

(1) *Health.* An important implication of the structural demand function for health is that health status and the demand for medical services are positively correlated because medical care serves as an input to produce the (optimal) stock of health. The empirical results of WAGSTAFF (1986b) and LEU AND GERFIN (1992) find a negative correlation. The latter study is particularly worrying because the authors modeled health stock as a latent variable reflected by several indicators, thus making every effort to filter out the permanent component of 'health' that should correspond to the target value at which optimizing individuals aim according to the Grossman model. However, all components of medical care distinguished exhibit a very definite and highly significant negative partial correlation with health so defined.

(2) *Education.* The structural demand function (3.15) predicts that a higher level of education lowers the demand for medical services. When estimating this function WAGSTAFF (1986b) found the opposite, i.e., $\alpha_E < 0$ in equation (3.21). However, the reduced-form function (3.20) had $(\kappa\alpha_E) > 0$. Since $0 < \kappa < 1$ by assumption, this implies $\alpha_E > 0$, a contradiction.

(3) *Age.* The multi-period Grossman model predicts that the demand for health decreases in the course of aging whereas the demand for medical services (given health) increases because optimizing individuals substitute medical care for their own efforts. Turning again to the empirical evidence, the prediction with regard to health stock is confirmed [LEU AND DOPPMANN (1986b), LEU AND GERFIN (1992)]. The prediction with regard to the demand for medical services (given indication of health), however, is consistently contradicted by empirical evidence in the case of ambulatory medical care. This holds true especially if the probability of seeing a physician at all is used as an indicator (on the grounds that the demand for medical services is not yet distorted by advice provided by a self-interested physician) [DUAN ET AL. (1984), NEWHOUSE AND PHELPS (1976), ZWEIFEL (1985)].

Several solutions have been proposed to deal with these shortcomings which are surveyed by GROSSMAN (2000). He also provides arguments in defense of the model. In particular, he points out that estimates of the structural demand function can be biased because health is not treated as endogenous.

A modification of the Grossman model by WAGSTAFF (1993) deserves closer attention. According to this reformulation, the desired stock of health capital cannot be reached immediately – a popular assumption in many stock adjustments models of investment behavior. The pertinent modification of the structural demand function (3.15) then does exhibit a significantly positive partial correlation between the demand for medical services and health, and education has the predicted negative sign as well. However, when individuals may be off their optimal health trajectory, the question arises as to why they permit this to happen. In the usual stock adjustment models, the justification is that getting immediately back to target is too costly. In the context of health, this makes sense if a change of lifestyle is considered; but then, inputs of consumer goods are neglected in the production functions of Appendix 3.A. Introducing adjustment costs makes much less sense when considering a sudden deterioration of health, e.g., due to an accident or the discovery of a life-threatening condition. In that event, it is often simply impossible to return to the desired health level.

Conclusion 3.4. *Some of the implications of the Grossman model are not consistent with available empirical evidence. Most importantly, the notion that expenditure on medical services constitutes a demand derived from an underlying demand for health cannot easily be upheld because permanent health status and demand for medical services are negatively rather than positively related.*

Admittedly, the final verdict on the Grossman model is not returned yet. More conclusive evidence may be expected from panel data tracing individuals over time in their efforts to keep health stock on the optimal trajectory prescribed by dynamic optimization. It seems safe to state at this point, however, that emphasis on long-run optimization generally tends to *neglect the uncertainty* surrounding health status and survival itself. Thus it entails the danger of overstating the degree of control individuals may have over their state of health in at least two ways:

(a) The Grossman model assumes that the rate of health capital depreciation δ in equation (3.2) is not affected by stochastic shocks such as accidents or major illnesses (in the multi-period version, it depends on age only). However, these events may impart very large values to δ. Indeed, δ may take on a value so large as to prevent the individual from returning to the optimal value of health stock because medical services simply are not effective enough to make up for such a large loss of health capital. Thus current health status may *deviate from optimal health status*, an eventuality excluded from the Grossman model, at least in its original form.

(b) The rate of depreciation and hence the loss of health capital may become so life-threatening as to let the *planning horizon shrink* to a few days or even hours.[5] In that event, rules of optimal long-term intertemporal allocation of the type described by condition (3.13) lose much of their relevance.

---

[5] Recall that the two-period formulation presented here is a simplified version of the original model, which comprises T periods (with T usually equal to remaining life expectancy).

For these reasons, an alternative approach will be proposed in the remainder of this chapter. In contrast to the Grossman model, it will emphasize *individuals' lack of control over their health status*. The starting point is provided by health status being governed by a stochastic process. The only thing individuals can influence in this process is the probabilities of transition from one state to another. This view opens the door to making willingness to pay for health state-dependent (Section 3.4.2). Even more important, the individual's production possibilities can be made state-dependent as well, with one technology (based on preventive efforts) prevailing in the healthy state but another technology (relying on medical care) in the sick state. The corresponding model will be presented in the Sections 3.4.3 and 3.4.4. An overview of the empirical research analyzing the production of health with regard to the two approaches discussed here will be given in Chapter 4.

3.4 The Production of Health as the Modification of a Stochastic Process

3.4.1 Conditional Health Production Functions

The health status of a given short period (e.g., a particular day) can be viewed as a sample taken from a sequence of states. In principle, the individual is subject to chance, deprived of a choice between two sequences such as

$$hhhhhssshhhhhhhhhhhhhs\dots \text{and} \dots hhssssshhhhhshhhhhh\dots$$

where (h) means healthy and (s) means sick.

All the individual can do is to influence the transition probabilities so as to increase the likelihood of the preferred sequence to be realized. Considering only two consecutive periods, there are four possible sequences, $hh, hs, sh,$ and ss (see Table 3.2). Accordingly, ϕ_{hs} symbolizes the probability of being sick in period 2 after having been healthy in period 1. If the probabilities entered in Table 3.2 remain constant over time, the sequence has the properties of a Markov process. Consider the probability of being healthy in period 2, $\pi_{h,2}$. This probability is given by (see Table 3.2)

$$\pi_{h,2} = \pi_{h,1}(1 - \phi_{hs}) + \pi_{s,1}(1 - \phi_{ss}). \tag{3.22}$$

The first term reflects the possibility of remaining in good health in period 2, after having been in good health during period 1, with $(1 - \phi_{hs})$ symbolizing the relevant transition probability. The second term reflects the case of a person who is sick in period 1 but turns healthy in period 2, with $(1 - \phi_{ss})$ denoting the transition probability and ϕ_{ss}, the probability of remaining sick.

Table 3.2. Transition and State Probabilities

	healthy in period 2	sick in period 2
healthy (h) in period 1	$1 - \phi_{hs}$	ϕ_{hs}
sick (s) in period 1	$1 - \phi_{ss}$	ϕ_{ss}
$\pi_{h,2} \, (= 1 - \pi)$	$\pi_{h,1}(1 - \phi_{hs}) + \pi_{s,1}(1 - \phi_{ss})$	
$\pi_{s,2} \, (= \pi)$		$\pi_{h,1}\phi_{hs} + \pi_{s,1}\phi_{ss}$

ϕ_{hs}: probability of transition from healthy to sick
ϕ_{ss}: probability of transition from sick to sick
$\pi_{h,t}$: state probability of being healthy in period t
$\pi_{s,t}$: state probability of being sick in period t

Now let the state of health in period 1 be known to the individual. In the case of good initial health, $\pi_{s,1} = 0$, the only way to influence $\pi_{h,2}$ is through ϕ_{hs} (ϕ_{ss} being irrelevant in this case). Being healthy, the individual has a wide choice of preventive measures at his or her disposal, ranging from nutrition to recreation.

However, all of these measures cost *time spent in favor of health*, symbolized by t^I. Conversely, given sickness in period 1, $\pi_{h,1} = 0$, the assumption is that only medical services M can contribute to reducing the probability ϕ_{ss} (ϕ_{hs} being irrelevant this time) and hence increasing the probability $\pi_{h,2}$ of being healthy again. Thus, the chance of health in period 2 depends on different factors, conditional upon health status prevailing in period 1,

$$\pi_{h,2} = \begin{cases} \pi_{h,2}[\phi_{hs}(t^I, \ldots)] & \text{if healthy in period 1;} \\ \pi_{h,2}[\phi_{ss}(M, \ldots)] & \text{if sick in period 1.} \end{cases} \tag{3.23}$$

Conclusion 3.5. *In a formulation that seems to be in accordance with everyday experience, the production function for health is dependent on the state of health prevailing during the decision period. Production of health amounts to a modification of transition probabilities in a sequence of states of health which is essentially governed by chance.*

In contrast to the Grossman model, the health production function is conditional. Depending on the initial state of health, only medical care or own effort has a positive productivity. Moreover, the output is a probability rather than the addition to a stock, in keeping with the modeling of prevention in Chapter 6.

3.4.2 Short-run Optimization and Willingness to Pay for Health

In Chapter 2, methods for estimating the marginal willingness to pay for improved health were discussed. Willingness to pay means nothing else but a willingness to go without other desirable things in favor of health. If these other things are understood to be consumer goods or, in short, 'consumption', then this willingness to pay is reflected by the ratio of marginal utilities between consumption C and health H, and therefore by the slope of the indifference curves in the (H, C)-space introduced in Chapter 1.

The considerations of the previous section imply that health itself cannot be controlled, but the probability of reaching a particular state of health in a future period can be modified. In full analogy to equation (3.23), which makes the production function state-dependent, the utility derived from consumption can be made *state-dependent* as well (see also Section 6.3.2). Let the objective function of an individual with a long-term planning horizon be written as (with π_t denoting the probability of being sick in period t),

$$EU = \sum_{t=0}^{T} \beta^t \left[(1 - \pi_t) u_h[C_{h,t}, H_t] + \pi_t u_s[C_{s,t}, H_t] \right]. \tag{3.24}$$

According to this equation, future streams of utility are summed up after being discounted by the individual using the subjective rate of time preference $\beta < 1$. In each period, the expected utility depends on consumption ($C_{h,t}$ and $C_{s,t}$) respectively. Moreover, the utility function itself may depend on health status in the following way, $u_h[C_{h,t}, h] > u_s[C_{s,t}, s]$, with $C_{h,t} = C_{s,t} \equiv C$ for all values of C and all t. A given quantity of consumption services thus always gives rise to more utility in the healthy state than in the sick state.

In the following, the planning horizon is shortened to comprise periods 1 and 2 only. Since the period is defined as a very short time span just long enough so that the transition probabilities of Table (3.2) can be changed marginally, time preference may be discarded ($\beta = 1$) and equation (3.24) simplified to

$$EU = (1 - \pi_1) u_h[C_{h,1}, h] + \pi_1 u_s[C_{s,1}, s] + (1 - \pi_2) u_h[C_{h,2}, h] + \pi_2 u_s[C_{s,2}, s]. \tag{3.25}$$

In the following, the argument H is dropped from the utility function because it will prove sufficient to discuss differences in health states in terms of their influence on the marginal utility of consumption, i.e., $\partial U_h / \partial C_h$ and $\partial U_s / \partial C_s$, respectively. As in the derivation of equation (3.23), let the state of health in period 1 be known. Consider first $\pi_1 = 0$ (healthy in period 1). Therefore, first period consumption $C_{h,1}$ is left as the one decision variable relating to the current period. As will be shown in Section 3.4.3, consuming less in period 1 serves to reduce the probability π_2 of being sick in the following period. Therefore, it is appropriate to determine the reduction of π_2 that would compensate for the sacrifice of one unit of $C_{h,1}$ or $C_{s,1}$ (consumption in period 1). In this calculation, consumption in period 2 is kept constant at $C_{h,2} = C_{s,2} \equiv C_2$.

The following relationship defines the marginal willingness to pay for improved health in the sense of reducing the risk of illness π_2,

$$dEU = 0 = \frac{\partial u_h[C_{h,1}]}{\partial C_{h,1}} dC_{h,1} - \{u_h[C_2] - u_s[C_2]\} d\pi_2. \tag{3.26}$$

In order to represent the subjective trade-off in preference (i.e., the indifference curve) between consumption and improved chances of health as two goods, we derive from equation (3.26) the slope of the indifference curve for the $(C_{h,1}, 1 - \pi_2)$-space:

$$\left. \frac{dC_{h,1}}{d(1 - \pi_2)} \right|_{dE_h=0} = - \left. \frac{dC_{h,1}}{d\pi_2} \right|_{dE_h=0} = - \frac{u_h[C_2] - u_s[C_2]}{\dfrac{\partial u_h[C_{h,1}]}{\partial C_{h,1}}}. \tag{3.27}$$

However, the individual could have been in a state of sickness in period 1. Giving up a unit of consumption $dC_{s,1}$ would again have to be compensated by an improvement in the chance of health $d(1 - \pi_2)$. Setting $\pi_1 = 1$ in equation (3.25) this time, one obtains the slope of this indifference curve due to the condition $dEU = 0$,

$$\frac{dC_{s,1}}{d(1 - \pi_2)} = - \frac{dC_{s,1}}{d\pi_2} = - \frac{u_h[C_2] - u_s[C_2]}{\dfrac{\partial u_s[C_{s,1}]}{\partial C_{s,1}}}. \tag{3.28}$$

Equations (3.27) and (3.28) can be interpreted as follows.

- Both equations indicate a *marginal rate of substitution* (MRS) between consumption and the probability of being healthy. The individual is willing to pay for a marginal improvement of his or her chances of being healthy in the following period by sacrificing some consumption during the current period.

- The MRS is given by the ratio of two differences of utility (which become marginal utilities in the limit) in the usual way. The greater the *difference between 'healthy' and 'sick'* in terms of utilities in the numerator of equations (3.27) and (3.28), the greater the absolute value of MRS and hence marginal willingness to pay for health. The greater the *loss in utility* occasioned by a sacrifice of consumption in the current period (denominator of the equations), the smaller the willingness to pay for an improvement of one's chance of health.

- The MRS *may well be state-dependent.* The reason for this is that the marginal utility of consumption takes on a different value according to health state. It could be large in times of good health [denominator of equation (3.27)] while small in times of bad health [denominator of equation (3.28)].

This last point is illustrated in Figure 3.1. For simplicity, C is henceforth used as the common symbol for a unit of consumption services, regardless of the state of health and period. Accordingly, indifference curves are shown in a $[C, 1 - \pi]$-space, one having index h, the other s. Both have high absolute slopes, reflecting considerable marginal willingness to pay for health throughout. However, the indifference

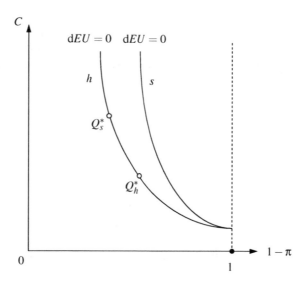

Fig. 3.1. Marginal Willingness to Pay for Health (Short Term)

curve with index *s* (initial state sick) has a more marked (negative) slope, defining an even *higher marginal willingness to pay for health*. Again, the reason is that additional consumption has a lower marginal utility in the denominator of equation (3.28) compared to equation (3.27). In this way, a behavior can be modeled that patients are often criticized for by their physicians, 'Do not care much about health as long as it is good, sacrifice everything for health as soon as it is bad'.

In the remainder of this section, this alleged instability of preferences with regard to health will not be pursued any further, for three reasons.

(1) The argument that marginal utility of consumption is *lower in the state of sickness* than in the state of health is *not fully convincing*. Quite possibly, sick persons have to rely to a particularly high degree on high quality accommodation and nutrition, implying that additional consumption services are of very high utility to them (see Section 6.3.2).

(2) *Health insurance* enables individuals to redistribute their income between health states in a way as to cause the marginal utilities of additional income or consumption to *converge*; under certain conditions, they will even become equal (see again Section 6.3.2).

(3) MRS also varies along a *stable indifference curve*. In Figure 3.1, it is sufficient that a point like Q_h^* is realized in good health and a point like Q_s^* in bad health for creating the impression of a volatile valuation of health.

Summarizing our findings leads to

Conclusion 3.6. *Short-run marginal willingness to pay for health can be represented by a subjective trade-off between 'consumption in the current period' against 'probability of being healthy in the subsequent period'. It may be regarded as state-dependent, but there is no necessity to do so.*

Since this chapter deals primarily with the individual as a producer and not as a demander of health, it will be shown in the following section that the seemingly volatile valuation of health may be due to the stochastic nature of individual production possibilities.

3.4.3 A Model with State-Dependent Production Possibilities: The Short Term

3.4.3.1 State-Dependent Optimization of a Stochastic Process

The production of health was defined above as the influence exerted on probabilities characterizing a stochastic process. The subjective valuation of improved chances of health was introduced, using terms such as transition probabilities, state probabilities, and expected utilities. These terms will now be used to describe the short-term decision situation of the individual, which will give rise to state-dependent trade-offs.

A sample taken from a sequence of health states is shown in Figure 3.2. In a previous period 0, the health status of the individual was determined. By assumption, this also determines his or her possibilities of influencing transition probabilities during period 1 in order to control the state probabilities of period 2. If the individual is initially healthy (upper branch of Figure 3.2), he or she can spend time in favor of health (t^I), lowering the probability of falling ill ϕ_{hs} and hence the probability π of being sick in period 2 (see Table 3.2). The utility payoff amounts to $u_h(C_h)$ with probability $[1 - \pi(t^I)]$. With probability $\pi(t^I)$, the lower payoff $u_s(C_s)$ materializes. The *short-run objective* is to select a value t^I such that expected utility EU, calculated over the conditional payoffs of period 2, is maximized.

If the initial state in period 1 is 'sickness', then efforts will be made to reduce the probability ϕ_{ss} in order to avoid spending period 2 in the state of bad health as well. By assumption, this is only possible through the *utilization of medical services* M but not using one's own means t^I. Accordingly, there is the probability $[1 - \pi(M)]$ of attaining a utility payoff amounting to $u_h(C_h)$ in period 2. With probability $\pi(M)$, however, no more than the utility payoff from consumption in the state of sickness, $u_s(C_s)$ can be attained. The individual will try to maximize expected utility again, this time by optimizing the use of medical services.

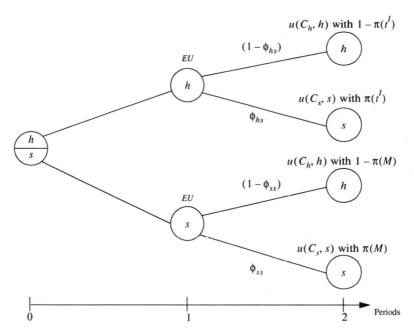

Fig. 3.2. Sequence of Health States as a Stochastic Process

The peculiarities of the production process as shown in Figure 3.2 can be seen in the following three points, which express in economic terms why 'health is different'.

(1) The role and responsibility of individuals as producers of their own health is limited to an influence on *probabilities*;

(2) Only in a *state of good health* can this influence take the form of the deployment of one's own efforts, whereas inputs provided by a third party are indispensable in a state of sickness;

(3) Health status is not only the result of a production process but has also the effect of a *stochastic input factor*, viz. initial health status, causing the production function to be conditional on health.

Conclusion 3.7. *From an economic point of view, the peculiarity of health can be seen in its dual role as an output of a production process and as a stochastic determinant of the individual's possibilities to contribute to this production process.*

3.4.3.2 The Elements of the Model

In the model presented in this section, the individuals are presumed to distinguish two states of health, 'healthy' and 'sick', and to limit their planning horizon to the current and one subsequent period. While the production possibilities are different between the two states, a joint objective function is postulated as given by equation (3.25). Therefore, the model described below (and shown in Box 3.2) is in the tradition of 'contingent claims', the analysis of which was pioneered by ARROW (1951) and DEBREU (1959, Chapter 7).

As long as individuals are *healthy*, they can themselves have an influence on their chance of health, while medical services have no effect. In particular, this means that additional input of time in favor of health t^I can serve to reduce the probability π of being sick in the following period, with π remaining strictly positive. With subscripts h, s dropped whenever there is no risk of ambiguity, one has

$$\pi = \pi(t^I) \qquad \text{with } \partial\pi/\partial t^H < 0 \text{ and } \pi > 0. \tag{3.29}$$

Consumption services produced depend not only on the input of consumption goods X but also on time available for consumption t^C, in keeping with household production theory as developed by BECKER (1965).

$$C_h = C_h(X, t^C) \qquad \text{with } \partial C_h/\partial X > 0, \partial C_h/\partial t^C > 0. \tag{3.30}$$

If healthy (and active in the labor force), individuals earn *labor income* given by multiplying working time t^W by the wage rate w (which for simplicity is considered exogenous rather than dependent on health status). By assumption, this income is just sufficient for financing the purchases of consumption goods at price c,

$$wt^W = cX_h. \tag{3.31}$$

Finally, time normalized to 1 is available for consumption t^C, health maintenance t^I and work t^W,

$$1 = t^C + t^I + t^W. \tag{3.32}$$

Turning to the *production possibilities in the state of sickness*, the equations reveal several differences. First, the probability π of spending the subsequent period in sickness can only be lowered by using medical services M. It is still, however, not possible to reduce this probability π to zero,

$$\pi = \pi(M) \quad \text{with } \partial\pi/\partial M < 0 \text{ and } \pi > 0. \tag{3.33}$$

The *production of consumption services* requires both time and consumption goods, exactly as in the healthy state. However, these two inputs have a lower value, since illness restricts the productive activities of the household,

$$C_s = C_s(X, t^C) \quad \text{with } \partial C_s/\partial X > 0, \partial C_s/\partial t^C > 0. \tag{3.34}$$

Box 3.2. A Model of State-Dependent Production of Health

INITIAL SITUATION HEALTHY $(1-\pi)$	INITIAL SITUATION SICK (π)
$\pi = \pi(t^I)$ with $\partial\pi/\partial t^I < 0$ and $\pi > 0$ $\qquad$ (3.29)	$\pi = \pi(M)$ with $\partial\pi/\partial M < 0$ and $\pi > 0$ $\qquad$ (3.33)
$C_h = C_h(X, t^C)$ with $\partial C_h/\partial X > 0,\ \partial C_h/\partial t^C > 0$ $\qquad$ (3.30)	$C_s = C_s(X, t^C)$ with $\partial C_s/\partial X > 0,\ \partial C_s/\partial t^C > 0$ $\qquad$ (3.34)
$wt^w = cX_h$ $\qquad$ (3.31)	$\overline{Y} = cX + pM$ $\qquad$ (3.35)
$1 = t^c + t^I + t^w$ $\qquad$ (3.32)	$1 = t^c + \mu M$ $\qquad$ (3.36)

C: $\quad$ consumption services
h: $\quad$ state of good health (subscript)
s: $\quad$ state of sickness (subscript)
M: $\quad$ medical services
μ: $\quad$ time cost per unit of medical services
p: $\quad$ price of consumer goods
π: $\quad$ probability of being sick in the subsequent period
q: $\quad$ net price of medical services
t^C: $\quad$ time spent on consumption
t^I: $\quad$ time spent in favor of health
t^W: $\quad$ working time
w: $\quad$ wage rate
X: $\quad$ consumer goods
$\overline{Y}$: $\quad$ social security income in case of sickness

Of crucial importance is the fact that in today's industrial countries *income in the event of sickness* does not depend on working time but is equal to a replacement income $\overline{Y}$ guaranteed by social security. This income is used to finance the purchase of consumption goods and of medical services (at price p). At this point, no difference is made between the gross price and the net price after health insurance,

$$\overline{Y} = cX + pM. \qquad (3.35)$$

Since working time is zero in the state of sickness, the *time constraint* comprises only time for consumption and for utilizing medical services. Individuals, as patients, view each physician hour or each day in hospital as costing μ hours or days of their own time. By assumption, working time (t^W) as well as time invested in health (t^I) are also zero, because of social security and due to lack of effectiveness, respectively,

$$1 = t^C + \mu M. \qquad (3.36)$$

The two sets of equations [(3.29) – (3.32), (3.33) – (3.36)] admittedly *overstate* the differences between the two health states. For example, healthy individuals also visit a physician, mostly in the hope of detecting a potential threat to their health. Clearly, they perceive the probability of falling ill ϕ_{hs} and hence π as dependent on medical services M in the healthy state as well. Conversely, health enhancing efforts t^I by the individual (reducing ϕ_{ss} and hence π) may also be worthwhile in the state of sickness, contrary to assumptions. Finally, especially the self-employed frequently continue working even though they are ill, causing t^W to appear in their time constraint independently of the state of health. These qualifications will be neglected, however, in the aim of sharpening.

> **Conclusion 3.8.** *The productive possibilities of individuals depend on the health status inherited from the previous period in many ways. If in good health, they can contribute themselves to an increase of their chance of health while earning a labor income. If in bad health, they must rely on medical services, do not work, and receive a transfer income that must cover expenditures on consumption goods as well as the cost of medical care.*

3.4.3.3 Conditional Short-term Production Frontiers

This section is devoted to the analysis of two production frontiers (trade-offs),

(1) Trade-off between consumption and the probability of being healthy in the subsequent period, given *good health* in the current period;

(2) Trade-off between consumption and the probability of being healthy in the subsequent period, given *bad health* in the current period.

The Short-Term Trade-Off Given Good Health

The trade-off between health and consumption can be illustrated by the case of a pedestrian ignoring a red light. Such a person does not directly opt for a worse state of health but for a probability distribution containing *unfavorable states with increased probability*. In terms of Table 3.2, he or she accepts an increased probability of becoming ill (due to an accident) ϕ_{hs}, which implies a smaller probability $(1 - \pi)$ of being in good health during the next period. On the other hand, the reduced waiting time at the light (amounting to a reduction of t^I) is now available for additional consumption C_h. Therefore, the trade-off confronting our pedestrian can be depicted as a transformation curve in a $(C_h, 1 - \pi)$-space (see Figure 3.3a). The shape of this curve is given by its slope, the marginal rate of transformation (MRT). Total differentiation of equations (3.29) to (3.32) yields [see Appendix 3.A.2, equation (3.A.23)]:

$$\frac{dC_h}{d(1 - \pi)} = \frac{\dfrac{\partial C}{\partial t^C}}{\dfrac{\partial \pi}{\partial t^I}} < 0. \tag{3.37}$$

The concavity of the production possibility frontier in Figure 3.3a is derived in the Appendix [equation (3.A.24)]. The two indifference curves could generally be members of different families [see equations (3.27) and (3.28) above]. In order to focus on the impact of conditional production possibilities, however, they are assumed

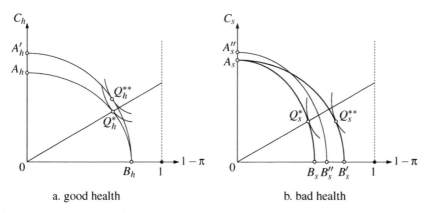

a. good health   b. bad health

Fig. 3.3. Trade-Offs Between Consumption and Health, Influenced by Exogenous Changes

to be *homothetic*, i.e., exhibiting the same slope (MRS) along a radial line from the origin. If the individual is healthy, he or she will attain Q_h^*, where the marginal rates of transformation MRT and substitution MRS are equal.

The following parameters appearing in equation (3.38) are discussed here.

- *Increase in the real wage rate (w/c).* As a first approximation, this change does not have an immediate influence on the transformation curve [see the explanation of equation (3.A.23) in the appendix for a justification]. Basically, an increase in the real wage serves to boost both labor income and the time cost of consumption in this simplified model, resulting in a cancelation of the two effects.[6] Therefore, the trade-off between health chances and consumption is identical for 'poor' and 'rich' individuals.

- *Technological change in the household.* Being mainly labor-saving, this type of technological change results in an increase of $\partial C/\partial t^C$. Under the presumption that the marginal productivity $\partial \pi/\partial t^I$ remains unaffected, the transformation curve becomes steeper, running from A_h' to B_h in Figure 3.3a. Given high marginal willingness to pay for an improved chance of health, the initial optimum would have to be close to point B_h, such as Q_h^*. There, the production possibility set changes comparatively little horizontally. The new optimum accordingly must be like Q_h^{**}, indicating that consumption rather than health benefits from the change in this case. Thus the diffusion of labor-saving consumption technology should have little impact on the health behavior of individuals – at least as long as they are healthy (see below).

---

[6] This is in contrast to the Grossman model, which distinguishes a negative wage effect on the demand for health stock in its 'pure consumption version' from a positive wage effect in its 'pure investment version'.

The Short-Term Trade-Off Given Bad Health

On the basis of equations (3.33) to (3.36), one obtains for the production possibility frontier [see equation (3.A.30) of the appendix]:

$$
\frac{\mathrm{d}C_s}{\mathrm{d}(1-\pi)} = \frac{\overset{(+)}{\dfrac{\partial C_s}{\partial t^C}\mu}}{\underset{(-)}{\dfrac{\partial \pi}{\partial M}}} + \frac{\overset{(+)}{\dfrac{\partial C_s}{\partial X}\dfrac{p}{c}}}{\underset{(-)}{\dfrac{\partial \pi}{\partial M}}} < 0. \tag{3.38}
$$

Equation (3.38) shows that an improved chance of health can only be achieved at the price of a sacrifice of consumption services, since both terms of the sum are unambiguously negative. One the one hand, utilization of medical services requires time to be spent by the patient (first term); on the other hand, medical services and consumption goods compete for the fixed income (second term). The opportunity cost of an improved chance of health depends crucially on $\partial C_s/\partial t^C$ and $\partial C_s/\partial X$. The first quantity (the individual's productivity in producing consumption services) is low in the state of sickness, whereas the second quantity (productivity of purchased goods and services) may be higher than in good health.

The transformation curve appears in Figure 3.3b. It is influenced by the following parameters.

- *Technological change in the household.* As in the 'healthy' state, this serves to increase the (absolute value of the) slope of the transformation curve. (This change is not shown in Figure 3.3b). Therefore, the diffusion of new consumption technology is predicted to have little effect on behavior with regard to health in the 'sick' state as well.

- *Technological change in medicine.* This can be symbolized by an increased absolute value of $\partial \pi/\partial M$. Both terms of equation (3.38) therefore decrease in absolute value, resulting in a flatter frontier, symbolized by the shift from A_sB_s to A_sB_s' in Figure 3.3b. The extreme point on the C-axis remains unchanged because the production possibilities of the current period are not affected by technological change in medicine. However, the extreme point on the $(1-\pi)$-axis *moves away from the origin* because the maximum attainable probability of being healthy in the subsequent period increases. The shift towards the frontier A_sB_s' implies the prediction of a notable improvement of health chances, illustrated by the new optimum Q_s^{**}.

- *Increased density of supply.* This amounts to a reduction of μ, because the patient has to spend less time when using medical services. With respect to the time constraint (3.38), t^C and/or M may take on higher values, which means that both extreme points move away from the origin. To the extent that medical services are subject to decreasing marginal returns, the new extreme point B_s'' will remain to the left of B_s', obtained for the case of technological change in medicine (see the previous paragraph). And according to equation (3.38), the new transformation curve has a flatter slope, resulting in the dashed curve $A_s''B_s''$ in Figure 3.3b. A limited improvement of the chance of health is achieved in conjunction with additional outlay on medical services in this case.

- *Extended coverage by health insurance.* This serves to decrease p/c because the insured have to bear a smaller share of the true cost of a physician hour, a drug, or a hospital day. Therefore, income can be spent on additional consumption goods and/or medical services. In terms of (Figure 3.3b), the transformation curve again shifts away from the origin, to a position such as $A_s''B_s''$, because decreasing marginal returns continue to set in as early as before given an unchanged state of technology in medicine.

Conclusion 3.9. *In both states 'health' and 'sickness', the short-term transformation curve is decreasing and concave from the origin. Technological change in the household serves to increase its steepness with respect to both states. Technological change in medicine, increased density of supply, and extended coverage by health insurance serve to make it flatter and to move it away from the origin, resulting in improved chances of health in the state of 'sickness'.*

3.4.3.4 Alleged Instability of Health Behavior

In Section 3.4.2, the claim was made that the observed instability of health behavior need not reflect a volatile valuation of health but can be traced to the stochastic nature of individual production possibilities. The validity of this claim can be shown now, subject to two assumptions:

(1) The expected utility function is homothetic in $(C, 1 - \pi)$-space, e.g., the indifference curves have identical slopes along a ray through the origin;

(2) The difference between the states 'healthy' and 'sick' has a stronger impact on the maximum attainable chance of health $(1 - \pi)$ than on the maximum attainable amount of consumption (C).

Under these two assumptions, the individual opts for Q_h^* when healthy (see Figure 3.4). MRS_h and MRT_h have the same value in this optimum. In the state of sickness, the individual must settle for point Q_s^*; at that point, MRS_s and MRS_s are again equal. In the majority of cases, this new optimum must lie above the ray $0Q_h^*$ (as marked in Figure 3.4) because the transformation curve A_sB_s runs steeper on average than A_hB_h, in keeping with Assumption 3.2. In particular, point $\overline{Q}_s$ having the same MRS as in point Q_h^*, cannot be an optimum. The MRS must take on a higher value in order to satisfy the condition $\text{MRS}_s = \text{MRS}_s$.

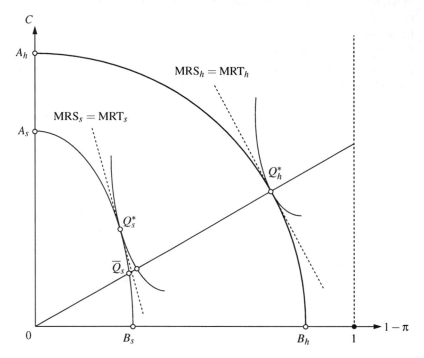

Fig. 3.4. 'Instability' of Health Behavior

This comparison among state-dependent production possibilities therefore leads to the prediction that in the *state of sickness a higher absolute value* of the marginal rates of substitution MRS as well as of transformation MRT will be realized. The observable health behavior of individuals accordingly suggests that an improvement of their chance of health is valued more highly in the event of illness than in good health. This 'inconsistency' was already explained in Section 3.4.2, using economic terms. The usual explanation by physicians, however, points to the aforementioned *inconsistency of preferences*, that people care too little about their health as long as they are healthy while being prepared to sacrifice almost everything as soon as they fall ill.

By way of contrast, Figure 3.4 shows that the observable increase of willingness to pay for an improved chance of health when 'sick' need not be related to a volatility of preferences at all. Rather it can be traced to objective production possibilities and their stochastic changes, which are occasioned by the instability of health itself. Moreover, physicians only observe the revealed willingness to pay for medical services. To the extent that the assumption made above holds true, viz. that medical services do not contribute to an improvement of chances of health as long as the healthy state prevails, willingness to pay for such services should be small. Therefore, the demand for *medical services* becomes state-dependent even if the demand for health is stable. This fact is of crucial importance to empirical research dealing with the demand for health care services, as will be shown in Section 4.4.

Conclusion 3.10. *The alleged instability of individual health behavior does not permit to conclude that there is a lack of rationality but may simply reflect state-dependent production possibilities of the individual.*

This conclusion is important because health is a non-tradable commodity, which makes the separation of subjective preferences from objective production possibilities difficult. If chances of health could be traded between buyers and sellers, one would observe not only optimal points such as Q_h^* and Q_s^* of Figure 3.4, but also the associated terms of trade. Therefore, relative prices could be compared with MRT, i.e., the relative marginal costs in the production of consumption services and health, for finding out whether individuals are at their optimum indeed and what factors are responsible for any systematic deviation from that optimum. However, the lack of tradability of health renders relative prices non-observable, causing a lack of objective information that could contribute to an evaluation of health-related policies. Recently, experimental evidence has increasingly been used to estimate MRS values in general and willingness-to-pay values in particular (see Chapter 2).

3.4.4 State-Dependent Production Possibilities: The Longer Run

If individuals succeed in improving their chances of health permanently, they modify their longer-run time constraint. The reason is that an increased probability of spending subsequent periods in good health results in an accumulation of healthy periods. The *healthy time thus gained* can in turn be used to produce more consumption services and/or spend additional effort in favor of health, a notion that is also prominent in the Grossman model [see equation (3.2) in Section 3.3.1]. Conversely, an increase in the probability of being sick in subsequent periods results in an increased number of periods spent in bad health.

For simplicity, individuals are assumed to simply extrapolate their current state of health. Their optimization thus remains *myopic* in that it does not contain a strategy for the event that the state of health should change again at the end of the current phase of good or bad health. For example, sick people might commit to stepping up their preventive efforts if they should ever become healthy again. Accordingly, the two short-run trade-offs are simply extrapolated as follows.

(1) Trade-off between average duration of a future phase of good health and consumption, current state *'healthy'*;

(2) Trade-off between average duration of a future phase of sickness and consumption, current period *'sick'*.

3.4.4.1 The Longer-Run Trade-Off Given Good Health

In order to analyze the longer run, the Markov process described in Figure 3.2 above is now extended to more than two periods. If the state probability π (the risk of sickness) remains constant after a once-and-for-all modification by the individual, then the Markov process becomes a binomial process [sick with probability π, healthy with probability $(1 - \pi)$]. A binomial process can be transformed into a geometric distribution of waiting times. The *mean number of periods* that elapse before the event 'sickness' materializes is given by[7]

$$T_h = \frac{1}{\pi} \qquad T_h : \text{mean number of periods lived in good health.} \qquad (3.39)$$

Accordingly, the time constraint is changed in that t_h^C, t^I and t^W are not limited by the current time period as in equation (3.32) of Table 3.2, but by T_h, such that

$$T_h = t^C + t^I + t^W. \qquad (3.40)$$

By means of total differentiation of equations (3.29) to (3.31) and (3.40), the slope of the transformation curve can be determined, which is now defined in (C_h, T_h)-space rather than in $(C_h, 1 - \pi)$-space [see the Appendix to this chapter, equation (3.A.36)],

$$\frac{dC_H}{dT_h} = \frac{\overset{(+)}{\dfrac{\partial C_h}{\partial t^C}} \overset{(+/-)}{\left[\dfrac{\partial T_h}{\partial \pi} \dfrac{\partial \pi}{\partial t^I} - 1 \right]}}{\underset{(-)\,(-)}{\dfrac{\partial T_h}{\partial \pi} \dfrac{\partial \pi}{\partial t^I}}} \gtreqless 0. \qquad (3.41)$$

For small values of T_h, this transformation curve has a *positive slope* (see Figure 3.5a). In this situation, time spent on health is still small, while its marginal productivity $\partial \pi / \partial t^H$ is large (in absolute value). The product of $\partial T_h / \partial \pi$ and $\partial \pi / \partial t^H$ in the bracket of equation (3.41) indicates whether an additional hour spent returns more or less than an hour of time in good health. As long as it returns more than one hour of healthy time, the numerator of equation (3.41) is positive, resulting in a positive slope of the transformation curve. Thus, efforts in favor of maintaining or enhancing health constitute an *investment*, making more health and more consumption possible at the same time. This view corresponds to an early strand of thought in health economics, especially as applied to developing countries [see SALA-I-MARTIN (2005)]. It has recently revived in the so-called new growth theory which emphasizes the contribution of human capital (education, but also health) to economic growth.

The shape of the longer-run transformation curve is shown in Figure 3.5a. It is valid also at the *aggregate level* because the majority of a given population is healthy, capable of extending the duration of their current phase of good health

---

[7] See BHATTACHARYYA AND JOHNSON (1977, p. 154).

by spending time on preventive efforts. This serves to increase aggregate productivity, with the potential of both improved health and more consumption. For this reason, the macroeconomic trade-off between consumption and health presented in Chapter 1 is similar to the one shown in Figure 3.5a.

Sooner or later, however, the law of diminishing marginal returns sets in, causing marginal productivity of time spent in favor of health to fall. The location of the maximum point can be determined by setting the numerator of equation (3.41) equal to zero. From equation (3.39) one obtains for $\partial T_h/\partial \pi$:

$$\frac{\partial T_h}{\partial \pi} = \frac{\partial}{\partial \pi}\left[\frac{1}{\pi}\right] = -\frac{1}{\pi^2}, \tag{3.42}$$

$$\text{or} \quad \frac{\partial T_h}{\partial(1-\pi)} = \frac{1}{\pi^2}.$$

Upon substitution into equation (3.41), a *critical value* of $\partial \pi/\partial t^I$ is implicitly defined by the condition

$$\frac{dC_h}{dT_h} \gtrless 0 \quad \Leftrightarrow \quad \left|\frac{\partial \pi}{\partial t^I}\right| \gtrless \left|-\pi^2\right|. \tag{3.43}$$

Condition (3.43) shows that for an individual with excellent health prospects (π small), the critical value of $\partial \pi/\partial t^I$ is quite small, implying that t^I and here T_h may attain high values before health becomes a consumption good. For an individual with a higher probability of future illness ($\pi=0.3$, say), the required marginal effectiveness already attains 0.09, which is substantial. Defining the intermediate term to be 90 days (say), a marginal variation of t^I might be 1 day or 15 minutes per day ($90 \times 1/4 = 22.5$ hours ≈ 1 day) spent on prevention. This effort would have to reduce π from 0.3 to 0.21 or more for health and consumption to be still positively related rather than presenting a trade-off.

The critical value of $\partial \pi/\partial t^I$ corresponds to the maximum point A_h in Figure 3.5a. Beyond point A_h, the impact of health-enhancing time on the risk of sickness, while still present, is too small (too close to zero) to be compensated by a longer duration of the phase of good health. Concavity of the frontier of production possibilities from the origin is derived in the Appendix [equation (3.A.24)].

On the preference side, the indifference curves of Figures 3.1 and 3.3 respectively can be transformed into the (C_h, T_h)-space of Figure 3.5a because T_h increases monotonically with $(1 - \pi)$, as can be seen from equation (3.42). This implies that the optimal point Q_h^* must lie beyond the maximum point A_h. There health is a *consumer good*. A situation in which health still amounts to an investment cannot be optimal (point $\overline{Q}_h$ of Figure 3.5a is not admissible), since nobody will purposefully opt for a short phase of health with $T_h < T_h'$.

In the healthy state, the marginal productivity of preventive effort is usually so small that the case $\left|\partial \pi/\partial t^I\right| < \left|-\pi^2\right|$ of equation (3.43) obtains. It necessarily characterizes the first *short-term trade-off* of Section 3.4.3.3 since there T_h is equal to one. Accordingly, the opportunity cost for additional improvement of health chances

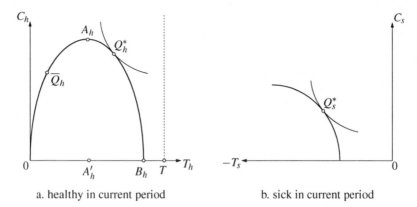

a. healthy in current period   b. sick in current period

Fig. 3.5. Long-Run Trade-Offs Between Consumption and Time Spent in Good Health

appears to be high [see equation (3.37)]. Therefore, the short-term optimum Q_h^* of Figure 3.3a has been put where the absolute value of the MRT and thus the opportunity cost of improved chances of health is high.

> **Conclusion 3.11.** *At the individual level, time spent in good health has the property of a consumption good rather than an investment good because the returns of time invested in favor of health in terms of healthy time are not sufficiently high at the consumer's optimum. At the same time, the consumption good property also means that individuals try to attain long phases of good health.*

A final detail may be noteworthy. At an advanced age, the upper limit T of Figure 3.5a (being healthy for the rest of one's lifetime) becomes more and more binding because death is approaching. Yet, at a given age individuals still differ with regard to their remaining life expectancy [while they can estimate it with a considerable degree of precision, see PHILIPSON AND BECKER (1998)]. This means that observed differences in health become marked although preferences are similar. More generally, it may well be that closeness to death rather than calendar age determines health behavior (see Chapter 14 for some evidence).

3.4.4.2 The Longer-Run Trade-Off Given Bad Health

If the current period is in the 'sick' state, the individual must settle for a phase of sickness the mean duration of which in analogy to equation (3.39) is given by

$$T_s = \frac{1}{1-\pi} \qquad T_s : \text{mean number of periods lived in bad health.} \qquad (3.44)$$

The time constraint of equation (3.36) in Box 3.2 is replaced by

$$T_s = t_s^C + \mu M. \tag{3.45}$$

It will be in the interest of the individual to keep this phase of sickness as short as possible; therefore the trade-off derived below is presented in $(C_s, -T_s)$-space (see Figure 3.5b). The slope of the production possibility frontier is given by [see Appendix, equation (3.A.41)]

$$-\frac{dC_s}{dT_s} = -\frac{\dfrac{\partial C_s}{\partial t^C}\left[\dfrac{\partial T_s}{\partial \pi}\dfrac{\partial \pi}{\partial M} - \mu\right]}{\dfrac{\partial T_s}{\partial \pi}\dfrac{\partial \pi}{\partial M}} + \frac{\dfrac{\partial C_s}{\partial X}\dfrac{p}{c}}{\dfrac{\partial T_s}{\partial \pi}\dfrac{\partial \pi}{\partial M}} < 0. \tag{3.46}$$

This slope is negative throughout, implying that the transformation curve of Figure 3.5b is *strictly decreasing*. In bad health, an improvement of the chance of health therefore will never have the property of an investment because it can only be brought about by the use of medical services. While medical care contributes to a shortening of the phase of sickness, it does cost time that would have been available for consumption [according to the parameter μ in the numerator of the first term of equation (3.46)]. Depending on the value of the relative net price (p/c), it also costs money that is not available for consumption goods [second term of equation (3.46)]. Finally, equation (3.46) resembles closely equation (3.38), and therefore the parameters influencing both location and shape of the transformation curve considered in Section 3.4.3.3 need not be discussed again.

3.4.5 Complementarity or Substitutability in the Production of Health?

3.4.5.1 Significance of the Issue

The theory of production importantly concerns the relationship between inputs. If a factor of production becomes more expensive and must therefore be used less, does this necessarily lead to an increased use of all other factors? On the one hand, given only *two production factors* and profit maximization by a firm, the answer to this question is clearly 'yes', i.e., substitutability prevails. On the other hand, with three or more production factors, complementary relationships become possible. There is some evidence suggesting that the increase in the price of energy in the 1970s led to a more labor-intensive style of production, whilst at the same time slowing the introduction of new technologies and therefore investment. Thus, one may say that substitutability exists between energy and labor but complementarity between energy and capital [see MAGNUS (1979)].

A similar issue is of considerable interest for health policy. One possibility of dampening the surge in health care expenditure is to reduce the demand for medical services. Increasing the amount of cost sharing in health insurance results in an increase in the net price of medical services, which would serve to curtail demand. Since this measure would meet with resistance, particularly amongst the older groups of the population who constitute the majority of voters in today's industrialized countries, *substitution of medical services* by the individual's own efforts (particularly preventive ones) offers a possible solution. Reducing the labor cost of the individual is out of the question, since this would amount to a reduction of the wage rate of the working population. Moreover, this measure would fail to be effective among the retired, who are considered to be heavy users of medical services. The use of a production factor can however be encouraged not only through a lowering of its price but also by an increase of its (marginal) productivity. One is therefore led to ask whether an *improved productivity of the individuals' own efforts* in favor of health would help to save medical services.

At first sight, the model developed in Section 3.4.4 does not seem to give an answer to this question. Since consumption goods X do not have any influence on health status by assumption, there is only *one factor of production* in each state. In good health, this is one's own time t^I, in bad health, the utilization of medical services M [see Box 3.2, equations (3.29) and (3.33)]. Therefore, the two inputs appear to be entirely unrelated. However, there is an indirect relationship which takes on different quality depending on the initial situation, to be discussed in the next two sections.

3.4.5.2 Substitutability in the Healthy State

In the previous section it was assumed that the marginal productivity of one's health-enhancing efforts can be increased, through more education in particular. This results in an improved productivity in both market and non-market activities. Even if it were possible to limit the effect of education to the non-market domain, the time restriction (3.32) of the model highlights the fact that time allocation may not only change in favor of t^I, but of t^C as well, i.e., in favor of the production of consumption services. In addition, having acquired marketable skills, the individual can obtain a higher wage in the labor market. This effect has caused, for example, women to increasingly enter the labor market, changing their time budget in favor of t^W, possibly to the detriment of t^I.

Should an increase in t^I occur despite these reservations, the probability of sickness π would fall, and with it the probability of future utilization of medical services. In addition, phases of good health would be lengthened and hence the demand for medical services deferred. Since, as a result of this, *remaining life expectancy* increases, total medical care consumed during the entire life cycle need not necessarily decrease. This is an effect reminiscent of the so-called Sisyphus syndrome in health care (see Section 14.4.1). Nevertheless, demand for medical services would be reduced in the short and medium term as a result of substitution.

3.4.5.3 Complementarity in the Sick State

If the initial state is one of sickness, an improvement in the individual's productivity is without effect. On the other hand, by increasing the chance of recovery, medical care provides individuals with additional opportunity to contribute their own time t^I to the maintenance of health. The expected duration of the sick period is reduced, permitting health-enhancing efforts to become effective sooner. Thus, t^I and M turn out to be complements rather than substitutes.

> **Conclusion 3.12.** *The relationship between one's own efforts and medical inputs in the production of health is state-dependent. If the initial state is 'healthy', the two inputs are substitutes and may become complements in the very long term. If the initial state is 'sick', they are complements.*

For empirical research into the production of health (to be discussed in Chapter 4), this conclusion leads to very differentiated predictions. For groups of basically healthy, young people, the relationship between their own health-enhancing efforts and the demand for medical services should unambiguously be one of substitutability. If the sample contains older and less healthy individuals, complementarity between the two inputs should prevail. At a regional or national level of aggregation, complementarity rather than substitutability may again be observed, because the published data reflect cases of very intensive medical treatment, which are typically absent from samples of individuals participating in surveys.

3.5 Summary

(1) The concept of a production function enables one to evaluate the optimality of the individual's behavior and the efficient use of scarce resources. Admittedly, health is also determined by chance, it is neither storable nor tradable. However, this does not rule out considering health as being the result of a production process.

(2) According to the Grossman model, health and wealth are optimally managed over time by the individual. The marginal utility of holding an additional unit of health stock has a consumption and an investment component. The marginal cost consists of interest, depreciation, and a possible change in the value of the capital good 'health' over time.

(3) From the Grossman model, demand functions for health and medical services can be derived. For this purpose, it is necessary to assume specific functional forms. Both types of demand depend on the relative price of medical care, the real wage rate, wealth, age, and nonmarket productivity (determined by education).

(4) In the alternative formulation emphasizing the stochastic nature of health, the short-term marginal willingness to pay for health can be defined as a subjective trade-off between 'consumption in the current period' and the 'probability of being healthy in the following period'. It becomes state-dependent as soon as the marginal utility of consumption varies between the 'healthy' and the 'sick' state; no inconsistencies of preferences are involved.

(5) An individual's productive possibilities also depend on the current state of health in various ways. If 'healthy', individuals themselves are able to increase the probability of being healthy in the short term and to extend the 'healthy' phase on the longer term through their own efforts.

(6) In both states the short-term transformation curve between consumption services and health is decreasing and concave. Technological change in the household causes the marginal rate of transformation to change in favor of consumption, with only small effects on health. In the sick state, individuals are predicted to benefit from technological change in medicine and higher physician density by mainly opting for improved chances of health.

(7) In the longer term, consumption and health are positively related at low levels if the initial state is 'healthy'. At the aggregate level, this holds for the majority of the population, giving rise to the notion of health being an investment good. However, optimizing individuals will push health to the point where the trade-off with consumption is negative, causing health to be a consumption good.

(8) In the short run, one's own health-enhancing efforts and medical care are un-related by assumption. In the longer run, their relationship as inputs into the production of health becomes state-dependent. If the current state is 'healthy' (relevant for the majority of the population), the two inputs are substitutes and may become complements only in the very long run. If the current state is 'sick', they are complements.

3.6 Further Reading

The article by GROSSMAN (2000) in the HANDBOOK OF HEALTH ECONOMICS deals with the intra- and intertemporal allocation of time and wealth. A rare example of a model version where individuals can also influence their time of death (calling for taking into account the so-called transversality condition of optimal control) has been NOCERA AND ZWEIFEL (1998).

3.A Appendix to Chapter 3

This appendix is devoted to the derivation of the demand functions in the Grossman model. Moreover, the production possibility frontier of the model outlined in Section 3.4 is illustrated. First, its short-term version is established for the states of health and sickness. Then, the longer term is considered as an extrapolation of the specific current state.

3.A.1 Appendix to Section 3.3

The Structural Demand Curve for Medical Services

To derive the structural demand curve for medical services, first logarithmize the investment function (3.14). This leads to

$$\ln I = \alpha_M \ln M + (1 - \alpha_M) \ln t^I + \alpha_E E. \tag{3.A.1}$$

Note that α_M and $(1 - \alpha_M)$ are the production elasticities of M and t^I,

$$\partial \ln I / \partial \ln M = (\partial I / \partial M)(M/I) = \alpha_M; \tag{3.A.2}$$

$$\partial \ln I / \partial \ln t^I = (\partial I / \partial t^I)(t^I / I) = (1 - \alpha_M). \tag{3.A.3}$$

Equation (3.9) can thus be rewritten as [with $w \equiv w_0 = w_1$ as stated in (3.17)]

$$\frac{M}{t^I} \times \frac{1 - \alpha_M}{\alpha_M} = \frac{w}{p}. \tag{3.A.4}$$

Taking logarithms results in

$$\ln M - \ln t^I + \ln \frac{1 - \alpha_M}{\alpha_M} = \ln w - \ln p. \tag{3.A.5}$$

This yields an expression for $\ln t^I$ which can be substituted into equation (3.A.1),

$$\ln I - \ln M - (1 - \alpha_M) \ln w + (1 - \alpha_M) \ln p + \alpha_E E + (1 - \alpha_M) \ln \left(\frac{1 - \alpha_M}{\alpha_M} \right). \tag{3.A.6}$$

Solving this equation for $\ln M$ and neglecting the constant last term, one has

$$\ln M = \ln I - (1 - \alpha_M) \ln p + (1 - \alpha_M) \ln w - \alpha_E E. \tag{3.A.7}$$

Since we assume $\delta = 1$, we have $\ln I = \ln H_1$ by equation (3.2). Using this expression in equation (3.A.7) gives the *structural demand function for medical services* in the investment model,

$$\ln M = const. + \ln H_1 - (1 - \alpha_M) \ln p + (1 - \alpha_M) \ln w_0 - \alpha_E E. \tag{3.15}$$

Derivation of the Demand Functions in the Investment Model

In the pure investment model, $\partial U/\partial t^s = 0$. Thus, equation (3.13) becomes

$$-\frac{\partial t^s}{\partial H_1}w_1\frac{\beta\partial U/\partial X_1}{c} = \frac{\partial U/\partial X_0}{\partial I/\partial M}\frac{p}{c}.$$

(3.A.8)

Setting $\beta = R = 1$, using (3.10) and simplifying yields

$$-\frac{\partial t_s}{\partial H_1}w_1 = \frac{p}{\partial I/\partial M}.$$

(3.A.9)

From equation (3.16), one obtains

$$\frac{\partial t^s}{\partial H_1} = -\theta_1\theta_2 H_1^{-\theta_2-1}.$$

(3.A.10)

The demand function for health can be derived from equations (3.A.9) and (3.A.10), using $\partial I/\partial M = \alpha_M(I/M)$ from (3.A.2), and taking logarithms to obtain

$$\ln p = \ln w_1 + \ln\alpha_M + (\ln I - \ln M) + \ln\theta_1 + \ln\theta_2 + (-\theta_2 - 1)\ln H_1.$$

(3.A.11)

From (3.A.7), one has

$$\ln I - \ln M = (1-\alpha_M)\ln p - (1-\alpha_M)\ln w_0 + \alpha_E E.$$

(3.A.12)

Substituting this into (3.A.11), defining $\varepsilon \equiv 1/(\theta_2 + 1) < 1$, using again $w \equiv w_0 = w_1$, and solving for $\ln H_1$ yields the *demand function for health in the pure investment model*,

$$\ln H_1 = const. - \varepsilon\alpha_M\ln p + \varepsilon\alpha_M\ln w + \varepsilon\alpha_E E.$$

(3.17)

Inserting (3.17) in (3.15) yields the *reduced demand function for medical services*

$$\ln M = const. - (1+\alpha_M(\varepsilon-1))\ln p + (1+\alpha_M(\varepsilon-1))\ln w - (1-\varepsilon)\alpha_E E.$$ (3.18)

Derivation of the Demand Functions in the Consumption Model

With $\beta = 1$, equation (3.13) in the pure consumption model simplifies to

$$\frac{\partial t^s}{\partial H_1}\frac{\partial U}{\partial t^s} = \mu = \lambda\frac{p}{\partial I/\partial M}.$$

(3.A.13)

With (3.16) and the utility function (3.19), one obtains

$$\frac{\partial U}{\partial t^s} = \alpha_1\alpha_2(t^s)^{\alpha_2-1} = \alpha_1\alpha_2\theta_1 H_1^{\theta_2(1-\alpha_2)} = const.\, H_1^{\theta_2(1-\alpha_2)}.$$

(3.A.14)

Substituting (3.A.14) in (3.A.13) and using (3.A.10) leads to

$$\frac{\partial t^s}{\partial H_1} const. \, H_1^{\theta_2(1-\alpha_2)} = const. \, H_1^{-\theta_2-1} H_1^{\theta_2(1-\alpha_2)} \tag{3.A.15}$$

$$= const. H_1^{-(1+\alpha_2\theta_2)} = \lambda \frac{p}{\partial I / \partial M}. \tag{3.A.16}$$

Writing $\kappa \equiv 1/(1+\alpha_2\theta_2) < 1$, using $\partial I/\partial M = \alpha_M(I/M)$ from (3.A.2) and taking logarithms, one obtains

$$\ln H_1 = const. - \kappa[\ln p + \ln M - \ln I - \ln \alpha_M + \ln \lambda]. \tag{3.A.17}$$

Using equation (3.A.6) finally yields the *demand function for health in the pure consumption model*,

$$\ln H_1 = const. - \kappa\alpha_M \ln p - \kappa(1-\alpha_M) \ln w_0 + \kappa\alpha_E E - \kappa \ln \lambda. \tag{3.20}$$

The *reduced demand function for medical services* in the pure consumption model is obtained by inserting (3.20) in the structural demand curve (3.15). This yields

$$\ln M = const. - [1 + \alpha_M(\kappa-1)] \ln p + (1-\kappa)(1-\alpha_M) \ln w_0 \tag{3.21}$$
$$- (1-\kappa)\alpha_E E - \kappa \ln \lambda.$$

3.A.2 Appendix to Section 3.4

Production in the Healthy State, Short Run

In this section, we aim at determining the sign of $dC_h/d(1-\pi)$. For this purpose, differentiate equation (3.29),

$$d(1-\pi) = -d\pi = -\frac{\partial \pi}{\partial t^I} dt^I \tag{3.A.18}$$

Total differentiation of the production function for consumption services, given by equation (3.30), yields (dropping the subscript h for the sake of simplicity where there is no risk of ambiguity),

$$dC_h = \frac{\partial C_h}{\partial X} dX + \frac{\partial C_h}{\partial t^C} dt^C. \tag{3.A.19}$$

The budget constraint (3.31) implies that additional consumption goods can only be financed out of additional labor income, which requires more working time,

$$dX = \frac{w}{c} dt^w. \tag{3.A.20}$$

The change of time available for consumption (dt^C) is derived from the time constraint (3.32), yielding

$$dt^C = -dt^l - dt^w.$$ (3.A.21)

Substitution of the expressions (3.A.20) and (3.A.21) into equation (3.A.19) for dC_h results in

$$
\begin{aligned}
dC_h &= \frac{\partial C_h}{\partial X}\left[\frac{w}{c}dt^w\right] - \frac{\partial C_h}{\partial t^C}(dt^l + dt^w) \\
&= -\frac{\partial C_h}{\partial t^C}dt^l + \left[\frac{\partial C_h}{\partial X}\frac{w}{c} - \frac{\partial C_h}{\partial t^C}\right]dt^w.
\end{aligned}
$$ (3.A.22)

If the individual uses time and goods for producing consumption services in an optimal manner, the ratio of marginal productivities $[(\partial C/\partial t^C)/(\partial C/\partial X)]$ is equal to the price ratio w/c, with w indicating the so-called shadow price of time (which could be used for earning additional labor income). Given this assumption, the second term of equation (3.A.22) is zero, and after dividing by equation (3.A.18) we obtain the expression discussed in the body of the text [equation (3.37)]

$$\frac{dC_h}{d(1-\pi)} = \frac{\dfrac{\partial C_h}{\partial t^C}}{\dfrac{\partial \pi}{\partial t^l}} < 0.$$ (3.A.23)

The curvature of the transformation curve is given by the sign of $d^2C_h/d(1-\pi)^2$. Treating $\partial C/\partial t^C$ as a constant and using (3.A.18) and (3.A.23), one obtains

$$
\frac{d^2C_h}{d(1-\pi)^2} = \frac{d}{dt^l}\left[\frac{dC_h}{d(1-\pi)}\right]\frac{dt^l}{d(1-\pi)} = \frac{d}{dt^l}\underset{(+)\quad(+)}{\left[\frac{\dfrac{\partial C_h}{\partial t^C}}{\dfrac{\partial \pi}{\partial t^l}}\right]}\frac{(-1)}{\dfrac{\partial \pi}{\partial t^l}}
$$

$$
= \frac{0\times\dfrac{\partial \pi}{\partial t^l} - \dfrac{\partial C_h}{\partial t^C}\dfrac{\partial^2 \pi}{(\partial t^l)^2}}{\left[\dfrac{\partial \pi}{\partial t^l}\right]^2}\frac{(-1)}{\dfrac{\partial \pi}{\partial t^l}} = \underset{(-)}{\frac{\dfrac{\partial C_h}{\partial t^C}\dfrac{\partial^2 \pi}{(\partial t^l)^2}}{\left[\dfrac{\partial \pi}{\partial t^l}\right]^3}} < 0.
$$ (3.A.24)

This shows that the transformation curve must be concave from the origin.

Production in the Sick State, Short Run

According to the assumption, the probability of being healthy in the subsequent period can only be increased by the use of medical services. Hence, differentiation of equation (3.33) yields

$$d(1 - \pi) = -d\pi = -\frac{\partial \pi}{\partial M} dM.$$

(3.A.25)

With regard to the production function for consumption services, there are no modifications except for the fact that marginal productivity of consumption goods as well as of time are likely to be smaller than in the healthy state:

$$dC_s = \frac{\partial C_s}{\partial X} dX + \frac{\partial C_s}{\partial t^C} dt^C.$$

(3.A.26)

Due to the budget constraint of equation (3.35), the purchase of additional consumption goods entails a sacrifice of medical services:

$$dX = \frac{-p}{c} dM.$$

(3.A.27)

Finally, total differentiation of the time constraint (3.36) yields

$$dt^C = -\mu dM.$$

(3.A.28)

Now, the two expressions (3.A.27) and (3.A.28) can be substituted into equation (3.A.26), resulting in

$$dC_s = \frac{-\partial C_s}{\partial X} \frac{p}{c} dM - \mu \frac{\partial C_s}{\partial t^C} dM.$$

(3.A.29)

Dividing this by (3.A.25), one obtains equation(3.33):

$$\frac{dC_s}{d(1 - \pi)} = \frac{\overset{(+)}{\frac{\partial C_s}{\partial t^C}} \mu}{\underset{(-)}{\frac{\partial \pi}{\partial M}}} + \frac{\overset{(+)}{\frac{\partial C_s}{\partial X}} \frac{p}{c}}{\underset{(-)}{\frac{\partial \pi}{\partial M}}} < 0.$$

(3.A.30)

The sign of this expression is unambiguously negative. Assuming $\partial C/\partial X, q/p$ and $\partial C/\partial t^C$ to be independent of M, it is possible to show in full analogy to equation (3.A.24) that

$$\frac{d^2 C_s}{d(1 - \pi)^2} < 0;$$

(3.A.31)

thus, the transformation curve is again concave from the origin.

Production in the Healthy State, Longer Run

On the longer run, the time constraint (3.32) is replaced by (3.40), which is given by

$$T_h\{\pi(t^H)\} = t_h^C + t^I + t^W. \tag{3.A.32}$$

The mean duration of a phase in good health therefore can be increased by spending additional health-enhancing time t^H. This increase is given by

$$dT_h = \frac{\partial T_h}{\partial \pi}\frac{\partial \pi}{\partial t^I}dt^I. \tag{3.A.33}$$

Total differentiation of equation (3.A.32) and solving for dt^C (dropping the subscript h for simplicity) yields, due to (3.A.33)

$$dt^C = dT_h - dt^H - dt^W = dT_h - \frac{1}{\frac{\partial T_h}{\partial \pi}\frac{\partial \pi}{\partial t^I}}dT_h - dt^W.$$

Thus,

$$dt^C = \left[\frac{\frac{\partial T_h}{\partial \pi}\frac{\partial \pi}{\partial t^I} - 1}{\frac{\partial T_h}{\partial \pi}\frac{\partial \pi}{\partial t^I}}\right]dT_h - dt^W. \tag{3.A.34}$$

Substituting expressions (3.A.20) and (3.A.34) into (3.A.19) for dC_h, one obtains

$$dC_h = \frac{\partial C_h}{\partial X}\left[\frac{w}{p}dt^W\right] + \frac{\partial C_h}{\partial t^C}\left[\frac{\frac{\partial T_h}{\partial \pi}\frac{\partial \pi}{\partial t^I} - 1}{\frac{\partial T_h}{\partial \pi}\frac{\partial \pi}{\partial t^I}}dT_h - dt^W\right] \tag{3.A.35}$$

$$= \left[\frac{\frac{\partial C_h}{\partial t^C}\left[\frac{\partial T_h}{\partial \pi}\frac{\partial \pi}{\partial t^I} - 1\right]}{\frac{\partial T_h}{\partial \pi}\frac{\partial \pi}{\partial t^I}}\right]dT_h + \left[\frac{\partial C_h}{\partial X}\frac{w}{p} - \frac{\partial C_h}{\partial t^C}\right]dt^W.$$

Again, in the neighborhood of an optimum, the term involving dt^W can be neglected [see the justification of equation (3.A.23)] resulting in [see equation (3.41) in the text]

$$\frac{dC_H}{dT_h} = \frac{\overset{(+)}{\frac{\partial C_h}{\partial t^C}}\overset{(+/-)}{\left[\frac{\partial T_h}{\partial \pi}\frac{\partial \pi}{\partial t^I} - 1\right]}}{\underset{(-)\,(-)}{\frac{\partial T_h}{\partial \pi}\frac{\partial \pi}{\partial t^I}}} \gtreqless 0. \tag{3.A.36}$$

The curvature of this transformation curve depends on the sign of d^2C_h/dT_h^2. In spite of the change in the time constraint we consider $\partial C/\partial t^C$ as independent from t^I.

Using equation (3.A.33) and substituting $\partial T_h/\partial \pi = -1/\pi^2$ according to equation (3.42), we obtain

$$\frac{d^2 C_h}{dT_h^2} = \frac{d}{dt^l}\left[\frac{dC_h}{dT_h}\right]\frac{dt^l}{dT_h}$$

$$= \frac{d}{dt^l}\left[\frac{\frac{\partial C_h}{\partial t^C}\left[\frac{-1}{\pi^2}\frac{\partial \pi}{\partial t^l} - 1\right]}{\frac{-1}{\pi^2}\frac{\partial \pi}{\partial t^l}}\right]\frac{1}{\frac{\partial T_h}{\partial \pi}\frac{\partial \pi}{\partial t^l}}$$

$$= \frac{\partial C_h}{\partial t^C}\frac{d}{dt^l}\left[1 + \frac{\pi^2}{\frac{\partial \pi}{\partial t^l}}\right]\frac{1}{\frac{\partial T_h}{\partial \pi}\frac{\partial \pi}{\partial t^l}}$$

$$= \frac{\partial C_h}{\partial t^C}\left[2\pi\frac{\partial \pi}{\partial t^l} - \pi^2\frac{\partial^2 \pi}{\partial t^{l2}}\right]\left[\frac{1}{\frac{\partial \pi}{\partial t^l}}\right]^2\frac{1}{\frac{-1}{\pi^2}\frac{\partial \pi}{\partial t^l}} < 0. \qquad (3.A.37)$$

$$\quad(+)\qquad(-)\qquad\quad(+)\qquad(+)\qquad(+)$$

This proves concavity from the origin for this transformation curve as well.

Production in the Sick State, Longer Run

With the time constraint (3.36) being replaced by (3.45), its differentiation results in

$$dT_s = \frac{\partial T_s}{\partial \pi}\frac{\partial \pi}{\partial M}dM. \qquad (3.A.38)$$

The second modification concerns the time available for consumption. Here, using equation (3.A.38), equation (3.A.28) is replaced by

$$dt^C = dT_s - \mu dM = \left[\frac{\partial T_s}{\partial \pi}\frac{\partial \pi}{\partial M} - \mu\right]dM. \qquad (3.A.39)$$

Combined with (3.A.27) for dX, the change in consumption goods follows from equation (3.A.26),

$$dC_s = \frac{-\partial C_s}{\partial X}\frac{p}{c}dM + \frac{\partial C_s}{\partial t^C}\left[\frac{\partial T_s}{\partial \pi}\frac{\partial \pi}{\partial M} - \mu\right]dM. \qquad (3.A.40)$$

Dividing this expression by equation (3.A.38) yields

$$\qquad\qquad(+)\qquad(-)\qquad\qquad(+)$$

$$\frac{dC_s}{-dT_s} = -\frac{\frac{\partial C_s}{\partial t^C}\left[\frac{\partial T_s}{\partial \pi}\frac{\partial \pi}{\partial M} - \mu\right]}{\frac{\partial T_s}{\partial \pi}\frac{\partial \pi}{\partial M}} + \frac{\frac{\partial C_s}{\partial X}\frac{p}{c}}{\frac{\partial T_s}{\partial \pi}\frac{\partial \pi}{\partial M}} < 0. \qquad (3.A.41)$$

$$\qquad\qquad\qquad(+)(-)\qquad\qquad\quad(+)(-)$$

In the denominator of this expression, the negative value of T_s appears in order to facilitate comparison with expression (3.A.36) for the case of good health.

3.E Exercises

3.1. Answer the following questions related to the Grossman model.

(a) Explain the difference between health being considered as (i) investment good and as (ii) consumption good.

(b) One can derive demand functions for health and for medical services from the Grossman model. Explain the differences between the two demand functions. Why does demand for health and for medical services depend on age?

(c) In richer societies, expenditure on medical services is higher. Explain this fact using the Grossman model.

3.2. Interpret the following functions:

$$U = \alpha_1 (t^s)^{\alpha_2} + g(X), \qquad \alpha_1 > 0, 0 < \alpha_2 < 1, g'(X) > 0, g''(X) < 0,$$
$$t^s(H) = H^{\frac{\varepsilon-1}{\varepsilon}}, \quad 0 < \varepsilon < 1,$$
$$I = M^{\alpha_M} (t^I)^{1-\alpha_M} e^{\alpha_E E}, \quad 0 < \alpha_M < 1, \alpha_E > 0.$$

3.3. Considering the pure investment model and the pure consumption model respectively try to determine the demand function for health in terms of the Grossman model if the investments in health only depend on (i) medical services or on (ii) the individual input of time. How would you interpret the result?

3.4. Consider Figure 3.1.

(a) Which condition determines that the indifference curve becomes vertical? Is a horizontal curve possible as well?

(b) What would be the consequences of these two extreme cases for observed behavior?

3.5. A policy maker suggests increasing sick pay, to be financed by a deduction from the wage of employed people. What would be the expected effects on the population's health behavior and health status?

4

Empirical Studies of the Production of Health

4.1 Introduction

The concept of a transformation curve for consumption services and health, introduced in the previous chapter, raises a number of questions which are of considerable importance for health policy. To illustrate this, consider the increase in life expectancy in industrialized countries (see Table 4.1).

Between 1900 and 1930, average life expectancy at birth increased. In the United States, for example, it grew by more than 0.3 years annually. However, the annual increase between 1980 and 1998 amounted to less than 0.2 years. With the exception of women in Germany, all countries shown in Table 4.1 register a considerable *slowdown of the increase in life expectancy*.

Since the utilization of health care per person in the population increased in all OECD countries during the period 1950–1998, many observers have come to the conclusion that the marginal contribution of medicine to health has gone towards zero ('flat-of-the-curve' medicine). Can this conclusion be upheld if the economic concept of the production of health is applied?

The transformation curve reminds one that other factors could be responsible for the observed development, both on the input and the output side.

(1) *Choice of output indicator.* Neither life expectancies nor mortality rates (another frequently used indicator) provide direct information about health status, i.e., the variable of interest to the individual. If one takes QALYs (as described in Section 2.3.2) as the measure, then additional life years only count fully if spent in a state of perfect health. Some epidemiologists doubt that additional life years fully translate into QALYs, pointing to the prevalence of chronic illnesses in the later part of the life span [see VERBRUGGE (1984)]. Rheumatic illnesses, for example, rarely result in death but reduce the quality of life. Moreover, they cause absence from work and thus considerable losses to the economy. By the same token, the state of health of the population may improve even though life expectancy no longer increases or only increases at a slower rate.

P. Zweifel et al., *Health Economics*, 2nd ed., DOI 10.1007/978-3-540-68540-1_4,
© Springer-Verlag Berlin Heidelberg 2009

Table 4.1. Development of Life Expectancy at Birth in Selected Countries

		Annual increase (in years)			
		1900–1930	1930–1950	1950–1980	1980–1998
Germany[a]	M	0.503	0.225	0.203	0.164
	F	0.483	0.275	0.303	0.139
France	M	0.300	0.480	0.226	0.157
	F	0.343	0.535	0.303	0.136
United Kingdom	M	0.343	0.385	0.150	0.136
	F	0.350	0.420	0.188	0.096
Japan	M	0.027	0.635	0.509	0.136
	F	0.057	0.715	0.585	0.186
Switzerland	M	0.330	0.385	0.203	0.150
	F	0.363	0.410	0.279	0.132
United States	M	0.327	0.395	0.166	0.139
	F	0.343	0.510	0.225	0.071

a) Including former Eastern Germany after reunification (from 1992).

Source: OECD (1987, 2001)

(2) *Consumption and health as outputs.* If individuals are allowed to optimize in spite of the many regulations restricting their health behavior [alcohol, tobacco, addictive substances; for a comparative survey of two countries see ZWEIFEL ET AL. (1998)], then additional consumption services must have an opportunity cost in terms of health[1] (see Figure 3.5 in Section 3.4.4). If preferences vary between different time periods or individuals, there is a risk of spurious correlation. An observed decline in the state of health may be the consequence of an intensified quest for consumption, whose negative side effects fail to be balanced by an increase in the productivity of medical services.

(3) *Relative productivity of inputs.* The fact that life expectancy has been increasing at a lower rate while health care expenditure (HCE) has continued to surge does not imply that the marginal productivity of medical services has been dropping. Individuals' health-enhancing effort may have decreased or other, previously not considered factors, in particular environmental ones, may have become more important. This is equivalent to saying that *relative* (not absolute) marginal productivity determines (together with relative marginal cost) the optimal mix of factors in production. Particularly in recent years, the marginal productivity of road safety or air quality in terms of health may have increased, serving to obviate to some extent preventive effort on the part of individuals and hence encouraging reliance on health care services.

---

[1] In the model of Section 3.4.3, consumption goods have no effect on health. This assumption considerably simplifies the mathematical analysis.

(4) *Composition of the population.* The larger the proportion of elderly people approaching death, the more trade-offs occur in the state of bad health.[2] Hence, the productivity of medical services relative to its alternatives is very high while being rather limited in absolute terms. To the extent that aging of the population goes along with an increased concentration of medical care expenditure in the upper age groups, it is spent precisely where its returns are low, at least if measured in terms of additional life expectancy.

In the following, some of these issues will at least partly be resolved by empirical studies. First, studies based on aggregate data will be presented, since they date back further and because they raise a few questions which can then be addressed by research based on more detailed individual data.

4.2 Studies Based on Aggregate Data

4.2.1 Mortality Rates and Life Expectancy as Measures of Output?

Since official population statistics typically register deaths but not episodes of illness, there is a limited choice of indicators to describe aggregate 'output' of the production of health. The measures available are mortality rates (classified according to age and sex) as well as life expectancies, which can be calculated from the mortality table.

From the individual's point of view, a mortality rate that is not age-specific makes little sense as an output measure, as the *long-run probability of death* equals one. It is only slightly more informative if defined for a particular subset of the population. The probability of a randomly selected person not to be alive at the end of the current year has little relevance for individual decision making, since almost everyone differs from the statistical average in one or several aspects. This objection is less applicable to infants who are still in the process of developing their personal characteristics. In this respect, the habit of using infant mortality rates for comparing the performance of health care systems does make some sense.

Even in the case of infants, however, the mortality rate selects an extreme 'state of health', providing information only about its probability weight π_h. This is very little indeed when compared to the QALY benchmark for describing health (see Section 2.3.2). Yet, mortality rates continue to serve as output indicators for empirical studies in the production of health, since they are derived from official statistics and can be compared across regions and countries.

As an alternative one may consider *life expectancy*, particularly at the time of birth. This indicator is an aggregate of all possible states of health with the exception

---

[2] There is an increasing amount of evidence suggesting that not age per se but proximity to death determines HCE [the so-called 'Red Herring' hypothesis, see ZWEIFEL ET AL. (1999a), and, e.g., ZWEIFEL ET AL. (2004a)].

of death. It simply sums the amounts of time the individual finds himself in one of these states, thus mirroring the fact that the attainment of a particular age depends not only on the current survival probability but on the entire sequence of survival probabilities since birth. Life expectancy is therefore subject to influences on the state of health which occurred in the past, and in order to catch their impact, lags need to be introduced in cause and effect relationships.

4.2.2 Marginal Productivity of a Health Care System

For the economic classics it was obvious that the health status and especially the mortality of a population depended substantially on economic influences [see MALTHUS (1798)]. Only towards the end of the 19th century did medicine receive scientific foundations, paving the way for its successes in fighting infectious disease. However, the first drugs permitting causal rather than symptomatic treatment (sulphonamides) appeared on the market as late as in the 1930s. Within a few years, they essentially eradicated tuberculosis. This miracle served to establish the conviction that medical care can improve health at the level of entire populations.

4.2.2.1 Early Evidence from the United States

AUSTER ET AL. (1969) were the first to examine the effectiveness of medicine, adopting the economic concept of a production function. The authors used the states of the United States as their unit of observation. They replaced the observed mortality rates by values standardized for age and sex, i.e., the value they would obtain if the state's population had the same age and sex structure as the United States as a whole. They thus took into account item (4) (composition of the population) mentioned in Section 4.1. Without such a standardization, Florida, e.g., with its many pensioners, would come off badly. Four groups of factors were distinguished in order to explain the remaining differences in standardized mortality rates (S). These factors enter a generalized Cobb-Douglas production function, given by

$$S_i = cZ_i^{\alpha}X_i^{\beta}M_i^{\gamma}e^{D_i\delta}e^{u_i}. \tag{4.1}$$

In this equation, Z_i represent economic input factors, X_i input factors linked to consumption, and M_i medical input factors, where D_i symbolizes additional influences emanating from the organization of health care (see Table 4.2 for more details). Finally, the variable u_i is a stochastic variable reflecting all those influences upon 'output' S_i in a particular state which were not recorded by the researchers. The seemingly complicated form of the function (4.1) boils down to a linear equation after taking logarithms,

$$\ln S_i = \ln c + \alpha\ln Z_i + \beta\ln X_i + \gamma\ln M_i + \delta D_i + u_i, \tag{4.2}$$

$$\text{with, e.g.,} \qquad \frac{\partial\ln S_i}{\partial\ln Z_i} = \frac{\partial S_i/S_i}{\partial Z_i/Z_i} \equiv \varepsilon(S,Z) = \alpha,$$

where ln denotes the natural logarithm. The parameter α indicates the *elasticity of mortality* with respect to economic influences (e.g., income). The variable D_i, in contrast to the others, appears in arithmetic form, since it also contains a so-called dummy variable or categorical variable, which can only take on the values 1 (characteristic present in the state) and 0 (characteristic not present).

The variables of equation (4.2) were further differentiated by AUSTER ET AL. (1969) into a total of 12 explanatory variables, also called regressors (see Table 4.2).

- *Economic factors Z_i.* Income per capita stands for a number of influences. On the one hand, it may reflect differences in preference, i.e., a marginal rate of substitution between consumption and health that depends on income. On the other hand, income may also influence the aggregate marginal rate of transformation between consumption and health (see Section 1.2.2). Second, average number of years of schooling plays a role because improved education presumably increases the productivity of individuals, not only in the market domain but also in the non-market domain, maintenance of their health in particular. Third, the degrees of urbanization and industrialization, serve as indicators of environmental influences on health.

- *Factors related to consumption X_i.* From the large number of consumable goods and services, the two whose health-damaging effects presumably weigh most heavily at the aggregate level are alcohol and cigarette consumption per capita.[3]

- *Medical factors M_i.* In view of the successes of drug therapy starting in the 1930s it is expected that pharmaceutical outlay per person contributes to a lowering of the mortality rate. The second component is physician density, internationally the most frequently used indicator of (potential) provision of medical services. The authors also include medical auxiliary staff in the production function, since many tasks in medical practices and in the hospitals are performed by nurses and auxiliary staff. The fourth factor is the per capita amount of capital available to the hospitals in the state concerned. According to widespread opinion, equipping hospitals with capital goods is the prerequisite for offering top quality medical care.

- *Organizational factors D_i.* In addition to the four medical inputs, two aspects of the organization of medical care are also considered. In particular, group practice held the promise of improved information exchange between the physicians of different specialties, and also of a certain mutual quality control. Accordingly, their share in the total number of practices in the state appears as an explanatory variable. The last regressor is a dummy variable, indicating whether a medical school exists within the state concerned ($= 1$) or not ($= 0$).

---

[3] In this way, item (2) of Section 4.1 is taken into account. Consumption (and with it consumption goods X_i) and health are two quantities that are simultaneously set by the individual. However, this also means that the X_i strictly speaking are not exogenous variables but, like S_i, endogenous ones that contain a stochastic error. This complication will be pursued in Section 4.3.4.

Table 4.2. Determinants of Mortality in 48 States of the United States, 1960[a]

Explanatory variable[b]	OLS[c]		2SLS[c]	
Constant	−0.065	(0.157)	0.037	(0.251)
Income per capita	0.105	(0.079)	0.183	(0.116)
Average no. of years of schooling	−0.161	(0.121)	−0.288	(0.216)
Share of population in urban areas	−0.001	(0.005)	−0.001	(0.005)
Share of industry in total employment	0.051**	(0.023)	0.042	(0.040)
Alcohol consumption per capita	−0.002	(0.037)	0.013	(0.044)
Cigarette consumption per capita	0.094*	(0.053)	0.097	(0.058)
Pharmaceutical outlay per capita[d]	−0.070*	(0.040)	−0.076	(0.066)
No. of physicians per capita[d]	0.143**	(0.064)	0.044	(0.111)
Medical auxiliary staff per capita[d]	−0.190**	(0.076)	−0.031	(0.195)
Capital stock of hospitals per capita[d]	−0.004	(0.048)	−0.109	(0.141)
Share of group practices	0.007	(0.012)	0.007	(0.021)
Existence of a medical school (1=yes, 0=no)	−0.034***	(0.012)	−0.024	(0.019)
R^2	0.639		0.586	
Elasticity with respect to medical services (pharmaceutical outlay, no. of physicians, medical auxiliary staff and capital stock of hospitals, each per capita)	−0.121		−0.172	

*,**,*** significant at the 10, 5 and 1 percent level, respectively.
  a) Natural logarithm of mortality rates, standardized according to age and sex.
  b) Natural logarithm, except the dummy variable 'existence of a medical school'; the coefficients presented are therefore elasticities [see also equation (4.2)].
  c) Standard errors of the estimated coefficients in parentheses.
  d) These regressors are endogenous and are replaced by their estimated values (see also Box 4.2).

Source: AUSTER ET AL. (1969, Table 6)

An Ordinary Least Squares (OLS) estimate of equation (4.2) yielded surprising results (see first column of Table 4.2; for an explanation of test statistics see Boxes 4.1 and 4.2).

- Contrary to popular belief and findings from development economics, a higher *average income* does not contribute to a lower mortality rate but possibly to a higher one. However, the elasticity estimate of 0.105 does not clearly differ from zero because of its large standard error of 0.079.

- Prolonged *schooling* appears to contribute to a reduction of the mortality rate, with an elasticity of −0.16. But this estimate is again not significantly different from zero. Among the two variables of the set which can be counted as environmental influences (degree of urbanization and industrialization), only industrialization has a discernible effect on mortality.

Box 4.1. A Simple Production Function of Health and its Empirical Estimation, Part 1

Ordinary Least Squares (OLS)

$$s_i = c' + \alpha z_i + \beta x_i + \gamma m_i + \delta D_i + u_i \qquad (4.2)$$

where $s_i \equiv \ln S_i, c' \equiv \ln c, z_i \equiv \ln Z_i, x_i \equiv \ln X_i$ und $m_i \equiv \ln M_i$.

u_i is a normally distributed random variable with an expected value of $E(u_i) = 0$ and a constant variance $Var(u_i)$ in every state i; u_i is assumed to be *independent* from all regressors (z_i, x_i, m_i, D_i).

- The parameters $\hat{c}, \hat{\alpha}, \hat{\beta}, \hat{\gamma}, \hat{\delta}$ are to be determined such that the sum of squared deviations between observed (s_i) and calculated values $(\hat{s}_i)$ of the dependent variables are minimized,

$$\min \sum_i \hat{u}_i^2 = \sum_i (s_i - \hat{s}_i)^2 = \sum_i (s_i - \hat{c}' - \hat{\alpha} z_i - \hat{\beta} x_i - \hat{\gamma} m_i - \hat{\delta} D_i)^2.$$

- As s_i contains the random variable u_i, the estimates $\hat{c}, \hat{\alpha}, \hat{\beta}, \hat{\gamma}, \hat{\delta}$ themselves are random variables and have a variance or a standard error $(\sigma_{\hat{\alpha}})$ respectively, that can be estimated. *Example* in Table 4.2: $\hat{\alpha} = 0.1443, \hat{\sigma}_{\hat{\alpha}} = 0.079$ for the variable 'number of physicians per capita'.
- The standardized estimated coefficients (e.g., $\hat{\alpha}/\hat{\sigma}_{\hat{\alpha}}$) are t-distributed. For example, in the regression by AUSTER ET AL. (1969) presented in Table 4.2, the number of degrees of freedom is 35 (48 observations minus 13 estimated parameters). This means that a deviation from zero of $|\hat{\alpha}/\hat{\sigma}_{\hat{\alpha}}| - 0 \geq 1.690$ can only occur in 10 percent of all cases, provided that $\alpha = 0$. Deviations of $|\hat{\alpha}/\hat{\sigma}_{\hat{\alpha}}| - 0 \geq 2.030$ should only occur in 5 percent and of $|\hat{\alpha}/\hat{\sigma}_{\hat{\alpha}}| - 0 \geq 2.724$ in 1 percent of all cases (significance levels of 10 percent, 5 percent, 1 percent). *Example* in Table 4.2: $\hat{\alpha}/\hat{\sigma}_{\hat{\alpha}} = 0.143/0.064 = 2.234$; the coefficient of variable number of physicians per capita is different from zero with an error probability of 5 percent but not with an error probability of 1 percent
- The quality of the achieved adjustment to the observed values of the dependent variable is expressed by the *coefficient of determination* R^2, i.e., the part of the variance of the dependent variable not attributed to the random variable u_i (= 0.639 or 64 percent in Table 4.2).

- Turning to medical inputs, the claim could be made that in the 'Fight against Death' medical auxiliary staff and pharmaceutical outlay have a recognizable success, with an elasticity of -0.19 and -0.07, respectively. By way of contrast, increased *physician density* seems to result not in a lower but a *higher* rate of mortality in the state, ceteris paribus.

Unexpected results such as these give rise to critical objections. One such objection can be immediately gleaned from Section 4.2.1, where it was pointed out that life expectancies (and presumably also mortality rates) of the current period depend on influences which are to be found way back in the lifespan of the deceased. The mortality rates of a state of the United States in 1960 may therefore be determined by circumstances which *date back many years*.

Box 4.2. A Simple Production Function of Health and its Empirical Estimation, Part 2

Two-Stage Least Squares (2SLS)

$$m_i = c'' + \alpha'' z_i + \kappa r_i + \tau s_i(u_i) + u_i'$$

- This equation represents the assumed reverse influence of mortality on m_i (e.g., physician density, whereas r_i symbolizes the other determinants of m_i and u_i' another random variable, with properties as the u_i of Box 4.1.

- Thus m_i is a regressor *depending*, via s_i, on the *error term* u_i of equation (4.2) and is therefore endogenous.

- A purging of m_i of its error component can be achieved by a preliminary regression on all exogenous variables (first stage), resulting in the parameters $\hat{c}''$, $\alpha'' z_i$ and $\hat{\kappa}$ estimated using OLS. The purged values of m_i are thus given by

$$\hat{m}_i = \hat{c}'' + \hat{\alpha}' z_i + \hat{\kappa} r_i. \qquad (4.3)$$

- Equation (4.2) is estimated with $\hat{m}_i$ instead of m_i, again using OLS (second stage).

Further explanations can be found in most textbooks of econometrics [see, e.g., GREENE (2008, Chapter 12)].

Another important objection concerns the assumed *direction of causality*. The OLS estimate of Table 4.2 suggests that additional physicians cause mortality rates to increase, for example through an excessive intensity of treatment due to supplier-induced demand (see Section 8.3). Causality could, however, just as well run the *other way round*. In areas where people are exposed to an increased risk of death, their demand for physician services may be particularly high, causing physicians to set up practice in the high-mortality state. A similar reversal of causality might also apply to the remaining three components of medical services.

Following this argument, additional regression equations for the four components of medical care can be postulated. In these equations, medical inputs M_i are linked to their determinants, among them, mortality S_i (see Box 4.2). This implies that through equation (4.2), M_i depend on u_i, i.e., on the same error term u_i which appears in the equation (4.2) to be estimated. This means that the distinction between systematic and random determinants which is so crucial for regression analysis breaks down. The standard approach to dealing with this problem is called Two-Stage Least Squares. In a first stage, all variables suspected of endogeneity (i.e., to depend on the error term u_i) are regressed on all exogenous variables (taken from Box 4.1, but complemented by additional ones not shown in the present study). The predicted values from these regressors can be said to be purged of their error component. Using these purged values in a second-stage regression, one obtains coefficients that are corrected for possible reversed causation (see Box 4.2 for some more explanation). These corrected coefficients appear in the second column of Table 4.2, labeled, 'Two-Stage Least Squares'. This two-stage estimation procedure (2SLS) yields the following results.

- The detrimental effect of income and the health-enhancing effect of schooling now differ even more markedly, although again neither elasticity quite reaches customary levels of statistical significance.

- Both environmental variables (urbanization, industrialization) remain statistically insignificant.

- Those variables most directly linked to individual health behavior, alcohol and cigarette consumption, fail to contribute to the explanation of mortality rates in a statistically significant way.

- Three out of four components of the medical infrastructure display a negative relationship with mortality, as one would expect if medical inputs are effective. The one exception might be physician density, whose elasticity cannot be distinguished from zero. The overall productivity of medical amounts to an elasticity of about -0.172 (-0.121 according to OLS estimates). However, the productivity of length of schooling is -0.288 (not clearly distinguishable from zero).

Conclusion 4.1. *If the contribution of different inputs to the production of health is measured by their influence on mortality, then there are indications suggesting a low marginal productivity of U.S. medical infrastructure.*

As a qualification it must be noted that this conclusion is based on observations from almost fifty years ago, which fail to reflect technological change in medicine that has occurred in the meantime.

4.2.2.2 Recent Evidence from the United States

Many changes have taken place in the health care system of the United States over the past decades. Medical care expenditure has multiplied from US$26.9 billion in 1960 to US$1,700 billion in 2003, its share in the GDP going from 5.1 to 15.2 percent [WHO, 2007; THORNTON (2002)]. AUSTER ET AL. (1969), SILVER (1972) and HADLEY (1982) find that the marginal contribution of medical care to reducing mortality is relatively small, with an estimated elasticity between -0.10 and -0.15. THORNTON (2002) presents a reestimation using 1990 data. However, additional health-related factors as well as race are incorporated and both medical care and income treated as endogenous variables.

The aggregate health production function is therefore given by:

$$\ln S_i = \beta_0 + \beta_M \ln M_i + \beta_S \ln X_i + \beta_L \ln L_i + \beta_E \ln E_i + \beta_C R_i + u_i \qquad (4.4)$$

where S_i denotes the age-adjusted mortality rate in state i, M_i medical care expenditure, X_i a vector of socioeconomic variables, L_i a vector of lifestyle variables, E_i a vector of environmental variables, R_i race and gender, and u_i a classical error term. These variables are defined as follows.

- *Medical care M_i.* Medical care expenditure per capita is deemed more appropriate than stocks (contrary to Section 4.2.2.1 above), because it better reflects differences in the quality and quantity of services between the states. Since M_i depends on wealth, it must be purged of its endogeneity (see Box 4.2 for an introduction to Two-Stage Least Squares).

- *Socioeconomic status S_i.* Education and income are included to represent socioeconomic status. Education is measured as the percentage of the population 25 years of age or older that has schooling beyond a high school degree. Income is measured as personal income per capita and treated as an exogenous variable.

- *Lifestyle factors L_i.* The indicators used are cigarette consumption, alcohol consumption per capita, the percentage of married households.

- *Environmental factors E_i.* Here, urbanization is measured as the percentage of the population residing in a standard metropolitan statistical area. The percentage of workers employed in manufacturing serves as an indicator of industrialization, capturing the health risks associated with, e.g., exposure to hazardous agents. Finally, the number of violent crimes per 100,000 people has an immediate effect on health.

- *Race and gender R_i.* The first variable is the percentage of non-whites in the state population, the second, that of women.

The estimation result is presented in Table 4.3. It may be interpreted as follows.

- Although medical care expenditure does have a negative estimated elasticity, it fails to be significant, confirming the findings of AUSTER ET AL. (1969) who used stocks of physicians, nurses, and capital invested in hospitals. Since HCE multiplied between 1960 and 1990, this does suggest diminishing returns to medical care ('flat-of-the-curve' medicine).

- Income now serves to lower mortality, in keeping with international studies but in contrast to AUSTER ET AL. (1969).

- With an estimated elasticity of -0.2, education again turns out to be the policy variable with maximum impact.

- Now cigarette consumption can be claimed to increase mortality, although the estimated elasticity of 0.08 is small. This result differs from AUSTER ET AL. (1969), where the 2SLS estimate was not significantly different from zero. Alcohol consumption again cannot be said to influence mortality.

Table 4.3. Determinants of Mortality in the United States, 1990[a]

Explanatory variable	2SLS		Comparison with Table 4.2 (2SLS)
Constant	6.590***	(1.430)	now significant
Medical care expendit.	−0.065	(0.151)	new variable
Income[a]	−0.179*	(0.096)	change from insignificant to −
Education[b]	−0.200**	(0.083)	new definition of variable[b]
Cigarette consumption	0.077***	(0.024)	change from insignificant to +
Alcohol consumption	0.038	(0.040)	again insignificant
Married households	−0.572***	(0.195)	new variable
Urbanization	−0.025	(0.025)	again insignificant
Manufacturing	0.013	(0.019)	again insignificant
Crime	0.038***	(0.013)	new variable
R^2 unadjusted	0.800		
R^2 adjusted	0.740		larger value

*,**,*** significant at the 10, 5 and 1 percent level, respectively.

a) Age-adjusted mortality rates; endogenous regressors, replaced by their estimated values.

b) Defined as share of individuals with higher education, contrary to Table 4.2 of Section 4.2.2.1, (years of schooling).

Source: THORNTON (2002, Table 1)

- Martial status has the largest impact on the death rate. A 10 percent increase (from a share of 0.6 to 0.66, say) serves to lower the mortality rate by no less than 3.4 percent in married households.

- As in the original study, urbanization and industrialization cannot be said to visibly influence mortality. However, crime does have a recognizable effect, albeit it is small, comparable to alcohol consumption.

To sum up, as already indicated by AUSTER ET AL. (1969) medical care expenditure does not contribute significantly to the reduction of the death rate. From a point of view emphasizing population health, tripling its share in the GDP between 1960 and 2003 cannot be justified. However, the willingness to pay of citizens for medical care may continue to exceed its marginal cost for other reasons (see Chapter 2 for some preliminary evidence).

4.2.2.3 Evidence from Industrialized Countries

MILLER AND FRECH (2000) investigate the production of health in 21 industrialized countries. Using aggregate OECD data for 1996, they relate life expectancy at birth, at age 40 and age 60 respectively to economic and medical inputs. Like THORNTON (2002), their explanatory variable is health care expenditure (HCE) rather than stocks of personnel and capital, made comparable by purchasing power parity (PPP)

Table 4.4. Production of Health, OECD Countries, 1985

Explanatory variable	Remaining life expectancy at birth	at age of 40	at age of 60
Constant	−0.534*	−0.026	−0.895
Women (=1, Men=0)	0.039***	0.100***	0.137***
Pharmaceutical outlays[a]	0.005	0.017*	0.040**
Non-pharmaceutical outlays[c]	0.005	−0.011	−0.015
Income per capita	0.012	0.057**	0.088**
Share of Smokers	−0.007	−0.010	0.002
Alcohol per capita, in liters	−0.009**	−0.014	−0.019
(Alcohol)×(Women)	0.017***	0.015**	0.031***
Animal fat consumption per capita	1.404***	0.955***	0.910**
Animal fat consumption per capita, squared	−0.105***	−0.073***	−0.071**
Adjusted R^2	0.952	0.911	0.909
Sample size	42	42	42

*,**,*** significant at the 10, 5 and 1 percent level, respectively.

a) Pharmaceutical outlays transformed to US$ according to pharmaceutical purchasing power parity, Source: OECD.

b) Nonpharmaceutical outlays transformed to US$ according to medical purchasing power parity, Source: OECD.

Source: MILLER AND FRECH (2000, Table 3)

calculations performed by the OECD. A new feature of their work is the distinction between pharmaceutical and nonpharmaceutical outlays, relating back to the pioneering study by AUSTER ET AL. (1969), discussed in Section 4.2.2.1. The following conclusions may be drawn from the estimates presented in Table 4.4.

- At birth, girls have a 4 percent (i.e., some 3 years, calculated on 75 years) higher life expectancy than boys. However, the differential increases to about 10 percent (i.e., some 3.5 years, calculated on 35 years) at age 40 and 14 percent (i.e., some 2.8 years, calculated on 20 years, say) at age 60. Observed differentials are higher and are due to differences in lifestyle (see below).

- Pharmaceuticals have a considerable impact on remaining life expectancy, especially at higher ages. A doubling would result in a 1.7 percent increase at the age of 40 and 4 percent at the age of 60.

- The marginal effect of increasing pharmaceutical expenditure by one US$ is greatest in those countries where it is low. This follows from the double-logarithmic specification because the elasticity $\varepsilon(y,P) = (\partial y/\partial P) \times (P/y)$ with remaining life expectancy (y) and pharmaceutical outlay (P) is a constant by assumption. Therefore, a lower value of (P/y) requires a high value of ($\partial y/\partial P$).

The impact of the other regressors can be summarized as follows.

- Income per capita has a positive and significant influence on remaining life expectancy (except for life expectancy at birth). This vindicates THORNTON (2002) as well as other studies using OECD country data such as GERDTHAM AND RUHM (2006) and ZWEIFEL ET AL. (2005) but contradicts AUSTER ET AL. (1969). It suggests that traditional emphasis both on the extreme event 'death' (mortality) and life expectancy at birth may be misplaced.

- Nonpharmaceutical expenditure does not have a statistically relevant influence on remaining life expectancy, suggesting that OECD countries are indeed on the 'flat-of-the-curve' medicine, or a misspecification of the regression equation. Specifically, health care expenditure might be endogenous, depending on remaining life expectancy. This would make economic sense since these outlays may be regarded as an investment (as in the Grossman model) whose payoff increases with the number of years a rate of return can be expected.

4.2.2.4 Evidence from a Comparison of Two Neighboring Areas

Sometimes it is possible to learn a great deal from a direct comparison between two areas of almost identical characteristics [see FUCHS (1974)]. Utah and Nevada are suitable for such a comparison, as they are neighboring states of the U.S. both sparsely populated and having the same desert climate. Therefore, environmental influences cannot account for any differences in health status. Nevertheless, mortality rates are quite different. As of 1970, infant mortality in Nevada was 42 percent (boys) and 35 percent (girls) in excess of Utah (see part A of Table 4.5). In the 40–49 years age group, the relative mortality rate in Nevada was even higher, by 54 percent (men) and 69 percent (women).

Rates of mortality due to particular causes of death are even more informative (see part B of Table 4.5). Deaths of cirrhosis of the liver and lung cancer (so-called 'malignant neoplasm of the respiratory tract') occur almost 7 times more frequently in Nevada in the male age group 30–39 than in Utah. This can hardly be the result of inadequate provision of medical services in Nevada, since Nevada and Utah have comparable densities of physicians and other health workers (variables No. 1 and 2 in part C of Table 4.5).

Considering the economic factors, median income (variable No. 3) is indeed 16 percent higher in Nevada than in Utah. However, applying the elasticity estimates presented in Table 4.2, this could raise the mortality rate by 1.6 percentage points to 2.9 percent at the most, which is not sufficient to explain the difference between Nevada and Utah. Finally, length of schooling is the same in both states (variable No. 4), and the inhabitants of both states demonstrate the same preference for living on the countryside (variable No. 5).

Table 4.5. Mortality in Nevada and Utah and Some Possible Determinants, 1970

| | | Age groups | | | | | | |
		< 1	1–19	20–29	30–39	40–49	50–59	60–69
A.	Mortality in Nevada	M	142	116	144	137	154	138	126
	(Utah=100)	F	135	126	142	148	169	128	117
B.	Mortality resulting from	M				690	211	306	217
	cirrhosis of the liver	F				543	396	305	327
	and lung cancer								
	(Utah=100)								

C.	Possible determinants of mortality	Nevada	Utah
	1. Physicians per 10,000 inhabitants	11.3	13.8
	2. Nonmedical staff per 10,000 inhabitants	161.0	180.0
	3. Median value of income per capita (US$)	10,942	9,356
	4. Median value of years of schooling	12.4	12.5
	5. Proportion of rural population, in percent	19.1	19.4
	6. Proportion of over 20 years old born in the same state, in percent	10.0	63.0
	7. Proportion of over 5 years old having the same place of residence in 1970 as in 1965, in percent	36.0	54.0
	8. Proportion of 35 – 64 years old who were single, separated or remarried, in percent	47.4	25.5

Source: FUCHS (1974)

In search for an explanation, one comes across things which reflect a very different *lifestyle* in the two states. Nevada was evidently marked by strong immigration right up to the 1970s, the proportion of adults also born in Nevada being only 10 percent, compared to 63 percent in Utah (see variable No. 6). After five years of residence, only 36 percent of Nevada's population still lives in the same place (variable No. 7), while almost half of the 35-64 year old men are single or no longer married to their first wife (variable No. 8). These details paint a picture of an extraordinarily *mobile, even unstable society in Nevada* – and in fact, Las Vegas and Reno with their casinos are cities of Nevada, whilst the tone in neighboring Utah is set by the Mormons with their emphasis on abstinence. In all, this comparison supports the conclusion that lifestyle and habits may have a much greater influence on mortality rates than medical care.

4.2.2.5 Evidence from a Developing Region (Sub-Saharan Africa)

According to the WORLD BANK (2008), a new infant born in Sub-Saharan Africa is expected to live for 50 years. The same infant would be expected to live at least 70 years if he or she were born in a high-income country during the same period. Between the 1960s and the 1990s, average life expectancy at birth in Sub-Saharan Africa has improved by only 7 life years, which is far below the world average of about 11 years. FAYISSA AND GUTEMA (2005) estimate a health production function for 31 Sub-Saharan African countries over the period 1990–2000 using two economic (Y_i), one medical (M), three lifestyle or social (L_j) and two environmental factors (E_k) as inputs. The health production function is given by

$$\ln H = \ln \Omega + \sum \alpha_i (\ln Y_i) + \beta \ln M + \sum \gamma_j (\ln L_j) + \sum \delta_k (\ln E_k) + u \qquad (4.5)$$

where $i = 1,2$, $j = 1,2,3$ and $k = 1,2$ denote the number of indicators used, H symbolizes realized health, and Ω initial health of the region. All variables are in natural logs, therefore coefficients amount to elasticities. The variables are defined as follows.

- *Health H.* The dependent variable is life expectancy at birth. It indicates the number of years a newborn infant would live if prevailing patterns of mortality at the time of its birth were to stay the same throughout its life.

- *Economic factors Y_i.* GDP per capita (Y_1) calculated in constant US\$ is expected to have a positive coefficient, a higher level of income permitting more access to consumption of higher quality of goods and services, better housing, and medical services, all of which favorably influence health status. Moreover, as income increases, there is a general tendency to move away from jobs with higher stress which may adversely affect health status. Beyond some threshold level of affluence, increasing income may no longer buy better health. However, since income per capita is generally low in Sub-Saharan Africa, the sign of the income coefficient is expected to be positive. Food availability (Y_2), is singled out as a separate influence.

- *Medical factor M.* This is simply per capita HCE, comprising both public and private expenditure. Its sign cannot be determined a priori. On the one hand, higher levels of HCE may contribute to life expectancy, while on the other hand, HCE may squeeze out outlay on food, clothing, and housing – things that are crucial for survival in subsistence societies.

- *Lifestyle and social factors L_j.* Here, adult illiteracy (L_1) is used as a proxy for lack of education. It is the percentage of people above 15 years who cannot read, write, and understand a simple statement concerning their daily activities. GROSSMAN (1972b) and others have argued that education influences many decisions (such as a choice of job, healthy diet, avoidance of unhealthy habits, efficient use of medical care) which impacts on the quality of life. The second factor is adult alcohol consumption per capita (L_2). Finally, a larger population (L_3) is hypothesized to reduce food availability resulting in a decreased life expectancy.[4]

---

[4] This is the explanation given by the authors. It is puzzling because food availability already is taken into account (Y_2). However, a larger population may have other influences on health. For instance, it may be the result of migration, with immigrants obtaining a reduced benefit from HCE due to their lack of familiarity with the host country's health care system.

Table 4.6. Health Production Function for Sub-Saharan African Countries, 1990–2000

Explanatory variable	Dependent variable: life expectancy at birth	
	Elasticity	s.e.
Constant	3.3206***	(0.3639)
GDP per capita (Y_1)	0.0482**	(0.0235)
Food availability (Y_2)	0.1397***	(0.0496)
HCE per capita (M)	−0.0947***	(0.0273)
Illiteracy rate (L_1)	−0.0028**	(0.0011)
Adult alcohol consumption per capita (L_2)	−0.0196	(0.0120)
Population (L_3)	−0.0084	(0.0141)
Urbanization (E_1)	0.0011	(0.0016)
CO2 emissions per capita (E_2)	0.0000	(0.0001)

*,**,*** significant at the 10, 5 and 1 percent level, respectively.

Source: FAYISSA AND GUTEMA (2005, Table 2)

- *Environmental factors E_k.* The sign of urbanization (E_1) cannot be determined a priori. On the positive side, clinics are more effective in urban areas. On the negative side, urbanization is associated with pollution and congestion, which have adverse effects on health. In particular, carbon dioxide emissions per capita (E_2) are used as a proxy here.

Since the data have panel structure (Sub-Saharan countries observed between 1990 and 2000), FAYISSA AND GUTEMA (2005) estimate a so-called two-way random effects model. In fact, the error term u of equation (4.5) is split up into a component that is country-specific (μ_c) and a component that varies between countries and over time (v_{ct}) such that

$$u = \mu_c + v_{ct}. \tag{4.6}$$

The component μ_c induces a degree of autocorrelation over time that is reflected by the coefficient of first-order autocorrelation.

The estimation result is shown in Table 4.6. The key results are the following.

- GDP per capita and food availability, have a significant favorable effect on life expectancy.

- HCE has a marked negative relationship with life expectancy, possibly due to an inefficient provision of health care services.

- The rate of illiteracy has a small but significant effect on life expectancy. It is negative, as hypothesized.

- Alcohol consumption, population, urbanization, and CO_2 concentration fail to attain conventional levels of statistical significance; their effects have the expected signs, however.

Overall, the results suggest that a primary focus on the provision of health care services may do little to improve the health status in the 31 countries making up Sub-Saharan Africa. Rather, policies fostering food availability and economic growth may be decisive for extending life expectancy.

4.2.3 Marginal Productivity of Selected Medical Interventions

Health economics research has concerned itself comparatively little with the contribution of individual medical interventions to the health status of the person treated, and for two reasons. First, the internationally observed 'cost explosion' gave rise to the suspicion that HCE had exceeded its optimum amount at any rate. Second, economists rarely had access to clinical data, and if they did, the objective of the study often was to prove an advantageous benefit-cost ratio for a specific pharmaceutical or technological innovation.

The gap between the macroeconomic view and product-specific studies has been filled primarily by epidemiologists and medical sociologists. They categorize global mortality according to *cause of death*, estimate the possible contribution of single medical measures, and aggregate the specific effects into a total effect. MCKEOWN (1976), for example, investigated the historical development of mortality due to infectious diseases. He found that at a time when the respective diseases (ranging from typhus, small pox, scarlet fever to tuberculosis and pneumonia) could not yet be treated medically, the pertinent mortality rates were already declining in several industrial countries. MCKINLAY ET AL. (1989) limited their study to the United States, in return, they covered a broad range of disease categories. The main results are the following.

- *Infectious diseases.* Better control of infection was responsible for about 40 percent of the mortality decline between 1900 and 1973. Among the ten illnesses in this group, only three (influenza, whooping cough, and polio) showed a reduction in the specific mortality rates of 25 percent or more, that could be causally linked to a medical innovation (vaccinations). If one aggregates these three categories, no more than 3.5 percent of the drop in total U.S. mortality since 1900 can be attributed to medical advances in fighting infectious disease.

- *Chronic illnesses.* Here, one can distinguish two main groups, cardiovascular disease (which currently accounts for one third of all deaths) and cancer. In the first group, mortality rates have been falling in the United States since 1978, whilst in Western Germany for example, they continued to increase until the mid-1980s, possibly due to a different lifestyle [see KANNEL AND THOM (1984)]. In the same vein, only about 9 percent of the reduction in mortality can be attributed to the treatment of high blood pressure. The fact that the decrease mainly occurred outside the hospital may be interpreted as pointing to successful preventive efforts. In the case of cancer, medical success was limited to the treatment of testicular cancer in young men, and lymphatic leukemia in children, which together only make up about 8 percent of the incidence of these illnesses. By contrast, an increasing proportion of deaths is due to lung cancer, with cigarette smoking being the decisive risk factor. The decrease in mortality from heart attack seems in the main to reflect a reduced *frequency of circulatory disease* (where again preventive effort is important) rather than reduced lethality of the disease (where the effectiveness of medical treatment is important).

MCKINLAY ET AL. (1989) complement the picture of a limited success of modern medicine with two surprising facts. First of all, the number of lost workdays per person as well as the frequency of long-term health-related limitations of usual activity have been increasing since the 1950s in the United States.[5] Second, while life expectancy did grow between 1964 and 1985 by around 4.4 years for men and 4.5 years for women in the United States, *expected life years free from handicap* did not. These result from weighting the probability of survival by the conditional probability of being able to live without handicap. Between 1964 and 1985, this expected value even showed a decline of no less than 7.3 years (men) and 7.6 years (women at birth). Gains of 3.9 and 3.2 years respectively resulted in the over 65-year old age group only.

In sum, these estimates establish a correspondence between the weak or even counter-intuitive links connecting health and medicine found at the national level and the development of mortality in certain disease categories. In a predominantly healthy population, inputs other than medical ones must play a more important role in the production of health (see Sections 3.4.3 and 3.4.4).

4.2.4 Environmental Determinants of Health Status

Since the pioneering study by AUSTER ET AL. (1969), causality was hypothesized to run from industrialization to health, with limited success in terms of statistically significant relationships. By way of contrast, the study by LOPEZ ET AL. (1992) recognizes that industrialization may well be endogenous. Especially in an emerging economy, individuals have to weigh, e.g., *consumption* and *water pollution* against each other while having an influence upon both.

- On the one hand, the creation of jobs in industry expands consumption possibilities, yet aggravates the problem of water pollution;

- On the other hand, the installation of running water and sewage relieves problems of water pollution but limits consumption possibilities.

The authors use data on empirical evidence for the existence of a trade-off between consumption and life expectancy. Surprisingly, and in contradiction to the

---

[5] Part of this increase may be due to improved insurance coverage in the case of illness, reflecting a moral hazard effect that is discussed in Section 6.4. However, MCKINLAY ET AL. (1989) judge moral hazard effects to be insignificant.

study by FAYISSA AND GUTEMA (2005) for Sub-Saharan Africa, a high degree of illiteracy and high population density appear to go along with a low rate of cancer deaths.

4.2.5 Economic Instability and Health

At the level of aggregate data, the effects of economic instability on health have received considerable attention. The debate was started by BRENNER (1979), who, using annual data from 1936 to 1976, found a significant statistical connection between the *mortality rate* and the *unemployment rate* in England and Wales. The two other most important explanatory variables were the trend value of real income per capita and the deviation of current income from this trend.

In the framework of the model developed in Section 3.5, the influence of economic instability can be represented by a sudden change in several productivities. In the healthy state, the sudden income loss due to unemployment could cause a decrease in individuals' contribution to health in the guise of controlling their risk of illness $(\partial \pi / \partial t')$ [see Section 3.4.4.1, equation (3.41)]. This change serves to decrease longer-run production possibilities in the (C_h, T_h)-space; the second in particular serves to move the attainable maximum on the T_h-axis inwards, which ceteris paribus leads to a marked loss of healthy time (see Figure 3.5). In the sick state, worsening economic conditions could limit the contribution of medical services to recovery $[(\partial \pi / \partial M)$ smaller in absolute value in equation (3.33)], resulting in an increased minimal duration of a spell of illness. In extreme cases, these effects may conceivably combine to *increase the rate of mortality*. In this way, the findings of BRENNER (1983) can be said to have a theoretical foundation.

Table 4.7 contains evidence concerning mortality rates of England and Wales as well as Scotland, both separately and combined from BRENNER (1983). At first sight, it looks convincing.

- There is statistical evidence to the effect that the aggregate economic unemployment rate and, even more markedly, the unemployment ratio of over 20-year old men, *increases the mortality rate*, with a lag of up to two years.

- Cigarette consumption and (in Scotland) spirits consumption make a statistically recognizable contribution to the explanation of mortality rates.

- The regression equation of Table 4.7 also performs well in the analysis of mortality resulting from cardiovascular disease, heart disease following brain stroke, cirrhosis of the liver, suicide, murder, car accidents and infant deaths, since very high coefficients of determination R^2 are obtained throughout (not shown).

However, closer inspection of estimation results gives rise to concern. First, the coefficients relating to unemployment are highly unstable, ranging from 0.035 in the combined sample to 31.62 (a factor of one thousand) in Scotland. Differences of a factor of seven also are found in the coefficients relating to unemployment among

Table 4.7. Mortality Rates in England, Wales and Scotland

	[Lag][a]	England and Wales 1954–76	Scotland 1954–76	Combined sample 1955–79
Constant		−3.53	32.76[†††]	15.42[†††]
Real income per capita, trend		−0.013[†††]	−0.025[†††]	−0.013[†††]
Real income, Δ previous year		−0.003[†]	φ	−
Unemployment rate[b]	[1-6]	0.355[††]	31.62[††]	0.035[†]
Unemployment ratio, 20–40-year-old men	[1-2]	5.10[†††]	0.704[†]	0.986[††]
Unemployment ratio, 40+-year-old-men	[0-2]	7.25[†††]	0.840[†]	0.981[†]
Weekly working time, industrial		φ	−0.344[††]	−
Cigarette consumption per capita	[2-5]	0.0027[†††]	0.0030[†††]	0.001[†]
Spirits consumption per capita		φ	10.10[†††]	−
Health expenditure & public exp.	[0-1]	−20.56[†††]	−14.02	−4.53[†]
Average temperature in February		−	−	−0.016[†]
Regional income ratio		−	−	−3.33[††]
R^2		0.97	0.95	0.96
DW after Cochran-Orcutt transformation[c]		1.90	2.68	2.08
N		23	23	50

†, ††, †††: significant at the 5, 1 and 0.1 percent level, respectively.
− : not estimated.
φ: excluded from regression due to closeness of t value to zero.
a) [Lag] = Lag in years used in the estimated equations.
b) The rate of unemployment in Scotland is not known throughout; it is partially replaced by the one from the U.K.
c) The Cochran-Orcutt transformation is a method to free the estimated equation from the so-called autocorrelation in the error terms. A high value of $\hat{\rho} = \text{corr}(\hat{u}_t, \hat{u}_{t-1})$, i.e., a high correlation of the residual terms over time is an indicator of such autocorrelation. The test measure of Durbin and Watson (DW) takes on the value 2 if $\rho = 0$. If the DW value is significantly different from 2, the estimated equation can be multiplied with $(1 - \hat{\rho})$ (Cochran-Orcutt transformation). This results in estimated values of the regressions coefficients and their standard errors which are freed from autocorrelation [see, e.g., GREENE (2008, Chapter 19)].

Source: BRENNER (1983, Tables 1 and 19)

20–40 and 40+-year-old-men. Second, it is not HCE but HCE and public expenditure that is claimed to reduce mortality. Apart from widely different estimates of the negative regression coefficient, this implies that any increase of public expenditure that leaves HCE unaffected causes mortality to increase. Finally, very different lags occur, ranging for example in cigarette consumption from two to five years. In a comparable study of four industrial countries [see BRENNER (1983)], lagged effects even go from zero (Sweden) to 16 years (France) and 18 (Denmark).

Apart from these weaknesses, GRAVELLE (1984) raised three criticisms that apply to many investigations of this type.

(1) *Inaccurate theoretical foundation.* According to Table 4.7, consumption affects health through goods such as alcohol and tobacco, whose purchase must be financed out of disposable income. Thus income itself does not belong in the equation, unless it is used as an indicator of general lifestyle. For example, the role of income is not clear in the study by FAYISSA AND GUTEMA (2005) either, because food availability serves as an additional explanatory variable there.

(2) *Simultaneity problem.* Changes in health status (which lie at the basis of changes in mortality) have an impact on labor income. Therefore, income cannot be treated as predetermined but contains a stochastic component which is positively correlated with mortality. This positive correlation causes one to overestimate the influence of income fluctuations on the mortality rate. The impact of unemployment on health is also exaggerated, since income fluctuations and unemployment are closely linked. In fact, this criticism applies to just about all studies presented so far, with the exception of THORNTON (2002).

(3) *Functional form.* The trend value of income can increase with time (even at an accelerated rate because an exponential trend is assumed). This means that at some point of time in the future, the model will predict *negative* mortality rates. Moreover, the dependent variable amounts to a linear combination of two mortality rates, one characterizing the unemployed, the other, the rest of the population, while the theory revolves around the mortality rate of the unemployed. Since the weights of this linear combination are given by the rate of unemployment (UN_t) and its complement $(1 - UN_t)$,[6] the equation should contain regressors such as UN_t^2 and $UN_t \Delta Y_t$, with ΔY_t symbolizing change in real income. Quite generally, the composition of the population studied receives little consideration in many studies at the macro level. It may call for interaction terms, such as (Alcohol times women) in MILLER AND FRECH (2004a).

Conclusion 4.2. *A negative impact of economic instability and unemployment in particular on the individual's health-enhancing productivity as well as on the productivity of medical services is theoretically plausible. The statistical evidence supporting such a relationship is at present not very strong, however, not least because the estimation equation is not specified in a careful manner.*

---

[6] The rate of unemployment usually refers to the active population rather than to the total population. This difference is neglected here for the sake of simplicity.

4.3 Studies Based on Individual Data

4.3.1 Measurement of Health Status

At the aggregate level, the choice of output variable in a production function of health is severely limited by the availability of statistical data. Individual measurements based on surveys, however, open up a broad range of possible definitions of output. The theoretical guideline is equation 2.3 of Section 2.3.2, which defines (subjective) health status by a probability distribution over various possible states. One of them materializes at the time of measurement. The ambiguity then arises whether this state is to be understood prior to or after the input of medical care (or the individual's own effort).

As already established in Section 1.3 and in Table 3.7, health has a *double function*. On the one hand, it is a variable of crucial importance for explaining the utilization of medical care; on the other hand, it represents the outcome of a production process. This double function creates no problems as long as inputs are defined as potential ones such as physician density, number of beds etc. As soon as the inputs turn into effective consumption of medical services, beginning and end of the production process must be kept apart in the measurement of health status. Therefore, measurements of health should preferably refer to a particular healthy phase or sickness episode. This type of temporal disaggregation has rarely been undertaken [see KEELER (1987)].

Apart from the timing of the measurement, the source of measurement also is a far more important issue in the case of individual data than with aggregate data. In particular, a distinction needs to be made between

(a) Information provided by individuals themselves;

(b) Information provided by a third party, in particular by physicians and nursing staff.

The category (a) of information is often subjective and therefore deemed less reliable. For some purposes, however, the answer of a hypochondriac to the question, 'How are you at the moment?' can be quite informative. It may betray a particularly high marginal willingness to pay for better health, from which a high probability of utilization of medical services can be inferred. Information belonging to category (b) is indeed objective, being at least partially based on clinical measurement. Distinguishing between latent variables and their fallible indicators [see GOLDBERGER (1974) and JÖRESKOG (1973)], one may say that clinical measurement gives rise to indicators having a small share of measurement error variance in their total variance. On the other hand, they frequently fail to have a strong, significant relationship with the latent variable of primary interest, 'health'.

However, the search for an 'objective' output measure which is independent of the individual's willingness to pay (and also ability to pay) is hardly worthwhile in this context. It hinges on the questionable premise that *health ought to be maximized regardless of competing objectives.*[7] As soon as one is to allow other competing objectives, an improvement in health would need to be evaluated according to marginal willingness to pay. Inasmuch as willingness to pay depends on the current subjective state of health, information provided by individuals themselves becomes very suitable.

4.3.2 Marginal Productivity of Medical Infrastructure at the Individual Level

In the United States, a National Health Examination Survey was conducted around 1960, in the course of which over 6,000 individuals from 39 randomly selected areas were examined for various physiological aspects of the health state. These measurements thus belong to category (b) of the sources of information mentioned in Section 4.3.1. They were related, by NEWHOUSE AND FRIEDLANDER (1980), to the available regional medical infrastructure on the one hand and to variables characterizing these individuals and their environment on the other. Apart from the explanatory variables presented in Table 4.8, categorical variables for occupation, family status, family size, self employment and sex enter the regression equations. Age appears in linear and squared form.

The first five clinical indicators shown in Table 4.8 refer to blood pressure and lipid concentration in the blood, conditions which evidently contribute to cardiovascular mortality according to the findings of large-scale epidemiological studies (see Section 4.3.3 below). The following observations are of particular interest.

- Neither *medical infrastructure*, nor education or income of the individual examined have a statistically proven influence on the first four indicators.

- In the case of the other three indicators, viz. *X-rays, periodontal index* and *age index*, more schooling appears to turn individuals into better producers of health, without an increased income becoming counterproductive. In terms of the age index, a 10 percent increase in the length of schooling makes individuals 0.5 percent younger physiologically than their calendar age, other things kept equal.

- With regard to the degree of urbanization, only the occurrence of an *abnormal X-ray* is affected positively and significantly.

- *Race* is the variable having statistical significance most often. Non-whites, when compared with white people, appear less healthy. While differences in blood

---

[7] This does not deny that non-financial (medical) measures of health status may contribute to an optimal allocation in health care, e.g., when it comes to the choice between various treatment alternatives within a previously established health budget (see the discussion in Chapter 2).

Table 4.8. Estimated Influences on Clinical Health Indicators, United States, around 1960[a]

Clinical indicators	Medical infrastructure[b]			Individual productivity[c]		Environmental factors[d]	
	PHYS	OTH	BEDS	EDU	INC	URB	RACE
Diastol. blood pressure, conditional[f]	−0.02	−0.003	0.009	0.01	−0.003	−0.007	2.48**
Excess lipid concentration in the blood[e]	0.39	−0.03	−0.13	−0.08	0.05	−0.000	−0.02**
Lipid concentration in the blood, conditional[g]	0.02	−0.02	0.03	0.02	−0.003	0.031	−1.01
Abnormal ECG[e]	0.03	−0.06	0.06	−0.02	−0.04	0.000	0.15***
Hypertension[e]	−0.06	0.20**	0.32*	−0.25*	−0.006	−0.001***	0.12***
Abnormal X-ray[e]	−0.04	−0.07***	0.07**	−0.09***	−0.03**	0.002***	−0.082*
Varicose veins[e]	0.13	0.002	−0.44***	−0.19	−0.04	0.003	−0.05***
Periodontal index				−0.77***	−0.21***	−0.002	0.19***
Aging index[h]	−0.004	0.001	0.01	−0.05***	−0.01***	0.002	0.72**

*,**,*** significant at the 10, 5 and 1 percent level (one-tailed test), respectively. $N = 4,769$.

a) The values shown are elasticities calculated using sample means, except for URB and RACE, where regression coefficients are shown.

b) PHYS = general practitioners, internists, and gynecologists, OTH = other physicians, BEDS = hospital beds, all per 100,000 inhabitants. Two additional regressors (beds in hospitals run by the federal government and dentist density) are not listed. All regressions contain age, $(age)^2$ and a categorical variable for sex.

c) EDU = number of years of schooling, INC = family income.

d) URB = Proportion of the examined living in communities having more than 2,500 inhabitants; RACE = 1 for non-whites, = 0 for whites.

e) Logit estimate, as the dependent variable can only take on the values 0 and 1.

f) Only cases of hypertension.

g) Only cases of excess lipid concentration.

h) Based on regressions of age on the clinical indicators (without *hypertension* and *excess of lipid concentration*); every individual is assigned a 'clinical age' using the average of the eight calculated expected values.

Source: NEWHOUSE AND FRIEDLANDER (1980)

pressure and lipid concentration may be due to genetic differences, the periodontal index points to differences in behavior and even preferences.

4.3.3 The Productivity of Medical Interventions at the Individual Level

In the 1960s, cardiovascular diseases were the most important cause of death in the United States. High blood pressure, high lipid concentration in the blood, and tobacco consumption were suspected to constitute the decisive risk factors. At that time, many long-term studies were initiated, among them, the *Framingham study*. Conducted in Massachusetts, it is the most famous, having an observation period of up to 18 years. The results of this study give insights into the 'production of health' in a very concrete, almost technical sense. Output may be defined as a reduction in the cholesterol level of the blood which in turn results in lowered blood pressure. The medical input consists of treatment with an appropriate drug, while the patient's own contribution consists in maintaining a particular diet. Is the maintenance of the diet alone sufficient for reducing cholesterol, or is it effective only in the combination with a drug?

Since hypertensive patients can continue their normal life as if healthy, the conditional production possibility frontier model [in particular Conclusion 3.12 in Section 3.4.5] leads to the presumption that individual efforts could *substitute* for the use of drugs. However, participants in these long-term studies do live through periods of illness during the period of observation, and may also use drugs during these periods. Therefore, medical inputs may well contribute to survival. Surprisingly, HOUSTON (1989, p. 928) in his extensive survey comes to the conclusion that drug therapy has no definite influence on mortality in the case of cardiovascular diseases. Indeed, certain forms of therapy can even *undermine the success of a diet* [HOUSTON (1989, p. 929)]. This conclusion provides an excellent illustration of the idea developed in Section 3.4.3, according to which medical services cannot be substituted by individual efforts to improve health in the event of illness, while substitution becomes possible in the longer run.

Conclusion 4.3. *The concept of the production of health, with the individual's own contribution and medical services as inputs, can also be applied to individual data, exhibiting considerable extent of substitutability in the case of specific diseases.*

4.3.4 Environmental Quality and the State of Health

In the studies based on individual data presented so far, environmental influences have been neglected, or they have proved statistically insignificant. The first systematic attempt to assess the effects at least of air pollution on human health was made by LAVE AND SESKIN (1977). However, they had to work with English counties as their unit of observation, with no indicators available describing individual productivity such as education or income. Usually, [as in LOPEZ ET AL. (1992), see Section 4.2.4], population density must assume the role of both an (inverse) income indicator and a factor favoring the spreading of communicable disease. This often leads to instability of estimated coefficients or even implausible results.

4.3.4.1 Air Quality and Smoking as Exogenous Factors

The problems associated with the use of aggregate data were first overcome by OSTRO (1983), who combined *individual responses* to the health survey of 1976 in the United States with measurements of the air quality in 84 metropolitan areas. *TSP* (Total Suspended Particles) and *SULF* (Sulfuric Compounds) were selected from a large number of measurements to serve as regressors. Since both indicators had been consistently measured over a long period of time, their use ensured comparability with earlier studies. Indicators of health status were the number of days of restricted activity due to health reasons and the number of workdays lost during the two weeks preceding the survey (see Table 4.9).

The regression coefficients entered in column *A* of Table 4.9 suggest that *TSP* has the expected positive influence upon the number of restricted activity days, whereas *SULF* shows no significant effect. More relevant to economics in the more traditional sense, the number of lost workdays is shown in column *B*. Again, *TSP* concentration plays a statistically significant role, with an elasticity of 0.45 (calculated at the sample mean). An increase in TSP concentration of 10 percent thus is estimated to result in a 4.5 percent increase in the number of workdays lost – a value which according to OSTRO (1983) is ten times that found in previous investigations.

In analyzing the connection between air quality and health, the concept of health production proves useful once more. In *avoiding tobacco consumption*, individuals can improve substantially the quality of the air they breathe. Accordingly, the number of cigarettes smoked (*CIGARETTES*) appears in the equations of columns *A* and *B* of Table 4.9. The corresponding regression coefficient proves both times to be statistically insignificant, however. Yet, the low coefficients of determination of 0.09 and 0.01 point to the possibility of misspecification in that the regression equation fails to account for many determinants of the dependent variables. Specifically, differences between smokers and non-smokers may not be sufficiently represented by the number of cigarettes smoked (*CIGARETTES*). For instance, the number of chronic health problems (*CHRONIC*) probably has a completely different (also sex-specific) significance to smokers with their frequent respiratory diseases than to non-smokers. In analogy to the case of measurement error in a regressor, the likely effect would be to bias the estimate of the influence of air quality on health status toward zero.

In order to estimate the effects of air pollution on the number of lost workdays without such bias, columns *C* and *D* of Table 4.9 refer exclusively to male, employed non-smokers. A full 94 percent of these had no absences from work in the two weeks before investigation, while 6 percent had lost one or more workdays.[8] This calls for first estimating the *probability* of absence from work (column *C* of Table 4.9) prior to estimating the length of an absence when applicable (column *D*). Accordingly, the dependent variable of column *C* is a dummy variable, which takes on the value of 1 when at least one workday was lost for health reasons, and 0 otherwise. This restriction on the range of the dependent variable can be removed by means of the so-called Logit transformation. The consequence is, though, that the values entered in column *C* are coefficients of a logistic regression, which cannot be interpreted as partial influences on probability [see GREENE (2008, Chapter 23)]. The values in column *D*, by contrast, are Ordinary Least Squares estimates.

---

[8] This means that the dependent variable is extremely skewed to the left, which does not square well with the customary assumption of a normally distributed error term, the normal distribution being symmetrical around the expected value (see also Boxes 4.1 and 4.2 in Section 4.2.2.1).

Table 4.9. Influence of Air Quality on Health, United States, 1976

Variable[a]	Restricted activity days (A)[b]	Workdays lost (B)[c]	Probability of $B > 0$ (C)[d]	Workdays lost if $B > 0$ (D)[d]
Constant	−0.83***	−0.47***	−3.66***	−0.39
TSP	0.00282***	0.00145**	0.0071**	0.002
SULF	−0.00008	−0.001	−0.051*	−0.009
CHRONIC	1.25***	0.25***	0.48***	0.93**
AGE	0.0063***	0.0033***	−0.0048	0.075***
INCOME	−0.009***	−0.002	−0.004	0.012
MARRIED	−0.011	−0.011	0.227*	−1.24***
RACE	0.17***	0.045	−0.04	−0.46
TEMPERATURE	0.013***	0.0065***	0.003	0.097**
BLUE-COLLAR WORKER		−0.046*	0.29	−1.26***
EMPLOYED	−0.114***			
POP.DENSITY	0.0057	0.0056*	0.030**	−0.050
PRECIPITATION	−0.0004	−0.0004	0.0097	−0.040*
SEXF	0.093**	0.067***		
CIGARETTES	0.0032	−0.0006		
R^2	0.09	0.01		0.17
χ^2			25.8***	
N	13,230	8,294	4,473	263

*,**,*** significant at the 10, 5 and 1 percent level (one-tailed test), respectively.

a) TSP = concentration of total suspended particles in the air, annual average (in microgram/m^3); $SULF$ = concentration of sulfuric compounds in the air, annual average (in microgram/m^3); $CHRONIC$ = number of chronic diseases; AGE = age in years; $INCOME$ = family income (in thousands of US\$); $MARRIED$ = 1, if individual is married, = 0 otherwise; $RACE$ = 1, if non-white, = 0 otherwise; $TEMPERATURE$ = annual average temperature (in degrees Fahrenheit); $EMPLOYED$ = 1 if employed, = 0 otherwise; $BLUE$-$COLLAR$ $WORKER$ = 1 if blue-collar worker, = 0 otherwise; $POP.DENSITY$ = population of the metropolitan area (in 1,000 per square mile); $PRECIPITATION$ = annual average precipitation; $SEXF$ = 1 if female, = 0 otherwise; $CIGARETTES$ = number of cigarettes smoked per day.
b) Sample of 18–65 year old persons in 84 metropolitan areas.
c) Sample only includes employed ($EMPLOYED$ = 1).
d) Sample only includes male employed non-smokers.

Source: OSTRO (1983, Tables I and III)

Since columns C and D of Table 4.9 refer to non-smokers only, they should provide information about the influence of air quality upon work capability independently of the behavior of the individual, viz., choice of smoking status. The concentration of total suspended particles (TSP) has a statistically significant influence on the *probability of absence from work*, but not on the *length* of this period. The influence of the other component of air quality, that of sulfuric compounds ($SULF$), cannot be proved. Furthermore, other environmental factors such as average air temperature of rainfall do not seem to have an influence on the absence from work (both probability of occurrence and duration of absence).

4.3.4.2 Smoking as an Endogenous Factor

All studies discussed so far (including those using aggregate data of Section 4.2) have a common flaw because they analyze influences on health only, whilst the model of health behavior developed in Section 3.4.3 simultaneously explains *consumption* and *health*. Analyzing health becomes problematic as soon as the consumption decision has an immediate impact on health, as in the case of smoking (see item (2) of Section 4.1). In an attempt to control for this impact, the number of cigarettes smoked appeared as a regressor in Table 4.9. However, ROSENZWEIG AND SCHULTZ (1983) argue that this solution fails to do justice to the theoretical model, calling attention to background variables that may well have an effect both on health (particularly respiratory diseases) and on tobacco consumption. If, for example, anxious people hardly ever smoke, but nevertheless are more ill than others, then an *artificial positive correlation* between illness and tobacco consumption arises. This bias serves to neutralize the expected negative correlation (i.e., the disease-enhancing effect of tobacco). It could be the reason for the lack of statistical significance of the regressor *CIGARETTES* in Table 4.9.

Evidently the explanatory variable *CIGARETTES* must be purged of an error component that is due to its endogeneity. This can be done through a first-stage regression (as part of a Two-Stage Least Squares estimation, see Box 4.2), in which the observed values of *CIGARETTES* are replaced by their expected conditional values.

MULLAHY AND PORTNEY (1990) applied a procedure of this type, the so-called Generalized Method of Moments (GMM) [see GREENE (2008, Chapter 15)] to the same sample as OSTRO (1983), but using data for 1979 instead of 1976. The dependent variable is the number of restricted activity days during the two weeks prior to the investigation, but only if occurring as a result of *respiratory diseases*. This variable should thus bear a closer relationship to air quality than the dependent variable of Table 4.9, the number of restricted activity days for (all) health reasons. Since 96 percent of those interviewed had no such days, the probability of having days with health-related limitations is examined in columns *A* of Table 4.10. The parameter estimates of an equation explaining the duration of these limitations are shown in columns *B*. To demonstrate the importance of purging the variable *CIGARETTES* of its endogeneity, the OLS and GMM estimates appear next to each other in Table 4.10.

The results presented in Table 4.10 can be summarized in the following statements.

(1) *Influence of tobacco consumption.* If tobacco consumption is treated as an exogenous variable beyond the influence of the individual (like ozone concentration), then there is no indication of any impact on health status, exactly as in the study by OSTRO (1983). This holds true even if tobacco consumption is specifically

Table 4.10. Air Quality and Smoking in the Production of Health, United States, 1979

Variable[a]	Probability of nonzero restricted activity days[b] (A)		Number of restricted activity days, conditional on $A > 0$ (B)	
	OLS	GMM[c]	OLS	GMM[c]
Constant	0.035	0.185***	0.0078	0.789***
$CIGARETTES$	−0.060	−1.91***	−0.034	−8.44***
$CIGARETTES^2$	0.25	5.81***	1.09	27.95***
$OZONE$	0.064	0.51	4.25**	6.64**
$OZONE^2$	−1.60	−3.97	−23.7**	−35.8**
$SULF$	−0.20	−0.20	−1.52	−1.77
$SULF^2$	0.65	0.56	4.87	5.07
$TEMPERATURE$	−0.055*	−0.090**	−0.44***	−0.61***
$PRECIPITATION$	−0.017	−0.034	0.033	−0.028
AGE	0.35	−0.16	2.14**	−0.90
AGE^2	−0.48*	0.077	−2.82**	0.60
$DCHRONIC$	0.011	−0.0066	0.19	0.094
$SEXM$	−0.00089	−0.032***	−0.045	−0.17***
N	2,331	2,331	89	89

*,**,*** significant at the 10, 5 and 1 percent level, respectively.

a) $CIGARETTES$ = Number of cigarettes smoked per day (/100); $CIGARETTES^2$ = Squared value of $CIGARETTES$; $OZONE$ = Ozone concentration based on daily maximum values during the 14 days prior to the investigation (in PPM, parts per million); $OZONE^2$ = Squared value of $OZONE$; $SULF$ = Concentration of sulfuric compounds, mean of measurements taken during 14 days prior to the investigation; $SULF^2$ = Squared value of $SULF$; $TEMPERATURE$ = Average temperature based on the maximum values of 14 days (in degrees Fahrenheit, /100); $PRECIPITATION$ = Mean value of the measurements taken during 14 days (in inches), AGE = Age in years; AGE^2 = Squared value of AGE; $DCHRONIC$ = 1 if individual is restricted in his activity due to chronic diseases , = 0 otherwise; $SEXM$ = 1 if individual is male, = 0 otherwise.

b) Although the dependent variable can take on the values 0 and 1 only, it is treated like a continuous variable here. The resulting coefficients can therefore be interpreted as estimated partial effects on the probability of the corresponding regressors.

c) GMM = Generalized Method of Moments; method generalizing the two-stage estimates of Box 4.2.

Source: MULLAHY AND PORTNEY (1990, Table 3)

related to respiratory health (see OLS estimates of the variables $CIGARETTES$ and $CIGARETTES^2$). On the other hand, once $CIGARETTES$ is cleared of its endogeneity, it proves a *highly significant* determinant of health (see GMM estimates of the two variables measuring the consumption of cigarettes). Actually, smoking a few cigarettes a day seems to have a positive effect on health (negative coefficients of $CIGARETTES$), but beyond about 16 cigarettes, the negative effects on the respiratory tract become predominant.

(2) *Influence of air quality.* Ozone has to be recognized as a relevant substance in air pollution. Its effects on health, in contrast to tobacco consumption, tend to decrease with increased concentration (i.e., beyond about 0.06 microgram/m^3, the average value in the sample being 0.043); this follows from the negative coefficients of variable $OZONE^2$. A high ozone concentration *increases the probability* of spending a period of restricted activity and prolongs its duration (see part *B* of Table 4.10).

(3) *Sulfuric compound concentration as an indicator of air quality.* Despite a narrowly defined dependent variable and improved estimation methods, no influence of sulfuric compounds (SULF) on respiratory health can be proved (see variables $SULF$ and $SULF^2$). On this point, the earlier investigation of OSTRO (1983) is confirmed (see Table 4.9, variable $SULF$).

(4) *Comparison of magnitudes of influences.* Using the parameter values estimated with the GMM method and the respective sample means, values of elasticities can be calculated. For example, with an increase in daily cigarette consumption of around 10 percent, the probability of having a period of restricted activity increases by around 33 percent, in contrast to only 13 percent in the case of an increase in ozone concentration of around 10 percent. The length of such a period increases by around 44 percent following increased smoking, and by about 28 percent as a result of 10 percent more ozone in the air. Therefore, the estimated relative productivities in enhancing health of the respiratory tracts *shift* from the exogenous influence of air quality *towards smoking as an input* in the production of health, which is under the individual's control.

Conclusion 4.4. *By means of individual data, a relationship between air quality and the state of health becomes evident. However, the input 'tobacco consumption' plays a crucial role in the simultaneous production of consumption services and respiratory health.*

This conclusion supports the notion that the observed slowdown of the increase of life expectancy can be traced only to a rather limited extent to a change in relative productivity of the input factors in the production of health due to a deterioration of the environment (see item (3) of Section 4.1). Rather, it may be caused by the health behavior of consumers.

4.4 Demand for Health, Demand for Health Services

The model of health related behavior introduced in Section 3.4.3 assumes that the individual is a demander of and a supplier or producer of health at the same time. So far it has been implicitly assumed that the empirical relationships reflect the production side of individual behavior. This section deals with the questions of whether a differentiation between supply and demand is necessary at all, how it could be achieved, and whether certain puzzles emerging in the production function for health literature can be explained.

One might claim that investigating the demand for health separately from its production by the individual is unnecessary. Given state-independent average preferences and production possibilities with regard to consumption and health, the Marginal Rate of Substitution (MRS) can be simply inferred from the observed Marginal Rate of Transformation (MRT). Indeed, Figure 1.1 of Section 1.2 shows that these two values coincide at the optimum (point R^*). While the location of this optimal point does depend on the preferences of the observed individual, this does not preclude an unbiased estimation of the parameters of the individual's production function as long as preferences differ *randomly* between individuals. In this case, they only affect the error term of the estimated equation (the variable u_i in Boxes 4.1 and 4.2), causing a loss of statistical fit but having no further consequences. This is the 'classical view' based on GROSSMAN (1972b) [see ROSENZWEIG AND SCHULTZ (1983)].

This view, however, cannot be upheld within the framework of the model developed in Section 3.4.3. According to that model, individuals are not really able to choose their state of health. Rather, their options are limited to *influencing the probability* of a certain state of health occurring. Consequently, they choose an optimal probability $(1 - \pi_i^*)$ to remain in good health or to be in good health again, with $0 < (1 - \pi_i^*) < 1$. During a given period of time, they are (given only two possible states) either healthy $[h_i = 1]$ *or* sick $[h_i = 0]$. This means that the target is missed by most of the people most of the time. These deviations compensate one another when taking the average, but only for a large group or a large number of periods. At the level of the single individual and during a shorter observation period, the deviations between actual health h_i and targeted chance of being healthy $(1 - \pi_i^*)$ give rise to an additional error term $\tilde{u}_i$, which does not exist in the 'classical view'. However, one can posit a feedback from this error term to the inputs of the production function of health as follows.

- $h_i - 1 > (1 - \pi_i^*) \rightarrow \tilde{u}_i > 0$: the individual is in good health, while aiming at a chance of being healthy amounting to $(1 - \pi_i^*) < 1 = 1 - \varepsilon_i$ with ε_i usually a very small number. Accordingly, efforts to maintain this state of health (t_i^I in Box 3.2) will be reduced. This induces a *negative* correlation between t_i^I and $\tilde{u}_i$ (being too healthy goes together with neglecting prevention).

- $h_i = 0 < (1 - \pi_i^*) \rightarrow \tilde{u}_i < 0$: the individual is sick, although aiming at a probability of being healthy of $(1 - \pi_i^*) = 1 - \varepsilon_i$. Accordingly, there will be a demand for medical services (M in Box 3.2). This induces a *negative* correlation between M_i and $\tilde{u}_i$ (being sicker than expected goes together with a reliance on medicine).

These considerations show that not only discrepancies between MRT and MRS can be expected when observing individual behavior but also that these discrepancies *feed back* onto the production of health. Causality not only runs from M_i and t_i^I to $(1 - \pi_i^*)$ but also from the discrepancies $\{h_i - (1 - \pi_i^*)\}$ back to M_i and t_i^I. In order to avoid biases in estimating the production function of health, two possible tracks can be pursued.

First, the regressors M_i and t_i^f can be purged of their error components due to endogeneity, by using, e.g., a two-stage estimation method (see Box 4.2). A second approach is to purge the error term of the component $\tilde{u}_i = h_i - (1 - \pi_i^*)$ that is correlated with the regressors. This procedure obviously requires a measure of 'target health status' $(1 - \pi_i^*)$ which is independent of 'actual health status' h_i.[9] As the quality of health status measurement is continuously improving, the second method will be analyzed more closely here. Thus, an equation of the form

$$h_i = c + \alpha M_i + \beta t_i^f + (u_i + \tilde{u}_i), \quad \text{where} \quad \tilde{u}_i = h_i - (1 - \pi_i^*) \qquad (4.7)$$

is to be estimated, the component $\tilde{u}_i$ of the error term being (negatively) correlated with the regressors M_i and t_i^f. If measurements of $\tilde{u}_i$ are available, however, $\tilde{u}_i$ can be singled out from the error term to become an *additional regressor*,

$$h_i = c + \alpha M_i + \beta t_i^f + \gamma\{h_i - (1 - \pi_i^*)\} + u_i, \quad \text{where} \quad \gamma = 1. \qquad (4.8)$$

Solving this equation for the input factor M_i, results in

$$M_i = -\frac{c}{\alpha} - \frac{\beta}{\alpha}t_i^f - \frac{1}{\alpha}\left\{h_i - (1 - \pi_i^*)\right\} + \frac{1}{\alpha}h_i - \frac{1}{\alpha}u_i. \qquad (4.9)$$

Estimation of this equation can lead to different results, depending on what health status measurement actually means.

(a) If one succeeds in measuring target health status $(1 - \pi_i^*)$, the third term of equation (4.9) can be split up into $(1/\alpha)(1 - \pi_i^*)$ and $-(1/\alpha)u_i$. Therefore, terms in u_i cancel out. As $\alpha > 0$, the correlation of medical services and the state of health should be *positive*, as predicted by the GROSSMAN (1972b) model.

(b) If respondents rate their health as 'good' when it was better than expected at the time of measurement, the estimated equation (4.9) does contain the term $(-1/\alpha)\{h_i - (1 - \pi_i^*)\}$. As $u_i > 1 - \pi_i$, there will be a *negative* estimated correlation between measured state of health and medical services in the sample, a possibility encompassed by the stochastic formulation presented in Section 3.4

(c) If the survey is limited to measuring actual health status, the term $(1/\alpha)h_i$ enters equation (4.9) as an explanatory variable, basically causing correlation between medical services and health. However, $(-1/\alpha)\{h_i - (1 - \pi_i^*)\}$ is added to the error term in this case, resulting in equation (4.7) again, which means that α and $(1/\alpha)$ respectively cannot be estimated without bias. The result may well be a negative correlation, especially if α is small. Again, this is a possibility encompassed by the stochastic formulation of Section 3.4.

One of the most ambitious attempts ever at filtering out desired health status in order to assure case (a) was undertaken by LEU AND DOPPMANN (1986a). The authors defined health as a latent variable that is reflected by several indicators, each of

---

[9] As soon as individuals only have an influence on the probability of occurrence of various states, their optimal target health status is defined by this very probability, [see Figure 3.3 of Section 3.4.3.3]. Therefore $(1 - \pi_i^*)$ equals target and h_i actual health status, respectively.

which may not vary 1:1 with health and moreover contain measurement error. This type of statistical modeling is reminiscent of factor analysis. It differs from factor analysis in that identifying restrictions exclude multiplication of the system by an arbitrary definite matrix (called 'factor rotation' in factor analysis). It can be estimated by Maximum Likelihood methods [LISREL, see JÖRESKOG (1973)]. In the course of a health survey conducted in Switzerland in 1980, a very comprehensive set of indicators related to health were collected for 3,155 adult persons. However, when LEU AND DOPPMANN (1986a) analyzed ambulatory care visits, days in hospital, and days at a health resort, they consistently found negative elasticities w.r.t. their latent variable 'health'. Therefore, in spite of considerable effort to assure that case (a) above obtains (where the partial correlation between medical services and health should be positive in keeping with the GROSSMAN (1972b) model), they obtained highly significantly negative ones. This contradiction also was found by GERFIN ET AL. (1992).

Conclusion 4.5. *The concept of a transformation curve with consumption services and health care as outputs that is conditional on current health status is supported by empirical investigations based on individual data. In particular, it predicts the negative partial correlation between health and medical inputs that is to be expected when individuals are below their desired probability of being healthy in the future when currently sick.*

Since in the sick state individuals crucially rely on medical inputs for the production of health, the question arises as to who performs the function of coordination only (choice of doctor, preference for drug, termination of treatment). Depending on the severity of the illness and the amount of information available, they frequently delegate authority to a physician in charge. This gives physicians leeway to pursue their own objectives.

This consideration calls for an investigation into the decision situation of the physician, which is undertaken in Chapter 8. In a certain sense, this analysis in unsatisfactory, as it fails to fully portray the interaction between physician and patient. Through comparing and combining empirically tested implications of such partial models, however, it is possible to approximately predict the effects of particular health policies.

4.5 Summary

(1) This chapter revolves around the empirical implementation of the production function of health, and more generally, of the transformation curve in terms of health and consumption services.

(2) There are indications based on the analysis of aggregate data suggesting that in several countries (among them the United States), the marginal productivity of medical infrastructure in terms of longevity may well fall short of that of education.

(3) Studies based on national as well as regional data support the view that differences in mortality rates can only very partially be traced to medical infrastructure (and physician density in particular). Individuals' productivity in maintaining their health seems to be of greater importance.

(4) A negative impact of economic instability on the individual's health-enhancing productivity as well as on the productivity of medical services is theoretically plausible. However, the statistical evidence supporting such a relationship is not firm at present, not least because it is subject to faulty specification of the regression equations.

(5) The concept of health production with the individual's own contribution and medical services as inputs can also be applied to individual data, exhibiting considerable extent of substitutability in the case of specific diseases.

(6) In individual data, relationships between air quality and health have become evident. However, the input 'tobacco consumption' appears to play a role of at least equal importance once the simultaneous production of consumption services and respiratory health is accounted for.

(7) The concept of a situation-dependent transformation curve in terms of consumption services and health is confirmed by disaggregate data. State dependence is illustrated by the negative partial correlation between health and medical care.

4.6 Further Reading

We recommend the World Development Report published by the World Bank in 1993 [see WORLD BANK (1993)]. Further empirical studies of the production of health can be found in MILLER AND FRECH (2004b) and COMANOR ET AL. (2006).

4.E Exercises

4.1. One criticism of the estimated equation developed by BRENNER (1983) states that it should include regressors such as $UN_t \Delta Y_t$ and UN_t^2, because the dependent variable is not the mortality rate of the unemployed people but rather the one of the total (active) population. This would imply that the relationship between the mortality rate and the rate of unemployment does not remain constant but varies over time.

Prove these statements by formulating two simplified estimated equations [one for S^u (mortality rate of the unemployed) and one for S^e (mortality rate of the employed)] using the regressors No. 1–3 of Table 4.7 for each one. Then form their linear combination, as mentioned in the text.

4.2. The comment on the study by MULLAHY AND PORTNEY (1990) says that more than 16 cigarettes a day of additional tobacco consumption is damaging to health, whereas beyond 0.06 micrograms/m^3, an increase ozone concentration has no negative effect.

(a) Try to explain how these results come about, using the coefficients of Table 4.10. Draw the graph of the partial functions $P = f(CIGARETTES)$ and $P = g(OZONE)$, with P = probability of a phase of restricted activity.

(b) Write down the estimated equation underlying Table 4.10 and determine by means of partial differentiation the algebraic value of $CIGARETTES$ where additional consumption turns from a health-enhancing into a health-damaging effect.

(c) Insert the GMM estimated coefficients of Table 4.10 and calculate this extreme point algebraically, taking into account that $CIGARETTES$ is the effective number divided by 100. Determine the extreme point in the case of $OZONE$ in analogous manner.

5

Health Goods, Market Failure and Justice

5.1 Introduction

The allocation of health goods frequently deviates from the principles of a market economy. This holds true particularly of medical services, even in Western industrialized countries, which claim to be market economies. In general, neither the decision to offer a medical service (e.g., an appendectomy) nor the decision to demand that service are made by sovereign individuals or firms who bear the full financial consequences of their choices. Moreover, the price mechanism is not permitted to coordinate choices in health care by signaling varying degrees of scarcity. The decision-making process is thus completely different from that characterizing the production and purchase of refrigerators, for example.

The United Kingdom and Italy, for example, have tax-financed national health services with permanently employed physicians who provide their services to patients free of charge. In other countries, social health insurance covers all or at least the majority of citizens, who often do not have a choice of insurer. In addition, benefits are usually laid down by law, while the prices of medical services are regulated by fee schedules enforced by public authorities.

These deviations from market allocation are generally justified by claiming that health goods present particular features rendering them different from other goods. These features are said to cause a 'market failure', i.e., to result in an equilibrium that does not correspond to a Pareto-optimal allocation in non-regulated markets. In addition, equity concerns provide a reason to reject the market mechanism.

The appropriate point of departure for the theory of market failure is the First Theorem of Welfare Economics. This proposition states that in the absence of external effects and public goods, every competitive equilibrium constitutes a

P. Zweifel et al., *Health Economics*, 2nd ed., DOI 10.1007/978-3-540-68540-1_5,
© Springer-Verlag Berlin Heidelberg 2009

Pareto optimum. In order to justify the regulation of the market for health goods, one needs to show that at least one of the requirements cited in this theorem are violated, notably because

- health goods have the characteristics of public goods;
- the consumption of health goods gives rise to external effects;
- the criteria of a perfectly competitive market, specifically market transparency and consumer sovereignty, are not met.

In the following, the most important peculiarities of health goods cited in the literature will be discussed in the light of these three points. Even if a market failure surfaces, however, it is still appropriate to examine the suitability of alternative social institutions (e.g., public provision of goods or compulsory insurance) to check whether they secure a higher degree of efficiency than the market. In doing so, one has to bear in mind that health goods are not homogeneous. This makes it possible that the market presents a suitable form of allocation in one case but may fail in another.

A distinction between market failure at different levels in the production process will turn out to be useful,

(a) failure in the market for medical services;
(b) failure in private insurance markets providing coverage against the financial risks associated with illness.

Note, however, that the discussion will be limited to criteria for static efficiency, thereby holding health care technology constant at the existing level. We thus ignore problems of dynamic efficiency arising from the impact of health care financing on the development of health care technology (this issue is addressed in Chapter 14).

This chapter is structured accordingly. Section 5.2 is devoted to a discussion of the peculiar features of health goods that may cause failure in the market for these goods. Section 5.3 deals with characteristics of private markets for health insurance suggesting market failure.

At first, market outcomes will be evaluated in terms of efficiency. Inefficiency, however, does not constitute the only or even main motivation for the regulation of markets both for health goods and health insurance. Therefore, Section 5.4 reviews considerations of justice as a reason for government intervention in health care. Recently, this intervention has increasingly resulted in the rationing of at least some types of health care services. Accordingly, Section 5.5 deals with the concept of rationing in health care.

5.2 Market Failure in Markets for Health Goods

5.2.1 Externalities and the Problem of Public Goods

If the consumption of a good h by individual i has direct effects on the utility of individual j, giving rise to an externality, then the market mechanism does not lead to a Pareto-optimal allocation in a situation of perfect competition. The reason is that in this case, consumer i optimally buys a quantity of good h such that his or her own marginal utility (measured in monetary units) derived from the last unit of the good is equal to its price. In doing this, she or he does not take the potential effects on j's marginal utility into account.

Positive externalities are therefore, as a rule, associated with under-consumption of the good, while negative externalities are associated with over-consumption in a market economy, relative to the Pareto-optimal solution. In the case of health goods, positive externalities are more relevant. We can distinguish two varieties. The consumption of health good h by the individual i can either

- directly improve the health of individual j [these are called 'physical externalities', see CULYER (1971)] or

- simply lead to increased satisfaction for individual j ['psychological externalities'].

Physical externalities. Physical externalities arise in the context of communicable diseases. If individual i seeks treatment or tries to prevent that she or he contracts such a disease, the probability of individual j getting infected is reduced. In a two-person case involving i and j only (e.g., a vaccination), a Pareto optimum could easily be brought about by j voluntarily subsidizing the vaccination costs of i. In reality, externalities are of course spread over many people, giving rise to their collective-good property, a complication that can be explained as follows.

A 'collective good' (also called 'public good') is characterized by non-rivalry in consumption. If consumer i obtains a unit of good h, then another consumer j can also use the same unit without diminishing i's enjoyment of the good. This condition is satisfied in an ideal way in the case of the external benefit created by the vaccination (good h) of individual i, since this affects several other individuals, even without a diminishing effect if their number increases.

Moreover, the exclusion principle cannot as a rule be applied to collective goods, meaning that nobody can be barred from using them, even though she or he has not contributed to their provision. In a perfectly competitive market, these goods will be under-provided. The reason is that the individual consumer has no incentive to contribute to the financing of such a good (in the present case to participate in subsidizing the vaccination of individual i), being able to benefit from the advantages of a reduced risk of infection while others take over the financing.

These considerations suggest that compulsory vaccinations to prevent communicable diseases (such as polio or dangerous flu viruses) or measures designed to prevent epidemics (typhus, cholera) should be provided by the government and subsidized (possibly financed entirely) using general tax revenue. The appropriate level of implementation (community, provincial, federal or international level) should be chosen depending on the spatial distribution of the external benefit.

In view of the low share of total health care expenditure attributable to infectious diseases, however, this line of argument cannot be used to justify free provision of much or even all medical care by the government in present times. First, epidemics and pandemics have become very rare, at least in industrial countries. Second, not all citizens are exposed to the danger of infectious disease to the same extent. The positive externality of fighting an epidemic vanishes for example when individuals can effectively protect themselves from infection at a sufficiently low cost. Conversely, if those who are not themselves at risk are forced to contribute to the cost of controlling an epidemic through their tax payment, then public provision no longer leads to a Pareto improvement relative to the market solution.

Psychological externalities. For psychological external benefits, the term 'altruism' is frequently used. The utility level of the altruistic individual j not only depends on her or his own consumption, but also (again positively) on the consumption of individual i. As a rule, a positive externality may arise only as long as the consumption of a fellow citizen is perceived as being 'unbearably' low. Indeed, it causes most people to be distressed when seeing others die from starvation or lack of medical care, particularly if their suffering was not caused by their own actions.

The existence of altruistic attitudes in society now raises the question of whether the corresponding positive externalities

(1) can be internalized through private action or whether some public intervention is required for attaining a Pareto improvement, and

(2) require subsidization or even free provision of certain goods (e.g., medical treatment), or whether they can be settled using money transfers, i.e., whether 'transfers in kind' are considered superior to 'transfers in cash' according to welfare criteria.

In a society with many wealthy members, everyone benefits when someone else supports the poor. In the absence of organization by the government, this situation would result in under-provision of relief for the needy. Charity therefore has the properties of a collective good which provides an argument for the government to organize support for the poor who cannot afford medical treatment.

At first sight, free provision of transfers in kind seems to be inferior to transfers in cash as transfers in kind distort relative prices, inducing the needy to consume the subsidized good in excess of the Pareto optimum. This argument however overlooks the specific effects of recipient's consumption on the donor. If donors are not interested in increasing recipients' utility *per se* but rather their consumption of a particular good,[1] then their willingness to make the transfer increases if they can earmark it. The increased size of the transfer may serve to raise the utility of the recipient above the maximum level attainable with the (smaller) income transfer, therefore resulting in a Pareto-superior outcome.

This argument seems to apply primarily to nutrition, appropriate housing, and life-saving medical care, the consumption of which is deemed worthy of support by donors, calling for earmarked transfers in their interest. This does not imply, however, that the government needs to provide medical services. The 'market failure' associated with external effects and collective goods affects the demand side exclusively, and not the supply side of the market for health goods.

5.2.2 Option-Good Property of Medical Services

Another peculiarity of most medical services is that at the individual level, their demand is frequently not predictable. When it arises, however, it may often be of extreme urgency, while capacities for providing medical services, particularly in the hospital, cannot be created at such short notice. The existence of a certain reserve capacity therefore constitutes an option good, meaning that the mere existence of the good yields utility to consumers. In order to create an incentive for hospitals to hold capacity on reserve, this must be paid for separately, implying that the hospital's revenue must not depend on bed occupancy only.

Does this imply the necessity of organization by the government? The answer is in the negative, since option demand can be completely met within the domain of (private) health insurance. The insurer simply guarantees that a hospital bed will be available to the insured in case of need. Part of the premium revenue is then used to pay a hospital in the insured person's area of residence for holding reserve capacity.[2]

Only to the extent that the option in its turn has the character of a collective good would financing reserve hospital capacity through taxes be appropriate. In fact, the condition of non-rivalry is fulfilled, since one and the same hospital bed can provide several potential patients with the utility of secure access at the same time. The remaining issue is whether or not the exclusion principle holds, requiring that in the case of a shortage, those who have failed to conclude an appropriate insurance contract must be discriminated against. Since in an emergency, the exclusion principle must presumably be waived for humanitarian reasons, it is justified to force all citizens to carry insurance for emergency access to a hospital. Such a mandate is not equivalent to financing emerging departments using tax money because competing health insurers can negotiate for their provision.

---

[1] This case is referred to as a 'good externality', distinct from a 'utility externality'.

[2] It may be argued that a hospital may contract with several insurers, conjuring up the risk of insufficient capacity as soon as several insured wish to exercise their option (e.g., in the wake of an epidemic). While this is true, this still does not justify public ownership of hospitals because the public hospital is confronted with exactly the same problem.

Conclusion 5.1. *The market 'fails' in its allocation of health goods if these goods exhibit collective-good properties (vaccinations, hospital beds held in reserve) or give rise to externalities. In the case of vaccination, the government can use taxes and transfers, possibly in kind, to remedy the market failure. In the case of emergency hospital services, insurers can negotiate for their provision. There is no need for the government to finance these services, let alone to act as the supplier of health goods.*

5.2.3 Lack of Consumer Sovereignty

Another frequently cited reason for the 'failure' of free markets for health goods is consumers' inability of deciding about their demand for medical care rationally. The most widespread arguments in support of this allegation are discussed in the following.

5.2.3.1 Incapability of Rational Decision Making

The state of illness presents an exceptional human situation, in the extreme life may be at stake. Accordingly, the notion of 'consumer sovereignty' is challenged by many. They doubt that individuals in this situation are capable of seeking out the treatment alternative maximizing their utility, taking into account the associated costs in a rational balancing process. Indeed, a person in a state of unconsciousness, great pain, or mental illness admittedly cannot make a rational decision. Close relatives or a guardian must decide for her or him, on the understanding that they act in the same ways as the affected person would if in a position to do so.

A related problem arises if a disease is life-threatening while not limiting mental capacity. Here, patients are in a weak position relative to the supplier of health services, since they will frequently be prepared to pay any amount of money to recover their health. They will therefore hardly seek out reasonable treatment offers in terms of cost as soon as an alternative (seemingly) entails a greater risk of failure. The purchase of health insurance, however, takes care of such a situation provided coverage is sufficient to protect the insured from costs of treatment that jeopardize economic survival. Thus, health insurance serves to remedy patients' structural inferiority to the provider of care. The downside is that patients have a diminished interest in seeking out low-cost treatment alternatives (see Section 6.4 on moral hazard).

Consequently, there is no reason to presume that a form of allocation other than the competitive market results in a higher degree of efficiency. Ex ante, i.e., before a life-threatening situation arises, individuals can take care by selecting someone close to make the decision for them or by purchasing health insurance which protects them from being exploited by health care providers. Public bureaucrats, who lack both incentive and capability to find out about individual preferences, would likely deal with this task in a less satisfactory way. The arguments cited above provide even less support for having the government organize the supply of medical services.

5.2.3.2 Excess Discounting of Future Needs

By nature, frequency and severity of illness increase with age, causing the likelihood of treatment costs that cannot be paid out of current income to increase as well. A rational individual will, even without public intervention, provide for this risk by saving, or better still, by buying insurance. Since most people value future consumption less than present consumption, however, many will only attach limited importance to this eventuality, causing their coverage to be insufficient. This implies a lack of means in old age, resulting in – so the argument goes – a systematic underprovision of health goods.

This argument has a paternalistic undertone, since evidently the preferences of individuals with 'excessive' discounting of future needs are not acknowledged as their 'true' preferences. But who should have the right to decide what these true preferences are? The argument outlined also fails to point out alternative institutional arrangements that may be expected to produce a 'better' outcome.

But assume that politicians were allowed to decide the appropriate amount of provision (e.g., as part of compulsory health insurance), and that they have to run for office in a democracy. Then, more provision for the future could only be expected if a corresponding platform is supported by the majority of voters. Younger individuals, however, would have to disagree unless they behave schizophrenically in this respect. Acting as voters, they would have to discount future wants to a lesser degree than when acting as consumers on the market. Older voters, on the other hand, while considering such provision necessary in view of their own (negative) experience, would not benefit from such a program anymore. Therefore, they would also have insufficient motivation to support it.[3]

5.2.4 Lack of Perfect Information in Markets for Health Goods

For the First Theorem of Welfare Economics (as stated in Section 5.1) to hold, perfect market transparency constitutes another requirement that does not seem to be fully satisfied in the case of health goods. Market transparency means that potential buyers are informed about qualities offered and prices quoted by all suppliers on the market. Indeed, perfect knowledge of product quality is generally precluded in the case of services, where production and consumption occur simultaneously ('uno actu principle'). The various offers cannot be inspected and compared before making the decision.

Medical services, however, are not unique in this respect. Incomplete information about quality also characterizes the services of hairdressers, banks (investment advice), restaurants, and artistic performances, to name just a few. Nevertheless, three additional features can be identified which distinguish health goods from most other services.

---

[3] The tendency of governments in democracies to finance expenditures through public debt shows that their discounting of future needs may be as marked as of the citizenry at large.

(1) *Lack of opportunity for sampling.* The quality of the work of a hairdresser or of an innkeeper can be experienced through trial and error, and, within certain limits, by relying on the judgment of others who have already tried it. By contrast, medical services, particularly the ones crucial for survival in the case of life-threatening illness, are often consumed only once in a lifetime, causing a lack of experience for evaluation. Furthermore, experience of others does not help much since health problems are never completely comparable, while treatment processes contain a strong individual physician-patient component. The importance of this interaction also makes an objective evaluation of quality (e.g., by testing agencies) difficult, in contradistinction to other goods that are bought infrequently such as washing machines.

(2) *Unclear cause-effect relationships.* Frequently, the quality of a medical service cannot be judged correctly even after utilization, since the causality between treatment and change of health status may be blurred by other biological processes, such as the self-healing powers of the body. Health goods therefore tend to be 'credence goods' whose quality is rarely learned [DARBY AND KARNI (1973)] as opposed to 'search goods' and 'experience goods' whose quality can be ascertained either before or after utilization [NELSON (1970)].

(3) *Asymmetric information.* In the case of diagnostic services in particular, the good demanded is information. This makes it impossible for patients to evaluate the quality of the service prior to its purchase because this would require them to already be in possession of the desired information. Of course, the information advantage of suppliers gives them a certain degree of power over the buyers (see the analysis of supplier-induced demand in Chapter 8). Again, however, medical services are far from unique in this respect. One may think, for example, of the services of a car repair shop. Mechanics begin with diagnosing the failure and defining the repair needs. Lawyers likewise have an information advantage with regard to clients' prospects of winning a trial.

Specific interventions in health care markets may be justified if they aim at securing a minimum level of quality, e.g., through licensure of physicians and other health professions.[4] Medical liability (malpractice lawsuits) can to some extent prevent skimping on quality which is to be expected in view of patients' incapability of evaluating service quality.[5] Furthermore, health information campaigns can help consumers to better judge the quality of health goods.

On the other hand, none of the features of health services mentioned above justify the belief that organization of supply by the government would result in better

---

[4] Another reason for 'market failure' is seen in consumers' incapability of making rational decisions about their demand for health services. However, this does not provide justification for public provision of medical services, but rather of information to consumers.

[5] Nevertheless, this approach should be used with care. If physician liability is excessive, physicians may respond by practicing 'defensive medicine', i.e., by taking too many tests and by avoiding risky procedures which may be in the patient's interest [see DANZON (2000, 1368–69)].

welfare than coordination through the market. Bureaucratically structured institutions, which inevitably come with government organization, are ill-suited to control service quality.

Conclusion 5.2. *Another reason for 'market failure' is seen in consumers' incapability of making rational decisions about their demand for health services. However, this does not provide justification for public provision, but rather for measures to improve the information of consumers and to secure product quality.*

5.3 Market Failure in Health Insurance Markets

While the peculiarities of health goods outlined in Section 5.2 suggest that a few targeted policy measures may be welfare-enhancing, they do not justify either the monopolization of supply through a national health service nor the financing of services through tax revenue. Consequently, health goods should be paid for by individual consumers. Since the costs of illness occur stochastically, they can hedge their disposable income against inevitable uncertainty by buying health insurance. The question to be answered in the following is whether private insurance markets may be expected to deal with this demand in an optimal way, or whether there is reason to fear market failure. Finally, one has to check whether this market failure should be accepted or whether it could in fact be remedied by public intervention, in particular compulsory health insurance. Before discussing arguments in favor of government intervention, we first present a simple insurance model that serves as the basis of the analysis.

5.3.1 The Basic Model

Our basic model assumes that an individual is sick with probability π and remains in good health with probability $1 - \pi$ $(0 < \pi < 1)$. When ill, the individual needs medical treatment which restores her or his health completely. The cost of treatment takes on the fixed value M. Health insurance is characterized by two parameters, the premium P (to be paid in any event) and insurance benefits I received in the event of illness I $(0 \leq I \leq M)$.

The individual earns an exogenously given gross income Y and derives utility $u(y)$ from disposable income y.[6] Assume that $u'(y) > 0$ and $u''(y) < 0$, which implies that individuals are risk averse. If the individual is healthy, disposable income is $y_h = Y - P$, in case of sickness, it is given by $y_s = Y - P - M + I$.

---

[6] This utility function defined on sure amounts of money is often called von-Neumann-Morgenstern utility function [see, e.g., LAFFONT (1989, Chapter 1)] or Bernoulli utility function [see, e.g., MAS-COLELL ET AL. (1995, Chapter 6)]. It is a cardinal utility function, i.e., unique up to a positive affine transformation.

Box 5.1. A Basic Insurance Model

$$EU = (1 - \pi)u(y_h) + \pi u(y_s) \tag{5.1}$$

$$y_h = Y - P = Y - \pi I$$
$$y_s = Y - P - M + I = Y - M + (1 - \pi)I. \tag{5.4}$$

$$u'[Y - \pi I^*] = u'[Y - M + (1 - \pi)I^*] \quad \Rightarrow \quad I^* = M \tag{5.3}$$

EU:	expected utility of the individual
$u(y)$:	utility function, $u'(y) > 0, u''(y) < 0$
y_h:	disposable income when healthy
y_s:	disposable income when sick
π:	probability of being sick
Y:	gross income
M:	cost of treatment
I:	insurance benefit
$P = \pi I$:	actuarially fair health insurance premium

The individual is presumed to maximize expected utility which is given by

$$EU = (1 - \pi)u(y_h) + \pi u(y_s) = (1 - \pi)u(Y - P) + \pi u(Y - P - M + I). \tag{5.1}$$

We assume that insurers incur no administrative expenses and maximize expected profits. The market for health insurance is characterized by perfect competition. Insurers therefore offer *actuarially fair* contracts with $P = \pi I$, i.e., the premium is equal to the expected benefit.

With $P = \pi I$, the optimal quantity of insurance benefits I can be found by solving

$$\max_I EU = (1 - \pi)u(Y - \pi I) + \pi u(Y - M + (1 - \pi)I). \tag{5.2}$$

The first-order condition for an interior solution is given by

$$\frac{dEU}{dI} = (1 - \pi)u'[Y - \pi I^*](-\pi) + \pi u'[Y - M + (1 - \pi)I^*](1 - \pi) = 0.$$

Note that the second-order condition is met due to $u''(y) < 0$. Rearranging the first-order condition yields

$$u'[Y - \pi I^*] = u'[Y - M + (1 - \pi)I^*], \tag{5.3}$$

i.e., marginal utility must be the same in both states. As $u''(y) < 0$, this implies that also disposable income must be identical. Therefore full insurance with $I^* = M$ is optimal and the individual has a certain income $y_h = y_s = Y - \pi M$. This result characterizes an efficient outcome. If insurance is actuarially fair, i.e., if insurers can insure risk at no cost, then it is optimal that consumers are fully insured (see also Section 6.3.1.1).

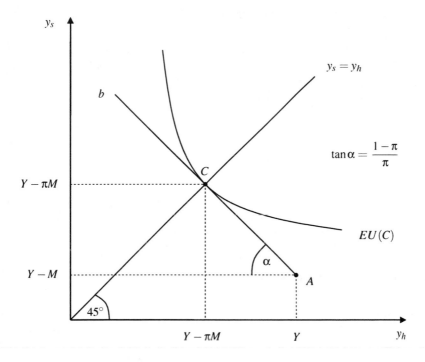

Fig. 5.1. Optimal Insurance Coverage

Figure 5.1 illustrates the individual's optimal choice in a (y_h, y_s) diagram. The individual's initial situation is given by point A, where $y_h = Y$ and $y_s = Y - M$. The purchase of insurance changes state-contingent incomes to

$$y_h = Y - P = Y - \pi I$$
$$y_s = Y - P - M + I = Y - M + (1 - \pi)I. \tag{5.4}$$

Solving one equation for I and substituting into the other yields the budget line b:

$$y_s = \frac{Y}{\pi} - M - \frac{1 - \pi}{\pi} y_h. \tag{5.5}$$

Turning to the individual's indifference curves, their slope is given by

$$\left. \frac{dy_s}{dy_h} \right|_{dEU=0} = -\frac{\dfrac{\partial EU}{\partial y_h}}{\dfrac{\partial EU}{\partial y_s}} = -\frac{1 - \pi}{\pi} \frac{u'(y_h)}{u'(y_s)} < 0. \tag{5.6}$$

Furthermore, $u''(y) < 0$ implies that the indifference curves are strictly convex:

$$\frac{d^2 y_s}{dy_h^2}\bigg|_{dEU=0} = -\frac{1-\pi}{\pi} \times \frac{u''(y_h)u'(y_s) - u'(y_h)u''(y_s)\dfrac{dy_s}{dy_h}\bigg|_{dEU=0}}{[u'(y_s(y_h))]^2} > 0. \qquad (5.7)$$

On the certainty line where $y_s = y_h$, the slope of the indifference curve reduces to

$$\frac{dy_s}{dy_h}\bigg|_{dEU=0, y_h=y_s} = -\frac{1-\pi}{\pi}. \qquad (5.8)$$

Therefore, on the certainty line the slopes of the budget line and the indifference curve are equal implying that the optimum is given by point C on the certainty line, where the indifference curve is tangent to the budget line. From equation (5.5), one obtains that the individual has a certain income $Y - \pi M$.

5.3.2 The Free-Rider Problem

In Subsection 5.2.1, the theory of externalities was used to show that in a wealthy society, there likely is a consensus that life-saving medical care should be made available to citizens who are in need without fault of their own. Since it is difficult to check whether the 'no fault' case applies, low income and lack of wealth usually serve as substitute criteria for claiming subsidized or free treatment. But there is the danger that individuals who are close to the limit value where the subsidy kicks in lose all incentive to insure against the cost of illness. By not buying insurance, they save the premium, enjoying a higher level of consumption as long as they remain in good health. As soon as sizable payments for medical care occur, however, these individuals very quickly satisfy the criteria for free treatment. This means that ex ante, under the veil of ignorance regarding their future demand for health goods, they can reach a higher level of expected utility without buying insurance, i.e., acting as a free rider on the rest of society.

One way of dealing with this problem would be to deny treatment to individuals who failed to buy health insurance. To a rich society, however, it is not acceptable to make the provision of medical care dependent on the patient's ability to pay if, for example, the victim of an accident or a seriously ill person is rushed to hospital. In fact, anyone denying medical care for this reason risks to be sued for failure to provide assistance. If subsequently the patient turns out to lack health insurance or means for payment, the bill has to be settled by a transfer.

To analyze the free-rider problem, the basic model presented above is extended by the following assumptions.[7]

---

[7] For further analysis, the reader is referred to COATE (1995). He provides an analysis which explicitly considers altruistic behavior and determines the minimum income in society endogenously.

(1) All citizens are guaranteed a minimum income Y_{min};

(2) Citizens differ in gross income Y, while the probability of illness π and treatment cost M are identical for all individuals;

(3) Treatment cannot be denied to anyone. In principle, individuals must pay for their treatment. But because their net income cannot fall below Y_{min}, the government needs to step in if

$$Y - P - M + I < Y_{min}.$$

In this case, the government incurs expenses of $Y_{min} - (Y - P - M + I)$.

The fact that income cannot fall below Y_{min} implies that income when ill is

$$y_s = \max\{Y - P - M + I; Y_{min}\}.$$

With the premium $P = \pi I$, expected utility is given by

$$EU = (1 - \pi)u(Y - \pi I) + \pi u(\max\{Y - \pi I - M + I; Y_{min}\}). \qquad (5.9)$$

We first analyze the optimal amount of insurance I^* depending on the individual's gross income. If $Y - M \geq Y_{min}$, the results from the basic model apply. In this case, income when ill is always above Y_{min}, i.e., $\max\{Y - \pi I - M + I; Y_{min}\} = Y - \pi I - M + I$, and the individual's decision problem is the same as stated in equation (5.2). The individual will therefore choose full insurance with $I^* = M$.

If $Y - M < Y_{min}$, however, it can be optimal for an individual not to buy insurance. Consider the change in expected utility associated with an increase in I. As long as

$$I < \frac{Y_{min} - Y + M}{1 - \pi} \equiv \hat{I},$$

income with insurance is smaller than minimum income, i.e., $Y - \pi I - M + I < Y_{min}$. In this case, the second term of equation (5.9) is not a function of I, causing the derivative to boil down to

$$\left.\frac{dEU}{dI}\right|_{I \leq \hat{I}} = (1 - \pi)u'(y_h)(-\pi) < 0. \qquad (5.10)$$

Since disposable income when ill remains at Y_{min} while income when healthy falls, buying more insurance lowers expected utility if $I \leq \hat{I}$.

For $I > \hat{I}$, however, expected utility starts rising again with I until a local maximum is reached at $I = M$ since now

$$\left.\frac{dEU}{dI}\right|_{\hat{I} < I < M} = (1 - \pi)\pi\{u'(y_s) - u'(y_h)\} > 0 \qquad (5.11)$$

as $u'(y_s)$ is larger than $u'(y_h)$ as long as $I < M$ due to $u''(y) < 0$.

Equations (5.10) and (5.11) imply that there are two local optima, $I = 0$ and $I = M$. Therefore, the question is whether

$$EU[I = M] - EU[I = 0] = u[Y - \pi M] - \{(1 - \pi)u[Y] + \pi u[Y_{\min}]\} \gtreqless 0.$$

Since this difference is increasing in gross income Y, one obtains

$$\frac{d\,[EU[I = M] - EU[I = 0]]}{dY} = u'(Y - \pi M) - (1 - \pi)u'(Y) > 0.$$

Hence, there must be a critical income level $\tilde{Y}$ such that individuals with income above $\tilde{Y}$ prefer to buy full insurance and those with lower income to buy no insurance at all, i.e.,

$$I^*(Y) = \begin{cases} 0 & \text{if} \quad Y < \tilde{Y} \\ M & \text{if} \quad Y \geq \tilde{Y}. \end{cases}$$

The fact that low-income individuals do not buy health insurance may be a reason for concern. Individuals whose gross income is below $Y_{\min}$, however, are insured completely anyhow since they always receive government transfers. This is desired, as minimum income $Y_{\min}$ is there to protect those individuals. Things are different, however, for individuals with income $Y > Y_{\min}$. In particular, individuals who can in principle afford to buy health insurance, i.e., those with $Y - \pi M \geq Y_{\min}$ may also prefer not to buy insurance. Indeed, for individuals with income $Y = Y_{\min} + \pi M$, one finds

$$EU[I = M] - EU[I = 0] = u[Y_{\min}] - \{(1 - \pi)u[Y_{\min} + \pi M] + \pi u[Y_{\min}]\} < 0.$$

These individuals will therefore act as 'free riders' on the implicit insurance provided by the government's minimum income guarantee. This result also holds for some individuals whose income strictly exceeds $Y_{\min} + \pi M$ if they buy full insurance. Finally, individuals with gross income between $Y_{\min}$ and $Y_{\min} + \pi M$ also fail to buy insurance. They would qualify for public assistance if they bought full insurance but prefer the implicit insurance provided by the government free of charge.

Making insurance compulsory can solve these problems.[8] In particular, it prevents those who can in principle afford to buy health insurance from free riding. For those with gross income below $Y_{\min}$, compulsory insurance which is fully financed by the government can be preferred for administrative reasons. In this case, the government fully finances the health insurance premium while delegating the payment of claims to health insurers.

---

[8] Alternatively, a sufficiently large subsidy of insurance premiums for the needy would serve the same purpose. This conception was realized in Switzerland between 1911 and 1994. However, subsidies continued to be paid per enrollee regardless of income, resulting in some 97 percent of the population being voluntary members of sickness funds. This in turn paved the way to general compulsory insurance (with free choice of sickness funds as a rule) combined with premium subsidies for the poor which was introduced in 1994 [see ZWEIFEL AND BREUER (2006)].

In the remainder of this section, we demonstrate that there is also an efficiency rationale for compulsory insurance. It allows to achieve a Pareto improvement if combined with a transfer τ which is paid regardless of whether an individual is healthy or sick. To show this, first calculate the expected transfer for free riders. They contribute only $Y - Y_{min}$ to their cost of treatment. The government covers the rest and therefore pays a transfer $T = M - (Y - Y_{min})$ whose expected value ET in the absence of compulsory insurance is given by

$$ET = \pi [M - (Y - Y_{min})]. \tag{5.12}$$

A free rider has expected utility

$$EU_{FR} = (1 - \pi)u[Y] + \pi u[Y_{min}]. \tag{5.13}$$

The free rider's expected income is

$$EY_{FR} = (1 - \pi)Y + \pi Y_{min} = Y - \pi M + ET. \tag{5.14}$$

Now consider a free rider's situation given compulsory insurance. Since individuals are risk averse, they derive a benefit from security, causing free riders to demand a relatively low compensation (denoted by τ) to accept the mandate. With full compulsory insurance at premium πM, τ is given by

$$u[Y - \pi M + \tau] = (1 - \pi)u[Y] + \pi u[Y_{min}]. \tag{5.15}$$

Risk-averse individuals are willing to pay a positive risk premium ρ in exchange for a certain income. This risk premium is defined by

$$u[EY_{FR} - \rho] = (1 - \pi)u[Y] + \pi u[Y_{min}]. \tag{5.16}$$

Equations (5.15) and (5.16) imply $Y - \pi M + \tau = EY_{FR} - \rho$. Inserting for EY_{FR} from equation (5.14) yields

$$Y - \pi M + \tau = Y - \pi M + ET - \rho \quad \Leftrightarrow \quad \tau = ET - \rho.$$

Since $\rho > 0$, one obtains

$$\tau < ET.$$

This condition can be interpreted as follows. Without compulsory insurance, free riders must be paid a transfer ET to keep their income above Y_{min}. With compulsory insurance, they must be paid τ so they accept the mandate. The second transfer is smaller while keeping free riders' utility at the same level. Since transfers have to be financed by taxpayers, the introduction of compulsory health insurance achieves a Pareto improvement. The reason is that it prevents an inefficiency. For free riders,

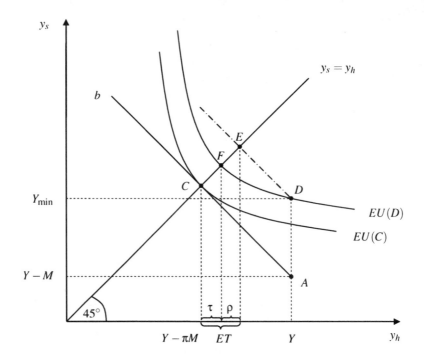

Fig. 5.2. Free Riding and Efficiency Gains through Compulsory Insurance

income is lower in the case of sickness than in health. In the presence of actuarially fair insurance, this risk allocation is not optimal. But purchasing insurance is not rational for low-income persons because it lowers their income in the state of health without increasing it in the state of sickness since all insurance does is to reduce the transfer received from the government in the state of sickness. By forcing them to purchase health insurance, while paying them a compensating transfer, taxpayers can be made better off at no loss to free riders, which constitutes a Pareto improvement.[9]

Figure 5.2 illustrates the argument. Without compulsory insurance, free riders are at point D. They obtain higher expected utility than under full insurance (point C) because they receive a transfer that raises their income from $Y - M$ to Y_{min} in the event of sickness. The expected value ET of this transfer can be read off by drawing line ED, which runs parallel to the budget line b. At E, income is EY_{FR} in both states; at C, by contrast, income is $Y - \pi M$. The difference between these incomes is ET [see also equation (5.14)]. If insurance is made compulsory and former free riders receive transfer τ which keeps them at the same utility as at point D, they reach point

---

[9] The transition to compulsory health insurance in Switzerland noted in footnote 8 fell in a time when the federal government was strongly committed to reducing the subsidies devoted to health insurance. It could thus have represented a Pareto improvement provided the savings in subsidies had been used to reduce taxation (which was not the case).

F with certain income $Y - \pi M + \tau$. The transition from point D with risk to point E without risk (the optimum given actuarially fair insurance), though, yields a benefit corresponding to FE on the security line, or the risk premium ρ on the y_h axis. Clearly, τ is smaller than ET, with the difference being equal to the risk premium ρ.

Conclusion 5.3. *Compulsory health insurance prevents society from being exploited by 'free riders'. Furthermore, if combined with a state-independent transfer to compensate free riders, it achieves a Pareto improvement over an institutional arrangement where free riders fail to buy insurance but are guaranteed some minimum income when sick.*

The free-rider problem therefore provides a rationale for making health insurance mandatory. A health insurance market without such a mandate 'fails' in the sense that some individuals with low income don't buy insurance since they can count on receiving a transfer when sick, designed to guarantee them a minimum income. It needs to be emphasized, however, that this is no inherent market failure but rather a problem caused by government interference in the first place. Without the implicit insurance provided by the government in the form of a minimum income, more individuals could be expected to buy full insurance. But those who are unable to afford health insurance would not be able to finance their treatment costs.

5.3.3 Asymmetric Information in the Health Insurance Market

We now turn to a form of market failure which is not due to government interference. It arises if individuals are heterogeneous in terms of the risk to be insured and are the only ones to know their risk. This *information asymmetry* was explored by ROTH SCHILD AND STIGLITZ (1976) and WILSON (1977). Their analysis is presented in this section.

5.3.3.1 Risk Types

We extend the basic model presented in Section 5.3.1 and now allow for two groups H and L who are characterized by different probabilities of being sick π_L and π_H, with $\pi_L < \pi_H$. The share λ of the total population belongs to 'low risk type' L, the share $(1 - \lambda)$ to 'high risk type' H. Let y_k^i be the net income of an individual of type i ($i = H, L$) in state k ($k = h, s$). Expected utility of risk type i is given by

$$EU_i = \pi_i u(y_s^i) + (1 - \pi_i) u(y_h^i), \quad i = H, L. \tag{5.17}$$

All individuals have the same gross income Y. Before turning to the problem of asymmetric information, we first analyze the reference scenario in which information is symmetric and insurers are able to observe π_i.

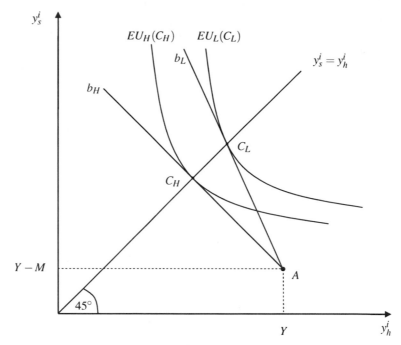

Fig. 5.3. Insurance Contracts under Symmetric Information

5.3.3.2 Market Equilibrium under Symmetric Information

As above assume actuarially fair insurance contracts. If insurers can identify the risk types, the premium for type i is then given by

$$P_i = \pi_i l_i, \quad i = L, H. \tag{5.18}$$

As shown in Section 5.3.1, individuals will buy full insurance given this premium. The premium for H-types, however, is higher for a given amount of benefits I because their probability of being sick in the future is higher than that of L-types.

Figure 5.3 illustrates this result in (y_h^i, y_s^i) space, in which A describes the identical endowment point for both risk types. In analogy to equation (5.5), the budget lines b_L and b_H for risk types L and H are given by

$$y_s^i = \frac{y}{\pi_i} - M - \frac{1 - \pi_i}{\pi_i} y_h^i, \quad i = L, H.$$

Therefore, the budget lines have slopes

$$\frac{dy_s^i}{dy_h^i} = -\frac{1 - \pi_i}{\pi_i}, \quad i = L, H.$$

Due to $\pi_H > \pi_L$, the budget line of low-risk types runs steeper than the one for the high-risk types. The utility-maximizing contracts C_H and C_L for each type must as always satisfy the tangency condition, i.e., the slope of the budget line must be equal to the slope of the indifference curve of type i [see equation (5.6)],

$$\left. \frac{dy_s^i}{dy_h^i} \right|_{dEU_i=0} = -\frac{1-\pi_i}{\pi_i} \frac{u'(y_h^i)}{u'(y_s^i)}. \tag{5.19}$$

In view of equation (5.8), the right-hand side of (5.19) becomes $-(1-\pi_i)/\pi_i$ if $y_s^i = y_h^i$. Therefore, it is again on the certainty line that the slope of the indifference curve of risk type i is equal to the slope of the respective budget line. This means that the two optima C_H and C_L lie on the certainty line. Also note that equation (5.19) implies that the indifference curve for a given combination of state-contingent income y_s and y_h is flatter for high risk types as $(1-\pi_i)/\pi_i$ is decreasing in π_i.

Conclusion 5.4. *If loss probabilities are known to insurers and premiums are actuarially fair, all risk types are predicted to opt for full insurance, albeit at different premiums.*

5.3.3.3 Market Equilibrium under Asymmetric Information

We now assume that only individuals themselves have information about their risk type. Insurers cannot identify the risk type but know the percentage λ of low-risk types in the total population. Furthermore, we make two additional assumptions.

(a) insurers offer contracts (P, I) consisting of a fixed reimbursement level I and premium P. These contracts correspond to a point in (y_h, y_s) space;

(b) each individual buys exactly one insurance contract.

In the context of asymmetric information, the definition of a market equilibrium plays a crucial role. We first employ the definition used by ROTHSCHILD AND STIGLITZ (1976).

Definition 5.1. *A Rothschild-Stiglitz (RS) equilibrium in the health insurance market consists of a set of contracts with the following properties,*

    (i)   all individuals choose the contract which maximizes their expected utility;

    (ii)   each contract leads to nonnegative expected profits for insurers;

    (iii)   no contract outside the set of equilibrium contracts yields nonnegative expected profits.

A *separating equilibrium* exists if the risk types choose different contracts. A *pooling equilibrium* arises if all types opt for the same contract.

Clearly, the market equilibrium with full insurance and differentiated premia, derived in the preceding section and symbolized by the contracts C_L and C_H in Figure 5.3 is no RS equilibrium. High-risk individuals, who cannot be identified by insurers, would buy the contract designed for low-risk types, causing expected losses to insurers.

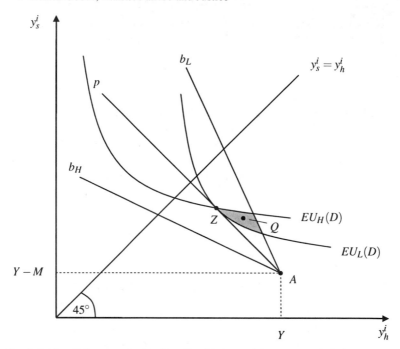

Fig. 5.4. Non-Existence of a Pooling Equilibrium with Asymmetric Information

Non-Existence of a Pooling Equilibrium

We first examine whether a pooling equilibrium can exist. A possible candidate is the contract Z with (P_Z, I_Z) having the property

$$P_Z = \bar{\pi} I_Z \quad \text{with} \quad \bar{\pi} = \lambda \pi_L + (1 - \lambda) \pi_H. \tag{5.20}$$

Being based on the average probability of loss, $\bar{\pi}$, this contract breaks even if chosen by all individuals. In Figure 5.4, contract Z lies on the pooling-line p with slope $-(1 - \bar{\pi})/\bar{\pi}$. Since this pooling contract is not actuarially fair to low-risk types, they will opt for less than full coverage, i.e., some degree of cost sharing. This can be seen from the fact that point Z does not lie on the security line anymore. However, since the indifference curves of the high-risk types run flatter than those of the low-risk types throughout, they must cross the indifference curve of high risks from the right in Z.

Now consider a contract in the shaded area, e.g., contract Q. It has the following properties.

(1) Low risks prefer contract Q to contract Z because it lies above their indifference curve through Z which implies higher expected utility;
(2) High risks prefer contract Z because a contract in the shaded area lies below their (flatter) indifference curve through Z;
(3) contract Q makes a positive expected profit since it is chosen by low risks only and lies below the budget line for low risks.

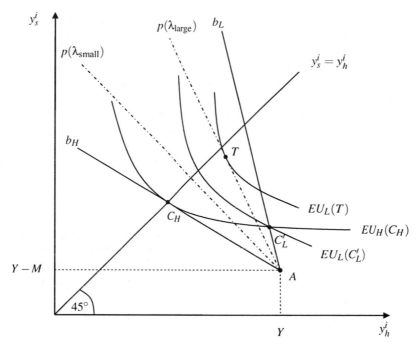

Fig. 5.5. Separating Equilibrium with Asymmetric Information

If contract Z is on the market, it is profitable to offer contract Q. This implies that contract Z cannot be an equilibrium contract as requirement (*iii*) of Definition 5.1 is violated. A shaded area with the properties (1) to (3) above exists for every possible pooling equilibrium. This type of equilibrium can therefore be excluded.

Possible Existence of a Separating Equilibrium

By contrast, a separating equilibrium may exist. In such an equilibrium two different contracts are offered. Each is designed for one risk type, with the individuals selecting themselves into the respective contract. Incentive compatibility requires that H-types prefer the contract 'meant' for them, and L-types vice versa.

This is illustrated in Figure 5.5. Although the process of risk separation is not explicitly described in the model, it can be envisaged as follows. Let insurers offer a contract at a high premium. If one group of consumers buys full coverage nonetheless, they must be high risks. This means that point C_H establishes a benchmark for them; in particular, they would migrate to any contract designed for the low risks that is closer to the certainty line than C'_L. Therefore, in order to preserve incentive compatibility, insurers can offer only partial insurance to low-risk types, albeit at a fair premium. Low risks are rationed in the sense that they cannot obtain the amount of insurance they want although they are willing to pay the price that covers the marginal cost of insuring them (i.e., the expected value of future health care expenditure $\pi_L M$).

Whether the contracts C_H and C'_L actually constitute a separating equilibrium depends on the share of low risks λ. If λ is relatively large, then the pooling line crosses the indifference curve $EU_L(C'_L)$ of low risks, e.g., the pooling $p(\lambda_{\text{large}})$ in Figure 5.5. In this case, a contract on the pooling line such as T exists which makes both types better off while yielding nonnegative expected profits. By requirement (*iii*) of Definition 5.1, the contracts C_H and C'_L cannot form an equilibrium in this case. The pooling contract T can in turn be challenged by an alternative that attracts only low risks. Therefore, no equilibrium exists in this case.[10] If the share of low risks λ is small, however, the pooling line does not cross the indifference curve $EU_L(C'_L)$ of low risks (e.g., the pooling $p(\lambda_{\text{small}})$ in Figure 5.5). No pooling contract exists that the low risks prefer to C'_L, establishing the pair C_H and C'_L as a separating equilibrium.

The case in which no market equilibrium exists is sometimes interpreted in the sense that the 'market fails entirely' [see, e.g., BARR (2004, p. 110)]. But this is an extreme interpretation. From a methodological point of view, the model fails to yield a prediction for a certain range of the parameter λ. The appropriate response is to alter the model. In particular, the definition of equilibrium needs to be adjusted to the inherently game-theoretic context, a point taken up in Section 5.3.3.5 below.

Assuming that a separating equilibrium exists, it is worth emphasizing the importance of the assumptions that (a) insurers offer price-quantity contracts and (b) that each individual buys exactly one insurance contract. First, if insurers allow individuals to choose their indemnity I at a price p per unit of coverage such that the premium equals $P = pI$, it is not possible to constrain low risk types to the coverage of contract C'_L. As this contract is on the zero-profit line for L-types, its price would need to be $p = \pi_L$. At this fair premium, however, L-types will extend their coverage up to M. This causes coverage designed for L-types to become attractive for H-types, undermining the separating equilibrium. Likewise, if individuals can buy several contracts, incentive compatibility is violated. In particular, high-risk types can accept partial coverage from any given insurer, who takes this as a sign of low-risk status. By piecing together several contracts, they are able to obtain extensive coverage. For example, if contract C'_L specifies an indemnity $I_{C'_L} = M/3$, everyone could obtain full coverage at price $\pi_L M$ by buying three contracts. Clearly, contract C'_L would not be sustainable. In practice, however, the possibility of getting reimbursed more than once can be ruled out by requiring individuals to hand in original bills, or by permitting insurers to share information about their customers [see JAYNES (1978)].

5.3.3.4 Welfare-Enhancing Government Intervention in Insurance Markets

Assume for now that the share of low risks is sufficiently small for a separating equilibrium to exist. Since the low risks are rationed in this type of equilibrium, there may be scope for Pareto improvement. In particular, the question arises of whether

---

[10] To be more precise, no equilibrium in 'pure strategies' exists. DASGUPTA AND MASKIN (1986) show that there is always an equilibrium in 'mixed strategies'. It seems unlikely, however, that insurers will randomize the offering of their contracts.

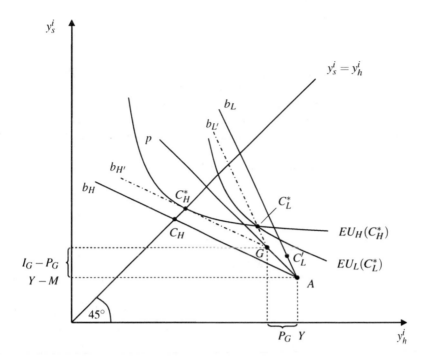

Fig. 5.6. Pareto Improvement through Compulsory Partial Insurance

the government can achieve such an improvement by introducing compulsory public insurance coverage. To answer this question, consider point G in Figure 5.6. It reflects a mandatory public policy (P_G, I_G) which will just break even because it lies on the pooling line pertinent to the population at large. Now if individuals are allowed to buy supplementary health insurance, the set of contracts that can be offered in a RS equilibrium in the private market must constitute a pair (C_H^*, C_L^*) with the following properties,

(1) C_H^* lies at the intersection of the budget line $b_{H'}$ through G and the certainty line;

(2) C_L^* lies at the intersection of the H-indifference curve through $EU_H(C_H^*)$ and the budget line $b_{L'}$ through G.

Figure 5.6 shows the case in which the resulting pair of contracts (compulsory plus voluntary part) Pareto-dominates the RS equilibrium in the absence of social insurance.[11] The intuition for this result is that high-risk types benefit from the cross-subsidization within the public insurance contract, while low-risk types are better off due to the relaxation of the rationing restriction, allowing an increased overall coverage as compared to the absence of mandatory public insurance with partial

---

[11] See WILSON (1977, p. 200) and DAHLBY (1981).

coverage.[12] It can be shown that this result holds if the share of low risks is larger than some critical value which is compatible with the existence of a RS equilibrium [see CROCKER AND SNOW (1985a)].

This property of the model by ROTHSCHILD AND STIGLITZ (1976) and WIL-SON (1977) has received wide-spread attention in the literature. In particular, it is frequently used as an argument in favor of government intervention in insurance markets. Before drawing such a conclusion, however, we want to emphasize that the desirability of a compulsory public health insurance scheme has been established on the basis of a particular equilibrium concept, viz. the Rothschild-Stiglitz equilibrium. It needs to be examined for its robustness with respect to changes in the definition of equilibrium.

5.3.3.5 Alternative Equilibrium Definitions

In Section 5.3.3.3, it was shown that no RS equilibrium exists if the share of low risks is too large. In this case, the model is unable to predict the outcome of a competitive insurance market under asymmetric information. In the literature, a number of approaches have been taken to overcome this problem.[13] In the following, we want to focus on two extensions of the equilibrium concept. First, WILSON (1977) has proposed an alternative (subsequently called W equilibrium) in which property (*iii*) of the RS equilibrium in Definition 5.1 is replaced by

(*iii'*)   *no other contract outside the set of equilibrium contracts yields nonnegative expected profits even if all contracts that have been rendered unprofitable by this contract have been withdrawn from the market.*

The idea is that insurers anticipate the reactions of competitors and will not offer contracts which yield losses if these reactions are taken into account. This change in the third property of the equilibrium notion has no consequence if the share λ of low risks is sufficiently small for a RS equilibrium to exist since property (*iii'*) adds a requirement which does not apply in this case. However, if λ is too large to guarantee a RS equilibrium, it induces a W equilibrium of the pooling type. In Figure 5.4, for example, contract Z on the pooling line is a W equilibrium in this case. As opposed to requirement (*iii*), contracts in the shaded area do not violate the requirement (*iii'*). Anticipating that contract Z would be withdrawn, causing high risks to also choose their contracts, insurers abstain from offering contracts in this area. Note that contract Z must be the best pooling contract for low risks. Other pooling contracts cannot form an equilibrium since better contracts for low risks could be offered which make positive expected profits even if these contracts are withdrawn from the market.

---

[12] CROCKER AND SNOW (1985b) have shown that an equivalent policy is to tax partial insurance and to subsidize full insurance.

[13] See DIONNE AND DOHERTY (1992) for an overview.

From a welfare-theoretic point of view, the W equilibrium does not require a reassessment of our result from the previous section. Since the W equilibrium is identical with a RS equilibrium if it exists, the finding that introducing compulsory public insurance coverage can bring about a Pareto-improvement continues to hold.

The second extension of the RS equilibrium concept lifts the requirement that every single insurance contract offered must guarantee non-negative expected profits. This requirement can be regarded as an unrealistic behavioral assumption since insurance companies may well perform cross-subsidization among different contracts if thereby total profits are increased. This possibility was already considered by WILSON (1977) and examined in detail by MIYAZAKI (1977) and SPENCE (1978). Their approach can be captured in the following equilibrium concept which combines the anticipatory element of the W equilibrium and the possibility of cross-subsidization between insurance contracts.

Definition 5.2. *A Wilson-Miyazaki-Spence (WMS) equilibrium in the health insurance market consists of a set of contracts with the following properties,*

(*i*)   *all individuals choose the contract which maximizes their expected utility;*

(*ii*)   *every insurance company offers a set of contracts which, taken together, guarantees a non-negative expected profit;*

(*iii*) *no set of insurance contracts outside the sets mentioned in (ii) yields nonnegative expected profits even if those sets of contracts that have become unprofitable by the introduction of the new set have been withdrawn from the market.*

This concept shares the property of the W equilibrium that an equilibrium always exists. The implications for the efficiency of private health insurance markets differ sharply, however. As CROCKER AND SNOW (1985a) show, such an equilibrium is always second-best efficient. Given the self-selection and resource constraints, no Pareto improvement is possible. The intuition of this result is that cross-subsidization gives insurers the same means as the government to make individuals better off. Similar to the contracts C_L^* and C_H^* in Figure 5.6, this will generally imply that the contract for low risks will be below line b_L and therefore leads to expected profits which are used to subsidize the contract for H-types. But competing insurers will not exploit this by offering a better contract for L-types because the subsidized contract for H-types would then be withdrawn and H-types would make their offer unprofitable. Note that without the anticipatory element, cross-subsidization would not be possible and one would obtain the same results as for the RS equilibrium concept.

The implications of the RS and the WMS equilibrium concepts therefore differ considerably. Unfortunately, the question which equilibrium definition best describes the market for health insurance is hard to resolve. The possibility of cross-subsidization seems plausible as insurers can use this is a means to increase expected profits. But the assumption that insurers anticipate the withdrawal of competing contracts in response to their own contract offer remains controversial. HELLWIG (1987) has analyzed this issue in a game-theoretic framework which explicitly allows for withdrawals. He finds that the order in which firms move is crucial. It is not clear, however, that such an order can be observed in the market for health insurance; indeed, it may not exist at all.

Conclusion 5.5. *Whether the government can achieve a Pareto improvement by interfering in the health insurance market depends on the equilibrium concept employed. In particular, it makes a difference whether insurers anticipate the withdrawal of unprofitable contracts in response to their own actions and whether they cross-subsidize between contracts. If both conditions obtain, a private health insurance market yields a second-best efficient outcome. Otherwise, a Pareto improvement by mandating partial public insurance coverage is possible.*

5.3.4 Premium Risk

In the previous section, the possibility of market failure arose because insurers are unable to observe risk types. By contrast, we now focus on a problem which arises precisely because insurers can observe risk characteristics of individuals, e.g., their age, gender, and easily observable medical conditions. In a private health insurance market in which premiums reflect expected health care expenditure, insurers charge different premiums according to these criteria. Since some of these characteristics are uncertain, in particular health status, individuals face the risk of uncertain premiums. This is the *premium risk problem*.

As before, the existence of a problem does not per se justify government intervention. Indeed, private insurers may cover premium risk in two major ways. First, they can offer *guaranteed renewable contracts* which provide a premium guarantee to individuals in exchange for a prepayment [PAULY ET AL. (1995)]. Second, COCHRANE (1995) proposes to insure premium risk by a separate insurance which pays an indemnity to individuals who become a high risk. Under this *premium insurance*, the indemnity would exactly cover the higher health insurance premium that a high-risk individual has to pay. Finally, government regulation may be efficiency-enhancing in the presence of premium risk. In particular, the question is whether *community rating*, i.e., the requirement for health insurers to set a uniform premium for all individuals regardless of risk, is a sensible approach to insure premium risk.

5.3.4.1 Pure-Market Solutions

In order to illustrate the advantages and disadvantages of a pure-market solution to the premium risk problem, it is helpful to consider a simple model. Let all individuals be identical initially and live for two periods. In each period, they face the risk of being ill with health care expenditure M. In period 1, everyone has the same probability π_L of being ill. In period 2, individuals remain an L-type with probability λ and become a high-risk type with $\pi_H > \pi_L$ otherwise. The average probability of being ill in period 2 is therefore $\bar{\pi} \equiv \lambda \pi_L + (1 - \lambda)\pi_H$.

As above, assume that insurers incur no administrative expenses and maximize expected profits. The market for health insurance is characterized by perfect competition. This implies that insurance contracts are actuarially fair and that consumers will always buy full insurance. Insurers can observe the risk type of individuals. In period 2, they will therefore charge a premium equal to each risk type's expected cost. Thus, individuals who sign only one-period insurance contracts are subject to premium risk because their premium in period 2 is uncertain. With probability λ, their premium is $P_L = \pi_L M$, with probability $1 - \lambda$, it is $P_H = \pi_H M$, exposing them to an expected loss of $(\pi_H - \pi_L)M$. Risk-averse consumers would like to insure this premium risk.

A straightforward solution is to sign a long-term contract for both periods in period 1. Since the risk type is not known ex ante, health insurers would sell such insurance at a fair premium equal to average health care expenditure in each period, i.e., charge premium $P_1 = \pi_L M$ in period 1 and premium $P_2 = \bar{\pi} M$ in period 2. As a consequence, individuals would face no premium risk. This solution, however, has two problems.

- In period 2, individuals who turn out to be low risk types have an incentive to cancel the contract, replacing it by a one-period contract with a premium equal to their expected costs of $\pi_L M$. They would save $(\bar{\pi} - \pi_L)M$ in period 2. Only high-risk types keep their original contract causing insurers to make losses. Of course, insurers could insist on the execution of the long-term contract; however, courts may not enforce it. In this case, insurers would never offer such long-term contracts.

- Consumers must select their health insurer in period 1 already. However, they may wish to wait with their choice. Their preferences may change, or new insurers may enter the market. In addition, insurers may exploit the fact that individuals can only switch at a cost. For instance, they may deny payment, arguing that the loss occurred does not fall under the terms of the contract. Under managed care, switching is costly because the new insurer may not contract with certain providers of care. In addition, insurers may not be up-to-date with the latest developments in health care technology.

The first problem is a *commitment problem* on the part of consumers. Those who wish to insure against premium risk would like to commit themselves in period 1, guaranteeing that they will not defect if they turn out to be low risks. Whether they can in fact commit this way depends on the behavior of courts. If courts interpret contracts ex post in favor of consumers seeking to renege, premium risk cannot be insured using a long-term contract.

The second problem is a *lock-in problem*. In period 2, consumers may find themselves locked in with a contract that does not suit their changed preferences. Moreover, insurers may exploit the fact that ex post it is costly to switch. Whether they do so, will depend on how detailed contracts can be drafted and therefore be enforced by consumers. It is difficult, however, to include every possible contingency in a health insurance contract, causing contracts to be incomplete and hence costly to enforce. Nevertheless, insurers may abstain from acting opportunistically if they risk to lose their reputation for being a high quality insurer. This incentive is strong if new customers can judge whether insurers treat their current customers fairly.[14] The second problem can therefore also be interpreted as a commitment problem, this time on the part of the insurer.

Guaranteed renewable contracts and premium insurance try to overcome these problems. Whereas guaranteed renewable contracts focus on the commitment problem, premium insurance seeks to solve both problems.

Guaranteed Renewable Contracts

PAULY ET AL. (1995) propose to insure premium risk through guaranteed renewable (GR) contracts. The basic idea is that health insurers provide a premium guarantee against a prepayment. Consumers are free to switch insurers after disclosure of their type. Yet, nobody will switch, as shown below. Assuming a zero interest rate for simplicity, the GR contract can be described by the following properties:[15]

- In period 2, the premium P_2^{GR} cannot exceed $\pi_L M$. Otherwise, low-risk types would buy a one-period contract from a different health insurer. In the following, assume that P_2^{GR} is set as high as possible, implying $P_2^{GR} = \pi_L M$.
- The premium in period 1, P_1, has to be set such that insurers make zero expected profits, i.e.,

$$P_1^{GR} + P_2^{GR} = \pi_L M + \bar{\pi} M. \tag{5.21}$$

With $P_2^{GR} = \pi_L M$, one therefore obtains

$$P_1^{GR} = \bar{\pi} M. \tag{5.22}$$

Since expected health care expenditure in period 1 is only $\pi_L M$, individuals therefore make a prepayment amounting to

$$Pre^{GR} = (\bar{\pi} - \pi_L)M. \tag{5.23}$$

---

[14] Note that ex ante they have an interest to guarantee not to take advantage of this lock-in situation in order to attract consumers.

[15] The GR concept can easily be generalized to more than two periods [see PAULY ET AL. (1995)].

The main advantage of GR contracts is that low risks do not have an incentive to opt out, causing them to be self-enforcing (the high risks will hold on to them at any rate).[16] GR contracts therefore solve the commitment problem. Nevertheless, the lock-in problem remains. As under simple long-term contracts, individuals have to commit themselves to an insurer before their type can change, a situation that might be exploited by the insurer.[17]

Finally, some consumers may have problems to finance the prepayment required by GR contracts. Consider the following numerical example. An individual has an income of € 5,000 in period 1 and of € 10,000 in period 2. Let $\pi_L = 0.2$, $\pi_H = 0.6$, $\lambda = 0.75$, implying $\bar{\pi} = 0.3$. With $M = €\,10,000$, this yields $P_1^{GR} = €\,3,000$ and $P_2^{GR} = €\,2,000$, respectively. The prepayment in period 1 therefore amounts to € 1,000. For a consumer who has the same utility function across the two periods and no time preference, optimal expenditure on consumption is equal in all periods and amounts to € 5,000. With an income of € 5,000 in the first period, this consumer would have to take out a € 3,000 loan to finance her or his GR contract in order to be able to enjoy consumption as planned. In the presence of asymmetric information in credit markets, however, an income stream of (€ 5,000; € 10,000) is likely to induce a borrowing constraint. Let this constraint amount to € 2,000. In this case, the GR prepayment of € 1,000 forces a trade-off between intertemporal consumption smoothing and insuring premium risk.[18]

GR contracts are used in Australian and German private health insurance. Insurers are by law required to calculate premiums in such a way that they remain constant (save for technological changes in medicine) over a policyholder's lifetime. Since health care expenditure rises with age, the premium is higher than expected costs at young age, thus containing a prepayment.

Premium Insurance

While GR contracts can only solve the commitment problem, the concept of premium insurance (PI) developed by COCHRANE (1995) can in principle address both the commitment and the lock-in problem. The idea is simple. PI is a separate insurance contract contingent on individuals' risk type complementing their one-period policy. Those turning out to be high risks receive an indemnity, or, following COCHRANE, a severance payment, which exactly compensates for the higher pre-

---

[16] However, they may want to go to court to recover their prepayment. If courts are willing to recognize such claims, then GR contracts do not have an advantage over simple long-term contracts.

[17] If the premium in period 2 is $P_2^{GR} = \pi_L M$, then L-types are not locked in as they can change insurers at no cost. H-types, however, face additional costs of $(\pi_H - \pi_L)M$ if they switch insurers.

[18] FRICK (1998) shows that credit-constrained consumers may either buy partial GR contracts, i.e., contracts with a guaranteed premium above the expected costs of low risks but below expected costs of high risks, or no GR contracts at all. The subjective rate of time preference is crucial in this decision. Individuals with a marked time preference (who are relatively impatient) will not buy GR contracts if subject to a borrowing constraint.

mium. Consumers are then free to choose again. They are not locked in since the premium risk is fully covered.

In the model presented above, a simple form of premium insurance operates as follows. In period 2, the health insurance premiums for high and low risk types equals $\pi_H M$ and $\pi_L M$, respectively. Premium insurance obliges low risks to pay a surcharge $(\bar{\pi} - \pi_L)M$ which is used to finance the reduction $(\pi_H - \bar{\pi})M$ to high risks. Thus, everyone effectively pays the same premium $\bar{\pi}M$.

As COCHRANE points out, this simple form of premium insurance fails if low risk types cannot be obliged ex post to pay $(\bar{\pi} - \pi_L)M$. They may want to spend most of their wealth once they find out that they are low risks to avoid cross-subsidizing high risks. He therefore proposes to design PI such that low risk types pay the surcharge up front in period 1. Since the share $(1 - \lambda)$ of high risks receive the indemnity $(\pi_H - \pi_L)M$, this surcharge (assuming a zero interest rate) thus amounts to

$$Pre^{PI} = (1 - \lambda)(\pi_H - \pi_L)M = (\bar{\pi} - \pi_L)M. \qquad (5.24)$$

A comparison with (5.23) shows that PI calls for the same prepayment as GR contracts. This implies that PI can prevent credit-constrained consumers to deviate from their optimal consumption plan in the same way as GR does.

In principle, PI is superior to GR because it solves both the commitment and the lock-in problem. But PI is also more demanding than GR in that contracts contingent on risk type must be enforceable. While it has been assumed in the analysis that risk types are observable, it may be difficult to describe them ex ante in a contract. In contrast to other forms of insurance, payment is not contingent upon the actual occurrence of a loss but the mere redefinition of health status. The only two indicators available are the health condition of the individual (which may be subject to interpretation) and the health insurance premium paid. COCHRANE therefore proposed to tie the indemnity to the premium paid which reveals the risk type. This, however, creates incentives for low-risk types to conspire with their health insurer against the premium insurer. By officially paying a high premium but actually paying a low premium (or obtaining additional benefits for a given premium), they could obtain a higher indemnity from the premium insurer.

The Achilles' heel of PI insurance is therefore the type-measurement problem. Clearly, there exist a number of diagnoses which are indisputable and can be assigned a cost of treatment. For instance, a patient with kidney failure needs regular dialysis whose expected cost can easily be determined. Still, there are also many health conditions which can hardly be written into a contract in a satisfactory manner and therefore unverifiable in court. Not only the presence but also the severity of changes in health status would have to be specified. Take depression as an example. An insured might demand intensive psychotherapy while the insurer deems occasional counseling sufficient. It is difficult for a court to resolve a conflict of this type. Premium insurance contracts therefore are likely to be incomplete, giving rise to skepticism concerning their viability.

Unfortunately, there is no empirical evidence as premium insurance does not even exist in the United States where private health insurance covers most of the population. On the one hand, this may be due to the impossibility of premium insurance. On the other hand, existing regulation may obstruct the development of premium insurance. For example, U.S. employer-sponsored health insurance is a tax-exempt fringe benefit, which causes the market for individually contracted health insurance to be limited. In addition, there are only few other countries with private health insurance and even where it exists market its share is small.[19]

> **Conclusion 5.6.** *Both pure-market approaches to insuring premium risk suffer from problems. Guaranteed renewable contracts lock consumers in. Premium insurance contracts are likely to be incomplete since it is difficult to define the risk type with sufficient precision. Both solutions require a premium surcharge at young age.*

5.3.4.2 Community Rating as a Solution

Premium risk is not an issue in countries with extensive public coverage. In the United Kingdom, for example, most health care is provided through the tax-financed National Health Service (NHS). Individuals obtain services free of charge, while their tax contributions do not vary with health status. The downside of this alternative is that in the absence of competition, the NHS has only weak incentives to provide services at low cost and in accordance with citizens' preferences. For this reason, private health insurance may be a desirable. But private insurers are typically constrained when it comes to premium setting by the mandate to apply *community rating* (CR). This approach requires a given insurer's premiums to be uniform for all individuals who enroll in a particular health plan. A desirable side effect of CR is that it relieves consumers from uncertainty with regard to future premiums.

Unlike the pure-market approaches to the premium risk problem, CR also imposes ex-ante redistribution between high and low risks. In most industrial countries, however, this redistribution is regarded as fair because, to a large extent, health is considered to be beyond citizens' responsibility. Risk-based premiums would unjustly put a higher burden on people with a poor health status. Furthermore, if the premium is not raised too much by ex-ante redistribution, everyone can be in favor of community rating in the absence of other possibilities to insure premium risk. Consider that in period 1 a fraction μ of individuals are high risk individuals who remain also high risks in period 2. The fraction $1 - \mu$ are low risks. In period 2, they remain a low risk with probability λ and become a high risk with probability $1 - \lambda$. Community rating then leads to the following premiums in periods 1 and 2:

$$P_1^{CR} = \left[\mu\pi_H + (1-\mu)\pi_L\right]M > \pi_L M$$
$$P_2^{CR} = \left[(\mu + (1-\mu)(1-\lambda))\pi_H + (1-\mu)\lambda\pi_L\right]M > \left[\lambda\pi_L + (1-\lambda)\pi_H\right]M.$$

---

[19] See CHOLLET AND LEWIS (1997).

In both cases, the premium is higher than expected expenditure of low risks in period 1. Whether these will nevertheless prefer community rating depends on the share μ of initially high risks and their degree of risk aversion. In particular, if μ is not too large, the increase in expected expenditure will not exceed the risk premium that low risks are willing to pay for the elimination of premium risk.

In practice, community-rated health insurance systems also prohibit age-based premium differentiation, thereby inducing pay-as-you-go finance of health insurance. As a consequence, the young must pay part of the health care expenditure of the old. Assuming a stationary population and abstracting from individuals who are initially high risks, this leads to a constant premium

$$P_1^{CR} = P_2^{CR} = \frac{(\pi_L + \bar{\pi})M}{2} = \pi_L M + \frac{(\bar{\pi} - \pi_L)M}{2} \tag{5.25}$$

Community rating therefore also induces a surcharge at young age, amounting to $[(\bar{\pi} - \pi_L)M]/2$. Compared to GR and PI, this surcharge is smaller [see equations (5.23) and (5.24)]. Furthermore, community-rated systems frequently link premiums to income. Since the young on average earn less than the old, this tends to reduce the surcharge at young age. A possible drawback of pay-as-you-go finance, however, is that it implies redistribution from young to old which intensifies in response to population ageing (see Section 14.3.1.2).

CR is typically accompanied by two additional interventions in the market for health insurance.

- *Open enrollment* requires health insurers to accept any individual who applies. Otherwise insurers would have the incentive to reject high risks who therefore might not find coverage.

- *Compulsory insurance* is imposed; else low risks may prefer not buy any health insurance to avoid cross-subsidizing high risks.

The threefold regulation of community rating, open enrollment, and compulsory insurance can be found in Belgium, Germany, the Netherlands, and Switzerland. It is also part of ENTHOVEN's (1988) proposal to reform the health care system of the United States.

The main problem involved in community rating is the gap between a person's contribution and expected health care expenditure. This creates an incentive for insurers to concentrate their efforts not on an efficient provision of services but on *risk selection* by designing benefit packages that are attractive to low risks but unattractive to high risks. For example, low risks can be lured by including services related to wellness and fitness. At the same time, high risks can be scared off by high nonfinancial hurdles for the utilization of medical services or by low payments to service providers for expensive chronic diseases such as diabetes.[20] This practice of risk selection or 'cream-skimming' can be controlled by regulation of the benefit package

---

[20] Additional examples can be found in VAN DE VEN AND VAN VLIET (1992).

and a *risk adjustment scheme*. The latter taxes insurers with a favorable risk structure and pays transfers to insurers with a less favorable risk structure. How exactly this serves to mitigate incentives for risk selection will be discussed in Chapter 7.

Conclusion 5.7. *Community rating requires an insurer's premiums to be uniform for all individuals who enrol in a health plan. This avoids a premium for the type risk but also induces ex-ante redistribution. To mitigate incentives for risk selection, further intervention is necessary, in particular, the regulation of benefits and a risk adjustment scheme.*

5.3.4.3 Comparing the Solutions

Whether community rating works better than the two proposals which do not require government intervention depends on the economic environment. In the following, we identify the most important factors.

(1) *Are payments contingent on risk types possible?*

If it is not possible or very costly to specify risk types in contracts, then premium insurance (PI) cannot work well while guaranteed renewability (GR) is not affected. Community rating (CR) does not require contracts contingent on risk types. But risk adjustment schemes need information on risk types which is difficult to come by. Still, as shown by SELDEN (1998) and GLAZER AND MCGUIRE (2000) imperfect indicators of risk types may be used (see Chapter 7).

(2) *How complete are long-term health insurance contracts?*

Complete specification of contracts is important for GR which relies on long-term health insurance contracts. In particular, contracts could include sanctions for insurers if they do not operate efficiently, e.g., by not being up-to-date with the developments in medical technology. Under PI and CR, this problem is less severe since contracts are short-term, permitting consumers to sanction insurers for shirking by switching.

(3) *How easily can the benefit package be regulated?*

If product differentiation is possible, price regulation needs to be complemented by product regulation to prevent producers from varying effective price by adjusting quality. CR amounts to premium regulation; it calls for regulation of the benefit package because insurers have an incentive to attract low-risk types (who contribute the same marginal revenue for less expected future marginal cost than high-risk types). This holds true unless risk adjustment is perfect. Both PI and GR do not require regulation of the benefit package since they allow insurers to set risk-based premiums and therefore do not create an incentive for risk selection.

Table 5.1. Efficiency Problems of the Solutions to the Premium Risk Problem

	Criterion	GR	PI	CR
1.	Specification of risk types	n	y	o
2.	Specification of long-term health insurance	y	n	n
3.	Regulation of benefits	n	n	y
4.	Heterogeneous preferences	o	n	y
5.	Borrowing constraints	y	y	o

(4) *How heterogeneous are preferences?*

Product regulation restricts consumer choice, causing a loss of efficiency. This is a downside of CR but not PI and GR (see item (3) above). It weighs the more heavily, the more heterogeneous are preferences. So-called market experiments can be used to measure preferences. Applying this tool, ZWEIFEL ET AL. (2006) find substantial preference heterogeneity with regard to the provision of health care in Switzerland. Both systems under risk-based premiums do better in this respect. Under PI, individuals can choose their desired health insurance contract and even switch insurers. Under GR, they have an initial choice. Owing to the lock-in problem, however, their choice is restricted at a later stage.

(5) *Do individuals face borrowing constraints?*

The prepayment required by GR and PI may be large enough to obviate life-time consumption plans of individuals who face borrowing constraints. Even in rich countries, the majority of citizens has almost no savings apart from social security wealth, potentially causing them to rely on consumer credit to finance GR and PI contracts. Banks on the other hand usually limit credit to one year's income and its duration to 36 months. The argument applies less to CR, which burdens consumers later in this life cycle, when they are able to generate some savings. Borrowing constraints do not have the same relevance in this case.

Table 5.1 provides an overview of the presence (y) and absence (n) of the problems associated with 'o' indicating an intermediate position. No alternatives dominates the others implying that their ranking will depend on the specific circumstances characterizing a health care system.

A further aspect is whether ex-ante redistribution is desired or not. Here, CR is the only system which necessarily introduces ex-ante redistribution between risk types. Under GR and PI, individuals initially pay a premium according to risk type. Those who argue that there is too much redistribution of income and wealth to begin with, will therefore tend to favor these solutions. CR will be supported by those who prefer more redistribution or prefer health insurance over other instruments (e.g., income taxation) to achieve this goal.

Conclusion 5.8. *Premium risk can be addressed by pure-market solutions (Guaranteed Renewability, Premium Insurance) or public regulation (Community Rating). Apart from a preference for redistribution, the assessment of these alternatives hinges on efficiency issues such as problems with the specification of risk types, writing long-term contracts, regulation of benefits, heterogeneity of preferences, and the frequency of borrowing constraints. No alternative a priori dominates the others.*

5.4 Justice as an Argument in Favor of Government Intervention in Health Care

Often considerations of justice are invoked to justify government intervention in health care. For example, in many Anglo-Saxon countries, 'equal access' to health care constitutes a goal of health policy besides efficiency. In France and Germany, the principles of equality (égalité) or 'comparable living conditions' play a prominent role. Frequently, the access to medical services is regarded as a 'right' which implies that willingness to pay (and a fortiori ability to pay) of an individual or a group (e.g., inhabitants of a region of a country) must not constitute a criterion for the allocation of health care services.

5.4.1 Willingness and Ability to Pay and Access to Health Care

With respect to willingness and ability to pay, two postulates are commonly made when it comes to access to health care services. The first says that access should not depend upon *ability to pay*, i.e., income or wealth of a person. The second goes even further by requiring that not even *willingness to pay* should play a role, i.e., the amount of money that a person is willing to give up for the service. Instead medical criteria alone are to govern access to health care.

To assess these postulates, first notice that willingness to pay simply reflects preferences for health as opposed to other goods if two persons with the same ability to pay are compared. To exclude willingness to pay as a criterion for access to health care services therefore implies that preferences must not play a role. Given equal ability to pay, this is ethically questionable and not compatible with the idea of a liberal society. Thus, if one were to agree on excluding willingness to pay, one would want to limit application of this principle to persons who differ in their ability to pay.

The mere fact that ability to pay differs between patients, however, is not sufficient reason to ban it as a criterion governing access to health care services. The crucial point is whether differences in ability to pay are to be considered as unjust. To answer this question, one may consider the factors causing such differences, in particular

(a) unequal personal effort,

(b) unequal initial opportunities,

(c) unequal 'luck' in life.

If only unequal personal effort were responsible for the differences in ability to pay, then there would be no reason to call the distribution of ability to pay unjust. A different verdict obtains if unequal initial opportunities and luck in life are predominant. In reality, it is likely that all three factors play a role, justifying a policy of redistribution in principle. But this does not imply that the access to health care services should be made completely independent of ability to pay. Rather, it seems more appropriate to treat ability to pay as such the primary target variable of social policy by paying transfers to the lowest income groups. To get political support from taxpayers, tying these transfers to the purchase of (social) health insurance may be advantageous (see Section 5.3.2), which guarantees access to health care services.

On the other hand, if ability to pay is to be completely disregarded as a criterion for access, there are only two ways to accomplish this. First, one can try to completely equalize ability to pay. But this alternative seems hardly desirable because it involves high efficiency losses through taxation and transfers that cause important distortions in economic decisions, particularly with respect to labor supply and capital formation. Furthermore, it can be argued that enforcing an equal distribution of income and wealth gives rise to injustice to the extent that differences in income reflect differences in effort and services provided to other members of society, rather than the other two factors cited above.

Secondly, one can attempt to suppress willingness to pay and thus ability to pay as a determinant of access to health care services. This idea of a *specific egalitarianism* has been advocated by WILLIAMS (1962), TOBIN (1970) and WALZER (1983). A consequence of this view is that greater personal effort does not serve to obtain more health care services. A key argument in favor of specific egalitarianism is that in emergency situations involving life and death, ability and willingness to pay often coincide. In the face of death, however, citizens should be equal. Another situation calling for specific egalitarianism is an incident of a scale so large that available resources do not permit all victims to be treated. In such a situation, only an allocation of scarce resources according to medical criteria, in particular urgency and chance of survival, is deemed ethically acceptable. Failure to enforce specific egalitarianism would result in ability to pay only to decide who obtains treatment.

An important question is how frequently such 'life or death' situations occur. More importantly still, resources available for health care are not exogenously given, but determined by demand and supply. For example, if the demand for physiotherapy by people with high ability to pay rises, the market mechanism will lead to an expansion of the supply of physiotherapeutic services, through more services provided by existing physiotherapists or entry of new providers. Therefore, the quantity of services and with it consumer surplus rises. These beneficial effects cannot be achieved if willingness to pay is excluded as a determinant of the allocation of health care.

There are additional arguments against the concept of a specific egalitarianism with respect to health care,

- Copayments create incentives for health-related behavior (see Chapter 6). However, they are more easily borne by individuals who have a high willingness to pay. This means that copayments are not compatible with specific egalitarianism and must be ruled out if willingness to pay is to be excluded from the criteria determining access to health care services. As a consequence, people will ignore the financial consequences of their nutrition, exercise, smoking and drinking habits. To avoid an explosion of health care expenditure, the government would have to control health-related behavior through compulsion, thus risking a conflict with basic values of a liberal society.

- As shown in Chapters 3 and 4, medical services are not the only (and perhaps not even the most important) goods that have an impact on health. Other things such as adequate nutrition and housing play a comparable role. Thus, they should be allocated free of charge according to specific egalitarianism. Withdrawing such a wide spectrum of goods from the discipline of market mechanisms, however, would jeopardize the allocative efficiency of the economy as a whole.

- The freedom of patients to decide on their own matters would be curtailed since decisions to treat would be based solely upon criteria emanating from a collective (and most probably bureaucratic) decision process or else the individual preferences of attending physicians.

For these reasons, proposals to exclude willingness to pay as a criterion governing the access to health care services appear to be misguided. Only in emergencies where it is impossible to treat everybody in an adequate way does willingness to pay constitute an ethically questionable criterion for the allocation of health care services. In all other situations, the health care system is not a zero-sum game in which the well-to-do impose their demands at the expense of the poorer members of society. Therefore, if ability to pay is inequitably distributed, it is a better strategy to influence it directly through taxes and transfers in order to guarantee an adequate provision of health care services for all citizens.

Conclusion 5.9. *A general exclusion of ability to pay or even willingness to pay from the criteria governing access to medical services is not desirable as it runs counter to the principles of a liberal society and would lead to an important loss of efficiency. Differences in ability to pay due to factors that are deemed unjustified can be addressed by taxes and income transfers. Only in emergency situations where a fixed amount of resources is available which is insufficient to treat everyone affected should willingness to pay be neglected in the allocation of health care services.*

5.4.2 Congenital Differences in Health and Access to Health Insurance

5.4.2.1 Redistribution and the Veil of Ignorance

In a private market for health insurance, the insured pays a premium which – given the amount of coverage – reflects the expected value of future health care costs. Those with a higher risk of illness thus have to pay higher premiums than those with a lower risk. This market solution can be considered 'unjust' if differences in health risk are entirely due to inequality in health endowments (e.g., congenital diseases or handicaps) and not to differences in the persons' health-related behavior. As a remedy, financial transfers from 'low risks' to 'high risks' are recommended which compensate the latter for the excess in their health insurance premiums.

Such cross-subsidies between low and high risks can be justified using the concept of the *veil of ignorance* introduced by HARSANYI (1955) and RAWLS (1971). According to their argument, a distribution is considered as just if it can be unanimously agreed upon in a hypothetical situation in which nobody knows whether she or he will belong to the advantaged or disadvantaged. In the present context, people behind the veil of ignorance do not know whether they will be born as high or low risks. On top of their health risk as such, they face a lottery concerning their expected health care costs and thus their health insurance premiums. Given the plausible assumption of risk aversion behind the veil of ignorance, they would be willing to insure against this premium risk. Hence, if the hypothetical veil of ignorance is accepted as the basis of a fair decision, not guided by particular interests, equalization of health insurance premiums between high and low risks appears desirable.[21]

There will be a trade-off between equity and efficiency, however, if differences in health states depend not only on genetic endowments but also on health-related behavior such as nutrition, smoking, drinking and exercise. In this case, a complete equalization of health insurance premiums induces *ex-ante moral hazard* (see Section 6.4.1). This efficiency loss can be mitigated by making patients pay a fraction of their bill out of pocket or permitting experience rating of premiums, i.e., letting insurers adjust their premiums to past health care expenditure. Taking moral hazard effects into account, citizens would presumably agree on a partial equalization of premiums across risk groups only [see BOADWAY ET AL. (2003) for a formal analysis].

> **Conclusion 5.10.** *Behind a veil of ignorance, risk-averse individuals would consent to insuring the risk of high expected health care expenditure (and hence health insurance premiums). In the presence of ex-ante moral hazard, however, only a partial equalization of premiums across risk groups would be optimal.*

---

[21] A further argument in favor of cross-subsidies between low and high risks can be made if health risks are negatively correlated with ability. Then equalizing health insurance premiums implies redistribution from high- to low-ability individuals which may allow to reduce the efficiency loss due to income taxation [see CREMER AND PESTIEAU (1996)].

5.4.2.2 Implementing Cross-Subsidies between High and Low Risks

The equity problem posed by congenital health differences is closely related to the premium risk problem discussed in Section 5.3.4. Both call for cross-subsidies between high and low risks. The only difference is that premium risk can in principle be insured by the market since individuals are able to buy insurance contracts before their risk type changes. Implementing cross-subsidies between individuals who differ in their health status at birth, requires government intervention. This intervention takes on two main forms, a national health service and community rating. As pointed out in Section 5.3.4.2, both have their drawbacks. The problem of a national health service is lack of competition and limited freedom of choice while community rating has to deal with the risk-selection problem.

In the literature, additional solutions requiring less market intervention have been proposed. In particular, they allow insurers to charge risk-based premiums. The task of subsidizing high risks is delegated to the tax and transfer system. For example, PAULY ET AL. (1992) propose to introduce refundable tax credits reflecting a household's risk category and inversely related to household income. Citizens with little or no tax liability would receive a transfer payment.[22] This scheme is similar to the concept of premium insurance (see Section 5.3.4.1), with the government acting as the premium insurer. In a similar vein, ZWEIFEL AND BREUER (2006) propose to subsidize risk-based premiums to the extent that they exceed a certain percentage of household income. In this way, they aim at seeking out those individuals who are both high-risk and low-income types, arguing that high risks with high incomes need not be subsidized.

The scheme by PAULY ET AL. (1992) requires risk-adjusted transfers. As with premium insurance, the crucial question is how precisely these transfers are to reflect risk type. In the context of premium insurance (Section 5.3.4.1), it was found that specifying risk types with sufficient precision poses major problems. In practice, only a few diseases which are easily diagnosed would probably be used to determine the transfers. As an alternative to a direct measurement of risk, the premium itself could be used as an indicator of risk. This approach is taken by ZWEIFEL AND BREUER (2006). A premium subsidy, however, creates an incentive for both the insurer and the insured to include additional services in the contract in order to increase the transfer. This can be avoided by defining the benefit package in detail. Then, however, an important advantage of competition in the health insurance market would be lost. Alternatively, the subsidy could be scaled not to the individual premium but to an average defined over a broadly defined risk class.

Furthermore, means-tested subsidization of health insurance is not without its problematic incentive effects. When a great number of welfare benefits, ranging from housing subsidies to food stamps and educational grants hinge or a threshold level of income, earning more in the labor market may result in a loss of benefits and a fall in net income, with unfavorable effects on labor supply. Finally, risk-based premiums

---

[22] See also VAN DE VEN ET AL. (2000) for a discussion of this approach.

may require a safety net. Therefore, both PAULY ET AL. (1992) and ZWEIFEL AND BREUER (2006) envisage a government-run fallback insurance scheme similar to the assigned risk pool in the U.S. auto liability insurance which provides basic coverage at a uniform contribution.

The proposals by PAULY ET AL. (1992) and ZWEIFEL AND BREUER (2006) show that it is not necessary to interfere in the price mechanism to achieve cross-subsidies between high and low risks. A comparison with the standard solutions to this problem shows that society faces a trade-off. If priority is given to equalizing the premiums of high and low risks, community rating and a national health service are both appropriate. But these two solutions suffer from a high degree of regulation and limited freedom of choice. Community rating has the advantage that it is compatible with insurer competition. Its drawback are the incentives for risk-selection. If the freedom of individuals to choose their own most preferred insurance plan is given priority, then risk-based premiums are a necessary consequence, calling for transfers that are unlikely to always benefit the target groups.

> **Conclusion 5.11.** *Cross-subsidies between risk groups can be achieved through a national health service, community rating, or risk-adjusted transfers. The first solution facilitates the attainment of distributional objectives but does not allow competition. Community rating assigns the goal of redistribution to insurers. Risk-based premiums shift this task to the government, which is called upon to implement risk-adjustment transfers which in turn may miss distributional objectives. The preferred position on this equity-efficiency trade-off ultimately depends on citizens' preferences.*

5.5 Rationing of Health Care Services

Political debates on the design of health care systems often focus on the concept of 'rationing' medical care. While some experts warn that in view of rapid medical progress (see Chapter 14) and scarce resources health care services will soon have to be rationed, cabinet ministers who are responsible for the health sector frequently promise that, as long as they are in charge, rationing will never occur. Typically both sides agree in equating the very concept of rationing with 'denying or withholding necessary or at least potentially beneficial medical services' from patients. Not surprisingly, debates on rationing often become heated, in particular when its compatibility with ethics is at issue. To mitigate controversy, it is sometimes proposed to avoid the 'R word' and use the term 'priority setting' instead. For clarity, however, it is preferable to define the term 'rationing' in accordance with its general meaning in economics.

5.5.1 The Concept of Rationing

In its wide sense, 'rationing' is synonymous to 'allocating', i.e., deciding which of several competing wants is to be satisfied whenever a resource is scarce. This concept can be best explained using the example of a non-augmentable resource such as human organs (e.g., hearts). In the short run, i.e., taking the legal rules for organ procurement as fixed, the supply of hearts is given by the rate of brain-dead patients and their previous willingness to donate their hearts post-mortem. The demand for hearts is determined by the number of patients with chronic heart failure on the waiting list. 'Allocating' or 'rationing' the available hearts among the potential beneficiaries can now be performed either

(a) by auctioning them off according to willingness to pay ('price rationing'), or
(b) by distributing them according to other criteria such as medical urgency or waiting time ('non-price rationing').

No matter which of the two mechanisms is applied, nobody would claim that a heart allocated to patient A is 'withheld' from patient B. When people speak of rationing, they normally use the term as a short-hand for non-price rationing.[23] We prefer to call this type of non-price rationing 'secondary', because the need to allocate derives from the natural scarcity of a medical resource.

In the long run, the quantity of almost all medical resources can be increased. The relevant question now becomes how much of its scarce resources a society wants to devote to the production of health care services as opposed to other commodities. Here again, one possibility is the use of the price mechanism, resulting in medical services to be produced and utilized according to willingness and ability to pay. Since the need for medical services is stochastic, insurance companies will offer health insurance contracts to cover the costs of these services. In an unregulated insurance market, insurers will offer a variety of contracts, some with generous benefits and high premiums and others with limits on the scope and amount of benefits and lower premiums. Thus consumers have the opportunity to trade off some limitations against reductions in premium in accordance with their preferences. In a way, they ration themselves through their choice of insurance contract. Abstracting from special programs such as Medicare (for the aged) and Medicaid (for the poor), this type of price-rationing describes the situation in the United States of America.

Medicare and Medicaid as well as major parts of all health care systems in the OECD constitute another possibility. Here, it is the role of the government to finance health care by levying taxes or mandatory health insurance contributions to provide

---

[23] The word rationing emanates from the wartime economy when the government's increasing claim to resources and thus a shrinking supply of consumer goods would have led to a tremendous hike in prices of consumer goods. To avoid severe inequalities in consumption of essential goods, governments suspended the price mechanism and introduced alternative modes of distributing goods among consumers.

medical services to patients either free of charge or at least below market price. As it is impossible to give unlimited amounts of anything for free to all citizens,[24] there are usually some limits to the provision of these services, and these limits are defined in the benefit package of the collectively financed health care system. We prefer to call this definition '(primary) rationing':

> **Definition 5.3.** *'(Primary) Rationing' means determining the benefit package of a collectively financed health care system in a political decision.*

Common criteria for inclusion of a service in the benefit package of such a health system may be the cost-utility ratio (see Chapter 2) or the severity of the respective disease.

5.5.2 Types of Primary Rationing

As soon as collective financing of health care is combined with a uniformly regulated benefit package, the inevitable result is 'non-price rationing'. Thus the question becomes not whether but how health care services are being rationed. The modes of rationing can be distinguished according to two criteria (see Figure 5.7), namely

(1) hard versus soft rationing, and

(2) explicit versus implicit rationing.

'Soft' rationing means that markets are admitted in which people are allowed to purchase additional services not covered by the collectively financed health care system. 'Hard' rationing, by contrast, means that these markets are prohibited. For a discussion of these two options, see Section 5.4.1 above.

'Explicit' rationing means that the benefit package is defined by clear and transparent rules, whereas 'implicit' rationing (also called 'bedside' rationing) means that such rules do not exist but allocation decisions are taken by health care providers on a case-by-case basis. As they are usually not allowed to employ the price system, this amounts to secondary rationing. Implicit rationing is often the consequence of budgetary allocations by the government. For example, the National Health Service of the United Kingdom does not necessarily limit the quantity of open heart surgeries that can be performed by a public hospital. By setting spending limits, however, it causes hospitals to stop performing this type of intervention towards the end of the year because they run out of money.

In the choice between explicit and implicit rationing, it is clear that it is not possible to avoid implicit rationing completely. In particular, it is not feasible to devise rules for each contingency that can arise when physicians must decide on whom to

---

[24] For a limited number of individuals, such as the President of the Unites States, unlimited access to health care is possible but as VICTOR FUCHS (1984a) points out 'presidential medicine' is clearly not feasible for everybody.

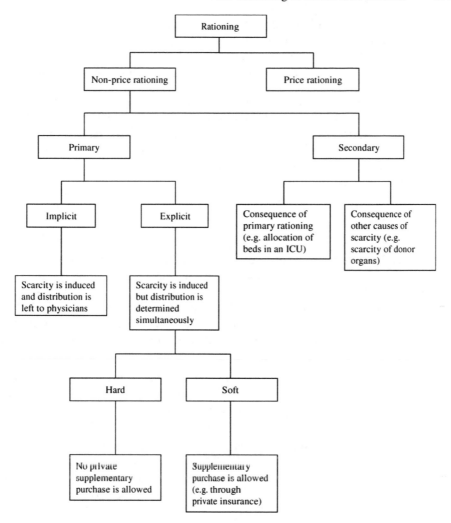

Fig. 5.7. Types of Rationing

treat. Furthermore, many people seem to favor implicit over explicit rationing rules because the former help to maintain the belief that death is caused by bad luck and is not the result of specific rationing decisions including one's own decision not to insure against the costs of certain services. This attitude, however, comes at a price since in the absence of explicit rules personal preferences may decide who is treated. For this reason, explicit rationing can be useful in many instances. For example, in distributing donor hearts, explicit rules exclude that hearts are allocated according to a physicians' sympathy for certain patients. A further argument in favor of explicit rationing is related to the choice between hard and soft rationing discussed above. If it is agreed that the right type of rationing is the soft one, then the logical consequence is to make rationing explicit because only if the limitations of coverage in the mandatory insurance plan are transparently specified, can these gaps be filled by purchasing private supplementary insurance contracts at a time when it is not yet predictable who will need the respective services for a prolongation of her or his life.

> **Conclusion 5.12.** *In a wide sense of the word, 'rationing' means 'allocating'. Thus, by definition health services are always rationed. In the more narrow sense of 'non-price rationing', health services are rationed in those countries which run some type of collectively financed health care system. Therefore not the presence, but only the type of rationing (hard vs. soft, explicit vs. implicit) can be a matter of debate.*

5.6 Summary

(1) The market fails in its allocation of health goods if these goods exhibit collective-good properties (vaccinations, hospital beds held in reserve) or give rise to externalities. In the case of vaccination, the government can use taxes and transfers, possibly in kind, to remedy the market failure. In the case of emergency hospital services, insurers can negotiate for their provision. There is no need for the government to finance these services, let alone to act as the supplier of health goods.

(2) Another reason for market failure is seen in consumers' incapability of making rational decisions about their demand for health services. However, this does not provide justification for public provision, but rather for measures to improve the information of consumers and to secure product quality.

(3) Compulsory health insurance prevents society from being exploited by 'free riders'. Furthermore, if combined with a state-independent transfer to compensate 'free riders', it achieves a Pareto improvement over an institutional arrangement where 'free riders' fail to buy insurance but are guaranteed some minimum income when sick.

(4) Health insurance markets may fail if individuals are heterogeneous in terms of the risk to be insured and are the only ones to know their risk. Whether the government can achieve a Pareto improvement by interfering in the health insurance market depends on the equilibrium concept employed. In particular, it makes a difference whether insurers anticipate the withdrawal of unprofitable contracts in response to their own actions and whether they cross-subsidize between contracts. If both conditions obtain, a private health insurance market yields a second-best efficient outcome. Otherwise, a Pareto improvement by mandating partial public insurance coverage is possible.

(5) In a private health insurance market in which premiums reflect expected health care expenditure, insurers charge different premiums according to these criteria. Since some of these characteristics are uncertain, in particular health status, individuals face 'premium risk', i.e., the risk of uncertain premiums.

(6) Premium risk can be addressed by pure-market solutions (Guaranteed Renewability, Premium Insurance) or public regulation (Community Rating). Apart from a preference for redistribution, the assessment of these alternatives hinges on efficiency issues such as problems with the specification of risk types, writing long-term contracts, regulation of benefits, heterogeneity of preferences, and the frequency of borrowing constraints. No alternative a priori dominates the others.

(7) A general exclusion of ability to pay or even willingness to pay from the criteria governing access to medical services is not desirable as it runs counter to the principles of a liberal society and would lead to an important loss of efficiency. Differences in ability to pay due to factors that are deemed unjustified can be addressed by taxes and income transfers. Only in emergency situations where a fixed amount of resources is available which is insufficient to treat everyone affected should willingness to pay be neglected in the allocation of health care services.

(8) Behind a veil of ignorance, risk-averse individuals would consent to insuring the risk of high expected health care expenditure (and hence health insurance premiums). In the presence of ex-ante moral hazard, however, only a partial equalization of premiums across risk groups would be optimal. Cross-subsidies between risk groups can be achieved through a national health service, community rating, or risk-adjusted transfers. The first solution facilitates the attainment of distributional objectives but does not allow competition. Community rating assigns the goal of redistribution to insurers. Risk-based premiums shift this task to the government, which is called upon to implement risk-adjustment transfers which in turn may miss distributional objectives. The preferred position on this equity-efficiency trade-off ultimately depends on citizens' preferences.

(9) In a wide sense of the word, 'rationing' means 'allocating'. Thus, by definition health services are always rationed. In the more narrow sense of 'non-price rationing', health services are rationed in those countries which run some type of collectively financed health care system. Therefore not the presence, but only the type of rationing (hard vs. soft, explicit vs. implicit) can be a matter of debate.

5.7 Further Reading

ARROW (1963) and PAULY (1988) are classical articles which discuss the special characteristics of health care goods. A proof of the First Theorem of Welfare Economics can be found in Chapter 13 of GRAVELLE AND REES (2004) and in Chapter 10 of MAS-COLELL ET AL. (1995). DIONNE AND DOHERTY (1992) provide an excellent review of the literature on adverse selection in insurance market. McGUIRE ET AL. (1988) and HURLEY (2000) review arguments of justice with respect to health goods. The various concepts of rationing are explained in BREYER AND SCHULTHEISS (2002). Ethical arguments on the respective types of rationing can be found in BUTLER (1999), MENZEL (1990), UBEL (2000) and the contributions to BREYER ET AL. (2001).

5.E Exercises

5.1. Consider the following questions:

(a) What are possible reasons for market failure on the markets for health goods? How may the government intervene appropriately?

(b) What arguments serve to justify compulsory health insurance?

5.2. Consider the 'free rider' model in Section 5.3.2 and assume that $\pi = 0.5$, $M = €25,000$ and $Y_{min} = €2,500$. Individuals derive utility $u(y) = y^{0.5}$ from disposable income y.

(a) Calculate the critical income level $\tilde{Y}$ below which an individual will choose no insurance coverage.

(b) An individual earns gross income $Y = €20,000$. Show that compulsory insurance in combination with a state-independent transfer τ can (i) raise expected utility of the individual and (ii) lower the expected transfer payment by the government. Explain your result.

5.3. Consider the model of an insurance market with asymmetric information presented in Section 5.3.3.3. All individuals have the utility function $u(y) = -e^{-0.1y}$, gross income $Y = 100$ and face treatment costs $M = 80$. High risks have a probability of illness $\pi_H = 0.8$; for low risks this probability is $\pi_L = 0.2$. The share of low risks in the population is λ. In the following, base your analysis on the RS equilibrium concept.

(a) Consider the contracts in a possible separating equilibrium.

(i) Consider the following equation:

$$(1 - \pi_H)u(Y - \pi_L\hat{I}) + \pi_H u(Y - \pi_L\hat{I} - M + \hat{I}) = u(Y - \pi_H M).$$

Interpret this equation and $\hat{I}$.

(ii) Show that $\hat{I} \approx 17.21$ (e.g., use a spreadsheet program and vary $\hat{I}$ until both sides of the equation are equal).

(iii) Determine the expected utility of both risk types in a possible separating equilibrium.

(b) What is the critical value of λ_{crit} up to which a separating equilibrium exists?

Hint: first determine the optimal insurance coverage $I^*(\lambda)$ for low risks in a pooling contract with price $p = \bar{\pi} \equiv \lambda\pi_L + (1-\lambda)\pi_H$ per unit insurance coverage. Inserting $I^*(\lambda)$ in the low risks' utility function yields the maximum utility of low risks in a pooling contract. Furthermore, determine the utility of low risks in a possible separating equilibrium. Use these results (and a spreadsheet program) to show that $\lambda_{crit} \approx 0.17$.

(c) Assume that $\lambda = 0.1$. The government introduces compulsory insurance with coverage $I_G = 20$ and a premium $P_G = \bar{\pi} I_G$.

  (i) Consider the following equation:

$$(1 - \pi_H)u\left(Y - \pi_L \tilde{I} - \bar{\pi} I_G\right) + \pi_H u\left(Y - \pi_L \tilde{I} - \bar{\pi} I_G - M + \tilde{I} + I_G\right)$$

$$= u\left(Y - \pi_H\left(M - I_G\right) - \bar{\pi} I_G\right).$$

Interpret this equation and $\tilde{I}$. Use a spreadsheet programm to show that $\tilde{I} \approx 12.23$.

  (ii) Determine the utility of both risk types in a possible separating equilibrium and compare these with the situation without compulsory insurance.

  (iii) Show that the separating equilibrium exists.

  (iv) Illustrate your result in a diagram.

5.4. In the German private health insurance system, insurers must charge a constant premium over the life-cycle.

(a) Use the premium risk model of Section 5.3.4.1 to calculate the constant premium P_{const} which yields zero profits under the assumption that no individuals switch in period 2.

(b) Compare the constant premium to the premiums of a guaranteed renewable contract and show that

$$P_1^{GR} > P_{const} > P_2^{GR}.$$

What are the implications of this result for a contract which guarantees a constant premium P_{const}?

(c) Suppose that everybody experiences a deterioration of the health status in period 2. With probability ϕ, individuals have a probability of $\pi_M > \pi_L$ of becoming ill, with probability $1 - \phi$ the probability is $\pi_H > \pi_M$. Show that for a sufficiently high value of π_M, we must have $P_{const} < P_2^{GR}$. Comment on your result.

6

Optimal Health Insurance Contracts

6.1 Introduction

In Chapter 5, several reasons were presented and discussed as to why a developed society may decide to have social health insurance with compulsory membership. This means that individuals are not completely free in deciding the amount of their insurance coverage against the cost of illness, since they are not permitted to have less than a minimum level of protection.

Such compulsion can only be justified if the insurance protection prescribed by law has certain *optimal properties* with regard to its type and extent. Specifically, it should be designed such that it would be voluntarily selected by an individual which behaves rationally but abstains from the free-rider behavior described in Subsection 5.3.2 of the previous chapter.

This consideration raises the issue of optimal design of health insurance contracts from the point of view of the person to be insured. Of course, in a free market, people would choose different contracts according to their risk characteristics, and the government can take this into account by specifying different contents of the compulsory insurance coverage for different groups of the population. Above all, the discussion will focus on the conditions under which a complete shifting of risk by means of a comprehensive insurance policy is optimal, and the conditions under which cost-sharing clauses are optimal for the insured.

In dealing with this question, the general findings of insurance theory as well as the peculiarities of the risk 'illness' must be considered, in particular the dual loss in the event of illness and the 'moral hazard' problem:

(1) *Dual loss in the event of illness.* The onset of an illness leads to two different types of loss with it. On the one hand, individuals suffer a financial loss in terms of the cost of treatment made necessary by the illness in addition to forgone earnings. On the other hand, they suffer the non-financial loss of health itself, in

P. Zweifel et al., *Health Economics*, 2nd ed., DOI 10.1007/978-3-540-68540-1_6,
© Springer-Verlag Berlin Heidelberg 2009

particular if the initial health status cannot be recovered. Illness therefore simultaneously entails an insurable and an uninsurable risk, and as we shall see, this fact has implications for the optimal protection against the insurable risk.

(2) *Dual moral hazard.* The phenomenon of 'moral hazard', well-known in insurance theory, describes the incentive of insured individuals to behave opportunistically after signing the insurance contract. The crucial point is that the insurer cannot observe the actions of the insured ('hidden action'). In the case of health risks, moral hazard occurs in two different forms:

  (a) *Ex-ante moral hazard.* As ARROW (1970, p. 142) has pointed out, moral hazard entails that 'the insurance policy might itself change incentives and therefore the probabilities upon which the insurance company has relied'. With respect to health risks, individuals can influence their probability of being ill through prevention, e.g., a general change in lifestyle.

  (b) *Ex-post moral hazard.* In the event of illness, the associated financial loss (cost of treatment) is not necessarily obvious to the insurer, who cannot observe the exact severity of the illness. Therefore insured individuals and their doctors often have the choice between cheaper and more expensive treatments.

In case (a), individuals act in a sense prior to 'nature', the realization of chance, and therefore 'ex ante'. In case (b), individuals act after nature ('ex post'). The 'hidden action' problem of the increased demand for health services is in this case a consequence of the 'hidden information' problem of the insurer, who is not able to observe the illness and its adequate therapy. This reflects the fact that the benefit of health insurance cannot simply be expressed by a fixed amount of money (e.g., the current value of a stolen object) when writing the contract. Rather, it must be circumscribed, e.g., as 'the cost of sufficient, appropriate and economical treatment.' One of the key questions addressed in this chapter will be to see under what conditions a complete shifting of the cost of treatment from individuals to the health insurer becomes optimal, rather than having the insured contribute to them (copayment, cost sharing).

This chapter is structured accordingly. First of all, an overview of possible and currently observed types of cost sharing is given in Section 6.2, complemented by a description of some other characteristics of health insurance policies. A few preliminary considerations regarding the implied incentives governing the demand for health services will also be offered. In the three following sections, the optimal design of health insurance will be investigated in various settings (see Figure 6.1). Section 6.3 deals with the case of no moral hazard, i.e., the case in which the loss distribution cannot be influenced by the insured. In Section 6.4, the occurrence of moral hazard in its two versions (a) and (b) defined above is discussed. In Section 6.5, we draw some conclusions for the design of compulsory health insurance.

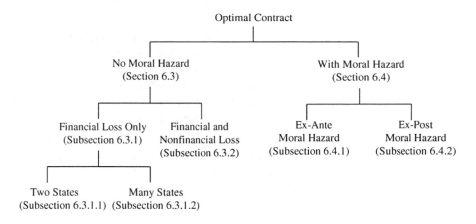

Fig. 6.1. Overview of Health Insurance Settings

In accordance with the introductory character of this text, a number of simplifying assumptions are made. The formal models are therefore all *static*, i.e., the conclusion of the insurance contract, possible prevention, and the stochastic event 'illness' all take place within the same time period. Furthermore, it is presumed that only one case of illness may occur during the period considered. Additional uncertainties, e.g., regarding the effectiveness of prevention and medical treatment, are also ignored. Nevertheless, the models provide many general and basic insights into the structure of optimal health insurance. Finally, a fundamental assumption is that health insurance does not have to take over the task of income redistribution. The insurance premium of each insured thus bears a well-defined relationship to the expected value of his or her claims.

6.2 Types of Health Insurance Contracts

The simplest type of insurance is that of *full coverage*. In this case, the insurer reimburses the full cost of medical care to the insured. Health services therefore have an effective price of zero to the insured persons, who have an incentive to extend their demand to the point where their marginal utility is zero ('satiation quantity'). Deviations from full coverage relate (1) to the type of health service provided, (2) to the person providing the service, and (3) to the extent of compensation paid by the insurer.

(1) The differentiation of insurance benefits according to *health services covered* may take the following forms:

    (a) Exclusion of entire categories of services (inpatient, outpatient, or dental care): in private health insurance, separate plans for different service categories are common. A few decades ago, many plans in the United States only covered hospital treatment, while in Switzerland dental care is not part of social health insurance. Such exclusions create incentives to substitute insured services for non-insured ones, wherever possible.

    (b) Exclusion of specific items: usually, so-called 'convenience drugs' and non-medical treatment methods are excluded from insurance coverage. Again, this creates an incentive, e.g., to replace drugs that are not reimbursed by those that have comparable therapeutic effects but are reimbursed.

(2) The insurance contract can stipulate that cost reimbursement is only granted if the service is provided *by a certain supplier* or a group of suppliers. Social health insurance in Germany pays only for medical treatment by accredited physicians. It is also possible for health insurers to employ salaried doctors for treating their members,[1] who therefore do not have the free choice of physicians. This accounts for the fact that patients often do not decide themselves about their demand for medical treatment, but rather in cooperation with the doctor. For this reason there should be incentives to behave economically for physicians as well (see Chapter 10).

(3) With respect to the extent of reimbursement, insurance policies can include limitations of (a) the quantity of services consumed, (b) the price of the service, or (c) the product of quantity and price, i.e., total expenditure:

    (a) Limitations concerning the quantity of a particular medical service per unit of time are used, e.g., in the case of psychotherapeutic treatment and eyeglasses.

    (b) Limitations of price may consist in the use of fee schedules. However, the plan may simply fix the compensation per unit of medical service, permitting service providers to 'balance-bill' (so-called indemnity plans). One instance of this is provided by the Canadian national health insurance in the province of Ontario, another by the public health insurance system in Germany, where fixed indemnities for drugs of a given therapeutic class were introduced in 1989. As the difference between the actual price and the indemnity has to be paid by the patient out-of-pocket, limitations of this type conserve consumers' incentives to search for a low-cost provider while giving providers an incentive to remain within the price limit, but if they do, there is no effect on the quantity demanded. Imposing an absolute per-unit fee (e.g., a fixed copayment per prescription) similarly leads to a nonzero effective price for

---

[1] This corresponds approximately to the Health Maintenance Organization (HMO) in the United States and Switzerland, where participating doctors get a salary and bonuses linked to the profits of the plan (see Chapter 11).

the patient. Its incentive effect, however, differs since the patient pays more the larger the quantity consumed, independently of actual price.

(c) Limitations in terms of *expenditure* present the most general case and are commonly referred to as 'cost sharing' by the insured. The following forms may be distinguished:

(i) *Proportional cost sharing.* In this case the insurer generally bears a fraction k of all treatment costs $(0 < k < 1)$. The fraction $(1 - k) = c$ ('coinsurance rate') is borne by patients. The effective price of the treatment to the insured thus equals the proportion c of the price set by the service provider. Accordingly, their interest in the cost-effectiveness of care increases with an increase in the rate of coinsurance.

(ii) *Absolute per-period deductible.* In this case, insured persons pay the first €D of their total health care cost per period (quarter or year) out of their own pocket. The effective price of health care cost therefore amounts to the supply price as long as total expenditure is relatively low (up to €D). Above this threshold, however, it drops to zero. If the insured expects to exceed this level in the course of the period anyway, then the incentive for cost-effectiveness in consumption vanishes from the beginning. Nevertheless, this form of copayment is widespread because it relieves the insurer from the processing of petty claims, as claims with total value below €D will never be submitted.

(iii) Per-period *caps* on benefits provided have exactly the opposite incentive effect, but are not very common because they limit insurance in exactly those situations where it is most needed, namely when the cost of treatment is jeopardizing economic survival. Nevertheless many insurance contracts for example in the United States have caps on the benefits provided over the whole lifespan of the insured individual. The caps lie typically between US$250,000 and 1 million.

(iv) So-called 'indemnity insurance' represents a borderline case of category (c). Here, benefits are not tied to the costs of treatment at all. Rather, they consist of a lump-sum payment in the event of illness, differentiated according to type of illness. This means that the efficiency incentives for the insured remain intact, since their marginal share in the cost of treatment amounts to 100 percent as soon as the cost exceeds the indemnity payment.

Of course, variations of these 'pure' forms of cost sharing are conceivable, for example a copayment which somehow depends on the amount of expenditure (i.e., more or less than proportional coinsurance), or mixed forms, e.g., a deductible combined with coinsurance on expenditures in excess of the deductible.

Apart from differentiations on the benefit side, incentives can also be created on the premium side. The simplest example of this is the *fixed bonus* where €x per year are paid back for not filing any claims. However, this does not need to be considered further, since in this simple model defined for a single time-period and perfectly rational behavior, the incentive effects of such a bonus do not differ from those of a fixed deductible of equal amount.[2] The premium can, however, be differentiated according to particular features relevant to health behavior, such as body weight or smoking habits, creating incentives to give up patterns of behavior damaging to health.

6.3 Optimal Insurance Protection in the Absence of Moral Hazard

In this section, we abstract from the phenomenon of moral hazard. Thus, the financial (and non-financial, if applicable) loss resulting from sickness is assumed to have the character of a pure random variable, whose distribution is not influenced by the insured, neither by lowering the probability of illness through prevention nor by limiting the cost of treatment in the event of illness. As a result of these restrictive assumptions, the conclusions to be drawn from the models dealt with here can only provide preliminary insights, which can, however, serve as a point of reference for models incorporating moral hazard effects in Section 6.4.

6.3.1 Financial Consequences of Illness Only

We first assume that medical treatment completely eliminates the non-financial consequences of illness so that the remaining loss is of exclusively financial nature. The cost of treatment M is a random variable that takes different values M_s depending on the state of nature $s \in \{0, 1, \ldots, S\}$ which is not known at the beginning of the period. For example, state $s = 0$ can denote the case of perfect health and the other states may be ordered by the cost of treatment M_s:

$$0 = M_0 < M_1 < \ldots < M_S. \tag{6.1}$$

Let Y denote gross income of the individual and y *income disposable* for consumption. In the absence of health insurance, y is itself a random variable, given by the equation

$$y_s = Y - M_s. \tag{6.2}$$

---

[2] Actual experience of insurers suggests that saving one's bonus represents a value in itself to many, causing physicians to take into account an increased resistance against excessive bills on the part of patients. Apart from this, bonus options permit the insured to move the incidence of the financial consequences of illness out of the period of incidence of the illness itself. These differences as well as the effects of dynamic (experience-rated) bonus options, which make premium rebates increase with the number of claim-free years, will not be discussed here any further. Interested readers are referred to ZWEIFEL AND WASER (1992).

An *insurance contract* is generally characterized by the *benefit schedule* $I(M)$ as a function of the loss M and the *premium P*. With health insurance, equation (6.2) for disposable income becomes

$$y_s = Y - P - M_s + I(M_s). \tag{6.3}$$

In the case considered here, where non-financial consequences of illness are absent, the utility of the individual depends only on the consumption of goods and not directly on health status. If we assume constant prices of consumption goods and utility-maximizing behavior, then the maximum achievable utility u (in the sense of the indirect utility function) can be expressed as a function of disposable income y. As usual, 'marginal utility of money' is positive but decreasing, i.e., the function u is assumed to have the properties:

$$u = u(y),\ u'(y) > 0,\ u''(y) < 0. \tag{6.4}$$

The latter property ('strict concavity') $u''(y) < 0$ implies that the individual is *risk averse*.

Finally, the individual is assumed to maximize *expected utility* $EU \equiv E[u(y)]$. The symbol E represents the expected value which results from multiplying each utility value u (associated with the value y_s by the random variable y in state s) with the accompanying probability π_s and forming the sum,

$$EU = \sum_{s=0}^{S} \pi_s u(y_s). \tag{6.5}$$

Box 6.1 gives an overview over the main equations of this section and the abbreviations used.

6.3.1.1 A Model with Two Health States

In the simplest case, there are only two states of health: with probability π $(0 \leq \pi \leq 1)$, the individual will be ill, with the cost of treatment M taking on the value L. With probability $1 - \pi$, the individual remains in good health and thus $M = 0$. Consequently, all possible insurance contracts can be characterized by two parameters only, the premium P (to be paid in any event) and insurance benefits I received in the event of sickness I $(0 \leq I \leq L)$.

The premium P depends on insurance benefits I,

$$P = P(I),\quad P'(I) > 0. \tag{6.6}$$

Using equation (6.3) for both states, defined as 'sickness' $(M = L > 0, I > 0)$ and 'health' $(M = 0, I = 0)$, expected utility EU can be expressed as a function of I,

$$\begin{aligned}
EU(I) &= EU\{y(I)\} \\
&= \pi u[Y - P(I) - L + I] + (1 - \pi)u[Y - P(I)].
\end{aligned} \tag{6.7}$$

Box 6.1. Basic Model of Optimal Health Insurance in the Absence of Moral Hazard

$$y = Y - P - M + I(M) \tag{6.3}$$

$$EU(I) = EU\{y(I)\}$$
$$= \pi u[Y - P(I) - L + I] + (1 - \pi)u[Y - P(I)] \tag{6.7}$$

$$\frac{dEU}{dI} = \pi\{1 - P'[I^o]\}u'\{Y - P[I^o] - L + I^o\}$$

$$-(1-\pi)P'[I^o]u'\{Y - P[I^o]\}
\begin{cases}
\leq 0 \text{ if } & I^o = 0 \\
= 0 \text{ if } 0 < I^o < L \\
\geq 0 \text{ if } & I^o = L
\end{cases} \tag{6.8}$$

$$P(I) = P^n(I) + C(I) = C_0 + \rho\pi + (1+\lambda)\pi I \tag{6.11}$$

y:	disposable income
Y:	gross income
M:	cost of treatment (general)
L:	cost of treatment in the state of illness
π:	probability of being ill
$u(y)$:	utility of disposable income y
EU:	expected utility
I:	insurance benefits
P:	insurance premium
P^n:	net premium, expected value of claims
$C(I)$:	benefits-related administrative expense
C_0:	fixed component of administrative expense
λ:	proportional surcharge on net premium
ρ:	loading for settlement of claims

In this simple case, the choice of optimal health insurance reduces to the choice of the value of I that maximizes expected utility EU in (6.7), which is denoted by I^o. One obtains the necessary condition for an optimum by differentiating EU and applying the Kuhn-Tucker theorem:[3]

$$\frac{dEU}{dI} = \pi\{1 - P'[I^o]\}u'\{Y - P[I^o] - L + I^o\} \tag{6.8}$$

$$-(1-\pi)P'[I^o]u'\{Y - P[I^o]\}
\begin{cases}
\leq 0 & I^o = 0 \\
= 0 & \text{if} \quad 0 < I^o < L \\
\geq 0 & I^o = L
\end{cases}$$

---

[3] See, e.g., HOY ET AL. (2001, Chapter 15).

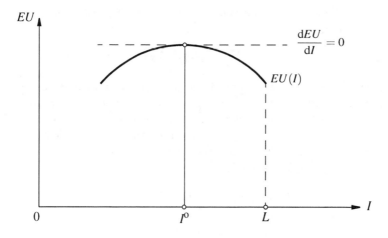

(a) Interior Optimum: $0 < I^0 < L$

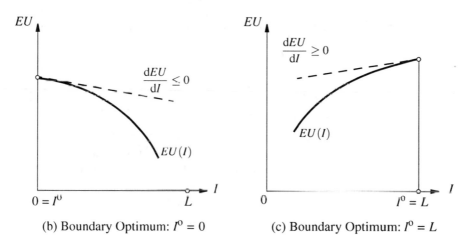

(b) Boundary Optimum: $I^0 = 0$ (c) Boundary Optimum: $I^0 = L$

Fig. 6.2. Types of Optima

Figure 6.2 illustrates how the necessary first-order condition for an interior optimum (I^0 strictly between 0 and L) differs from that characterizing an optimum at the
lower boundary ($I^0 = 0$) or at the upper boundary ($I^0 = L$) of the admissible domain
of I.

Following (6.8), the optimal value I^0 depends on the nature of the utility function
u, but also on the shape of the premium function $P(I)$. Therefore, a plausible form of
the premium function is proposed in order to gain additional insights. In the case of
a nonprofit organization typical of compulsory health insurance, the premium must

cover expected claims plus all administrative expenses. The first component, the *net premium*, covers the expected value of benefits. It is given by

$$P^n(I) = E\{I(M)\} = \pi I. \tag{6.9}$$

With reference to the second component, the *loading*, one may assume that it consists of three elements, the first (C_0) being a fixed amount ('cost of negotiating an insurance contract'), the second being proportional (with factor ρ) to the individual's probability of filing a claim ('costs of claims processing'), and the third being proportional (with factor λ) to the net premium (e.g., risk surcharge and commission). The total loading is therefore given by

$$C(I) = C_0 + \rho\pi + \lambda\pi I, \quad C_0, \rho, \lambda \geq 0. \tag{6.10}$$

Thus, the *gross premium* amounts to

$$P(I) = P^n(I) + C(I) = C_0 + \rho\pi + (1+\lambda)\pi I. \tag{6.11}$$

Note that it increases with benefits which have a strictly positive probability ($\pi > 0$) of being claimed,

$$P'(I) = (1+\lambda)\pi > 0. \tag{6.12}$$

An insurance contract is called *actuarially fair* if the premium is equal to the net premium, i.e., if there are no administrative expenses. It is called 'marginally fair' if the surcharge does not increase with the expected value of claims, i.e., if $\lambda = 0$.

In the following, we concentrate on the conditions under which *full reimbursement* of health care expenditure, i.e., $I^\circ = L$ is optimal. Substituting this value into the optimality condition (6.8) and rearranging terms in $P'(L)$ yields the following inequality:

$$\{\pi - P'[L]\}u'[Y - P[L]] \geq 0. \tag{6.13}$$

Since u' is always positive, inequality is equivalent to

$$\pi - (1+\lambda)\pi \geq 0. \tag{6.14}$$

due to (6.13). Condition (6.14) is satisfied if $\lambda \leq 0$. Therefore, according to (6.8) full coverage is optimal if there are *no* proportional expenses related to the expected value of claims, i.e., if insurance is 'marginally fair'. If, on the other hand, $\lambda > 0$, at most partial coverage can be optimal.

Strictly speaking, however, the fulfillment of the optimality condition (6.8) only states that the individual cannot increase expected utility by varying insurance coverage I by a small amount. If $\lambda = 0$, the option 'full coverage' therefore needs to be compared in terms of expected utility with the option 'no insurance', bearing in mind that expected utility is discontinuous at $I = 0$, since fixed costs are only paid if insurance is taken out. Full coverage is preferred to no coverage, if $EU[I = L] \geq EU[I = 0]$, i.e., if

$$u[Y - P[L]] = u[Y - (C_0 + \rho\pi + (1+\lambda)\pi L)] \geq \pi u[Y - L] + (1 - \pi)u[Y]. \quad (6.15)$$

From the definition of risk aversion in (6.4) it follows that the individual always prefers *actuarially fair* insurance to the alternative of no insurance.[4] Strict concavity of the utility function implies

$$u[Y - \pi L] > \pi u[Y - L] + (1 - \pi)u[Y]. \quad (6.16)$$

Thus, a comparison of (6.16) and (6.15) shows that an individual's likelihood of opting for no insurance (rather than full coverage) is greater

- the larger the fixed component C_0 of administrative expenses,
- the greater the probability of loss π (whenever $\rho > 0$).

The second result may seem somewhat surprising at first sight. But one should bear in mind that for a given expected value of claims, coverage of a small but highly probable loss is more expensive for the policyholder than coverage of a large but rather unlikely loss as soon as the insurer charges a loading for claims processing.

The Access Motive

So far, the purchase of health insurance was motivated by the assumption that the individual is risk averse. But risk aversion is not a necessary condition for the purchase of health insurance. Another possible reason is that treatment costs in the case of a particular illness exceed the individual's gross income Y but the person would die without treatment. In this case, health insurance is important because it provides 'access' to a treatment [see NYMAN (1999b)]. To see this, suppose that the cost of treatment is $L > Y$ and that the individual cannot borrow. Utility when healthy, u_h, is linear in disposable income which implies that the individual is risk neutral. Being sick and untreated leads to immediate death, which we express by a utility value u_d of minus k, where k can be a large number.[5] Hence,

$$u = \begin{cases} u_h = y & \text{when healthy (not sick or sick and treated)} \\ u_d = -k & \text{when sick and not treated.} \end{cases} \quad (6.17)$$

---

[4] Combined with the result that for the case of $C_0 = 0$ and $\lambda > 0$ only partial coverage can be optimal, this result is sometimes referred to as *Mossin's theorem* after MOSSIN (1968). These findings were also derived independently by SMITH (1968).

[5] Note that this presupposes that individuals cannot count on external help if they are sick. If this were the case, individuals may lose the incentive to buy insurance, causing them to 'free ride' on the rest of society. Making insurance compulsory can solve this problem. As we show in Section 5.3.2, even a Pareto improvement can be achieved by combining compulsory insurance with a state-independent transfer if individuals are risk averse.

Assume in addition that full insurance is available, which bears the full costs of treatment in case of illness, L, at a fair premium of $P = \pi L$. Then expected utility with insurance is

$$EU(I = L) = Y - \pi L, \tag{6.18}$$

whereas without insurance we obtain

$$EU(I = 0) = (1 - \pi)Y - \pi k = Y - \pi(Y + k), \tag{6.19}$$

so that whenever $L < Y + k$, it is always better to buy insurance even though the individual is not risk averse as with utility (6.4). The main reason for the access motive to become valid is that medical treatment is assumed to be indivisible so that there is a minimum quantity below which the individual does not benefit from it but suffers a large loss in the case of illness. This reasoning can also explain why risk-averse individuals may still buy insurance even though the loading λ is high (see Exercise 6.4).

For a model with two health states, the findings may be summarized in

Conclusion 6.1. *In the absence of moral hazard,*

- *the necessary condition for full insurance coverage requires that the contract offered be marginally fair, i.e., that the premium does not include a proportional loading on top of the net premium, otherwise less than full insurance will generally be chosen;*

- *the sufficient condition for a risk-averse individual to opt for full insurance coverage is that the insurance be 'actuarially fair' i.e., that its premium be equal to the net premium;*

- *the decision to buy no insurance rather than full coverage against the financial risk of illness is more likely to be optimal the greater the cost of insurance (the fixed fee and the loading for claims processing) and the greater the individual's probability of illness;*

- *even a risk-neutral individual will buy health insurance if some health services are indivisible and necessary for survival and their cost exceeds the individual's wealth. Examples are renal dialysis and organ transplants.*

6.3.1.2 A Model with an Arbitrary Number of Health States

We now turn to the more realistic case where many different health states exist and therefore the cost of treatment M can take on any positive value.[6] This case can be dealt with in two ways:

(a) M is a continuously distributed random variable with a known density function $f(M)$.

(b) M takes on a finite number of values M_s $(s = 0, ..., S)$, including the value zero, with fixed positive probabilities π_s.

Case (a) is a borderline case of (b) if the number of possible states S (and hence of possible values of loss) tends to infinity. But monetary units are not infinitely divisible, and even more importantly, there will always be an upper limit for the individual's health care expenditure (the country's GDP). This makes variant (b) the more realistic of the two. Moreover, variant (b) permits the use of the Lagrange method instead of the more complicated control theory without affecting results substantively.

Thus, let the risk neutral insurance company offer a policy giving the individual a choice of benefit I_s for every loss of value M_s, imposing only the restriction[7]

$$0 \leq I_s \leq M_s \quad \text{for} \quad s = 0, ..., S \tag{6.20}$$

from which we get $I_0 = M_0 = 0$. With each vector $I = (I_1, ..., I_S)$, a premium P is associated which is determined by the following function:

$$P(I) = C_0 + \sum_{s=1}^{S} \pi_s (I_s + C_I(I_s)) \tag{6.21}$$

The premium therefore consists of the expense related to signing the contract, C_0, the net premium $P^n(I) = \sum_{s=1}^{S} \pi_s I_s$ and a loading of $C_I(I_s)$ for each benefit I_s. Total loadings are therefore given by $\sum_{s=1}^{S} \pi_s C_I(I_s)$. Concerning the common loading function C_I we assume that $C_I[0] = 0$ and $C_I' \geq 0$. In the following, four cases will be treated in more detail:

(i) $C_I' = 0$: the variable loading is zero, resulting in marginally fair insurance.

(ii) $C_I' > 0, C_I'' = 0$: the variable loading is proportional to benefits and therefore proportional to the net premium.

(iii) $C_I' > 0, C_I'' > 0$: the variable loading increases more than in proportion with the insurance benefits.

(iv) $C_I' > 0, C_I'' < 0$: the variable loading increases less than in proportion with the insurance benefits.

---

[6] This case was investigated by GOULD (1969), ARROW (1974), RAVIV (1979) as well as HUBERMAN ET AL. (1983).

[7] See GOLLIER (1987) and BREUER (2006) for an analysis which allows for negative payments I_s.

Individuals are assumed to be risk averse. Their expected utility function may be formulated in analogy to equations (6.3) and (6.5),

$$EU = E[u(y)] = \sum_{s=0}^{S} \pi_s u(Y - M_s + I_s - P).\tag{6.22}$$

The Lagrangian function for expected utility maximization, involving the decision variables $I_1, ..., I_S, P$ and the Lagrange multiplier μ for the constraint (6.21) reads as follows,

$$\Phi = \sum_{s=0}^{S} \pi_s u(Y - M_s + I_s - P) + \mu\{P - C_0 - \sum_{s=1}^{S} \pi_s(I_s + C_I(I_s))\}.\tag{6.23}$$

Due to the nonnegativity condition (6.20) on I_s, the Kuhn-Tucker theorem must be applied, yielding the following necessary conditions,

$$\frac{\partial \Phi}{\partial I_s} = \pi_s u'(Y - M_s + I_s^o - P^o) - \mu^o \pi_s(1 + C_I') \begin{cases} \leq 0 & I_s^o = 0 \\ = 0 \text{ if } 0 < I_s^o < M_s \\ \geq 0 & I_s^o = M_s \end{cases} \tag{6.24}$$
$$(s = 1, ..., S)$$

$$\frac{\partial \Phi}{\partial P} = -\sum_{s=0}^{S} \pi_s u'(Y - M_s + I_s^o - P^o) + \mu^o \begin{cases} \leq 0 \text{ if } P^o = 0 \\ = 0 \text{ if } P^o > 0 \end{cases} \tag{6.25}$$

In the following we assume that it is optimal for the individual to choose at least some coverage, i.e., that $P^o > 0$. Therefore, condition (6.25) is satisfied as an equality.

In the case of full coverage ($I_s^o = M_s$), the result from the model with two health states is easily generalized: the income is then $Y - P^o$ in all states of the world. Thus the first-order conditions with $P^o > 0$ have to look as follows,

$$\frac{\partial \Phi}{\partial I_s} = \pi_s u'[Y - P^o] - \mu^o \pi_s(1 + C_I') \geq 0 \tag{6.26}$$

$$\frac{\partial \Phi}{\partial P} = -u'[Y - P^o] + \mu^o = 0. \tag{6.27}$$

Therefore,

$$u'[Y - P^o] \geq (1 + C_I')u'[Y - P^o].\tag{6.28}$$

This is only possible in case (i), i.e., if insurance is marginally fair. In cases (ii) to (iv) partial insurance must therefore be optimal.

To identify the structure of the optimal insurance contracts for the four cases mentioned above, we look at two states z and t with $M_z > M_t$. We first investigate the two cases where the marginal loading is constant ($C_I'' = 0$).

Cases (i) & (ii): Constant Marginal Loading, i.e., $C_I'' = 0$

In the case of an interior solution, it follows from the assumptions $\pi_z > 0, \pi_t > 0$ and equation (6.24):

$$u'[Y - M_z + I_z^o - P^o] = \mu^o(1 + C_I') = u'[Y - M_t + I_t^o - P^o].\tag{6.29}$$

Due to the strict concavity of the utility function ($u'' < 0$), marginal utility of income in the two states z and t can only be the same if disposable *incomes* y_z, y_t *themselves are equal* [see equation (6.2)]:

$$y_z \equiv Y - M_z + I_z^o - P^o = Y - M_t + I_t^o - P^o \equiv y_t \tag{6.30}$$

and hence

$$M_z - I_z^o = M_t - I_t^o \equiv D. \tag{6.31}$$

D is the difference between the cost of treatment and the insurance benefit; it is the same across all states with positive benefits. Because of equation (6.20), we have $D \geq 0$. The vector of optimal benefits I^o can be characterized as follows:

$$I_s^o = \begin{cases} 0 & \text{if } M_s \leq D, \\ M_s - D & \text{if } M_s > D. \end{cases} \tag{6.32}$$

Thus D may be interpreted as a *deductible*. The insurer agrees to pay all the health care expenditure in excess of the threshold D. In all cases s where expenditure M_s amounts to at least D, insurance benefits I_s^o allow the individual to attain the same disposable income y^*. Whenever $M_s < D$, benefits are zero, resulting in a value of y_s greater than y^*:

$$y_s = \begin{cases} Y - P - D \equiv y^* & \text{if } M_s \geq D, \\ Y - P - M_s > y^* & \text{if } M_s < D. \end{cases} \tag{6.33}$$

Due to such a deductible, disposable income cannot fall below y^* while utility cannot fall below $u[y^*]$. On the other hand, marginal utility has an upper limit given by $u'[y^*] = \mu^o(1 + C_I')$ [see equation (6.29)], since (6.24) and (6.31) imply

$$u'[y_s] \leq u'[y^*] = \mu^o(1 + C_I'). \tag{6.34}$$

Next we will investigate under what circumstances the *optimal deductible* is positive. We already know that a zero deductible implies that the policy must be marginally fair. The reverse is also true: all Kuhn-Tucker conditions are satisfied for $C_I' = 0$, if $I_s^o = M_s$ in all states s. In this case it follows from (6.25) that $u'[Y - P^o] = \mu^o$ and hence condition (6.24) is satisfied for all states s. This is the only solution since the objective function is strictly concave due to risk aversion and the constraints are also concave. Consequently full coverage is optimal. This in turn means that a zero deductible is optimal if and only if insurance is marginally fair.

In case (i) with $C_I' = 0$, the optimal insurance contract thus implies full coverage. By contrast, in case (ii) with $C_I' > 0, C_I'' = 0$ the optimal deductible must be positive since full coverage cannot be optimal. This can also be seen from the fact that the individual's expected utility at $D = 0$ is increasing in D. Using (6.32) we get

$$EU(D)\big|_{D=0} = \pi_0 u(Y - P(D)) + \sum_{s=1}^{S} \pi_s u(Y - D - P(D)). \tag{6.35}$$

Differentiating with respect to D yields

$$
\begin{aligned}
\left.\frac{dEU}{dD}\right|_{D=0} &= -\pi_0 u'(Y - P(D)) \left.\frac{dP}{dD}\right|_{D=0} - \sum_{s=1}^{S} \pi_s u'(Y - D - P(D)) \left(1 + \left.\frac{dP}{dD}\right|_{D=0}\right) \\
&= -\pi_0 u'(Y - P(0)) \left.\frac{dP}{dD}\right|_{D=0} - \left(1 + \left.\frac{dP}{dD}\right|_{D=0}\right) u'(Y - P(0)) \sum_{s=1}^{S} \pi_s \\
&= -u'(Y - P(0)) \left(\sum_{s=1}^{S} \pi_s + \left.\frac{dP}{dD}\right|_{D=0}\right) \quad\quad (6.36)
\end{aligned}
$$

since $\sum_{s=0}^{S} \pi_s = 1$. For the premium we obtain

$$
P(D)\big|_{D=0} = C_0 + \sum_{s=1}^{S} \pi_s(M_s - D + C_I(M_s - D))
$$

and therefore

$$
\left.\frac{dP}{dD}\right|_{D=0} = -\sum_{s=1}^{S} \pi_s - \sum_{s=1}^{S} \pi_s C_I'(M_s).
$$

Inserting into (6.36) leads to

$$
\left.\frac{dEU}{dD}\right|_{D=0} = u'(Y - P(0)) \sum_{s=1}^{S} \pi_s C_I'(M_s) \begin{cases} = 0 & \text{if } C_I' = 0, \\ > 0 & \text{if } C_I' > 0. \end{cases} \quad\quad (6.37)
$$

Therefore the optimal deductible is positive if $C_I' > 0$.

We summarize our results for the case $C_I'' = 0$ in

Conclusion 6.2. *With constant marginal loading, the optimal insurance contract is characterized by a deductible and full coverage of expenditures in excess of the deductible. The optimal deductible is positive if and only if the marginal loading itself is positive.*

Figures 6.3 (i) and (ii) show the optimal benefit function for both cases.

Case (iii) – Positive and Increasing Marginal Loading, i.e., $C_I' > 0, C_I'' > 0$

From condition (6.24), we have for an interior solution

$$
\frac{u'[Y - M_z + I_z^o - P^o]}{u'[Y - M_t + I_t^o - P^o]} = \frac{1 + C_I'(I_z^o)}{1 + C_I'(I_t^o)}. \quad\quad (6.38)
$$

If $M_z > M_t$ the solution $I_t^o = I_z^o$ is obviously not possible because the utility function is strictly concave. Neither can $I_t^o > I_z^o$ be optimal. In this case, income in the state t would be higher than in state z. Because of the strict concavity of the utility function, the left-hand side of the equation would be greater than one, while the right-hand

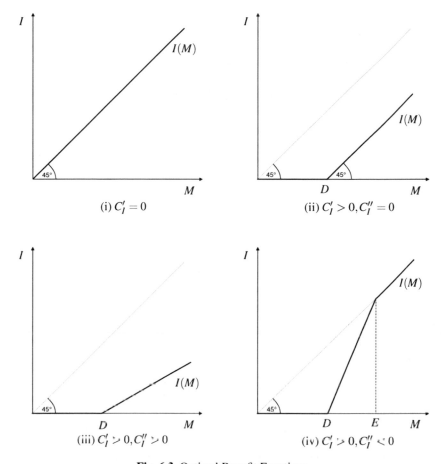

Fig. 6.3. Optimal Benefit Functions

side would be smaller than one because of the convexity of the cost function. Consequently, $I_z^o > I_t^o$. Finally we consider

$$I_z^o - M_z \geq I_t^o - M_t.$$

In this case, the left-hand side of (6.38) would be at most one. Because of $I_z^o > I_t^o$, however, the right-hand side would be greater than one. Consequently, this solution to (6.38) can be excluded, and the relevant interior solution must be characterized by $I_z^o - M_z < I_t^o - M_t$ or

$$I_z^o - I_t^o = \Delta I^o < \Delta M = M_z - M_t.$$

Differences in health care expenditure translate in smaller differences of optimal benefits. Thus, with increasing marginal loading the optimal insurance contract features a positive *marginal copayment*, which means that in states with higher treatment costs, copayment is also higher.

It follows from the assumptions $C_I[0] = 0, C'_I > 0$ and $C''_I > 0$ that the contract cannot be marginally fair. This in turn excludes full coverage as the optimal solution. From condition (6.37), we know that a deductible is optimal if $C'_I > 0$. Thus, the optimal insurance contract includes a positive deductible D and partial coverage beyond this value [see Figure 6.3 (iii)]. This can be explained as follows. On the one hand, a positive marginal loading implies that it is worthwhile to insure medical expenditures only if they exceed a certain level. If they are below that level, the loading exceeds possible advantages in terms of relief from risk. On the other hand, a loading that increases progressively makes full coverage beyond the deductible too costly and calls for partial coverage only. Full coverage at the margin cannot be optimal because the cost of insurance increases more than proportionally, outweighing the advantage of protection against risk.[8]

Case (iv): Positive but Decreasing Marginal Loading, i.e., $C'_I > 0, C''_I < 0$

In this case, an interior solution characterized by

$$\Delta I^o > \Delta M$$

can be derived from condition (6.38).[9] This calls for *marginal overinsurance*: a one-Euro increase in health care expenditure is associated with an increase of the insurance benefit by more than one Euro. Condition (6.37) states that a deductible is optimal if $C'_I > 0$. Assuming for simplicity that $\Delta I^o = \gamma \Delta M$ with $\gamma > 1$ holds for an interior solution [see HUBERMAN ET AL. (1983, p. 423)], the optimal benefit function for case (iv) takes the following form [see Figure 6.3 (iv)]:

$$I_s = \begin{cases} 0 & \text{if} \quad M_s \leq D \\ \gamma(M_s - D) & \text{if} \quad D < M_s \leq E \\ M_s & \text{if} \quad M_s > E. \end{cases} \tag{6.39}$$

with $E \equiv \gamma D/(\gamma - 1)$. Therefore, benefits increase more than proportionally until they are equal to medical expenditure. For still higher expenditures, there is full coverage at the margin. This is referred to as the *disappearing deductible*, since the deductible becomes irrelevant for high expenditures. This can be motivated in the following way: insurance is not worthwhile for low expenditures because of the positive loading $C_I(I_S)$; high expenditures, however, can be insured at low cost because of a loading that rises less than proportionally. As to the problems engendered by this type of contract, the major one may be that the insured (and with them, health care providers if paid fee-for-service) face an incentive to artificially increase cost of treatment, e.g., by opting for the newest medical technology (moral hazard of the ex-post

---

[8] RAVIV (1979) shows that this result can also occur when the insurer is risk averse. The intuition behind this result is that it is optimal to marginally share the risk if both partners to the contract are risk averse.

[9] In addition, it needs to be checked here whether the second-order conditions of the optimization problem (6.23) are satisfied. This is not guaranteed if $C''_I < 0$.

Table 6.1. Optimal Insurance Type in the Presence of a Variable Loading

		deductible		marginal insurance coverage		
		$D=0$	$D>0$	partial	full	>1
(i)	$C_I' = 0$	×			×	
(ii)	$C_I' > 0, C_I'' = 0$		×		×	
(iii)	$C_I' > 0, C_I'' > 0$		×	×		
(iv)	$C_I' > 0, C_I'' < 0$		×		×	×

variety, see Section 6.4.2).[10] This incentive could be neutralized by imposing the additional restriction $\Delta I \leq \Delta M$. However, this reduces to case (ii) with constant marginal loading, making full coverage at the margin optimal. In addition, the deductible would be positive according to condition (6.37).

Conclusion 6.3. *A positive deductible is always optimal in the presence of a positive marginal loading. If marginal loading is increasing, the deductible is to be followed by partial coverage, i.e., a positive rate of coinsurance. With decreasing marginal loading, however, benefits beyond the deductible increase more than proportionally with expenditures until they equal expenditures. This insurance contract, however, creates the incentive to raise expenditures artificially.*

Table 6.1 summarizes the results for the four cases.

6.3.2 Direct Utility Effects of Illness

In the following, we drop the assumption that the occurrence of illness has no effects on the individual apart from the costs of treatment. Rather, utility is supposed to be state dependent with the health status H appearing directly as an argument in the utility function in addition to disposable income y:

$$u = u(y, H). \tag{6.40}$$

To simplify, we limit ourselves to the case in which the health status can take on only two values, $H = b$ ('bad health') and $H = g$ ('good health'). Furthermore, $u(y, b)$ and $u(y, g)$ are replaced by $u_b(y)$ and $u_g(y)$. In this way, the utility function continues to have only y as its argument. In return, its slope now depends upon the realization of the binary variable H.[11]

When the probability of illness is again represented by π, expected utility is given by

$$EU = E[u(y)] = \pi u_b(y) + (1 - \pi)u_g(y). \tag{6.41}$$

---

[10] Strictly speaking, this possibility is assumed away in this section which is entitled "Optimal Insurance Protection *in the Absence of Moral Hazard*".

[11] This model was first investigated by COOK AND GRAHAM (1977).

Let Y be gross income and L the cost of treatment in state b. Furthermore, let I be the insurance benefit and $P(I)$ the associated premium. In contrast to the former model, we now allow for the possibility that I exceeds the cost of treatment because illness also entails a non-financial loss. Thus, payment in excess of L may be interpreted as damages, i.e., compensation for suffering.

The individual's problem is to find the value of I that maximizes expected utility

$$EU(I) = \pi u_b[Y - P(I) - L + I] + (1 - \pi)u_g[Y - P(I)]. \qquad (6.42)$$

The necessary condition for a maximum reads

$$\frac{dEU}{dI} = \pi\{1 - P'(I^\circ)\}u_b'[Y - P(I^\circ) - L + I^\circ] - (1 - \pi)P'(I^\circ)u_g'[Y - P(I^\circ)]$$

$$\begin{cases} \leq 0 \text{ if } I^\circ = 0 \\ = 0 \text{ if } I^\circ > 0. \end{cases} \qquad (6.43)$$

Focusing on the case of an interior solution, this condition can be simplified by writing the arguments of u_b' and u_g' as disposable incomes y_b° and y_g°, respectively,

$$\pi u_b'[y_b^\circ] = P'(I)\{\pi u_b'[y_b^\circ] + (1 - \pi)u_g'[y_g^\circ]\} \qquad (6.44)$$
$$= P'(I)E[u'(y)].$$

The left-hand side of (6.44) shows the expected utility gain from increasing benefits I by a (marginal) monetary unit, while the right-hand side shows the expected utility loss due to the increase in premium. The two effects must balance in an interior optimum. If the premium function is a simplified version of equation (6.11),

$$P(I) = C_0 + (1 + \lambda)\pi I, \quad (C_0, \lambda \geq 0) \qquad (6.45)$$

then

$$P'(I) = (1 + \lambda)\pi > 0. \qquad (6.46)$$

Given these specifications, condition (6.44) reduces to

$$u_b'[y_b^\circ] = (1 + \lambda)\{\pi u_b'[y_b^\circ] + (1 - \pi)u_g'[y_g^\circ]\}. \qquad (6.47)$$

This can be rewritten as

$$u_b'[y_b^\circ]\{1 - \pi(1 + \lambda)\} = (1 - \pi)(1 + \lambda)u_g'[y_g^\circ]. \qquad (6.48)$$

From this condition, the following conclusions can be drawn for the optimal health insurance contract in the case where the utility function depends on health status.

(1) If insurance is *marginally fair*, i.e., $\lambda = 0$, then (6.48) becomes

$$u_b'[y_b^\circ] = u_g'[y_g^\circ]. \qquad (6.49)$$

Thus, benefits will be chosen such that the marginal utility of income is *equal* in both health states. In contrast to the model of Subsection 6.3.1.1, however, this does *not* mean that disposable incomes are equalized (by setting $I = L$), since u_b' and u_g' derive from different utility functions. Thus we can make the following distinction:

(a) If illness implies that an individual is *less able to enjoy* consumption,[12] i.e., if $u_b'[y] < u_g'[y]$ holds at a given disposable income y, then (6.49) is satisfied if $y_b^o < y_g^o$ because of the concavity of u_b and u_g. This calls for $I^o < L$, implying optimality of *partial insurance coverage*, i.e., *cost sharing*. For example, one may think of an enthusiastic golf player who is prepared to spend a lot of money on his hobby as long as he is in good health. If unable to play because of illness, he has no way in which money could yield him comparable utility; therefore he is not interested in completely equalizing his disposable income across states of health.

(b) On the other hand, it is conceivable that, in the case of sickness, marginal utility of income even *increases*, i.e., that $u_b'[y] > u_g'[y]$. Then (6.49) requires $y_b^o > y_g^o$ and thus $I^o > L$: being *overinsured* and *contracting for damages* (i.e., compensation of non-financial loss) is optimal for such an individual. An economic reason for this case would be that in the event of illness, an additional need arises for certain consumer goods that are not medical services in a strict sense, such as an apartment that is suitable for handicapped persons. This case may actually be the more common one of the two.

(2) If the policy is *not marginally fair*, i.e., if $\lambda > 0$, then (6.48) is only satisfied for $u_b'[y_b] > u_g'[y_g]$. Marginal utility of income must be greater in the sick state than in the healthy state. This in turn means that because of the strict concavity of the utility functions ($u_b'', u_g'' < 0$), *less* coverage I^o is demanded than in the case of marginally fair insurance. In combination with the above-mentioned case (a), $I^o < L$ holds a fortiori. In case (b), however, this may imply full coverage.

(3) The preceding points relate to the necessary condition for an *interior* optimum. This condition is also sufficient if the insurance premium does not contain a fixed component of administrative expense. If $C_0 > 0$, however, the solution resulting from (6.48) and calling for I^o has to be compared with the decision to have no insurance at all ($I = 0$). Having no insurance at all is preferred if

$$\pi u_b[Y - L] + (1 - \pi)u_g[Y] > \pi u_b[Y - L + (1 - (1 + \lambda)\pi)I^o - C_0] \quad (6.50)$$
$$+ (1 - \pi)u_g[Y - (1 + \lambda)\pi I^o - C_0].$$

This condition is more likely to be satisfied the lower the cost of treatment L and the greater the fixed component of administrative expense C_0.

Conclusion 6.4. *If an illness gives rise to an immaterial loss in addition to the financial loss due to the cost of treatment, then marginal utility of income is equalized across health states, provided the premium is 'marginally fair'. Still, the optimal amount of insurance coverage may exceed or fall short of the cost of treatment.*

---

[12] See VISCUSI AND EVANS (1990) for evidence for this hypothesis.

6.3.3 Summary

Even ignoring the possible incentive effects due to the existence of an insurance contract ('moral hazard'), there are two separate reasons for the optimal health insurance policy not to simply cover the cost of treatment, namely (a) the existence of *loading*, and (b) the fact that illness entails a *non-financial loss* in addition to the financial loss.

The loading may be constant or depend on the expected value of benefits paid. A fixed component may cause the individual not to take out any insurance, but it does not influence the extent of coverage if insurance is purchased. Given a positive marginal loading, it is generally optimal – in the absence of immaterial losses due to illness – to choose a *deductible*, resulting in a smaller disposable income in the state of sickness than in good health. If the marginal loading is constant, insurance providing full coverage beyond the deductible is warranted. With an increasing marginal loading, however, it is optimal that insured persons bear part of their health care expenditure in excess of the deductible.

Conversely, if illness entails immaterial as well as financial loss, i.e., if it changes the marginal utility of other consumption, then even if insurance free of transaction costs is available, the optimal policy may provide coverage falling short of or exceeding the cost of treatment.

6.4 Optimal Insurance Coverage with Moral Hazard

6.4.1 Ex-Ante Moral Hazard

The analysis of Section 6.3 rested on the assumption that the cost of treatment is a random variable with a distribution that cannot be influenced by the individual. However, individuals can usually influence the probability of illness and its course through their lifestyle. This fact is taken into account in the model to be discussed below, focusing on the ex-ante version of moral hazard. Through prevention, the individual is assumed to be able to influence the *probability distribution* of health care expenditure. But once the event 'illness' has occurred, the cost of treatment is exogenously fixed. The problem of moral hazard in its ex-ante version is that prevention cannot be observed and thus cannot be rewarded by the insurer.

6.4.1.1 Assumptions

We presuppose that the prevention of illness costs money but has no other direct impact on the individual's utility. Thus, health-enhancing activities such as physical exercise, which for some may be a pleasure and for others a pain, is excluded. The same holds true for other non-financial sacrifices such as the abstinence from alcohol, tobacco and 'decadent' (i.e., delicious but unhealthy) food. In addition, expenditures on prevention are assumed to reduce the income of the insured to their full extent as they are not reimbursable under the insurance contract. For one, this is justified by the fact that such expenditures are decided upon by the individual rather than being a random variable and hence do not constitute an 'insurable risk'. On the other hand, prevention costs are often incurred for goods other than pure health care services, such as expensive health foods or vacations in a healthy climate. Health insurers typically do not reimburse this type of expenditure.

To make the analysis as simple as possible, we take the model in Subsection 6.3.1.1 with only two health states ('sick' and 'healthy') as point of departure. In this model, the prevention of illness may affect

(a) the *probability of illness* with cost of treatment L constant in the event of illness,

(b) the value of health care expenditure L given a certain probability of illness π.

Type (b) is somewhat less plausible in the case of illness.[13] In the following, we will therefore deal with case (a), making the probability of ill health π a function of preventive effort V with the following properties:

$$\pi = \pi(V) = \begin{cases} \pi_0 & \text{if } V = V_0 = 0 \\ \pi_1 & \text{if } V = V_1 > 0 \end{cases} \quad \text{with} \quad \pi_0 > \pi_1 > 0. \tag{6.51}$$

The individual can thus choose between two levels of prevention.[14] In the case of no prevention, $V = V_0 = 0$ and the probability of illness is $\pi_0 = \pi[V_0]$. On the other hand, the individual can choose to spend $V_1 > 0$ on prevention. This will lower the probability of illness to $\pi_1 = \pi[V_1] < \pi_0$.

An important feature distinguishing the different models is whether or not the insurer can *observe* the preventive effort of the insured, which would allow to *reward* them in setting the premium. Prior to making this distinction, however, we determine the optimal level of prevention in the absence of health insurance (Subsection 6.4.1.2). This analysis will provide a benchmark for establishing the relationship between prevention and insurance coverage. Box 6.2 provides an overview of the model and the main equations of this section.

---

[13] The intensity of medical treatment is largely decided by the physician. In other areas, the insured may have more influence on the size of the loss once it occurs. The purchase of a fire extinguisher is a case in point: the probability that a fire breaks out is in no way influenced by the purchase, but certainly the possible damage given that a fire breaks out.

[14] The case of a continuous level of prevention is analyzed, e.g., by WINTER (2000).

6.4.1.2 Optimal Prevention without Insurance

Expenditure on prevention diminishes the individual's disposable income in all states of nature because by definition it has to be made prior to the occurrence of the probabilistic event 'sickness'. Referring to equations (6.5) and (6.51), expected utility in the absence of health insurance is given by

$$EU_j = E[u(y(V_j))] \tag{6.52}$$
$$= \pi_j u[Y - V_j - L] + (1 - \pi_j)u[Y - V_j], \quad j = 0, 1.$$

Therefore, when insurance is not available, the condition for a positive amount of prevention is $\Delta EU \equiv EU_1 - EU_0 > 0$, or

$$\pi_1 u[Y - V_1 - L] + (1 - \pi_1)u[Y - V_1] - \left(\pi_0 u[Y - L] + (1 - \pi_0)u[Y]\right) > 0.$$

Using $\Delta\pi \equiv \pi_1 - \pi_0$ leads to

$$\Delta EU = \pi_0 \left(u[Y - V_1 - L] - u[Y - L] \right) + \Delta\pi u[Y - V_1 - L]$$
$$+ (1 - \pi_0) \left(u[Y - V_1] - u[Y] \right) - \Delta\pi u[Y - V_1].$$

For marginal changes $d\pi \equiv \pi_1 - \pi_0$ and $dV \equiv V_1 - V_0$ we get

$$dEU = -\pi_0 u'[Y - L]dV + u[Y - V_1 - L]d\pi - (1 - \pi_0)u'[Y]dV - u[Y - V_1]d\pi,$$

since

$$u[Y - V_1] - u[Y] = -u'[Y]dV \quad \text{and} \quad u[Y - V_1 - L] - u[Y - L] = -u'[Y - L]dV.$$

Considering that $\pi_0 u'[Y - L] + (1 - \pi_0)u'[Y]$ is the expected value of marginal utility, $EU'(y)$, the condition $dEU/dV > 0 \; \forall V$ simplifies to

$$\left(u[Y - V_1] - u[Y - V_1 - L] \right) \left| \frac{d\pi}{dV} \right| > \pi_0 u'[Y - L] + (1 - \pi_0)u'[Y] \equiv EU'(y). \tag{6.53}$$

The left-hand side of (6.53) measures the increase in expected utility due to a reduction in the probability of illness π brought about by an increase of V by a (marginal) Euro. The right-hand side shows the loss of expected utility as a result of the associated reduction of disposable income in both states. To calculate this loss of expected utility, marginal utility of income must be identified for each health status and then added after weighing them with the associated probabilities π_0 and $(1 - \pi_0)$, respectively. Consequently, prevention is more worthwhile,

- the larger $|d\pi/dV|$, i.e., the more effective prevention is in lowering the probability of illness;
- the larger the utility loss through illness $u[Y - V_1] - u[Y - V_1 - L]$;
- the smaller the expected loss in utility $EU'(y)$ caused by the reduction of disposable income in both states.

Box 6.2. A Model of Optimal Prevention and Optimal Insurance Coverage

---

Prevention and probability of illness:

$$\pi = \pi(V) = \begin{cases} \pi_0 & \text{if } V = V_0 = 0 \\ \pi_1 & \text{if } V = V_1 > 0 \end{cases} \quad \text{with} \quad \pi_0 > \pi_1 > 0. \tag{6.51}$$

Condition for prevention without the possibility of insurance:

$$\left(u[Y - V_1] - u[Y - V_1 - L] \right) \left| \frac{d\pi}{dV} \right| > EU'(y). \tag{6.53}$$

Condition for prevention with fair insurance and observable prevention:

$$Y - \pi_1 L - V_1 > Y - \pi_0 L \quad \Leftrightarrow \quad V_1 < (\pi_0 - \pi_1)L. \tag{6.57}$$

Conditions for prevention with fair insurance and unobservable prevention:

$$\begin{aligned} EU(V_1, I, P = \pi_1 I) &= (1 - \pi_1)u[Y - \pi_1 I - V_1] + \pi_1 u[Y + (1 - \pi_1)I - V_1 - L] \\ &\geq \underbrace{(1 - \pi_0)u[Y - \pi_1 I] + \pi_0 u[Y + (1 - \pi_1)I - L]}_{= EU(V_0, I, P = \pi_1 I)} \end{aligned} \tag{6.61}$$

$$\begin{aligned} EU(V_1, \tilde{I}, P = \pi_1 \tilde{I}) &= (1 - \pi_1)u[Y - \pi_1 \tilde{I} - V_1] + \pi_1 u[Y + (1 - \pi_1)\tilde{I} - L - V_1] \\ &> u[Y - \pi_0 L] = EU(V_0, L, P = \pi_0 L). \end{aligned} \tag{6.62}$$

Y:	gross income
y:	disposable income
L:	loss of income in the 'sick' state
V_j:	expenditures on prevention, $j = 0, 1$
π_j:	probability of 'sick' state, $j = 0, 1$
$u(y)$:	utility of the individual
EU:	expected utility
I:	insurance benefit
P:	insurance premium
$\tilde{I}$:	maximum value of I that satisfies (6.61)

6.4.1.3 The Optimum with Observable Prevention

Let the individual be in a position to take out an insurance policy that guarantees a benefit I $(0 \leq I \leq L)$ in the event of illness, with free choice of the value of I. Furthermore, let the insurance company be able to *observe* expenditure on prevention V and to adjust its premium accordingly. For simplicity, we assume that the premium is actuarially fair, i.e.,

$$P(V, I) = \pi(V)I. \tag{6.54}$$

Let the individual maximize expected utility by a suitable choice of the decision variables V (prevention) and I (insurance),

$$EU(V,I) = \pi(V)u[Y - P(V,I) - V - L + I] \tag{6.55}$$
$$+ (1 - \pi(V))u[Y - P(V,I) - V].$$

The optimality condition for a given level of prevention using (6.54) is

$$\frac{\partial EU(V,I)}{\partial I} = \pi(V)u'[Y - \pi(V)I^\circ - V - L + I^\circ](1 - \pi(V))$$
$$+ (1 - \pi(V))u'[Y - \pi(V)I^\circ - V](-\pi(V)) = 0.$$

Hence, we obtain

$$u'[Y - \pi(V)I^\circ - V - L + I] = u'[Y - \pi(V)I^\circ - V] \quad \Leftrightarrow \quad I^\circ = L, \tag{6.56}$$

i.e., full coverage is optimal in the case of actuarially fair insurance, as in Section 6.3.1.

By assumption, the insurer can observe the behavior of the insured and therefore adjust the premium accordingly. For the insured, it is thus optimal to choose V_1 rather than $V_0 = 0$ if and only if

$$u[Y - \pi_1 L - V_1] > u[Y - \pi_0 L]$$

or if

$$Y - \pi_1 L - V_1 > Y - \pi_0 L \quad \Leftrightarrow \quad V_1 < (\pi_0 - \pi_1)L. \tag{6.57}$$

This condition states that prevention is optimal if and only if it increases expected income. It is equivalent to the condition that expenditure on prevention is smaller than the reduction in expected health care expenditure.

Conclusion 6.5. *If the insurer is able to observe the extent of prevention and given fair premiums, the insured optimally engages in prevention if and only if prevention increases expected income. Full coverage continues to be optimal; it keeps net income constant across health states.*

6.4.1.4 The Optimum with Unobservable Prevention

We now investigate the more realistic case in which the insurer *cannot* observe whether the individual invests in prevention. Therefore, the insurance premium P does not depend on the level of prevention V but only on the amount of benefit I contracted,

$$P = P(I). \tag{6.58}$$

Does that mean that the insured has no incentive whatsoever to spend on prevention? Or is there still an opportunity to indirectly influence the choice of V by setting the premium function (6.58) in an appropriate way?

Indeed, prevention can be indirectly rewarded by noting that the more generous the insurance coverage, the smaller is the incentive for the insured to invest in prevention. Thus, an increase in coverage makes it more likely that the probability of illness is π_0, implying a higher price of fair insurance *per unit* of reimbursement I. The insurer, who is aware of this relationship, can respond by offering full coverage at a disproportionally higher premium than a contract with copayment. This may cause the individual to choose less than full coverage, which in turn preserves the interest in prevention at least to some degree. Alternatively, the insured could totally forgo prevention and pay a correspondingly higher premium.

In the following, we assume that $V_1 < (\pi_0 - \pi_1)L$, i.e., prevention is worthwhile in principle. In the case of fair insurance, the relation between insurance coverage and premium is given by (observe the impact of prevention on π)

$$P(I) = \pi(V(I))I. \tag{6.59}$$

Here, $V(I)$ is the chosen level of prevention, which depends on I. How large can the insurance benefit I be so that the insured still has an incentive to opt for V_1, even though prevention is not observable? It is intuitively clear that I has to be smaller than health care expenditure in the state of illness L. For with $I = L$, the insured would never invest in prevention, since independently of the premium P it holds true that

$$EU_0[I = L] = u[Y - P - V_0] > u[Y - P - V_1] = EU_1[I = L]. \tag{6.60}$$

Clearly, expected utility given V_1 has to be at least as high as expected utility given V_0 for a given value of I. Using equation (6.59), this condition can be written as

$$EU[V_1, I, P = \pi_1 I] = (1 - \pi_1)u[Y - \pi_1 I - V_1] + \pi_1 u[Y + (1 - \pi_1)I - V_1 - L]$$
$$\geq \underbrace{(1 - \pi_0)u[Y - \pi_1 I] + \pi_0 u[Y + (1 - \pi_1)I - L]}_{= EU[V_0, I, P = \pi_1 I]}. \tag{6.61}$$

It is easy to show that expected utility of the insured increases ceteris paribus with the insurance benefit I as long as $I < L$. Subject to the condition that the insured does invest in prevention, expected utility is thus at a maximum if I has the largest possible value that still satisfies condition (6.61). This value $\tilde{I}$ is the highest insurance benefit that is compatible with the insured voluntarily opting for prevention.

Finally, it has to be checked whether maximum expected utility given that the insured chooses V_1 is higher than expected utility with full coverage and no prevention. If

$$EU[V_1, \tilde{I}, P = \pi_1 \tilde{I}] = (1 - \pi_1)u[Y - \pi_1 \tilde{I} - V_1] + \pi_1 u[Y + (1 - \pi_1)\tilde{I} - L - V_1]$$
$$> u[Y - \pi_0 L] = EU[V_0, L, P = \pi_0 L], \tag{6.62}$$

then it is optimal for the insured to purchase partial coverage $\tilde{I} < L$ in the case where prevention is unobservable.

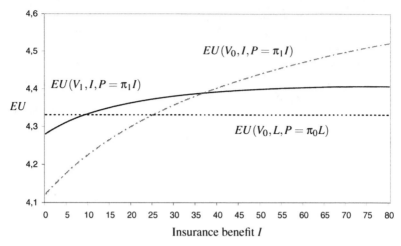

Fig. 6.4. Ex-Ante Moral Hazard: $V_1 = 10$

If condition (6.62) is not satisfied, however, a contract with full coverage – which provides no incentives for prevention – yields higher expected utility. From condition (6.62), it can be seen which factors matter. For a given value of $\tilde{I}$, the solution with prevention is more likely to be preferred the smaller π_1 and V_1, i.e., the more effectively prevention lowers the risk of illness. But in both cases the insured is still worse off than if prevention were observable [see condition 6.57]; therefore, we are dealing with a second-best optimum.

To illustrate the limited compatibility of prevention and insurance, consider the following example. Let the utility function be given by $u(y) = \ln(y)$. Without prevention, the probability of illness is $\pi_0 = 0.3$, with prevention $\pi_1 = 0.1$. The income of the individual is $Y = 100$. The cost of treatment in the event of illness is $L = 80$. Prevention costs $V_1 = 10$. Thus, prevention is efficient in principle, since $V_1 = 10 < (0.3 - 0.1) \times 80 = 16$.

Figure 6.4 shows $EU(V_0, I, P = \pi_1 I)$ and $EU(V_1, I, P = \pi_1 I)$ as functions of benefits I [see condition (6.61)]. Their intersection at $\tilde{I} = 37$ determines the maximum value of the insurance benefit that still induces the insured to voluntarily engage in prevention. The horizontal line shows the value of $EU[V_0, L, P = \pi_0 L]$, i.e., expected utility with full coverage and no prevention. Since $EU[V_1, \tilde{I}, P = \pi_1 \tilde{I}] > EU[V_0, L, P = \pi_0 L]$, the insurance contract with the benefit $\tilde{I} = 37$ and the premium $P = \pi_1 \tilde{I} = 3.7$ is the preferred one. It is associated with positive expenditure on prevention ($V_1 = 10$).

A different result prevails if the reduction of π by 20 percentage points can only be attained at a higher price of prevention, viz. $V_1 = 15$. With observable prevention it would still be efficient to invest in prevention, since $V_1 = 15 < 16$. If prevention is not observable, however, a policy with full coverage and no incentives for prevention is the preferred one. In Figure 6.5, the functions $EU(V_0, I, P = \pi_1 I)$ and

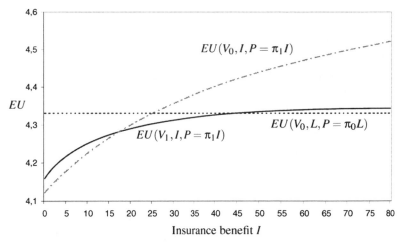

Fig. 6.5. Ex-Ante Moral Hazard: $V_1 = 15$

$EU(V_1, I, P = \pi_1 I)$ intersect already at $\tilde{I} = 17$. Expected utility $EU(V_1, I, P = \pi_1 I)$ is lower than in the first example because of the higher cost of prevention. Since $EU[V_1, \tilde{I}, P = \pi_1 \tilde{I}] < EU[V_0, L, P = \pi_0 L]$, it is optimal to forgo prevention. The individual thus prefers an insurance contract with full coverage and the premium $P = 0.3 \times 80 = 24$.

Conclusion 6.6. *If the insurer is not able to observe the extent of prevention, then it may be optimal to create incentives for prevention by means of a copayment. This is a 'second best' solution because the insured's expected utility is smaller ceteris paribus than in the case of observable prevention.*

Note that the insured does not have to be obliged to purchase the contract with partial coverage if prevention is sufficiently effective. Indeed, this type of policy is in insured's self-interest. Signing it is in fact a self-commitment in favor of prevention.

However, an enforcement problem connected with the second-best contract was identified already by PAULY (1974). If the insured is able to increase insurance coverage by combining several insurance policies, then the incentive effect of partial coverage is lost. For example, with $\tilde{I} = L/2$, the purchase of two contracts would add up to full coverage at the total premium $\pi_1 L$. The insured would then refrain from prevention, causing both insurance companies to incur losses. Anticipating this behavior, companies will not offer the insurance contract with benefit $\tilde{I}$ and premium $\pi_1 \tilde{I}$. Rather they will write policies based on the assumption that the insured will fail to exert preventive effort, charging a premium π_0 per unit of insurance benefit. The insured will indeed choose full coverage in this case. If condition (6.62) is satisfied, i.e., if positive expenditure on prevention is optimal in the 'second-best solution', the insured will be even worse off in the 'third-best solution' in which it cannot be proven that one does not hold additional insurance policies.

The argument can be summarized in

Conclusion 6.7. *If the insured can purchase coverage from several sources, then the second-best solution described in Conclusion 6.6 may not be reached. Given fair premiums, the insured will choose full coverage and zero prevention. Expected utility in this 'third-best solution' is even lower than in the second-best solution.*

One has to bear in mind that this 'third-best solution' is only relevant if there are several insurance companies offering health insurance. In the case of a monopolistic supplier, e.g., a national health service, this problem does not arise. For the case of several competing insurers, it can be solved by *mandatory registration* of health insurance policies. This permits insurers to set premiums according to total coverage contracted, which determines the extent of ex-ante moral hazard. Moreover, insurers can prevent fraudulent multiple claiming for a single loss by making reimbursement conditional on the submission of the original bill. This requirement is regularly imposed by private health insurers, e.g., in Germany and Switzerland.

6.4.1.5 Implications

We showed that less than full insurance coverage can also be motivated by the fact that the insured wishes to create incentives to himself to invest in prevention. But these incentives remain intact only if the insured can be prevented from secretly buying several insurance policies. Full insurance coverage and unfettered incentives for prevention are only compatible in the (unrealistic) case that the insurer can observe preventive effort, which permits to reward it through making the premium depend on effort. This would not even benefit insurers in the long run (recall the zero-expected-profit condition in competitive equilibrium), but it does benefit consumers, who achieve a higher level of welfare on average.

6.4.1.6 Empirical Evidence on Ex-Ante Moral Hazard

In other insurance contexts, e.g., automobile insurance, there is evidence that more generous coverage reduces the intensity of prevention and thus increases the frequency of accidents. In health insurance, such an effect appears less plausible due to the undesirability of the adverse health consequences per se. Moreover, it is difficult to study these effects because for most people health insurance coverage is not exogenous but self-selected.

However, a recent study by DAVE AND KAESTNER (2006) examines the behavior of a population group with an exogenous change in health insurance coverage, viz. previously uninsured Americans who turn 65 and thus become eligible to Medicare coverage. From the theory of ex-ante moral hazard, the authors infer that this change in coverage should have two different effects on the health-related behavior of members of the respective group (compared to previously insured persons):

- a pure moral hazard effect (less prevention) due to better coverage,
- more prevention due to more physician contacts and thus more physician advice on prevention because the price of these contacts has fallen.

To test their predictions, the authors first analyze a panel of individuals over the age bracket 60–69 and secondly a cross-section of persons in the same age bracket. Health behavior is measured by weight (body mass index, BMI), the frequency of vigorous exercise, smoking and alcohol use.

In line with the hypothesized price effect, the authors find that Medicare coverage increased the number of doctor visits of previously uninsured and low-educated men (women) by 35 (41) percent, and both effects were significant. The health behavior that reacted most strongly to the expansion of health insurance coverage was the probability of engaging in vigorous physical activity, which fell by 7.9 percentage points (or 21 percent of its previous level) for men and 3.6 percentage points (or 13 percent) for women. When the number of doctor visits was held constant, exercise decreased even by 13.1 percentage points (or 34 percent) for men and 13.7 percentage points (or 48 percent) for women. Similar but somewhat smaller and often insignificant effects were found for smoking and drinking. The authors conclude that both effects postulated above are in fact present.

6.4.2 Ex-Post Moral Hazard

This section is devoted to moral hazard in its ex-post variant. The individual is assumed to have a choice among different treatment options once an illness has occurred. The insurer is not able to observe how ill the individual is and can therefore not judge which treatment is adequate. Again, we study the optimal health insurance coverage. To focus on ex-post moral hazard, we abstract from the possibility of lowering the probability of illness.[15]

6.4.2.1 Assumptions

Consider a one-period situation with only two goods: a homogeneous health care service ('medical treatment') and other consumption. The relative price of medical treatment is supposed to be constant and can thus be normalized to 1. Accordingly, the respective *quantities* of the goods consumed by the individual may be replaced by the *expenditure* on medical treatment M and on other consumption y. With health insurance, I denotes benefits and P the premium, and if the individual has a gross income Y, the budget constraint implies

$$y = Y - P - M + I. \tag{6.63}$$

---

[15] Ex-post moral hazard was first investigated in a formal model by ZECKHAUSER (1970). Important extensions are SPENCE AND ZECKHAUSER (1971) and BLOMQVIST (1997).

The individual's state of health, θ, is a random variable whose realization is unknown to the individual at the beginning of the period. θ can have S different values $(\theta_1, ..., \theta_S)$, which occur with probabilities $(\pi_1, ..., \pi_S)$. Upon realization, health state θ_s can be improved with expenditures for medical treatment. For simplicity, let the resulting health state be given by

$$H_s = \theta_s + M_s, \quad s = 1, ..., S. \tag{6.64}$$

Thus, medical care has a marginal productivity in terms of health of one, regardless of the state of health (and hence type of sickness). While this assumption admittedly is not very realistic, another one importantly adds to realism. To the extent that gross income Y derives from labor, it depends on the individual's state of health. As already noted in the graphical analysis of Section 1.2.1, good health is a precondition for earning income on the labor market. It allows to be productive on the job, to work long hours, and to invest in continuous education. Therefore, the following relationship is introduced:

$$Y = f(H) \quad \text{with} \quad f'[\theta_{\max}] \geq 1 \quad \text{and} \quad f'' < 0, \tag{6.65}$$

where $\theta_{\max}$ is the best possible health state. A health state $\theta_s < \theta_{\max}$ can therefore be interpreted as a case of illness. The restriction $f'[\theta_{\max}] \geq 1$ ensures that there is a positive demand for medical care in all states. It simplifies the analysis greatly by obviating the need to check for corner solutions ($M_s^o = 0$). In fact, with this restriction, marginal productivity of medical care in terms of income is always at least as large as its price (which is normalized to one; also recall that its marginal productivity in terms of health is one as well).

The individual's disposable income in state s now becomes

$$\begin{aligned} y_s &= f(H_s) - P - M_s + I_s \\ &= f(\theta_s + M_s) - P - M_s + I_s \end{aligned} \tag{6.66}$$

Finally, utility of the individual is a strictly concave function of disposable income y, i.e.,

$$u = u(y) \quad \text{with} \quad u' > 0, u'' < 0. \tag{6.67}$$

Note that the state of health H has no direct influence on utility. For the individual, health is therefore a pure investment good.

An overview over the main equations of this section and the abbreviations used is given in Box 6.3.

Box 6.3. Optimal Insurance Coverage and Optimal Demand for Medical Care

---

Observable state of health:

$$EU = \sum_{s=1}^{S} \pi_s u(f(\theta_s + M_s) - M_s - P + I_s) \tag{6.68}$$

$$P = \sum_{s=1}^{S} \pi_s I_s \tag{6.69}$$

$$I_s^o = M_s^o + \alpha. \tag{6.77}$$

Unobservable state of health:

$$I = (1-c)M, \quad 0 \le c \le 1 \tag{6.82}$$

$$\frac{\partial M_s}{\partial c} = \frac{dH^o}{dc} < 0 \tag{6.89}$$

$$EU(c) = \sum_{s=1}^{S} \pi_s u(f(\theta_s + M_s(c,\theta_s)) - cM_s(c,\theta_s) - P(c)) \tag{6.90}$$

$$P(c) = \sum_{s=1}^{S} \pi_s (1-c) M_s(c,\theta_s) = (1-c) \sum_{s=1}^{S} \pi_s M_s(c,\theta_s). \tag{6.91}$$

y:	disposable income of the individual
Y:	gross income
θ_s:	state of health
π_s:	probability of state θ_s
M_s:	expenditures for medical treatment in state s
H_s:	realized state of health
$u(y)$:	utility of the individual
EU:	expected utility of the individual
I_s:	insurance benefit in state s
P:	insurance premium
c:	rate of copayment

6.4.2.2 Optimal Insurance Coverage with Observable State of Health

First, we investigate the reference case with no ex-post moral hazard, where the health state can be observed by the insurer. Due to the deterministic relationship between medical care and health, individuals can in fact determine the level of health in each future state s by the choice of medical care M_s. They are behind the 'veil of ignorance' only with regard to which state s will occur. Along with M_s they select insurance benefit I_s in a way that maximizes expected utility,

$$EU = \sum_{s=1}^{S} \pi_s u(f(\theta_s + M_s) - M_s - P + I_s). \tag{6.68}$$

In the following we assume that actuarially fair insurance is available. The premium then adds up to

$$P = \sum_{s=1}^{S} \pi_s I_s. \tag{6.69}$$

To identify the optimal insurance contract, consider the Lagrangian function,

$$\Phi\left((M_s, I_s)_{s=1}^{S}, P, \mu\right) = \sum_{s=1}^{S} \pi_s u(f(\theta_s + M_s) - M_s - P + I_s) + \mu \left[P - \sum_{s=1}^{S} \pi_s I_s\right]. \tag{6.70}$$

The first-order conditions for an interior solution are:[16]

$$\frac{\partial \Phi}{\partial M_s} = \pi_s u'[y_s^o][f'[H_s^o] - 1] = 0 \tag{6.71}$$

$$\frac{\partial \Phi}{\partial I_s} = \pi_s u'[y_s^o] - \mu^o \pi_s = 0 \tag{6.72}$$

$$\frac{\partial \Phi}{\partial P} = -\sum_{s=1}^{S} \pi_s u'[y_s^o] + \mu^o = 0 \tag{6.73}$$

$$\frac{\partial \Phi}{\partial \mu} = P^o - \sum_{s=1}^{S} \pi_s I_s^o = 0.[17] \tag{6.74}$$

From equation (6.71) we obtain the condition that the marginal benefit of medical care is equal to marginal cost,

$$f'[\theta_s + M_s^o] = 1. \tag{6.75}$$

Because of the assumption $f'[\theta_{max}] \geq 1$ (see equation (6.65)), the individual always demands a positive amount of medical services. The actually achieved state of health H_s is therefore identical in all states s. Defining H^o as the state of health that satisfies equation (6.75), one has

$$M_s^o = H^o - \theta_s. \tag{6.76}$$

Minimum health care expenditure thus amounts to $M_{min}^o = H^o - \theta_{max}$. Next, equation (6.72) implies $u'(y_s^o) = \mu^o$, i.e., marginal utility and thus disposable income are the same in all states. This implies that

$$I_s^o = M_s^o + \alpha, \tag{6.77}$$

where α is a constant. For example, $I_s^o = M_s^o$ or $I_s^o = M_s^o - M_{min}^o$ are possible insurance benefits.

Can we therefore conclude that with a fair premium the insurance benefit should simply cover health care expenditure? To answer this question, consider the utility-maximizing behavior of the individual in the ex-post situation, i.e., when health state

---

[16] The second-order conditions are satisfied because of the strict concavity of the functions $u(y)$ and $f(H)$.

θ_s has materialized, with insurance coverage and premium given. Assume that the insurance benefit depends on health care expenditure, i.e., that $I = I(M)$. The individual then chooses the value M_s that maximizes utility

$$u(f(\theta_s + M_s) - P - M_s + I(M_s)). \tag{6.78}$$

The first-order condition is

$$\frac{\partial u(y_s)}{\partial M_s} = u'[y_s](f'[\theta_s + M_s] - 1 + I'[M_s]) = 0. \tag{6.79}$$

This condition is compatible with the global optimality condition (6.71) if and only if $I'[M_s] = 0$ for all states s, i.e., if insurance benefits do *not at all* depend on health care expenditure. Note that in view of equation (6.76), the insurer must not only be able to observe health expenditure M_s but also the state of health prior to treatment, θ_s. The insurance benefit can then take the form of either an *in-kind benefit* with a value of M_s^o or of an *indemnity*, i.e., a lump-sum payment depending only on the state s. In the latter case the individual solves the problem

$$\max_{M_s} u(f(\theta_s + M_s) - P - M_s + I_s). \tag{6.80}$$

The first-order condition is

$$\frac{\partial u(y_s)}{\partial M_s} = u'(y_s)(f'(H_s) - 1) = 0 \quad \Rightarrow \quad f'(\theta_s + M_s) = 1. \tag{6.81}$$

Thus, the individual himself chooses the optimal expenditures M_s^o.

Conclusion 6.8. *If the insurer is able to observe the health state of the insured, optimal contract design calls for either an in-kind benefit amounting to the value of optimal health care expenditure or an indemnity, i.e., a lump-sum benefit which depends only on the health state prior to treatment.*

6.4.2.3 Optimal Insurance Coverage with Unobservable State of Health

The first-best optimum characterized above cannot be attained if the insurer is unable to observe the health state of the insured. Instead, medical expenditure must serve as an indicator of the sickness itself, causing insurance payments to depend on expenditure through a reimbursement function $I(M)$. To keep the search for an optimal reimbursement function simple, we consider in the following only insurance contracts with proportional coinsurance. Thus, the reimbursement function takes the form

$$I = (1 - c)M, \quad 0 \leq c \leq 1, \tag{6.82}$$

where $100 \times c$ is the coinsurance rate in percent.[18]

---

[18] In the absence of this restriction, the optimal reimbursement function is in general non-linear [see SPENCE AND ZECKHAUSER (1971) and BLOMQVIST (1997)].

The individual now faces a *two-stage optimization problem*. Ex post, i.e., after the realization of θ_s, utility-maximizing health care expenditure $M(c, \theta_s)$ is determined, where the copayment rate c is taken as exogenous. Ex ante the value of c has to be chosen so as to maximize expected utility, taking one's ex-post behavior into account.

Ex-Post Optimization

We start with the optimal demand for medical care, given coinsurance c and after realization of θ_s. The individual then faces the following problem:

$$\max_{M_s} u(f(\theta_s + M_s) - P - cM_s). \tag{6.83}$$

The first-order condition reads

$$\frac{du}{dM_s} = u'[y_s](f'[\theta_s + M_s^*] - c) = 0 \quad \Rightarrow \quad f'[\theta_s + M_s^*] = f'[H^*] = c. \tag{6.84}$$

It not only determines the optimal amount of medical care in the presence of ex-post moral hazard (M_s^*) but also the optimal level of health in each state, $H^*(c)$. The second-order condition is satisfied,

$$\frac{d^2u}{dM_s^2} = u''[y_s](f'[\theta_s + M_s^*] - c)^2 + u'(y_s)f''[\theta_s + M_s^*] < 0 \tag{6.85}$$

since $u'' < 0$ and $f'' < 0$. From $f'[\theta_s + M_s^*] = c$ and the implicit function theorem, we obtain,   using $H^* = \theta_s + M_s^*$,

$$\frac{dH^*}{dc} = \frac{1}{f''(H^*)} < 0 \tag{6.86}$$

as $f'' < 0$. For $c = 1$ (no insurance) H^* corresponds to the value of the first-best, H° (see equation (6.75)). For $c < 1$, expenditure on medical care is consequently larger than in the first-best. This demonstrates already the trade-off between insuring the risk of high expenditure on health care (calling for a value of c as small as possible before the occurrence of illness) and an efficient level of health care expenditure (c as high as possible after the occurrence of illness).

From equation (6.64) we can determine the utility-maximizing health expenditures depending on c and θ_s:

$$M_s(c, \theta_s) = H^*(c) - \theta_s. \tag{6.87}$$

The partial derivatives are:

$$\frac{\partial M_s}{\partial \theta_s} = -1 < 0 \tag{6.88}$$

$$\frac{\partial M_s}{\partial c} = \frac{dH^*}{dc} < 0. \tag{6.89}$$

Health care expenditure is predicted to be smaller, the better the health state θ_s. Furthermore, equation (6.89) gives rise to

Conclusion 6.9. *A utility-maximizing individual demands more medical services, the smaller the rate of copayment ('ex-post moral hazard').*

Ex-Ante Optimization

At the end of the last subsection, we identified the trade-off characterizing the determination of the optimal rate of copayment. Before the occurrence of sickness, it should ideally be zero. But after the occurrence of sickness, it should be one. Now, this conflict will be resolved ex-ante. Since the demand for medical services $M_s(c, \theta_s)$ and the insurance premium $P(c)$ depend on the rate of copayment c selected, expected utility of the individual as a function of c is

$$EU(c) = \sum_{s=1}^{S} \pi_s u[f(\theta_s + M_s(c, \theta_s)) - cM_s(c, \theta_s) - P(c)]. \tag{6.90}$$

In the case of fair insurance, the premium function reads

$$P(c) = \sum_{s=1}^{S} \pi_s (1 - c) M_s(c, \theta_s) = (1 - c) \sum_{s=1}^{S} \pi_s M_s(c, \theta_s). \tag{6.91}$$

After inserting (6.91) into (6.90), the optimal copayment rate is the solution to the following problem:

$$\max_c EU(c) = \sum_{s=1}^{S} \pi_s u\left[f(\theta_s + M_s(c, \theta_s)) - cM_s(c, \theta_s) - (1 - c)\sum_{s=1}^{S} \pi_s M_s(c, \theta_s)\right], \tag{6.92}$$

subject to the constraint $0 \leq c \leq 1$.

The Kuhn-Tucker conditions for problem (6.92) are

$$\frac{dEU}{dc} \begin{cases} \leq 0 \text{ if } & c^* = 0 \\ = 0 \text{ if } & 0 < c^* < 1 \\ \geq 0 \text{ if } & c^* = 1 \end{cases} \tag{6.93}$$

where

$$\frac{dEU}{dc} = \sum_{s=1}^{S} \pi_s u'(y_s) \left[f'\frac{\partial M_s}{\partial c} - c\frac{\partial M_s}{\partial c} - M_s + \sum_{s=1}^{S} \pi_s M_s - (1 - c)\sum_{s=1}^{S} \pi_s \frac{\partial M_s}{\partial c} \right].$$

Because of equation (6.84) this simplifies to

$$\frac{dEU}{dc} = \sum_{s=1}^{S} \pi_s u'(y_s) \left[-M_s + \sum_{s=1}^{S} \pi_s M_s - (1 - c)\sum_{s=1}^{S} \pi_s \frac{\partial M_s}{\partial c} \right]. \tag{6.94}$$

The terms in the squared brackets can be interpreted in the following way: the negative of M_s denotes the reduction in reimbursement in state s if the copayment rate c is marginally increased. $\sum_{s=1}^{S} \pi_s M_s$ reflects the decrease of the premium, ignoring the moral hazard effect. For positive values of c, the combined effect of these two terms is negative. By contrast, there is a positive effect due to the premium reduction of $-(1 - c)\sum_{s=1}^{S} \pi_s \frac{\partial M_s}{\partial c} > 0$ because of the drop in excess consumption.

In the Appendix to this chapter, we demonstrate that it is always optimal to sign an insurance contract. Furthermore, we show that

$$\frac{dEU}{dc}\bigg|_{c=0} = -u'(y) \sum_{s=1}^{S} \pi_s \frac{\partial M_s}{\partial c} > 0, \tag{6.95}$$

where y is certain income if the individual is fully covered. Since $\partial M_s/\partial c$ is negative, the derivative of expected utility at $c = 0$ must be positive. This implies that a positive copayment rate is always optimal. At $c = 0$, the individual has full coverage and therefore marginal exposure to risk does not matter. There is thus only a moral hazard effect which is mitigated by the increase of the copayment rate.

In the Appendix, we also derive

$$\frac{\partial EU}{\partial c} = \sum_{s=1}^{S} \pi_s u'(y_s) \left[\theta_s - \sum_{s=1}^{S} \pi_s \theta_s - \frac{1-c^*}{c^*} \eta_{H,c} H^*(c) \right] \equiv F(c^*, \eta_{H,c}). \tag{6.96}$$

where $\eta_{H,c} = \frac{dH^*}{dc} \frac{c}{H^*} < 0$ is the elasticity of the demand for health care with respect to the copayment rate which is assumed to be constant. We suppose that there is a unique optimal copayment rate c^*, which is characterized by the first-order condition $F(c^*, \eta_{H,c}) = 0$. With the help of the implicit function theorem, we obtain

$$\frac{dc^*}{d\eta_{H,c}} = -\frac{\dfrac{\partial F}{\partial \eta_{H,c}}}{\dfrac{\partial F}{\partial c^*}} = \frac{\displaystyle\sum_{s=1}^{S} \pi_s u'(y_s) \dfrac{1-c^*}{c^*} H^*}{\dfrac{\partial^2 EU}{\partial (c^*)^2}} < 0. \tag{6.97}$$

Note that a higher value of $\eta_{H,c}$ implies that demand for health care with respect to the coinsurance rate is less elastic, as $\eta_{H,c}$ is negative. Thus, equation (6.97) states that the more elastic the demand for health with respect to the coinsurance rate (which is also a price elasticity because 1 percent more coinsurance increases the net price of medical care by 1 percent), the larger is the optimal copayment rate.

Finally, $\eta_{H,c}$ can be translated into the price elasticity of the demand for medical care. Using equation (6.89) we get

$$\eta_{M,c} = \frac{\partial M}{\partial c} \frac{c}{M} = \frac{dH}{dc} \frac{c}{M} = \eta_{H,c} \frac{H^*}{M}. \tag{6.98}$$

Therefore $\eta_{M,c}$ is proportional to the elasticity $\eta_{H,c}$ for all M. Consequently, we obtain the intuitive result that the optimal copayment rate increases if the demand for medical care becomes more price elastic.

Conclusion 6.10. *The optimal rate of copayment is positive because it serves to limit ex-post moral hazard, which would be extreme without copayment. It is ceteris paribus higher, the more price elastic the demand for medical care.*

Note that in addition to the restrictive assumption that the individual derives no direct utility from health, we have also limited the analysis to insurance contracts with proportional coinsurance. A more general analysis can be found in BLOMQVIST (1997), who applies optimal control theory to determine the optimal non-linear co-payment function.

Finally, it has to be emphasized that health care expenditure is not the only possible indicator of unobservable health state θ_s. In practice, other sources of information are conceivable. In the model considered here, income depends on health and therefore might serve as an alternative. Not least because of tax concerns, income may not be fully revealed by the individual, however. Still another indicator is the type of medical treatment performed. For example, an appendectomy constitutes a strong indicator that the patient suffered from appendicitis. But a back massage does not necessarily imply that patients suffered from a severe back problem. Rather, they may have simply enjoyed the comfort of getting the massage. Accordingly, the copayment rate should depend on the information content of the service: for appendectomies, it should be zero, whereas for massages it should be relatively high.

6.4.2.4 Implications

We have learned that apart from the reasons stated in Subsections 6.3 and 6.4.1, there is still another important justification of refraining from full insurance coverage of health care expenditure. Full coverage is not optimal if the insured, in the attempt to maximize utility in the 'sick' state, is able to influence the amount of medical care obtained. In this case, it is to advantageous to choose an insurance contract with coinsurance, which creates an *incentive to use health services in a cost-conscious manner*.

Yet, full ex-ante optimality in the sense of maximum expected utility is attained only if the marginal utility of one unit of expenditure is equal in all possible types of use. This, however, requires that the insured bears the full marginal cost of medical care, i.e., benefits must not depend on the expenditure on health care but be simply linked to health status ('indemnity' insurance). But this would require the insurer to be able to observe the insured's health status.

These considerations show clearly that the above-mentioned choice of coinsurance in the case of unobservable health represents a *second-best solution*: in the event of illness, disposable income is still smaller and hence marginal utility of income larger than in good health. Thus, the first-best maximum of expected utility described in Subsection 6.4.2.2, which calls for equal marginal utility of consumption in all states, is not attained.

This failure derives from fact that the insured are forced to choose between two evils. By opting for a low rate of coinsurance, they induce themselves to consume a lot of costly medical services, causing them to face the 'Scylla' of a *high insurance premium*. Deciding in favor of a high rate of coinsurance, they run into the 'Charybdis' of an *incomplete shifting of risk* onto the insurer. The course of the 'golden middle path' between Scylla and Charybdis depends on the price elasticity of demand for health services. For instance, if demand is totally inelastic, incentives are ineffective anyway, permitting consumers to opt for a complete shifting of risk through a full-coverage contract. Of course, a private insurance purchaser will take these effects into account when choosing the most preferred insurance coverage.

By contrast, the above considerations are relevant for the design of mandatory social insurance and they highlight the great importance of empirical research into the price elasticity of demand for medical care. In general, the appropriate elasticity to be used in this analysis is the Hicksian or compensated price elasticity of the demand for health care services, which is not directly observable but can be inferred from the price elasticity of the observable Marshallian demand function via the Slutsky decomposition. In this particular model, in which health is a pure investment good, the demand for medical care has no income effect, causing the Hicksian and the Marshallian elasticities to coincide. But in a more general model they would have to be distinguished.[19]

Furthermore, ex-post moral hazard is often identified with the observation that insured persons use more medical services than uninsured ones. This may be true but it cannot be inferred that the extra services used by the insured are necessarily inefficient. Recall the 'access motive' introduced above (in Section 6.3.1.1), which applies to an indivisible treatment such as renal dialysis whose cost exceeds the individual's income. If some individuals buy insurance in order to be able to afford dialysis in the case of renal failure, it is quite natural that among all individuals with renal failure those who are insured obtain dialysis and the others don't. But of course this does not mean that renal dialysis constitutes an inefficient service. This example shows that empirical evidence indicating that insured persons use more services than uninsured ones is not sufficient to infer that insurance leads to over-consumption of medical care.

6.4.2.5 The Empirical Relationship Between Insurance Coverage and the Demand for Health Care Services

Already in the 1970s, numerous empirical studies dealing with the impact of health insurance on the utilization of medical services were published in the United States. In contrast to countries with mandatory health insurance where all or most citizens have the same insurance coverage, the United States are perfectly suitable for this type of investigation in view of the enormous variety of insurance contracts.

As the rate of coinsurance changes the (effective) price the insured has to pay for medical care, the primary goal of these surveys was to estimate the price elasticity of the demand for medical services. Of course, as many influencing factors as possible had to be considered, such as age, sex, income, and state of health, calling for

---

[19] This distinction lies at the heart of the criticism by NYMAN (1999a,2001) of some previous estimates of the 'welfare loss of excess health insurance' based on Marshallian demand elasticities.

multiple regression analysis in most cases. The price elasticities found in these studies [see, e.g., PHELPS AND NEWHOUSE (1972), SCITOVSKY AND SNIDER (1972)] mainly lie between 0 and -0.2. They thus had the expected sign, although they were relatively low. However, some studies found considerably higher values, up to -2.1 [see NEWHOUSE ET AL. (1980, p. 378)].

The methodology used in all these studies was criticized, however, on the grounds that the negative correlation between the deductible and the utilization of medical services might also be the consequence of the individual choice of the insurance contract. Individuals who expect only little utilization of medical services (due to their robust health or their aversion against orthodox medicine), may well have selected a higher deductible than others. These others in turn would be more likely to opt for full insurance coverage. Causality could thus be exactly reverse, running from low (expected) demand to cost sharing rather than from cost sharing to reduced demand [see NEWHOUSE ET AL. (1980)].

To exclude this effect of 'self-selection' when estimating the price elasticity of demand for medical care, the Rand Corporation initiated a large-scale 'Health Insurance Experiment' at the end of the 1970s costing over US$80 million. At six different locations, approximately representative of the entire United States, around 1,000 persons each were enrolled for 3 to 5 years in an insurance company especially created for the purpose of the study. Participants were assigned randomly to one of sixteen health insurance contracts. The rate of coinsurance varied from 0 to 95 percent. Some policies also featured fixed deductibles.

The statistical analysis of this experiment [see MANNING ET AL. (1987)] yielded estimates of the price elasticity of demand for medical services lying approximately between -0.1 and -0.2, i.e., within the range of earlier studies but towards the lower end. In particular, people confronted with a high deductible turned out to have a high probability of not seeing a doctor at all within a year. But given that a doctor has been consulted, the quantity of services demanded does not seem to vary much with insurance coverage [see KEELER AND ROLPH (1983)].

Furthermore, the experimental character of the study allowed to gather information about participants' health status at the beginning and at the end of the experiment. In this way, it was possible to test the widespread opinion that the financial barrier created by cost sharing would lead to an under-consumption of medical services and indirectly to a deterioration of health status.

Therefore six different indicators of health were measured [see BROOK ET AL. (1983)]. Three of these indicators (high blood pressure, myopia, and caries) actually showed a slight improvement among insured with low incomes when there was full insurance coverage. The authors argue, however, that the same outcome could have been achieved through comparably cheap targeted mass screening programs rather than costly '100 percent-insurance'. Nonetheless, it has to be conceded that the long-term health consequences of increased cost-sharing are not known with certainty.

Since then, advances in econometric methodology have permitted to sort out the two causal links referred to above. Specifically, one can try to first model the choice of insurance contract. A major health loss is likely to result in a changed estimate of the severity of a future illness, which in turn results in an increased demand for coverage. Therefore, causality also runs from (expected) health status to cost sharing. Next, one seeks to explain the demand for health care given the choice of contract [see, e.g., CAMERON ET AL. (1988)].

> **Conclusion 6.11.** *The demand for medical services, especially for initial physician visits, reacts in a statistically significant way to the extent of insurance coverage, although estimated price elasticities are generally low. The additional utilization induced by more extensive insurance coverage appears to result in a marginal health improvement only.*

We note in passing that moral hazard is not only present in the demand for medical services but also with respect to paid sick-leave, which is also included in many health insurance contracts. JOHANSSON AND PALME (2005) found that a reduction in the replacement rate of sick-leave payments in Sweden for short spells of absence due to sickness, which occurred in 1991, significantly reduced the incidence of this type of absence spells. It also increased the length of absence spells over 90 days because the reform increased the cost of returning to work by making it more costly to begin a new spell of absence.

6.5 Consequences for the Design of Social Health Insurance

In Chapter 5, we stated efficiency reasons for the existence of compulsory health insurance schemes. Specifically, compulsory insurance serves to tackle the 'free-rider problem' and to redistribute resources in favor of those who are disadvantaged in terms of their innate health. For its implementation, however, a minimum package must be defined to prevent the scheme from being circumvented by plans providing merely nominal coverage. In several countries, this problem is solved by providing health insurance coverage with no or very little cost sharing for most types of medical treatment.[20]

In view of the theoretical analysis provided in this chapter, full insurance coverage of this type cannot be considered optimal. The following points may be cited in support of this claim:

(1) Administrative costs do increase with benefits (see Section 6.3, Conclusion 6.1).

---

[20] For example, this holds true for Canada, the Czech Republic, Denmark, Hungary, the Netherlands prior to the 2006 reform, and Poland. In countries with a National Health Service, such as Italy, Portugal, Spain and the United Kingdom, the government implicitly acts as the insurer. However, the common feature with regard to moral hazard effects is that the money price of medical care is very low or even zero [see ZWEIFEL AND MANNING (2000)].

(2) With full coverage, there is a complete lack of incentive to invest in prevention as insurers usually have little means to observe preventive effort ('ex-ante moral hazard', see Section 6.4.1, Conclusion 6.6).

(3) The price elasticity of demand for health care services, although not very high, is different from zero ('ex-post moral hazard', see Sections 6.4.2 und 6.4.2.5, Conclusion 6.11).

To some extent, this problem can be tackled by introducing measures apart from copayments:

- Some countries such as Germany try to avoid administrative costs by providing benefits in kind. Thus, the insured do not submit their bills to their insurer, who instead receives a quarterly billing for all its members from the medical providers (aggregated by regional medical associations). Although cost-saving, this practice greatly affects transparency in that the insured cannot keep track of services consumed, let alone of the expenditures associated with them.

- Ex-ante moral hazard can to some extent be alleviated if preventive activities are subsidized. For example, many countries subsidize physical exercise. For instance, sickness funds in Germany offer courses in nordic walking and inline skating and provide dietary advice to encourage good nutrition. In addition, the consumption of goods associated with an unhealthy life-style, in particular tobacco, can be discouraged by taxes. Nevertheless, only a limited number of activities related to health can be influenced in this way.

- Ex-post moral hazard can also be reduced by giving physicians incentives to control health care expenditure. This strategy, however, has a number of negative side effects which will be discussed in Chapter 10. Specifically, physicians may lower the quality of treatment and try to avoid costly patients.

Overall, however, it seems unlikely that such measures fully eliminate the need for copayments in social health insurance. In particular, ex-post moral hazard calls for an optimal rate of copayment that varies across types of health services according to the price elasticity of demand. In line with this insight, many countries with mandatory health insurance schemes have higher rates of copayment for prescription drugs than, e.g., for hospital care (where most individuals delegate decision making authority to the attending physician, which serves to lower price elasticity of demand). Furthermore, the formal analysis showed that the optimal rate of copayment depends on individual health risk and individual preferences and thus can vary considerably among individuals. Therefore, uniform mandated insurance coverage may not be welfare-maximizing if preferences differ importantly.[21] It seems to be a better idea to let lawmakers determine a minimal extent of insurance coverage while leaving it up to the individuals to extend their coverage by buying complementary health insurance.

---

[21] ZWEIFEL ET AL. (2006) provide evidence for preference heterogeneity.

However, an important caveat has to be kept in mind when copayments are used in a social health insurance system. The more extensive the compulsory part of insurance coverage, the more redistribution can be achieved among different risk groups (see Chapter 5), which may be an important objective of policy makers (who shy away from redistributing income through taxation). On the other hand, extending mandatory coverage undermines incentives for prevention and for efficient utilization of health care services. Thus, a trade-off between efficiency and equity seems to emerge. As shown in BREYER (1991), however, it is generally not optimal to do without any efficiency incentives, mandating full coverage for everyone. This is because those benefiting from redistribution also benefit from the continuing existence of incentives encouraging the economic use of health care services.

6.6 Summary

In this chapter, we have analyzed the optimal design of health insurance contracts. The crucial question was under what circumstances copayment is optimal. Our main results are:

(1) In the absence of moral hazard,

- the necessary condition for full insurance coverage to be optimal is that the contract offered be *marginally fair*, i.e., that the premium does not include a proportional loading on the net premium;

- the sufficient condition for a risk-averse individual to opt for full insurance coverage is that the insurance be *actuarially fair* i.e., that its premium be equal to the net premium;

- the decision to buy no insurance rather than full coverage is more likely to be optimal the greater the cost of insurance (consisting of a fixed surcharge and a proportional loading for claims processing) and the greater the individual's probability of illness, which causes the loading to increase;

- even a risk-neutral individual will buy health insurance if some health services are indivisible and necessary for survival and their cost exceeds the individual's wealth. Examples are renal dialysis and organ transplants.

(2) If an illness gives rise to an immaterial loss in addition to the financial loss due to the cost of treatment, then the marginal utility of income is equalized across health states, provided the premium is marginally fair. However, optimal insurance benefits may exceed or fall short of the cost of treatment.

(3) If the individual can affect the probability of illness by preventive effort which is unobservable to the insurer, there is the problem of *ex-ante moral hazard*, meaning that with full coverage, the insured will refrain from prevention. Hence, copayment can be optimal because it provides incentives to engage in prevention.

(4) If the insurer can observe the state of health, the optimal health insurance contract has an in-kind benefit or an *indemnity*, i.e., a lump-sum payment which depends only on the health state.

(5) If health is unobservable to the insurer, then full coverage leads to over-consumption of health services (*ex-post moral hazard*). A positive rate of coinsurance then results in a higher expected utility than full coverage. The optimal rate of coinsurance is higher the more elastic the demand for medical services.

(6) Empirical studies show that the demand for medical services, especially for initial physician visits, reacts in a statistically significant way to the extent of insurance coverage, although the estimated price elasticity is generally low (-0.1 to -0.2). Exceptions are specific services of the 'consumption' type such as massages etc. with higher elasticities. The additional utilization induced by more extensive insurance coverage appears to result in a marginal health improvement only.

6.7 Further Reading

In the HANDBOOK OF HEALTH ECONOMICS, the chapters by CUTLER AND ZECK-HAUSER (2000), PAULY (2000) and ZWEIFEL AND MANNING (2000) deal with the design of insurance contracts and moral hazard. For a deeper introduction in the economics of insurance, we recommend the volumes of survey articles edited by Georges Dionne [see DIONNE (1992) and DIONNE (2000)]. In particular, the contributions by GOLLIER (2000), SCHLESINGER (2000) and WINTER (2000) analyze the optimal design of insurance contracts. EECKHOUDT ET AL. (2005) provide a general introduction to economic and financial decisions under risk.

6.A Appendix

In this Appendix, we show that the optimal coinsurance rate c^* in the ex-post moral hazard case of Section 6.4.2 must lie between zero and one. Furthermore, we derive equation (6.96).

We first demonstrate that it must be less than one, meaning that it is generally optimal to purchase insurance. From the first-order condition (6.94) we obtain for $c = 1$, i.e., no insurance,

$$\left. \frac{\mathrm{d}EU}{\mathrm{d}c} \right|_{c=1} = \sum_{s=1}^{S} \pi_s u'(y_s) \left[-M_s + \sum_{s=1}^{S} \pi_s M_s \right].$$

The term in squared brackets is positive for small values and negative for large values of M_s as $\sum_{s=1}^{S} \pi_s M_s$ is the expected value of M. Because of risk aversion ($u'' < 0$), $u'(y_s)$ increases with M_s in the absence of insurance. Let M_t be the largest value of M which is smaller than the expected value of M and y_t the corresponding income. Then, we have $u'(y_t) < u'(y_s)$ when the term in squared brackets is negative ($M_s > M_t$). Analogously, we have $u'(y_t) \geq u'(y_s)$ when the term in squared brackets is positive ($M_s \leq M_t$). Thus, it holds that

$$\left. \frac{\mathrm{d}EU}{\mathrm{d}c} \right|_{c=1} = \sum_{s=1}^{S} \pi_s u'(y_s) \left[-M_s + \sum_{s=1}^{S} \pi_s M_s \right] < \sum_{s=1}^{S} \pi_s u'(y_t) \left[-M_s + \sum_{s=1}^{S} \pi_s M_s \right].$$

From

$$\sum_{s=1}^{S} \pi_s u'(y_t) \left[-M_s + \sum_{s=1}^{S} \pi_s M_s \right] = u'(y_t) \sum_{s=1}^{S} \pi_s \left[-M_s + \sum_{s=1}^{S} \pi_s M_s \right]$$

$$= u'(y_t) \left[-\sum_{s=1}^{S} \pi_s M_s + \underbrace{\sum_{s=1}^{S} \pi_s}_{=1} \sum_{s=1}^{S} \pi_s M_s \right]$$

$$= 0,$$

it follows

$$\left. \frac{\mathrm{d}EU}{\mathrm{d}c} \right|_{c=1} < 0.$$

This implies $c^* < 1$, i.e., the individual will want to purchase health insurance also in the presence of ex-post moral hazard.

To demonstrate that full coverage cannot be optimal, we analyze the first-order condition (6.94) at $c = 0$. All of the individual's health care expenditures are reimbursed by the insurance company and disposable income is thus the same in all states, so that $u'(y_s) = u'(y)$. We obtain

$$
\frac{dEU}{dc}\bigg|_{c=0} = \sum_{s=1}^{S} \pi_s u'(y) \left[-M_s + \sum_{s=1}^{S} \pi_s M_s - \sum_{s=1}^{S} \pi_s \frac{\partial M_s}{\partial c} \right]
$$

$$
= u'(y) \left[-\sum_{s=1}^{S} \pi_s M_s + \sum_{s=1}^{S} \pi_s \sum_{s=1}^{S} \pi_s M_s - \sum_{s=1}^{S} \pi_s \sum_{s=1}^{S} \pi_s \frac{\partial M_s}{\partial c} \right]
$$

$$
= u'(y) \left[-\sum_{s=1}^{S} \pi_s M_s + \sum_{s=1}^{S} \pi_s M_s - \sum_{s=1}^{S} \pi_s \frac{\partial M_s}{\partial c} \right]
$$

and therefore

$$
\frac{dEU}{dc}\bigg|_{c=0} = -u'(y) \sum_{s=1}^{S} \pi_s \frac{\partial M_s}{\partial c} > 0, \tag{6.95}
$$

since $\partial M_s/\partial c$ is negative. Thus, the derivative of expected utility at $c = 0$ is positive, implying $c^* > 0$.

Finally, we derive equation (6.96). Inserting (6.64) and (6.89) into (6.94) and using $\sum_{s=1}^{S} \pi_s = 1$ yields

$$
\frac{dEU}{dc} = \sum_{s=1}^{S} \pi_s u'(y_s) \left[-M_s + \sum_{s=1}^{S} \pi_s M_s - (1-c) \sum_{s=1}^{S} \pi_s \frac{\partial M_s}{\partial c} \right]
$$

$$
= \sum_{s=1}^{S} \pi_s u'(y_s) \left[-(II^* - 0_s) + \sum_{s=1}^{S} \pi_s (II^* - 0_s) - (1-c) \sum_{s=1}^{S} \pi_s \frac{dH^*}{dc} \right]
$$

$$
- \sum_{s=1}^{S} \pi_s u'(y_s) \left[0_s - \sum_{s=1}^{S} \pi_s 0_s - (1-c) \frac{dH^*}{dc} \right].
$$

Assuming that the elasticity of the demand for health care with respect to the copayment rate, $\eta_{H,c} = \frac{dH^*}{dc} \frac{c}{H^*} < 0$, is constant, we obtain

$$
\frac{dEU}{dc} = \sum_{s=1}^{S} \pi_s u'(y_s) \left[0_s - \sum_{s=1}^{S} \pi_s 0_s - \frac{1-c^*}{c^*} \eta_{H,c} H^*(c) \right] \equiv F(c^*, \eta_{H,c}). \tag{6.96}
$$

6.E Exercises

6.1. Consider the following questions:

(a) What are the conditions rendering full insurance coverage optimal in the case of nonfinancial consequences of illness and no moral hazard? Under what conditions does the optimal insurance contract include a positive deductible?

(b) Why can it be optimal for those having a high health risk to go without insurance coverage?

(c) What characterizes an optimal health insurance contract, offered at a fair premium, if illness entails a non-financial loss? Give an economic explanation.

6.2. An individual with the utility function $u(y) = -e^{-ay}, a > 0$, and gross income Y faces the probability π of getting ill with health care expenditures L. Insurance coverage I is available at a unit price of $(1+\lambda)\pi$, $\lambda \geq 0$, so that the premium P is given by $(1+\lambda)\pi I$. Denote disposable income by y.

(a) Determine the optimal insurance coverage $I^\circ(Y, L, \pi, \lambda, a)$. What is the optimal coverage if $\lambda = 0$? How does it depend on gross income Y? Interpret your result.

(b) Assuming a positive loading $\lambda > 0$, determine the reaction of the demand for insurance to

(i) an increase in λ,

(ii) an increase in a.

Discuss your results.

6.3. Consider the same insurance problem as in Exercise 6.2 but assume a state-dependent utility function with $u_g(y) = -e^{-ay}, a > 0$ in the good and $u_b(y) = -\kappa e^{-ay}$, $\kappa > 0$ in the bad state of health.

(a) Determine the optimal insurance coverage $I^\circ(Y, L, \pi, \lambda, a, \kappa)$.

(b) For $\lambda = 0$ determine I° for $\kappa \gtrless 1$. Discuss your result.

(c) What problem can arise if an insurance contract specifies $I^\circ > L$?

6.4. An individual with gross income Y faces the probability $\pi = 25$ percent of getting ill. Treatment requires health care expenditures $L = 500$. Insurance coverage I is available at a unit price of 0.5, implying a premium $P = 0.5I$. Utility is given by

$$
u = \begin{cases} u_h = v(y) & \text{when healthy (not sick or sick and treated)} \\ u_d = -350 & \text{when sick and not treated,} \end{cases}
$$

where $y \geq 0$ is disposable income. Treatment must be financed by the individual. Borrowing is not possible.

(a) Assume that $v(y) = y$ and $Y = 400$. Show that the individual will buy insurance cover $I^* = 200$. Explain your result.

(b) Now let $v(y) = -e^{-0.002y}$.

  (i) Show that the individual will not buy insurance if $Y > 500$.

  (ii) Determine the optimal insurance coverage if $Y = 400$.

  Discuss your results.

6.5. An individual with the utility function $u(y) = \ln y$ and gross income $Y = 10.08$ can contract two exclusive diseases $s = 1, 2$. With probability $\pi_1 = 0.2$, the individual gets ill with disease 1, causing health care expenditures $M_1 = 4$. With probability $\pi_2 = 0.1$, the individual contracts disease 2, leading to health care expenditure $M_2 = 8$. Denote disposable income by y and insurance coverage for disease $s = 1, 2$ by I_s. The premium for insurance is given by

$$
P = 1.2(\pi_1 I_1 + \pi_2 I_2).
$$

(a) Assume that the insurance contract specifies a rate of copayment c such that $I_s = (1 - c)M_s$. Show that the optimal copayment rate is $c^o = 7.58$ percent and determine the corresponding value of expected utility.

(b) Now assume that there are no restrictions on insurance coverage. Determine the optimal values I_s^o and the corresponding value of expected utility.

(c) Compare your results with reference to Conclusion 6.3.

6.6. Consider the following questions:

(a) What is 'moral hazard' and in which forms can it take in the context of health?

(b) When does it matter for the optimal insurance contract whether an insurer is able to observe the extent of prevention?

(c) What can be said about the optimal rate of coinsurance given moral hazard in the ex-post form in the framework of the model considered here?

6.7. Assume that an individual with a utility function $u(y) = \ln(y)$ and income $y = 100$ can choose between a specific level of prevention $V_1 > 0$ and zero prevention. In the latter case, the probability of illness is $\pi_0 = 0.2$, in the former case it is $\pi_1 = 0.1$. In the case of illness, health care costs are $L = 80$. Assume in the following that expected utilities with a premium $\pi_1 I$ coincide for $V = 0$ und $V = V_1$ only for one value $I = \tilde{I}$.

(a) Let $V_1 = 4$.

   (i) Determine the optimal level of prevention if the insurer can observe the extent of prevention.

   (ii) Show that in the second-best case the critical level of insurance coverage $\tilde{I}$ lies between 40 and 50. Is it second-best optimal to engage in prevention?

(b) Now let $V_1 = 7$.

   (i) Determine the optimal level of prevention if the insurer can observe the extent of prevention for this case.

   (ii) Show that in the second best, the critical insurance coverage $\tilde{I}$ lies between 20 and 30. Is it second-best optimal to engage in prevention?

6.8. Consider the ex-post moral hazard model of Section 6.4.2 and assume the following functions:

$$f(H) = \ln H - H + 100$$

$$u(y) = \ln y$$

There are three states of the world with probabilities $\pi_1 = 0.2$, $\pi_2 = 0.5$ and $\pi_3 = 0.3$ and health states $\theta_1 = -10$, $\theta_2 = -15$ and $\theta_3 = -40$.

(a) Determine health state H^o, income $Y^o = f(H^o)$, health expenditures M_s^o and expected utility in the optimum with symmetric information.

(b) Now assume that the health state is unobservable and that only insurance contracts with constant coinsurance rates are offered.

   (i) Determine the state-dependent medical expenditures as a function of c and θ_s.

   (ii) Determine expected utility as a function of c.

   (iii) Calculate expected utility for different values of c between zero and one. Which value of the coinsurance rate maximizes expected utility?

7

Risk Selection in Health Insurance Markets

7.1 Introduction

In the 1990s, several countries exposed their social health insurers to an increased degree of competition in the hope of improving efficiency in health insurance and in their health care sectors. However, as shown in Section 5.4, competitive health insurers tend to charge a high premium to high risks and a low premium to low risks. This is nothing but a generalized version of the 'price equal to marginal cost' rule; after all, high risks are characterized by comparatively high expected cost of treatment due to a high probability of being sick. Moreover, for reasons spelled out in Chapter 5, the government wants all citizens to have health insurance.

One way to ensure universal access would be to subsidize the premiums of the poor. But governments traditionally have preferred premium regulation, prohibiting insurers to charge risk-based premiums, a practice called *community rating* in the United States. In addition, regulators usually require that insurers accept any applicant under an open enrollment policy. For example, public health insurance in Germany and Switzerland is organized according to these principles. In the United States, Medicare gives its beneficiaries a choice between the original Medicare Plan and competing health plans which receive a capitation payment.

For insurers the incentive for risk selection arises naturally in this type of system. The requirement to accept any individual at a uniform premium leads to expected losses with high-risk types and expected profits with low-risk types. Even if the health insurer is not for profit, it needs a sufficient number of low risks to balance its books and assure its economic survival. As always, 'more is better', calling for additional low-risk insured. Under competitive pressure, all insurers will engage in *cream-skimming*, i.e., attempt to attract favorable risks while excluding unfavorable ones.

Risk selection can take two different forms. On the one hand, health insurers can perform *direct risk selection* by influencing who signs a contract. For example, insurers may 'lose' the contract form handed in by a person who is considered expensive.

P. Zweifel et al., *Health Economics*, 2nd ed., DOI 10.1007/978-3-540-68540-1_7,
© Springer-Verlag Berlin Heidelberg 2009

Individuals who can be expected to require little health care may be encouraged to sign a contract by offering them supplementary services at a discount or, in the extreme case, outright payments. *Indirect risk selection*, on the other hand, consists in designing benefit packages or by contracting with service providers who are attractive for low risks but unattractive for high risks.[1]

Both forms of risk selection can only arise if insurers or consumers possess information about individual health care expenditure. Direct risk selection requires that insurers can observe characteristics of individuals which are correlated with their expected cost, e.g., gender and age, but also behavior. For instance, if healthy individuals use the internet more frequently, then a risk selection strategy is to market insurance contracts online. For direct risk selection to work, individuals need not know their risk type. For indirect risk selection, by contrast, this is a requirement. In particular, individuals must know their probabilities of using certain services. This allows insurers to design benefit packages and enlist service providers appealing to different risk types.

Direct and indirect risk selection can arise simultaneously. Measures which rule out one of the two need not affect the incentives for the other. For example, even if the benefit package is tightly regulated, preventing indirect risk selection, insurers will still be interested in attracting favorable risks, causing them to resort to direct risk selection. Conversely, if insurers have no possibility of direct risk selection, the incentive to design the benefit package in a way to attract low risks and to avoid high risks still remains.[2]

To avoid risk selection, three types of measures can be taken, the underlying assumption always being that health insurance is compulsory so that low risks cannot escape cross-subsidizing the high risks by not purchasing insurance at all:

(1) *Regulation of the enrollment process*

Open enrollment guarantees that high risks cannot simply be rejected by insurers. Furthermore, obvious methods of direct risk selection can be ruled out by law and controls. For example, financial and other rewards for low risks may be prohibited.

(2) *Regulation of the benefit package*

Regulation of the benefit package is a measure against indirect risk selection. On the one hand, minimum benefits can be stipulated, forcing insurers to offer benefits that are of importance for high risks, such as treatment of diabetes. On

---

[1] A similar distinction is made by GLAZER AND MCGUIRE (2002, p. 154) who refer to the *individual access problem* and the *quality problem*. The first problem corresponds to direct, the second to indirect risk selection.

[2] Indirect risk selection is closely related to the phenomenon of adverse selection in insurance markets which arises if individuals are better informed about their risk type than insurers (see Section 5.3.3). The difference is that adverse selection emerges without intervention by the government. Indirect risk selection, on the other hand, is a consequence of government premium regulation, as first pointed out by PAULY (1984).

the other hand, imposing an upper limit on benefits can prevent insurers from including services that are of particular interest to low risks, such as visits to fitness centers. In addition, certain types of benefits that are especially suited for risk selection may be 'carved out', i.e., offered by a separate scheme.

However, one aspect of the benefit package consists in the choice of contractual partners for the provision of services. Through this choice (which is particularly important in the context of Managed Care), insurers are capable of attracting favorable risks. For example, by enrolling many specialists in athletic medicine, they make hope to have additional sports-minded consumers on their books.

(3) *Risk adjustment and cost reimbursement*

The objective of a *risk adjustment scheme* (RAS) is to reward insurers who en-roll high risks by additional payments and to impose a financial sanction to those who 'skim the cream', i.e., who cream off the favorable risks. Payments depend on observable characteristics of individuals such as age and gender. A *cost re-imbursement scheme* (CRS) reimburses a share of the actual treatment costs of individuals. The idea is to reduce the gains from risk selection by mitigating the impact of costs on insurers' profits. The drawback of a CRS are weakened incentives for health insurers to control costs.

In this chapter, we explore how these measures can reduce the incentives for risk selection. We start by presenting the theory of risk selection in Section 7.2. Two ad-ditional justifications for risk adjustment and cost reimbursement are discussed in Section 7.3. The first refers to the possibility that insurers differ in terms of their insured population for historic reasons. In this case, risk adjustment and cost reim-bursement can avoid putting insurers with a favorable risk structure in a better start-ing position when a competitive system is introduced. Second, the health insurance market may become unstable if new insurers can enter the market and low risks tend to be more willing to switch insurers than high risks. The incentives for migration of course are mitigated when premium differentials between insurers are reduced by risk adjustment and cost reimbursement. The design of risk adjustment and cost re-imbursement schemes is presented in Sections 7.4 and 7.5. The results of this chapter are summarized in Section 7.6.

7.2 Modeling Risk Selection

7.2.1 Direct Risk Selection

Direct risk selection is the most obvious way to discriminate against high risks. It requires that insurers can observe characteristics of individuals that correlate with the expected cost of treatment. Furthermore, the insurer must have influence on whether the contract is signed or not in spite of open enrollment. For example, expensive individuals may be deterred by unfriendly behavior on the part of insurance agents or by a pedantic handling of contract forms. Low risks can by attracted by targeted advertising (e.g., in the context of sports events) or by offering them supplementary benefits at a discount [see KIFMANN (2006b)].

There are two ways to deal with the problem of direct risk selection. On the one hand, certain selection methods can be prohibited or limited by law, in particular offering supplementary benefits or outright payments to customers. The amount of contact between insurers and customers before signing the contract can be minimized by simplifying and standardizing contract forms. But less obvious methods like 'losing' applications are hard to rule out. Furthermore, it should be noted that regulation of this type makes the launching of product innovations that serve to better match contracts to consumer preferences more costly and sometimes impossible.

The second method to prevent direct risk selection is to implement a risk adjustment scheme (RAS) which, ideally, relies on the same individual characteristics that can be observed by insurers. A simple model may illustrate this approach. Assume that insurers can only observe one particular characteristic which allows them to categorize customers into two groups (e.g., gender). Formally, this corresponds to a signal s that takes the values 0 or 1. Average expected cost of a person with signal s amounts to M_s and the share of persons with signal $s = 1$ is μ. Average expected cost of all individuals is therefore given by $\overline{M} = (1 - \mu)M_0 + \mu M_1$. We assume $M_1 > M_0$, which gives insurers an incentive to discriminate against individuals with the signal $s = 1$ given that they must not charge those risks a higher premium.

If the regulator can observe the signal s, a RAS may be designed that neutralizes the incentive for direct risk selection. This is achieved by transfers $\hat{z}_s$ paid to the regulator ($\hat{z}_0 < 0$) or received from the regulator ($\hat{z}_1 > 0$) amounting to

$$\hat{z}_s = M_s - \overline{M}, \quad s = 0, 1. \tag{7.1}$$

These transfers make expected cost for each individual equal to $\overline{M}$ from the perspective of the insurer who pays $-\hat{z}_0 = \overline{M} - M_0 > 0$ for each person with $s = 0$ and receives $\hat{z}_1 = M_1 - \overline{M} > 0$ for each person with $s = 1$. Furthermore, the regulator's budget is balanced since

$$(1 - \mu)\hat{z}_0 + \mu\hat{z}_1 = (1 - \mu)M_0 + \mu M_1 - \overline{M} = 0. \tag{7.2}$$

In principle, a RAS can completely eliminate the incentives for direct risk selection, at least as long as the insurer's planning horizon coincides with that of the regulator.[3] However, a RAS requires the regulator to be able to observe the same signal as insurers. If not, a *cost reimbursement scheme* (CRS) is an alternative. The simplest possibility is to reimburse a fraction γ of costs. As this weakens insurers' incentives to control costs, expected cost M_s depends on γ, with $M_s'(\gamma) > 0$. If insurers pay a transfer $b(\gamma)$ per insured to finance the cost reimbursement scheme, expected cost for a person with signal s becomes $(1 - \gamma)M_s(\gamma) + b(\gamma)$ from the insurer's perspective.

---

[3] For a critical discussion of this assumption, see ZWEIFEL AND BREUER (2006).

Measuring the incentives for direct risk selection by the difference in expected cost between the two groups, $\Delta M_A(\gamma)$, we obtain

$$\Delta M_A(\gamma) = (1-\gamma)M_1(\gamma) + b(\gamma) - \left((1-\gamma)M_0(\gamma) + b(\gamma)\right) \qquad (7.3)$$
$$= (1-\gamma)(M_1(\gamma) - M_0(\gamma)).$$

If costs are reimbursed in full, then $\Delta M_A(1) = 0$, and no incentives for risk selection remain. But insurers lack any incentive to control costs in this case. In general, a CRS therefore leads to a trade-off between eliminating incentives for risk selection and preserving incentives to control costs. However, it may even increase the incentives for risk selection for some values of γ compared to no cost reimbursement. This can be shown by calculating the marginal effect of γ on the difference in expected costs. We obtain

$$\frac{d\Delta M_A(\gamma)}{d\gamma} = -(M_1(\gamma) - M_0(\gamma)) + (1-\gamma)(M_1{}'(\gamma) - M_0{}'(\gamma)) \gtrless 0. \qquad (7.4)$$

The first term $-(M_1(\gamma) - M_0(\gamma))$ is negative as long as $M_1(\gamma) > M_0(\gamma)$. The second term $(1-\gamma)(M_1{}'(\gamma) - M_0{}'(\gamma))$, however, is positive if $M_1{}'(\gamma) > M_0{}'(\gamma)$. In this case, expected cost of an individual with signal 1 are more sensitive to incentives to control costs. If this term is larger, the difference in expected costs actually increases in γ. It is therefore possible that a cost reimbursement scheme can make things worse both in terms of incentives for risk selection and cost control. Only if γ is sufficiently high, incentives for risk selection are sure to be lower than in the absence of cost reimbursement since $\Delta M_A(1) = 0$ (see Exercise 7.4).

> **Conclusion 7.1.** *Direct risk selection can be avoided by prohibiting selection methods such as selling supplementary benefits or offering outright payments to attractive risks. Both a risk adjustment scheme which relies on observable characteristics of individuals and a cost reimbursement scheme can decrease incentives for direct risk selection. The advantage of a risk adjustment scheme over a cost reimbursement scheme is that it does not affect the insurers' incentives to control costs and is sure to decrease incentives for risk selection.*

7.2.2 Indirect Risk Selection

Indirect risk selection is the more subtle variant of risk selection as it does not require that insurers actually observe any characteristics of individuals. All it takes is that

- insurers know that the population consists of different risk types, and
- individuals with different risk type differ in their preferences.

This opens up the possibility of designing a benefit package which is attractive for low risks but not for high risks. An example is a contract with a deductible. This is more appealing for low than for high risks since they face a lower probability of becoming ill and therefore of having to pay the deductible. The same reasoning applies to the design of the benefit package in general. For instance, an insurer who covers only few services for patients suffering from diabetes can expect these high risks to prefer another insurer.[4]

A straightforward counter strategy is to impose a maximum deductible and a minimum benefit package. This may not be sufficient, however, because insurers can still try to attract low risks by writing policies with ample coverage of athletic medicine and well-baby care. If included in the mandatory package, these benefits will also have to be financed by high risks who have no interest in them [see KIFMANN (2002)]. It may therefore be necessary to specify a maximum benefit package as well, thus increasingly limiting the scope of product innovation.

The fundamental question remains whether this type of regulation can actually be enforced. Considering the multitude of benefits which are available for medical treatment, this is doubtful. Furthermore, the insurers' ways of paying providers and organizing the delivery of health care would have to be analyzed because they determine the quality of treatment and who is treated (see Chapters 10 and 11). In particular, Managed Care may not only be a way to provide health care at lower cost but also a method to attract low risks.[5] Ultimately, indirect risk selection can only be ruled out if all insurers are required to provide identical benefits which are tightly regulated. Such a policy, however, risks throwing out the baby with the bath water as one of the main benefits of insurer competition is the efficient provision of benefits which requires that insurers have some freedom in the design of benefits.

In the following, we analyze indirect risk selection in two steps. In Section 7.2.2.1, we first treat the case where insurers offer only one benefit and perform indirect risk selection by the *quantity* of benefits. In Section 7.2.2.2 insurers offer two benefits, enabling them to select risks by the *structure* of benefits. For both cases, we discuss how the extent of risk selection can be reduced. Given the problems associated with regulating the benefit package, we pay particular attention to the optimal design of risk adjustment.

> **Conclusion 7.2.** *Regulation designed to avoid indirect risk selection requires the specification of the benefit package. These measures, however, may not be enforceable while stifling insurer competition through product innovation.*

---

[4] In economic theory, this type of behavior is called *screening* [see, e.g., MAS-COLELL ET AL. (1995, Chapter 13) for an exposition].

[5] See Section 11.4.2 for an empirical and KIFMANN (1999) for a theoretical analysis.

7.2.2.1 Indirect Risk Selection Using the Quantity of Benefits

Assume a population consisting of two risk types who differ in their probability of becoming ill $\pi_i, i = h, l$ (high and low risks), with $0 < \pi_l < \pi_h \leq 1$. The share of low-risk types is λ, with $0 < \lambda < 1$. The average probability of becoming ill is therefore given by $\bar{\pi} = \lambda\pi_l + (1 - \lambda)\pi_h$. If the individual remains healthy, her utility simply amounts to consumption C. If she becomes ill, her utility can be increased by medical expenditure M according to the function $v(M)$. Total utility when ill therefore is given by $C + v(M)$. We assume $v < 0$, $v' > 0$, $v'' < 0$, i.e., medical care cannot make up fully for the health loss and is characterized by decreasing marginal returns. Furthermore, $v'[0] > 1$, implying that initially, medical care is more important to the insured than consumption. Expected utility of an individual of type i is thus

$$EU_i(C,M) = C + \pi_i v(M).^6 \tag{7.5}$$

Uniform medical benefits are provided through health insurers. Initially, we allow the premium P_i to depend on the risk type i. With income Y, the budget constraint of an individual thus reads

$$Y = C + P_i, \quad i = h, l.$$

Substitution into equation (7.5) yields expected utility as a function of Y, P_i and M,

$$EU_i(Y, P_i, M) = Y - P_i + \pi_i v(M). \tag{7.6}$$

The health insurance market is assumed to be perfectly competitive. Since we abstract from administrative expenses incurred by insurers and normalize the price of medical benefits to one, insurers' costs equal benefits provided M. Furthermore, we suppose that each individual buys exactly one contract (P_i, M). We first analyze a scenario in which insurers charge risk-based premiums as a benchmark before turning to the market equilibrium with uniform premiums. An overview of the model is given in Box 7.1.

Equilibrium in an Unregulated Insurance Market

With insurers charging risk-based premiums, individuals are offered actuarially fair premiums in a competitive insurance market,

$$P_i = \pi_i M. \tag{7.7}$$

Substituting into equation (7.6) yields expected utility as a function of M. An individual of type i therefore faces the decision problem

$$\max_M \; EU_i(Y, M) = Y - \pi_i M + \pi_i v(M). \tag{7.8}$$

---

[6] Since utility is linear in consumption C, individuals are risk neutral and would therefore not be interested in being insured for risk protection. However, another important role of the health insurer is to organize the provision of health care, e.g., by negotiating payment systems with providers and by monitoring services provided. We focus on this determinant of the demand for health insurance in the following.

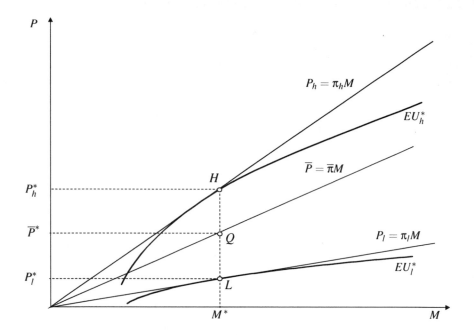

Fig. 7.1. Equilibrium in an Unregulated Insurance Market

Assuming that income Y is sufficiently high to guarantee positive consumption C in the optimum, the first-order condition is

$$\frac{dEU_i}{dM} = -\pi_i + \pi_i v'[M^*] = 0 \quad \Leftrightarrow \quad v'[M^*] = 1. \tag{7.9}$$

Note that the second-order condition is met since $v'' < 0$. Condition (7.9) implies that the optimal quantity M^* is independent of the risk type. Because of a constant marginal utility of consumption equal to one, it is optimal for both types to vary medical benefits until their marginal utility also equals one.

Figure 7.1 illustrates the market equilibrium with the optimal contracts (P_i^*, M^*). The straight lines $P_i = \pi_i M$ through the origin show the relationship between the quantity of benefits and the premium for each type. Due to $\pi_h > \pi_l$, the line for high risks has a steeper slope. The slopes of the indifference curves can be obtained by totally differentiating equation (7.6). This yields

$$\left.\frac{dP}{dM}\right|_{dEU_i=0} = \pi_i v'(M) > 0; \tag{7.10}$$

$$\left.\frac{d^2P}{dM^2}\right|_{dEU_i=0} = \pi_i v''(M) < 0. \tag{7.11}$$

Box 7.1. Risk Selection by the Quantity of Benefits

$$EU_i(Y, P_i, M) = Y - P_i + \pi_i v(M) \tag{7.6}$$

$$P_i = \pi_i M \tag{7.7}$$

$$\left.\frac{dP}{dM}\right|_{dEU_i=0} = \pi_i v'(M) > 0 \tag{7.10}$$

$$\left.\frac{d^2P}{dM^2}\right|_{dEU_i=0} = \pi_i v''(M) < 0 \tag{7.11}$$

$$\overline{P}^* = \overline{\pi} M^* \tag{7.12}$$

Y:	gross income
M:	medical benefits (at price equal to one)
M^*:	efficient quantity of medical benefits
π_i:	probability of being ill, $i = l, h$, $0 < \pi_l < \pi_h \leq 1$
$\overline{\pi}$:	average probability of being ill
$v(M)$:	utility increase due to medical benefits
EU_i:	expected utility
P_i:	insurance premium
$\overline{P}^*$:	average premium pertaining to M^*

The indifference curves are therefore positively sloped and strictly concave. They are steeper for high risks at each point: since their probability of being ill is higher, one unit of M leads to a larger increase in utility compared to low risks. Therefore, high risks remain indifferent with a larger premium increase in return for more M than do low risks. The optimal contracts are denoted by H and L, respectively. They call for $P_h^* > P_l^*$, i.e., high risks pay a higher premium for the same quantity of medical benefits than low risks.

The fact that high risks must pay a higher price for health insurance may be regarded as unjust, in particular if the difference in types is congenital. In this case, a scheme which redistributes between the types may be politically acceptable. We formulate two requirements for such a scheme.

(1) Both types should obtain the efficient quantity of medical benefits M^*.

(2) The cost of health insurance to consumers should not depend on the risk type.[7]

---

[7] This requirement can also be justified by a social welfare function with aversion to inequality in utilities. With a maximin social welfare function which depends on the utility of the worst-off, even over-compensating the high risks could be justified since we assume $v(M) < 0$.

These requirements imply that both risk types obtain contract Q in Figure 7.1 with benefits M^* and at a premium

$$\overline{P}^* = \overline{\pi}M^*. \tag{7.12}$$

In the following, we examine whether this solution can be implemented by imposing *community rating*, i.e., by prohibiting insurers from charging risk-based premiums. We also assume that insurance is compulsory and that insurers are required to accept any individual.[8]

Equilibrium in an Insurance Market with Community Rating

Community rating has similar consequences as asymmetric information about the risk type. In the first case, insurers cannot charge risk-based premiums because of regulation, while in the latter case they are unable to do so because they cannot identify the risk type. The analysis of community rating is therefore closely related to the model of an insurance market presented in Section 5.3.3. We use the same definition of a market equilibrium.

Definition 7.1. *An equilibrium in the health insurance market consists of a set of contracts with the following properties:*

(*i*)   *all individuals choose the contract which maximizes their expected utility;*

(*ii*)   *each contract results in nonnegative expected profits for insurers;*

(*iii*)   *no other contract outside the set of equilibrium contracts yields nonnegative expected profits.*

A *separating equilibrium* exists if the risk types choose different contracts. If all individuals buy the same contract, a *pooling equilibrium* arises.

We first examine whether community rating can lead to a pooling equilibrium. In this case, the equilibrium contract must lie on the pooling line $\overline{P}(M) = \overline{\pi}M$ in Figure 7.2. A possible candidate is contract D with (P_D, M_D). Since the indifference curves of high-risk types are steeper at that point, the indifference curve of low risks must cross the indifference curve of high risks from above in D. Any contract in the shaded area therefore has the following properties:

(1) it is preferred over contract D by low risks because it is below their indifference curve through D, which implies higher expected utility;

(2) it is rejected in favor of contract D by high risks because it lies above their indifference curve through D;

(3) it makes positive expected profits if chosen only by low risks because it lies above the line $P_l = \pi_l M$.

---

[8] An alternative solution is to introduce type-specific taxes and transfers. If low risks have to pay a tax $(\overline{\pi} - \pi_l)M^*$ while high risks receive a subsidy $(\pi_h - \overline{\pi})M^*$, then the optimal solution could be implemented. This solution, however, requires that the government can identify risk types.

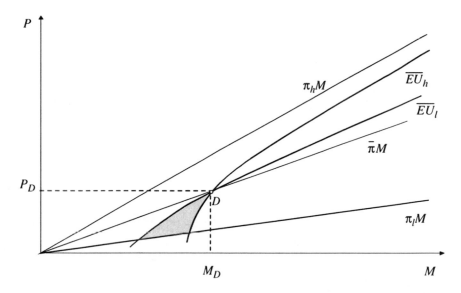

Fig. 7.2. Impossibility of a Pooling Equilibrium

Requirement (*iii*) for a market equilibrium is therefore violated. As a shaded area with the properties (1) through (3) exists for every possible pooling equilibrium, this type of equilibrium can therefore be excluded.

By contrast, a separating equilibrium may exist. In this type of equilibrium, the contracts offered for each type must yield zero expected profits. High risks receive the same contract *H* as when risk-based premiums are allowed (see Figure 7.3). A better contract for them, however, is not possible since insurers would make losses. Expected utility of high risks in a separating equilibrium is therefore given by

$$\overline{EU}_h = Y - \pi_h M^* + \pi_h v[M^*]. \tag{7.13}$$

The contract for low risks in a separating equilibrium cannot lie to the right of the indifference curve with expected utility $\overline{EU}_h$ lest it is chosen by high risks as well. Assuming that high risks opt for the contract with more benefits when indifferent, the contract *L′* in Figure 7.3 is the only candidate for a separating equilibrium. This contract will not be chosen by high risks while yielding the highest possible expected utility for low risks and satisfying the requirement that insurers make nonnegative expected profits.

Whether the contracts *H* and *L′* actually constitute a separating equilibrium depends on the share of low risks λ. Figure 7.3 shows two possible pooling lines. If λ is relatively large, then the pooling line $P(M) = \bar{\pi}M$ crosses the indifference curve of low risks corresponding to contract *L′*. Thus, a contract on the pooling line exists which makes both types better off while generating nonnegative expected profit.

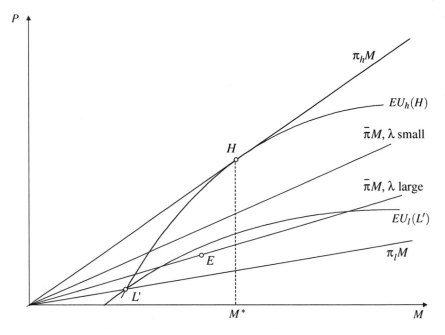

Fig. 7.3. Existence of a Separating Equilibrium

By requirement (*iii*) of Definition 7.1, contracts H and L' therefore cannot form an equilibrium. Since a pooling equilibrium is ruled out, no equilibrium exists in this case. If the share of low risks λ is small, however, no contract on the pooling line exists that would attract low risks. Hence, contracts H and L' constitute a separating equilibrium.

The problem of non-existence of equilibrium can be avoided by broadening the definition of equilibrium (see Section 5.3.3.5). In the following, we simply assume the share of low risks to be sufficiently small to guarantee a separating equilibrium. In that event, community rating, rather than inducing cross-subsidies between high and low risks, only makes low risks worse off. They obtain a lower amount of medical benefits while high risks obtain the same contract as with risk-based premiums. The intuition of this result is that contract L' allows insurers to practice risk selection by *reducing the quantity of benefits*. This deters high risks for whom benefits are more valuable than for low risks.

Conclusion 7.3. *In a model in which insurers offer one variable benefit with equilibrium described by Definition 7.1, community rating can only lead to a separating equilibrium. In such an equilibrium, no cross-subsidies between risk types occur. Low risks are selected by a lower quantity of benefits, causing them to be worse off than without regulation, while high-risk types obtain the same contract as in an unregulated insurance market.*

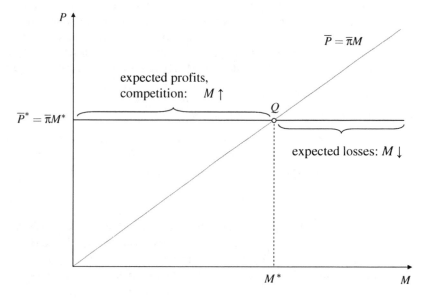

Fig. 7.4. Fixing the Premium

As community rating is not sufficient to induce insurers to offer contracts with benefits M^* at premium $\overline{P}^*$, additional measures need to be considered. Three proposals are of interest.

(1) *Enforcing the efficient benefit level.* The regulator can require each insurer to provide at least M^*. In an insurance market equilibrium, this quantity of medical benefits will be offered at premium $\overline{P}^* = \overline{\pi}M^*$. However, enforcing a given quantity of benefits is a difficult task. In particular, deviations from M^* must be verifiable.

(2) *Fixing the premium.* Community rating can be supplemented by fixing the premium at $\overline{P}^* = \overline{\pi}M^*$. This solution is illustrated in Figure 7.4. Since the premium now does not depend on actual benefits M, it is reflected as the horizontal straight line at level $\overline{P}^*$. It intersects the pooling line at point Q where $M = M^*$. Point Q is the equilibrium contract: to the right of Q, contracts would make losses on expectation because they are below the pooling line. Clearly, the level of benefits provided is too high; therefore, insurers will cut back. To the left of Q, insurers would make profits. But competition would force insurers to become more generous since consumers prefer more benefits given the premium $\overline{P}^* = \overline{\pi}M^*$. The equilibrium therefore is stable. By fixing the premium, the regulator therefore prevents insurers from attracting low risks by offering less benefits in return for lower premiums. In Section 7.2.2.2 below, however, we show that this result is not valid as soon as insurers offer several benefits.

(3) *Risk adjustment.* If the regulator observes risk types, then a risk adjustment scheme is simple. Insurers receive payment $(\pi_h - \overline{\pi})M^*$ for a high risk and pay $(\overline{\pi} - \pi_l)M^*$ for every low risk they enroll. The problem is that the observable characteristics are only imperfect indicators of risk types. This difficulty, examined by SELDEN (1998) and GLAZER AND MCGUIRE (2000), is analyzed in the following.

Risk adjustment with Imperfect Indicators of Risk Types

Assume that the regulator is able to observe a signal which is correlated with risk type. As in Section 7.2.1, the signal can take the values $s = 0, 1$ (e.g., gender or age). The probability q_i of a risk type $i = h, l$ transmitting the signal $s = 1$ is given by

$$0 \leq q_l < q_h \leq 1. \tag{7.14}$$

Hence a high risk is more likely to transmit the signal $s = 1$ than a low risk. We refer to the signal as perfect if $q_l = 0$ and $q_h = 1$. The risk adjustment scheme (RAS) consists of payments z_s^* from the regulator to the insurer which depend on the signal. To prevent risk selection, the RAS needs to be designed in such a way that an insurer who enrolls high risks only, offering them the efficient quantity of benefits M^*, is compensated for the cost difference $P_h^* - \overline{P}^*$, where $P_h^* = \pi_h M^*$ and $\overline{P}^* = \overline{\pi}M^*$. The payments z_0 and z_1 therefore have to satisfy

$$q_h z_1^* + (1 - q_h)z_0^* = P_h^* - \overline{P}^*. \tag{7.15}$$

Analogously, an insurer with low risks only should pay $\overline{P}^* - P_l^*$ into the RAS, where $P_l^* = \pi_l M^*$. This yields a second condition for payments z_0^* and z_1^*,

$$q_l z_1^* + (1 - q_l)z_0^* = -(\overline{P}^* - P_l^*). \tag{7.16}$$

If payments satisfy conditions (7.15) and (7.16), then in equilibrium an insurance contract with benefits M^* and premium $\overline{P}^*$ is written and chosen by all individuals. The contract yields expected profits of zero. There is also no other contract that is chosen by both risk types while yielding positive expected profits. This holds because the quantity of benefits M^* is efficient, and it is therefore not possible to increase the utility of both risk types given the constraint $\overline{P} = \overline{\pi}M$. Finally, we can rule out that there are profitable alternative contracts which are selected by one risk type only:

- For an insurer, a contract that is selected *only by high risks* would lead to a payment z_1^* with probability q_h and to a payment z_0^* with probability $(1 - q_h)$. For a high risk, M^* is the solution to the problem

$$\max_{M} EU_h(Y, M) = Y - P + \pi_h v(M)$$

$$\text{s.t.} \quad P = \pi_h M - [q_h z_1^* + (1 - q_h)z_0^*],$$

which implies that, at best, the contract would also offer benefits M^* at a premium $\overline{P}^*$. Consequently, there is no profitable alternative contract.

- Likewise, an alternative contract that is selected *only by low risks* leads to a payment z_1^* with probability q_l and to a payment z_0^* with probability $(1 - q_l)$ for the insurer. For a low risk, M^* is the solution to the problem

$$\max_M \; EU_l(Y,M) = Y - P + \pi_l v(M)$$

$$\text{s.t.} \quad P = \pi_l M - [q_l z_1^* + (1 - q_l) z_0^*].$$

Again, there is no profitable alternative contract.

We further examine the characteristics of the optimal RAS. This calls for solving equations (7.15) and (7.16) for z_0 and z_1. We obtain

$$z_0^* = \frac{q_h P_l^* - q_l P_h^*}{q_h - q_l} - \overline{P}^* \quad \text{and} \quad z_1^* = \frac{(1 - q_l)P_h^* - (1 - q_h)P_l^*}{q_h - q_l} - \overline{P}^*. \tag{7.17}$$

With perfect signals, $q_l = 0$ and $q_h = 1$, this reduces to

$$z_0^* = P_l^* - \overline{P}^* < 0 \quad \text{and} \quad z_1^* = P_h^* - \overline{P}^* > 0, \tag{7.18}$$

i.e., RAS payments are equal to the difference between expected expenditures according to observable risk type and average expenditure.

Of particular interest is the case of imperfect signals, i.e., $q_h < 1$ or $q_l > 0$. Differentiating z_0^* and z_1^* from equation (7.17) with respect to probabilities q_i yields

$$\frac{\partial z_0^*}{\partial q_h} = \frac{q_l(P_h^* - P_l^*)}{(q_h - q_l)^2} > 0, \tag{7.19}$$

$$\frac{\partial z_0^*}{\partial q_l} = \frac{q_h(P_l^* - P_h^*)}{(q_h - q_l)^2} < 0, \tag{7.20}$$

$$\frac{\partial z_1^*}{\partial q_h} = \frac{(1 - q_l)(P_l^* - P_h^*)}{(q_h - q_l)^2} < 0, \tag{7.21}$$

$$\frac{\partial z_1^*}{\partial q_l} = \frac{(1 - q_h)(P_h^* - P_l^*)}{(q_h - q_l)^2} > 0. \tag{7.22}$$

If the signal is imperfect, we therefore obtain

$$z_0^* < P_l^* - \overline{P}^* \quad \text{and} \quad z_1^* > P_h^* - \overline{P}^*, \tag{7.23}$$

i.e., the risk adjustment scheme compensates imperfect signals by spreading transfer payments. The intuition of this solution is that 'punishment' for risk selection, i.e., payment for individuals with the signal 0, has to be higher the lower the share of individuals with this signal. Analogously, the reward for abstaining from risk selection, i.e., payment for individuals with the signal 1, must be higher the lower the share of individuals with this signal, indicating a presumably high risk.

We summarize our results in

Conclusion 7.4. *In the case of a single benefit, risk selection can be prevented in two ways besides enforcing the efficient benefit level. First, the premium can be fixed at the average premium for an efficient benefit level. Second, a risk adjustment scheme based on observable characteristics of the risk type may be imposed. Payments based on these characteristics must be higher in absolute terms if these characteristics are only imperfect indicators of the risk type.*

Risk Adjustment Against Direct and Indirect Risk Selection Compared

In Section 7.2.1 we derived the optimal risk adjustment scheme designed to prevent direct risk selection. Here, the RAS is constructed to avoid indirect risk selection. It is of interest to compare the two cases in order to find out whether they give rise to a conflict of objectives. In the following, assume insurers to only be able to observe the signal s when performing direct risk selection. We start by specifying optimal RAS payments against direct risk selection and then compare them with the optimal RAS payments against indirect risk selection.

The RAS designed to prevent direct risk selection is based on average cost M_s of observable groups [see equation (7.1)]. Observed cost values depend on the shares of high and low risks with the respective signal. Let μ_s denote the share of high risks with signal s. Then, the average probability of being ill for individuals with this signal is given by $\mu_s \pi_h + (1 - \mu_s)\pi_l$. Given an efficient quantity of benefits, the observable cost for group s therefore is equal to

$$M_s = (\mu_s \pi_h + (1 - \mu_s)\pi_l)M^*, \quad s = 0, 1. \tag{7.24}$$

Using Bayes' theorem, we obtain

$$\mu_s = P(h|s) = \frac{P(s|h)P(h)}{P(s|h)P(h) + P(s|l)P(l)}. \tag{7.25}$$

According to the notation of the indirect risk selection model, $P(h) = 1 - \lambda$, $P(l) = \lambda$, $P(s = 1|h) = q_h$, $P(s = 1|l) = q_l$, $P(s = 0|h) = 1 - q_h$, and $P(s = 0|l) = 1 - q_l$. Consequently, we obtain

$$\mu_0 = \frac{(1 - q_h)(1 - \lambda)}{(1 - q_h)(1 - \lambda) + (1 - q_l)\lambda} \quad \text{and} \quad \mu_1 = \frac{q_h(1 - \lambda)}{q_h(1 - \lambda) + q_l\lambda}. \tag{7.26}$$

Perfect signals $q_l = 0$ and $q_h = 1$ imply $\mu_0 = 0$ and $\mu_1 = 1$ and therefore $M_0 = \pi_l M^*$ and $M_1 = \pi_h M^*$. If the signals are imperfect, however, then $\mu_0 > 0$ and $\mu_1 < 1$, which leads to $M_0 > \pi_l M^*$ and $M_1 < \pi_h M^*$. The assumption $q_h > q_l$ implies $M_1 > M_0$.

Box 7.2. Risk Adjustment with Imperfect Indicators for the Risk Type

$$z_0^* = \frac{q_h P_l^* - q_l P_h^*}{q_h - q_l} - \overline{P}^* \quad \text{and} \quad z_1^* = \frac{(1 - q_l) P_h^* - (1 - q_h) P_l^*}{q_h - q_l} - \overline{P}^* \tag{7.17}$$

$$M_s = (\mu_s \pi_h + (1 - \mu_s)\pi_l)M^*, \quad s = 0, 1 \tag{7.24}$$

$$\mu_0 = \frac{(1 - q_h)(1 - \lambda)}{(1 - q_h)(1 - \lambda) + (1 - q_l)\lambda} \quad \text{and} \quad \mu_1 = \frac{q_h(1 - \lambda)}{q_h(1 - \lambda) + q_l \lambda} \tag{7.26}$$

$$\hat{z}_s = M_s - \overline{M} = M_s - \overline{\pi} M^*, \quad s = 0, 1 \tag{7.27}$$

If the signals are perfect, i.e., $q_l = 0$ and $q_h = 1$, then

$$z_0^* = P_l^* - \overline{P}^* = \hat{z}_0 \quad \text{and} \quad z_1^* = P_h^* - \overline{P}^* = \hat{z}_1 \tag{7.29}$$

Otherwise

$$z_0^* < P_l^* - \overline{P}^* < \hat{z}_0 < 0 \quad \text{and} \quad z_1^* > P_h^* - \overline{P}^* > \hat{z}_1 > 0 \tag{7.30}$$

$s = 0, 1$:	signal, i.e., observable personal characteristic
P_i^*:	fair premium for risk type $i = l, h$ and $M = M^*$
$\overline{P}^*$:	average premium for $M = M^*$
M^*:	efficient quantity of medical benefits
z_s:	payments into the risk adjustment scheme
z_s^*:	payments which neutralize incentives for indirect risk selection
z_s^{DRS}:	payments which neutralize incentives for direct risk selection
q_i:	probability of risk type $i = h, l$ transmitting the signal $s = 1$
π_i:	probability of being ill
$\overline{\pi}$:	average probability of being ill
μ_s:	probability of a high risk having characteristic s
λ:	share of low-risk types

Now we are able to compare RAS payments designed to prevent direct ($\hat{z}_s$) and indirect risk selection (z_s^*). Equation (7.1) yields

$$\hat{z}_s = M_s - \overline{M} = M_s - \overline{\pi} M^*, \tag{7.27}$$

with $\overline{\pi} M^*$ denoting overall average cost when the quantity of benefits is efficient. If the signals are perfect, we have $M_0 = \pi_l M^*$ and $M_1 = \pi_h M^*$ and therefore

$$\hat{z}_0 = (\pi_l - \overline{\pi})M^* = P_l^* - \overline{P}^* \quad \text{and} \quad \hat{z}_1 = (\pi_h - \overline{\pi})M^* = P_h^* - \overline{P}^*. \tag{7.28}$$

RAS payments z_s^* needed to avoid indirect risk selection given perfect signals $q_l = 0$ and $q_h = 1$ are defined by equation (7.18). Thus,

$$z_0^* = P_l^* - \overline{P}^* = \hat{z}_0 \quad \text{and} \quad z_1^* = P_h^* - \overline{P}^* = \hat{z}_1. \tag{7.29}$$

Hence, payments against direct and indirect risk selection are identical, and the RAS can solve both problems simultaneously.

However, if the signals are imperfect, we have $M_0 > \pi_l M^*$ and $M_1 < \pi_h M^*$, and therefore

$$\hat{z}_0 > (\pi_l - \bar{\pi})M^* = P_l^* - \bar{P}^* \quad \text{and} \quad \hat{z}_1 < (\pi_h - \bar{\pi})M^* = P_h^* - \bar{P}^*.$$

Payments are lower in absolute terms compared to payments with perfect signals since the observable groups now include low as well as high risks.

Comparing these payments with those necessary to prevent indirect risk selection in equation (7.23), one finds

$$z_0^* < P_l^* - \bar{P}^* < \hat{z}_0 < 0 \quad \text{and} \quad z_1^* > P_h^* - \bar{P}^* > \hat{z}_1 > 0. \tag{7.30}$$

Thus with imperfect signals, direct and indirect risk selection require different RAS payments. Whereas indirect risk selection calls for spreading of payments, direct risk selection demands payments that are lower in absolute value than in the presence of perfect signals. This leads to a *trade-off between the prevention of direct and indirect risk selection* if insurers practice both. Only a second-best solution is possible which entails setting payments z_s between z_s^* and $\hat{z}_s$, reflecting the importance of the two types of risk selection. Note that the common practice of adjusting for cost differentials between observable groups is optimal only for the prevention of direct risk selection. If the RAS is intended to reduce indirect risk selection as well, payments have to be higher in absolute value.[9]

Conclusion 7.5. *RAS payments designed to prevent direct and indirect risk selection are identical only if risk types are observable. Given imperfect signals of risk types and insurers' capability of performing direct risk selection based on these signals, payments designed to prevent indirect risk selection are higher in absolute value than those designed to prevent direct risk selection. In this case, only a second-best solution is possible, and the two objectives have to be balanced against each other.*

7.2.2.2 Risk Selection Using the Structure of Benefits

So far, the case of a single benefit has been examined. In practice, insurers provide a range of benefits which differ in importance to risk types. For example, all individuals may face a similar probability of contracting an acute disease such as a flu but differ in their chance of becoming chronically ill. This opens up the possibility of risk selection using the structure of the benefit package. Specifically, the benefit

---

[9] GLAZER AND MCGUIRE (2000) focus exclusively on indirect risk selection and contrast 'optimal' risk adjustment payments z_s^* to 'conventional' risk adjustment with $\hat{z}_s$. If insurers also practice direct risk selection, however, payments z_s^* need not be optimal. Nevertheless, their criticism of the conventional approach remains valid as long as insurers practice indirect risk selection.

package can be expected to include extensive acute care benefits but few benefits for
the chronically ill.

We analyze risk selection by the structure of benefits using the model by GLAZER
AND MCGUIRE (2000), which extends the analysis of the previous section. Assume
two risk types who face an acute disease which can be cured using acute care benefits
M_a yielding utility $v_a(M_a)$, where $v_a < 0$, $v'_a > 0$, and $v''_a < 0$ as well as $v'_a[0] > 1$.
Both types have the same probability $0 < \rho \leq 1$ of demanding these benefits.[10] But
their probability of contracting a chronic disease is π_i, $i = l, h$, $0 < \pi_l < \pi_h \leq 1$. In
this event, medical benefits M_c yield utility $v_c(M_c)$, with $v_c < 0$, $v'_c > 0$, $v''_c < 0$, and
$v'_c[0] > 1$. Expected utility of an individual of type i is given by

$$EU_i(C, M_a, M_c) = C + \rho v_a(M_a) + \pi_i v_c(M_c). \tag{7.31}$$

With premium P_i for health insurance and income Y, the budget constraint is given
by $Y = C + P_i$. Substituting into (7.31), we can write expected utility of an individual
as

$$EU_i(Y, P_i, M_a, M_c) = Y - P_i + \rho v_a(M_a) + \pi_i v_c(M_c). \tag{7.32}$$

Again we assume perfect competition in the health insurance market and abstract
from additional expenses incurred by insurers. Each individual buys exactly one contract. Before turning to the issue of market equilibrium with community rating, we
analyze the benchmark case in which insurers are allowed to charge risk-based premiums.

Equilibrium in an Unregulated Insurance Market

The actuarially fair premium is given by

$$P_i = \rho M_a + \pi_i M_c. \tag{7.33}$$

Inserting this into (7.32), we obtain expected utility of an individual as a function of
M_a and M_c. A person of type i then solves the following problem,

$$\max_{M_a, M_c} EU_i(Y, M_a, M_c) = Y - \rho M_a - \pi_i M_c + \rho v_a(M_a) + \pi_i v_c(M_c). \tag{7.34}$$

Assuming that the income of the person is sufficiently high to ensure an interior
solution, the first-order conditions are

$$\frac{\partial EU_i}{\partial M_a} = -\rho + \rho v'_a[M^*_a] \Rightarrow v'_a[M^*_a] = 1 \tag{7.35}$$

$$\frac{\partial EU_i}{\partial M_c} = -\pi_i + \pi_i v'_c[M^*_c] \Rightarrow v'_c[M^*_c] = 1. \tag{7.36}$$

The efficient quantities M^*_a and M^*_c are independent of the risk type. Furthermore,
the second-order condition is met because $v''_a < 0$ and $v''_c < 0$.

---

[10] GLAZER AND MCGUIRE (2000) assume $\rho = 1$.

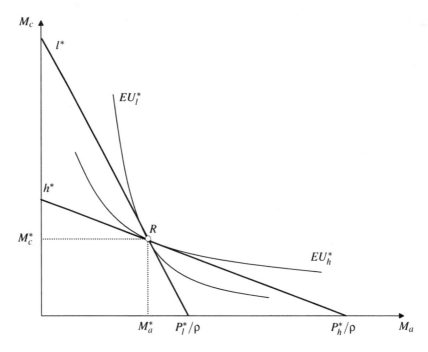

Fig. 7.5. Equilibrium in an Unregulated Market

Figure 7.5 illustrates the optimal contracts for both risk types. Along the lines labeled l^* and h^*, M_a and M_c vary in a way as to exhaust the premium on expected value, which in turn is set in a way such that it suffices to finance optimal benefits M_a^* and M_c^* on expectation, i.e.,

$$\rho M_a + \pi_i M_c = P_i^* \equiv \rho M_a^* + \pi_i M_c^* \quad \Leftrightarrow \quad M_c = \frac{P_i^*}{\pi_i} - \frac{\rho}{\pi_i} M_a. \tag{7.37}$$

Accordingly, the slopes of the respective budget lines i^* are given by $dM_c/dM_a = -\rho/\pi_i$. For $M_c = 0$, we obtain $M_a = P_i^*/\rho$.

From equation (7.32), we can derive the slopes of the indifference curves

$$\left. \frac{dM_c}{dM_a} \right|_{dEU_i=0} = -\frac{\rho v_a'(M_a)}{\pi_i v_c'(M_c)} < 0 \tag{7.38}$$

and their curvature, noting that (7.38) makes M_c a function of M_a,

$$\left. \frac{d^2 M_c}{dM_a^2} \right|_{dEU_i=0} = -\frac{\rho}{\pi_i} \frac{v_a''(M_a)v_c'(M_c) - v_a'(M_a)v_c''(M_c) \left. \frac{dM_c}{dM_a} \right|_{dEU_i=0}}{[v_c'(M_c)]^2} < 0. \tag{7.39}$$

The indifference curves are therefore falling and strictly convex from the origin. Furthermore, equation (7.38) implies that their slope is higher in absolute value for low risks at given quantities of benefits M_a and M_c.

Box 7.3. Risk Selection Using the Structure of Benefits

$$EU_i(Y, P_i, M_a, M_c) = Y - P_i + \rho v_a(M_a) + \pi_i v_c(M_c) \tag{7.32}$$

$$P_i = \rho M_a + \pi_i M_c \tag{7.33}$$

$$\left.\frac{dM_c}{dM_a}\right|_{dEU_i=0} = -\frac{\rho v_a'(M_a)}{\pi_i v_c'(M_c)} < 0 \tag{7.38}$$

$$\left.\frac{d^2 M_c}{dM_a^2}\right|_{dEU_i=0} = -\frac{\rho}{\pi_i} \frac{v_a''(M_a)v_c'(M_c) - v_a'(M_a)v_c''(M_c)\left.\frac{dM_c}{dM_a}\right|_{dEU_i=0}}{[v_c'(M_c)]^2} > 0 \tag{7.39}$$

$$\overline{P}^* = \rho M_a^* + \overline{\pi} M_c^* \tag{7.40}$$

Y:	gross income
M_a:	medical benefits for acute diseases
M_c:	medical benefits for chronic diseases
M_j^*:	efficient quantity of medical benefits $j = a, c$
ρ:	probability of being acutely ill
π_i:	probability of being chronically ill, $i = l, h$, $0 < \pi_l < \pi_h \leq 1$
$\overline{p}$:	average probability of being ill
$v_a(M_a)$:	utility due to medical benefits for acute diseases
$v_c(M_c)$:	utility due to medical benefits for chronic diseases
EU_i:	expected utility
P_l:	insurance premium
$\overline{P}^*$	average premium sufficient to finance M_a^*, M_c^*

At the optimum, the indifference curve of a high risk is tangent to the budget line h^*. The same result applies to low risks with respect to the budget line l^*. For both risk types, the optimal solution is therefore given by point R where l^* and h^* intersect. Note, however, that equation (7.33) implies

$$P_h^* = \rho M_a^* + \pi_h M_c^* > P_l^* = \rho M_a^* + \pi_l M_c^*,$$

i.e., high-risk types pay a higher premium.

Equilibrium in an Insurance Market with Community Rating

Again we examine whether community rating can induce cross-subsidies between high and low risks in such a way that both risks are offered efficient benefit levels M_a^* and M_c^* while paying the average premium

$$\overline{P}^* = \rho M_a^* + \overline{\pi} M_c^*. \tag{7.40}$$

To rule out risk selection by the level of benefits, we assume that the premium is fixed at the average level for an efficient benefit level $\overline{P}^*$. In the model with one benefit only, this measure was sufficient to prevent risk selection. From the zero expected profit condition for each risk type $i = h, l$, we obtain the following relationship between M_c and M_a,

$$\overline{P}^* = \rho M_a + \pi_i M_c \Leftrightarrow M_c = \frac{\overline{P}^*}{\pi_i} - \frac{\rho}{\pi_i} M_a. \tag{7.41}$$

The lines l' and h' in Figure 7.6 show this function for each risk type. They run parallel to the zero-profit lines l^* and h^* implied by premiums P_i^* that obtain in an unregulated insurance market [see equation (7.37)]. The zero-profit line l' for low risks is located to the right of line l^* due to $\overline{P}^* > P_l^*$. Likewise, $\overline{P}^* < P_h^*$ implies that the zero-profit line h' for high risks runs to the left of line h^*. As can be seen from equation (7.41), l' and h' intersect at $M_c = 0$ because they share the same value for $M_a (= \overline{P}^*/\rho)$.

Similar to the model with one benefit, only a separating equilibrium can exist. Again, it is necessary that the share of low risks be sufficiently small. In the following, we assume that this condition is met to examine the properties of the separating equilibrium. High risks obtain the optimal contract under the constraint (7.41) for their risk type. In Figure 7.6 this contract is denoted by A. At this point, the indifference curves of high risks are tangent to the zero-profit line h'. Point B characterizes the contract for low risks. It yields zero expected profits and is not chosen by high risks. Thus, the separating equilibrium is characterized by contracts A and B.

In the separating equilibrium, no cross-subsidies between risk types occur. Contract B is used to risk select low risks using the structure of benefits. As Figure 7.6 shows, $M_a^l > M_a^*$ and $M_c^l < M_c^*$, i.e., low risks receive more acute medical care and less benefits for chronic illness, making the contract unattractive for high risks. Compared to an unregulated insurance market, both risk types are worse off: high risks obtain suboptimal insurance coverage $M_j^h < M_j^*$, $j = a, c$. They would prefer to spend more on health insurance. Low risks are worse off as well because they pay more for health insurance than they desire and because their benefit structure is distorted.

We therefore find that it is not sufficient to fix the premium if the insurance policy contains several benefits. To the contrary, this measure is counterproductive as it does not induce any cross-subsidies. Without fixing the premium, one could at least ensure that high risks obtain their preferred benefit package M_j^*, $j = a, c$ at price P_h^*.[11]

---

[11] In this case, insurers would always offer contracts with the efficient quantity M_a^*. However, the benefits for chronic illnesses would still be used for risk selection. As in the model with one benefit, low risks have to settle for a contract with $M_c^l < M_c^*$ in a separating equilibrium, whereas high risks obtain a contract with the efficient quantity M_c^* [see GLAZER AND MCGUIRE (2000, p. 1069)]. Thus, high risks end up with the same contract as with risk-based premiums. As in the model with one benefit, community rating would only make low risks worse off.

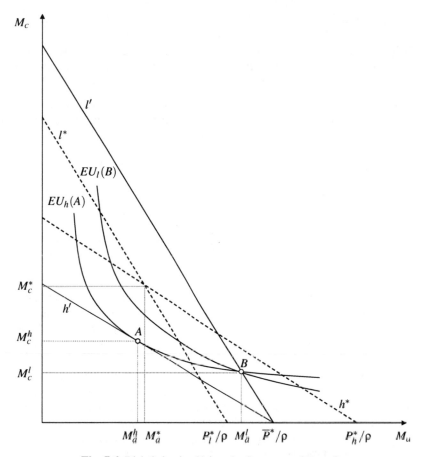

Fig. 7.6. Risk Selection Using the Structure of Benefits

Conclusion 7.6. *If health insurers offer two benefits, where the first is demanded by both risk types with the same probability but the second with different probabilities, then it is not possible to avoid risk selection by fixing the premium. Insurers use the structure of benefits to perform risk selection.*

Three ways remain to induce cross-subsidies between high and low risks in such a way that both obtain the efficient amount of benefits.

(1) *Regulation of the benefit package.* If the regulator is able to enforce the quantities M_a^* and M_c^*, indirect risk selection can be prevented. However, this is a very demanding task. In particular, insurers could try to camouflage acute medical care of interest to low risks by claiming it to benefit the chronically ill.

(2) *Institutional separation of benefits.* A *carveout*, i.e., the provision of benefits for the chronically ill by a separate institution, can avoid risk selection using the benefit structure. The regulator simply has to fix the premium for chronic benefits

as in the model with a single benefit. Insurers would then supply the efficient quantity M_c^* at the premium $\bar{\pi}M_c^*$. Should there be economies of scope in the design of health insurance, however, this solution causes inefficiency. Moreover, it burdens any substitution of the two types of medical services in the delivery of health care with transaction costs.

(3) *Risk adjustment.* As in the previous section, a RAS can induce insurers to offer an insurance contract with an efficient benefit package at a uniform price $\bar{P}^*$. The variables $\bar{P}^*$ and P_i^* merely need to be redefined as

$$\bar{P}^* = \rho M_a^* + \bar{\pi}M_c^* \quad \text{and} \quad P_i^* = \rho M_a^* + \pi_i M_c^*. \tag{7.42}$$

As above, the RAS payments z_0 and z_1 are the solution to the equations (7.15) and (7.16) repeated here for convenience,

$$q_h z_1 + (1 - q_h)z_0 = P_h^* - \bar{P}^* \tag{7.15}$$

$$q_l z_1 + (1 - q_l)z_0 = -(\bar{P}^* - P_l^*), \tag{7.16}$$

where q_i is the probability that a risk type $i = h, l$ sends the signal $s = 1$. In equilibrium, a contract with benefits M_a^* and M_c^* is offered at the premium $\bar{P}^*$, the line of argument being the same as in the case with only one benefit. However, this also means that these payments fail to get rid of any direct risk selection.

Conclusion 7.7. *If it is not possible to regulate benefits directly, risk selection using the structure of benefits can be prevented in two different ways. On the one hand, the benefit which is more likely to be demanded by high-risk types can be assigned to a carveout. On the other hand, a risk adjustment scheme can succeed to neutralize insurers' incentives to perform indirect (but not direct) risk selection.*

The model presented in this section considers only two benefits, a strong simplification. FRANK ET AL. (2000) and GLAZER AND MCGUIRE (2002) extend the analysis to derive a RAS that prevents indirect risk selection in the case of several benefits.

7.3 Further Arguments in Favor of Risk Adjustment and Cost Reimbursement

Two more arguments for risk adjustment and cost reimbursement have been advanced. First, these schemes may be useful in establishing fair competition in the insurance market if insurers have inherited widely differing populations with respect to health risks at the time before competition is introduced. Secondly, they can prevent market entry by insurers who merely seek to exploit the higher switching propensity of lower risks.

7.3.1 Fair Competition in the Health Insurance Market

For historic reasons, insurers may differ in terms of their risk structure. Without a system of transfers in place, insurers with a particularly high share of favorable risks have a better starting position when pro-competitive reform permits them to compete for consumers. This is problematic for fairness as well as for efficiency reasons, since those insurers enrolling the high risks in the absence of competition may not be the least efficient ones that should be driven out of the market. In Germany and Switzerland, this was a central motivation to implement a RAS well before the introduction of competition among sickness funds. Initially, the most expensive German insurers charged a contribution rate twice the rate of the least expensive funds, mainly because of differences in risk structures.[12]

7.3.2 Stabilization of the Health Insurance Market

An additional rationale for risk adjustment and cost reimbursement exists if low risks are more likely to switch insurers than high risks. Insurers who enter the market can therefore expect to insure mainly low risks, causing the health insurance market to be characterized by a high amount of *churning*, i.e., by individuals changing insurers frequently. Since established insurers will be stuck with high-risk types, they will eventually have to increase premiums or file for bankruptcy. Such a scenario is a reason for concern since insurers have little incentive to invest in an efficient provision of benefits under these circumstances.

For the German health insurance market, LAUTERBACH AND WILLE (2000) find evidence for higher mobility of low risks. They compare health care expenditure (HCE) of those who switch insurers and those who stay. Depending on the age category, individuals who switch cause on average 45 to 85 percent lower HCE than comparable individuals who do not switch. Especially among adults, the difference is striking. A study by NUSCHELER AND KNAUS (2005) based on the German socio-economic panel (SOEP) arrives at a similar conclusion showing that individuals who remain loyal to their insurer have a significantly worse state of health than those who switch. For the United States, there is the famous case study be CUTLER AND REBER (1998), who analyzed the effect of Harvard University's decisions to make employers contribute more to premiums unless they chose the least costly alternative (a HMO plan). Within one year; the risk types began to separate. Those who left the most expensive plans for a HMO were 46 years old and had HCE of 9 percent above the general average, those who stayed, 50 years old and had HCE 16 percent above the general average. Indeed, the exodus of the low risks from the most comprehensive plan was so fast that it had to be discontinued.

---

[12] In addition, the fact that in Germany contributions are proportional to wage income put insurers with high-income members at an advantage. For this reason, the German RAS also compensates for income differences.

We summarize the additional arguments in favor of risk adjustment and cost reimbursement in

Conclusion 7.8. *Risk adjustment and cost reimbursement can also help to secure a level playing field during the transition to a competitive market and to stabilize the health insurance market. Otherwise the most efficient insurer may not prevail in the market.*

7.4 Designing Risk Adjustment Schemes

7.4.1 An Overview of Risk Adjusters

A RAS is based on risk adjusters, i.e., observable characteristics of individuals. A starting point for the search for risk adjusters is to examine empirically their ability to predict HCE. The following variables have proven to be useful.

(1) *Socio-demographic variables.* The most commonly used demographic variables are age and gender. However, their explanatory power is relatively small [see, e.g., NEWHOUSE ET AL. (1989) and VAN DE VEN AND VAN VLIET (1992)]. Other socio-demographic variables are marital, retirement, and disability status, educational level, and income. Using data from German sickness funds, BREYER ET AL. (2003) and BEHREND ET AL. (2004) find that old-age and disability pensioners have significantly higher HCE. BREYER ET AL. (2003) furthermore report that single retirees and individuals with low income show higher HCE.

(2) *Health care expenditure in previous periods.* An obvious indicator for morbidity is HCE in the past. Studies by NEWHOUSE ET AL. (1989), VAN DE VEN AND VAN VLIET (1992) and ASH ET AL. (1998) show that an increase of HCE by one monetary unit leads to an increase of expenditure in the following period by 0.2 to 0.3 units. The associated gain in explanatory power has to be weighed, however, against a weakening of incentives for keeping down costs, since higher HCE incurred now will be reimbursed to some extent later. Nevertheless, this can be a sensible approach because it emulates the way insurers try to screen favorable risks [LEHMANN AND ZWEIFEL (2004)]; in addition, better adjusters may not be available [see MARCHAND ET AL. (2003)]. A related indicator which predicts HCE is the previous *use of prescription drugs* [see, e.g., CLARK ET AL. (1995)].

(3) *Diagnostic information.* Morbidity can be measured by collecting or using available diagnostic information to identify chronically ill and to categorize individuals according to their expected HCE.[13] Empirical studies [see GREENWALD

---

[13] See VAN DE VEN AND ELLIS (2000, p. 798) for an overview of various methods to categorize diagnostic information.

ET AL. (1998), LAMERS (1999)] demonstrate that diagnostic information contributes to forecasting HCE. However, its collection can be costly. As insurers have an interest in profitable diagnoses for their members, they are also tempted to manipulate this information, a phenomenon called 'upcoding'. They might even encourage their members to consult physicians frequently in order to gather as many diagnoses as possible. An argument in favor of diagnostic information is that it is a strong predictor of HCE. Moreover, many countries and health care systems use diagnostic information to determine provider reimbursement, making the required information readily available (see Section 10.4.3.3 on DRG-based payment).

(4) *Self-reported health status.* Empirical studies show that self-reported health status (obtained from interviews) significantly contributes to the prediction of HCE [see, e.g., NEWHOUSE ET AL. (1989) and VAN DE VEN AND VAN VLIET (1992)]. An obvious disadvantage of this method is the considerable effort required to collect the data. Another problem is the possibility of manipulation, in particular if the interviews can be influenced by insurers.

(5) *Mortality.* A substantial amount of HCE occurs during the last two years of a person's life. Empirical studies show that the fact that a person has died is associated with a significant surge in HCE [see, e.g., VAN VLIET AND LAMERS (1998) and BECK AND ZWEIFEL (1998)]. A lump-sum payment for death-related expenses might therefore be useful to prevent risk selection hurting the deathbound.

(6) *Switching behavior.* As mentioned above, the propensity to switch insurers likely depends on the risk type of an individual with supporting evidence from LAUTERBACH AND WILLE (2000) and NUSCHELER AND KNAUS (2005) for Germany and CUTLER AND REBER (1998) and STROMBOM ET AL. (2002) for the United States.

(7) *Regional differences.* Another significant explanation for differences in HCE is the place of residence [see, e.g., VAN DE VEN ET AL. (2000)]. One reason are differences in the price of medical care [VAN DE VEN AND ELLIS (2000)], another, differences in morbidity and the density of health care providers. In the latter case, it is questionable that a RAS should use the place of residence as a risk adjuster, as this may serve to reinforce undesired regional discrepancies in the access to health care.

An important question is the part of total variance of HCE that can be attributed to the various explanatory variables. Indeed, the predictable fraction of the total variance can be divided into the *between-person variance*, which is due to differences between individuals (e.g., gender), and the *within-person variance* which emerges from fluctuations of HCE of one and the same person over time. Volatility of HCE may well increase with age, reflecting loss of control over one's health status. Empirical studies suggest that the first component (between-person variance) is the dominant one, constituting about 15 to 20 percent of the total [see, e.g., NEWHOUSE ET AL. (1989) and VAN VLIET (1992a)]. Another 4 to 5 percent of variance can be traced to the predictable part of within-person variance. Hence at most between 20 and 25 percent of total variance in HCE is predictable [see NEWHOUSE (1996, p. 1256)], the remainder being due to random fluctuations.

A general result of empirical studies is that socio-demographic variables explain only a small fraction of the variance in HCE. Estimates range from 1 to 5 percent [see, e.g., NEWHOUSE ET AL. (1989), VAN DE VEN AND VAN VLIET (1992), VAN BARNEVELD ET AL. (1998), GREENWALD ET AL. (1998)]. Including HCE lagged one year serves to increase the explained part of the variance (measured by the determination coefficient R^2) considerably. For example, NEWHOUSE ET AL. (1989) report increases from 1.6 to 6.4 percentage points, VAN DE VEN AND VAN VLIET (1992) from 2.4 to 7.2 percentage points. Adding self-reported health yields similar increases over a purely socio-demographic specification, e.g., 1.2 percentage points in NEWHOUSE ET AL. (1989) and up to 3.4 points in VAN DE VEN AND VAN VLIET (1992). Finally, diagnostic information is very effective in explaining HCE. A study by GREENWALD ET AL. (1998) finds that R^2 rises by more than 7 percentage points, i.e., from 1.0 up to 8.6 percent, compared to the socio-demographic model.

Conclusion 7.9. *Due to stochastic fluctuations over time, only between 20 and 25 percent of the total variance of HCE can be predicted. Demographic variables such as age and gender have little explanatory value. Lagged HCE, self-reported health, and diagnostic information increase explanatory power considerably. However, using lagged HCE as a risk adjuster reduces incentives to provide health benefits efficiently since higher HCE will be reimbursed to some extent later. In the case of diagnostic information, collecting the data can be costly and open to manipulation.*

7.4.2 Costs and Payment Flows

Once the set of risk adjusters is selected, it has to be decided how RAS payments are to be determined. A first problem concerns the cost concept to be used. The *actual cost approach* relies on actual HCE, whereas the *normative cost approach* uses HCE values as deemed adequate for different groups of persons. The normative cost approach is superior from a conceptual point of view. For practical reasons, however, RAS payments usually are based on actual cost. This approach is problematic since existing over- or undersupply may be reinforced.

Second, it needs to be decided whether RAS payments should be calculated *prospectively*, i.e., at the beginning of the period and based on predicted HCE, or *retrospectively*, i.e., at the end of the period and based on actual HCE incurred. A first rationale for a prospective calculation is that it shifts cost responsibility to health insurers, thus preserving incentives for cost containment. Another is the consideration that insurers who perform risk selection must use information that is available at the beginning of the period [see VAN DE VEN AND ELLIS (2000, p. 786)]. However, a possible advantage of the retrospective method is that it introduces a reinsurance element into the RAS. For example, HCE for a certain group of insured may turn out to be higher than expected because of a medical innovation. Under the retrospective method, insurers with a relatively large share of this group receive higher payments from the scheme and are therefore insured against this event to some extent. Once more, the downside is that incentives for cost efficiency may be weakened if RAS payments for an insurer depend in a non-negligible way on this insurer's costs. Specifically, this can happen under the cell-based approach discussed below.

A further issue concerns payment flows between individuals, insurers and the central agency in charge of the RAS. To address this question, let us first summarize the characteristics of a person i in a vector e_i to the extent that they are relevant for the RAS. For example, if age and gender are used as adjusters, a forty-year-old woman would be described by the vector $(40, F)$. The RAS formula defines a payment z_i for each person i as a function of e_i,

$$z_i = z(e_i). \tag{7.43}$$

RAS payments need to satisfy a budget constraint

$$\sum_i z(e_i) = B, \tag{7.44}$$

with B depending on the design of the RAS. If individuals pay their insurance contribution directly to insurers, the sum of all transfer payments must be zero, implying $B = 0$. Alternatively, all or a share of contributions can initially be paid to a central fund, which allocates them to insurers according to their risk structure. The budget B of this fund is positive in this case, amounting to the sum of contributions to the central fund, possibly augmented by a tax-financed subsidy. Such a system is in place in Germany and the Netherlands. For a RAS, the differences between payments for individuals with different characteristics matter. As long as all payments z_i are increased by the average contribution from the central fund, these remain the same.

Conclusion 7.10. *A risk adjustment scheme (RAS) can be based on actual or normative HCE and can be calculated prospectively or retrospectively. A RAS is compatible both with a pure transfer scheme between insurers and a system where a central fund distributes contributions to insurers.*

Note that direct payments from individuals to health insurers will be lower if a central fund has its own budget. This can have an effect on individual choice of health insurer. Consider an insurer whose costs are 10 percent below average of all insurers. If individuals pay their contribution directly to insurers, it can therefore charge a premium 10 percent below average as well. If a central fund finances one-half of HCE, however, the premium can be decreased by 20 percent, possibly resulting in a stronger demand increase.

7.4.3 Calculating Risk Adjustment Payments

Last but not least, the relationship between RAS payments and the retained risk adjusters needs to be defined. Here, two approaches can be distinguished. The *statistical approach* is based on a regression model to predict HCE and builds directly on the research presented in Section 7.4.1. It is widely used in practice and has been termed 'conventional risk adjustment' by GLAZER AND MCGUIRE (2000). The *incentive approach*, by contrast, regards risk adjustment as a method to induce providers to act according to the regulator's objectives. GLAZER AND MCGUIRE (2000) refer to this approach as 'optimal risk adjustment'.

7.4.3.1 The Statistical Approach to Risk Adjustment

Under this approach, RAS payments are based on predicted HCE conditional on the values of regressors – independent of whether they are continuous or discrete. In this way, a large number of risk adjusters can be taken into account. This is an important consideration if diagnostic information is to be part of the RAS formula. The price one pays is that a functional form must be assumed. The simplest and most frequently used model is linear and employs least-squares estimation. Non-linear models have been developed by DUAN (1983) and MANNING ET AL. (1987).[14]

A special case of the statistical approach is the *cell approach* (also referred to as *matrix approach*). Groups are formed for each risk adjuster, for age, e.g., the 0 to 10 years old, 11 to 20 years old, etc. The RAS cells are defined by combining the levels of the different risk adjusters. Each individual is associated exactly with one cell. The number of cells is given by the product of the number of groups for each risk adjuster. For example, 10 age groups, 2 gender groups, and 5 income groups give rise to $10 \times 2 \times 5 = 100$ RAS cells. RAS payments are determined by average HCE in the respective cell. The cell approach is equivalent to the prediction of a least-squares regression model if dummy variables for each group (except for a reference group for each risk adjuster) are used as regressors (including interaction terms). The estimated coefficients allow to calculate average HCE of each cell.

The major advantage of the cell approach is its simplicity. The number of cells, however, increases rapidly with the number of risk adjusters and levels per risk adjuster, causing the number of observations per cell to become small and hence imparting large standard errors to cell-specific HCE. In the limit, RAS payment degenerates into cost reimbursement if RAS payments are calculated retrospectively.

---

[14] See JONES (2000, Section 4) for a detailed discussion. These models explicitly consider that HCE cannot be negative. Since retransformation involves the standard error of the regression, heteroskedasticity, i.e., a nonconstant error, may severely bias retransformed estimates [see MANNING (1998) and MULLAHY (1998)].

Indeed, in a cell containing only one individual, average and actual HCE coincide. As a consequence, the insurer is fully compensated for all HCE of this person.[15]

When judging the merits of a RAS formula, the objectives of such a scheme should be kept in mind. In particular, a RAS should reduce incentives for risk selection. To avoid direct risk selection, the RAS formula should ideally replicate the model that insurers use to predict HCE. For example, if insurers classify individuals into four groups depending on gender and age above and below 30 years, then the cell approach can perfectly neutralize incentives for direct risk selection. However, if they use a regression model with age defined continuously, the cell approach will fail to fully eliminate incentives for risk selection. Conversely, if the RAS administrator bases payments on the regression model yielding the highest value of R^2, he may miss the objective of the scheme because a major insurer happens to prefer another regression model (for its own insured population) or rely on a cell approach.

A further consideration are variables that can be manipulated by insurers and can therefore not be used as risk adjusters. For instance, insurers may encourage physicians to mark multiple diagnostic codes if multimorbidity triggers a special RAS payment. In addition, it may be argued that life-style variables such as drinking or smoking behavior should not be included in the formula because insurers would lose interest in fostering prevention among their members.[16]

7.4.3.2 The Incentive Approach to Risk Adjustment

The incentive approach is based on the idea that risk adjustment should motivate insurers to behave in the regulator's interest. The starting point is an analysis of the problems risk adjustment is intended to solve. In particular, these are the objectives discussed above, viz. avoiding direct and indirect selection, ensuring fair competition and stabilizing the insurance market. Such an analysis also considers to what extent other forms of regulation are available. For example, open enrollment may be sufficient to rule out direct risk selection.

A next step involves setting up a model of insurer behavior and competition. Together with the available data, a RAS can then be designed which changes insurers' constraints to govern their behavior. In general, such a RAS differs from a RAS determined by a regression model. For instance, we showed in Section 7.2.2 that RAS payments based on observable characteristics must be higher in absolute terms if these characteristics are only imperfect indicators of the risk type (see Conclusion 7.4). A linear regression, by contrast, would yield optimal payments only if perfect indicators were available.

---

[15] A prospective RAS can lead to a similar result unless the individual is assigned to a new cell in the following period. In this case, current HCE is simply reimbursed in the following period.

[16] To the extent that such variables are determinants of HCE and correlated with variables in the regression (a likely event since, e.g., women are less likely to smoke), estimates suffer from omitted variables bias [see SCHOKKAERT AND VAN DE VOORDE (2004)].

From a conceptual point of view, the incentive approach is superior to the statistical approach. But it requires a model which adequately captures insurer behavior. FRANK ET AL. (2000) and GLAZER AND MCGUIRE (2002) have developed a model in which insurers practice indirect risk selection by rationing at the service level. An alternative approach has been explored by JACK (2006), who assumes that insurers are able to ration services by individual type. SHEN AND ELLIS (2002) focus on direct risk selection in the form of explicit dumping of individuals who are expected to be unprofitable. Based on their analysis of insurer behavior, these models characterize optimal risk adjustment which differs considerable from a scheme based on a regression. The incentive approach to risk adjustment can yield considerable welfare gains. SHEN AND ELLIS (2002) find that their optimal scheme can reduce the regulator's cost by up to 25.6 percent compared to regression-based risk adjustment.

The incentive approach to risk adjustment is still under development. It is therefore not surprising that the statistical approach to risk adjustment remains dominant, the trend being the incorporation of diagnostic data. However, collecting and monitoring this data comes at considerable cost. Incentive-based risk adjustment, by contrast, promises to use available data more efficiently in advancing the regulator's objectives.

Conclusion 7.11. *The statistical approach to risk adjustment is based on regression models to predict health care expenditure whereas the incentive approach regards risk adjustment as a method to induce insurers to act according to the regulator's objectives. The incentive approach is superior on conceptual grounds but requires carefully specified models of insurer behavior. In general, the two approaches differ in their recommendations.*

7.5 Designing Cost Reimbursement Schemes

Cost reimbursement can in principle advance all objectives discussed above. This can be seen by considering a cost reimbursement scheme (CRS) that reimburses all costs. Then no incentives for risk selection remain and fairness of competition as well as stability of the health insurance market is ensured. However, no incentives remain to provide services cost-effectively. Hence, competition among insurers will have no positive effects on HCE.[17] Furthermore, a CRS serves to relieve insurers from risk, which is of value to them to the extent that they exhibit risk aversion (caused, e.g., by regulation placing a high priority on maintaining solvency).

In general, cost reimbursement schemes need to strike a balance between the possible benefits and incentives for cost efficiency. Apart from the extent of cost

---

[17] If excessive cost responsibility reduces the quality of medical care, then less incentives for containing costs can be desirable. In Section 10.3.1, this result is established for the reimbursement of health care providers if these have a self-interest in higher quality. Whether such concerns also apply to insurers is an open question.

reimbursement, the types of cost reimbursed are of key importance. Furthermore, the share of costs to be reimbursed must be specified, e.g., only costs exceeding a threshold. The possible options are discussed in the following.

7.5.1 The Basis of Cost Reimbursement

Depending on the quality of cost data, a CRS can be based on three possible definitions of costs.

(1) *Total cost of an insurer.* In this case the total amount of costs is the basis for the CRS. If, by contrast, all costs above a threshold are reimbursed, the scheme can be called *stop-loss cost sharing*.

(2) *Individual HCE.* This variant requires that costs can be assigned to individuals. For instance, the share of the HCE above a certain threshold can be covered by the CRS. It is also possible to reimburse only the costs of a specific group of individuals.

(3) *Costs by service type.* When costs can be assigned to certain types of service, the cost reimbursement scheme can focus on the costs of selected benefits which are especially prone to risk selection (e.g., renal dialysis).

Note that a CRS that is based on individual HCE or costs of selected benefits requires more monitoring by the regulator as insurers have the incentive to attribute costs to certain people or benefit types. For example, if HCE above a certain threshold are reimbursed, insurers can increase their cost reimbursement by assigning costs to the least possible number of individuals. When costs cannot be attributed to individuals or benefits, only the first type of CRS is feasible.

7.5.2 The Structure of Cost Reimbursement

Several proposals have been advanced in the literature how to structure cost reimbursement. Most of them refer to the compensation of individual HCE. The individuals whose HCE will be reimbursed are either selected at the beginning or at the end of the period.

(1) *Prospective selection of individuals whose costs will be reimbursed.* VAN DE VEN AND VAN VLIET (1992) have developed the concept of *risk sharing for high risks*. Under this scheme, insurers assign a certain percentage of their members to a *prospective high-risk pool* at the beginning of each period. All costs of these individuals are reimbursed.

(2) *Retrospective selection of individuals whose costs will be reimbursed.* Under this approach, the level of costs of an individual is the criterion according to which costs are reimbursed. Two versions can be distinguished:

(a) *Full cost reimbursement for the individuals with the highest HCE.* This approach of *risk sharing for high costs* has been proposed by VAN BARNEVELD ET AL. (2001).

(b) *Cost Reimbursement according to a general cost reimbursement function.* Here, functional forms are often borrowed from reinsurance. For such contracts, ARROW (1974) and RAVIV (1979) have shown that full or partial coverage above a deductible is optimal (see Section 6.3). For optimal cost reimbursement, this implies that HCE should only be reimbursed above a threshold. This *outlier risk sharing* [VAN DE VEN AND ELLIS (2000)] is used in practice. In Germany, for example, 60 percent of individual health care costs which exceed €21,051 were reimbursed in 2007.

An important question is the extent to which principles of reinsurance can be applied to the problem of preventing risk selection. The rationale given by insurance theory for contracts with deductibles and partial reimbursement of higher losses relies on risk-averse reinsurers or convex cost functions. The problem of risk selection, however, is of a different nature. The principles of optimal insurance contracts may therefore not be valid in the context of risk selection. For example, KIFMANN AND LORENZ (2009) find in a theoretical model that *a priori* all functional forms can be optimal to reduce incentives for direct risk selection. The precise shape of the optimal cost reimbursement function depends on how health care costs for each risk type are distributed.

> **Conclusion 7.12.** *Cost reimbursement schemes can be based on total cost, costs by service type, and individual HCE. In the latter case, the individuals whose HCE are reimbursed can be determined prospectively or retrospectively. Various functional forms of reimbursement can be employed. Although principles of reinsurance are advocated, it is unclear whether they can be applied to the problem of preventing risk selection.*

7.5.3 Findings of Empirical Studies

Empirical studies by VAN BARNEVELD ET AL. (1996, 1998, 2001) and KIFMANN AND LORENZ (2009) have compared different approaches to cost reimbursement. The studies of VAN BARNEVELD ET AL. focus on two aspects.

(1) *Risk sharing for high risks.* In their first study, VAN BARNEVELD ET AL. analyze the cost data of 69,000 members of a Dutch health insurer. They find that the 1 percent of the members with the highest costs in 1992 account for about 10 percent of all costs in 1993. If the highest 4 percent are considered, this value rises to 25 percent [see VAN BARNEVELD ET AL. (1996)]. These findings are confirmed by a second study that compares the 1992 costs of 245,000 members

of a Dutch health insurance fund [VAN BARNEVELD ET AL. (1998)]. 2 percent of the members with the highest costs in the previous year account for 14 percent of all costs.

(2) *Comparison between different cost reimbursement schemes.* The study of VAN BARNEVELD ET AL. (1998) compares 'risk sharing for high risks' with a proportional CRS and cost reimbursement above a threshold. In addition, VAN BARNEVELD ET AL. (2001) examine the concept of 'risk sharing for high costs'. Based on several indicators, the authors measure the incentives for risk selection and cost effectiveness. They conclude that 'risk sharing for high risks' and 'risk sharing for high costs' are superior to proportional cost reimbursement and reimbursement above a threshold.

KIFMANN AND LORENZ (2009) use data of a Swiss health insurer compromising 104,000 adults. Their hypothesis is that insurers practice risk selection according to whether a person has stayed in a hospital in the previous year. Furthermore, they assume that insurers control costs to some extent. They derive an optimal cost reimbursement formula which balances the incentives for risk selection and cost control. Applying this formula to the data set, they find that risk selection can most effectively be prevented if costs are reimbursed only up to a limit. A scheme which partially reimburses costs above a threshold performs significantly worse.

Conclusion 7.13. *Empirical studies demonstrate that cost reimbursement can be useful in preventing risk selection. Particularly, the variants 'risk sharing for high risks', 'risk sharing for high costs', and a scheme which reimburses total cost only up to a limit perform well. More research on their relative merit is needed, however.*

7.6 Summary

(1) The incentive to risk select is a consequence of government intervention in the health insurance market. The requirement to accept any individual at a uniform premium leads to expected losses with high-risk types and a contribution margin with low-risk types.

(2) Risk selection can take two forms. On the one hand, health insurers can perform *direct risk selection* by influencing who signs a contract. This requires that insurers can observe characteristics of individuals which are correlated with their expected cost, e.g., gender and age, but also behavior. *Indirect risk selection*, on the other hand, consists in designing benefit packages or by signing up with service providers that are attractive for low risks but unattractive for high risks. Individuals must therefore know their probabilities of needing certain services.

(3) Direct risk selection can be avoided by prohibiting selection methods such as selling supplementary benefits or offering outright payments to attractive risks. Both a risk adjustment scheme which relies on observable characteristics of individuals and a cost reimbursement scheme can decrease incentives for direct risk selection. The advantage of a risk adjustment scheme over a cost reimbursement scheme is that it does not affect the insurers' incentives to control costs and is sure to decrease incentives for risk selection.

(4) Regulation designed to avoid indirect risk selection requires the specification of the benefit package. However, these measures may not be enforceable while stifling insurer competition through product innovation.

(5) In a model in which insurers offer one variable benefit, community rating can lead to a separating equilibrium. In such an equilibrium, no cross-subsidies between risk types occur. Low risks are selected by a lower quantity of benefits, causing them to be worse off than without regulation, while high-risk types obtain the same contract as in an unregulated insurance market. In this case, risk selection can be prevented in two ways besides enforcing the efficient benefit level. First, the premium can be fixed at the average premium for an efficient benefit level. Second, a risk adjustment scheme based on observable characteristics of the risk type may be imposed. Payments based on these characteristics must be higher in absolute terms if these characteristics are only imperfect indicators of risk type.

(6) If health insurers offer two benefits, where the first is demanded by both risk types with the same probability but the second with different probabilities, then it is not possible to avoid risk selection by fixing the premium. Insurers use the structure of benefits to perform risk selection. If it is not possible to regulate benefits directly, risk selection using the structure of benefits can be prevented by assigning the benefit which is more likely to be demanded by high-risk types to a carve-out or by a risk adjustment scheme designed to neutralize insurers' incentives to perform indirect risk selection.

(7) Risk adjustment schemes designed to prevent direct and indirect risk selection are identical only if risk types are observable. Given imperfect signals of risk types and insurers' capability of performing direct risk selection based on these signals, payments designed to prevent indirect risk selection are higher in absolute value than those designed to prevent direct risk selection. In this case, only a second-best solution is possible and both objectives have to be balanced against each other.

(8) Risk adjustment and cost reimbursement can also help to secure a level playing field during the transition to a competitive market and to stabilize the health insurance market. Otherwise the most efficient insurer may not prevail in the market.

(9) Due to stochastic fluctuations over time, only between 20 and 25 percent of the total variance of health care expenditure can be predicted. Demographic variables such as age and gender have little explanatory value. Lagged health care

expenditure, self-reported health, and diagnostic information increase explanatory power considerably. However, using lagged health care expenditure as a risk adjuster reduces incentives to provide health benefits efficiently since higher health care expenditure will be reimbursed to some extent later. In the case of diagnostic information, collecting the data can be costly and open to manipulation.

(10) A risk adjustment scheme can be based on actual or normative health care expenditure and can be calculated prospectively or retrospectively. A risk adjustment scheme is compatible both with a pure transfer scheme between insurers and a system where a central fund distributes contributions to insurers.

(11) The statistical approach to risk adjustment is based on regression models to predict health care expenditure. The incentive approach, by contrast, regards risk adjustment as a method to induce insurers to act according to the regulator's objectives. While the incentive approach is superior on conceptual grounds, it requires carefully specified models of insurer behavior. In general, the two approaches differ in their recommendations.

(12) Cost reimbursement schemes can be based on total cost, costs by service type, and individual health care expenditure. In the latter case, the individuals whose health care expenditure is reimbursed can be determined prospectively or retrospectively. Various functional forms of reimbursing costs can be employed. Empirical studies demonstrate that cost reimbursement schemes can be useful in preventing risk selection. Particularly, the variants 'risk sharing for high risks', 'risk sharing for high costs', and a scheme which reimburses total cost only up to a limit perform well.

7.7 Further Reading

We recommend the survey articles by VAN DE VEN AND ELLIS (2000) and ELLIS (2008). GLAZER AND MCGUIRE (2006) present the case for the incentive approach to risk adjustment.

7.E Exercises

7.1. What causes incentives for risk selection in the health insurance market?

7.2. Define direct and indirect risk selection. Which information do insurers and individuals need to be able to perform risk selection of either type?

7.3. Which measures can prevent insurers from direct risk selection? How can indirect risk selection be avoided?

7.4. Assume that health insurers practice direct risk selection on the basis of a signal $s = 0, 1$. The regulator uses a cost reimbursement scheme to prevent risk selection. This scheme reimburses the share γ of an insurer's HCE. The average HCE of a person with the signal s are given by

$$M_0(\gamma) = 110 + \alpha\gamma \quad \text{and} \quad M_1(\gamma) = 120 + \beta\gamma.$$

Incentives for risk selection increase with the difference in HCE $\Delta M_A = (1 - \gamma)(M_1(\gamma) - M_0(\gamma))$.

(a) Assume $\alpha = \beta = 10$. Determine the difference in HCE as a function of γ. What problem emerges if γ is increased?

(b) Assume that $\alpha = 10$ and $\beta = 30$. Show how ΔM_A depends on γ. Determine the minimum value of γ that decreases the incentives for risk selection. When are incentives for risk selection lower than for $\gamma = 0$? Explain your findings.

(c) Assume $\alpha = 30$ and $\beta = 10$. Again, show how ΔM_A depends on γ. Which is the minimum value of γ that eliminates the incentive for risk selection? Discuss your result.

7.5. Assume that in the model of section 7.2.2.1 with one benefit, the utility function is given by

$$V_i(M, C) = C + \pi_i(4M^{0.5} - 8).$$

The probabilities of illness are $\pi_h = 0.5$ and $\pi_l = 0.2$. One-half of the individuals are high risks.

(a) Determine the efficient amount of M^* and the premium P_i in absence of regulation.

(b) Determine the contracts making up a separating equilibrium if the regulator requires community rating. Illustrate your results in a diagram.

(c) How can the regulator achieve that both risk types receive the efficient quantity M^* of medical care while paying premiums independent of risk type?

7.6. Assume that in the model of Section 7.2.2.2 with two benefits, the utility function is given by

$$V_i(M_a, M_c, C) = C + (2M_a^{0.5} - 2) + \pi_i(4M_c^{0.5} - 8).$$

The probabilities of illness are $\pi_h = 0.5$ and $\pi_l = 0.2$. One-half of the individuals are high risks. Determine

(a) the efficient amounts of M_a and M_c;

(b) the premiums P_i in the absence of regulation;

(c) the contracts in a separating equilibrium if the regulator fixes the premium at $\overline{P}^* = M_a^* + \overline{\pi} M_c^*$ (use a spreadsheet or mathematics program to calculate the contract for low risks). Interpret your results and illustrate them in a diagram.

7.7. Assume an equal number of high and low risks, respectively. If medical services are provided efficiently, HCE is €3,000 for high-risk types and €1,800 for low-risk types. The regulator can only observe whether an individual is old or young. 30 percent of the high risks and 20 percent of the low risks are old.

(a) Determine age-specific RAS payments to avoid direct risk selection based on age;

(b) Calculate age-specific RAS payments if incentives for indirect risk selection are to be neutralized.

Explain the difference between your results.

8

Physicians as Suppliers of Medical Services

8.1 Introduction

Private-practice physicians play a key role in the production and distribution of medical services. Most people first see a physician when they seek help for a health problem. This makes the physician the first agent to decide upon diagnosis, treatment, prescription of drugs, and referral to other providers of medical services (specialists, hospitals, pharmacists, and different types of therapists). Consequently, physicians are regarded by many as gatekeepers to the health care system.

In this chapter, we will look only at those services that practicing physicians supply themselves or in collaboration with their aides, using their own medical supplies and technical devices.[1] The objective is to find out whether one can expect the production and allocation of ambulatory care services to be performed according to basic principles of efficiency, ensuring that a given treatment outcome is achieved using the smallest possible amount of scarce resources. The achievement of efficiency is doubtful because of the dual role of physicians in relation to their patients, acting both as providers of medical services and as an advisors concerning the services to be demanded by patients.

This peculiarity (which does not exclusively apply to physicians but to lawyers and other professions as well) has caused a fierce debate among economists whether or not physicians use their informational advantage to secure a high volume of business even in circumstances where one would expect to see idle capacity because of high physician density. First, the predicted effects of an increase of supply in a competitive market are derived in Section 8.2 in order to establish a benchmark for testing the 'supplier-induced demand' (SID) hypothesis. Section 8.3 contains the important distinction between supplier-determined and supply-induced demand. In Section 8.4, a model of physician behavior is presented that permits to predict the circumstances in which SID is likely to occur. Section 8.5 is devoted to the discussion of alternative explanations for the puzzling observation that an increased physician density often goes along with a higher rather than lower per-capita utilization of medical services.

---

[1] Services initiated by physicians in other areas will be addressed in Chapters 9 and 12.

P. Zweifel et al., *Health Economics*, 2nd ed., DOI 10.1007/978-3-540-68540-1_8,
© Springer-Verlag Berlin Heidelberg 2009

An important finding is that SID crucially depends on the way physicians are paid for their services. Finally, results of empirical studies will be outlined in Section 8.6. Basically, physician behavior is decisively shaped by incentives that result from the way they are paid for their services. These issues will be addressed in Chapter 10.

8.2 The Relationship Between Physician Density and the Utilization of Medical Services

In most industrialized countries, the medical profession enjoys great popularity as an occupational choice, perhaps more than any other academic profession. It combines two features that attract many young people, viz. the fulfilment of the desire to help other people and the expectation to earn an above-average income. Due to the rush to the medical schools, the number of physicians has greatly increased during the past few decades (not only in absolute terms but also relative to population) and continues to rise. During the period 1970–2000, the total number of practising physicians in the Federal Republic of Germany increased from 16 to 36 for every 10,000 inhabitants and the number of physicians in surgeries from 8 to 13.[2] In Switzerland the number of physicians working in surgeries rose from 9 to 19 for every 10,000 inhabitants during the same period.[3]

Surprisingly, the continuous growth in the number of practices *did not cause underemployment* among physicians because the demand for ambulatory care services kept growing as well. Cross-section studies indicate that a greater supply of physicians goes hand-in-hand with an increased utilization of medical services per capita, as measured by health insurers' expenditures on ambulatory care for their beneficiaries. Far-reaching conclusions were drawn from this observation, viz. that the market for medical services 'does not function' and that health care will remain affordable only if the number of physicians is limited through licensing restrictions.

The mere fact that utilization of medical services increases with the number of suppliers is not at all surprising, however. If the market for ambulatory care were competitive, then an increase in the number of suppliers should lead to an outward shift of the market supply function. Combined with a downward-sloping demand curve, the quantity transacted M is predicted to increase, accompanied by a fall in price p (see Figure 8.1). The effect on the total expenditure (pM) is a priori uncertain and depends on the price elasticity of demand.

In many countries, however, the utilization of medical services per capita rises with an increase in physician density even though *fees do not drop*. Using data covering the years 1963 and 1970 for different regions of the United States, FUCHS (1978) found that a 10 percent increase in surgeon density ceteris paribus led to 3

---

[2] See BUNDESMINISTERIUM FÜR GESUNDHEIT (2001) and FEDERAL STATISTICAL OFFICE OF GERMANY (2001, p. 444).

[3] See BUNDESAMT FÜR STATISTIK (1973, p. 502) and VERBINDUNG DER SCHWEIZER ÄRZTINNEN UND ÄRZTE (2002).

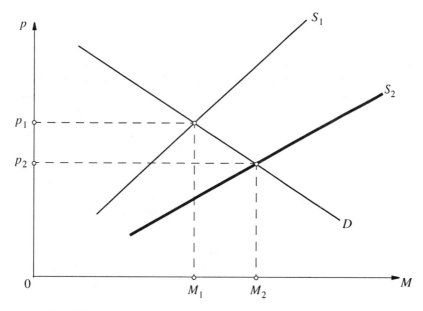

Fig. 8.1. Impact of an Increase in Physician Supply, 'Standard Case'

percent more operations per capita while *surgical fees* increased. A positive correlation between physician density and per capita utilization of medical services also exists in countries like Germany, where fees are fixed at a uniform rate across regions so that an increase in supply cannot reduce prices. Of course, in these countries total medical expenditure rises in step with an increase in physician density.

8.3 The Hypothesis of Supplier-Induced Demand for Ambulatory Medical Services

The relationship between supplier (physician) and demander (patient) that is peculiar to health care (see Chapter 5) may play a key role in the existence of supplier-induced demand.

The most striking feature of the physician-patient relationship is the demanders' *incomplete information* about true needs. Many patients who consult their doctor know only that they require some medical treatment (of the diagnostic or therapeutic type) because they are not satisfied with their health status. Thus, they delegate the choice of treatment to the better-informed doctor while deciding merely whether or not to follow the doctors's advice and comply with his or her prescriptions. Not even in this decision are patients completely sovereign, as there is a consensus among physicians and patients that the patient's confidence in the doctor's competence is an important precondition for successful treatment. This means that the demand curve, which depicts the volume of planned utilization of medical treatment at alternative prices, predominantly mirrors the *decisions of suppliers*, not of demanders of medical care. In the limit, the demand for medical services is thus supplier *determined*.

The fact remains without consequences as long as the doctors act as *perfect agents of their patients*, choosing what patients would have chosen had they possessed the necessary technological knowledge. It does become a problem, however, as soon as doctors' decisions on behalf of their patients are influenced by their own interests. If doctors vary the information provided to their patients systematically with an increase in physician density so as to secure their own full employment, then supplier-*determined* demand becomes supplier-*induced* demand (SID).

The case of SID is illustrated in Figure 8.2, assuming full insurance coverage of patients. Therefore, demand does not depend on price. Let D_0 denote 'primary demand', that is, the volume of services that meets the ideal standard of medical care given the number of patients in the catchment area, prevalence of health conditions, and the decisions of patients to contact the doctor. Let governmental regulation fix the unit price at p_0, assumed to equate primary demand and supply of medical services given initial physician density (the S_0 curve).

Now assume that due to an increase in the number of physicians, the supply curve shifts outward (to S_1). If providers had no direct influence on demand or if they acted as perfect agents of their patients, the demand curve would remain stable. At the regulated price, the quantity of services actually transacted would remain constant at $D_0 = M_0$. Evidently, providers produce fewer services than they would like to at this price; there is underutilization of their capacity at the level of $M_1 - M_0$.

Assume, however, that physicians do *not* act as *perfect* agents, but in advising their patients pursue their own interests. In this case they would recommend their patients medically unnecessary, marginally effective, or totally ineffective services such that the planned quantities of supply $M_1 = S_1(p_0)$ *will actually be 'demanded'*. In terms of Figure 8.2, the demand curve would shift outward to the point where the quantity demanded (at any price, here at the regulated price level p_0) equals supply S_1 planned at price p_0.

If it is possible for the doctors to boost the demand for their services at their own discretion, then the *distinction* between 'supply' and 'demand' loses its relevance. According to the 'SID' hypothesis, the amount of services transacted on the market is exclusively determined by supply as desired by the physicians. The 'demand' required to match supply is created artificially ('induced') through the advice to patients, whether medically appropriate or not.

Evidently, there are conditions facilitating the inducement of demand. The two most important ones are

(1) *Comprehensive health insurance*. If patients are fully *insured* for the cost of medical treatment (in Germany, e.g., medical services are insured close to 100 percent), their own willingness to pay, which would put a limit to the consumption of services, is no longer relevant. The only reason to resist demand inducement is the time cost associated with the consumption of medical care.

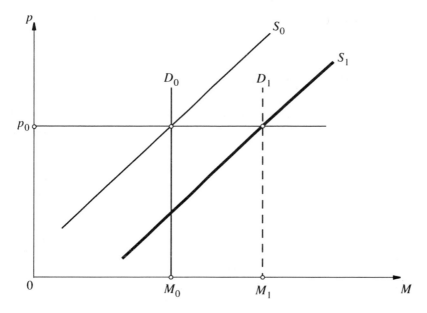

Fig. 8.2. Supplier-Induced Demand as a Response to an Increase of Physician Density

(2) *Riskless medical technology.* If doctors have services at their disposal that, though providing only minimal benefits, do no harm (e.g., diagnostic procedures that serve to exclude the existence of a concomitant disease causing similar symptoms), they have little reason to refrain from creating demand.

Conclusion 8.1. *Due to their superior information, physicians exert considerable influence on patient demand. Supplier-induced demand (SID), however, prevails only if physicians act not as perfect agents but according to their own interests, in particular by systematically modifying the information provided to patients in response to an increase in physician density in the aim of securing their own employment.*

The occurrence of such a marked deviation from perfect agency would have important implications for health policy, especially in a system providing full insurance coverage while striving to contain health care expenditure. In particular, it may create pressure to limit access to the medical profession. This calls for an empirical examination of the SID hypothesis under conditions of full insurance. We develop a formal model of physician behavior in the following Section 8.4. This model implies empirically testable hypotheses concerning the relationship between physician density and per capita utilization of medical services. Other explanations for this relationship are examined in Section 8.5. In Section 8.6 we will present the results of empirical tests of the SID hypothesis.

8.4 Utility Maximization of the Physician and Supplier-Induced Demand

8.4.1 A Model of Physician Behavior

Assume that a utility-maximizing physician decides on the amount of services to be provided to his or her patients.[4] Medical treatment is considered a homogeneous good. Let there be one consumer good which is used as numeraire. The price per unit medical care is a regulated fee, which we denote by p. There are a identical physicians in the area with n inhabitants. Thus

$$\delta = a/n \tag{8.1}$$

denotes the physician-population ratio or *physician density*. Patients are fully insured which implies that their demand does not depend on p. If there is no demand inducement, each inhabitant demands M units of physician services, measured in units of physician working time, so that primary demand per physician is $nM/a = M/\delta$. In addition to this primary demand, each physician can create s units of 'induced' demand so that total demand per physician for working time is given by

$$h(\delta,s) = M/\delta + s, \quad s \geq 0. \tag{8.2}$$

Actual working time t, expressed as a fraction of total available time ($0 \leq t \leq 1$), is given by

$$t = \min[h(\delta,s),1]. \tag{8.3}$$

This states that physicians adjust their working time to demand unless they reach the upper limit of available time.

Disposable income of the physician, y, is given by the difference between revenue, pt, and practice expenses and taxes. When practice expenses are a fixed share of revenues and taxes are progressive, disposable income is an increasing and concave function of gross revenues,

$$y = y(pt) \quad \text{with} \quad y' > 0 \quad \text{and} \quad y'' < 0. \tag{8.4}$$

Because the price of the only consumer good is normalized to unity, y also denotes the physician's consumption.

Let the physician's utility function be strictly concave, depending positively on consumption y but negatively on working hours t and on demand inducement s. The latter is valued negatively because provision of marginally effective (or even superfluous) services is incompatible with professional ethics. One therefore obtains

---

[4] For an alternative formulation, in which physicians retain a varying amount of demand for themselves rather than referring borderline patients, with consequences reminiscent of supplier-induced demand [see ZWEIFEL (1981)].

$$u = u(y,t,s) \quad \text{with} \quad u_y > 0, u_{yy} < 0, u_t < 0, u_{tt} \leq 0, u_s < 0, u_{ss} \leq 0.^5 \tag{8.5}$$

Furthermore, assume that

$$u_{yt} \leq 0, u_{ys} \leq 0, u_{st} = 0. \tag{8.6}$$

The first inequality asserts that consumption and leisure are complementary goods, while the second states that professional ethics become more important the higher physician's income. Finally, we assume that workload t has no effect on the physician's attitude towards professional ethics.

The physician maximizes utility as given by equation (8.5) by choosing consumption level y, working hours t, and the amount of demand inducement s subject to the constraints (8.2) and (8.3). There are four types of optima, depending upon market conditions and the physician's preferences,

(a) a boundary optimum with $s = 0$ and $t = 1$, which occurs whenever physician density is so low that primary demand cannot be met even with all physicians working the maximum amount of time ($M/\delta \geq 1$);

(b) an optimum with $s = 0$ and $t < 1$, which occurs when ethics or preferences for leisure are very strong, causing physicians to just meet primary demand while working below capacity;

(c) an interior optimum with $s > 0$ and $t < 1$, which occurs when physician density is so high that physicians are not fully occupied even with (the optimum amount of) demand inducement;

(d) an optimum with $s > 0$ but $t = 1$, which occurs when the income motive is strong enough for physicians to induce demand up to the point of a full workload.

The latter three cases can be analyzed by inserting (8.2) into the utility function, so that it can be expressed as function of s only. As the physician maximizes utility subject to the constraint (8.3), we can form the Lagrangean

$$Z(s,\lambda) = u[y(p(M/\delta+s)), M/\delta + s, s] + \lambda[1 - M/\delta - s] \tag{8.7}$$

with the necessary Kuhn-Tucker conditions

$$\frac{\partial Z}{\partial s} = py'u_y + u_t + u_s - \lambda \leq 0, \quad s \geq 0, \quad s\frac{\partial Z}{\partial s} = 0, \tag{8.8}$$

$$\frac{\partial Z}{\partial \lambda} = 1 - M/\delta - s \geq 0, \quad \lambda \geq 0, \quad \lambda\frac{\partial Z}{\partial \lambda} = 0. \tag{8.9}$$

The assumptions in (8.5) and (8.6) ensure that the second-order conditions are met. Condition (8.8) shows that demand inducement requires a positive fee p and is therefore a consequence of fee-for-service payment.

---

[5] We write u_y for $\frac{\partial u}{\partial y}$ etc.

In the optima of type (b) and (c), the constraint (8.3) is not binding, implying $\lambda = 0$. In a type (c) optimum, condition (8.8) can be rewritten as

$$F(s,\delta,p,M) = py'u_y + u_t + u_s = 0. \tag{8.10}$$

This equation implicitly defines s as a function of the exogenous variables δ, p and M, i.e., $s(\delta, p, M)$. This condition is easy to interpret. Demand is induced to the point where the marginal benefit of additional consumption equals the marginal utility loss of the additional working hours and the 'bad conscience' resulting from demand inducement.

In a type (d) optimum, the constraint (8.3) is binding, $\lambda > 0$, and one obtains

$$s = 1 - M/\delta \tag{8.11}$$

Box 8.1 provides an overview of the model.

The theory of SID is concerned with physicians' reactions to changes in the physician density and the level of regulated fees. In the following, we therefore examine the comparative statics of the model with respect to these parameters.

8.4.2 Increasing Physician Density

We first examine how an increase in physician density δ affects the amount of services provided per patient. To do this, categorize the four optima mentioned above as follows.

Type (a) or (d) optimum ($t = 1$)

If physician density is very low so that $M/\delta \geq 1$, primary demand exceeds physicians' working capacity and the constraint $t \leq 1$ is binding. The same is true for $M/\delta < 1$ if physicians have a strong income motive, causing them to induce demand up to the full workload. Since we measure physician services in units of physician working time and we have $t = 1$ in both cases, physicians supply $a \times 1$ units. The amount of services provided per patient then becomes

$$q = \frac{a}{n} = \delta \tag{8.12}$$

and consequently

$$\frac{dq}{d\delta} = 1, \tag{8.13}$$

i.e., billings per patient are proportional to physician density as long as all physicians work at full capacity.

Box 8.1. A Model of Physician Behavior

$$\delta = a/n \tag{8.1}$$

$$h(\delta,s) = M/\delta + s \tag{8.2}$$

$$t = \min[h(\delta,s),1] \tag{8.3}$$

$$y = y(pt) \quad \text{with} \quad y' > 0 \quad \text{and} \quad y'' < 0 \tag{8.4}$$

$$u = u(y,t,s) \quad \text{with} \quad u_y > 0, u_{yy} < 0, u_t < 0, u_{tt} \leq 0, u_s < 0, u_{ss} \leq 0 \tag{8.5}$$

$$u_{yt} \leq 0, u_{ys} \leq 0, u_{st} = 0 \tag{8.6}$$

$$F(s,\delta,p,M) = py'u_y + u_t + u_s = 0 \tag{8.10}$$

n: population size
a: number of physicians
δ: physician density
M: primary demand per capita of population
y: disposable income (consumption) of physician
p: regulated fee per unit medical care
t: physician's working time
s: demand inducement by physician
u: utility of physician
h: total demand for a physician's services
q: amount of services provided per patient

Type (b) optimum ($s = 0, t < 1, M/\delta < 1$)

In this equilibrium, physicians do not induce demand because of preferences for leisure or an ethical orientation. In this situation, the amount of services provided per patient is

$$q = M. \tag{8.14}$$

Consequently,

$$\frac{dq}{d\delta} = 0, \tag{8.15}$$

i.e., billings per patient do not depend upon physician density in this range of δ.

Type (c) optimum $(s > 0, 0 < t < 1, M/\delta < 1)$

In that case, physicians have spare capacity even if they induce the optimal amount of demand $s(\delta, p, M)$ as implicitly defined by the first-order condition (8.10). The amount of services provided per patient is then given by

$$q(\delta, s) = M + \frac{as(\delta, p, M)}{n} = M + s(\delta, p, M)\delta. \tag{8.16}$$

We thus obtain from (8.16),

$$\frac{dq}{d\delta} = s + \delta \frac{ds}{d\delta} \tag{8.17}$$

i.e., the total reaction of observed utilization to an increase of physician density is composed of a direct and an indirect effect. The direct effect is positive as long as every doctor performs some amount of demand inducement. The indirect effect depends upon the impact of physician density on the demand inducement at the individual level, $ds/d\delta$. Thus a sufficient condition for a positive total effect is that the latter expression is positive. As the necessary first-order condition (8.10) has to be satisfied before and after the change, we get from the implicit function theorem

$$\frac{ds}{d\delta} = -\frac{\dfrac{\partial F(s, \delta, p, M)}{\partial \delta}}{\dfrac{\partial F(s, \delta, p, M)}{\partial s}}. \tag{8.18}$$

The denominator in (8.18) is negative because of the second-order condition of utility maximization. The term $ds/d\delta$ therefore has the same sign as the partial derivative of $F(s, \delta, p, M)$ with respect to δ. To obtain this derivative, write (8.8) explicitly as function of δ,

$$\begin{aligned}
F(s, \delta, p, M) = {} & py'[p(M/\delta + s)]u_y[y(p(M/\delta + s)), M/\delta + s, s] \\
& + u_t[y(p(M/\delta + s)), M/\delta + s, s] \\
& + u_s[y(p(M/\delta + s)), M/\delta + s, s] = 0.
\end{aligned} \tag{8.19}$$

Partial differentiation of equation (8.19) with respect to δ then yields:

$$\frac{\partial F(s, \delta, p, M)}{\partial \delta} = -M\delta^{-2}\left\{ p^2 y'' u_y + p^2 (y')^2 u_{yy} + 2py' u_{yt} + u_{tt} + py' u_{ys} + u_{st} \right\} > 0$$

due to the assumptions on the utility function (8.5) and (8.6). In economic terms, the increase in the physician density exerts an income effect on the physician's choice variables. At an unchanged value of demand inducement s, gross revenue pt and consumption y both fall. This raises marginal disposable income when revenue rises (y' goes up) and marginal utility of consumption (u_y goes up), while both disutility from labor and disutility from demand inducement shrink in absolute value (u_t and u_s, both negative, go towards zero).

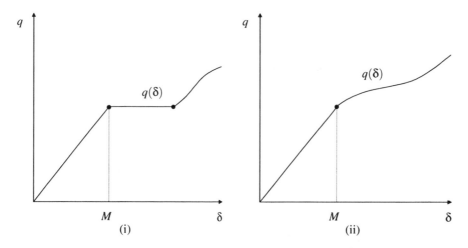

Fig. 8.3. Physician Density and Predicted Physician Billings per Patient

In sum, the economic model of physician behavior proposed here generates the prediction of demand inducement, i.e., a monotonous relation between billings per patient and the physician-population ratio when the latter is sufficiently high. But recall the assumption that patients are fully insured. With partial coverage, they are exposed to the financial consequences of demand inducement, giving rise to resistance on their part. Moreover, the effect depends upon the mode of payment, where we assumed fee-for-service. By contrast, payment modes typical of Managed Care such as capitation give no incentive to demand inducement. On the other hand, at very low values of physician density, demand is rationed and billings per patient are simply proportional to physician density. In addition, there might be an intermediate range of physician density in which no demand inducement occurs and thus billings per patient do not change when physician density increases. Large values of physician density, however, cause physician income to decline. Unless physicians have very strong objections against inducing demand, the marginal benefit of additional consumption is likely to exceed the marginal utility loss due to the additional working hours and demand inducement, causing billings per patient to rise again.

The theoretical predictions are graphically presented in Figure 8.3. Panel (i) depicts the case in which for an intermediate range of physician density above M a type (b) optimum without demand inducement exists, whereas panel (ii) shows the case in which demand inducement occurs as soon as there are enough physicians to meet primary demand.

8.4.3 Increasing Fee Level

We now examine how the amount of demand inducement reacts to a change in the level of regulated fees, assuming an interior optimum. By the same reasoning as above, the sign of the partial derivative ds/dp is identical to the sign of the following expression,

$$\frac{\partial F(s,\delta,p,M)}{\partial p} = y'u_y + py''tu_y + p(y')^2 u_{yy} + y'tu_{yt} + y'tu_{ys}. \tag{8.20}$$

The sign of expression (8.20) is ambiguous because the first term is positive, while the remaining four terms are negative due to the assumptions on the utility function (8.5) and (8.6). The first term measures the substitution effect of an increase in the fee level, which makes it worthwhile for the physician to provide more (unnecessary) services. The size of this effect depends upon the strength of the physician's income motive and the degree to which disposable income rises with increasing gross revenue. The other four terms measure the income effect, which by itself dampens the degree of demand inducement when the fee rises. It is stronger the more concave is the net income schedule and the faster marginal utility of consumption falls when consumption, working time and the amount of demand inducement rise.

An interesting implication follows from the model for the case in which there are either several types of services (e.g., office visits and laboratory tests) or several types of payers (e.g., Medicare and private insurance) and the fee change is limited to some services/payers, while other fees stay constant. In this case, there is no substitution effect for the set of 'other' services, and only the (negative) income effect prevails [see McGuire and Pauly (1991)]. Thus a suitable test of the SID hypothesis would be that a fee change in one market should imply a reverse change in service volume in all other markets.

> **Conclusion 8.2.** *In a world in which patients are fully insured and fees are exogenously fixed, rational physicians whose utility depends on income, working hours, and demand inducement are predicted to induce demand, resulting in a positive relationship between physician density and per capita volume of medical services; in the limiting case of very low physician density this is due to a relaxation of rationing, causing the relationship to be strictly proportional. Moreover, the reaction of services per capita to the fee level is ambiguous because the substitution effect calls for an increase whereas the income effect calls for a decrease in service volume.*

8.5 Physician Density and Utilization of Medical Services: Alternative Explanations

SID for medical services constitutes only one explanation of the phenomenon of increasing utilization of medical services per capita with increasing physician density, while the price of medical services does not fall. This explanation is based on the hypothesis that physicians exploit the delegation of decision-making powers by

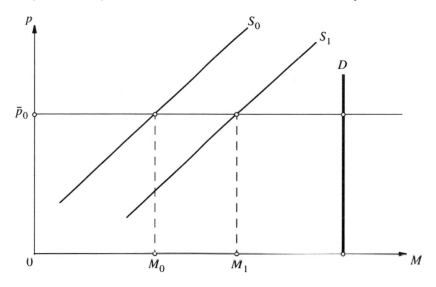

Fig. 8.4. Effects of a Supply Extension at Regulated Prices and Excess Demand

their patients by prescribing medically useless (ineffective) or economically inappropriate (inefficient) services in striving to protect their incomes from the pressures of competition. However, there are *alternative explanations* of the same empirical phenomenon. They include the following:

(1) *Permanent excess demand.* The observed correlation between physician density and utilization of medical services may result from permanent excess demand on the market for medical services, which in turn is caused by price regulation. In this situation, physicians work to capacity but still must turn away some patients. In the price-quantity-diagram of Figure 8.4, demand is rationed. Therefore, observed price-quantity observations lie on the (shifting) supply curve rather than on the (stable) demand curve. When supply increases, the observed quantity of services provided increases as well, from M_0 to M_1. This case corresponds to the type (a) optimum in the model of Subsection 8.4.1.

(2) *Decreasing indirect cost, improved quality of treatment.* The growth of service volume associated with increasing physician density can also be the result of demand decisions by rational patients. It could be particularly the result of the outward shift of the demand curve, when one considers that demand for medical services is closely linked to *indirect costs* for the patients, and that these decrease, when there is an increased availability of physicians. The opening of new practices, particularly in rural areas, reduces the non-financial cost in terms of getting an appointment, travel time, and waiting in the practice. Also, physicians who are less busy are able to devote more time to each patient. Time devoted to a case often serves as an indicator of quality. Therefore, these changes amount to a reduction in the total cost of medical care or an increase in its quality, causing

patients' demand to shift outward at a given money price (especially so at a zero money price) in response to an increased physician density ('availability effect').

(3) *Reverse causality.* The third explanation for the observed positive statistical correlation between physician density and per capita utilization hinges on the argument that causality may run the other way round. When choosing a location for their practice, young doctors presumably try to determine whether demand will be strong enough to generate a sufficient amount of revenue. Regions with high demand for medical services should thus attract more physicians than those with low demand. Consequently, a high (exogenous) per capita utilization of medical services leads to a high (endogenous) physician density on average.[6]

Conclusion 8.3. *The joint occurrence of rising per capita utilization of medical services with rising physician density does not prove that physicians induce demand. There are other explanations of the same phenomenon in that pre-existing excess demand may be reduced, total cost of utilization to patients may have fallen, and variations in physician density itself could be the result of variations in the demand for medical care.*

8.6 Empirical Examination of the Supplier-Induced Demand Hypothesis

8.6.1 Physician Density and Volume of Services

A careful empirical study of the SID hypothesis based on the relationship between number of physicians and volume of services per capita should ideally provide discriminating evidence with regard to the three explanations given in the preceding subsection by taking the following implications into account.

(a) If there is only *excess demand* but no demand inducement, we should observe a positive (and proportional) correlation between physician density and the service volume at *low physician densities* that *vanishes* once a certain density is reached.

(b) Patients' *time costs* should be controlled for to rule out the 'rational demand shift' explanation.

(c) Locational choice by physicians should be *controlled* for to rule out the 'reverse causality' explanation.

One of the earliest empirical tests of the SID hypothesis was performed by FUCHS (1978) in a cross-section study of the United States between 1963 and 1970. To take point (c) into account, the author uses two-stage-least-squares estimation to explain the supply of surgeons as well as the frequency of surgery. He also shows

---

[6] In contrast to the first explanation, each region is in an equilibrium situation here.

that surgeons had a low degree of capacity utilization in his sample, which rules out reason (a). As operations are usually scheduled well in advance, differences in time cost should be low, ruling out explanation (b). Thus FUCHS's finding that an increase of 10 percent in surgeon density leads ceteris paribus to a 3 percent increase in the frequency of surgery strongly supports the *SID hypothesis*.

The methodology used by Fuchs was criticized later by DRANOVE AND WEHNER (1994) who used two-stage-least-squares to produce a similar result in a market where SID most certainly does not exist, namely the market for childbirths. In their sample of U.S. county data from 1988, the number of childbirths is significantly positively related to the predicted number of obstetricians. The authors come up with two possible explanations for this apparently absurd correlation: (i) the demand equation may not be correctly identified, and (ii) there may have been border-crossing of patients into counties with a large supply of obstetricians.

More convincing evidence for SID can be found in cases in which physicians react to a sudden downward shift in demand by increasing the intensity of services provided. Such a natural experiment was provided by the drastic decline in fertility in the U.S. during the 1970s, which was accompanied by a large increase in the share of the most highly reimbursed type of delivery, the caesarean section. In particular, this type of delivery was chosen more frequently in states in which fertility was the lowest and the density of obstetricians the highest although the size of the effects was much too small to offset the income loss due to the decline in births [see GRUBER AND OWINGS (1996)].

A more recent study with Norwegian data from 1995 [CARLSEN AND GRYTTEN (1998)] demonstrated a fairly strong effect of physician density on office visits and laboratory tests per patient but the slope of the relationship was found to be significantly larger in the part of the data set where physicians were relatively scarce so that the effect can be more plausibly explained as a result of rationing (or at least, availability of doctors) than as a result of SID.

8.6.2 Regulated Fees and Volume of Services

A number of other studies examined the reaction of utilization to changes in regulated fees. RICE (1983) analyzed data from a natural experiment that occurred in Colorado in 1977, when Medicare reimbursement rates were sharply raised in nonurban areas relative to those in urban areas. The author found a significant negative relationship between changes in service intensity and changes in fees thus providing evidence for the existence of a strong income effect, which is a necessary condition for SID to hold. More recently, YIP (1998) looked at the effects of the 1988 Medicare fee reform in which reimbursement rates for certain procedures performed by thoracic surgeons were drastically reduced, and she found sizable and highly significant income effects of these fee cuts on the volumes of bypass surgery performed both to Medicare patients and to private patients so that surgeons could make up 70 percent of the income loss from reduced fees by an increase in volume.

Conclusion 8.4. *Empirical studies from the United States and Europe show a statistically significant correlation between physician density and per capita expenditure on medical services. In most cases, however, the alternative hypotheses of reverse causality or rationing cannot be definitely excluded. Studies of the relationship between fees for physician services and service volume, however, provide evidence of a strong income effect, which is a necessary prerequisite for the SID hypothesis to hold.*

We would like to stress once more that there is one crucial condition for demand inducement in ambulatory medical care to prevail, resulting in a squandering of scarce resources. Medical revenues must rise sufficiently with the amount of services supplied, which is true in the presence of fee-for-service payment for medical services. This indicates that SID is not really the key issue for efficient resource use, but rather the choice of *payment system*. The problem of economic efficiency would be solved if physicians were paid in a way that induces them to use the resources under their control efficiently. Chapter 10 will therefore deal with the influence of payment systems on the physicians' behavior, highlighting the implications for rational resource use in ambulatory medical care.

8.7 Summary

(1) Due to their superior information, physicians exert considerable influence on patient demand. Supplier-induced demand, however, prevails only if physicians act not as perfect agents but according to their own interests, in particular by systematically modifying the information provided to patients in response to an increase in physician density in the aim of securing their own employment.

(2) In a world in which patients are fully insured and fees are exogenously fixed, rational physicians whose utility depends on income, working hours, and demand inducement are predicted to induce demand, resulting in a positive relationship between physician density and per capita volume of medical services; in the limiting case of very low physician density this is due to a relaxation of rationing, causing the relationship to be strictly proportional. Moreover, the reaction of services per capita to the fee level is ambiguous because the substitution effect calls for an increase whereas the income effect calls for a decrease in service volume.

(3) The joint occurrence of rising per capita utilization of medical services with rising physician density does not prove that physicians induce demand. There are other explanations of the same phenomenon in that pre-existing excess demand may be reduced, total cost of utilization to patients may have fallen, and variations in physician density itself could be the result of variations in the demand for medical care.

(4) Empirical studies from the United States and Europe show a statistically significant correlation between physician density and per capita expenditure on medical services. In most cases, however, the alternative hypotheses of reverse causality or rationing cannot be definitely excluded. Studies of the relationship between fees for physician services and service volume, however, provide evidence of a strong income effect, which is a necessary prerequisite for the supplier-induced demand hypothesis to hold.

8.8 Further Reading

EVANS (1974) first proposed the hypothesis of supplier-induced demand. LABELLE ET AL. (1994) and PAULY (1994) give an overview of the following discussion. We also recommend the survey on physician agency by MCGUIRE (2000) published in the HANDBOOK OF HEALTH ECONOMICS.

8.E Exercises

8.1. Discuss the difference between supplier-determined and supplier-induced demand.

8.2. Describe the different explanations for the observed empirical phenomenon, that the per capita utilization of medical services rises with increasing physician density. How can be discriminated between the different explanations considering the empirical studies?

8.3. Let a physician's utility function be $u(y,t,s) = \alpha y^{0.5} - t - s$. The physician's disposable income is $y(t) = 64t$, where t is working time $(0 \leq t \leq 1)$. The demand for his services is given by $M/\delta + s$, where δ denotes physician density and M corresponds to 'primary' demand per capita. s denotes demand inducement.

(a) What is the first-order condition for the optimal value of s?

(b) Suppose $M = 0.02$ and $\alpha = 0.4$. For what values of δ does the physician induce demand? Check the second-order condition.

(c) For what values of δ is the time constraint binding?

(d) Describe the relationship between physician density δ and amount of services provided per patient, q.

(e) How are the results affected if the parameter α in the utility function is raised to 0.6? Explain.

9

Hospital Services and Efficiency

9.1 Introduction

In debates about the economic problems of health care, the hospital plays a key role. This is due to the quantitative importance of the hospital industry. In many industrialized countries, hospital services account for the largest single block of health care expenditure. In 2005, most OECD countries spend more than a third of health care expenditure on hospital services [see OECD (2008)].

As stated in Chapter 1, however, not the *amount* of health care expenditure is of primary interest to economists but the *rules* that determine the allocation of re sources. Here, one feature of the hospital sector deserves particular attention: to a large extent hospitals are *non-profit* institutions. Therefore, hospitals may not be interested in operating in a cost-efficient manner. From the point of view of a regulatory agency whose objective is to control hospital efficiency, this creates the need to gather and evaluate information on the production process of hospitals. Since the production function of a hospital is not known, the standard approach is to compare hospitals in a *benchmarking* study. Several methods have been proposed to conduct such studies. With the estimation of a hospital cost function and Data Envelopment Analysis (DEA), we present both a parametric and a nonparametric method for comparing the efficiency of hospitals.

To determine the efficiency of a hospital, the inputs and outputs need to be defined and measured. Inputs comprise the use of productive resources such as human labor, energy and raw materials – inputs that are usually straightforward to define and measure. The definition of hospital output, though, is far from self-evident. In particular, it is difficult to state what exactly a hospital is supposed to produce. And once output has been defined, the problem of measurement is not trivial. In Section 9.2, we therefore discuss the definition and measurement of hospital output in detail. Section 9.3 is devoted to the comparison of hospital efficiency.

P. Zweifel et al., *Health Economics*, 2nd ed., DOI 10.1007/978-3-540-68540-1_9,
© Springer-Verlag Berlin Heidelberg 2009

In addition to the measurement of hospital efficiency, the design of hospital reimbursement systems is of crucial importance for the efficiency of the hospital sector. How a hospital is paid for its services determines its admissions policy and the intensity of treatment to a great extent. Since the problem of reimbursement applies to providers of health services in general, we devote Chapter 10 to this topic. In Sections 10.2 and 10.3, we present the economic theory of provider reimbursement. Section 10.4.3 discusses the implications for the hospital sector.

9.2 The Hospital as a Productive Unit

9.2.1 Hospital Output: Health as a Latent Variable

In order to measure hospital output, it is not enough to describe the tasks that are carried out (surgery, radiotherapy, medication, wound dressing, and accommodation, to name a few) or bundles of tasks such as medical, nursing or hotel services. All of these tasks are only a means to an end. One gets closer to true output by asking the question of what the patients (or referring physicians acting on their behalf) want, what they expect from hospitalization, and what taxpayers expect to obtain in return for their contribution to the financing of the hospital.

In the majority of cases, expectations are in terms of a positive *contribution to the patient's state of health*, that is, the curing of disease (or control of its development) and the alleviation of pain. Even though there is little disagreement with regard to these objectives, the degree of their realization nevertheless may hardly serve as a basis for the payment of hospital services. The difficulties lie with the measurement as well as the imputation of outputs to services performed.

In order to measure the extent of recovery of patients, their state of health would have to be evaluated not only at the beginning and at the end of hospital treatment but frequently years after the stay, using objective criteria. This is – except for obvious indicators such as survival and complication rates – a fairly hopeless undertaking because health is not only multi-dimensional but also contains a considerable subjective component. Even if this difficulty is surmounted, one should not simply tie payment for hospital services to the measured change in the state of health achieved during the period of hospitalization. For the relevant benchmark for assessing hospital performance is not the patient's actual state before admission, but the (hypothetical) state that *would have been realized without hospital treatment* at the end of the observation period. The importance of this distinction becomes very clear in cases where hospital treatment can only slow down the progressive course of an incurable disease. However, the extent of 'deterioration averted' usually defies measurement.[1]

---

[1] Prognoses from 'comparable' cases are not very reliable, because no two cases are ever the same.

Patients hold expectations not only with regard to the final state of their health after hospital treatment but also with regard to their physical and mental well-being *during hospitalization* (to the extent that the disease will permit), as life goes on in the hospital. This aspect takes on special significance if the disease itself can no longer be fought and only suffering can be alleviated, that is, when dealing with incurable and terminally ill patients. Objective and reliable measurement of subjective well-being during hospitalization, however, is just as difficult as measuring the influence of hospitalization on the patient's health status.

Finally, the customers of a hospital not just cover people that will actually be treated as patients, but the whole population of its catchment area. The mere existence of a hospital provides people with the security that in case of accident or serious illness inpatient treatment will be available. This so called 'option demand' is satisfied by hospital beds held on reserve, along with the necessary staff and equipment.

> **Conclusion 9.1.** *Hospital output consists of improving or maintaining the patient's state of health on the one hand and the capacity to satisfy an option demand on the other hand. The former part of output is particularly difficult to operationalize and can only partially be attributed to the hospital.*

9.2.2 The Multi-Stage Character of Production in the Hospital

As the final outcome of hospital activity (particularly the improvement of a patient's health status) can only be measured imperfectly, observable quantities suitable to serve as *output indicators* have to be identified for obtaining an operational definition of the term, 'efficient use of resources'. In the present context, it seems appropriate to list various indicators of hospital activity and to classify them according to the stage of production, using a scheme that may help to describe hospital activity from an economic perspective.

The indicators most commonly used are:

- Quantities of *factors of production* (hours worked by physicians, by the nursing staff and by other employees, drugs and dressings, electricity, fuel etc.);

- Quantities of *individual medical and nursing services* performed (examinations, operations, medications, injections, physical therapies, temperature measurements, meals etc.);

- The *number of patients* or *cases* treated, possibly differentiated according to various types of diseases (see Section 9.2.3);

- The *number of patient days*, possibly differentiated according to intensity of care.

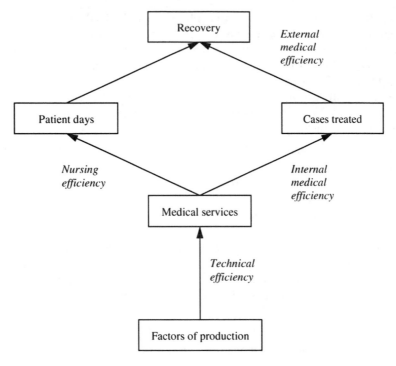

Fig. 9.1. Patient Days and Cases Treated as Intermediate Hospital Products

Figures 9.1 and 9.2 show two alternative views of the different stages of hospital production involving these quantities. In both of them, the factors of production, which can be interpreted as the primary input, appear at the bottom level. With their help, various medical services are produced, which are therefore located at the second level (secondary inputs). The concept of minimization of factor inputs for producing a given bundle of services may be called 'technical efficiency'.

With regard to the two remaining indicators, cases treated and hospital days, there are two different views.

(1) Cases treated and days in hospital may be seen as indicators of different *intermediate products*, located at the same stage (Figure 9.1), which thus enter immediately prior to the true output 'recovery'. The number of cases treated reflects the medical component and the number of patient days, the nursing component of hospital services, respectively. Different types of services in the form of (direct) inputs may be assigned to the two components. This view thus results in two different types of efficiency, viz. the use of the least amount of nursing services possible per day ('nursing efficiency') and the least amount of medical services possible per case ('internal medical efficiency') for a given improvement. In addition, the economic objective of the health system as a whole is to achieve a

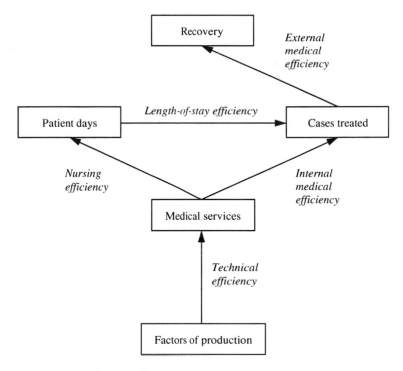

Fig. 9.2. Patient Days as an Input to the Treatment Process

given degree of health improvement at the lowest cost possible (for hospitalization as well as other services). This enters as 'external' medical efficiency in Figure 9.1.

(2) Alternatively, one may argue that hospitalization per se neither gives rise to utility (because patients are removed from their normal environment) nor improves patients' health status as such. In contradistinction to view (1), *days spent in hospital may themselves be considered as an input* into the treatment process (Figure 9.2). In this view, minimizing the length of stay for a given spectrum of diseases constitutes a type of efficiency of its own ('length-of-stay efficiency').

This second approach obviously presupposes the existence of binding norms for measuring health status at discharge because otherwise it would be possible to increase the length-of-stay efficiency by simply sending patients home 'quicker but sicker'.

In this context, the question arises as how to characterize 'beds'. At first sight, beds seem to be an input to the production of hospital services simply because a hospital cannot exist without beds. But with a given (maximum) number of cases simultaneously treated in the hospital, the required input of the factor 'beds' is uniquely determined, causing additional beds to have a marginal productivity of zero. A fur-

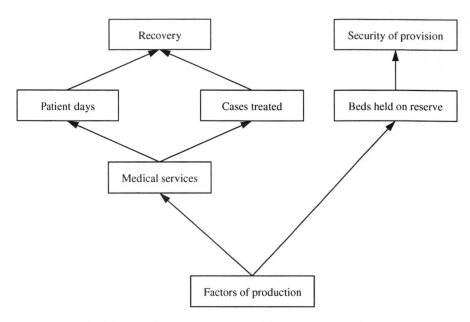

Fig. 9.3. Beds Held on Reserve as an Additional Hospital Output

ther problem with this approach is that almost no costs of current operation are associated with the factor 'beds'. One could possibly regard depreciation and interest on the purchase price of beds as a user cost of beds, in analogy of user cost of capital.

By contrast, the notion of option demand discussed in Section 9.2.1 provides a justification for regarding an empty bed as an output of the hospital in question. This holds true as long as the number of empty beds or beds occupied by patients ready for discharge remains within the bounds defined by the requirements in the event of a catastrophic incident.

Following this latter approach, that part of a hospital's factor endowment which must be allocated independently of the number of patients is assigned to the service capacity held on reserve, making the number of beds another indicator of a hospital's output. Completing the scheme of Figure 9.1 in this way results in Figure 9.3.

Conclusion 9.2. *A hospital's 'output' can be described as the outcome of a multi-stage process, with each stage being assigned its specific concept of efficiency.*

9.2.3 The Heterogeneity of Hospital Output

Another problem with defining and measuring the output of a hospital stems from a considerable amount of heterogeneity, be it at the level of output indicators or of intermediate products. Consider the number of cases treated in a hospital in the course of a year. Is it possible to describe adequately a hospital's output simply by counting the number of cases? Is it appropriate to say that a hospital that treats 1,000 cases achieves more than the one that treats 995? Obviously, the 1,000 cases of the first hospital might consist of 500 minor fractures and 500 uncomplicated tonsillectomies whereas the second hospital might be a heart unit specializing in transplantations.

One must therefore take into consideration that the 'case treated' does not constitute a homogeneous quantity but a mental construct that needs to be specified through its characteristics. This means that a treatment case must be differentiated along various dimensions, for example:

- The *type of illness* that has called for hospital treatment (principal diagnosis);
- The *severity of the illness* and *complications* arising during treatment;
- The *stage of the disease* (e.g., in the case of cancer);
- *Concomitant diseases* (secondary diagnosis);
- *Patient characteristics* reflecting her or his contribution to the 'production of recovery', such as age and possibly sex.

In view of these distinctions, to which still more could be added, a purist must come to the conclusion that heterogeneity of casemix can only adequately be taken into account by considering each patient as an output category of her or his own. Following this principle, however, one would forego the possibility of comparing the output vectors of two or more hospitals. This would put an end to the economic analysis of the hospital in the quest of, for example, measuring the degree of efficiency or determining a performance-based payment system.

A reasonable compromise between the rigorous approach just outlined and the total abandonment of case differentiation may be achieved by dividing patients into a manageable number of groups, using the distinguishing characteristics mentioned above. This division is known as *patient classification* and purports to form a manageable number of patient groups that are as homogeneous as possible. Moreover, assignment to a group should be unique and reproducible using objective criteria. Obviously, there is a conflict between the criteria 'manageable number' and 'greatest possible homogeneity within each group' which can only be resolved by weighing the relative disadvantages caused by their violation.

The three most common patient classification systems are:

(1) The *International Classification of Diseases* (ICD), originally developed as a basis for mortality statistics and thus solely referring to (principal) diagnoses. In its three-digit version, the ICD consists of more than 900 groups, while aggregation to the level of 110 main groups is already very coarse. For instance, all benign neoplasms form one single group in this categorization.

(2) *Diagnosis Related Groups* (DRGs), developed at Yale University in the 1970s with the explicit objective to create relatively cost-homogeneous groups. Besides the principal diagnosis, DRGs take into account the existence of concomitant disease and complications, the age of the patient, and the type of treatment (surgical or conservative), getting by with approximately 500 groups [see FETTER ET AL. (1980) and HEALTH CARE FINANCING ADMINISTRATION (1983)].

(3) *Patient Management Categories* (PMCs), also developed in the United States (Pittsburgh) and consisting of a total of 840 groups. Compared to DRGs, PMCs put greater emphasis on concomitant diseases as well as the treatment strategies chosen by the hospital [see, e.g., YOUNG (1991)].

Conclusion 9.3. *Patient classification systems try to do justice to the heterogeneity of the hospital output while making comparisons between hospitals possible. All systems seek to describe hospital output in some detail, if not with regard to treatment outcomes, that is, the improvement of health status, at least with regard to the difficulty of the task.*

9.3 Comparing Hospital Efficiency

9.3.1 Regulation and Asymmetric Information

In a competitive market, there is no reason to measure the efficiency of firms. Only efficient firms make sufficient profits to cover their costs. The market for hospital services is different. Even though competition has been introduced in the hospital sector in a number of countries (e.g., the United States, Germany, the Netherlands, and Switzerland), hospitals continue to be subsidized by tax-payers undermining the incentives for efficiency. In addition, market entry is difficult because of public regulation (such as participation in the supply emergency services and capacity limitation schemes) and political opposition of public hospitals, who want to avoid competition. Conversely, market exit is frequently a highly unpopular political decision, in particular for public hospitals. For the majority of hospitals, their economic environment therefore cannot be expected to create incentives for efficiency.

An alternative approach to ensure the efficiency of hospitals is *regulation*. A regulatory agency that is fully informed about a hospital's technology and efforts to control costs could easily achieve this objective. But providers typically have an information advantage. *Asymmetric information* can exist both with respect to efforts to control cost ('hidden action') and with respect to the technology used ('hidden information'). The 'new economics of regulation' which applies the principal-agent methodology to the contractual relationship between regulators and regulated firms [see LAFFONT AND TIROLE (1993)] has shown how the presence of asymmetric information prevents regulators from implementing an efficient ('first-best') solution since efficient providers have both incentives and possibilities to imitate inefficient providers in order to get a favorable deal, allowing them to gain an *information rent*.

Faced with this problem, regulators have two options.

(1) They can design contracts to obtain a second-best solution, striking a compromise between the reduction of the information rent and incentives for providers to control costs. We present this approach in Section 10.2.3.

(2) The regulatory agency can try to alleviate the information asymmetry which would limit the hospitals' possibilities to obtain information rents. In particular, information about the efficiency of a hospital can be gained by comparing it to other hospitals. Economists have developed two basic methods to conduct such a comparison. In Section 9.3.2 we present the parametric approach, which is based on the estimation of a hospital cost function. Section 9.3.3 is devoted to the most popular nonparametric approach called 'Data Envelopment Analysis' (DEA).

9.3.2 Hospital Cost Functions

Considering the hospital as a productive unit suggests the application of elementary concepts of production theory to hospitals. One of the core concepts of production theory, which has great empirical relevance, is the cost function. It assigns *minimal costs of production to each output bundle* and contains the same information as the production function.[2] The quantities on the right-hand side of the cost function are factor prices and output quantities. These variables – and in the case of a short-term cost function, the amount of fixed factors – may be considered exogenous, provided perfect competition prevails in the factor markets. This makes the cost function more easily amenable to econometric estimation than the production function which depends on input quantities. As these are chosen by the firm, they cannot be considered as exogenous.

---

[2] This is a key result of duality theory [see, e.g., DIEWERT (1974) and VARIAN (1992, Chapter 6)]. Note that a cost function is a sequence of minimal cost points where the isoquant (representing the production function) is tangent to the budget constraint (representing cost). At these tangency points, relative factor prices are equal to relative marginal factor productivities, hence the equality of information.

The empirical estimation of cost functions is helpful for answering a number of important economic questions:

(1) From the shape of the cost function, one may recognize *economies or diseconomies of scale*, which are important for determining the optimal size of the unit. Optimal size is of relevance to policy because in some countries the hospital industry is subject to public regulation which prevents hospitals from freely choosing their number of beds.

(2) Differentiation of the cost function with respect to the number of patients of a given category yields the *marginal costs of treatment* of this patient type. This information is useful for calculating prices in the context of performance-based payment.

(3) Residuals of an estimated cost function are the difference between a hospital's actual and estimated cost. From their size, one may hope to derive statements about their *relative efficiency*. This may facilitate the monitoring of hospital performance under cost-based payment. These possibilities will be further explored below.

Following BAUMOL ET AL. (1982), a cost function should satisfy the following requirements:

- As predicted by microeconomic theory, the cost function should be continuous, linear-homogeneous, non-decreasing, and concave in prices [see VARIAN (1992, p. 72)].

- In the multi-output case, the cost function should allow for *zero values* for some outputs lest all hospitals failing to produce all outputs must be dropped from the sample. This may lead to a sample selection problem. In addition, it would not be possible to derive results about economies of scope.

- The cost function should be sufficiently *flexible*. For example, it should allow for different degrees of economies of scale and scope. Such a flexible cost function is the translog cost function [CHRISTENSEN ET AL. (1973)] which is a second-order Taylor-approximation of an arbitrary cost function.

Most importantly, the estimation of a microeconomic cost function proceeds on the assumption that the hospitals included in the sample all aim to minimize costs and that deviations from this target have the same property as an error term. This assumption is hardly sustainable for hospitals due to the predominance of government and community ownership, since the absence of the profit motive serves to diminish the pressure to minimize costs.

To deal with the problem of non-cost-minimizing firms, *stochastic frontier estimation* has been developed. This approach specifies the estimation equation for total hospital cost as

$$C_i = C(Y_i, W_i) + V_i + U_i, \tag{9.1}$$

where C_i denotes total cost of hospital i, Y_i a vector of output quantities, W_i a vector of input prices, V_i a normally distributed error term which measures statistical noise such as measurement error in the cost variable, and U_i a positive term which measures 'errors' in decision making which result in inefficiency and thus higher than minimum costs. To estimate equation (9.1), an assumption must be made concerning the distribution of the positive error term (such as half-normal, truncated normal or exponential) so that the equation can be estimated using maximum likelihood methods.[3]

In a second step, the inefficiency measures retrieved from this estimation can be regressed against various characteristics of the hospital and its market such as ownership type, teaching status, and the number of competing hospitals within its catchment area, to explore sources of hospital inefficiency.

In estimating a cost function such as (9.1), a number of econometric issues have to be addressed:

(1) Choosing total cost as the dependent variable leads to heteroskedasticity, if the error term is positively correlated with the output variable. Furthermore, the regression can suffer from multicollinearity among the output variables if these vary directly with hospital size. To avoid these problems, both sides of the equation can be divided by an appropriate output measure, making *average cost* the dependent variable. But this makes the output variable appear on both sides of the equation so that the estimation may be biased. Also, when hospitals are considered as multi-product firms, it is unclear which output category should be used.

(2) An appropriate functional form must be chosen for the function $C(\cdot)$. Candidates are the translog or the homothetic form, which are both flexible functional forms. A disadvantage of the translog function is that it does not allow for zero output and thus can only be used with broad output categories.

(3) Hospitals are multi-product firms with several hundreds of different outputs even if patients are only classified by diagnosis-related groups. Especially with flexible functional forms the number of regressors (which is on the order of n^2 when there are n outputs) can easily exceed the number of observations. Thus in past applications, the available output information was usually condensed into a small number of output categories such as the number of cases in the various hospital departments or just the number of inpatient and outpatient cases. In the latter case, often a scalar case-mix index (such as the average DRG weight) is added to control for output severity.

(4) A further problem is the availability of information on factor prices which ideally should be used in the estimation of a cost function. In the health care sector, this information is frequently difficult to obtain.

---

[3] A classic article using this approach is ZUCKERMANN ET AL. (1994).

HOLLINGSWORTH (2003) provides a comprehensive overview of stochastic frontier studies which attempted to measure efficiency in hospitals or other health services. Estimated mean inefficiency scores differ widely from 13 percent in some studies to 28 percent and more in others. These results cast doubt on whether estimated positive error terms can really be interpreted as measures of 'inefficiency'. In particular, as very few studies have good measures for output quality (case severity within a diagnostic group), there is the danger of interpreting cost differences due to higher quality as inefficiencies. The same qualification applies to the cost of holding spare capacity (empty hospital beds). These can be interpreted as sheer waste unless the spare capacity is provided to meet stochastic demand in cases of emergency. Therefore, NEWHOUSE (1994) explicitly warns against basing hospital payment on average cost estimates from stochastic frontier studies. However, HADLEY AND ZUCKERMANN (1994) argue that the studies may at least be used to identify the 10 to 25 percent least efficient hospitals in order to exclude their cost values from the calculation of payment rates.

> **Conclusion 9.4.** *The stochastic frontier approach to measuring hospital efficiency is adequate if the data is subject to measurement error and stochastic influences. As hospital output and quality are difficult to measure, however, it is problematic to simply equate the error term of this estimation with inefficiency.*

9.3.3 Data Envelopment Analysis

9.3.3.1 Introduction

An alternative approach to measure the efficiency of a production process is nonparametric, with *Data Envelopment Analysis* (DEA) constituting the most widely used approach (Free Disposable Hull Analysis is one of the alternatives). The DEA method was developed by CHARNES ET AL. (1978) and neither assumes cost-minimizing behavior nor knowledge about factor prices. Input and output *quantities*, for which reliable data is usually available, form the basis for this method. In addition, several inputs and outputs can be considered without requiring that each hospital uses all inputs or produces all outputs.

DEA determines an *empirical frontier* of production possibilities based on the most efficient input-output combinations. The relative efficiency of hospital $i = 1, \ldots, n$ can then be obtained by measuring the distance of its input-output combination to the frontier. This corresponds to finding a 'virtual hospital' as a linear combination of all n hospitals which produces at least as much output as hospital i and uses as little inputs as possible. Assuming that hospitals use varying amounts of m inputs to produce k different outputs and denoting the ratio of inputs of the virtual hospital and the actual inputs of hospital i by θ_i, the input-oriented linear (envelopment) program in the case of constant returns to scale (CRS) is

$$\min_{\theta_i, \lambda} \theta_i$$

$$\text{s.t. } \sum_{j=1}^{n} \lambda_j y_{rj} \geq y_{ri}, \; r = 1, \ldots, k \qquad\qquad\qquad Y\lambda \geq Y_i$$

$$\theta_i x_{zi} \geq \sum_{j=1}^{n} \lambda_j x_{zj}, \; z = 1, \ldots, m \quad \text{or, in matrix notation,} \quad \theta_i X_i \geq X\lambda \quad (9.2)$$

$$\lambda_j \geq 0, \; j = 1, \ldots, n \qquad\qquad\qquad\qquad\qquad\quad \lambda \geq 0.$$

For hospital i, Y_i is the vector of k outputs y_{ri}. X_i corresponds to the vector of m inputs x_{zi} (X and Y are the input and output matrices, respectively, which contain the n input and output vectors of all hospitals). λ_j is the weight assigned to hospital j in the virtual hospital (λ is the vector containing all λ_j). The higher λ_j, the more strongly the virtual hospital is related to hospital j.

The first constraint in program (9.2) ensures that the virtual hospital produces at least as much of each output as hospital i. The right-hand side of the second constraint is equal to the use of each input by the virtual hospital which should not exceed a fraction θ_i of the input use of hospital i. Thus, $1 - \theta_i$ can be interpreted as the factor by which all inputs of hospital i can be reduced without affecting its output.[4] The third constraint restricts the weights given to actual hospitals in the virtual hospital to be nonnegative.

Problem (9.2) requires that θ_i and all λ_j are chosen such that the virtual hospital uses the smallest fraction θ_i possible of the inputs of hospital i. If hospital i is efficient, the solution is $\lambda_i^* = 1, \lambda_{j \neq i}^* = 0$ and $\theta_i^* = 1$ since it is not possible to use less inputs for a given output. For an inefficient hospital, however, we obtain $\theta_i^* < 1$. In this case, it is possible to construct a virtual hospital which only uses $\theta_i^* X_i < X_i$ inputs to produce the same output as hospital i.

Figure 9.4 illustrates the DEA approach. Five hospitals are shown which produce the same output with two inputs. The efficient frontier is defined by observations 1 to 4. The optimal solution of program (9.2) is therefore $\theta_i^* = 1, i = 1, \ldots, 4$. The shaded area shows the technology set, i.e., the set of all permissible input-output combinations. Observation 5 is obviously inefficient since it is possible to produce the same output with less inputs. DEA yields $\lambda_2^* = 0.3, \lambda_3^* = 0.7$ and $\theta_5^* = 0.5$, i.e., a linear combination of hospitals 3 (30 percent) and hospital 5 (70 percent) leads to the same output using only 50 percent of inputs. The efficient combination of inputs is given by point 5'.

DEA can also take into account variable returns to scale (VRS) if one imposes the additional constraint $\sum_i \lambda_i = 1$ [see BANKER ET AL. (1984)]. This permits to test for *scale efficiency*. Figure 9.5 illustrates the procedure for the case of one input and one

---

[4] An alternative to input-oriented DEA is output-oriented DEA which maximizes outputs for a given quantity of inputs [see SEIFORD AND THRALL (1990)].

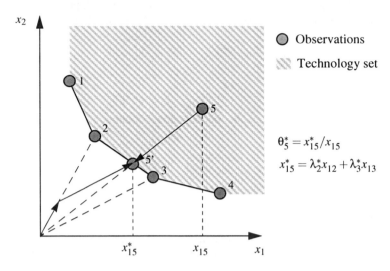

Fig. 9.4. The DEA Approach

output. The ray through the origin and observations 2 and 3 shows the technology set for constant returns to scale. The technology set under variable returns is given by the shaded area below observations 1 to 4. A comparison of both solutions, i.e., θ_i^* with constant and variable returns to scale, allows to determine scale efficiency in addition to technical efficiency. For observations 2 and 3, the result is one in both cases since they are on both frontiers. This implies that these observations are characterized by both technical and scale efficiency. By contrast, observation 5 meets neither criteria. First, this hospital is technically inefficient since the same output could be produced with less inputs ($x_{i=5}$ minus $x'_{i=5}$). Second, this hospital is too large. This scale inefficiency is captured by the difference of $x'_{i=5}$ and $x''_{i=5}$: even if hospital 5 were technically efficient and used only inputs $x'_{i=5}$, splitting the output between two hospitals (e.g., hospitals 2 und 3) would require only inputs $x''_{i=5}$. This information can be particularly valuable if new hospitals are planned.

Conclusion 9.5 . *Data Envelopment Analysis (DEA) is a nonparametric method to determine the efficiency of hospitals which does not require that hospitals minimize costs. DEA allows for multiple outputs and does not need information on factor prices which is usually difficult to obtain.*

9.3.3.2 Comparing the Efficiency of Swiss Hospitals

STEINMANN AND ZWEIFEL (2003) conduct a DEA study to examine the efficiency of 89 Swiss hospitals from 1993 to 1996 with a total of 310 observations. They adopt the usual 'two-stage approach'. First, they perform DEA according to the linear

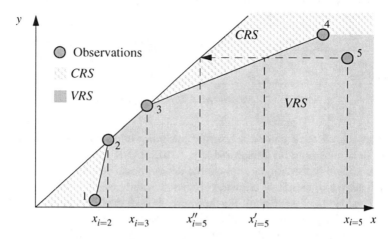

Fig. 9.5. Scale Inefficiency and Pure Technical Inefficiency

program (9.2). Second, they analyze the determinants of efficiency with a random-effects regression.

The study distinguishes three different categories of labor as inputs (medical, nursing, and administrative staff). Furthermore, non-labor expenses (at prices of 1990) and patient days are classified as inputs (see Section 9.2.2). On the output side, only in-patient services were considered even though hospitals in cities also provide some out-patient services. Five categories were used to capture the outputs of hospitals: medical, pediatric, surgical, gynecological, and intensive care discharges.

DEA implicitly assigns shadow prices to inputs and outputs (in Figure 9.4 the slope of the isoquant correspond to the shadow price ratio). Although the exact prices for inputs and outputs in the Swiss hospital sector are not known, it makes sense to restrict the ratio of shadow prices to reasonable values. This implies that only observations which operate under realistic shadow price ratios turn out to be efficient whereas observations with unrealistic shadow price ratios appear inefficient. The study therefore restricted all marginal rates of substitution and transformation. Marginal productivities, however, were not restricted. Furthermore, the analysis allowed for variable returns to scale.

DEA classifies 34 out of 310 observations as efficient. These 34 efficient observations are from 11 hospitals. Table 9.1 shows the distribution according to the type of hospital. Overall, efficient units occur among the largest and smallest hospitals in terms of beds. On the other hand, the category 249–499 beds does not contain a single efficient observation. This suggests constant returns to scale over a wide range, at least for the five specified outputs. Globally, increasing returns to scale are possible.

Compared to parametric methods, DEA does not directly consider the different conditions under which hospitals operate. A hospital classified as efficient (ineffi-

Table 9.1. Efficient and Inefficient Observations, Swiss Hospitals 1993–1996

| | Teaching hospital | Number of beds | | | | | |
		< 75	75–124	125–248	249–499	> 499	Total
Efficient	3	10	13	6	0	2	34
Inefficient	3	58	72	101	33	9	276

Source: STEINMANN AND ZWEIFEL (2003, Table 2)

cient) may therefore in fact be a hospital operating under favorable (adverse) conditions. To compensate for this drawback, STEINMANN AND ZWEIFEL (2003) use a random-effects regression to analyze the determinants of DEA inefficiency.[5] This approach allows to calculate adjusted efficiency scores which take into account the specific conditions of a hospital. Furthermore, the effect of conditions which can in principle be influenced by the regulator can be analyzed. For example, if a particular way of financing hospitals enhances efficiency, the regulator can implement this way in all hospitals.

Table 9.2 shows the result from the random-effects estimation of inefficiency of the 276 observations from 78 hospitals that are always inefficient. The following insights can be obtained.

- Subsidized hospitals are significantly less efficient.

- Further variables which could capture the incentives for hospital efficiency (deficit coverage, subsidization without deficit coverage, hospitals incorporated under public law, private hospitals) have the predicted sign but the coefficients are not significantly different from zero.

- Hospitals with emergency admission have significantly lower efficiency. This may be a consequence of not including out-patient cases as outputs in DEA.

- Inefficiency was decreasing over time (1993 is the reference year). A possible explanation is the revised health insurance law which became effective in 1995 and may have lead to a general increase in cost consciousness.

- The share of interns, i.e., medical or nursing interns or clerical apprentices, significantly increased efficiency at a decreasing rate as long as it does not exceed 12 percent.

- Hospitals with a higher share of private patient days are significantly less efficient.

- The incentives and conditions under which hospitals operate can only explain a small part of the differences in efficiency between the Swiss hospitals. However, this may be a consequence of the generally weak incentives for Swiss hospitals to operate efficiently.

---

[5] The random-effects model is an approach to take into account correlations between observations of the same unit in panel data [see, e.g., GREENE (2008, Chapter 9)].

Table 9.2. Random Effects Estimation, Swiss Hospitals 1993–1996

	Predicted Sign	Coefficient	P>z
Subsidized hospital	+	3.740	0.051
Deficit coverage	+	2.152	0.221
Subsidized without deficit coverage	−	−1.376	0.622
Hospital inc. under public law	+	1.015	0.705
Private hospital	?	0.735	0.868
Percentage interns	+	−0.451	0.061
Percentage interns, squared	+	0.018	0.072
Percentage private patient days	+	0.134	0.004
Emergency admissions	?	8.124	0.022
Dummyvariable for 1994	?	−3.008	0.000
Dummyvariable for 1995	?	−3.948	0.000
Dummyvariable for 1996	?	−5.527	0.000
Hospital with more than 500 beds	?	−9.069	0.360
Hospital with 250-499 beds	?	−7.280	0.377
Hospital with 125-249 beds	?	−7.975	0.315
Hospital with 75-124 beds	?	−5.629	0.480
Hospital with less than 75 beds	?	−3.678	0.647
Constant		14.599	0.103
$\hat{\sigma}_u$		10.120	0.000
$\hat{\sigma}_\varepsilon$		4.235	0.000
Log-likelihood		−912.798	
Hausman specification test		Prob $> \chi^2 = 0.300$	

Source: STEINMANN AND ZWEIFEL (2003, Table 5)

We summarize our results in

Conclusion 9.6. *A comparison of the efficiency of Swiss hospitals shows that subsidized hospitals and hospitals with emergency admission are significantly less efficient. There was a statistically significant increase in efficiency between 1993 and 1996.*

Finally, we want to point out possible problems of DEA. Measurement errors and stochastic influences can lead to outliers which may distort the efficient frontier and therefore the efficiency evaluation. In addition, the relation between the number of inputs and outputs and the size of the sample is relevant. In a small sample, average efficiency tends to be higher. It is therefore in the interest of the hospitals which are to be evaluated to demand a (too) high number of inputs and outputs.

9.3.4 Potential and Limits of Efficiency Measurement

The heterogeneity and complexity of hospital output makes it difficult to assess the efficiency of a hospital. The methods presented in this section approach this task by providing a measure of *relative efficiency*. Hospitals are compared to the 'best' observations in the sample. An assessment about absolute efficiency cannot be provided. Neither is it possible to compare the results about relative efficiency between different studies.

Furthermore, it should be kept in mind that the methods assume that all inputs and outputs are homogeneous. This assumption is needed to keep the number of inputs and outputs at a tractable level or simply because it is not possible to obtain the necessary information. Finally, it should be noted that the results about relative efficiency pertain to a specific period of time. For a regulatory agency it is also of interest how efficiency changes over time. For instance, innovations may bring about an increase in inefficiency in the short run but enhance efficiency in the long run.

Nevertheless, it needs to be emphasized that the methods presented here provide valuable information about the efficiency of hospitals. In any case, for a hospital which is classified as inefficient it should be checked in detail whether any of the aforementioned limitations applies or if it produces its output inefficiently as predicted by the study.

9.4 Summary

(1) Hospital output consists of improving or maintaining the patient's state of health on the one hand and the capacity to satisfy an option demand on the other hand. The former part of output is particularly difficult to operationalize and can only partially be attributed to the hospital.

(2) A hospital's 'output' can be described as the outcome of a multi-stage process, with each stage being assigned its specific concept of efficiency.

(3) A patient classification system represents the attempt to do justice to the heterogeneity of the hospital output while making comparisons among hospitals possible. All systems share the idea of describing hospital output in some detail, if not with reference to the outcome of treatment, i.e., the improvement of health status, still with reference to the difficulty associated with achieving this outcome.

(4) The stochastic frontier approach to the comparison of hospital efficiency is adequate if the data is subject to measurement error and stochastic influences. As hospital output and quality are difficult to measure, however, it is problematic to interpret the error term of this estimation solely as inefficiency.

(5) Data Envelopment Analysis (DEA) is a nonparametric method to determine the efficiency of hospitals which does not require that hospitals minimize costs. DEA allows for multiple outputs and does not need information on factor prices which is usually difficult to obtain.

(6) A comparison of the efficiency of Swiss hospitals shows that subsidized hospitals and hospitals with emergency admission are significantly less efficient. Efficiency increased to a statistically significant extent between 1993 and 1996.

9.5 Further Reading

In the HANDBOOK OF HEALTH ECONOMICS the chapters by SLOAN (2000) and SALKEVER (2000) are devoted to hospital behavior and regulation. An introduction to parametric and nonparametric methods of measuring efficiency can be found in COELLI ET AL. (1998). KUMBHAKAR AND LOVELL (2000) give an overview over parametric frontier approaches. COOPER ET AL. (2006) discuss nonparametric methods in detail. The results of a large number of studies of both types are summarized in HOLLINGSWORTH (2003).

9.E Exercises

9.1. Which problems arise when trying to measure the output of a hospital? Which approaches can be taken to solve these problems?

9.2. Compare the pros and cons of the methods of measuring hospital efficiency. Under which conditions is each method superior?

9.3. The technology in the hospital sector is characterized by constant returns to scale and two inputs x_1 and x_2.

(a) Five hospitals with identical outputs use the following inputs:

Hospital	1	2	3	4	5
x_1	4	1	6	2	9
x_2	2	6	3	4	9

Which hospitals operate efficiently? Find the value of θ_i for each hospital (see the optimization problem (9.2)).

(b) Now consider two additional hospitals 6 and 7. They produce twice the output with inputs $x_1^6 = 14$, $x_2^6 = 3.5$ and $x_1^7 = 16$, $x_2^7 = 2$. Are these hospitals efficient? Would your answer change if you only observed hospital 6?

10

Paying Providers

10.1 Introduction

One of the guiding themes of this book is the optimal design of incentives for patients and providers. In Chapter 6, we concentrated on the demand side. In case of moral hazard, we found that complete insurance coverage encourages excessive use of health care services by the insured. For this reason, *demand-side cost sharing* in the form of copayments will usually be optimal. In this chapter, we turn to the supply side to examine optimal incentives for providers of health care services who are prone to moral hazard as well. After all, they are guaranteed reimbursement regardless of cost by an insurer paying fee-for-service. Incentives to control costs under such a payment system are weak, calling for some kind of *supply-side cost sharing*.[1]

The general hypothesis of this chapter is that *payment systems* determine provider incentives to a large extent. This is not to say that professional ethics should be neglected. Indeed, as will become clear in the following, professional ethics importantly contribute to the quality of health care when quality is not verifiable. But some providers may lack an ethical orientation, and ethics could wear out in the course of a long professional life that typically brings with it a certain disillusionment. Therefore, a payment system must be designed in a way as to provide appropriate incentives to service providers who do not fully act in the overall interest of the insured.

With regard to the incentive to control costs noted above, payment systems can be characterized as *prospective* or *retrospective*. Under a fully retrospective system, the payer reimburses all costs incurred by providers, who therefore are relieved of the risk of having to bear even part of a cost overrun. Fee-for-service payment falls into the category that clearly provides little incentive for providers to control costs. By way of contrast, a prospective system establishes complete supply-side cost sharing and reimburses providers independently of cost.

---

[1] In addition, one is likely to have to deal with the problem of *supplier-induced demand* as long as an increase in the volume of services supplied causes provider income to increase, as is the case with fee-for-service payment (see Chapter 8).

P. Zweifel et al., *Health Economics*, 2nd ed., DOI 10.1007/978-3-540-68540-1_10,
© Springer-Verlag Berlin Heidelberg 2009

The increase in health care expenditure has led to a shift in favor of supply-side cost sharing. Especially in the hospital sector, payment systems with prospective elements have replaced the practice of covering costs. Already in 1984, Medicare, the public health insurance system for the elderly of the United States, introduced a per-case payment system based on Diagnosis Related Groups (DRGs). DRG payment means that hospitals receive a sum of money for the treatment of a patient that mainly depends on the diagnosis established at admission. It thus shifts to a considerable extent the risk of cost overruns to hospitals, causing them to be interested in controlling their cost of treatment.

While prospective payment eradicates moral hazard with respect to cost control, it is subject to a very basic criticism. After all, insurers and not single providers specialize in managing and ultimately bearing risk in other walks of life, and it is difficult to see why health insurance should constitute an exception to this rule. For this reason, it is hardly surprising that in actual practice, insurers and providers negotiate for a *mixed system* in which reimbursement reflects cost of treatment incurred to some degree, implying that insurers bear part of the financial risk that is necessarily associated with treatment processes that contain an important chance element.

Furthermore, a payment system should make providers perform in the best interest of consumers. Microeconomic theory predicts that consumers do not seek to minimize cost but to maximize utility. And in the context of health care, utility importantly depends on quality of treatment, which may be compromised if the incentives to control costs are too strong. In addition, if providers bear the risk of cost exceeding payment received, they may want to avoid costly patients. Thus, a payment system with strong emphasis on cost control may induce patient selection. These side effects would be of little relevance if payers (i.e., health insurers or a government agency) were able to monitor health care providers. But they typically suffer from an information asymmetry, possibly as much as patients themselves. A further complication arises if providers are better informed about the casemix than the payer. A fully prospective payment system is suboptimal in this case because it requires high payments to ensure that providers accept to treat patients, resulting in an excessive *information rent* to efficient providers.

These considerations make it clear that any payment system must strike a difficult balance between competing objectives. The analysis provided in this chapter will reveal that this balance is governed by parameters that are hardly observable such as the degree of risk aversion characterizing an individual service provider. It does indicate, however, how payment needs to be structured in order to accommodate concerns that go beyond cost control.

In keeping with the issues outlined, inducing providers to care about cost control is assumed to be the objective of overriding importance in Section 10.2. A basic model (that will be generalized later on) is presented in Section 10.2.1 to establish the *principle of full cost responsibility*. In Section 10.2.2, we assume that providers are risk averse, which already motivates a departure from the principle of full cost responsibility. The consequences of asymmetric information about the case mix are analyzed in Section 10.2.3. Section 10.3 is devoted to concerns that go beyond mere cost control. Section 10.3.1 analyzes how quality of treatment is affected by the payment system. A distinction of crucial importance is whether quality is verifiable or not. In Section 10.3.2, the second additional issue is addressed, viz. patient selection by health care providers. The basic model is modified to deal with the cases of symmetry and asymmetry of information about the cost types of patients. Section 10.4 spells out the implications of the theoretical analysis, first in general terms (Section 10.4.1), then for physician payment (Section 10.4.2), and finally for hospital payment (Section 10.4.3). A summary of the main insights is provided in Section 10.5.

Throughout the chapter, the payer is assumed to act as a *complementary agent* for patients (be it a national health service or a private health insurer). For simplicity, we abstract from possible principle-agent problems between patients and the payer. These are discussed in Chapter 11, where the pros and cons of different institutions acting as complementary agents are considered.

10.2 Paying Providers to Achieve Cost Control

10.2.1 The Principle of Full Cost Responsibility

10.2.1.1 The Basic Model

Let a risk-neutral payer maximize the difference between patients' benefit from treatment B and the payment to providers P.[2] In the basic model, the patient population to be treated is predetermined. Welfare W is given by

$$W = B - P, \tag{10.1}$$

where B is measured in monetary units. In the basic model, providers are assumed to be risk neutral, their preferences being described by the following (common) utility function

$$u(P,e) = P - C(e) - V(e) \quad \text{with} \quad e \geq 0, V(0) = 0, V'(e) > 0, V''(e) > 0. \tag{10.2}$$

e measures the effort exerted by the provider to control costs while $C(e)$ corresponds to the monetary cost of treatment, such as the costs of diagnostic tests and auxiliary services.[3] The payer is assumed to observe $C(e)$. This rules out that providers can

---

[2] Alternatively, the agent could maximize a utilitarian social welfare function which includes both patient and provider welfare as in LAFFONT AND TIROLE (1993) und CHALKLEY AND MALCOMSON (2000). This leads to the same qualitative results.

[3] $C(e)$ therefore differs from the notion of minimum cost used in standard microeconomic theory.

manipulate cost data. Otherwise the problem of *cost padding* arises, i.e., the manipulation of cost accounting data in order to obtain higher reimbursement [see LAFFONT AND TIROLE (1993, Chapter 12)].[4]

The function $V(e)$ captures the corresponding loss of utility as well as providers' opportunity cost of time and is assumed to be convex in e. This cost component is not verifiable in court and can therefore not be part of a payment system. Providers who do not accept the contract offered by the payer obtain reservation utility $\bar{u}$.

Costs C are uncertain, which implies that cost-reducing effort e cannot be inferred from observation. But their expected value, $EC(e)$, depends on effort e in the following way,

$$EC(e) \equiv E(C(e)), \quad \text{with} \quad EC'(e) < 0, EC''(e) \geq 0. \tag{10.3}$$

An increase in e therefore lowers expected costs $EC(e)$ at a non-increasing rate.

The objective of the payer is to design a payment system which maximizes welfare. To reduce complexity, we consider linear payment systems only, which serves to limit the problem to the optimization of parameters. The loss of generality is negligible because in practice provider payment uses linear relationships anyway. Specifically assume a linear payment system of the form

$$P = F + np + \gamma C. \tag{10.4}$$

Total payment P consists of a flat component F, a capitation payment p for each of the n patients treated, and a payment γC proportional to observed costs. The parameter γ is the share of actual costs borne by the payer. Correspondingly, $1 - \gamma$ can be interpreted as the degree of supply-side cost sharing. Providers bear full cost responsibility if $\gamma = 0$. In this case, the payment system is fully prospective. If $\gamma = 1$, the payer reimburses costs as evidenced. This amounts to a fully retrospective payment system. A mixed system is characterized by $0 < \gamma < 1$. Until the end of Section 10.3.1, we take the number of patients as given and set the capitation payment to zero, therefore neglecting possible provider influence on the number of patients. An overview over the basic model is given in Box 10.1.

10.2.1.2 The First-Best Payment System

The optimal values of P and e for the payer can be found by maximizing expected welfare

$$EW = B - EP, \tag{10.5}$$

where EP denotes the expected value of payment (which can in principle contain a stochastic component). The payer is restricted by the participation constraint for

---

[4] This implies that reliable cost data must not depend on easily manipulable factor quantities such as working time or use of equipment. Instead, it must be based on services which can be verified. These services can then be valued with prices to obtain a measure of cost.

Box 10.1. The Basic Model

$$W = B - P \tag{10.1}$$

$$U(P,e) = P - C(e) - V(e), \text{ with}$$
$$e \geq 0, \; V(0) = 0, \; V'(e) > 0, \; V''(e) > 0 \tag{10.2}$$

$$EC(e) \equiv E(C(e)), \; EC'(e) < 0, \; EC''(e) \geq 0 \tag{10.3}$$

$$P = F + np + \gamma C \tag{10.4}$$

$$V'[e_{FB}] = -EC'[e_{FB}] \tag{10.8}$$

$$EP = \bar{u} + V[e_{FB}] + EC[e_{FB}] \tag{10.9}$$

W:	payer's welfare
B:	patients' benefit from treatment
P:	payment to the provider
u:	utility of the provider
e:	provider effort devoted to cost control
$C(e)$:	monetary cost of treating a group of patients
$EC(e)$:	expected monetary costs of treating a defined group of patients
$V(e)$:	utility loss of provider due to effort e, inclusive of opportunity cost
$\bar{u}$:	reservation utility of the provider
F:	flat component of payment
n:	number of patients treated
p:	capitation payment
γ:	share of actual costs borne by the payer
FB:	first-best

providers which ensures that they will accept the contract offered by the payer. This will be the case if a provider's expected utility is at least as high as reservation utility $\bar{u}$,[5] i.e., if

$$EU(P,e) = E(u(P,e)) = EP - EC(e) - V(e) \geq \bar{u}. \tag{10.6}$$

Solving this equation on the left-hand side for EP and inserting into the objective function (10.5), one obtains

$$\max_{e,EU} EW = B - EC(e) - V(e) - EU \quad \text{s.t.} \quad EU \geq \bar{u}. \tag{10.7}$$

Now a payer acting on behalf of consumers should never 'leave money on the table' by guaranteeing providers more utility than is necessary to get them sign the contract. Therefore, $EU = \bar{u}$ holds. The first-order condition with respect to e defines the first-best (FB) level of effort e_{FB} to control costs,

$$V'[e_{FB}] = -EC'[e_{FB}]. \tag{10.8}$$

---

[5] In the following, we assume that it is always worthwhile to induce the provider to accept the contract.

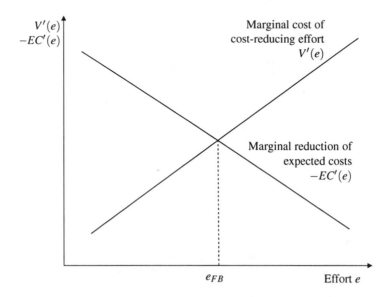

Fig. 10.1. Optimal Effort Level to Control Costs

At the optimum, marginal cost of effort devoted to control costs $V'(e)$ therefore equals the expected value of cost reduction achieved $-EC'(e)$ (see Figure 10.1). For the first-best payment system, we obtain from (10.6), using the condition $EU = \bar{u}$,

$$EP = EC[e_{FB}] + V[e_{FB}] + \bar{u}. \tag{10.9}$$

10.2.1.3 Implementing the First-Best Solution

To implement the first-best solution, a contract must be designed to yield expected utility $EU = \bar{u}$ to providers while creating incentives to exert effort e_{FB}. One possibility is to make the contract contingent on the effort level e, specifying the following payment rule,

$$P = \begin{cases} \bar{u} + V[e_{FB}] + C & \text{if } e \geq e_{FB} \\ -z & \text{if } e < e_{FB}. \end{cases} \tag{10.10}$$

The penalty z needs to be high enough to guarantee that it is in the provider's own interest to opt for e_{FB}; in return, actual costs incurred can be reimbursed because they reflect optimal effort (from the payer's and ultimately the patients' point of view) under all circumstances.

Note, however, that the rule (10.10) works only if effort is 'contractible', i.e., observable and verifiable in court – a condition unlikely to be satisfied in most cases. An alternative is the *principle of full cost responsibility*. Consider

$$P = F_{FB} = EC[e_{FB}] + V[e_{FB}] + \bar{u}, \tag{10.11}$$

i.e., providers receive a flat payment F_{FB} that is sufficient to cover their financial plus their opportunity cost of effort plus the money equivalent of their outside option. Therefore, they are fully responsible for all costs. Their expected utility is

$$
\begin{aligned}
EU(P,e) &= EP - EC(e) - V(e) \\
&= F_{FB} - EC(e) - V(e).
\end{aligned}
$$

Thus, they solve the problem

$$\max_{e} EU = F_{FB} - EC(e) - V(e).$$

The first-order condition is

$$-EC'(e) - V'(e) = 0 \Rightarrow e = e_{FB}. \tag{10.12}$$

Providers therefore choose first-best effort e_{FB}, attaining expected utility

$$EU(P,e) = F_{FB} - EC[e_{FB}] - V[e_{FB}] = \bar{u},$$

and the first-best solution is implemented. This establishes that the *principle of full cost responsibility* can implement the first-best solution.

Conclusion 10.1. *If providers are risk neutral and only have to pursue cost control, the first-best solution can be implemented by a prospective payment system placing full cost responsibility on providers. If effort devoted to cost control cannot be observed or specified sufficiently in a contract, prospective payment is the only payment system capable of implementing the first-best solution.*

It is important to keep in mind the obstacles that still need to be surmounted when trying to make this conclusion operational. Specifically, equation (10.11) is written without subscripts for notational simplicity. Yet each of the three components of payment depends on provider characteristics. Some physicians and hospitals are more effective than others when it comes to keeping costs low, causing $EC[e_{FB}]$ to differ between them. In addition, their psychic and opportunity cost $V[e_{FB}]$ is unlikely to be the same. Providers also have vastly different outside options $\bar{u}$; some of them may be flexible enough to move to a different country (value of $\bar{u}$ high) while others are 'married' to their local community ($\bar{u}$ low). Thus, the payer needs to have the know-how (and in the case of private insurers, the legal right) to set (negotiate, respectively) payment levels that are tailored to the characteristics of individual providers or at least provider groups [for some evidence concerning variability of physician preferences with regard to payment, see ZWEIFEL AND BRAENDLE (2008)].

10.2.2 Paying Risk-Averse Providers

Up to this point, health care providers were assumed to be risk neutral. This would be quite acceptable if one were dealing with corporations whose shares are held by investors who are amply diversified. The management of such a corporation would be acting in the best interest of its owners by taking decisions in a risk-neutral manner. However, only hospitals that are part of a chain come close to this state of affairs, let alone physicians in single practice who are hardly diversified at all because their principal asset is their human capital, which is tied to the practice. For this reason, taking account of risk aversion is of considerable importance.

Let providers have a strictly concave utility function,

$$u(P,e) = u(P - C(e) - V(e)), \quad \text{with} \quad u' > 0, u'' < 0. \tag{10.13}$$

Providers who do not sign up with the payer pursue an alternative activity guaranteeing them an income equivalent to a certain payment s. This certainty equivalent defines their reservation utility

$$\bar{u} \equiv u[s]. \tag{10.14}$$

In the following, a distinction will turn out to be crucial. Provider effort to control costs may be contractible (the easier yet unrealistic case), or noncontractible (the more difficult but realistic case). In the latter variant, the payer cannot observe effort or is unable to verify in court that provider effort has been insufficient.

10.2.2.1 Contractible Effort to Control Costs

As above, the payer's optimization problem is

$$\max EW = B - EP \tag{10.15}$$

subject to

$$EU(P,e) \geq \bar{u} = u[s]. \tag{10.16}$$

This participation constraint continues to be binding at the optimum.

Given that cost-reducing effort is contractible, the payer can cover observed costs $C(e)$ as in Section 10.2.1.3, implying a payment system

$$P = F + C. \tag{10.17}$$

After all, $EC[e_{FB}]$ can always be enforced in this event. Indeed, it would not make sense to expose providers to uncertainty by making them responsible even for part of observed costs. Being risk averse, they would have to be compensated for this through a *risk premium*.

Using (10.13), (10.14) and (10.17), the binding participation constraint (10.16) can be simplified to

$$u(F - V(e)) = u[s],$$

and thus

$$F = s + V(e). \tag{10.18}$$

Equation (10.17) implies $EP = F + EC(e)$. Hence, together with equation (10.18), the payer's objective function (10.15) can be formulated as

$$\max_e EW = B - EC(e) - V(e) - s. \tag{10.19}$$

The first-order condition yields

$$V'[e_{FB}] = -EC'[e_{FB}]. \tag{10.20}$$

This equation has the same structure as condition (10.8). Therefore, while payment is retrospective, making contracts contingent on cost-reducing effort enables the first-best solution to be attained. Accordingly, providers receive a flat payment amounting to

$$F_{FB} = V[e_{FB}] + s, \tag{10.21}$$

resulting in a first-best payment of

$$P = C[e_{FB}] + V[e_{FB}] + s. \tag{10.22}$$

Analogously to the payment rule in equation (10.10), the contract specifies a payment F_{FB} contingent on $e \geq e_{FR}$. If $e < e_{FR}$ is observed, the provider has to pay a contract penalty z:

$$P = \begin{cases} C[e_{FB}] + V[e_{FB}] + s & \text{if } e \geq e_{FB} \\ -z & \text{if } e < e_{FB}. \end{cases}$$

In practice, however, it is unlikely that such a contract can be enforced since the payer is not able to observe provider effort. Even if this were the case, it is difficult to prove in court that effort has been insufficient, i.e., effort is likely to be unverifiable. To create incentives for cost control, the contract must therefore depend on actual costs. This, however, creates a trade-off between efficient incentives to control costs and efficient risk-sharing, which we explore in the following section.

10.2.2.2 Noncontractible Effort to Control Costs

To analyze this case, we make a number of simplifying assumptions (a summary of the model is provided in Box 10.2).

(1) The cost function takes the following form,

$$C(e) = a - e + \sigma\varepsilon, \quad \text{with} \quad a > 0, E\varepsilon = 0, \text{Var}(\varepsilon) = 1,^6 \tag{10.23}$$

where ε is a random variable and $\sigma > 0$ corresponds to the standard deviation of costs. Expected costs are

$$EC(e) = a - e. \tag{10.24}$$

Each unit of effort e therefore decreases expected costs by one monetary unit.

(2) The utility loss due to cost-reducing effort e is given by

$$V(e) = \frac{1}{2}e^2. \tag{10.25}$$

Using (10.24), the first-best condition $V'[e_{FB}] = -EC'[e_{FB}]$ therefore implies $e_{FB} = 1$.

(3) With y as the provider's income net of cost of effort,

$$y \equiv P - C(e) - V(e), \tag{10.26}$$

expected utility is assumed to depend only on the expected value μ_y and the variance σ_y^2 of y.[7] Specifically, let expected utility take the following functional form,

$$EU = \mu_y - \frac{r}{2}\sigma_y^2, \tag{10.27}$$

where r is a measure of risk aversion. The provider is risk neutral if $r = 0$ and risk averse if $r > 0$.

Given these three simplifying assumptions, consider the payer's choice of the flat payment F and the degree of cost reimbursement γ in the linear payment system

$$P(C) = F + \gamma C. \tag{10.28}$$

To solve this problem, we first express provider's expected utility as a function of F and γ. We then use this relationship as a restriction in the payer's expected welfare function. Since this function now depends on F and γ, the optimal values of these two parameters can be determined.

---

[6] Assuming that the random variable ε is bounded from below, nonnegative treatment costs can be ensured by a suffiently high value of the parameter a .

[7] With the cost function (10.23) and a linear payment system, this assumption does not entail a loss of generality [see SINN (1983) and MEYER (1987)].

Box 10.2. Paying Risk-Averse Providers when Effort is Noncontractible

$$u(P,e) = u(P - C(e) - V(e)) \quad \text{with} \quad u' > 0, u'' < 0 \tag{10.13}$$

$$\bar{u} = u[s] \tag{10.14}$$

$$EW = B - EP \tag{10.15}$$

$$C(e) = a - e + \sigma\varepsilon \quad \text{with} \quad a > 0, E\varepsilon = 0, Var(\varepsilon) = 1 \tag{10.23}$$

$$V(e) = \frac{1}{2}e^2 \tag{10.25}$$

$$y = P - C(e) - V(e) \tag{10.26}$$

$$EU = \mu_y - \frac{r}{2}\sigma_y^2 \tag{10.27}$$

$$P(C) = F + \gamma C \tag{10.28}$$

$$\gamma^* = \frac{r\sigma^2}{1 + r\sigma^2} \tag{10.38}$$

$$e^* = \frac{1}{1 + r\sigma^2} \tag{10.39}$$

$$F^* = s + \frac{a}{1 + r\sigma^2} + \frac{r\sigma^2 - 1}{2(1 + r\sigma^2)^2} \tag{10.40}$$

EW:	expected welfare of payer
EU:	expected utility of provider
s:	certainty equivalent income under alternative employment
σ:	standard deviation of costs
y:	provider income net of cost of effort
μ_y:	expected value of y
σ_y^2:	variance of y
r:	measure of risk aversion
γ^*:	optimal degree of cost reimbursement by payer
e^*:	optimal provider effort
F^*:	optimal flat payment

Provider's expected utility

Inserting (10.28) into (10.26), one obtains for provider's income net of effort cost

$$y = F - (1 - \gamma)C(e) - V(e).$$

In view of (10.24) and (10.25), the expected value of y is given by

$$\mu_y = F - (1 - \gamma)EC(e) - V(e) = F - (1 - \gamma)a + (1 - \gamma)e - \frac{1}{2}e^2. \tag{10.29}$$

From (10.23), one has for the variance of y

$$\sigma_y^2 = (1 - \gamma)^2\sigma^2. \tag{10.30}$$

Substituting these two expressions into (10.27), provider's expected utility depends in the following way on effort e,

$$EU(e) = F - (1-\gamma)(a-e) - \frac{1}{2}e^2 - \frac{r}{2}(1-\gamma)^2\sigma^2. \tag{10.31}$$

The first two terms correspond to the expected value of the payment to be received from the payer. The cost of effort is captured by $\frac{1}{2}e^2$. The final term is a premium for risk bearing which increases in $1-\gamma$, the degree of provider's cost responsibility. This *risk premium* must be financed by the payer as well, a consideration that will prove important below.

The provider's first-order condition for optimal effort e is $1-\gamma-e = 0$. Thus,

$$e(\gamma) = 1-\gamma. \tag{10.32}$$

Substituting into (10.31) yields provider's expected utility as a function of the flat payment F and the degree of cost responsibility γ,

$$EU(F,\gamma) = F - a(1-\gamma) + \frac{(1-\gamma)^2}{2} - \frac{r}{2}(1-\gamma)^2\sigma^2. \tag{10.33}$$

The payer's problem

Using (10.24), (10.28) and (10.32), *payer's expected welfare* can be written as

$$\begin{aligned} EW(F,\gamma) &= E(B - P(C)) \\ &= B - F - \gamma EC(e(\gamma)) \\ &= B - F - a\gamma + \gamma(1-\gamma). \end{aligned} \tag{10.34}$$

The payer maximizes this function subject to the provider's participation constraint. With the utility function (10.27), expected utility under alternative employment is given by the certainty equivalent s. At the optimum, the participation constraint is binding, and $EU = s$. Inserting this restriction into equation (10.33) yields the following expression for F,

$$F = a(1-\gamma) - \frac{(1-\gamma)^2}{2} + \frac{r}{2}(1-\gamma)^2\sigma^2 + s. \tag{10.35}$$

Substituting (10.35) into (10.34) leads to

$$EW(\gamma) = B - a + \gamma(1-\gamma) + \frac{(1-\gamma)^2}{2} - \frac{r}{2}(1-\gamma)^2\sigma^2 - s. \tag{10.36}$$

The payer's problem is therefore reduced to the determination of the optimal degree of cost reimbursement γ. From the first-order condition $EW'(\gamma) = 0$, one obtains

$$\gamma^* = r\sigma^2(1-\gamma^*). \tag{10.37}$$

The optimal value of γ can be found by solving (10.37) for γ^*. The optimal effort level e^* is obtained by substituting γ^* into equation (10.32). This yields

$$\gamma^* = \frac{r\sigma^2}{1+r\sigma^2} > 0 \quad \text{if } r > 0,$$

(10.38)

$$e^* = \frac{1}{1+r\sigma^2} < 1 \quad \text{if } r > 0.$$

(10.39)

These results can be interpreted as follows.

- *Only partial cost responsibility of providers.* For a risk-averse provider ($r > 0$), we find $\gamma^* > 0$, with the departure from $\gamma = 0$ increasing with σ^2 [$\partial\gamma^*/\partial\sigma^2 = r/(1+r\sigma^2)^2 > 0$] and r [$\partial\gamma^*/\partial r = \sigma^2/(1+r\sigma^2)^2 > 0$]. Therefore, the greater the uncertainty surrounding the costs of treatment and the more marked providers' risk aversion, the more the payer should optimally reimburse actual costs.

- *Less than first-best effort.* Effort is below the first-best level $e_{FB} = 1$ if providers are risk averse. This is the moral hazard effect that must be expected as soon as providers are not fully responsible for costs incurred. Therefore, $\partial e^*/\partial\sigma^2 = -r(1+r\sigma^2)^2 < 0$ and $\partial e^*/\partial r = -\sigma^2(1+r\sigma^2)^2 < 0$ come as little surprise. The more marked cost uncertainty and provider risk aversion, the smaller optimal cost-reducing effort (since providers are increasingly relieved of cost responsibility).

The payer is willing to accept these distortions because the risk premium and therefore the expected payment to the provider is reduced. Note that γ^* must lie between zero and one, which implies that a mixed system is generally optimal.

Using γ^* from equation (10.38) in equation (10.35), one obtains the optimal flat payment

$$F^* = s + \frac{a}{1+r\sigma^2} + \frac{r\sigma^2 - 1}{2(1+r\sigma^2)^2}.$$

It depends on the provider's outside option as measured by s and the level of costs as measured by a. Furthermore, risk aversion and cost uncertainty influence F^* since these parameters affect the share of costs reimbursed by the payer.

> **Conclusion 10.2.** *If providers are risk averse and costs of treatment are uncertain, the first-best solution can be implemented if provider effort is contractible. Otherwise, it is optimal to deviate from full cost responsibility and to accept less than first-best effort. This allows to reduce the risk premium which must be paid to the provider.*

In general, cost uncertainty σ^2 and therefore the optimal level of cost reimbursement will differ between types of treatment and between providers. In that event, the question arises of whether this is due to provider characteristics (e.g., lack of experience) or to the patient mix. In addition, providers may be heterogeneous with regard to their risk aversion parameter r, which potentially could be established by making them participate in experiments involving choices under risk. This points to tailoring payment to these personal characteristics if possible. In particular, providers facing large cost risks should not be exposed to excessive cost responsibility. Otherwise, they may prefer not to carry out their task unless they are compensated by high flat payments.

10.2.3 Casemix and Information Rent

The basic model assumes that payers and providers have the same amount of information about the expected costs of treating a group of patients. In practice, however, providers are likely to be better informed because they can better assess the group's *casemix*. In analyzing the consequences of this for the optimal payment system, we continue to take the group of patients to be treated as given.[8] For simplicity, providers are assumed to be risk neutral as in the basic model. Box 10.3 provides an overview of this extension of the model.

Expected treatment costs are assumed to take the following form,

$$EC(\beta, e) = \beta - e. \qquad (10.40)$$

The parameter β reflects the casemix and can take any value in the interval $[\underline{\beta}, \overline{\beta}]$, with $\overline{\beta}$ indicating the most expensive casemix and $EC(\beta, e) > 0$ for all values of β.

10.2.3.1 Symmetric Information about Casemix

Given symmetric information about casemix, the payer can implement the first-best solution by assigning full cost responsibility to providers. The flat payment F that ensures that providers accept the contract [see equation (10.11)] is given by

$$\begin{aligned} F(\beta) &= EC[\beta, e_{FB}] + V[e_{FB}] + \overline{u} \\ &= \beta - e_{FB} + V[e_{FB}] + \overline{u}. \end{aligned} \qquad (10.41)$$

Note that the flat remuneration component depends on β as providers must be compensated for their expected costs.

10.2.3.2 Asymmetric Information about Casemix

As long as providers can make a contract contingent on effort e to control costs, asymmetric information about casemix does not lead to a welfare loss. The payer can implement the first-best solution by imposing a contract penalty if $e < e_{FB}$ [see

---

[8] In Section 10.3.2 we will discuss the case in which the provider is better informed about the expected costs of treating *each* patient and can decide whether to treat the patient.

Box 10.3. Asymmetric Information about Casemix

$$EC(\beta, e) = \beta - e \tag{10.40}$$

$$F(\gamma) = (1 - \gamma)(\bar{\beta} - e(\gamma)) + V(e(\gamma)) + \bar{u} \tag{10.47}$$

$$EI(\gamma) = (1 - \gamma)(\bar{\beta} - E\beta) \tag{10.48}$$

$$EW(\gamma) = B - (1 - \gamma)(\bar{\beta} - E\beta) - (E\beta - e(\gamma)) - V(e(\gamma)) - \bar{u} \tag{10.49}$$

$$\gamma^* = \frac{\bar{\beta} - E\beta}{-e'(\gamma^*)} \tag{10.51}$$

$\beta \in [\underline{\beta}, \bar{\beta}]$:	parameter measuring casemix-specific costs
$E\beta$:	average casemix
$F(\gamma)$:	basic remuneration as a function of γ
$EI(\gamma)$:	expected information rent of the provider as a function of γ
$e(\gamma)$:	optimal provider effort to control costs as a function of γ
γ^*:	optimal degree of cost reimbursement by the provider

equation (10.10)] while reimbursing all costs. With asymmetric information about casemix and noncontractible effort e, however, the first-best solution cannot be attained. To see this, consider that the payer wants to induce first-best cost-reducing effort. This requires full cost responsibility on the part of providers. To determine the flat payment, the payer needs to know the casemix parameter β [see equation (10.41)]. Clearly, provider information cannot be relied upon because they have every incentive to claim their casemix to be of type $\bar{\beta}$ in order to obtain the highest possible flat payment. The payer can therefore not be sure that providers accept the contract unless the flat payment amounts to $F[\bar{\beta}]$. This implies that all providers with casemix $\beta < \bar{\beta}$ obtain an *information rent* at the payer's expense. This information rent corresponds to the difference between provider's expected utility

$$EU(F[\bar{\beta}], \beta, e_{FB}) = F[\bar{\beta}] - EC[\beta, e_{FB}] - V[e_{FB}]$$
$$= F[\bar{\beta}] - (\beta - e_{FB}) - V[e_{FB}]$$

and reservation utility $\bar{u}$. Its expected value EI is

$$EI = E[EU(F[\bar{\beta}], \beta, e_{FB}) - \bar{u}]$$
$$= F[\bar{\beta}] - (E\beta - e_{FB}) - V[e_{FB}] - \bar{u}.$$

Using $F[\bar{\beta}] = \bar{\beta} - e_{FB} + V[e_{FB}] + \bar{u}$ from (10.41), this simplifies to

$$EI = \bar{\beta} - E\beta, \tag{10.42}$$

where $E\beta$ is the average casemix.

If casemix varies widely among providers, $\bar{\beta} - E\beta$ is large and hence information rent takes on a high value. In this case, trying to induce first-best cost-reducing effort is costly. Therefore, we consider again a deviation from $\gamma = 0$ in the basic payment formula $P(C) = F + \gamma C$. First, we determine the provider's optimal choice of effort and the flat payment which guarantees that the provider will accept the contract. We then use these results to derive the optimal degree of cost reimbursement by the payer.

Provider's expected utility

With the linear payment system $P(C) = F + \gamma C$, the provider's problem is

$$\max_{e} EU = F - (1 - \gamma)EC(\beta, e) - V(e) \qquad (10.43)$$
$$= F - (1 - \gamma)(\beta - e) - V(e)$$

The first-order condition

$$1 - \gamma - V'[e] = 0 \qquad (10.44)$$

defines $e(\gamma)$. The slope of this function can be established by totally differentiating (10.44). This yields $-d\gamma - V''[e]de = 0$, which can be solved to yield

$$\frac{de}{d\gamma} = -1/V''(e) < 0 \quad \text{since} \quad V''(e) > 0. \qquad (10.45)$$

If the participation constraint has to hold for a provider regardless of the casemix, it must be met for the most expensive casemix $\bar{\beta}$, i.e.,

$$EU(\bar{\beta}, \gamma) = F(\bar{\beta}, \gamma) - (1 - \gamma)(\bar{\beta} - e(\gamma)) - V(e(\gamma)) \geq \bar{u}. \qquad (10.46)$$

At the optimum, this constraint is binding, which implies that the flat payment

$$F(\bar{\beta}, \gamma) = (1 - \gamma)(\bar{\beta} - e(\gamma)) + V(e(\gamma)) + \bar{u} \qquad (10.47)$$

ensures that the provider will accept the contract. With $e(\gamma)$ and $F(\bar{\beta}, \gamma)$, expected utility of a provider with casemix β can be expressed as a function of γ,

$$EU(\beta, \gamma) = F(\bar{\beta}, \gamma) - (1 - \gamma)(\beta - e(\gamma)) - V(e(\gamma)).$$

Using (10.47), this simplifies to

$$EU(\beta, \gamma) = (1 - \gamma)(\bar{\beta} - \beta) + \bar{u}.$$

The first term is nothing but the information rent of the provider. Therefore, we obtain for the expected information rent

$$EI(\gamma) = E\left[EU(F(\bar{\beta}), \beta, e_{FB}) - \bar{u}\right] \qquad (10.48)$$
$$= (1 - \gamma)(\bar{\beta} - E\beta).$$

Thus, the expected value of information rent can be reduced by setting $\gamma > 0$. Intuitively, providers are able to use their superior information only for their cost share $(1 - \gamma)$.

The payer's problem

In order to determine the optimal value of γ, consider the payer's expected welfare $EW = B - EP$, with the expectation operator now defined over $\beta \in [\underline{\beta}, \overline{\beta}]$. Inserting $e(\gamma)$ and the flat payment $F(\overline{\beta}, \gamma)$ from (10.47), the expected payment to the provider is given by

$$EP(\gamma) = E[F(\overline{\beta}, \gamma) + \gamma EC(\beta, e(\gamma))]$$
$$= (1 - \gamma)(\overline{\beta} - e(\gamma)) + V(e(\gamma)) + \overline{u} + \gamma(E\beta - e(\gamma)).$$

Rearranging yields

$$EP(\gamma) = (1 - \gamma)(\overline{\beta} - E\beta) + (E\beta - e(\gamma)) + V(e(\gamma)) + \overline{u}.$$

Expected payment therefore consists of the expected information rent $(1 - \gamma)(\overline{\beta} - E\beta)$, the expected monetary costs of treatment $E\beta - e(\gamma)$, providers' utility loss due to cost-reducing effort $V(e(\gamma))$, and reservation utility $\overline{u}$.

Thus, the payer's welfare depends in the following way on γ,

$$EW(\gamma) = B - EP(\gamma) \tag{10.49}$$
$$= B - (1 - \gamma)(\overline{\beta} - E\beta) - (E\beta - e(\gamma)) - V(e(\gamma)) - \overline{u}.$$

The first-order condition of the optimal degree of cost reimbursement γ^* is[9]

$$\frac{dEW}{d\gamma} = \overline{\beta} - E\beta + e'[\gamma^*] - V'(e[\gamma^*])e'[\gamma^*] = 0,$$

which yields

$$\overline{\beta} - E\beta = -e'[\gamma^*] + V'(e[\gamma^*])e'[\gamma^*]. \tag{10.50}$$

The term on the left-hand side of equation (10.50) corresponds to the marginal decrease of the expected information rent. The right-hand side measures the marginal cost for the payer caused by weakened incentives for cost efficiency: $-e'[\gamma^*] > 0$ is the increase in the expected monetary costs of treatment, while $V'(e[\gamma^*])e'[\gamma^*] < 0$ captures the reduction in compensation due to cost-reducing effort on the part of providers. Now equation (10.44) implies $V'(e[\gamma^*]) = 1 - \gamma^*$. Therefore, the marginal cost of an increase in γ amounts to

$$-e'[\gamma^*] + V'(e[\gamma^*])e'[\gamma^*] = -\gamma^* e'[\gamma^*] > 0.$$

Substituting into (10.50) and solving for γ^* yields

$$\gamma^* = \frac{\overline{\beta} - E\beta}{-e'[\gamma^*]}, \tag{10.51}$$

which is positive because $e'[\gamma^*] < 0$ and $\overline{\beta} > E\beta$.

---

[9] The sufficient condition for a maximum $e''(\gamma) \leq 0$ is assumed to hold.

Equation (10.51) shows that it is optimal to deviate from the principle of full cost responsibility of providers. The deviation is the more marked

- the greater the expected value of the information rent that would have to be paid to providers with casemix $\beta < \overline{\beta}$ when trying to impose this principle;
- the less providers lower their cost-reducing effort in response to a deviation from this principle.

Conclusion 10.3. *In the presence of asymmetric information about casemix, it is optimal for the payer to deviate from the principle of full cost responsibility in the interest of reducing providers' expected information rent.*

The problem of asymmetric information about the cost function of providers has been further examined by LAFFONT AND TIROLE (1993). They show that a linear cost sharing scheme is generally not optimal. The payer can increase expected welfare by offering a menu of contracts of the form $P(\beta) = F(\beta) + \gamma(\beta)C$. Providers with casemix β select the contract with the optimal mix of flat payment and cost responsibility from their point of view. If the contract can be given to several providers, information rent can be reduced further by an *auction* in which providers bid for the contract. The basic insight that the payer should reimburse observed costs to some degree remains valid, however.

10.3 Concerns Beyond Cost Control

10.3.1 Quality of Treatment

A key concern in health care is the *quality* of treatment, which summarizes all aspects of the provider's service that affect the well-being of patients during and after treatment. A payer faces the problem of specifying the aspects of the quality providers are expected to deliver. Ideally, the contract would have to describe the appropriate quality for every possible health condition of patients. This is usually an unsurmountable task, however, implying that contracts are incomplete. Many aspects of quality are therefore *unverifiable*, i.e., they cannot be enforced in court. Instead, incentives for quality must be provided indirectly through the design of the payment system which must continue to induce cost-reducing effort on part of provides. The payer therefore faces what HOLMSTRÖM AND MILGROM (1991) term a *multi-task principal-agent problem*.

10.3.1.1 Extending the Basic Model

Extending the basic model of Section 10.2.1, let now the payer's welfare from the treatment of a group of patients $B(q)$ be increasing in a one-dimensional measure of quality q, i.e., $B'(q) = B_q > 0$. Expected costs of treatment $EC(q,e)$ depend on q and effort to control costs e with $EC_q > 0, EC_e < 0$ for all (q,e). With P denoting the payment to the provider, the objective function of the payer is[10]

$$EW = B(q) - EP. \tag{10.52}$$

The provider chooses both quality and cost-reducing effort. Treating patients lowers the provider's utility by $V(q,e)$. For all (q,e), we assume $V_e \geq 0$. With respect to V_q, the full range of assumptions is possible. If $V_q > 0$, providers' disutility increases with higher quality; providers' professional ethics are therefore insufficient to compensate for time and effort involved in providing quality. If $V_q = 0$, providers would still not be willing to give up any income in return for a better quality of treatment. If $V_q < 0$, however, providers' disutility decreases with higher quality, implying that they are ethically motivated.[11]

Assuming risk neutrality, provider's expected utility is given by

$$EU = EP - EC(q,e) - V(q,e). \tag{10.53}$$

The first-best values q_{FB} and e_{FB} can be found by maximizing (10.52) subject to (10.53) and $EU \geq \bar{u}$. As above, the providers' participation constraint is binding at the optimum, implying

$$EP = EC(q,e) + V(q,e) + \bar{u}.$$

Inserting into (10.52) yields the problem

$$\max_{q,e} EW = B(q) - EC(q,e) - V(q,e) - \bar{u}. \tag{10.54}$$

The first-order conditions are

$$B_q[q_{FB}] - EC_q[q_{FB}, e_{FB}] - V_q[q_{FB}, e_{FB}] = 0, \tag{10.55}$$

$$-EC_e[q_{FB}, e_{FB}] - V_e[q_{FB}, e_{FB}] = 0. \tag{10.56}$$

Assuming that $f(q,e) \equiv B(q) - EC(q,e) - V(q,e)$ is strictly concave in (q,e) ensures that the second-order condition is met.

In the following, we focus on the realistic case that the payer cannot enforce effort to control costs directly through a contract. Provided that either quality or treatment outcome are verifiable, the first-best solution can be implemented by shifting cost responsibility to provider (Section 10.3.1.2). But if neither quality nor treatment outcome can be specified explicitly in the contract with the provider, only a second-best solution is feasible (Section 10.3.1.3). An overview of the model is given in Box 10.4.

---

[10] A similar model with a utilitarian payer is analyzed by CHALKLEY AND MALCOMSON (1998a, 2000).

[11] Evidence from market experiments conducted with Swiss general practitioners points to a lack of willingness-to-pay for participation in quality circles and critical incident reporting, two activities that are considered crucial for quality assurance [see ZWEIFEL AND BRAENDLE (2008)].

10.3.1.2 Verifiable Quality or Treatment Outcomes

If either quality of treatment q or outcome $B(q)$ (but not effort to control costs) is verifiable, the first-best solution can be implemented in the following ways.

(1) If quality is verifiable, then a contract can simply prescribe the quality level q_{FB} and impose full provider cost responsibility. With a flat payment F, the provider solves the problem

$$\max_{e} EU = F - EC(q_{FB}, e) - V(q_{FB}, e). \tag{10.57}$$

The first-order condition

$$-EC_e[q_{FB}, e_{FB}] - V_e[q_{FB}, e_{FB}] = 0$$

is identical to the condition for the first-best solution [see equation (10.56)]. Therefore, providers opt for cost-reducing effort e_{FB}. If the basic remuneration is set at

$$F^{**} = EC[q_{FB}, e_{FB}] + V[q_{FB}, e_{FB}] + \bar{u}, \tag{10.58}$$

full cost responsibility combined with control of quality can implement the first-best solution.

(2) If treatment outcome B is verifiable, a contract can likewise specify the optimal treatment outcome $B[q_{FB}]$. Furthermore, a payment system of the type

$$P = F + B, \quad \text{with} \quad F = EC[q_{FB}, e_{FB}] + V[q_{FB}, e_{FB}] + \bar{u} - B[q_{FB}] \tag{10.59}$$

can be used. As is easily shown, this system implements the optimal values q_{FB} and e_{FB}, yielding expected utility $EU = \bar{u}$ for providers.

If providers are risk neutral, it does not matter whether the contract is contingent on quality or treatment outcome. For risk-averse providers, however, this equivalence only holds if the relationship between B and q is deterministic. Realistically, this relationship must be assumed to be stochastic, meaning that the quality of treatment can only influence but not determine outcomes. In this event, the payer must pay a risk premium to providers if payment is to be contingent on treatment outcome. Making payment depend on quality is therefore preferable in this case. The first-best solution, however, can only be reached if effort e is contractible. Otherwise, no more than the second-best solution derived in Section 10.2.2 is possible.

Conclusion 10.4. *If treatment quality or outcome is verifiable, then the first-best solution can be implemented by imposing full cost responsibility on providers. In the case of risk-averse providers and stochastic treatment outcomes, contractually prescribing quality is preferable to making payment dependent on treatment outcome.*

In practice, however, it is hardly possible to design contracts which specify quality or treatment outcome with sufficient precision. For this reason, neither quality nor treatment outcome are verifiable in the next section.

Box 10.4. Variable Quality

$$EW = B(q) - EP, \ B_q(q) > 0 \tag{10.52}$$

$$EU = EP - EC(q,e) - V(q,e) \tag{10.53}$$

$$B_q[q_{FB}] - EC_q[q_{FB}, e_{FB}] - V_q[q_{FB}, e_{FB}] = 0 \tag{10.55}$$

$$-EC_e[q_{FB}, e_{FB}] - V_e[q_{FB}, e_{FB}] = 0 \tag{10.56}$$

$$\hat{\gamma} \equiv \frac{B_q[q_{FB}]}{EC_q[q_{FB}, e_{FB}]} \tag{10.64}$$

$$\left. \frac{dE(W)}{d\gamma} \right|_{\gamma=0} = B_q q_\gamma \tag{10.73}$$

$$p_{FB} = \frac{B_q[q_{FB}]}{n_q[q_{FB}]} \tag{10.79}$$

q:	quality of treatment
$B(q)$:	welfare of treatment, $B_q > 0$
$\hat{\gamma}$:	optimal degree of cost sharing if $V_q < 0$ and $V_e = 0$
$n(q)$:	patient's demand for treatment, $n_q > 0$
p_{FB}:	optimal capitation payment if patients' demand depends on quality

10.3.1.3 Unverifiable Quality and Treatment Outcomes

If neither treatment quality nor outcome are verifiable, then there is the danger of full cost responsibility having an adverse effect on quality. Nevertheless, ELLIS AND MCGUIRE (1986) show that it may still be possible to implement the first-best solution. They assume that providers care about quality and abstract from efforts to control costs. Their result can be replicated in the present model by assuming $V_q < 0$ and $V_e = 0$.[12] Consider the payment system

$$P = F + \gamma C. \tag{10.60}$$

Then, the provider's problem is

$$\max_{q,e} EU = F - (1 - \gamma)EC(q,e) - V(q) \tag{10.61}$$

with the first-order conditions

$$\gamma EC_q(q,e) - EC_q(q,e) - V_q(q) = 0, \tag{10.62}$$

$$-(1 - \gamma)EC_e(q,e) = 0. \tag{10.63}$$

---

[12] Assuming that the provider can make the contract contingent on effort e, the following result also holds for $V_e > 0$ (see Exercise 10.6).

Since $V_e = 0$, conditions (10.62) and (10.63) correspond to the first-order conditions (10.55) and (10.56) of the payer if

$$\gamma = \hat{\gamma} \equiv \frac{B_q[q_{FB}]}{EC_q[q_{FB}, e_{FB}]}, \tag{10.64}$$

implying that the provider chooses e_{FB} und q_{FB}. Note that $\hat{\gamma}$ is positive because $B_q > 0$ and $EC_q > 0$. Furthermore, $\hat{\gamma} < 1$ since condition (10.55) and $V_q < 0$ imply

$$B_q[q_{FB}] = EC_q[q_{FB}, e_{FB}] + V_q[q_{FB}] < EC_q[q_{FB}, e_{FB}].$$

A payment system with partial cost reimbursement is therefore optimal. On the one hand, full cost responsibility ($\gamma = 0$) of providers is not optimal because this would cause them to neglect the payer's concern about quality. On the other hand, no cost responsibility ($\gamma = 1$) is not adequate either because this would induce providers to focus on quality without taking costs into account. An intermediate solution manages to reconcile both concerns.

This result, however, depends crucially on the assumption $V_e = 0$. Realistically, efforts to control costs decrease providers' utility. One therefore needs to take the analysis further to include the case $V_e > 0$. The optimal solution will then depend decisively on providers' preferences with respect to quality, i.e., the sign of V_q. Moreover, providers will in general deviate from the first-best values (q_{FB}, e_{FB}). Three cases are possible (recall that V denotes provider's disutility).

(1) *Providers incur disutility from providing higher quality* $(V_q > 0)$

In this case, providers will lower quality to some limit value $\underline{q}$ for any degree of cost reimbursement $\gamma \leq 1$. Setting $\gamma > 1$ would induce providers to supply quality but cause them not to exert any effort to control costs. Furthermore, being rewarded for higher costs, they would have the incentive to artificially inflate costs.

(2) *Providers are indifferent about quality* $(V_q = 0)$

Here, two solutions are possible. First, no cost responsibility ($\gamma = 1$) can be optimal now. Although providers exert no effort to control costs ($e = 0$), they opt for the optimal level of quality conditional on $e = 0$, provided they act in the payer's interest given that this is costless to them. Second, full cost responsibility ($\gamma = 0$) can be the preferred solution, too. While this induces providers to offer only minimum quality $\underline{q}$, they at least seek to minimize the costs of this low-quality treatment. A value of γ between zero and one cannot be optimal because providers would opt for minimum quality $\underline{q}$ without exerting an efficient amount of cost control.[13]

---

[13] If cost-reducing effort is contractible and providers maximize payer's welfare if indifferent, then a contract combining a penalty for low effort e and full cost reimbursement can implement the first-best solution, causing providers to exert effort e_{FB} to avoid the penalty. In addition, they opt for first-best quality q_{FB} as well since costs are fully reimbursed by the payer. If $V_q < 0$, however, this solution does not work because providers aim at an excessive level of quality.

(3) *Providers care about quality* $(V_q < 0)$

This scenario is in line with the professional ethics of physicians. To determine the optimal degree of cost reimbursement γ^* by the payer, first solve the provider's problem,

$$\max_{q,e} EU = F - (1 - \gamma)EC(q,e) - V(q,e). \tag{10.65}$$

The first-order conditions read

$$-(1 - \gamma)EC_q(q,e) - V_q(q,e) = 0, \tag{10.66}$$
$$-(1 - \gamma)EC_e(q,e) - V_e(q,e) = 0. \tag{10.67}$$

They define the functions $q(\gamma)$ und $e(\gamma)$. However, the signs of $dq/d\gamma$ and $de/d\gamma$ cannot generally be determined even if the second-order condition is met.[14] We make the plausible assumption that $dq/d\gamma > 0$ and $de/d\gamma < 0$. A higher degree of cost reimbursement by the payer therefore leads to higher quality and lower cost-reducing effort.

Expected welfare of the payer is

$$EW = B(q(\gamma)) - \gamma EC(q(\gamma),e(\gamma)) - F. \tag{10.68}$$

At the optimum, F is set to make the participation constraint binding, i.e.,

$$EU = F - (1 - \gamma)EC(q(\gamma),e(\gamma)) - V(q(\gamma),e(\gamma)) = \bar{u}. \tag{10.69}$$

Solving this equation for F and substituting into equation (10.68) yields the payer's expected welfare as a function of γ,

$$EW(\gamma) = B(q(\gamma)) - EC(q(\gamma),e(\gamma)) - V(q(\gamma),e(\gamma)) - \bar{u}. \tag{10.70}$$

Differentiating with respect to γ leads to

$$\frac{dEW}{d\gamma} = B_q\frac{dq}{d\gamma} - EC_q\frac{dq}{d\gamma} - EC_e\frac{de}{d\gamma} - V_q\frac{dq}{d\gamma} - V_e\frac{de}{d\gamma}. \tag{10.71}$$

Using equations (10.66) and (10.67), one can replace the last two terms to obtain

$$\frac{dEW}{d\gamma} = B_q\frac{dq}{d\gamma} - \gamma EC_q\frac{dq}{d\gamma} - \gamma EC_e\frac{de}{d\gamma}. \tag{10.72}$$

At $\gamma = 0$, we therefore have

$$\left.\frac{dEW}{d\gamma}\right|_{\gamma=0} = B_q\frac{dq}{d\gamma}. \tag{10.73}$$

---

[14] This amounts to the Hessian matrix of second-order derivatives being negative-definite [see, e.g., HOY ET AL. (2001, p. 562)].

Equation (10.73) shows that it is optimal to deviate from the principle of full cost responsibility of providers given the assumption $dq/d\gamma > 0$. This can be interpreted as follows [see also CHALKLEY AND MALCOMSON (1998a)]. At $\gamma = 0$, increasing γ has a positive first-order effect on quality whereas the effect on cost efficiency is negligible. Imposing full cost responsibility on providers is therefore not optimal because the loss in quality would be excessive.

In summary, only a second-best solution is possible if one makes the plausible assumption $V_e > 0$. If $V_q \geq 0$, either full or no cost responsibility is optimal. If $V_q < 0$, condition (10.73) calls for $\gamma^* > 0$. A mixed system weighing incentives for cost-efficiency against those for providing quality is likely to be optimal (see also Exercise 10.6). Only in the special case $V_e = 0$, where providers are indifferent with respect to cost-reducing effort, can the first-best solution be reached by setting $\gamma^* = \hat{\gamma}$.

Conclusion 10.5. *If neither quality nor treatment outcome are verifiable while the providers value quality, imposing full cost responsibility is not optimal. In general, only a second-best solution is possible which trades off incentives to control costs and to provide quality.*

Finally, let us examine the case that demand for treatment depends on quality which continues to be non-verifiable. Thus, patients react to differences in quality while courts are unable to ascertain then. As shown by MA (1994), the first-best solution can then be implemented by a capitation payment combined with full cost responsibility for providers. With n as the number of patients treated and p as the capitation payment, the payment system takes the following form

$$P = F + pn. \tag{10.74}$$

Aggregate demand for treatment by an individual provider is given by

$$n(q) \quad \text{with} \quad n_q(q) > 0. \tag{10.75}$$

The provider therefore faces the following problem,

$$\max_{q,e} EU = F + pn(q) - EC(q,e) - V(q,e) \tag{10.76}$$

yielding the first-order conditions

$$pn_q - EC_q(q,e) - V_q(q,e) = 0, \tag{10.77}$$
$$-EC_e(q,e) - V_e(q,e) = 0. \tag{10.78}$$

By setting the capitation at a value such that

$$p_{FB}n_q[q_{FB}] = B_q[q_{FB}], \tag{10.79}$$

the payer can obtain the first-best solution by inducing providers to opt for $[q_{FB}, e_{FB}]$. To see this, substitute (10.79) into (10.77). Conditions (10.77) and (10.78) become identical to the first-best conditions (10.55) and (10.56). Therefore, a capitation can create incentives for quality provision in absence of legal means to enforce quality.

The result by MA (1994) should be interpreted with caution, however. On the one hand, it is not obvious that patients can adequately judge the quality of providers. For example, if they base their judgment on easily observable characteristics such as the hotel service offered by a hospital, tying payment to patient demand can cause hospitals to invest in this type of service at the expense of other dimensions of quality [see CHALKLEY AND MALCOMSON (1998b)]. Precisely for this reason, a payer is needed to design a payment system which creates the right incentives.

On the other hand, demand is independent of quality in some situations, in particular if patients require treatment very urgently. In addition, many authors consider demand for treatment as a 'need' which is independent of quality, neglecting the fact that in non-emergency situations, individuals do decide not to see a physician or to avoid a hospital stay. Of course, this extreme response becomes less likely as soon as there are many competing providers.[15] Conversely, the problem of quality assurance can be expected to be most acute when there is only one provider. In this situation, however, it will be difficult to observe the demand response n_q because this would require the monopoly provider to vary quality over time or between groups of patients with everything else held constant. The payer may therefore have to give up on the first-best solution, settling for a trade-off between incentives for cost efficiency and quality provision.

Conclusion 10.6. *If demand for treatment depends on quality, the payer may be able to implement the first best using a capitation payment. However, patients may have difficulties in judging the quality of providers. Furthermore, the payer may not be able to identify patients' response to quality, as, e.g., in the presence of a monopolistic provider. Then only a second-best solution is feasible.*

10.3.2 Patient Selection

Up to this point, the population to be served by a provider was exogenously determined. But providers can exercise some discretion about whom to treat. Under purely prospective payment, they have an incentive to concentrate on patients who can easily be treated, a practice referred to as *creaming* or *cream skimming*. Severe cases can be rejected or *dumped* by pretending that a treatment has little chance of success.[16]

---

[15] For example, POPE (1989) examines quality competition among several providers. In his model with a fixed total demand for treatment, market share of providers depends on their quality of treatment relative to other providers. He shows that average quality is increasing with the intensity of competition.

[16] The incentive to dump patients was first examined by DRANOVE (1987), ALLEN AND GERTLER (1991), MA (1994, Section 5) and ELLIS (1998) analyze how providers can

For providers who can select patients, capitation payments play a crucial role. The extent to which they can give proper incentives to treat patients is examined in the following. First, the basic model is extended in Section 10.3.2.1. In Section 10.3.2.2, payer and providers have the same information about patients' expected costs of treatment. Capitation payments are shown to be suitable for implementing the first-best solution. Section 10.3.2.3 is devoted to the case in which providers are better informed than the payer about patients' cost types. The main result in that case is that reimbursing costs in addition to capitation payments can be optimal to avoid undesirable selection effects. Box 10.5 gives an overview of the model.

10.3.2.1 Extending the Basic Model

Let the expected costs of treating a patient of type θ be given by

$$Ec(\theta, e) = \theta - e \tag{10.80}$$

The lowercase letter c denotes *individual cost* of treatment as opposed to the costs of treating a group of patients (which was symbolized by C in the previous analysis). Patients differ in the parameter θ and therefore in their expected costs of treatment. Assume that

$$\theta \in [\underline{\theta}, \overline{\theta}], \ \underline{\theta} < \overline{\theta}. \tag{10.81}$$

In addition, let the *individual utility of treatment b* vary among patients as follows,

$$b \in [\underline{b}, \overline{b}], \quad \underline{b} < \overline{b}. \tag{10.82}$$

In the following, suppose that θ and b are distributed independently of each other, with distribution functions $F(\theta)$ and $H(b)$, respectively. For b, a uniform distribution is assumed implying a constant density function $h(b)$ over the interval $[\underline{b}, \overline{b}]$.

Providers derive utility αb from treating a patient, with $\alpha > 0$ measuring providers' ethical orientation.[17] Their disutility from effort e to control a patient's costs of treatment is given by $v(e)$, with $v[0] = 0, v'(e) > 0$ and $v''(e) > 0$. The payer maximizes a utilitarian welfare function, being in favor of treating a patient if total utility, i.e., the sum of payer's and provider's utility $b + \alpha b$, at least equals the opportunity cost of treatment.[18] A patient who is treated cost-efficiently should therefore receive treatment if and only if

$$(1 + \alpha)b \geq Ec[\theta, e_{FB}] + v[e_{FB}]. \tag{10.83}$$

---

select patients by varying their quality of treatment. For severe cases, quality is reduced, (a practice labeled *skimping*), while for easy cases, it is increased (an instance of creaming).

[17] In Exercise 10.8, you are asked to analyze the case $\alpha = 0$ in which providers do not derive utility from treating patients.

[18] Alternatively, the payer could only consider utility b, disregarding the provider's utility αb. This does not change the results with respect to the trade-off between treating too many low-cost and too few high-cost patients if the provider is an imperfect agent ($\alpha < 1$) from the payer's point of view. Only if the provider is a perfect agent ($\alpha = 1$) can the first-best solution be reached even if there is asymmetric information about patients' costs (see Exercise 10.9).

Box 10.5. Patient Selection

$$Ec(\theta,e) = \theta - e \tag{10.80}$$

$$\tilde{b}_{FB}(\theta) = \frac{\theta - e_{FB} + v[e_{FB}]}{1+\alpha} \tag{10.84}$$

$$p_{FB}(\theta) = \frac{\theta - e_{FB} + v[e_{FB}]}{1+\alpha} = \tilde{b}^{FB}(\theta) \tag{10.88}$$

$$EW(p,\gamma) = \int_{\underline{\theta}}^{\overline{\theta}} \int_{\tilde{b}^P(\theta.p(\gamma).\gamma)}^{\overline{b}} \left\{(1+\alpha)b - (\theta - e(\gamma)) - v[e(\gamma)]\right\} dH(b)dF(\theta) \tag{10.91}$$

$$p^*(\gamma) = \frac{((1+\alpha)(1-\gamma)-\alpha)(E\theta - e(\gamma)) + v[e(\gamma)]}{1+\alpha} \tag{10.92}$$

$$\left.\frac{d\tilde{b}^P}{d\gamma}\right|_{\gamma=0} = \frac{E\theta - \theta}{\alpha} \tag{10.97}$$

$$\left.\frac{\partial EW}{\partial\gamma}\right|_{\gamma=0} = \frac{h[\tilde{b}^P]}{\alpha^2}\sigma_\theta^2 > 0 \tag{10.98}$$

$\theta \in [\underline{\theta},\overline{\theta}]$:	patient's cost type
$E\theta$:	average cost type
$F(\theta)$:	distribution function of θ
$b \in [\underline{b},\overline{b}]$:	patient's utility of treatment
$H(b),h(b)$:	distribution, density function of b
$Ec(\theta,e)$:	expected monetary cost of treating patient of type θ
$v(e)$:	utility loss of controlling a patient's cost of treatment
αb:	provider's utility of treatment
$\tilde{b}^{FB}$:	first-best treatment threshold
$\tilde{b}^P$:	treatment threshold, provider
p_{FB}:	optimal capitation per patient under symmetric information
p^*:	optimal capitation per patient under asymmetric information

Using equation (10.80), the critical threshold $\tilde{b}_{FB}(\theta)$ for which the payer prefers treatment is given by

$$\tilde{b}_{FB}(\theta) = \frac{\theta - e_{FB} + v[e_{FB}]}{1+\alpha}. \tag{10.84}$$

A patient with expected cost $\theta - e$ should be treated if $b \geq \tilde{b}_{FB}(\theta)$. No treatment is adequate if $b < \tilde{b}_{FB}(\theta)$. Furthermore, note that

$$\frac{\partial \tilde{b}_{FB}(\theta)}{\partial\theta} = \frac{1}{1+\alpha} > 0, \tag{10.85}$$

i.e., the utility of patients with high expected costs must be high to justify treatment. Figure 10.2 shows payer preferences for treatment, the dividing line between treatment and no treatment being given by equation (10.84).

How can the payer induce providers to treat exactly those patients with $b \geq \tilde{b}_{FB}(\theta)$? A payer who observes b and θ could simply make the decision about

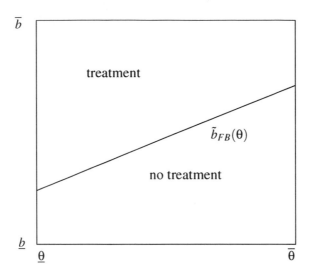

Fig. 10.2. Payer Treatment Preferences

treatment itself. In practice, however, only providers can observe b. In the following, information about b is therefore assumed to be asymmetric. Section 10.3.2.2 deals with the case where the payer can still observe θ. Here, the first-best solution can be implemented by making the capitation payment depend on θ. If there is asymmetric information about both b and θ, however, only a second-best solution is possible. As demonstrated in Section 10.3.2.3, it is optimal for the payer to deviate from the principle of full cost responsibility by partially reimbursing the actual costs of treatment.

10.3.2.2 Symmetric Information about Patients' Cost Types

As always, the case of symmetric information is treated first in order to derive the first-best solution as a benchmark. By assumption, payment continues to consist of a flat payment F and a capitation p per patient. The payer imposes full cost responsibility on providers, who then opt for optimal effort $e = e_{FB}$ as defined by the condition $-Ec_e[\theta, e_{FB}] = v'[e_{FB}]$. A provider who considers treating a patient of type (b, θ) evaluates the associated change in expected utility, which amounts to

$$\Delta EU = p - Ec[\theta, e_{FB}] - v[e_{FB}] + \alpha b$$
$$= p - (\theta - e_{FB}) - v[e_{FB}] + \alpha b.$$

The decision is to treat if and only if

$$\Delta EU \geq 0 \Leftrightarrow p + \alpha b \geq \theta - e_{FB} + v[e_{FB}]. \qquad (10.86)$$

The provider's critical threshold value $\tilde{b}_P(\theta)$ is thus given by

$$\tilde{b}_P(\theta) = \frac{\theta - e_{FB} + v[e_{FB}] - p}{\alpha}. \qquad (10.87)$$

It is increasing in costs of treatment and disability of effort but decreasing in capitation payment and ethical orientation α. By equating $\tilde{b}_P(\theta)$ to the payer's critical threshold $\tilde{b}_{FB}(\theta)$ from equation (10.84) and solving for p, one obtains the optimal capitation payment

$$p_{FB}(\theta) = \frac{\theta - e_{FB} + v[e_{FB}]}{1 + \alpha} = \tilde{b}_{FB}(\theta). \qquad (10.88)$$

Thus, by paying providers a capitation payment equal to the threshold $\tilde{b}_{FB}(\theta)$, the first-best treatment decision can be induced. Providers will then internalize the payer's preferences with respect to treatment. Note that the capitation increases with the patient's cost type θ and decreases with the ethical orientation of the provider α. Finally, payment must also ensure that the participation constraint $EU \geq \bar{u}$ is satisfied. With n denoting the expected number of patients to be treated, the optimal flat payment F_{FB} is determined by

$$EU = F_{FB} + n \left[\int_{\underline{\theta}}^{\overline{\theta}} \left(p_{FB}(\theta) - (\theta - e_{FB}) - v[e_{FB}] \right) dF(\theta) + \int_{\underline{b}}^{\overline{b}} \alpha b \, dH(b) \right] - \bar{u}.$$

Conclusion 10.7. *With symmetric information about patients' cost types, capitation payments contingent on the cost type can induce providers to make first-best treatment decisions.*

10.3.2.3 Asymmetric Information about Patients' Cost Types

If the expected cost of treating a patient can be observed by the provider only, first-best treatment decisions cannot be brought about by an appropriate capitation anymore. Being unable to scale capitation payments according to patients' cost type, the payer now faces a trade-off between creaming and dumping, i.e., the treatment of too many low-cost patients and too few high-cost patients. Consider, e.g., the capitation payment $p = p_{FB}(\overline{\theta})$ which guarantees that patients with the highest expected costs are treated adequately. But this payment is so high as to induce creaming on the part of providers, who thus accept patients with $b < \tilde{b}_{FB}$ for all cost types $\theta < \overline{\theta}$. A lower capitation, by contrast, makes them dump high-cost patients with $b \geq \tilde{b}_{FB}$ for high-cost types. To modify this trade-off, the payer may want to deviate from the principle of full cost responsibility of providers, i.e., by reimbursing part of the costs actually incurred. To examine this possibility, consider the following payment formula

$$P = F + np + \gamma C, \tag{10.89}$$

with C denoting the provider's total actual costs. The flat payment F is used to ensure that $EU = \bar{u}$.

Turning first to the providers' treatment decision, note that formula (10.89) implies that they have to bear only a share $(1 - \gamma)$ of each patient's costs. Thus, a patient with the characteristics (b, θ) is treated if and only if

$$\Delta EU = p - (1 - \gamma)(\theta - e(\gamma)) - v(e(\gamma)) + \alpha b \geq 0,$$

where $e(\gamma)$ is determined by $v'[e] = 1 - \gamma$, the condition for the provider's optimal cost-reducing effort. The provider's critical threshold is therefore given by

$$\tilde{b}_P(\theta, p, \gamma) = \frac{(1 - \gamma)(\theta - e(\gamma)) + v[e(\gamma)] - p}{\alpha}, \tag{10.90}$$

with

$$\frac{\partial \tilde{b}_P}{\partial \theta} = \frac{1 - \gamma}{\alpha} > 0, \quad \frac{\partial \tilde{b}_P}{\partial p} = -\frac{1}{\alpha} < 0, \quad \frac{\partial \tilde{b}_P}{\partial \gamma} = -\frac{\theta - e(\gamma)}{\alpha} < 0.$$

The utilitarian payer's expected welfare depends on the capitation payment p and the degree of cost reimbursement γ in the following way,

$$EW(p, \gamma) = \int_{\underline{\theta}}^{\bar{\theta}} \int_{\tilde{b}_P(\theta, p(\gamma), \gamma)}^{\bar{b}} \left\{ (1 + \alpha)b - (\theta - e(\gamma)) - v[e(\gamma)] \right\} dH(b) dF(\theta). \tag{10.91}$$

The payer's problem is to choose p and γ to induce providers to act in its interest. To solve this problem, the optimal capitation p^* for a given value of γ is determined first. As shown in the Appendix, this function reads

$$p^*(\gamma) = \frac{((1 + \alpha)(1 - \gamma) - \alpha)(E\theta - e(\gamma)) + v[e(\gamma)]}{1 + \alpha} \tag{10.92}$$

with $E\theta$ denoting the average value of θ.

Substituting $p^*(\gamma)$ in equation (10.90), one obtains the provider's critical threshold $\tilde{b}_P(\theta, p^*(\gamma), \gamma)$ given that the capitation payment is chosen optimally,

$$\tilde{b}_P(\theta, p^*(\gamma), \gamma) = \frac{(1 + \alpha)(1 - \gamma)\theta - ((1 + \alpha)(1 - \gamma) - \alpha)E\theta - \alpha e(\gamma) + \alpha v[e(\gamma)]}{\alpha(1 + \alpha)}$$

$$= \frac{(1 + \alpha)(1 - \gamma)(\theta - E\theta) + \alpha(E\theta - e(\gamma) + v[e(\gamma)])}{\alpha(1 + \alpha)}. \tag{10.93}$$

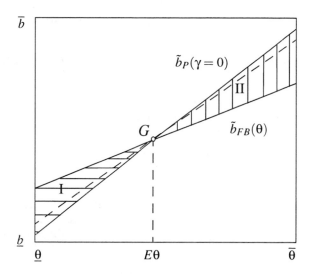

Fig. 10.3. The Provider's Treatment Decision

For $\gamma = 0$, equation (10.93) simplifies to

$$\tilde{b}_P[\theta, p^*[0], 0] = \frac{(1+\alpha)\theta - E\theta - \alpha e_{FB} + \alpha v[e_{FB}]}{\alpha(1+\alpha)}$$

$$= \frac{\frac{1+\alpha}{\alpha}\theta - \frac{E\theta}{\alpha} - e_{FB} + v[e_{FB}]}{1+\alpha}. \tag{10.94}$$

This value may be compared with the payer's first-best threshold, $\tilde{b}_{FB}(\theta)$ [see equation (10.84)]:

$$\tilde{b}_P(\theta, p^*[0], 0) \begin{cases} < \tilde{b}_{FB}(\theta) & \text{if } \theta < E\theta \\ = \tilde{b}_{FB}(\theta) & \text{if } \theta = E\theta \\ > \tilde{b}_{FB}(\theta) & \text{if } \theta > E\theta \end{cases}. \tag{10.95}$$

The optimal capitation for $\gamma = 0$ therefore solves the trade-off between creaming and dumping in the following way. Providers treat average-cost patients as prescribed by the first-best solution. However, they treat less costly patients too often and high-cost patients too seldom. Figure 10.3 illustrates this result. Between cost levels $\underline{\theta}$ and $E\theta$, creaming is the problem. Area I indicates the associated loss in terms of expected patients' benefit. Conversely, between cost levels $E\theta$ and $\bar{\theta}$, patients are dumped, resulting in the benefit loss as indicated by area II.

Now the question can be raised whether the payer should reimburse some of the provider's costs. Differentiating $\tilde{b}_P(\theta, p^*(\gamma), \gamma)$ with respect to γ and using $v'[e] = 1 - \gamma$ yields

$$\frac{\partial \tilde{b}_P(\theta, p^*(\gamma), \gamma)}{\partial \gamma} = \frac{-(1+\alpha)(\theta - E\theta) - \alpha e'(\gamma) + \alpha v'(e(\gamma))e'(\gamma)}{\alpha(1+\alpha)}$$

$$= \frac{(1+\alpha)(E\theta - \theta) - \alpha\gamma e'(\gamma)}{\alpha(1+\alpha)}$$

$$= \frac{E\theta - \theta}{\alpha} - \frac{\gamma e'(\gamma)}{1+\alpha}. \tag{10.96}$$

These two terms can be interpreted as follows.

- The first term in (10.96) is a *structural effect:* reimbursing costs lowers providers' critical threshold for expensive patients ($\theta > E\theta$) while raising it for low-cost patients ($\theta < E\theta$). This simultaneous reduction of creaming and dumping is in the payer's interest.

- The second term in (10.96) captures a *level effect:* recall that $e(\gamma)$ is determined by the condition $v'[e] = 1 - \gamma$. Since $v''(e) < 0$, $e'(\gamma)$ must be negative, i.e., cost-reducing effort is lower with cost reimbursement. Therefore, the second term in (10.96) serves to increase providers' critical threshold irrespective of θ. Overall, fewer patients are treated because cost reimbursement raises the expected costs of treatment.

At $\gamma = 0$, only the structural effect obtains,

$$\frac{d\tilde{b}_P}{d\gamma}\bigg|_{\gamma=0} = \frac{E\theta - \theta}{\alpha}. \tag{10.97}$$

This suggests that it may be in the payer's interest to partly reimburse the costs of treatment. As shown in the Appendix, one indeed obtains

$$\frac{\partial EW}{\partial \gamma}\bigg|_{\gamma=0} = \frac{h[\tilde{b}_P]}{\alpha^2}\sigma_\theta^2 > 0, \tag{10.98}$$

where $\sigma_\theta^2 > 0$ is the variance of θ. Deviating from the principle of full cost responsibility therefore increases the payer's expected welfare, calling for $\gamma^* > 0$ as a second-best solution.

This result can be traced back to the structural effect in equation (10.97). Figure 10.3 illustrates once more. The dashed line shows that increasing γ from the initial value zero leads to a clockwise rotation around point G, i.e., fewer patients for whom treatment is inappropriate and more patients for whom treatment is worthwhile are treated. This explains the increase in welfare from the payer's point of view. For larger values of γ, however, the negative level effect $-\gamma e'(\gamma)/(1+\alpha)$ arises, causing the payer to face a trade-off between creating incentives for treating the right patients and cost-efficiency.

Conclusion 10.8. *Asymmetric information about patients' cost types leads to a trade-off between treating too many low-cost and too few high-cost patients. In addition to a capitation payment, partial reimbursement of costs can be useful to induce providers to treat the right patients.*

SAPPINGTON AND LEWIS (1999) furthermore show that the payer's expected welfare can be increased by 'subjective risk adjustment', meaning that providers are allowed to choose between prospective payment and partial cost reimbursement.

10.4 Implications for the Design of Payment Systems

10.4.1 General Considerations

The preceding analysis has yielded some insights on how to design a payment system. The starting point was the principle of full cost responsibility, which calls for a purely prospective payment system. Summarizing results from the previous sections, this principle holds under the following conditions.

(1) Providers are risk neutral (Conclusion 10.1);

(2) Information about patients' casemix is symmetric (Conclusion 10.3);

(3) Either quality of treatment or outcome is verifiable (Conclusion 10.4), or demand for treatment depends on quality (Conclusion 10.6);[19]

(4) Providers select patients but the payer knows their expected cost of treatment, too, and can scale the capitation according to patients' cost type (Conclusion 10.7).

If one of these conditions is violated, the principle of full cost responsibility does not hold. Under some circumstances, it may be possible to implement the first-best solution by making the contract contingent on provider's cost-reducing effort, provided this effort is contractible, i.e., observable and verifiable in court.[20] In general, however, payers cannot write contracts contingent on cost-reducing effort. Then only a second-best solution can be reached, with the payer reimbursing part of the costs.[21] Deviating from the principle of full cost responsibility allows to

(1′) decrease the risk premium which has to be paid to risk-averse providers (Conclusion 10.2);

---

[19] In addition, there is the special case where providers derive no utility (or even a disutility) from providing quality that makes a first-best solution impossible. Nevertheless, the principle of full cost responsibility holds (see Section 10.3.1.3).

[20] This is the (unlikely) preferred solution when providers are risk averse or there is asymmetric information about casemix.

[21] In the special case where providers care about quality ($V_q < 0$) and derive no disutility from cost-reducing effort ($V_e = 0$), the first-best solution can be reached (see Section 10.3.1.3).

(2′) lower the expected information rent which arises if providers are better informed about patient casemix (Conclusion 10.3);

(3′) increase quality if neither treatment quality nor outcome are verifiable (Conclusion 10.5);

(4′) induce providers to select patients in accordance with the objectives of a payer who does not know the expected cost of treating a particular patient (Conclusion 10.8).

Note that the payer can to some extent overcome the lack of information that prevents application of the principle of full cost responsibility. Continuous monitoring is of key importance. Payers can track providers over time and compare their performance, using, e.g., Data Envelopment Analysis or estimating cost functions (see Chapter 9). The sheer mass of their administrative records enables them to engage in 'data mining' of this type to zero in on cost-reducing effort of providers. In addition, the frequency of repeated treatment for the same condition as well as of repeated referrals to specialists and hospital admissions can be recorded. Relating this data to patient characteristics permits payers to learn about the quality of treatment in the long run. Board certification of providers can also be used as an indicator of effort to supply quality.

However, all these efforts are costly. Optimization calls for their marginal cost to equal expected marginal return. And marginal return is zero if the payer cannot sanction non-performing providers by reducing payment or (in the extreme) excluding them from the list of contractual partners. Indeed, in most countries outside the United States, (social) health insurers are bound by so-called 'any willing provider' clauses, forcing them to contract with all providers who are willing to abide with certain (loosely defined) legal norms regulating their professional activity. Finally, competitive pressure is often insufficient to make insurers act as perfect agents of their clientele (as has been assumed throughout this chapter for simplicity). For all these reasons, it is unlikely that the conditions for the application of the principle of full cost responsibility are satisfied in practice.

If the conditions for the principle of full cost responsibility are violated or too costly to be established, the question arises to what extent actual costs incurred by providers should be reimbursed. The general rule is as evident as it is difficult to implement: the optimal degree of cost reimbursement should be the lower, the more marked are moral hazard effects on the part of providers, i.e., the greater their ability to influence the costs and quality of treatment. It is important to recall at this juncture that these parameters may differ between providers. Practice styles differ vastly, and with them marginal effectiveness of cost-reducing and quality-enhancing efforts. It is only for notational simplicity, that these differences have not been indicated by subscripts.

These considerations suggest that in most circumstances a *mixed payment system* is optimal. A *flat payment* is necessary to make providers conclude the contract at all. This is even true of a monopsony like a national health service because students can opt for something else than medicine and physicians can emigrate. The *capitation* component is important because it puts a price on the additional patient, influencing providers to admit or dump patients and causing them to be responsive to demand for treatment in general. Finally, the payer may be well advised to partly *reimburse the actual costs of treatment* incurred in an attempt to elicit quality that can be neither perfectly observed nor verified. But this deviation from the principle of full cost responsibility in fact introduces a fee-for-service component into the payment formula.

Conclusion 10.9. *In general, a mixed payment system containing a flat payment, a capitation component, and partial reimbursement of actual costs of treatment incurred by providers is optimal from the point of view of consumers.*

It should be noted that politicians who seek to reduce the health bill falling on their budget might want to break away entirely from the fee-for-service component implied by this conclusion, which strictly adopts the point of view of an insured and potential patient (neglecting, e.g., that of a taxpayer).

10.4.2 Paying Physicians

10.4.2.1 Overview of Payment Systems

Before discussing the implications of the previous analysis, we briefly review how they can be remunerated for their services. Employed physicians receive a salary, possibly supplemented by bonus payments. Physicians working in their own practice typically face a payment system consisting of two elements, a payment base and a payment schedule.

Payment Base

The payment base defines the attributes of medical practice that are remunerated. The main attributes are the following.

(1) *Factors of production employed* (the working time of the physician and his staff, use of equipment, drugs and other medical goods administered, space occupied, and heating and lighting of the surgery). The basic idea underlying this mode of payment is to reimburse costs incurred.

(2) *Types and quantities of services provided* (e.g., consultations, injections, radiation treatments, ultrasonic examinations). This 'fee-for-service' mode is usually based on a fee schedule that values each service with an absolute or a relative price.

(3) *Number of treatment episodes.* This usually amounts to a flat rate per treatment, possibly differentiated according to diagnosis (e.g., using Diagnosis Related Groups DRGs).

(4) *Number of patients treated.* Traditionally, patients had to obtain a treatment voucher either from the health insurer or from treating physicians. Increasingly, it is sufficient for them to present their membership card. Either way, physician payment depends on the number of treatment episodes recorded.

(5) *Number of potential patients.* At the beginning of the accounting period, every insured has to register with a particular physician who is in turn paid according to the number of registrations.[22]

(6) *Period of activity.* Here, payment is for the option to have access to a physician in the advent of illness. Usually, this amounts to a fixed per-period payment which is independent of all other attributes listed above.[23]

Payment Schedule

A payment schedule is the function that connects revenue P with the attributes defining the payment base, $Z_1, \ldots, Z_n$. In its most general form, it can be written as

$$P = P(Z_1, \ldots, Z_n).$$

The functional form of $P(Z_1, \ldots, Z_n)$ determines whether gross earnings are proportional, progressive, or regressive with respect to attributes. Accordingly, average payment per unit may decrease, be constant, or even increase. Note that the payment function (10.4) used throughout this chapter is a linear variant of this more general function $P(\cdot)$. In this context, an important feature repeatedly emphasized is whether the arguments of the function are predicted or past values. In the first case, the risk of deviation from predicted values is borne by the physician, while in the second case, it is borne by the payer.[24]

10.4.2.2 Optimal Physician Payment

Some general recommendations for the design of physician payment can be derived by checking the extent to which the principle of full cost responsibility is applicable, giving rise to the following observations based on the general considerations in Section 10.4.1.

(1) Physicians have most of their assets tied up in their practice, both in the guise of physical and human capital (medical skills). Being little diversified, they must assumed to be risk averse. In addition, observing their cost-reducing effort tends to be difficult.

---

[22] This payment base is reminiscent of Old China, where physicians were only paid as long as their patients were healthy.

[23] This differs from a salary since physicians must cover their practice expenses themselves.

[24] Payment based on predicted values is frequently referred to as prospective, that based on past values retrospective. This distinction, however, should not be confounded with the use of 'prospective' and 'retrospective' in the context of reimbursing costs.

(2) Physicians are usually better able to judge the casemix of their patients than the institution that pays them. Variation in the casemix may be limited, however, as difficult cases are usually referred to specialists or hospitals.

(3) Controlling a physician's quality of treatment or monitoring outcomes is often difficult. At the same time, demand for a physician's services tends to be highly dependent on quality as perceived by patients.

(4) Physicians have a number of means to select patients. For example, high-cost patients can be deterred by unfriendly behavior or long waiting times. Furthermore, a payer will frequently not know the expected cost of a patient.

In sum, these considerations suggest not to impose full cost responsibility on physicians. Rather, they provide support for a *mixed payment system* which reimburses some of physicians' costs. Costs can in principle be measured by the factors of production employed, the number of services provided, or the number of treatment episodes. Incentives for quality can be given by tying remuneration to the number of patients treated as well as the number of potential patients. Finally, payment can include a flat component. Therefore, the payment base can in principle contain all attributes discussed in the previous section. Their choice importantly depends on the reliability of measurement.

One solution can be to employ physicians, paying them a fixed salary and relieving them of any risk with respect to costs. Of course, this encourages moral hazard; on the other hand, an insurer may find it easier to monitor employed physicians than independent ones. This insurer-driven vertical integration usually is resisted by physicians, who prefer physician-driven vertical integration where they (possibly through their medical association) impose restrictions on health insurers or take over the insurance function themselves, as, e.g., in the United States in the guise of Blue Cross/Blue Shield. The factors favoring one type of vertical integration over the other are examined by ZWEIFEL ET AL. (2007). A high degree of concentration in the market for health insurance is found to facilitate insurer-driven vertical integration. It is maximum in a monopoly such as a national health service, which may explain why physicians tend to be employed there. Another instance of insurer-driven vertical integration is the Health Maintenance Organization, which is discussed in Section 11.4.

Conclusion 10.10. *Mixed physician payment can be optimal for several reasons. By reimbursing part of actual costs, the payer can save on the risk premium and mitigate incentives to select patients. By tying remuneration to the number of patients treated and the number of potential patients, it can induce quality-enhancing effort. Full insurer-driven vertical integration calls for employing physicians and possibly paying them a fixed salary.*

10.4.3 Paying Hospitals

10.4.3.1 Overview of Payment Systems

Hospital payment systems can be characterized by payment base and schedule as well.

Payment Base

The following attributes define the payment base.

(1) *Factors of production* employed (working time of physicians and nursing staff, hours of use of facilities such as operating rooms, amount of medication used).

(2) *Number of beds.*

(3) *Number of treatment episodes* (increasingly, payment is differentiated according to diagnosis, see Section 10.4.3.3 below).

(4) *Types and quantities of services provided* (nursing services, injections, radiation treatments, diagnostic examinations, surgical interventions).

(5) *Number of patient days*, possibly differentiated according to type of care provided (basic or intensive care) or to the hospital department involved (internal medicine, gynecology, psychiatry).

(6) *Number of patients* treated, possibly differentiated according to diagnosis and method of treatment (cardiac, trauma, burns).

(7) *Number of potential patients.* The hospital is given a budget depending on its catchment area.

(8) *Period of activity.* Here, it is the option of having access to the hospital during a year (say) that is being paid for. Usually, this amounts to a per-period fixed budget, which however is adjusted for some of the other attributes listed above, such as the number of beds or the types of services provided.

Payment Schedule

A payment function can be defined in full analogy to Section 10.4.2.1.

10.4.3.2 Optimal Hospital Payment

Again, we check the extent to which the principle of full cost responsibility is applicable. For the hospital sector, this gives rise to the following observations based on the general considerations in Section 10.4.1.

(1) Whether a hospital can be regarded as risk averse depends on its degree of diversification and its ownership. With regard to the first dimension, a psychiatric clinic typically has a few patients with length of stay in excess of one year, who

in addition require intensive custody. For such a clinic, it is difficult to balance these high-cost patients with those who merely stay for a few days only because they usually need medication that is expensive, too. More generally, however, larger hospitals have a more varied casemix than smaller ones, enabling them to benefit from diversification effects resulting in a diminished variance of costs. With regard to ownership, a chain controlling many hospitals can count on losses in one unit to be neutralized by surpluses in another, an impossibility for a free-standing community hospital. In addition, such a chain may be owned by shareholders who have stocks of many other companies, whereas a community hospital represents a major part of the assets of a city or the group of physician owning it.

(2) Whether a payer can judge the casemix of a hospital depends on its access to reliable diagnostic data. Comparing the hospital over time may enable the payer to gauge both cost-reducing and quality-enhancing efforts, e.g., by the methods discussed in Chapter 9.

(3) A hospital's quality can be controlled by quality assurance programs and external evaluations. In addition, demand from patients and referring physicians acting on their behalf depends on the hospital's reputation for quality. This is true in particular for procedures that are elective or can be planned in advance.

(4) Hospitals can easily select patients through their admissions policy, using excessive capacity utilization ("No beds are available, sorry") as an argument to refuse high-cost patients.

Compared to physicians, the arguments in favor of deviating from the principle of full cost responsibility seem less convincing for hospitals. Cost per patient is usually much higher in hospitals, however, creating the potential for high welfare losses due to creaming and dumping (see Section 10.3.2). The crucial question therefore is whether the payer has the diagnostic information necessary to predict the treatment cost of patients. If this is the case, *diagnosis-based capitation payments* are to be recommended. Nevertheless, partial reimbursement of actual costs may be necessary if hospitals are risk averse or incentives for quality must be provided. If the payer is unable to collect reliable data about the expected costs of patients, the principle of full cost responsibility must be given up in order to avoid unwanted patient selection. In addition, it can be optimal to pay hospitals for holding reserve capacity, in keeping with the arguments advanced in Section 5.2.2.

Conclusion 10.11. *Capitation payments should play a prominent role in financing hospitals. If the payer has reliable diagnostic information to predict expected costs, reimbursing costs is only appropriate if the hospital is risk averse or incentives for quality provision must be provided. Otherwise, cost reimbursement is also useful to avoid patient selection.*

10.4.3.3 Hospital Payment Based on Diagnosis Related Groups

During the past decades, hospital payment systems with prospective elements have been replacing the practice of cost reimbursement. The pioneer was Medicare in the United States which introduced per-case payment based on Diagnosis Related Groups (DRGs) in 1984. Since then, many countries (among them, Australia, Austria, Germany, Finland, Ireland, Italy, Portugal, and Sweden) have adopted DRG payment entirely or in part.

DRGs were initially designed to describe the output of a hospital in terms of patients treated who are as homogeneous as possible with respect to resource use and cost (see Section 9.2). Besides the principal diagnosis, DRGs take account of concomitant diseases and complications, the age of the patient, and the type of treatment. Therefore, they are not exclusively based on a diagnosis, causing them to be partially retrospective. While the diagnosis is the prospective component of payment, type of treatment and therefore costs actually incurred constitute a retrospective element. For example, payment for a cesarian section is higher than for a natural delivery. In addition, the payer reimburses very expensive cases ('outliers') separately, which serves to further reduce the prospective character of DRG-based payment. In an empirical study, MCCLELLAN (1997) estimates the extent of cost reimbursement. Using Medicare data from 1990, he finds that 55 percent of hospitals' actual costs of treatment was in fact reimbursed. Excluding outlier payments, this share still amounts to 32 percent, i.e., about a third of hospitals' actual costs were reimbursed by Medicare.

Conclusion 10.12. *DRG-based payment does not only rely on a patient's diagnosis but also on the type of treatment as an indicator. It therefore amounts to a mix between prospective capitation and retrospective cost reimbursement.*

The arguments detailed in the previous section support the basic idea of basing payment on DRGs. For two reasons, however, a crucial issue is the ability of DRGs to capture differences in expected costs among patients. First, the DRG classification may fail to sufficiently reflect patient heterogeneity. As shown in Section 10.3.2, this would induce hospitals to engage in creaming and dumping. Second, hospitals commonly perform *upcoding*, i.e., they assign patients to DRGs that pay well [see, e.g., DAFNY (2005)]. To the extent they succeed, they have an incentive to treat too many patients. The payer's foreseeable response is to reduce payment levels in order to stay within budget. But this invites dumping, i.e., the refusal to treat high-cost patients. Unless the initial degree of cost reimbursement was excessive, it would need to be increased for mitigating these incentives.

10.5 Summary

(1) Payment systems can be characterized as prospective or retrospective. A prospective system reimburses providers independently of costs actually incurred and therefore assigns cost responsibility entirely to them. A retrospective system reimburses all costs, mixed systems part of them.

(2) According to the principle of full cost responsibility, a prospective payment system is optimal. It applies under the following conditions.

   (a) Providers are risk neutral;

   (b) Information about patient casemix is symmetric, i.e., available to payer and providers;

   (c) Either quality of treatment or outcome is verifiable, or demand for treatment depends on quality;

   (d) Information about the expected costs of treatment is symmetric if providers can select patients. In this case, the first-best solution can be implemented by capitation payments dependent on patients' cost type.

(3) Under realistic circumstances, the conditions for the principle of full cost responsibility to be applicable do not hold. As a second-best solution, a mixed payment system consisting of a flat payment, a capitation payment, and partial reimbursement of actual costs is likely to be optimal. Deviating from prospective payment allows the payer to

   (a) lower the risk premium which has to be paid to risk-averse providers;

   (b) lower the expected information rent paid to providers who are better informed about patient casemix than the payer;

   (c) increase quality if neither quality of treatment nor outcome are verifiable;

   (d) induce providers to select patients according to the payer's objective if information about expected costs of treatment is asymmetric.

(4) Mixed physician payment can be optimal for several reasons. By reimbursing part of actual cost, the payer can save on the risk premium and mitigate incentives to select patients. By tying remuneration to the number of patients treated and the number of potential patients, it can induce quality-enhancing effort. Full insurer-driven vertical integration calls for employing physicians and possibly paying them a fixed salary.

(5) Capitation payments should play a prominent role in the financing of hospitals. If the payer has reliable diagnostic information to predict expected costs, full cost responsibility is appropriate unless hospitals are risk averse, need to be provided incentives for quality-enhancing effort or must be prevented from performing patient selection. DRG-based payment may qualify, although it is partially retrospective, taking into account the type of treatment provided. Thus, DRG payment amounts to a mixed system, combining prospective capitation and retrospective partial cost reimbursement.

10.6 Further Reading

In the HANDBOOK OF HEALTH ECONOMICS, the chapters by CHALKLEY AND MALCOMSON (2000) and DRANOVE AND SATTERTHWAITE (2000) review the literature on provider payment. We also recommend the contributions by LÉGER (2008) and ROBINSON (2001). LAFFONT AND TIROLE (1993) provide a general treatment of optimal contracts in procurement.

10.A Appendix

Derivation of Equation (10.92)

To derive the optimal capitation payment stated in equation (10.92), note that payer's welfare is given by (10.91),

$$EW(p,\gamma) = \int_{\underline{\theta}}^{\overline{\theta}} \int_{\tilde{b}_P(\theta,p(\gamma),\gamma)}^{\overline{b}} \left\{ (1+\alpha)b - (\theta - e(\gamma)) - v[e(\gamma)] \right\} dH(b) dF(\theta).$$

According to Leibniz's formula [see SYDSÆTER ET AL. (2005, p. 60)], it is true for an integrable function $g(\cdot)$ that

$$\frac{d}{dp} \int_{\tilde{b}_P(p)}^{\overline{b}} g(p,b) db = -g(p,\tilde{b}_P(p)) \frac{\partial \tilde{b}_P}{\partial p} + \int_{\tilde{b}_P(p)}^{\overline{b}} g_p(p,b) db.$$

In the present case, $g(p,b) = [(1+\alpha)b - (\theta - e(\gamma)) - v(e(\gamma))]h(b)$, yielding

$$\frac{d}{dp} \int_{\tilde{b}_P(p)}^{\overline{b}} g(p,b) db = -[(1+\alpha)\tilde{b}_P(p) - (\theta - e(\gamma)) - v(e(\gamma))]h[\tilde{b}_P] \frac{\partial \tilde{b}_P}{\partial p} + \int_{\tilde{b}_P(p)}^{\overline{b}} 0 \, db.$$

Therefore, the first-order condition for a maximum reads

$$\frac{\partial EW}{\partial p} = -\int_{\underline{\theta}}^{\overline{\theta}} [(1+\alpha)\tilde{b}_P(\theta,p,\gamma) - (\theta - e(\gamma)) - v[e(\gamma)]]h[\tilde{b}_P] \frac{\partial \tilde{b}_P}{\partial p} dF(\theta) = 0.$$

The uniform distribution of b (note that $h[\tilde{b}_P(\theta,p,\gamma)]$ is a constant) and $\partial \tilde{b}_P/\partial p = -1/\alpha$ lead to the equivalent condition,

$$\int_{\underline{\theta}}^{\overline{\theta}} [(1+\alpha)\tilde{b}_P(\theta,p,\gamma) - (\theta - e(\gamma)) - v[e(\gamma)]] dF(\theta) = 0.$$

Substituting for $\tilde{b}_P$ from (10.90), one obtains

$$\int\limits_{\underline{\theta}}^{\overline{\theta}} [((1+\alpha)(1-\gamma)-\alpha)(\theta-e(\gamma))+v[e(\gamma)]-(1+\alpha)p]dF(\theta)=0.$$

This can be solved for p to yield the optimal capitation as a function of γ,

$$p^*(\gamma)=\frac{((1+\alpha)(1-\gamma)-\alpha)(E\theta-e(\gamma))+v[e(\gamma)]}{1+\alpha} \tag{10.92}$$

with $E\theta=\int\limits_{\underline{\theta}}^{\overline{\theta}}\theta dF(\theta)$ denoting the average value of θ.

Derivation of Equation (10.98)

Substituting the optimal capitation from equation (10.93) into the payer's objective function (10.91) yields expected welfare as a function of the degree of cost reimbursement

$$EW(\gamma)=\int\limits_{\underline{\theta}}^{\overline{\theta}}\int\limits_{\tilde{b}_P(0,p(\gamma),\gamma)}^{\overline{b}}\left\{(1+\alpha)b-(\theta-e(\gamma))-v[e(\gamma)]\right\}dH(b)dF(\theta).$$

Differentiating with respect to γ, using the condition for the provider's optimal cost-reducing effort $v'[e]=1-\gamma$ and Leibniz's formula leads to

$$\frac{\partial EW}{\partial \gamma}=\int\limits_{\underline{\theta}}^{\overline{\theta}}\left\{(1+\alpha)\tilde{b}_P(\theta,p^*(\gamma),\gamma)-(\theta-e(\gamma))-v[e(\gamma)]\right\}h[\tilde{b}_P]\frac{d\tilde{b}_P}{d\gamma}dF(\theta)$$

$$+\int\limits_{\underline{\theta}}^{\overline{\theta}}\int\limits_{\tilde{b}_P}^{\overline{b}}\gamma e'(\gamma)dH(b)dF(\theta).$$

Substituting from (10.94) and noting that b is uniformly distributed, one obtains at $\gamma=0$,

$$\left.\frac{\partial EW}{\partial \gamma}\right|_{\gamma=0}=-\frac{h[\tilde{b}_P]}{\alpha}\int\limits_{\underline{\theta}}^{\overline{\theta}}(\theta-E\theta)\frac{d\tilde{b}_P}{d\gamma}dF(\theta).$$

Substituting from (10.97) finally gives

$$\left.\frac{\partial EW}{\partial \gamma}\right|_{\gamma=0}=\frac{h[\tilde{b}_P]}{\alpha^2}\int\limits_{\underline{\theta}}^{\overline{\theta}}(\theta-E\theta)^2 dF(\theta)=\frac{h[\tilde{b}_P]}{\alpha^2}\sigma_\theta^2>0, \tag{10.98}$$

with $\sigma_\theta^2>0$ denoting the variance of θ.

10.E Exercises

10.1. Can the principle of full cost responsibility be applied if

(a) providers determine the quality of treatment,

(b) providers decide whether or not a patient is treated?

10.2. What are the implications of asymmetric information between the payer and providers for the design of payment systems?

10.3. Discuss whether 'supply-side cost sharing' (shifting cost responsibility to providers) may serve as substitute to 'demand-side cost sharing' (coinsurance) to avoid moral hazard on part of the insured.

10.4. Let the treatment of a group of patients leads to utility $B = 5$. The payer maximizes expected welfare $EW = B - EP$, where P is the payment to the provider. Cost of treatment C is uncertain, depending on cost-reducing effort e in the following way,

$$C(e) = 1 - e + \varepsilon, \ \mathrm{E}(\varepsilon) = 0, \ \mathrm{Var}(\varepsilon) = 1.$$

The provider's utility loss due to effort is $V(e) = e^2$. An alternative activity would generate a certain income of 1 with effort $e = 0$.

(a) Assume that the provider is risk neutral, with utility $u = P - C(e) - V(e)$.

    (i) Find the optimal value of e, the payer's expected welfare and the provider's utility in the first-best solution.

    (ii) Describe two contracts which can implement the first-best solution if effort e is contractible.

    (iii) How can the first-best solution be implemented if the payer can only observe actual cost C?

(b) Now suppose that the provider is risk averse. Expected utility depends on the expected value μ_y and variance σ_y^2 of income net of the cost of effort $V(e)$ such that $EU = \mu_y - \sigma_y^2$.

    (i) Find the optimal value of e, the payer's expected welfare and the provider's utility in the first-best solution.

    (ii) Describe a contract which can implement the first-best solution if effort e is contractible.

    (iii) Assume that the payer can only observe actual cost C. The payment system takes the form $P = F + \gamma C$. Find the optimal degree of cost reimbursement γ, optimal effort e, payer's expected welfare, and the provider's expected utility. Compare your results with the case of risk neutrality and explain the difference.

10.5. Let the treatment of a group of patients result in utility $B = 20$. The payer maximizes expected welfare $EW = B(q) - EP$, where P is the payment to the provider. The expected total costs of treatment are $EC(\beta, e) = \beta - e$. The casemix parameter β is uniformly distributed over the interval $[9.5; 10.5]$. Cost-reducing effort e lowers the provider's utility according to $V(e) = 0.5e^2$. The provider treats the group of patients only if expected utility is at least zero. The payer cannot observe e.

(a) Determine expected welfare for a payer who observes β and pays the provider a flat payment $P = F$.

(b) Now assume that only the provider knows β. Calculate the payer's expected welfare if the payer

   (i) pays the provider a flat payment designed to guarantee that the group of patients is treated.

   (ii) uses mixed payment $P = F + \gamma C$ and chooses the optimal degree of cost reimbursement.

   For both cases, determine the provider's expected information rent, the expected monetary cost of treatment, and the provider's utility loss due to cost-reducing effort. Discuss your result.

10.6. Let the treatment of a group of patients result in utility $B(q) = 5 + q^{1/2}$, where q is the quality of treatment. The payer maximizes expected welfare $EW = B(q) - EP$, where P is payment to the provider. Expected costs of treatment $EC(q,e)$ depend on quality q and cost-reducing effort e in the following way,

$$EC(q,e) = 3 + q - 2e.$$

The provider's utility loss as a function of quality and effort is $V(q,e) = \eta e^2 - \kappa q^{1/2}$, $\eta \geq 0$. An alternative activity yields a certain income of 1 with $e = q = 0$. Expected utility is given by
$$EU = EP - EC(q,e) - V(q,e).$$

(a) Find the optimal values of q and e in the first-best solution. For $\kappa = \eta = 1$, determine expected welfare and the provider's expected utility.

(b) Assume that $\kappa = \eta = 1$ and that effort e is contractible. Show that a mixed payment system with a cost reimbursement rate $\hat{\gamma}$ as given by equation (10.64) combined with a requirement on e can implement the first-best solution.

(c) How can the first-best solution be implemented if quality is verifiable?

(d) Explain the payer's problem if neither treatment quality nor outcome nor effort to control costs are verifiable. Assuming that effort $e \in [0; 1.5]$ and that quality cannot fall below $\underline{q} = 0$, determine optimal contracts in the following cases.

   (i) $\kappa < 0$ und $\eta = 1$;   (ii) $\kappa = 1$ und $\eta = 0$;   (iii) $\kappa = 0$ und $\eta = 1$.

   Explain your results.

10.7. Let the treatment of a group of 10 patients result in utility

$$B(q) = 10 + 3q,$$

where q is the quality of treatment. The payer maximizes expected welfare $EW = B(q) - EP$ where P is the payment to the provider. Expected cost of treatment $EC(q,e)$ depends on quality q and cost-reducing effort e in the following way,

$$EC(q,e) = 7 + 2q - 2e.$$

The provider's utility loss as a function of quality and effort is $V(q,e) = q^2 - 2q + e^2$. An alternative activity yields a certain income of 1 with $e = q = 0$. Expected utility is given by

$$EU = EP - EC(q,e) - V(q,e).$$

(a) Determine the optimal values of q and e, the payer's expected welfare and the provider's expected utility in the first-best solution.

(b) Which types of contract can implement the first-best solution if treatment quality or outcome are verifiable but effort e is not observable?

(c) Now assume that neither treatment quality nor outcome are verifiable. The payer cannot observe effort e. The payment system is $P = F + \gamma C$, with C denoting actual cost. Determine the optimal values of F and γ and expected welfare.

(d) Suppose that patient demand depends on quality in the following way,

$$n(q) = \min\{4 + 4q; 10\}.$$

Let the payment system be $P = F + pn$, where p is a capitation per patient. Find the values of F and p that maximize expected welfare. Discuss your result.

10.8. Consider the model of patient selection in Section 10.3.2 but assume that $\alpha = 0$, i.e., providers do not care about patients' utility. However, they act in the payer's interest if this is costless to them.

(a) Show that the capitation payment $p_{FB}(\theta) = \theta - e_{FB} + v[e_{FB}]$ can implement the first-best solution if there is symmetric information about patients' cost types.

(b) Assuming asymmetric information about patients' cost types, show that

(i) the payer can only make the treatment decision dependent on θ but not on b;

(ii) no cost reimbursement is optimal;

(iii) the optimal capitation payment is $p^* = Eb$ where $Eb = \int_{\underline{b}}^{\overline{b}} b \, dH(b)$ is the average patient benefit b.

Discuss your results.

10.9. Consider the model of patient selection in Section 10.3.2 but assume that the payer only accounts for utility b in the utilitarian welfare function (disregarding provider utility αb). Determine the

(a) the critical threshold $\tilde{b}_{FB}(\theta)$ for which the payer prefers treatment;

(b) the optimal capitation payment $p_{FB}(\theta)$ if there is symmetric information about patients' cost types;

(c) the provider's critical threshold $\tilde{b}_P[\theta, p^*[0], 0]$ if there is asymmetric information about patients' cost types and no cost reimbursement.

Comment on the role of the provider's utility parameter α in this setting.

11

Forms of Delivery of Medical Care

11.1 Introduction

Forms of delivery of medical care differ considerably between countries. These differences ultimately reflect basic differences of philosophy. Where the state grants the citizen a right to health, government tends to be directly responsible for the provision of health care services. Examples include the former eastern bloc countries as well as the United Kingdom and Italy with their National Health Services. Conversely, in the United States it is the individuals themselves who in principle assume responsibility for their health. Nonetheless, the public purse finances 40 percent of total U.S. health care expenditure (HCE), supports public hospitals, and acts directly as a health insurer through the programs Medicare (for pensioners) and Medicaid (for the poor). While there is no National Health Service in Canada, the country has a national health insurance scheme. In the Netherlands, more than 30 percent of the population were members of a private health insurance scheme before the 2006 reform. Since then, formerly public and private health insurers compete for consumers side by side. Swedish hospitals, financed by district health authorities, play a key role in the provision of medical care.

This variety in the organization of medical care is in a sense surprising, since the relationship between the physician and his or her patient is the cornerstone of all health care systems. Acting as agents, physicians are expected to always put their knowledge and capabilities to the advantage and never to the detriment of their principal's health. This so-called *principal-agent relationship* between the patient (the principal) and the physician (the agent) fails, however, to serve the overall interest of the patient if only because the patient prefers to pay less rather than more for medical care, whereas the physician's economic interests calls for more rather than less HCE (see the Appendix to this chapter for a theoretical formulation). In solving this conflict, both parties may choose to enlist the help of a complementary agent. In this chapter, we focus on a few very crucial *complementary principal-agent relationships*. It is these complementary relationships which seem to be responsible for major differences in the delivery of medical care across countries.

P. Zweifel et al., *Health Economics*, 2nd ed., DOI 10.1007/978-3-540-68540-1_11,
© Springer-Verlag Berlin Heidelberg 2009

Table 11.1. Principal-Agent Relationships as a Characteristic of Health Care Systems

Principal	Delegation of authority to agent	System type, typical country
individual	physician, hospital (treatment) — policy maker ⟶ hospital (finance) — insurer ⟶ physician, hospital (fees)	*"Conventional Health Care Systems"* United States, Germany, Netherlands, Switzerland
individual	physician, hospital (treatment) — policy maker ⟶ physician, hospital (employment, finance)	*"National Health Service"* United Kingdom, Italy, Portugal, Spain
individual	physician, hospital (treatment) — policy maker ⟶ physician (fees) / hospital (finance)	*"National Health Insurance"* Canada, Sweden
individual ⟶ insurer ⟶ physician ⟶ hospital		*"Managed Care"* United States, Switzerland

Table 11.1 gives an overview of possible types of complementary principal-agent relationships in health. As far as *conventional health care* is concerned (first variant), which still constitutes the rule in western European countries and in the United States, consumers select a physician to act as their agent, who does not necessarily represent their interests in the hospital. Indeed, politicians enter as complementary agents who attempt to safeguard patient interests mainly by funding hospitals but also by regulating them.

In general, interventions in the health care system have an important advantage for politicians in their attempt to win votes. As a result of the key role played by health insurance, redistribution in favor of certain groups of voters is particularly easy to conceal. Redistribution is a main task of insurance, namely from the lucky ones who were spared a loss to those who suffered a loss. It is difficult for an individual insured voter to differentiate between this random, nonsystematic redistribution and a hidden systematic redistribution. It is for this reason that *politicians acting as complementary agents* have room for manipulation when it comes to structuring the other complementary principal-agent relationships in health care, resulting in a variety of health care systems.

In Sweden, e.g., where there are 26 health districts, local politicians have a comparatively large amount of power since they are able to raise taxes for public health in addition to overseeing hospitals. It is in these hospitals that the majority of medical services are provided, while physicians in private practice play only a marginal role in the health care system [see STAHL (1990)]. Conversely, in Germany the ban on establishing outpatient departments in hospitals has led to a marked division between ambulatory and hospital care, which serves to limit political agents' influence to hospitals in the main. In France, a significant share of medical care is provided in private hospitals, which grant community physicians access to their facilities [see ROSA AND LAUNOIS (1990)]. In Switzerland, there are publicly financed hospitals that admit physicians in private practice as consultants. Since cantonal governments are mainly responsible for health policy, voters use their direct democratic influence (popular initiatives, referenda) to assign differing authorities to the political stakeholders with regard to health care.

The affinity between *random and systematic redistribution* through insurance is also exploited in various ways in different countries. In Germany, for example, statutory health insurance was for many years forced to subsidize pensioners, whose contribution (paid by the government) fell far short of the cost of their medical care. Redistribution also comes into play when people with low incomes are not allowed to choose between statutory and private health insurance or are automatically tied to a certain health insurance scheme because of their occupation or employment in a particular company membership (as in Austria). In France everybody, even the self-employed, are members of social health insurance, which is integrated into the national budget [see ROSA AND LAUNOIS (1990)]. Conversely, prior to the reform of 1994/96 Swiss cantons had the right to decide whether or not to mandate health insurance for low income earners. In fact, most cantons left this decision to their citizens, with voluntary enrollment exceeding 95 percent by the 1980s. After all, signing up for health insurance was a way to benefit from the premium subsidy paid to the sick funds on a per capita basis. The Health Insurance Act of 1994 (which, having barely survived a popular referendum in December 1995 came into power in 1996) introduced a nation-wide mandate, combined however with a means-tested personal premium subsidy [see ZWEIFEL (2000)].

Political agents not only in the United Kindom and Italy, but also in Canada, have much more extensive powers (see Table 11.1, second variant). Health insurance no longer plays a major role in the United Kingdom, Italy, Spain, and Portugal, having been replaced by a *National Health Service* which is directly financed by the public purse. In Canada, politicians act as the voter's agent by overseeing *National Health Insurance*, which in its turn is responsible for physician payment and hospital finance (third variant).

Finally, Table 11.1 displays still another mode of organization, in which the health insurer becomes the most important agent of the individual in matters of health care. This concept, known as *Managed Care*, was developed in the 1970s (in the guise of *Health Maintenance Organizations* and *Preferred Provider Organizations*) in the United States. Managed Care is based on a bundle of measures to control HCE while ensuring quality by managing the behavior of both patients and service providers. The price to be paid is limited provider choice. Patients are on the list of a participating physician, who in turn can refer them only to a defined set of specialists and hospitals. Physicians usually have to follow guidelines in their medical treatment and accept so-called 'utilization reviews' monitoring their decisions. Finally, payment of service providers often, especially in Health Maintenance Organizations (HMOs), is structured in a way to make participating physicians bear part of the financial risk in order to limit the moral hazard effects inherent in fee-for-service payment (see Sections 6.4.2, 8.4, and Chapter 10). The Health Maintenance Organization (HMO) is the prototype of a *Managed Care Organization* (MCO), combining all of the elements mentioned in the preceding paragraph. However, a MCO may implement only some of the elements of Managed Care. For instance, Preferred Provider Organizations (PPOs) do not make participating physicians share in their financial risk, which also holds true of physician networks (where some form of utilization review is common).

Evidently, the form of delivery of medical care hinges on the principal-agent relationships complementing the basic physician-patient relationship. In order to explain the demand for such complementary agents, the basic theory of the principal-agent relationship needs to be expounded and its application to the physician-patient relationship is examined. This is done in Section 11.2, providing at least partial explanation of why individuals do not rely on a physician as their sole agent in health care but may prefer to also enlist the help of politicians ('the government'), insurers, or even employers. The possible role of the health insurer as a complementary agent in health care is further examined in Section 11.3. Finally Section 11.4 deals with MCOs, with much of the evidence relating to HMOs.

> **Conclusion 11.1.** *In addition to the basic principal-agent relationship between the physician and the patient, there exist complementary principal-agent relationships, which largely define the way medical care is delivered. In countries that have a national health service or a national health insurance, it is the government who acts as the main complementary agent. In other countries, this role is assumed by private insurers or even employers. The Managed Care approach amounts to a restriction of patients' choice of providers in return for lower contributions and possibly quality assurance.*

11.2 The Physician as the Patient's Agent

Patients generally do not know the optimal way to cure a disease. They have to rely on the physician to provide the pertinent information [and treatment as well as a rule; for an analysis of this joint function, see EMONS (1997)]. Most people agree that the patient's confidence in the physician is a crucial requirement for a successful treatment. Nevertheless, the physician-patient relationship cannot be based on trust only. According to the saying, 'trust is good, control is better', the patient may be interested in a complementary agent because of the following reasons.

(1) *Quality assurance.* Even if patients trust their physician, they may want his or her services be monitored by some independent expert just to avoid disappointment (and risk to health and life in the extreme). This calls for a complementary agent providing the necessary knowledge.

(2) *Remuneration.* Trusting one's physician in health matters does not imply trust in financial matters. Unless a physician is perfectly altruistic, more payment is better than less payment. This constitutes a conflict of interest with the patient which is not fully mitigated by health insurance. To the extent that health insurance imposes a positive rate of coinsurance (which is optimal in the presence of moral hazard, see Section 6.4), higher physician payment entails a sacrifice of income and wealth for the patient (see the Appendix for a formal statement). In addition, higher payment for all providers rather than one's own physician causes insurance premiums to rise, which constitutes a future financial burden to the patient. Again, it makes sense to have a complementary agent negotiate payment.

If a third party foots the bill, the conflict of interest between patients and physicians (and service providers more generally) appears to vanish. In the case of the health insurer, this presumption has been shown above to be wrong. However, it is wrong in the case of other sponsors as well. For instance, in the United States major employers offer (a contribution to) health insurance as a fringe benefit to workers. Evidently, employees must not cost more than their value marginal product, implying that the fringe benefit is balanced by less take-home pay. In addition, a sponsor has every interest to keep beneficiaries healthy. In terms of the model presented in Section 3.4, the sponsor seeks to push the probability of being healthy $(1 - \pi)$ towards one (π denotes the probability of being ill during a short period). By way of contrast, individuals are predicted to opt for $(1 - \pi^*) < 1$, with π^* as optimal probability of illness. Therefore, they do accept risk jeopardizing their health. This creates a conflict over health behavior with the sponsor induced by the basic conflict of interest between patients and physicians. Therefore, neither physicians nor complementary agents are perfect in the sense of fully representing patients' preferences.

Conclusion 11.2. *Two reasons explain patients' interest in a complementary agent besides the physician. The complementary agent can monitor the quality of services provided. In addition, it can negotiate for modes of payment that induce an optimal performance.*

11.3 Complementary Principal-Agent Relationships in Health Care

11.3.1 The Employer as Complementary Agent

Employers have a lot of experience regarding the design of contractual relationships. They could basically use this knowledge to conclude contracts for their employees with physicians and other service providers of health care. In fact, the first so-called *Health Maintenance Organization* was set up in the United States by Kaiser, a large building contractor (see Section 11.4).

The employees of a company will however have reservations with regard to their employer selecting physicians and hospitals for them. When negotiating their wages and employment, risk-averse workers have an interest in concealing fluctuations of their marginal productivity to preserve their jobs. As such fluctuations are closely related to the state of health, physicians constitute an important source of information. Usually, professional ethics safeguard the confidentiality of the information about patients. But the more strongly physicians and hospitals depend on the employer, the more likely they will have to yield to pressure to provide such information.

> **Conclusion 11.3.** *Employers can act as complementary agents shaping the contractual relationship with health care providers in the interest of their employees. Since they would be likely to obtain an informational advantage in wage bargaining, however, this solution is only accepted by workers in exceptional cases.*

This conclusion is the reason why employers are not listed in Table 11.1 among the viable combinations of principal-agent relationships. Only in exceptional situations (remote construction sites, factory towns, shift work) may the savings on transaction costs be so large as to cause the employer to take over the provision of medical services by hiring physicians.

As a rule, the employer's role is limited to providing health insurance, such as offering a company health insurance fund, as is the case in Germany and in the United States (where large firms are legally obliged to do so). Accordingly, employers may intervene in the negotiations of payment with providers of health care. In the case of so-called *Preferred Provider Organizations* in the United States, they strike preferential deals with groups of physicians and hospitals in order to obtain a discount on local fees.

11.3.2 The Government as Complementary Agent

In democracies, voters have the option of replacing market and bargaining allocation mechanisms by government-controlled ones. This might occur directly by popular initiatives as in some federal states of the United States and in Switzerland, or indirectly by electing a government that promises, for example, 'health for all' (the slogan of the World Health Organization since the 1980s). Two possible ways for the government to be the complementary agent are described here.

(1) The government directly organizes the provision of medical services establishing a *National Health Service* as it was the case, for example, in the former Eastern Bloc countries and is the case in the United Kingdom, Italy, Spain, and Portugal.

(2) The government assumes the role of a monopolistic *National Health Insurer*, as it is the case in Canada and Sweden.

11.3.2.1 National Health Service

In a national health service, public authorities act as a complementary agent of voters, taking over the task of contracting physicians and hospitals. By creating an optimal payment system, they can in principle achieve a favorable benefit-cost ratio in health care. This does not necessarily mean low HCE, but if the benefit-cost ratio is realized at low cost, citizens could benefit in the guise of reduced taxes or additional public goods. Whether this surplus is actually passed on to the electorate depends on the *intensity of political competition* (in full analogy to private markets).

Thus, the fact that for years spending on health care in the United Kingdom has been far below that of most other industrialized countries (see Table 1.1), is not a sufficient condition for the net burden on taxpayers to be low; the money saved in health care may well be channeled into other domains of public administration that are less valued by voters.

In spite of these reservations, the government may perform well as a complementary agent because of its power to shape the design of contracts in health care at will (see the Appendix to this chapter). As the demander of medical services on the market, it is also able to push down fees, by making alternatives outside the national health service unattractive to health care providers. Yet, such measures may prove counterproductive in the longer term. Within the national economy, health care competes with other industries for resources, especially for workers. If wages differ too much from wages paid in other industrial sectors, the health care sector loses out. In addition, international competition plays an important role because physicians in particular can easily find employment in another country.

Finally, if pressure resulting from competition between political parties is low, politicians may fail to design the payment of providers in a way to trigger much effort in favor of their patients.

11.3.2.2 National Health Insurance

A national health insurance scheme constitutes an intermediate solution between public health care and the use of private health insurers as complementary agents, an alternative to be examined in Section 11.3.3 below. An important issue is whether health care providers have to accept fees as payment in full or may 'balance-bill' patients (as, e.g., in the Canadian provinces of Alberta and Ontario). Although balance-billing is rejected by many out of a resentment against inequality of access, it can be seen as an instance of price discrimination. Providers charge higher fees to those having high willingness to pay and lower fees (usually negotiated with the government) to the remaining population. In this way, they are able to increase their income. At the same time, total volume of services and hence consumer surplus may well increase [in the case of linear demand functions, consumer surplus actually rises if the volume of services increases, see, e.g., VARIAN (1992, Section 14.8)]. An important difference from a private health insurer is that a national health insurer, being a monopolist not subject to the threat of entry by a challenger, does not have to actually pass on the savings achieved to citizens.

Conclusion 11.4. *Governments can negotiate for low fees for health care services, both directly as the organizer of a national health service and indirectly as the sponsor of national health insurance. This power, however, is limited both by competition from other industries and other countries' health care sectors. Finally, the intensity of competition for votes determines the degree to which governments are forced to pass on savings achieved to the citizenry.*

11.3.3 Private Health Insurers as Complementary Agents

Relying on private health insurers as a complementary agent dealing with providers of health care services seems to be an obvious alternative. In contrast to employers, the problem of misuse of confidential information is less severe. The danger of health insurers providing health information to other interested parties, e.g., life insurers or employers, can be dealt with through data protection legislation. Compared to public authorities or a national health insurer, private health insurers face competitive pressure causing them to negotiate for a favorable benefit-cost ratio and to pass on any savings to consumers [see ZWEIFEL (2004)]. An important downside springs up as soon as contributions are regulated, however. Since contributions are not sufficient to cover expected future HCE of high risks, competitive insurers have every incentive to avoid them and to enroll low risks instead (see Chapter 7). This means that high risks may have difficulty enlisting the support of an insurer as a complementary agent. In addition, insurers' efforts at risk selection compete with their efforts in favor of process, product, and organizational innovation.

As long as health insurers merely compensate patients for their HCE (as is typical of fee-for-service systems such as in Germany), product innovation is limited in the main to launching policies with different deductibles and rates of coinsurance, permitting consumers to control their moral hazard (see Chapter 6). If granted the freedom of contracting (as in the United States), insurers can assume a more comprehensive innovating role by negotiating modes of payment that convey incentives to service providers for achieving a favorable benefit-cost ratio. This may include developing Managed Care alternatives, which combine restrictions with regard to provider choice with a partial shifting of the risk of high cost of treatment to participating providers (see Section 11.4 below) in return for lower contributions. By comparing the performance of Managed Care with the conventional fee-for-service setting, health insurers can learn a lot about how to structure provider incentives in order to improve the benefit-cost ratio of the products they market to consumers.

Conclusion 11.5. *Compared to the government, private health insurers face competitive pressure forcing them to also invest in product innovation modifying incentives of both consumers and health service providers. Given premium regulation, however, risk selection efforts may have a higher return than innovation.*

11.4 The Managed Care Organization as an Alternative Form of Provision of Care

11.4.1 The Managed Care Organization as a Complementary Agent

Managed Care constitutes an alternative to conventional fee-for-service provision of health care. Originally it was implemented by Kaiser, a U.S. building contractor, who had to organize medical care for his employees on remote construction sites. Today, Managed Care Organizations (MCOs) comprise the Health Maintenance Organization (HMO) in which insurance and service provision are fully integrated, the Independent Practice Association (IPA) in which enrollees are restricted to participating health care providers, and the Preferred Provider Organization (PPO) which does not restrict the choice of providers but provides incentives to use 'preferred' providers and conducts utilization reviews.

MCOs impose vertical restraints in health care [ZWEIFEL ET AL. (2007)], with most often the health insurer taking the initiative. They are based on at least one of the following principles [see ENTHOVEN (1980)].

(i) The insured pay a monthly or yearly *fixed premium* in advance to the MCO;

(ii) In return, they are guaranteed comprehensive treatment as specified by the *Managed Care physician* in charge, with little or no copayment;

(iii) Patients must accept being treated by one of the participating health care providers;

(iv) Participating health care providers are *not* paid according to the quantity of services provided.

Among the MCOs, the Kaiser Foundation, which devotes itself exclusively to health insurance, is the largest single HMO, with more than 6 million total enrollment in

16 federal states of the United States. Since the turn of the century, the majority of Americans receive their health care through a MCO. This development was triggered by the HMO laws of 1973, which required employers to also include an HMO among the health insurance options offered.

The history of the HMO has been one of tension with the American Medical Association (AMA). The main reason for AMA opposition to HMOs seems to lie in the mode of payment. By not allowing fee-for-service payment, *price discrimination according to the insured's willingness to pay* is made difficult. Such price discrimination provides physicians with opportunities to increase their net incomes, which may serve to explain AMA's stance in favor of fee-for-service payment [see the pioneering analysis by KESSEL (1958)].

11.4.2 Cost Advantages of Managed Care

Managed Care (MC) physicians usually have a fixed budget per enrolled patient at their disposal. Moreover, they may receive a bonus if the MCO achieves a profit. These provisions come close to implementing the principle of full cost responsibility expounded in Chapter 10. In particular, MC physicians have an incentive to act as prudent purchasers of externally provided services. These external purchases may make up as much as 70 percent of the physician's total disposable budget, as estimated in an early study by MOORE (1979).

Due to these incentives, MC physicians are expected to achieve savings especially in terms of referrals to specialists and hospitals. This expectation has been confirmed in an extensive study by LUFT (1981). But low rates of hospitalization may also be due to *risk selection*, i.e., attracting healthy individuals. More generally, health status can be viewed as a latent variable governing both the choice of health insurance contract and the use of health care services after conclusion of the contract. However, HCE is also influenced by the changed incentives of MC providers. The issue then becomes to distinguish between the influence of latent health status (which may be called the 'risk selection effect') and that of changed contractual incentives in MC (the 'innovation effect').

LEHMANN AND ZWEIFEL (2004) sought to disentangle the two effects in the following way. They obtained individual records from a major Swiss health insurer HCE for the years 1997–2000, permitting them to simulate the selection process. For the years 1997–1999, they estimated three predicted HCE values given age, sex, region, and a dummy variable for receipt of a premium subsidy (an indicator of low income). On the one hand, this is the information legally available to the health insurer who therefore can verify whether an individual has average HCE in excess of the predicted value. If so, this would indicate unfavorable latent health, triggering efforts to make the client choose a contract other than MC (with a higher premium). On the other hand, clients with average HCE in excess of their predicted value may themselves infer that their health status is unfavorable, causing them to opt for a conventional rather than a more stingy MC contract. Therefore, past deviations of HCE from predicted values can serve as an indicator of latent health status that drives the risk selection process.

Table 11.2. Innovation and Risk Selection Components in Cost Reductions, Switzerland 2000

					Cost Reduction in Percent				
		HMO			IPA			PPO	
	Total	Innov-ation	Risk selec.	Total	Innov-ation	Risk selec.	Total	Innov-ation	Risk selec.
A	−62			−34			−39		
B	−53			−34			−39		
C	−9			0			0		
D		−3	−6		0	0		0	0
E		−37	−16		−10	−24		−21	−18
F		−40	−22		−10	−24		−21	−18

A: Gross differential (total HCE)
B: Gross differential (HCE given HCE>0)
C: Gross differential (likelihood of HCE>0)
D: Split differential (likelihood of HCE>0)
E: Split differential (HCE given HCE>0)
F: Split differential (total HCE)

Source: LEHMANN AND ZWEIFEL (2004)

Next, HCE in the year 2000 was related to the same predictors as before, complemented by the indicator of latent health status and type of contract (conventional fee-for-service vs. HMO, PPO, and IPA). Estimated differences in HCE according to type of contract must now be due to innovation effects, since latent health status controls for the selection effect. The evidence is presented in Table 11.2. The greatest cost savings (compared to the conventional contract) were achieved by HMOs, followed by the PPOs and the IPAs. This ordering corresponds to U.S. experience. Focusing on the HMO column, one sees that the gross cost reduction of no less than 62 percent (row A) can be split up into 53 percent due to less HCE given that there was some in the course of the year (row B) and 9 percent due to lowered likelihood of having positive HCE at all (row C). These 9 percent were attributable in smaller part to the innovation effect (3 percent, see row D) and in larger part to the risk selection effect (6 percent). The split is different when it comes to HCE given there was some HCE (row E), with 37 percent reduction attributable to innovation and 16 percent, to risk selection. Summing up, on obtains the overall split (row F). Of the total cost reduction of 62 percent, 40 percent is estimated to be due to the innovation effect and 22 percent, to the risk selection effect. Therefore, roughly two-thirds of the HMO savings could not be related to latent health status and therefore can be said to reflect 'true' savings due to contractual innovations. In case of IPAs, risk selection effects account for two-thirds of the cost advantage over conventional fee-for-service while the split is roughly 50:50 for PPOs. A weakness of this approach is that all differences in HCE that cannot be traced to risk selection effects are simply credited to 'innovation', although patients and providers may have changed their behavior for other unknown reasons.

Table 11.3. Comparison of the Structure of Medical Care Services and HCE, U.S. 1983

Type of organization	Hospital admissions per 100 enrollment	Days spent in hospital per 100 enrollment	Physician visits per enrollee	HCE in US$ per enrollee
HMO				
Participants in the experiment	8.4	49	4.3	439
Control group	8.3	38	4.7	469
Conventional insurance				
Without copayment	13.8	83	4.2	609

Source: MANNING ET AL. (1984)

Risk selection was even completely suppressed in the RAND Health Insurance Study [see DUAN ET AL. (1984)]. There, the initiators of the experiment bought off from participants the right to choose a contract for seven years in exchange for a lump sum payment. Participants were then randomly assigned to conventional contracts (with different deductibles and rates of coinsurance) or a HMO. From Table 11.3, it can be seen that people who were assigned to an HMO exhibit a number of hospital days quite similar to permanent HMO members, viz. 49 per 100 enrolled per year, compared to 83 per 100 for conventional insurance. This difference can be traced back to a 40 percent lower rate of hospitalization in HMOs.

The RAND Health Insurance Experiment also investigated whether MC savings were achieved at the expense of patients' health. While this did not prove true in general, low-income individuals with poor health at the beginning of the experiment were an exception. They benefited less from treatment in the HMO setting than those in the conventional setting [see WARE ET AL. (1986)].

Finally, the cost savings achieved by MCOs should result in lower premiums for the insured. As always, the pressure of competition is decisive. In a study by SCHLESINGER ET AL. (1986), it was found that in markets where a HMO is the only alternative to conventional health care, its premiums are higher, ceteris paribus.

Conclusion 11.6. *In comparison to conventional fee-for-service health care, Managed Care Organizations achieve substantial cost reductions that need not be at the expense of insured's health, with low-income individuals in bad health representing an exception. In strongly contested markets, Managed Care Organizations pass on these savings to consumers.*

11.4.3 Cost Effects of Managed Care Organizations at the System Level

If some suppliers succeed in producing their services at a lower cost due to an innovation, the usual presumption is that the cost of production decreases also at the level of the industry and even for the economy as a whole. However, this rule does not seem to hold in the case of health care. Critical observers point to the possibility of 'cost ballooning', that is, cost shifting between insurers and alternative modes of provision of medical care. There are at least two reasons for this to occur.

- The government as a purchaser of health care services may impose lower fees for itself while causing providers to compensate by charging *other purchasers* more. For instance, the introduction of hospital payment based on Diagnosis Related Groups in the mid-1980s (DRG, see Section 10.4.3.3) by the U.S. Medicare administration might have resulted in higher charges for other groups, such as higher fees for the privately insured and a curtailment of free services for the uninsured poor. Likewise, for many years the German government saved billions of Euros by not fully reimbursing the HCE of pensioners to statutory health insurance. This shortfall was compensated through higher contributions from the active population.

- The private sponsor of a new mode of provision is also suspected of *shifting cost rather than reducing cost* by putting pressure on prices of services purchased from external sources. For instance, physicians participating in a MCO may retain the right to compensate fee reductions negotiated with the MCO by charging higher fees to other patient groups. Similarly, a hospital might settle for low fees with a dominant purchaser such as a HMO while charging those having traditional insurance higher fees in compensation.

'Cost ballooning' between the suppliers of different insurance contracts and modes of provision is obviously of potential importance in health care. The *conditions* for such ballooning to occur can be studied using a model developed by DRANOVE (1988). To exemplify the situation, think of a hospital treating MC patients at fixed pre-negotiated fees as well as privately insured patients. Will a typical hospital actually charge private patients higher prices for comparable services if the MCO is capable of negotiating lower prices for their insured?

In order to answer this question, DRANOVE (1988) postulated an objective function for the hospital containing two groups of arguments. On the one hand, management seeks to make a profit consisting of a contribution from selling services to patients having traditional insurance (Π_T) and a contribution from treating HMO patients (Π_H) such that $\Pi = \Pi_T + \Pi_H$. On the other hand, the amounts of services (Y_T and Y_H, respectively) provided to the two patient groups also enter the utility function $u(\cdot)$,

$$u = u[\Pi_T(p_T, C_T) + \Pi_H(p_H, C_H); Y_T(p_T), Y_H(p_H)],$$

$$\text{with} \quad \frac{\partial u}{\partial \Pi_T} = \frac{\partial u}{\partial \Pi_H} \equiv \frac{\partial u}{\partial \Pi} > 0, \frac{\partial u}{\partial Y_T} > 0, \frac{\partial u}{\partial Y_H} > 0, \frac{\partial^2 Y_T}{\partial P_T^2} > 0, \quad (11.1)$$

$$\frac{\partial^2 u}{\partial \Pi_T \partial \Pi_T} = \frac{\partial^2 u}{\partial \Pi_H \partial \Pi_T} = \frac{\partial^2 u}{\partial \Pi^2} < 0.$$

The first two equalities in the second line of (11.1) mirror the assumption that the first argument of the objective function is the *sum* of profits. The management of the hospital is therefore viewed as being indifferent with regard to the source of profit. Partial differentiation of the equalities of the second line w.r.t. Π_T yields the equalities in the third line. Finally, the utility function is concave from below in profit, which may be justified by the assumption of risk aversion as soon as the model is generalized to include uncertainty (see Section 6.3.1).

Billed patient days (Y_T, Y_H) should generally depend negatively on the *price charged* (see, however, the assumptions (11.3) below). For patients having traditional health insurance, this is certainly plausible given the relatively high degree of cost sharing for hospital care in the United States. But also in the case of MC patients, physicians as prudent purchasers of hospital services are likely to respond to an increased price with a reduction of patient days ordered. For simplicity, the demand function is assumed to be linear $(\partial^2 Y_T / \partial p_T^2 = 0)$.

The following sign restrictions characterize the market for patients having traditional insurance from the point of view of the hospital (also see Box 11.1),

$$\frac{\partial \Pi_T}{\partial C_T} < 0, \ \frac{\partial^2 \Pi_T}{\partial p_T \partial C_T} > 0, \ \frac{\partial \Pi}{\partial p_T} > 0, \ \frac{\partial \Pi}{\partial p_H} > 0, \ \frac{\partial^2 \Pi}{\partial p_T^2} < 0. \tag{11.2}$$

According to (11.2), the contribution to profit from this market segment is reduced by cost increases. This effect is mitigated, however, if price can be raised at the same time $(\partial^2 \Pi / \partial p_T \partial C_T > 0)$. Since objectives as stipulated in equation (11.1) cause management to *deviate from profit maximization* $(\partial u / \partial Y_T > 0, \partial u / \partial Y_H > 0)$, there is scope for an increase of the service price to raise profits $(\partial \Pi / \partial p_T > 0)$, albeit at a decreasing rate $(\partial \Pi^2 / \partial p_T^2 < 0)$.

Additional assumptions serve to *characterize the MC market segment* from the point of view of the hospital,

$$C_T = C_H, \quad p_H = \bar{p}_H, \quad Y_H = \bar{Y}_H. \tag{11.3}$$

The first assumption indicates that treatment of a MC patient entails the same cost as that of a patient having traditional insurance. Consequently, cost differences are excluded as a reason for any ballooning of cost between the two patient groups. For the sake of simplicity, the price for MC patients $(\bar{p}_H)$ is considered exogenous, although – in contrast to the fees for Medicaid and Medicare patients which are determined by the government – this price results from a negotiating process. At this negotiated price, the MCO commits to paying for a fixed number of patient days $(\bar{Y}_H)$.

These additional assumptions leave the hospital with just p_T as its decision variable. The necessary condition for an (interior) optimum can thus be written as

$$\frac{\partial u}{\partial p_T} = \frac{\partial u}{\partial \Pi_T} \frac{\partial \Pi_T}{\partial p_T} + \frac{\partial u}{\partial Y_T} \frac{\partial Y_T}{\partial p_T} = 0. \tag{11.4}$$
$$ (+) \quad (+) \quad (+) \quad (-)$$

Box 11.1. Cost Shifting by the Hospital: The Model by DRANOVE (1988)

Objective function of the hospital:

$$u = u[\Pi_T(p_T, C_T) + \Pi_H(p_H, C_H); Y_T(p_T), Y_H(p_H)]$$

with $\dfrac{\partial u}{\partial \Pi_T} = \dfrac{\partial u}{\partial \Pi_H} \equiv \dfrac{\partial u}{\partial \Pi} > 0, \ \dfrac{\partial u}{\partial Y_T} > 0, \ \dfrac{\partial u}{\partial Y_H} > 0, \ \dfrac{\partial^2 u}{\partial \Pi_T \partial \Pi_T} = \dfrac{\partial^2 u}{\partial \Pi_H \partial \Pi_T} = \dfrac{\partial^2 u}{\partial \Pi^2} < 0$

$$(11.1)$$

Characteristics of the markets for patients having traditional health insurance:

$$\frac{\partial \Pi_T}{\partial C_T} < 0, \ \frac{\partial^2 \Pi_T}{\partial p_T \partial C_T} > 0, \ \frac{\partial \Pi}{\partial p_T} > 0, \ \frac{\partial \Pi}{\partial p_H} > 0, \ \frac{\partial^2 \Pi}{\partial p_T^2} < 0 \qquad (11.2)$$

Characteristics of the market for HMO patients:

$$C_T = C_H, p_H = \bar{p}_H, Y_H = \bar{Y}_H \qquad (11.3)$$

Π_T:	profit from treatment of patients having traditional insurance
Π_H:	profit from treatment of HMO patients
p_T, p_H:	prices to be charged to members of either group
C_T, C_H:	marginal cost (= average cost) of treating a member of the respective patient groups
Y_T, Y_H:	number of billed patient days

Increasing the price for those patients with traditional insurance has a positive effect on profit but a negative effect on the professional objective of providing services, since patients are deterred by the higher price.

Now let the optimum be disturbed by a *reduction of the fee* paid for MC patients. Evidently, the impact on the condition $\partial u / \partial p_T = 0$ must be compensated by a change in the decision variable p_T, in a way that the condition for the optimum is satisfied again after the adjustment. This requires

$$\frac{\partial^2 u}{\partial p_T^2} dp_T + \frac{\partial^2 u}{\partial p_T \partial p_H} d\bar{p}_H = 0. \qquad (11.5)$$

Solving (11.5) for $dp_T / d\bar{p}_H$, one obtains from (11.4) and (11.5),

$$\frac{dp_T}{d\bar{p}_H} = \frac{(-1)}{\dfrac{\partial^2 u}{\partial p_T^2}} \frac{\partial^2 u}{\partial p_T \partial p_H} \qquad (11.6)$$

$$= \frac{(-1)}{\dfrac{\partial^2 u}{\partial p_T^2}} \left[\frac{\partial^2 u}{\partial \Pi^2} \frac{\partial \Pi}{\partial p_T} \frac{\partial \Pi}{\partial \bar{p}_H} + \frac{\partial u}{\partial \Pi_T} \frac{\partial^2 \Pi_T}{\partial p_T^2} + \frac{\partial^2 u}{\partial Y_T \partial \Pi_H} \frac{\partial \Pi_H}{\partial \bar{p}_H} \frac{\partial Y_T}{\partial p_T} \right].$$

$$\quad (+) \quad (-) \ (+) \ (+) \qquad (+) \ (-) \qquad (+/-) \quad (+) \quad (-)$$

It is assumed that the sufficient condition for a maximum $\partial^2 u/\partial p_T^2 < 0$ holds. When interpreting equation (11.6), three cases may be distinguished.

(1) *Parallel movement of prices:* $\mathrm{d}p_T/\mathrm{d}\overline{p}_H > 0$. If the HMO has to be granted a reduction of prices, those having traditional insurance benefit from a reduced fee as well. This case may occur only if $\partial^2 u/\partial Y_T \partial \Pi_H \ll 0$. That is, the more services are provided to patients having traditional insurance, the smaller the management's marginal utility of profit from the treatment of HMO patients. This effect must be very marked in order to exceed the other two terms in the bracket, both of which are positive.

(2) *Independence of prices, no cost shifting:* $\mathrm{d}p_T/\mathrm{d}\overline{p}_H = 0$. A sufficient condition for this case to obtain is

$$\frac{\partial u}{\partial Y_T} = 0, \tag{11.7}$$

since due to equation (11.4), one obtains $\partial \Pi_T/\partial p_T = 0$; hence $\partial^2 \Pi_T/\partial p_T^2 = 0$ [the first two terms in the bracket of (11.6) may be dropped] and $\partial^2 u/\partial Y_T \partial \Pi_T = 0$ [the third term in (11.6) may be dropped]. In other words, as soon as the hospital pursues pure profit maximization, thus disregarding the objective of service provision ($\partial u/\partial Y_T = 0$), ballooning of cost ($\mathrm{d}p_T/\mathrm{d}p_H \neq 0$) can be ruled out. This is in accordance with the general result that states, "No cross-subsidization by profit-seeking competitive suppliers".

(3) *Compensating price movement, cost shifting:* $\mathrm{d}p_T/\mathrm{d}\overline{p}_H < 0$. A reduction of prices in favor of MC patients is compensated by a higher price charged to patients having traditional insurance. According to equation (11.6), it suffices for this case to occur that

- the marginal utility of additional profit from admitting MC patients $\partial u/\partial \Pi_H$ is *independent of the quantity of services* Y_T provided to patients having traditional insurance [implying $\partial^2 u/\partial \Pi_H \partial Y_T = 0$, so the third term in the bracket of (11.6) may be dropped], or

- the marginal utility of additional profit from admitting MC patients $\partial u/\partial \Pi_H$ *increases* with the quantity of services Y_T provided to patients having traditional insurance [implying $\partial^2 u/\partial \Pi_H \partial Y_T > 0$, causing the third term in the bracket of (11.6) to become negative]. This condition corresponds to the usual notion that a hospital which predominantly serves patients having traditional insurance (in particular the privately insured) is more likely to be profit-oriented.

Conclusion 11.7. *If service providers in health care were pure profit maximizers, there would be no reason to expect cost shifting (e.g., from Managed Care patients to patients having traditional insurance). Cost shifting may however occur if the profit orientation of the service providers is unaffected or becomes more important as they increasingly turn to patients having traditional insurance.*

The empirical relevance of cost shifting was tested by DRANOVE (1988). The evidence from hospitals in Illinois suggest that there was in fact a compensating increase in the price of services charged to patients having traditional insurance, amounting to 0.5 Dollar for every Dollar lost due to reduced charges for Medicaid and Medicare patients; that is, $dp_T/d\overline{p} = -0.5$.

11.4.4 Final Assessment of Managed Care Organizations

Relying on an MCO as a complementary agent may be advantageous to many individuals, who can obtain comprehensive health care at a lower cost, usually without a loss of health status. Therefore one may conclude that MCOs and HMOs in particular bring about an efficiency gain in health care. The price to be paid consists in a restricted choice of health care providers. If the cost savings lead to cost increases somewhere else in the health care sector (or the economy at large), however, this conclusion is unwarranted. Still, this cost increase would have to be weighted against the increasing consumer welfare through a widened range of choice among complementary agents in health care. This advantage is not achieved at the expense of physicians and hospitals as long as they *voluntarily* agree to the terms of contracts offered by the MCO.

Despite these advantages, it is questionable whether MC will acquire a significant market share outside the United States. In countries whose population is assigned to a national health service or to national health insurance without the freedom of choice, the monopoly insurer lacks the incentive to add MC to its services. However, even in countries such as France, Germany or Switzerland, where some competition exists between health insurers, it is difficult for MCOs to gain a large market share. As long as *hospitals in these countries are subsidized* by the government, permitting them to charge fees below actual cost, MCOs have a much smaller cost advantage than in the United States, where they achieve their savings mainly through fewer hospitalizations and patient days. This difference is reflected by the first European HMO which started business in Zurich (Switzerland) at the beginning of 1990. Its premiums were only 15 percent below those of conventional sick funds, compared to up to 30 percent in the United States. But even if MCOs attract only a minority of service providers of a health care system, their viability proves that modified financial incentives may make for a more economic use of resources without necessarily compromising quality of treatment.

11.5 Summary

(1) In addition to the core principal-agent relationship between the physician and the patient, there also exist complementary principal-agent relationships that cause national health care systems to differ a great deal. Countries opting for politicians as the main complementary agent are characterized by a national health service or national health insurance. Where competing health insurers take on this role, they may try to vertically integrate the provision of health care services, resulting in Managed Care Organizations (MCOs).

(2) There are at least two reasons why consumers may be interested in having a complementary agent besides the physician. One is monitoring the quality of services provided; the other, negotiating a payment system that induces a favorable performance-cost ratio in health care.

(3) Employers could in principle act as complementary agents, shaping contractual relationships with health care providers in the interest of their employees. However, they are accepted under exceptional circumstances only because employees fear the leaking of health information by health care providers.

(4) Due to its monopsony power, the government acting as the complementary agent can lower fees for health care services. This power, however, is limited because the health care sector competes with other industries and countries for resources. Moreover, a government is less constrained than competitive health insurers to pass on any cost savings to consumers.

(5) Compared to conventional insurance, Managed Care Organizations achieve substantial cost savings through vertically integrating the provision of health care services. With exceptions, these savings do not go along with worse health.

(6) If service providers in health care were pure profit maximizers, there would be no reason to expect any cost shifting from Managed Care patients to those with conventional insurance. However, cost shifting is predicted to occur if providers' profit orientation is independent of or even increases with services provided to Managed Care patients.

11.6 Further Reading

The articles by DRANOVE AND SATTERTHWAITE (2000) and GLIED (2000) published in the HANDBOOK OF HEALTH ECONOMICS deal with forms of delivery of medical care.

11.A Appendix

This appendix contains the derivation of the principal-agent relationship in the most simple case of one principal contracting with one agent. Both are assumed to be risk averse. There is no health insurer or government (who may step in as complementary agents to help resolve the difficulties noted below).

In terms of the general formulation of the principal-agent problem, the design of the contract amounts to a rule $p(\theta)$ that determines how the benefits of a planned transaction are shared between the two parties depending on the outcome θ. The principal's decision problem is to find the rule $p^*(\theta)$ maximizing his or her expected utility [see HOLMSTRÖM (1979) and LEVINTHAL (1988) for the ensuing development].

Accordingly, equation (11.A.1) below is a so-called objective functional. For (11.A.1) to be applicable to the physician-patient relationship, it must be assumed that health outcomes can be expressed in terms of money – a condition that may be considered satisfied in view of the willingness-to-pay approach to the evaluation of changes in health status developed in Chapter 2. The probability density function of possible outcomes $f(\theta|e^*)$ is conditional on the effort level of the agent, who can autonomously select the value e^* because the principal is unable to observe effort e by assumption. For simplicity, objectives other than income $[\theta - p(\theta)$ for the principal, valued according to u^P, $p(\theta)$ for the agent, valued according to $u^A]$ are neglected here. Thus, the principal's objective functional reads

$$\max_{p(\theta)} \int_{\theta} u^P\{\theta - p(\theta)\}f(\theta|e^*)\mathrm{d}\theta. \tag{11.A.1}$$

The agent will not strike the contract unless he or she benefits from it, the second-ranked alternative yielding some utility level $\overline{u}^A$. The agent too is supposed to maximize expected utility and to be risk averse (i.e., the second derivative of the utility function w.r.t. payment $p(\theta)$ is negative). With $v^A[e^*]$ denoting the cost of effort expressed in terms of utility,[1] the so-called *participation constraint* imposed by the agent reads

$$\int_0 u^A\{p(\theta)\}f(\theta|e^*)\mathrm{d}\theta - v^A[e^*] \geq \overline{u}^A. \tag{11.A.2}$$

Moreover, given the nonobservability of his or her effort, the agent is free to choose e such that expected utility less cost is maximized. This gives rise to the so-called *incentive compatibility constraint*, with $\arg\max\{\cdot\}$ rendering the value of e which maximizes the expression in braces,

$$e^* = \arg\max_{e} \left\{ \int_{\theta} u^A\{p(\theta)\}f(\theta|e)\mathrm{d}\theta - v^A(e) \right\}. \tag{11.A.3}$$

---

[1] The brackets indicate that the function has to be evaluated at the point indicated, i.e., $v^A[e^*]$ at the point $e = e^*$.

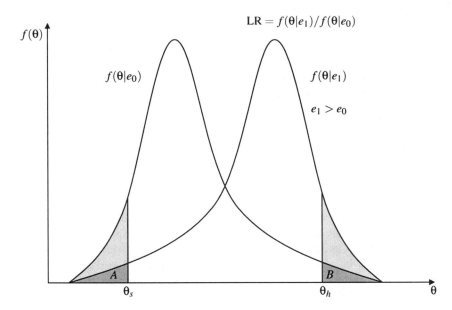

Fig. 11.A.1. Monotone Likelihood Ratio Property

The agent's choice e^* satisfies the first-order condition

$$\int_\theta u^A\{p(\theta)\}\frac{\mathrm{d}f(\theta|e^*)}{\mathrm{d}e}\mathrm{d}\theta - v'^A[e^*] = 0. \tag{11.A.4}$$

Optimal effort e^* is determined uniquely by condition (11.A.4) only if the probability of observing outcome θ given high effort, $f(\theta|e_1)$, increases with θ relative to the probability given low effort, $f(\theta|e_0)$ [see ROGERSON (1985)]. This is the so-called 'monotone likelihood ratio property'. Figure 11.A.1 illustrates. Let there be two density functions with common support, $f(\theta|e_0)$ and $f(\theta|e_1)$. The density function $f(\theta|e_1)$ is obtained by moving probability mass to the right while increasing effort from e_0 to e_1. At θ_s (sickness, unfavorable outcome), the likelihood ratio LR $= f(\theta|e_1)/f(\theta|e_0)$ is clearly below one. At θ_h (healthy, favorable outcome), $f(\theta|e_1)/f(\theta|e_0)$ exceeds one. Indeed, this ratio does not increase with θ throughout; thus, the situation depicted in Figure 11.A.1 satisfies the 'monotone likelihood ratio' requirement only locally.

The objective functional (11.A.1) and the constraints (11.A.2) and (11.A.3) may be combined to form a Lagrange functional, with θ below the integral sign indicating integration over all values of $\theta \in [\theta_s, \theta_h]$ and hence calculation of the expected value,

$$\mathcal{L} = \int_\theta u^P\{\theta - p(\theta)\}f(\theta|e^*)\mathrm{d}\theta + \lambda\left(\int_\theta u^A\{p(\theta)\}f(\theta|e^*)\mathrm{d}\theta - v^A[e^*] - \overline{u}^A\right)$$

$$+ \mu\left(\int_\theta u^A\{p(\theta)\}\frac{\mathrm{d}f(\theta|e^*)}{\mathrm{d}e}\mathrm{d}\theta - v'^A[e^*]\right). \tag{11.A.5}$$

Here, $\lambda, \mu \geq 0$ denote the Lagrange multipliers pertaining to the participation and the incentive compatibility constraint, respectively.

In order to avoid functional analysis, expression (11.A.5) is differentiated pointwise with respect to the value that the function p takes on at point θ [Gâteaux differentiation; see TIKHOMIROV (2001)]. Therefore, $p(\theta)$ in fact is treated like a scalar, which is admissible only if $p(\theta)$ is monotonously increasing or decreasing in θ. This means that at the optimum, each term under the integral must satisfy the first-order condition,

$$-u'^P[\theta - p^*(\theta)]f(\theta|e^*) + \lambda u'^A[p^*(\theta)]f(\theta|e^*) + \mu u'^A[p^*(\theta)]\frac{df(\theta|e^*)}{de} = 0 \quad (11.A.6)$$

with, for example, $u'^A[p^*(\theta)]$ symbolizing the agent's marginal utility if payment assumes the value $p^*(\theta)$. Dividing by $u'^A[p^*(\theta)]f(\theta|e^*)$, one obtains

$$\frac{u'^P[\theta - p^*(\theta)]}{u'^A[p^*(\theta)]} = \lambda + \mu\frac{\dfrac{df(\theta|e^*)}{de}}{f(\theta|e^*)} = \lambda + \mu E, \quad \text{with} \quad E \equiv \frac{\dfrac{df(\theta|e^*)}{de}}{f(\theta|e^*)}. \quad (11.A.7)$$

This condition holds for all possible values of θ and may be interpreted as follows. Its left-hand side represents the optimal sharing of the benefit accruing from the transaction between the principal and the agent, expressed in terms of subjective marginal utility units. The larger the party's marginal utility at the optimum, the smaller his or her share of the benefit because marginal utility decreases owing to risk-aversion ($u''^A, u''^P < 0$). Thus, the greater the value of the fraction on the left-hand side of equation (11.A.7), the smaller is the principal's 'net profit' compared to the agent's fee, and the greater is the agent's share of the benefit created by the transaction.

For the principal to be able to actually determine $p^*(\theta)$, he or she must know the right-hand side of equation (11.A.7). However, chances for having this knowledge are slim. First, in order to estimate λ, the principal would have to find out how strongly a relaxation or tightening of the participation constraint would affect his or her decision-making situation (partially differentiating (11.A.5) w.r.t. $\bar{u}^A$ yields λ). Second, a relaxation or tightening of the incentive compatibility constraint also affects the value of the Lagrangian (partially differentiating (11.A.5) w.r.t. $df(\theta|e^*)/de$ yields μ). And third, the principal (i.e., the prospective patient) would have to estimate the physician's stochastic effectiveness E that shows the extent to which marginal effort shifts probability mass towards more favorable health outcomes (see Figure 11.A.1 again). Needless to say that only few principals (i.e., prospective patients) could meet these requirements. Therefore, there is a market for the complementary agents described in Section 11.3 to mitigate or even remedy this potential market failure.

As a final remark, it may be worthwhile to emphasize that even if identifiable, this payment function is optimal on expectation only. In any single event, it has considerable potential for conflict and lack of incentive compatibility. To see this, refer back to Figure 11.A.1 and assume that the principal observes an outcome $\theta \leq \theta_s$. In keeping with equation (11.A.7), the principal would infer that the agent exerted (too) little effort, calling for deduction in payment. However, the shaded area marked A symbolizes the probability of an unfavorable outcome $\theta < \theta_s$ in spite of high effort e_1. The agent would certainly hate to be sanctioned in this situation and may decide to lower effort next time. Conversely, area B denotes the probability of a favorable outcome $\theta \geq \theta_h$ in spite of low effort e_0. According to equation (11.A.7), this would call for a bonus payment to the agent, who may again be tempted to lower effort next time because it was possible to obtain extra payment for no extra effort.

11.E Exercises

11.1. Discuss the difficulties to be expected when establishing a MCO in your own country.

11.2. 'Ballooning of cost' could also describe a situation in which an increase in the cost of treatment of MC patients results in higher prices charged the patients who are covered by conventional insurance. What does the occurrence of ballooning of cost of this type depend on? [Hint: eliminate the equality of costs $C_T = C_H$ in equation (11.3) and use $d\overline{C}_H$ instead of $d\overline{p}_H$ in equation (11.6)].

The Market for Pharmaceuticals

12.1 Introduction

One cannot possibly imagine present-day health care without pharmaceuticals. There are at least three reasons for this statement.

(1) Pharmaceuticals represent a form of therapy that does not involve *injuring or removing organs* while permitting causal treatment (not only aimed at alleviating symptoms) in several instances. Chemotherapy, employed in the treatment of tuberculosis, is the historic example of such causal treatment; vaccination against the AIDS virus may become a future example.

(2) Pharmaceuticals are generally in a dosed manner and may be replaced by other drugs in the event of adverse effects. Apart from organ transplants, surgical mistakes cannot be reversed. For example, once hysterectomy is performed, the womb cannot be restored to its previous condition.

(3) In contrast to nursing services, pharmaceuticals are industrially manufactured, providing them with a particularly large *potential of productivity increases* in the provision of health care services through saving the time not only of physicians and auxiliary staff, but of patients as well.

When held against these benefits, pharmaceuticals do not appear particularly expensive. On average, pharmaceuticals accounted for only 9.5 percent of total public health care expenditure (HCE) as of 1997 in OECD countries,[1] compared to 7.6 percent in 1970. Recently, this share has been on the increase especially in the United States, reaching 12.5 percent by 2006. By comparison, OECD member countries spend on average slightly less than one-half of their health care budget on hospitals. Moreover, LICHTENBERG (2005) presents evidence suggesting that pharmaceutical

---

[1] These percentages only include expenditure on pharmaceuticals that are traded via retail business (e.g., pharmacies). They exclude use of drugs by hospitals and by physicians for outpatient care.

P. Zweifel et al., *Health Economics*, 2nd ed., DOI 10.1007/978-3-540-68540-1_12,
© Springer-Verlag Berlin Heidelberg 2009

innovation is mainly responsible for the increase in survival time of HIV patients and increases in longevity in as many as 50 countries. Against this background, it seems surprising that the pharmaceutical industry of almost every western country faces so much criticism, which comprises four main points.

(1) Many drugs are branded *useless or even harmful*. In Germany for example only 30 percent of the newly introduced substances are classified as new and therapeutically significant [see SCHWABE AND PAFFRATH (2001, p. 22)]. In other words, approximately 70 percent of an already small number of new preparations are considered as marginal modifications of existing products, commonly called 'me-too' drugs.

(2) *Expenditure on advertising* is largely seen as excessive. In the late 1980s, 'advertisement and information' amounted to 26 percent of the total cost of the German pharmaceutical industry [see HOFFMEYER AND MCCARTHY (1994, p. 460)]. By contrast, expenditure on advertisement in German automotive manufacturing amounted only to approximately 6 percent of turnover [see TERPORTEN (1999, p. 132)].

(3) The pharmaceutical industry also has been under fire for its use of *animals* in testing new substances. In addition, its impact on the environment has been at issue since the pharmaceutical industry forms part of the chemical industry.

(4) As a result of what are considered *exorbitant prices*, revenues and profits are condemned as being excessive. The pharmaceutical industry of the OECD countries achieves a rate of return of 7 percent [see LICHTBLAU (1999)], the automobile industry, 2 percent [see TERPORTEN (1999, p. 463)].

While economic theory contributes to clarifying most of these points of criticism, it may not always result in conclusive suggestions for policy. This is mainly because the traditional criterion, 'price equal to marginal cost' cannot be applied directly. Suppliers do not so much compete with a given range of products but try to secure their economic survival through *innovation* – up to the point where the expected marginal revenue of an additional innovation covers its expected marginal cost – a condition not easily determined.

Evidently, the development of a new pharmaceutical – from the design of its desired therapeutic effects to its market launch and on to the end of its useful economic life – needs to be clearly understood. The pharmacological properties of a new substance constitute the starting point of Section 12.2, since they serve as the basis of assessment to regulators deciding about access to the market. Pharmaceutical innovation becomes an attractive investment only if there is a very good chance of market access being granted.

Returns to a pharmaceutical innovation will be examined in Section 12.3. They decisively depend on the length of patent protection granted by public authorities. Therefore, Section 12.4 is dedicated to the question of optimal patent life. Thanks to patent protection, pharmaceutical manufacturers obtain a monopoly position for a certain period of time, permitting them to charge prices well in excess of marginal cost. For this reason, a seemingly natural way to control pharmaceutical expenditure (and therefore HCE) is to regulate drug prices. The different forms of price regulation are analyzed in Section 12.5. After expiration of patent protection at the latest, price competition will be possible between drugs of the same diagnostic category. The extent to which this competition takes place shall be examined in Section 12.6.

12.2 The Development of a New Drug

Traditional microeconomic theory of demand takes an existing good with established characteristics of quality as the unit of analysis. Consequently, this theory is ill suited to describe so-called product innovation. In contrast to process innovation, which aims at lowering the cost of production of an already existing product, product innovation creates products with modified – and even completely new – characteristics. In the context of the development of a new pharmaceutical, it is therefore appropriate to make the characteristics of a pharmaceutical the basic element of analysis, as in the so-called *New Demand Theory* [see LANCASTER (1966, 1971) and BECKER (1965)].

12.2.1 The Consumption Technology of a Drug

Pharmaceuticals may be described along several quality dimensions, among them, e.g.,

- beneficial principal effect (per daily dose);
- adverse drug reaction;
- rate of absorption in the organism;
- convenience of handling (e.g., tablets instead of injection);
- storability.

For concreteness, consider a drug for the treatment of rheumatism. Let existing preparations act as pain relievers (featuring characteristic b_1), without however being able to stop the joints from degenerating. Therefore, they lack the characteristic, 'restoration of mobility of joints' (b_2). Let A be a product that is already on the market, with a daily dose that relieves pain during a period of four hours. Its so-called *consumption technology* is thus described by point $1A$ of Figure 12.1. Now consider first a 'me-too' innovation. This would be another pain killer, but effective for seven hours (say), represented by point $1N$. On a market with perfectly informed and fully insured patients, the producer of N would be able to conquer the market, since for fully insured patients (and their physicians) only the quality attributes of a drug matter, not its price.

12.2.2 Regulation of Market Access by Public Authorities

The innovation N of the preceding section was marginal in that it offered only more of the same quality attribute b_1, 'pain relief'. Patients suffering from rheumatism, however, typically are interested not only in pain relief but also in the restoration of mobility of their joints (b_2). In technical terms, both b_1 and b_2 are arguments of their utility function. In the following, an innovation which provides a good or service featuring additional characteristics relevant for demand will be called a *breakthrough innovation*. The consumption technology of such a breakthrough innovation is represented by point $1D$ of Figure 12.1.

Although D is pioneering, its access to the market is not certain, since in most industrialized countries, public authorities (e.g., the National Institute for Health and Clinical Excellence (NICE) in the United Kingdom) decide about admitting a new chemical entity (NCE) to the market. In the example of Figure 12.1, the agency regulating market access could easily assert that product D will not even guarantee the same pain relief as does A, let alone N. In fact, it would have to weigh restoring mobility of joints against pain relief, and it is questionable that it reflects patients' preferences in doing this.

Access to the market is only guaranteed to an innovator who succeeds in attaining *technological dominance* (e.g., point $1D'$ in Figure 12.1). A product is technologically dominant if it contains more of at least one and no less of the remaining characteristics per unit than its competitors. Since the price of a drug plays no role whatsoever for fully insured patients, such a breakthrough innovation has a guaranteed market success as well, provided health insurance coverage is comprehensive.

> **Conclusion 12.1.** *Apart from marginal ('me-too') innovations, which offer more of already existing characteristics, only those breakthrough innovations achieving technological dominance have guaranteed access to the market under traditional regulation. Given comprehensive health insurance, it also has guaranteed market success once access is granted.*

12.2.3 Effect of Copayment

As soon as patients do not have full insurance coverage and consequently have to bear part of the cost of pharmaceutical treatment (like in the United States, parts of the UK population, and increasingly Germany), product price in addition to quality becomes important. In the following, price is defined as the net amount the insured has to pay per daily defined dose.

The consumer's decision situation is presented in Figure 12.2 on the assumption that his or her budget for pharmaceutical treatment is a fixed amount of 12 money units (MU). If the traditional antirheumatic drug A costs 3 MU per dose, this budget buys 4 doses. Given a linear consumption technology, these 4 doses afford four times the effect of a single dose. Accordingly, point $1A$ of the consumption technology becomes the *economically relevant* point $4A$ of Figure 12.2 (note the smaller scale compared to Figure 12.1). Admittedly, this linearity assumption has its problems in many

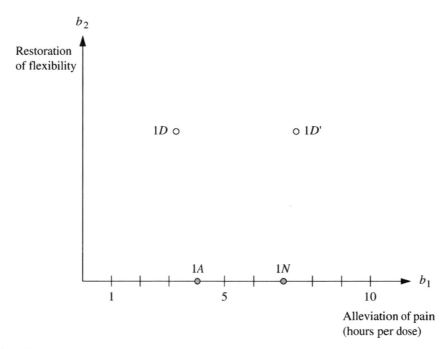

Fig. 12.1. Consumption Technology of Three Preparations for the Treatment of Rheumatism

cases. On the one hand, a drug may fully take effect after several applications only; on the other hand, some substances may be addictive, implying that their dose must be successively increased for achieving a given effect [see STIGLER AND BECKER (1977)]. In the first case, one may speak of a consumption technology exhibiting increasing returns to scale, while in the second case, it has decreasing returns to scale (with respect to the quantity of desired attributes).

Product N is more effective than A. If its price is the same as that of A, its superiority in terms of pharmacological effectiveness transforms into economic superiority. In general, however, the producer skims off at least part of the higher willingness to pay for the innovative product by charging a higher price. Let this price be 4 MU per dose, causing the budget of 12 MU to buy 3 doses of N only. At this price, product N still dominates product A on the market (see points $3N$ and $4A$ of Figure 12.2).

Now let the breakthrough innovation be even more expensive, costing 6 MU per dose. Assuming constant returns to scale, a patient using this preparation reaches point $2D$. Whether the patient actually chooses this point depends on *subjective preferences*, in keeping with the traditional theory of demand (except that these preferences may be influenced by medical advice). The indifference curve I_1 of Figure 12.2 thus represents patients who consider pain relief so important as to make them opt for the marginal innovation (point $3N$). Comparing points $3N$ and $4A$ of Figure 12.2, one finds that even this type of innovation (qualified as 'me too' above) confers a benefit upon consumers.

Other patients may be more interested in regaining mobility of joints (b_2). Accordingly, their indifference curves run flatter (like I_2), causing a combination of preparations D and N to be optimal. The optimum $(1.5N + 1D)$ indicated, however, cannot be realized if an integer number of doses is required (e.g., if the medicine is provided in the form of ampoules) or if the combined use of substances gives rise to adverse effects of interaction. If patients of type I_2 are numerous enough, it might be worthwhile for a producer to *combine* characteristics b_1 and b_2 in a new way, and setting a price such that its product lies on or beyond the existing efficiency boundary $2D3N$. Even if this means that 'only' a marginal product differentiation is performed, this producer still contributes to a better provision of rheumatic patients with drugs. To see this, just consider an indifference curve through $2D$ such as I_3, reflecting the situation where only the innovative drug is available. This advantage has to be weighed against the *cost of product differentiation*, however, since smaller lot sizes in the production of a given product specification drive up average cost. The problem of 'excessive' product differentiation mentioned at the beginning of the chapter can then be attributed to the fact that insured consumers only bear part of the cost of such product differentiation while fully reaping its benefits.

Figure 12.2 can also be used to demonstrate that the quantity demanded varies with a change in price also in the case of a breakthrough innovation; however, the price elasticity is closer to zero than for 'me-too' preparations. Consider the type of patient characterized by I_3, who is indifferent between $2D$ and $3N$ initially. If the producer of the 'me-too' preparation lowers price, the consumer can buy more than 3 doses of N given a budget of 12 MU. In this case, the breakthrough innovation loses its market with the I_3 type. Vice versa, if the producer of N increases price, there will be a critical price where the budget buys cN units (see point cN vertically below point $2D$). All types will have switched to $2D$ by then. There is no such critical price for the innovator; as long as the indifference curve is downward sloping, some type will always buy D. For example, the type characterized by I_4 is indifferent between $1D$ (where the price of the breakthrough innovation has doubled) and $2N$ (where the price of the 'me-too' has increased by a mere 50 percent). This implies that the price elasticity of demand must be closer to zero overall in the case of breakthrough innovation than for the conventional alternative, which is also completely substituted at some point.

Conclusion 12.2. *Suppliers of breakthrough innovations are faced with a falling demand curve for their product; the price elasticity for the innovation is closer to zero than for existing products.*

12.3 Pharmaceutical Innovation as an Investment

At first glance, one would be inclined to say that the development of a new drug has little to do with investment in property, buildings, or machinery. Nevertheless, all these activities entail expenditures that are certain and occur in the present, whereas the future promises uncertain returns. In this section, this similarity will be used to characterize drug innovation from an economic point of view.

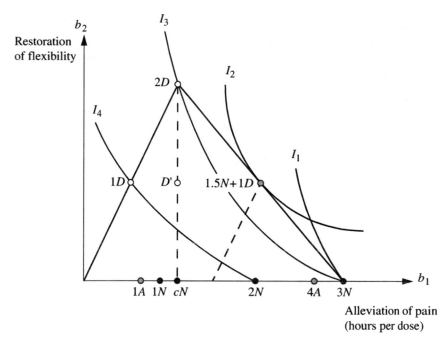

Fig. 12.2. Pharmacological and Economic Aspects of a Pharmaceutical Innovation

12.3.1 The Chronology of a Pharmaceutical Innovation

At present, the development of a new drug spans on average a period of more than ten years, from the point in time when, after thousands of synthesizing experiments involving 10,000 substances, there at last emerge about 20 promising ones (see Figure 12.3). Subsequent preclinical development takes about two years. Based on weeks or months of testing on animals, evidence accumulates as to whether the substance can be used in humans at all. This is followed by about three years of preclinical development that serves to establish the properties of the substance. Now a provisional registration with the regulatory authority (such as the Ministry of Health) can be made (New Drug Application (NDA) with the Food and Drug Administration (FDA) in the case of the United States).

Next, there are several years of clinical trials designed to prove the drug's efficacy and its safety not only in the short but also in the long term. Four phases can be distinguished (see again Figure 12.3). During phase I of clinical trials, substances are tested on healthy human volunteers. For this purpose, they need to be manufactured in large quantity for the first time. About one-half of them drop out at this point. In clinical trials II, the effects of the remaining substances are tested on a small number of select patients, while their long-term tolerance is examined on animals. Again about one-half of the substances fail. In phase III of clinical trials, these effects are tested on a larger number of patients under conditions that are similar to actual medical practice. During these three years, the documentation required for the official application of the drug is finalized as well. Also the drug is tested in several hospitals and countries in an attempt to discover any adverse drug reactions which may arise in its long-term use.

During the 1970s, this process *lengthened* considerably [see WALKER AND PARRISH (1988)] to about twelve years at present, compared to less than four years at the beginning of the 1960s. This extension is due to a tightening of requirements for registration, with the United States playing a leading role [see GRABOWSKI AND VERNON (2000)]. It was triggered by the Thalidomide tragedy (Contergan in Germany) when hundreds of babies with malformations were born because their mothers had used this sleeping drug. It is paradoxical that the added requirements for market access probably *cost more lives than they saved* because they caused effective drugs to become available with delay only. Many people died from diseases which could have been treated in the meantime [see PELTZMAN (1973)].

12.3.2 Probability of Success and the Cost of Innovation

The making of a pharmaceutical does not only take many years but is also subject to many setbacks. According to estimates prepared by WARDELL ET AL. (1980) for the United States, the synthesis of no less than 10,000 substances is necessary in order to develop one marketable drug. According to earlier estimates, the probability of success had been 1:3,000 during the 1960s [VANE (1964)]. At present, out of every 10,000 synthesized substances, only 15 to 40 will be tested for toxicity, of which only 2 to 3 will survive the long phase of clinical trials. In the course of investigations for long-term toxicity, this number reduces to one single New Chemical Entity (NCE) (see Figure 12.3). For Germany and Switzerland, a probability of success of 1:10,000 is assumed as well at present [see PHARMA INFORMATION (2001, p. 39)].

The simultaneous decrease in the probability of success and lengthening of the development phase caused a surge in the average cost of a new marketable drug. Discounted at 8 percent, development of a new product cost US$7.5 million during the 1950s [BAILY (1972)]. This figure rose to 54 million for products introduced during the 1970s [HANSEN (1979)] and on to 125 million during the 1980s [WIGGINS (1987)].[2] A more recent estimate amounts to roughly US$200 million [DIMASI ET AL. (1991)]; it refers to new substances which were tested during the period 1970–1982. Current estimates are around US$800 million [DIMASI ET AL. (2003)]. Since during the 1960s and 1970s sales did not increase as rapidly, the number of market introductions in the United States and some European countries fell [see REIS-ARNDT (1993)]. During the past two decades, sales increased mainly due to

---

[2] In this calculations, the accumulated costs at the time of market launch are discounted to the present value at the time of decision to develop, i.e., 10 years earlier.

Year

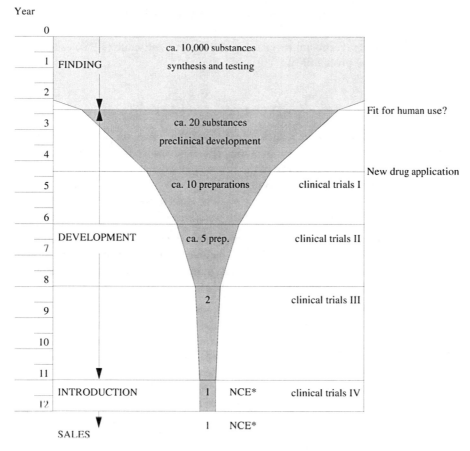

NCE*. New chemical entity

Fig. 12.3. The Development of a Pharmaceutical
Source: PHARMA INFORMATION (2001)

breakthrough innovations. Improved profit prospects triggered a surge of innovative effort, causing the number of market introductions to rise again [see GRABOWSKI AND VERNON (2000) and SCHWABE AND PAFFRATH (2001, p. 23)].

Conclusion 12.3. *Pharmaceutical innovation can be interpreted as an investment. Since the early 1960s, the cost of drug innovation has rapidly increased, while the number of newly introduced active substances tended to decrease worldwide. However, this trend was reversed in the 1980s.*

12.3.3 Excessive Returns to Pharmaceutical Innovation?

Since innovation represents an investment, the net present value (NPV) criterion is suitable for gauging profitability,

$$\text{NPV} = \sum_{t=0}^{T} \frac{R_t}{(1+r)^t} - \sum_{t=0}^{T} \frac{C_t}{(1+r)^t}. \tag{12.1}$$

In this formula, R_t represents a flow of revenues that takes on positive values no sooner than after twelve years on average. The expenditure flow, C_t, however, assumes high values at the beginning of the research and development phase but drops toward variable costs of production later on. If the NPV is positive, then the project contributes to the increase of the investor's assets. Both flows C_t and R_t as well as the interest rate r used for discounting can only be estimated at the moment of decision.

While the net present value criterion represents the theoretically preferred measure of profitability due to its unambiguity, the internal rate of return (IRR) is more popular. The *internal rate of return* is equal to the interest rate r^* that yields a net present value NPV $= 0$ in equation (12.1).

JOGLEKAR AND PATERSON (1986) were among the first to calculate the expected IRR of pharmaceutical innovations in the United States that were initiated in 1976 and to be registered in 1988. Based on trend extrapolations of the probable development of returns, they arrived at a value of 6.1 percent after taxes for the average NCE. This corresponds very well to the 5.5 percent that ZWEIFEL AND PEDRONI (1985) obtained, adjusting data provided by VIRTS AND WESTON (1981). According to GRABOWSKI AND VERNON (1990), the IRR rose by the end of the 1970s from 7.1 percent 1970–1974 to 10 percent in 1975–1979. Apparently this trend has continued to 11.1 percent for NCEs launched in the mid 1980s [GRABOWSKI AND VERNON (1994)], and to 11.5 percent for those launched in the 1990s [GRABOWSKI ET AL. (2002)].

In addition, JOGLEKAR AND PATERSON (1986) gave an impression of the *uncertainty* which an investor faced in the 1970s. Since the arithmetic mean is strongly influenced by outliers (i.e., the very few successful drugs in this case), the median IRR is far below the average value of 6.1 percent, amounting to –5.5 percent. One-half of the 218 innovations which were introduced in the United States during the period 1962–1977 will not have paid back their development costs even after 36 years. GRABOWSKI AND VERNON (1994) confirmed the extremely asymmetric distribution of present values. While the NPV was US$22.2 million on average (at prices of 1990), the top decile amounted to US$1 billion. However, the seven bottom deciles had all negative NPV values, i.e., revenues failed to recover the cost of development.

For an assessment of the social value of pharmaceutical innovation, *consumer surplus* must be added to the NPV, constituting the part of willingness to pay for the innovation not appropriated by its producer. For three particular pharmaceutical innovations, WU (1984) calculated total internal rates of return in excess of 25 percent, based on observed prices and quantities. However, drug prices paid on the

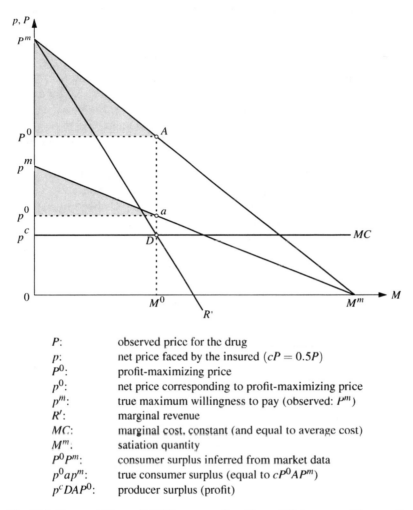

P:	observed price for the drug
p:	net price faced by the insured ($cP = 0.5P$)
P^0:	profit-maximizing price
p^0:	net price corresponding to profit-maximizing price
p^m:	true maximum willingness to pay (observed: P^m)
R':	marginal revenue
MC:	marginal cost, constant (and equal to average cost)
M^m:	satiation quantity
$P^0 P^m$:	consumer surplus inferred from market data
$p^0 a p^m$:	true consumer surplus (equal to $cP^0 A P^m$)
$p^c DA P^0$:	producer surplus (profit)

Fig. 12.4. True and Observed Willingness to Pay (Rate of Coinsurance 50 percent)

market exaggerate patients' willingness to pay in the presence of health insurance. This is demonstrated in Figure 12.4. Let patients' true marginal willingness to pay for the drug be represented by the demand function $p^m M^m$. With a copayment of 50 percent ($c = 0.5$), the observed market demand function $P^m M^m$ runs twice as steep. If, for example, a patient's true maximum willingness to pay is $p^m = 5$ MU, then the maximum price of the drug could be set at $P^m = 10$ MU. Assuming the innovator to have a monopoly, marginal revenue equals marginal cost. The price actually paid is P^0, resulting in M^0 as the quantity transacted.[3]

---

[3] For the sake of simplicity, the possibilities of reference prices and of price negotiations between pharmaceutical companies and health insurers (see Section 12.5.3) are neglected.

Based on price-quantity observations, an econometrician would estimate the demand function $P^m M^m$, obtaining a consumer surplus given by the area $P^0 A P^m$. This quantity would be added to the returns of the period $[0M^0 A P^0 - 0M^0 D p^c$, a typical element R_t of equation (12.1)] to calculate a social NPV or IRR.

Due to proportionality, the *true aggregate willingness to pay* for M^0 units of the drug amounts to only $0M^0 a p^m$, that is, one-half of the area in the case of $c = 0.5$. While costs remain the same, consumer surplus obviously also halves. So when WU (1984) estimated a social IRR of a pharmaceutical innovation to be around 200 percent of its private value, this multiplier must be reduced to 150 percent or less if the copayment is $c = 0.5$ (which was very common in the United States at the time) and to still lower values if c is lower (as in most other industrial countries). Widespread skepticism with regard to the social value of pharmaceutical innovation may well reflect this discrepancy between willingness to pay observed on the insured market and true willingness to pay on the part of the patient [see ZWEIFEL (1984)].

Conclusion 12.4. *Low real internal rates of return that average 5 to 10 percent for the innovator contrast with considerably higher social rates of return to pharmaceutical innovation. However, the consumer surplus component is overestimated due to the effect of health insurance.*

12.4 The Role of Patent Protection

12.4.1 Why Patent Protection?

Patent protection grants inventors of a new product or process a monopoly for the commercial use of their innovation. Although the monopoly has limited duration (20 years in most Western industrialized countries around 2000), it does contradict the principles of *perfect competition*. Perfect competition ensures that relative prices of commodities simultaneously reflect their relative marginal utilities on the demand side and their relative marginal cost of production on the supply side; this means that the economy is in a Pareto optimum. This crucial equality is disrupted by the existence of monopolies which cause relative commodity prices to differ from their relative marginal costs. Therefore, patent protection is responsible for long-term deviations from the optimal state of the economy.

This point of view, however, proves to be too narrow as soon as the commodity set contains not only products already in existence but also the ones *still to be invented in the future*. Patent protection serves to curtail the consumption of currently available goods (due to monopolization and its welfare losses) in the interest of the prospect of consuming newly developed goods in the future. In an ultimate sense, patent protection brings to the fore the latent willingness to pay for innovation, reflected by a price surcharge over and above the marginal cost of current output.

Through patent protection, innovators become *monopolists for a limited period of time* during which they can impose such a surcharge. It is easy to show that this surcharge usually is not socially optimal. The profit-maximizing price p^* is given by the equality of marginal revenue and marginal cost MC,

$$p^*(1 + 1/\eta) = MC, \quad \text{and thus} \quad \frac{p^*}{MC} = \frac{1}{1 + 1/\eta}. \tag{12.2}$$

Here, $\eta < 0$ represents the price elasticity of demand, which generally varies with output. Evidently the surcharge to marginal cost p^*/MC depends on η and hence on output. It is therefore variable, whereas the marginal cost of an innovation would optimally call for a *fixed* surcharge independent of the quantity of output.

Therefore, patent protection is a *second-best solution* to the problem of financing innovation. The problem stems from the fact that innovation is mainly based on information. The pharmaceutical industry is concerned with the search for knowledge that permits the creation or identification of an NCE with desirable characteristics. Once this knowledge is available in the form of a drug, its chemical structure can be found out at comparably low cost. Hence, the knowledge which makes the innovation possible becomes a public good.

Imitators do not have to bear the cost of innovation, enabling them to recover average cost at a lower price than the original manufacturer. They can therefore increase their market share at the innovator's expense through a reduction of price. Innovators will hesitate to lower price, not least because they would have difficulty justifying a high price for their next innovation in negotiations with health insurers and governments. Clinging to a high price, however, will sooner or later make them lose the market for this particular drug. This was the experience of innovators in 1989/90 when Germany introduced reference prices, causing patients to cover the gap between their actual price and the reference price [ZWEIFEL AND CRIVELLI (1996)]. Innovators thus have to lower price to the level of the imitator, that is, to marginal production cost. Whatever their pricing policy, innovators will come to the conclusion that innovation is not profitable in the absence of patent protection. Therefore it is the key function of patent protection to safeguard the incentives for innovation.

12.4.2 The Decision Situation of the Innovator

While patent protection constitutes a feasible (if suboptimal) solution to the problem of keeping technological change going, the question of its extent and duration remains. With regard to extent, novel drugs enjoy protection of substance rather than merely process. This allows innovators to reap the additional returns arising from new uses of a NCE. Since the scope of patent protection is so extensive in the case of drugs, the issue of its *duration* becomes all the more crucial, motivating the study of optimal length of patent protection in a simple model.

In the early literature [see ARROW (1962) and NORDHAUS (1969)], innovators are assumed to have already made their invention, their expenditure on research and development constituting sunk costs. They make their invention available to a firm, enabling it to produce at lower cost. The question to be answered was how long the acquiring firm should have to pay for the use of the invention. In these models, patent protection is not granted before the end of product development. But at least in the pharmaceutical industry, patents are applied for early in the process in order to benefit from the protection of substance right from the beginning. At this time, the *amount of investment is not determined yet*, implying that protection afforded by the patent will exert its influence on the incentive to invest in innovation to its full extent.

These facts are taken into account in a model developed by DEBROCK (1985), which is presented in the following. From the net present value criterion of equation (12.1), it follows that lengthening the useful life of an NCE (an increase of T) makes the innovation more profitable. On the other hand, increasing innovative effort I has an ambiguous influence on the net present value of profits NPV. More innovation yields more success after market launch and thus a higher present value of revenues R. However, the cost C of development and probably of production too will increase with rising I. The net present value of profits resulting from innovation therefore is given by,

$$NPV = R(I,T) - C(I). \tag{12.3}$$

The following assumptions are introduced.

Assumption 12.1. *Marginal returns to innovation are always positive and may even increase at first, reflecting the notion that innovative effort must exceed some threshold to really pay off.*

$$\frac{\partial R}{\partial I} > 0; \quad \frac{\partial^2 R}{\partial I^2} \begin{cases} > 0 \text{ for small values of } I \\ < 0 \text{ for large values of } I. \end{cases}$$

Assumption 12.2. *Additional innovative effort progressively costs more since this requires highly specialized resources (also to the extent that marginal cost increases progressively, i.e., $\partial^2 MC/\partial I^2 > 0$).*

$$\frac{\partial C}{\partial I} > 0; \quad \frac{\partial^2 C}{\partial I^2} > 0; \quad \frac{\partial^3 C}{\partial I^3} > 0. \tag{12.4}$$

Assumption 12.3. *The present value of revenues is higher the longer patent protection. Moreover, additional innovative efforts pay off with increasing duration of patent protection, or equivalently, patent protection is effective especially when the marginal return to innovative effort is high (as in the case of a breakthrough innovation).*

$$\frac{\partial R}{\partial T} > 0; \quad \frac{\partial^2 R}{\partial I \partial T} = \frac{\partial^2 R}{\partial T \partial I} > 0. \tag{12.5}$$

Thus, an increase in innovative effort I has an ambiguous impact on profit. On the one hand, additional innovation I results in additional revenues R but costs C rise with I as well.

Box 12.1. Simultaneous Determination of Innovation Effort and Length of Patent Protection

Innovator's problem:	max $NPV = R(I,T) - C(I)$
Regulator's problem:	max $W = S(I,T) + P(I,T)$

NPV: net present value of cash-flow from innovation
R: present value of returns from innovation
C: present value of cost of innovation
W: social welfare due to the innovation (social surplus)
S: present value of consumer's surplus after market launch
P: present value of producer's (private) surplus after market launch
I: innovative efforts; decision variable of the innovator
T: length of patent protection; decision variable of the Patent Office

The innovator's decision variable is innovative effort I, whereas the regulator (usually a Patent Office) determines the length of patent protection T (see also Box 12.1). The first step consists in deriving the innovator's reaction function, displaying its optimal adjustment of I to changes in T. For this purpose, consider the necessary optimum condition with respect to I,

$$\frac{\partial NPV}{\partial I} = \frac{\partial R}{\partial I}(I,T) - \frac{\partial C}{\partial I}(I) = 0. \tag{12.6}$$

Let this optimum be disturbed by a change in effective patent life dT. In order to restore the first-order optimum condition, the innovator's adjustment must satisfy the following condition,

$$\frac{\partial^2 R}{\partial I^2} dI + \frac{\partial^2 R}{\partial I \partial T} dT - \frac{\partial^2 C}{\partial I^2} dI = 0. \tag{12.7}$$

Solving for dI/dT, one obtains the slope of the innovator's reaction function,

$$\frac{dI}{dT} = -\frac{\overset{(+)}{\dfrac{\partial^2 R}{\partial I \partial T}}}{\underset{(-)}{\dfrac{\partial^2 R}{\partial I^2} - \dfrac{\partial^2 C}{\partial I^2}}} > 0. \tag{12.8}$$

The positive sign of equation (12.8) follows from Assumption 12.3 and the sufficient condition for maximum profit, $\partial^2 NPV/\partial I^2 = \partial^2 R/\partial I^2 - \partial^2 C/\partial I^2 < 0$.

The innovator's reaction function is graphically illustrated in Figure 12.5. The three curves showing the development of marginal revenue $(\partial R/\partial I)$ as a function of I hold for three different durations of patent protection, $T_1 < T_2 < T_3$. First, they rise with increasing I but for high values of I, they fall again in view of Assumption 12.1. The curve $\partial C/\partial I$ reflects progressively increasing marginal costs. Note that equality of marginal cost and marginal revenue at $\tilde{Q}$ does not qualify for an optimum because at this point the condition NPV $= \partial^2 R/\partial I^2 - \partial^2 C/\partial I^2 < 0$ is not satisfied yet. Due to convexity of the marginal cost function $(\partial^3 C/\partial I^3 > 0$, see Assumption 12.2) the optima $\{Q^*, Q^{**}, Q^{***}\}$ define a sequence of optimal innovation effort levels $\{I^*[T_1], I^*[T_2], I^*[T_3]\}$ that increase in T but at a decreasing rate. This expansion path appears as the $g(T)$ locus of Figure 12.6 below.

12.4.3 The Length of Patent Protection from the Regulator's Point of View

In this section, the viewpoint of the regulatory agency is adopted, assuming that it does not pursue its own objectives but has its eye on aggregate welfare. The agency's own interests would probably be served best by a long period of patent protection T, causing applicants to follow instructions with diligence because large stakes are involved. In the following, this institutional bias will be disregarded in favor of the assumption that the public authority seeks to maximize society's benefit from the innovation. If the economy as a whole profits, so does the government through its tax revenue. The gain in welfare W from an innovation that has been launched on the market has two components. First, there is the social component. Its present value S rises if the innovator's efforts I increase but diminishes with longer patent protection T. The second component of welfare gains is the private producer surplus with its present value P first depending positively on additional innovative efforts but then decreasing (see Section 12.4.2). Moreover, P is higher the longer effective patent protection. The function to be maximized by the regulator is thus (see also Box 12.1),

$$W = S(I,T) + P(I,T). \tag{12.9}$$

Two additional assumptions are introduced at this point.

Assumption 12.4. *The present value of the social component of the welfare gain increases with innovative effort but decreases with effective patent life. Thus, $\partial S/\partial I > 0$; $\partial S/\partial T < 0$.*

Assumption 12.5. *The present value of the private component of the welfare gain increases for low values of innovative effort but decreases for high values. However, it increases with effective patent life throughout,*

$$\frac{\partial P}{\partial I} \begin{cases} > 0 & \textit{for small values of } I \\ < 0 & \textit{for high values of } I \end{cases} \quad \textit{and} \quad \frac{\partial P}{\partial T} > 0.$$

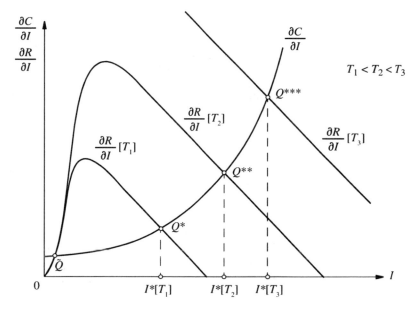

Fig. 12.5. Iso-profit Curves, Marginal Cost of Innovative Efforts and the Innovator's Reaction Function

An iso-welfare curve may be derived by totally differentiating the objective function (12.9),

$$dW = \frac{\partial S}{\partial I}dI + \frac{\partial S}{\partial T}dT + \frac{\partial P}{\partial I}dI + \frac{\partial P}{\partial T}dT = 0, \quad \text{so that}$$

$$\frac{dI}{dT} = -\frac{\frac{\partial S}{\partial T} + \frac{\partial P}{\partial T}}{\frac{\partial S}{\partial I} + \frac{\partial P}{\partial I}}, \quad \text{with} \quad \frac{\partial S}{\partial T} + \frac{\partial P}{\partial T} < 0. \tag{12.10}$$

The last inequality condition follows from the argument that an increase in T raises the so-called *welfare loss* because the loss in consumer surplus caused by monopolization cannot be fully transformed into additional producer surplus sooner or later. The slope of the iso-welfare curve thus depends on the denominator of (12.10), which in its turn hinges on $\partial P/\partial I$. For small values of innovative effort, the marginal effect of I on consumer as well as producer surplus is positive, causing the iso-welfare curves to be positively sloped (see Figure 12.6). For both innovator's profit and producer surplus it holds true that beyond some limit, additional innovative efforts are counterproductive. This causes the iso-welfare curve to bend back at the point where the loss of producer surplus is precisely compensated by the gain in consumer surplus.

If the regulator could choose T of Figure 12.6 according to its preferences without having to consider the reaction of the innovators, it would aim at reaching satiation point I_0^* as an *absolute optimum*, where the welfare loss is reduced to zero. But positive innovation efforts require a positive amount of patent protection, as argued in Section 12.4.1. Since point I_0^* is not on the innovator's reaction function $g(T)$, it cannot qualify for an equilibrium (the solution concept adopted here is the Nash equilibrium).

The equilibrium point R^* marked in Figure 12.6 is the outcome of a non-cooperative game between the regulator and the innovator, with the regulator taking the innovator's reaction function as given and seeking its optimum on that function.[4] The agency thus will strive for the highest attainable iso-welfare curve $W_2(> W_0)$ by granting patent protection of length T^*.

> **Conclusion 12.5.** *The optimal length of patent protection can be regarded as the result of a non-cooperative game between a regulator (e.g., the Patent Office) and an innovator. It assumes values that would still cause an increase in welfare if innovative efforts were intensified given a constant duration of patent protection T.*

Now consider an exogenous change that causes the NPV of a new drug to decrease, such as stiffer price regulation (see the next section), increased risk of product liability suits, or lowered barriers to entry for imitators. This would serve to shift the reaction function down, to $\bar{g}(T)$ in Figure 12.6. Under certain conditions (e.g., homotheticity of the $g(T)$ function), the new equilibrium is predicted to move to R^{**}. There, less innovation effort goes along with a longer effective patent life. Indeed, that was the solution adopted by the U.S. Drug and Price Competition and Patent Restoration Act of 1984. It increased the duration of patent protection from 17 to 20 years in return for abolishing the requirement for imitators to come up with the documentation prepared for the initial registration of the drug.

12.5 Price Regulation of Pharmaceuticals

12.5.1 Reasons for Price Regulation

In most countries, prices of pharmaceuticals are regulated by the government. From an economic point of view, this cannot be justified by the existence of a natural monopoly (as in the case of the power and telecommunication industries). The existing monopolies of the pharmaceutical industry are not natural but induced by the government guaranteeing patent protection on their products to create incentives for innovation (see Section 12.4.1).

---

[4] This equilibrium concept corresponds to the duopoly solution of Stackelberg with a leader and a follower. The regulator here assumes the role of the leader [see CARLTON AND PERLOFF (2000, Chapter 6)].

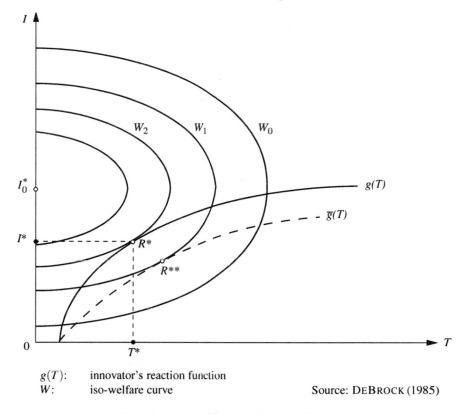

$g(T)$:   innovator's reaction function
W: iso-welfare curve   Source: DEBROCK (1985)

Fig. 12.6. Optimal Patent Life in Equilibrium

Rather, price regulation emanates from the government's (or social health insurer's) desire to *limit (public) expenditure on pharmaceuticals.* Insurance coverage induces moral hazard effects (see Chapter 6) because consumers do not have to bear the full cost and therefore overuse drugs. Service providers as well tend to perform too many services (at least in the case of fee-for-service payment). Thus, price regulation of pharmaceuticals can be seen as an attempt at mitigating moral hazard. In the absence of copayment (as it was the case, e.g., in Germany prior to 1989), a monopolistic innovator would be predicted to set an infinite price unless regulated. However, ZWEIFEL AND CRIVELLI (1996) show how the threat of transition to a regime with price regulation induces a finite price. From an economic point of view, strategies designed to limit moral hazard are generally desirable because they seek to relieve the insured from having to bear the high premiums to finance HCE in general.

Still, the moral hazard argument is not sufficient to justify price regulation of pharmaceuticals. First, there is always the alternative of limiting moral hazard by imposing copayment (see Chapter 6). Second, national price regulation may easily entail efficiency losses at the global level. Third, all existing variants of price regulation turn out to have negative side effects on innovation and competition, while need to be weighted against their benefits. And fourth, erosion of innovators' monopoly power might be fast enough to cast doubt on the logic of price regulation to begin with. These issues are taken up in the following.

12.5.2 The Conflict Between National Regulation and Global Optimization

Most pharmaceuticals constitute an internationally tradable good. The expenditure on research and development is a fixed cost that arises globally. It does not depend on the number of consumers and countries in which the drug is sold and thus cannot be attributed to a particular group of patients or countries. Therefore, it is not clear who is to bear the surcharge over marginal cost that is induced by patent protection in order to foster innovation. In addition, the cost of product development usually is sunk by the time the product is launched and prices are negotiated. Indeed, the marginal cost of production, wrapping, marketing, and distribution amount to no more than 30 percent of average total cost [see DANZON (1997b)].

Therefore, a regulation enforcing equality of price and marginal cost, while inducing the optimal consumption of existing drugs, fails to provide sufficient incentives for innovators to develop new products.[5] One way to redress this would be to levy a tax in favor of innovation, which however by necessity would be distortionary [see LAFFONT AND TIROLE (1993, p. 24)]. Another, possibly less distorting solution is to permit the monopolist so-called *Ramsey pricing* [see RAMSEY (1927) and BAUMOL AND BRADFORD (1970)]. The basic idea of Ramsey pricing is that the quantity transacted should deviate as little as possible from the optimum. This calls for charging a high price in markets with a price elasticity close to zero. In the case of a single product, the surcharge over marginal cost in percent (the so-called Lerner index) is optimally given by[6],

$$\frac{p_i - MC_i}{p_i} = \rho \left[\frac{1}{\eta_i} \right], \qquad (12.11)$$

where p_i denotes price, MC_i the marginal cost of the drug, and η_i the price elasticity of demand in market i. Finally, ρ is the Ramsey number lying between zero and one. If $\rho = 1$, the profit-maximizing price that follows from equation (12.11) corresponds to the one set by a price-discriminating monopolist. A value between zero and one indicates a certain extent of monopolistic pricing sufficient for the innovator to recoup expenditure on research and development. Finally, $\rho = 0$ corresponds to the classical optimality condition $p_i = MC_i$ for an existing product. It is worthwhile to point out that a low value of the price elasticity η_i often means that the patients affected are in great need of the product from a medical point of view. According to equation (12.11), it is precisely these patients that should be charged a high price for

---

[5] Problems caused by insurance coverage and incomplete information are not considered here.

[6] A model with monopolistic competition and positive cross price elasticity is described in DANZON (1997b).

efficiency – an implication that is unlikely to be acceptable in societies bent on equity in health care. Note, however, that the high price could be paid by a health insurer who (e.g., through Managed Care-type restraints imposed on health care providers) might try to channel pharmaceuticals to the seriously ill.

But the main problem of Ramsey pricing is that pharmaceuticals are traded worldwide because transportation costs are low. A price discrimination scheme implemented according to equation (12.11) therefore can easily be undermined by arbitrage (so-called parallel imports). Now parallel trade is particularly easy within a country. Still, DANZON (1997b) concludes in her empirical study that the price reductions on pharmaceuticals received by Managed Care consumers in the United States approximately correspond to the optimal Ramsey differential. This does not hold true of drug prices in the European Union (EU). Here, the European Commission sees a uniform price across the EU as the hallmark of open competitive markets where the law of one price prevails. Therefore, it tends to encourage parallel imports, which are also favored by most national governments who seek to lower public HCE in general and pharmaceutical expenditure in particular. Indeed, a company found to price differentiate between EU member countries runs the risk of being sanctioned.

Note that the Ramsey rule says that price discrimination may well yield higher social surplus compared to a uniform price. If marginal cost is the same across markets (which likely holds true within the EU), this criterion requires that the total transaction quantity of a pharmaceutical increases due to price discrimination. In the case of linear demand functions, it can be shown that an increase in the total transaction quantity is also sufficient for an increase in social surplus [see, e.g., VARIAN (1992, Section 14.8)]. On the whole, the second-best policy may well be to let the innovator set profit-maximizing differentiated prices but to impose reductions according to the Ramsey number ρ, which varies with the stringency of the constraint that sales must recover research expenditure along with production cost. The higher this expenditure, the higher the value of ρ.

However, this analysis assumes that the monopolist can perfectly separate markets. Since the cost of moving a drug from one country to another is low, arbitrage (i.e., parallel imports) is likely to occur. The task of the innovator then becomes the one of jointly optimizing the price structure and the amount of 'leakage' in the guise of parallel imports. The usual instrument for this is to impose vertical restraints on distributors.

This optimization is hampered by two sets of regulation in the case of the EU. First, as noted above, EU competition policy aims at implementing uniform prices. Accordingly, it views vertical restraints such as resale price maintenance and assignment of exclusive territories unfavorably [see ZWEIFEL AND ZAECH (2003)]. Second, in keeping with the EU subsidiarity principle, national governments retain authority in the domain of health policy, which includes the right to regulate the price of pharmaceuticals. Innovators could counter by credibly threatening to withdraw the drug if the regulated price deviates too much from its optimal value. Such a move, however, would entail a good deal of sunk costs, i.e., investment that cannot be recoupled when exiting from the market. Typically, it is less costly for the innovator to get its home government to prohibit parallel imports, thus substituting public intervention for its private efforts. This creates incentives for governments to act as *free riders* by imposing a low national price and relying on the others for the financing of research and development. In the ultimate analysis, domestic consumers are thus forced to cross-subsidize consumers in countries that use regulation to push down drug prices.

The current inefficient solution combining price regulation with limited amounts of parallel imports has been analyzed by VALLETTI (2006). He finds that once the innovation exists, it may well be welfare-enhancing for EU consumers overall to impose uniform prices combined with facilitating parallel trade because total transaction quantity increases. However, it is precisely this combination that causes a market reduction of the NPV of an investment in a new pharmaceutical. Thus, one ends up with the trade-off between static and dynamic efficiency evoked in the introductory section of this chapter. Note that permitting pharmaceutical companies (and suppliers in general) to pursue profit maximization does not pose a problem in a system of competing health insurers. Enrolling millions of consumers, these organizations have the resources and know-how to negotiate for prices on behalf of their clientele. This can be seen as part of their mission (emphasized in Managed Care) to act as prudent purchasers of goods and services. It is not a challenge for governments either, who are accustomed to deal with monopolists in public purchasing (armament, public transportation equipment).

> **Conclusion 12.6.** *The main motivation for regulation of pharmaceutical prices is governments' desire to reduce public expenditure on drugs. It likely results in a violation of the Ramsey rule for allocating the fixed cost of research and development to groups of consumers and countries.*

12.5.3 Types of Price Regulation and Their Consequences

Governments have developed a variety of ways to regulate drug prices, which all affect the incentive to innovate and hence dynamic efficiency.

12.5.3.1 Direct Price Regulation

According to this type of regulation, prices of new products and changes in prices of existing drugs that are to be reimbursed by social health insurance (or the national health service) require approval by a public authority. Often, wholesale and retail margins are regulated as well in order to control prices at the point of sale.

France, Italy, and Spain are the main representatives of this kind of regulation, whereas Canada, Switzerland, and the United States have less restrictive forms of direct price regulation. However, it holds true for all these countries that the criteria used fail to take the problem of global and substantial fixed costs arising in the development of pharmaceuticals into due account. Usually prices are negotiated, with international comparisons serving as a benchmark. Although international comparisons appear to be objective, they still are beset by a lot of discretion. First and most important, the choice of countries entering the comparison is arbitrary. In addition, the effective price depends on dosage and intensity of use, which differ between countries [see DANZON AND CHAO (2000)].

The negative consequences of direct price regulation are threefold. If administered, these prices typically do not reflect consumers' willingness to pay for the innovation. If negotiated, there is still the uncertainty about the outcome of the negotiation discouraging especially small innovators who are risk averse because they cannot hedge a failure using successes with other products. Finally, price negotiations may cause delay in the launching of new products, causing welfare losses to patients and pharmaceutical companies.

12.5.3.2 Reference Prices

Reference prices are known in Germany, the Netherlands, Denmark, New Zealand, and in some provinces of Canada. In this form of regulation, pharmaceuticals are grouped according to their therapeutic properties and a reference price fixed for each group. In theory, suppliers can charge prices in excess of the reference price, making patients pay the difference between reference and actual price out of pocket. Since net price jumps from zero to this difference (basically an infinite relative change), it does not take a very high price elasticity of demand to have a big impact on quantity sold [see ZWEIFEL AND CRIVELLI (1996) for an analysis of the German case].

While reference prices induce competition between pharmaceuticals within a therapeutic group if prices lie *above the reference price*, they weaken competition for prices below since the out-of-pocket cost to patients is zero at any rate. Therefore, patients do not have any incentive to switch to the cheaper drug. The impact on pharmaceutical expenditure depends on the breadth of the therapeutic group and on the reference price level. So far the German reference price system has not been successful in slowing down the increase in drug expenditure [see DANZON (1997a, p. 20–21)].

12.5.3.3 Rate-of-Return Regulation

Regulation of pharmaceuticals is different in the United Kingdom. Here, firms can set any price for a new product, provided the rate of return on investment from drugs supplied to the National Health Service (NHS) does not exceed a certain limit. Each firm negotiates with the government to obtain an individual maximum, ranging from 17 to 21 percent p.a. If return on investment exceeds the limit, excess profit must be returned to the NHS directly or through a price reduction. On the other hand, a firm can apply for a price adjustment if it fails to recover the permitted return on investment.

In contrast to other types of regulation, this alternative explicitly acknowledges that pharmaceutical firms must be able to gain a high return on their investment in research and development. However, rate-of-return regulation distorts incentives. By employing capital, firms can enlarge the base to which profits are compared in the calculation of the rate of return. This permits them to legally attain higher profits, provided the allowed rate of return is higher than the cost of capital [see AVERCH AND JOHNSON (1962) or LAFFONT AND TIROLE (1993, p. 33–34)]. On the whole, the UK system of regulation has not been more successful than that of the other OECD countries in limiting the growth of pharmaceutical expenditure [see OECD (2001)].

12.5.3.4 Pharmaceutical Budgets Imposed on Physicians

Imposing a budget for pharmaceutical prescriptions on physicians constitutes another variant of regulation. For example, the German Health Care Structure Act of 1993 stipulated a total budget of €12.27 billion for pharmaceutical prescriptions by medical practitioners. The first €143 million of the excess were to be charged against their drug budget for the following year. The next €143 million were to be slashed on the pharmaceutical industry, who would have to accept a price freeze [see HOFFMEYER AND MCCARTHY (1994, p. 467)]. Despite initial success, this instrument did not meet expectations [see DANZON (1997a, p. 24)]. During the nine years of its existence, physicians never were sanctioned although the budget was repeatedly exceeded. Opposition by physicians and the pharmaceutical industry simply proved too strong. In view of its lack of effectiveness, this regulation was repealed in 2002.

12.6 Price Competition on Pharmaceutical Markets

In the wake of the Thalidomide catastrophe, the U.S. pharmaceutical industry was examined by the Kefauver Committee of the Senate. The Committee found out that production cost in many cases did not exceed 15 percent of the selling price. If per-unit production cost is equated to marginal cost (MC), equation (12.2) indicates a considerable degree of monopolization (measured by the so-called *Lerner index* $1/|\eta|$) [see STEELE (1962)]. However, the Lerner index is only suitable for an industry characterized by a stable technology. As soon as the increase in output comes about as a result of product innovation involving a new technology, expenditure for developing and introducing this new technology becomes part of long-run the marginal cost. In addition, while only successes are observed on the market and reported by companies and the media, one must remember that the successful innovation constitutes the exception rather than the rule (see Section 12.3.1). Thus, when assessing the seemingly high profit margins contained in sales prices, one runs the risk of singling out the comparatively rare winners of a lottery [see COMANOR (1986)]. For this reason, the issue of price competition needs to be addressed with an emphasis not so much on static phenomena (as would be sufficient if the product set were given) but on dynamic developments, tracing the fate of a pharmaceutical innovation over time.

This fate crucially depends on the speed with which 'me-too' preparations and generics can enter the market. Generics are non-brand imitations containing the same substances as the originals. Their suppliers have to offer a lower price in order to gain market share. Insurance protection, however, has the side effect of weakening price competition. In Section 12.2.2, it was shown that a fully insured patient is only interested in the quality attributes of a pharmaceutical. Price becomes relevant as soon as patients face a copayment (i.e., a positive rate of coinsurance). But even if price matters to some extent, a low-price competitor cannot easily enter the market due to barriers to entry. The first and foremost barrier is patent protection. But during the life of the patent, drug companies themselves create scope for price competition by their willingness to supply their protected product to certain countries at a low administered price. In turn, some governments (notably Germany, Switzerland, and the United States) block this scope for price competition by prohibiting parallel imports. This amounts to market closure for patented drugs. As to EU countries permitting parallel imports, their importance has been increasing steadily since 1995, when the European Medicines Evaluation Agency (EMEA) led to a unification of registration procedures [see DARBÀ AND ROVIRA (1998)].

While the United States prohibit parallel imports, it has features that facilitate price competition. First, patients continue to face substantial rates of coinsurance, frequently amounting to 30 percent and more. Second, the Drug Price Competition and Patent Term Restoration Act of 1984 permits producers of generics to imitate drugs that go off patent without duplicating all the documentation required for the original application. The period 1983-1995 was examined in a study by the Congressional Budget Office of the United States [see CONGRESSIONAL BUDGET OFFICE (1998)]. It found a marked increase in the sales volume of generics. While in 1984 they accounted for only 19 percent of all prescribed drugs, their market share increased to 43 percent by 1995. The study investigated three types of competition, viz.

(1) Competition between original and 'me-too' preparations;

(2) Competition between original preparations and generic drugs;

(3) Competition among generic drugs.

Type (1) competition occurs if the original preparation, while still enjoying patent protection, is 'invented around', with the 'me too' product also protected by a patent. It takes only one to six years for this type of competition to spring up, which does not however prevent prices of the original preparations increasing faster than the rate of inflation. Still, the increase in price was slower when there were many competing 'me too' preparations. Moreover, producers of original preparations are known to grant higher reductions on list prices (which were analyzed in the study) if confronted with competition by imitators.

Type (2) competition does not occur before market entry of generic drugs, which cannot occur before the patent protecting the original preparation expires. In most cases, market entry lagged patent expiration by no more than one year. The price of the generic was four times lower than that of the original drug on average. This caused the original preparation to lose 44 percent of its market share within one year, without exerting much pressure on its price. Prices of original preparations continued to increase at a rate in excess of inflation, as noted above.

Type (3) competition, among different suppliers of generic drugs, was found to result in strong price competition. This is demonstrated by the fact that an increase in suppliers of generic drugs from one to ten resulted on average in a price reduction of 50 percent. An increase to twenty suppliers was estimated to cause a price reduction of even two-third.

On the whole, pressure of competition has been increasing dramatically in U.S. pharmaceutical markets since 1984. Average prices of pharmaceuticals that are offered by several suppliers have been kept down. In the year 1994 alone, U.S. consumers saved US$8-10 billion by substituting original preparations with cheaper generic drugs.

Manufacturers of generic drugs face stronger price competition than do innovators because highly insured patients are much more influenced by quality than by price. As soon as they share in the cost of treatment, however, innovators are subject to some degree of price competition as well, as predicted in Section 12.2 above.

Conclusion 12.7. *Pharmaceutical innovations are launched at prices which initially may be many times higher than the prices of already existing drugs. However, innovators face price competition from three sources, viz. 'me-too' preparations, generic drugs, and indirectly from competition among generics that drives down their prices even more.*

Early analysis of the price convergence between original and imitative drugs by REEKIE (1996, Chapter 3) unearthed important international differences. In the United States, convergence occurred much faster than in the Netherlands. In view of theory developed in Sections 12.2.2 and 12.2.3, a likely cause is the degree of health insurance coverage. While U.S. patients face a considerable copayment, Dutch patients (and those of most European countries) bear a small share of the price of a pharmaceutical, if at all. In a somewhat related yet different way, DANZON AND CHAO (2000) conclude that price competition by generic drugs is more effective in countries with less regulated markets than in more strongly regulated markets. They estimate a lower price elasticity of demand in regulated countries. This is little surprising because price and product regulation serves to curtail diversity. However, this means that search for high quality and low price has a reduced expected payoff.

12.7 Summary

(1) Pharmaceuticals differ in their quality characteristics. Breakthrough innovations are those that bestow a preparation with an entirely new attribute, while 'me-too' preparations combine existing attributes in new ways. Once regulators grant market access, breakthrough innovations have a guaranteed market success, provided patients are fully insured.

(2) As soon as patients share in the cost of drug treatment, both breakthrough innovators and imitators face falling demand curves; however, price elasticity of demand is higher for imitators.

(3) Pharmaceutical innovation constitutes a risky investment. Since the early 1960s, the cost of drug innovation has been increasing rapidly, with stiffer price regulation in major markets limiting returns. This caused the number of newly introduced active substances to decrease worldwide. However, the U.S. Food and Drug Administration has taken the lead in accelerating procedures regulating market access, serving to reverse the trend since the 1980s.

(4) Pharmaceutical innovations typically achieve a real internal rate of return between 5 and 10 percent. However, this figure reflects a small minority of successful products, while the majority of innovations fail to recover their cost of development.

(5) Patent protection is designed to enable innovators to recover the fixed costs caused by the development of the new drug, thus fostering incentives for innovation. The optimal length of patent life can be regarded as the outcome of a non-cooperative game between regulator and innovator.

(6) Governments of industrialized countries are involved in the financing of health care directly (national health service) or indirectly (social health insurance). That is why they seek to limit pharmaceutical expenditure, usually by imposing price regulation that contradicts Ramsey pricing which would call for charging a high price to patients with a low elasticity of demand. Rate-of-return regulation permits innovators to implement Ramsey prices to a first-order approximation.

(7) Price competition on markets for pharmaceuticals is limited not only because of market closure due to patent protection but also because of low price sensitivity of patients due to health insurance. However, three types of price competition cause the prices of innovative drugs to converge towards those of existing preparations, viz. 'me-too' drugs, generic alternatives, and generics among themselves.

12.8 Further Reading

The article by SCHERER (2000) in the HANDBOOK OF HEALTH ECONOMICS deals with research and development of new pharmaceuticals and covers issues such as patents, price regulation, and competition. Regarding the theory and practice of price regulation, an overview is provided by DANZON (1997a).

12.E Exercises

12.1. Figure 12.4 shows that consumer surplus is overestimated due to insurance coverage. Are there additional elements in that figure that change with health insurance coverage? What is their impact on the social rate of return to pharmaceutical innovation?

12.2. A pharmaceutical company produces a drug at constant marginal cost c. In addition fixed costs F for expenditure on research and development arise. Thus, the cost function reads,

$$K = F + \sum_{t=1}^{\infty} cx_t$$

where x_t denotes the amount produced in year t. Treat c like a present value by neglecting the rate of interest.

(a) Suppose that the company receives patent protection for T periods. It faces the linear demand function $p_t = a - bx_t$. After patent expiration competitors enter the market, causing its price to drop to $p_t = c$. Determine the optimal duration of patent life T^* that makes the company indifferent between developing the drug and not developing.

(b) Consider a regulated price $\bar{p}$. How does the result in (a) change if $c < \bar{p} < p_t$?

(c) Calculate optimal patent life for (a) and (b) assuming $a = 5$, $b = 1$ and $c = 1$. In (b) use different values for $\bar{p}$. Compare and interpret the results obtained.

12.3. In contrast to what has been assumed in Subsection 12.4.3, the regulator could be on the same level as the innovator (rather than being the Stackelberg leader). Try to derive a reaction function $h(I)$ for the regulatory agency in this case. Note that $\partial P/\partial T + \partial S/\partial T < 0$ for all values of T. Determine the so-called Cournot equilibrium determined by two reaction functions $g(T)$ and $h(T)$. What are the effects of an increase in the marginal cost of innovation in this variant of the model?

13

The Political Economy of Health Care

13.1 Introduction

Whenever a normative statement was made in Chapters 5 to 12, it was based on
the efficiency criteria of welfare economics. This left open the issue of whether a
Pareto-optimal design of a health care system might ever be achieved. Therefore,
this chapter raises the question of what determines the actual (rather than any desired) institutional structure of a health care system. This type of question is the
topic of 'Political Economy', also known as 'Public Choice'. This is a comparatively recent field of theoretical and empirical research into behavior in the political
domain.[1] With regard to health policy and regulation, the following agents can be
distinguished.

(1) *Citizens.* In a direct democracy, citizens may challenge a law that has been
    passed by a popular referendum. They may also force the legislature to deal
    with an issue through a popular initiative. In a purely representative democracy,
    voters have a mere indirect influence by voting for candidates for political of-
    fice or parties who promise to pursue a certain policy. Even in a dictatorship,
    however, citizens are not without influence because at least some of them must
    be won over to keep public administration and the economy functioning. The
    more closely the health policy adopted by a dictatorial government matches the
    preferences of the citizenry, the less costly it is for it to maintain its power.

(2) *Politicians.* These individuals want to be (re)elected. In a democracy (and even
    in most dictatorships), they need to obtain votes. Promising to organize the pro-
    vision of health care services (or at least the availability of health insurance) has
    been a selling proposition until recently. Meanwhile, especially younger voters
    seem to have become aware that these public programs typically place a heavy
    financial burden on them while benefitting mainly the elderly (see Chapter 14).

---

[1] For an overview, see, e.g., ROWLEY AND SCHNEIDER (2003) and PERSSON AND
TABELLINI (2000).

P. Zweifel et al., *Health Economics*, 2nd ed., DOI 10.1007/978-3-540-68540-1_13,
© Springer-Verlag Berlin Heidelberg 2009

(3) *Executive member of government.* Gaining or maintaining executive power usually calls for a great deal of financial support, which comes from large companies engaged in the health care sector (insurers, pharmaceutical companies) or professional associations (of physicians, nurses and hospitals). In general, the 'supply side' tends to prevail in health policy at the governmental level [FELDSTEIN (2005, Chapter 18)].

(4) *International organizations.* Here, the World Health Organization (WHO) has had considerable success in influencing national health policy by emphasizing the risks posed by epidemics (originally tuberculosis, later HIV/AIDS, mad cow disease, avian flu). Increasingly, decisions affecting health policy and regulation are made by the World Trade Organization (WTO) and in particular the European Union (EU). In both instances, the fact that traded commodities may have an impact on health while some health goods (above all, pharmaceuticals) are tradable provides a justification for intervention.

The focus of this chapter is on level (1), the viewpoint of citizens and voters. Their interests are decisive in countries with good governance because the other levels must take them into account in order to ensure their political survival. This is of course more true of level (2) than levels (3) and (4). A first question to be addressed is whether and how the existence and extent of the collectively financing of health care services can be explained. To this end, a simple model of a direct democracy is developed in Section 13.2. Even though such a model literally applies only to a few countries, in particular Switzerland, it generates a number of valuable insights that help to predict likely future developments at levels (2) and (3). Since professional association in health care have so much influence on regulative policy, it is worthwhile to study their objectives, which must reflect the interests of their members lest they lose market share. This is the topic of Section 13.3 which deals with the role of associations in the health sector, especially their function as political lobby-groups.

13.2 Collectively Financed Health Care in a Democracy

In many of the wealthy nations of Western Europe, collectively financed health care systems have been introduced during the last 125 years. Two main alternatives can be found.

(a) A *National Health Service* (associated with the UK politician William Beveridge) is usually financed out of general tax revenue. Medical treatment is more or less free of charge for all citizens. In addition to the UK, such systems can be found in Greece, Italy, Portugal, the Scandinavian countries and Spain.

(b) *Social Health Insurance* (first established by the German politician Otto von Bismarck) is financed by social insurance contributions that often amount to a payroll tax since they are levied on labor income while membership is compulsory.

In contrast to private health insurance, contributions are not based on risk; in particular, they do not depend on health status. They can either be uniform (as in Switzerland) or depend on income (as in Germany where contributions are proportional to labor income up to an income ceiling.)

The following analysis can be applied to both variants of a collectively financed public health care system.

An important question is whether citizens have the right to purchase health care not covered by the public system. If so, net payers, i.e., individuals whose contributions exceed their expected health care expenditure, tend to vote for a smaller public system than if they have to exclusively rely on it. Since in a country that respects civil liberties citizens can hardly be prevented from spending their own money on health care (if necessary abroad), a market for private health care services is assumed to exist in the following. Private insurers provide coverage for these services.

Three questions are at the center of the analysis.

(i)   Will a public health care system be introduced in a direct democracy?

(ii) If so, how large will the system be?

(iii) Will contributions be uniform or related to income?

The most important assumption is that citizens decide on the regime behind a veil of ignorance, i.e., a situation in which individuals do not yet know their risk of becoming ill. The decision on the quantity of health care in a given regime, however, occurs in full knowledge of one's state of health.

13.2.1 Basic Assumptions

Let citizens (and voters) of a society differ in two attributes, viz. income y and probability of being ill π, both assumed to be exogenous and observable. This allows to neglect incentive effects of taxation and of asymmetric information, viz. moral hazard and adverse selection problems. Furthermore, the characteristics are distributed independently of each other.

Each parameter can take on two values. Individuals are either poor or rich with $y_i, i = p, r$ and $y_p < y_r$. The proportion of poor individuals is θ, so the mean income is

$$\bar{y} = \theta y_p + (1 - \theta) y_r. \tag{13.1}$$

In the following, it is assumed that $\theta > 0.5$, which implies that median income is below mean income $\bar{y}$. This assumption captures the typical right-skewed income distribution in most countries. On the other hand, individuals will be ill with probability $\pi_j, j = l, h$, where $0 < \pi_l < \pi_h < 1$. The proportion of low risks is λ, implying an average probability of being ill

$$\bar{\pi} = \lambda \pi_l + (1 - \lambda) \pi_h. \tag{13.2}$$

We suppose $\lambda > 0.5$, which implies that the median type is an l-type and therefore has a lower illness probability than the average $\bar{\pi}$. This assumption is in line with the empirical distribution of health care expenditures.

Utility when healthy depends only on consumption c and is $u(c)$. We assume that $u(c)$ is a strictly concave function, which implies that individuals are risk averse. When ill, utility also depends on the amount of health insurance benefits z received and is $u(c) + v(z)$. These benefits are provided by the government (g) or can be purchased in the market (m) such that $z = g + m$. We assume that services bought in the market are supplementary and top up government health care.[2] The function $v(z)$ is assumed to be strictly concave and negative, expressing that illness reduces utility.

13.2.2 The Decision Process

Decisions are taken in the following sequence.

(1) Individuals decide by majority vote how the health care system is to be financed. The choice is between a public health care system with uniform contributions (UC) or income-related contributions (IR), or no public system with risk-based premiums. Individuals are assumed to know their income y_i but not their risk type π_j. This constitutional decision can only be revised unanimously at a later stage.

Now risk types π_j are revealed.

(2) The amount of public health care g is determined by majority vote.

(3) Individuals can buy additional private health insurance. Insurers observe the risk type and charge an actuarially fair premium of π_j per unit of health care provided in the state of illness.

At stage (1), when individuals do not yet know their risk type, they face the risk of being a high risk type who is charged a high premium by private insurers at stage (3). This is a case of *premium risk* which is discussed in Section 5.3.4. As pointed out there, market-based solutions to insure this risk may not work well. For this reason, we assume that insurance against premium risk is not available in the market.

In the following, the decisions to be made at the different stages are solved in reverse order, in keeping with the backward induction principle. In this way, individuals are modeled as anticipating the consequences of their decisions at later stages.

---

[2] For an analysis of the case where public and private provision are mutually exclusive, forcing consumers who want to use private health care to opt out of public provision, see EPPLE AND ROMANO (1996a) and GLOMM AND RAVIKUMAR (1998).

13.2.3 Purchase of Private Health Insurance and Demand for Health Care

As a point of reference, first consider the situation where the level of public health care is zero ($g = 0$). Private health insurers offer an individual of type ij the amount of health care m_{ij} at a variable premium

$$P_{ij} = \pi_j m_{ij}, \quad i = p, r; \; j = h, l. \tag{13.3}$$

Expected utility is given by

$$EU_{ij}^{g=0} = u(y_i - \pi_j m_{ij}) + \pi_j v(m_{ij}). \tag{13.4}$$

The problem of an individual of type ij is to choose the optimal value m_{ij}^*. The first-order condition for an interior maximum, $m_{ij}^* > 0$, yields

$$u'[y_i - \pi_j m_{ij}^*] = v'[m_{ij}^*], \tag{13.5}$$

i.e., individuals buy health insurance up to the point where the marginal utilities of consumption and health care are equalized. Using $u''(c) < 0$ and $v''(z) < 0$, one can see that the optimal amount of private health care is larger for the rich than for the poor,

$$m_{rj}^* > m_{pj}^*, \quad j = l, h. \tag{13.6}$$

Moreover, since low risk types pay a lower premium according to (13.3), they have a higher net income ceteris paribus, causing them to demand more private health care than the high risk types,

$$m_{il}^* > m_{ih}^*, \quad i = p, r. \tag{13.7}$$

Substituting (13.7) into the condition (13.5) and recalling the strict concavity of $v(\cdot)$, one obtains

$$u'[y_i - \pi_h m_{ih}^*] - v'[m_{ih}^*] > v'[m_{il}^*] - u'[y_i - \pi_l m_{il}^*]. \tag{13.8}$$

Therefore, the marginal utility of both consumption and health care is larger for high risks than low risks at the optimal point. Because of concavity, however, the level of utility attained by the high risks must be lower than that attained by high risks. This is the consequence of the higher premium they pay per unit of health care.

Condition (13.5) also holds in a modified form once one allows for a positive amount of public health care g. Let y_i^n be income net of the contribution to financing public health care. Then, the corresponding condition for an interior optimum is

$$u'[y_i^n - \pi_j m_{ij}^*] = v'[g + m_{ij}^*]. \tag{13.9}$$

Conclusion 13.1. *If private health insurance is available at an actuarially fair premium, individuals purchase private health insurance up to the point where marginal utilities of consumption and health care are equalized.*

13.2.4 Voting on Public Health Care for a Given Regime

This section is devoted to stage (2) of the decision process where the level of public health care g is decided upon by majority vote. The outcome of this vote depends on the choice of regime that was made at stage (1). There, voters had the possibility to vote for a public system with uniform contributions (UC) or with income-related contributions (IR).

Regime UC: Uniform Contribution

In regime UC, each individual contributes the same amount σ to the financing of the public health care system. For a given level of public health care g^{UC}, expected utility is

$$EU_{ij}^{UC} = u(y_i - \sigma - \pi_j m_{ij}) + \pi_j v(g^{UC} + m_{ij}). \tag{13.10}$$

The contribution σ necessary for budget balance is

$$\sigma = \bar{\pi} g^{UC}. \tag{13.11}$$

Thus, each individual faces a premium of $\bar{\pi}$ per unit of public health care. Private health insurance, by contrast, costs π_j, which implies that public health care is more expensive for low risks and less expensive for high risks than the private alternative. Since $\lambda > 1/2$, low risks make up the majority. Therefore, a majority vote will result in $g^{UC} = 0$.

> **Conclusion 13.2.** *If the public health care system is financed by a uniform contribution and if the majority is of the low-risk type, voting results in a rejection of public health care.*

Regime IR: Income-Related Contributions

In regime IR, public health insurance care is financed by an income or payroll tax. For simplicity, the tax rate t is assumed to be constant. Then, expected utility is

$$EU_{ij}^{IR} = u((1-t)y_i - \pi_j m_{ij}) + \pi_j v(g^{IR} + m_{ij}). \tag{13.12}$$

The budget constraint of the public health insurance system is given by

$$t\bar{y} = \bar{\pi} g^{IR}, \tag{13.13}$$

with $\bar{y}$ denoting average income. The price of one unit of public health care for an individual with income y_i therefore amounts to

$$\frac{ty_i}{g^{IR}} = \bar{\pi}\frac{y_i}{\bar{y}}. \tag{13.14}$$

Box 13.1. A Model of a Direct Democracy

$$\bar{y} = \theta y_p + (1 - \theta)y_r \tag{13.1}$$

$$\bar{\pi} = \lambda \pi_l + (1 - \lambda)\pi_h \tag{13.2}$$

$$P_{ij} = \pi_j m_{ij}, \quad i = p, r; \; j = h, l \tag{13.3}$$

$$EU_{ij}^{g=0} = u(y_i - \pi_j m_{ij}) + \pi_j v(m_{ij}) \tag{13.4}$$

$$EU_{ij}^{UC} = u(y_i - \sigma - \pi_j m_{ij}) + \pi_j v(g^{UC} + m_{ij}) \tag{13.10}$$

$$\sigma = \bar{\pi} g^{UC} \tag{13.11}$$

$$EU_{ij}^{IR} = u((1 - t)y_i - \pi_j m_{ij}) + \pi_j v(g^{IR} + m_{ij}) \tag{13.12}$$

$$t\bar{y} = \bar{\pi} g^{IR} \tag{13.13}$$

$i = p, r$:	index for poor and rich individuals
$j = h, l$:	index for high and low risks
$\theta > 0.5$:	proportion of poor individuals
$y_p < y_r$:	income of poor and rich individuals
$\bar{y}$:	average income
$\lambda > 0.5$:	proportion of low risks
$\pi_l < \pi_h$:	probability to be ill of low and high risks
$\bar{\pi}$:	average probability to be ill
m_{ij}:	health care purchased in the market
P_{ij}:	health insurance premium
g:	public health care
σ:	uniform contribution to finance public health care
t:	income tax rate to finance public health care
UC:	uniform contribution
IR:	income-related contributions

Comparing this to the market premium π_j per unit, one sees that only voters for whom the condition

$$\frac{\pi_j}{\bar{\pi}} \geq \frac{y_i}{\bar{y}} \tag{13.15}$$

is satisfied will be in favor of a positive amount of public health care.

Condition (13.15) shows that individuals of type ph ($y_p < \bar{y}$, $\pi_h > \bar{\pi}$) will always support public health care while those of type rl ($y_r > \bar{y}$, $\pi_l < \bar{\pi}$) will always prefer $g^{IR} = 0$. It is a priori unclear whether individuals of types pl and rh are in favor of public health care. The pivotal individuals, however, must be those of type pl, i.e., the 'poor low risks'. The assumptions $\theta, \lambda > 1/2$ imply that they form a majority with either group ph or group rl. A member of group pl is therefore the *median voter*, i.e., the individual who lies at the median of the voter distribution with respect to preferences for the amount of public health care. The outcome of the majority vote is determined by the solution to this individual's optimization problem. This is an application of the median voter theorem.[3]

Individuals of type pl will be in favor of public health care if

$$\frac{\pi_l}{\bar{\pi}} \geq \frac{y_p}{\bar{y}}. \tag{13.16}$$

Otherwise, the outcome of the majority vote is $g^{IR} = 0$. Condition (13.16) is more likely to be met,

- the more marked income inequality, indicated by a low value of y_p/y_r;
- the smaller the proportion of 'poor' individuals, θ, [see equation (13.1)];
- the smaller the inequality in the risk of ill health, i.e., the larger π_l compared to π_h;
- the larger the proportion of low risks, λ [see equation (13.2)].

Assuming that condition (13.16) holds, the preferred amount of public health care of a member of group pl is the solution to the optimization problem

$$\max_{g^{IR},t} EU_{pl} = u[(1-t)y_p] + \pi_l v(g^{IR}) \quad \text{s.t.} \quad t\bar{y} = \bar{\pi}g^{IR}. \tag{13.17}$$

Note that we do not have to consider that pl-types will buy supplementary health insurance. Condition (13.16) implies that private health care is more expensive for them than the public alternative. As can easily be shown, the condition

$$u'\left[\left(1 - \frac{\bar{\pi}}{\bar{y}}g^{IR}\right)y_p\right]\frac{y_p}{\bar{y}} = \frac{\pi_l}{\bar{\pi}}v'[g^{IR}] \tag{13.18}$$

characterizes the optimal amount of public health care and therefore the outcome of the majority vote if condition (13.16) is fulfilled.

> **Conclusion 13.3.** *If contributions are proportional to income, then the amount of public health care is equal to the preferred amount of a 'poor low-risk' person. A positive amount of public health care will be voted for if income inequality is large relative to inequality in risk types.*

13.2.5 Choice of Regime

Finally, we examine the choice of regime at stage (1) of the decision process. This choice is assumed to occur behind a veil of ignorance about the risk type, i.e., voters do not know their risk type.

If condition (13.16) is violated, no public health care is provided regardless of regime. We therefore concentrate on the case where (13.16) is met and g^{IR} is positive.

---

[3] In a one-dimensional policy space (the amount of public health care in the present context), the median voter theorem holds if voters' preferences are single-peaked [see, e.g., PERSSON AND TABELLINI (2000, p. 22) for a proof]. In the present case, this is ensured by the assumption of a concave utility function. An extensive discussion of the median voter theorem can be found in CONGLETON (2003).

This regime is preferred by all 'poor' individuals to a regime UC or, equivalently, a regime without public health insurance since they obtain at least part of their health insurance at a subsidized price.

- Individuals of type ph receive both an income transfer and a health care subsidy (see condition (13.15), where the left-hand side is larger and the right-hand side smaller than one);

- Individuals of type pl benefit from $g^{IR} > 0$ as well since condition (13.16) guarantees that their income transfer outweighs their health care subsidy to high risks.

Ex ante, poor voters can therefore be sure that ex post, i.e., after their risk type is revealed, they will be better off in regime IR than in regime UC. Thus, poor individuals will vote in favor of regime IR. Their share of the population is $\theta > 1/2$. Thus, regime IR is predicted to prevail in a majority vote at the first stage of the decision process.

Conclusion 13.4. *Behind a veil of ignorance about the risk type, a majority will vote for public health insurance with income-related contributions and will reject public health insurance with uniform fees or a regime without public health insurance if income inequality is large relative to inequality in risk types.*

It is possible that also the rich and therefore all individuals will vote for regime IR at the first stage [see KIFMANN (2006a)]. For the rich, this regime is attractive because it provides insurance against premium risk, i.e., the risk of having to pay a high health insurance premium if they turn out to be high risks. This premium insurance effect can dominate the transfer to poor individuals if income inequality is not too high (see Exercise 13.1).

13.2.6 Empirical Implications of the Analysis

According to the preceding analysis, public health care systems are predicted to exist in direct democracies and to be financed by contributions related to income rather than by uniform premiums. These results apply to direct democracies where voters have the right to directly decide political issues. They should also hold for democracies in general, provided that governance is good enough to tie higher level political agents to citizens' preferences. Indeed, almost all democracies have a public health care system financed by contributions linked to income. The fact that they are not always proportional to income is a minor deviation from an assumption introduced in the interest of simplicity. However, there are three prominent exceptions, viz. the United States, Switzerland and the majority of less developed counties (for whom the model was not designed to begin with).

(1) *The United States.* With the exception of the elderly (Medicare) and the poor (Medicaid), the U.S. population is not covered by a public health insurance sys-

tem. Employers provide health insurance for the majority of the rest of the population. This is encouraged by the tax code which exempts employer payments from payroll and income taxes. Premium risk is partially covered by employer-based health insurance as premiums are not adjusted to risk as long as individuals stay with their employer. Therefore, it is not surprising that Medicare is the only comprehensive health insurance program which found support in the political arena. This program sets in once employer-based health insurance ceases to work and covers a period in which premium risk is particularly severe. Moreover, the income distribution is highly skewed in the United States,[4] while upward mobility is high ('land of opportunity'). This makes for a majority of voters who expect to pay too much for health insurance with income-related contributions.

(2) *Switzerland.* In contradistinction to the United States, the choice of health insurance is made by the individual consumer; there is no employer involvement. Moreover, the retired are not assigned to a special scheme. At the same time, competitive social health insurers used to charge premiums according to age at entry until 1996, when a new law calling for uniform premiums for members of a given insurer passed a popular referendum. A minority had preferred income-related premiums following the German model. That was also a feature of a popular initiative proposing Canadian-style uniform national health insurance, which was defeated by a two-third majority in 2006. One may therefore justifiably argue that the Swiss system is the expression of citizens' preferences.

However, premiums actually paid are in fact income-related due to a 'premium reduction' scheme ('Prämienverbilligung') that was introduced as part of the 1996 reform. Depending on the canton of residence, a subsidy is granted as soon as health insurance costs more than 8 percent of taxable income (Genève) or as much as 12 percent (Zug). For recipients of the subsidy (who make up for one-third of the population nationwide), the contribution actually paid does increase with income. Subsidies are in great part financed by taxes that increase progressively with income. In sum, the Swiss experience suggests that citizens prefer means-tested, targeted subsidization of the poor while ensuring a good deal of competition between health insurers. Compared with the predictions of the model, the contradiction turns out to be limited in that net contributions vary with income at least in part.

(3) *Less developed countries.* The majority of less developed countries has a public health care system that however serves a minority of the population only. The scheme is reminiscent of that of the United States. Those in the work force realize that low probability of illness goes together with high income, and the income distribution is very skewed. Their interests are therefore served best by health insurance as a fringe benefit with a community-rated premium rather than contributions increasing with income. Contrary to the United States, however, political agents typically are less tied to citizens' preferences. This increases chances for a minority (often those working in the official sector of the econ-

---

[4] See ATKINSON ET AL. (1995) and GOTTSCHALK AND SMEEDING (1997).

omy, in particular public employees) to create a 'public' system in accordance with their interests. Little wonder therefore that a model of the type presented here fails to predict the outcome in these countries.

Conclusion 13.5. *The results of the political-economy model are supported by the fact that most democracies have a public health insurance system which is financed by income-dependent contributions. The flat-fee system in Switzerland is only an apparent contradiction because the system of 'premium reduction' leads de facto to income-dependent contributions. The fact that the United States are an outlier can be explained by high income inequality and the existence of employer-sponsored health insurance.*

13.3 The Role of Professional Associations in Health Care

This section is devoted to the objectives motivating professional associations in the health sector. In its first part, we show why there is a strong demand for the services provided by a professional association, in particular lobbying efforts. The second part reviews the possible directions of lobbying efforts. Finally, the third part investigates the case that professionals have a choice of associations. This creates potential for competition among associations that may be beneficial to some and disadvantageous to others.

13.3.1 Why Are Professional Associations so Important in Health Care?

Professional associations and especially medical associations play a crucial role in the health care systems of all industrialized countries. This observation may be interpreted as the result of particularly strong common interests of service providers [see ZWEIFEL AND EICHENBERGER (1992)]. Indeed, there is a small number of physicians within a given area and of the same specialty. In addition, their investments in medical technology and human capital are very specific. These factors ensure considerable homogeneity of interests which facilitates the creation and successful operation of an association. The mission of such an association is at least threefold.

(1) *Protection against competition.* According to the economic theory of cartels, associations have the task to limit price and quality competition among their members in order to keep their incomes high. Professional associations in health care have a much better chance of achieving this aim than associations in other industries because consumers, being covered by insurance, have little incentive to seek out a lower-priced outsider. Even if they search for one, it is difficult for them to compare cost due to fee schedules that permit one physician to issue a global invoice and the other a finely itemized one.

(2) *Access to public funds.* Medical associations serve as partners in negotiations not only with the health insurers but also with public authorities. Since health care accounts for eight percent or more of the Gross National Product (see Table 1.1 of Chapter 1), two-thirds of which or more is financed by public funds in most industrialized countries [see OECD (2008)], medical associations provide access to a much larger volume of public purchases than do, for example, bar associations of lawyers.

(3) *Control of market access.* A cartel seeks to restrict access to the market. A medical association is able to perform this service at particularly low cost. First, in view of the high cost of training (which is mainly borne by the public purse in most countries), authorities can be easily convinced of the need of limiting admission to medical schools. Second, quality assurance authorities and health insurers can be won over to the idea that only the medically trained should be allowed to provide certain health care services. These two stipulations make it difficult for a potential entrant to create a large medical firm as it would face high costs in finding a sufficient number of practitioners.

However, as pointed out by OLSON (1965), achievement of these objectives is a *public good*. Each member has therefore an incentive to contribute too little to the association or to free-ride, i.e., not to join the association at all. These problems would not be severe if the number of potential members were small, e.g., at the local level. Many common interests, however, are at the national level, involving hundreds or thousands of service providers.

According to OLSON, interest groups can nevertheless represent a large number of individuals if they are able to offer *separate and selective incentives* to limit free-riding. This explains why medical associations tend to provide their members with exclusive services such as advice on how to meet various regulations, e.g., on accounting, quality assurance and postgraduate training. Being actively involved in the design of these regulations, medical associations are usually better informed than outsiders on how to meet them. They also provide support in additional matters such as tax filing and liability insurance. In some countries, medical associations have even managed to make membership compulsory. In the German public health insurance system, for instance, all physicians in ambulatory care must be members of the local *Kassenärztliche Vereinigungen* (associations of physicians contracting with sickness funds). Similar considerations apply to other types of providers of health care, in particular dentists and pharmacists.

Conclusion 13.6. *Providers of health care services have strong common interests. Free riding on an association's achievements can be mitigated by the provision of exclusive services or by lobbying to make membership compulsory. This provides an explanation for the important role of professional associations in health care.*

Once an association has been set up, it acts as an agent of its members. Although members cannot monitor all activities of the association, the principal-agent problem is definitely not as severe as in the relationship between patient and physician. The chairman of the association is usually a fellow colleague who, after a limited term of service, joins the rank and file again. In this way, a divergence of interest between the leadership of the association and its members can be limited.

13.3.2 Tasks of Associations in Health Care

Professional associations in health care mainly have to deal with three groups, viz. their members, patients and politicians. One can associate a task with each group as follows:

- protecting the incomes of members;
- ensuring quality of treatment for patients;
- performing tasks of coordination in the interest of politicians.

Securing the Incomes of Members

From the point of view of its members, the principal task of a medical association is to protect and possibly increase their income. There are two main ways to reach these goals. One is to achieve market closure by obtaining the right to determine who is admitted to the practice of medicine (likewise nursing or dentistry). Competition can be restricted by limiting admissions to medical schools, controlling medical examinations, or erecting barriers to entry for foreign doctors. Second, given that there is a social insurance scheme or public health care system, a successful association has crucial influence on the delimitation of the benefit list. In particular, it is expected to lobby for an extension of this list because this serves to increase demand for its members' services. Furthermore, the association may try to make substitutes for their members' services less attractive. In particular, it has a strong interest in excluding alternative medicine from the benefit package of social health insurance or, if demand for these services is high, in securing its members exclusive rights for their provision.[5]

Quality Assurance on Behalf of Patients

Patients often have difficulty in judging the quality of treatment because their own experience is usually insufficient for interfering quality. Associations in health care therefore like to justify their existence by pointing out their contribution to the maintenance of professional ethics, guaranteeing a high standard of treatment.

---

[5] Members of a medical association may also have conflicting interests. General practitioners and specialists may compete for a larger share of the cake. Also, established physicians may use the medical association to implement seniority payments or to set high standards for medical education and low standards for training on the job in an attempt to limit competition from younger colleagues [see SELDER (2006)].

This claim does not appear credible. In their analysis of Canadian physicians, ROOS ET AL. (1977) found important differences in the style of practice within very small areas, which are hard to reconcile with the notion of uniform quality standards being enforced by local medical associations. BENHAM (1991) quotes several cases in which American chambers of medicine shied away from repealing the license to practice although the physician was patently incompetent. The reason for this failure may stem from the strong ties between the board of the association and its members. When members of the board resign from their position to become 'simple' physicians again, they must be prepared to face the consequences of unpopular decisions made during their time of service on the board. In addition, a proven way of quality assurance would be to subject health care professionals to relicensing. Pilots, who are also entrusted with the lives of many people, have to undergo regular tests to prove their skills. Medical associations, however, have never supported a repeal of license for members who fail to keep their skills up to date.

Performing Tasks of Coordination in the Interest of Politicians

In a democratic society, politicians need to win votes for elections, an objective to which professional associations in health care can contribute. This is true of medical associations in particular because their voting recommendations spread through tens of thousands of practices. In the longer run, they can also provide political support by guaranteeing the continued existence of redistribution in the health care system. This redistribution occurs not only through equal, age-independent contributions to social health insurance but also through charging lower fees to members of social than private health insurance. Such a fee structure is in the interest of the majority of physicians, as it amounts to the price differentiation of a profit-maximizing monopolist [see KESSEL (1958)].

Medical associations may also support governments who seek to stabilize the share of health in the GDP (see Section 1.2.3 for a critical review of this policy). To start with, such a policy requires information which in many cases can only be provided by professional associations. This especially applies to limiting admission to medical schools, which serves to keep health care expenditure low, at least in the short run. For administering the rationing process, medical associations have many experts who 'perfectly know' how to choose the 'right' candidates for a medical career. Furthermore, they can agree to exercise restraint in fee negotiations for a certain time, preventing the stabilization of the quantity of services from being offset by an increase in prices. In the longer run, however, they will want to use their increased market power to satisfy the income demands of their members.

Empirical Evidence

If medical associations exist primarily to serve their members' interest, one would expect countries with a strong medical association to be characterized by a slower increase in physician density than others. Second, given that an increase in physician density cannot be prevented, it should have a mitigated impact on physician income in a country with a powerful professional association, who is able to insulate their members from the tightened pressure of competition. These two hypotheses were tested by ZWEIFEL AND GRANDCHAMP (2002), who compare the development of physician density and physician income in France, Germany, Sweden, Switzerland, the United Kingdom and the United States between 1960 and 1998. With respect to the first hypothesis, they find that all countries show significant growth in physician density during the period, with the highest increase being in France, Germany, and Sweden and lowest in the United Kingdom (where general practitioners only were observed). Their analysis is in line with with indications that German medical associations at the regional level were losing influence to politicians as complementary agents from the 1960s. By way of contrast, they continue to wield substantial power in the United States and especially in the United Kingdom. There, medical associations jointly with the government control access to the National Health Service. In the United States, by way of contrast, the American Medical Association has until recently decided the accreditation of hospitals, permitting it to control both the number of medical schools and their capacity in terms of admission to the study of medicine. The one contradicting instance is Switzerland, whose rate of increase should have been comparable to that of Germany but turns out to be much lower. As to the second hypothesis, it is again in France, Germany, and Sweden that the increase in physician density goes along with a marked decrease in medical incomes relative to the average income of the active population. This downward pressure is less marked in the case of the United Kingdom, whereas U.S. physicians were even able to increase their relative income during the period of observation.

Conclusion 13.7. *Medical associations serve the interests of patients, politicians and their own membership. Their behavior, however, gives rise to the suspicion that the income interests of their members prevail since countries with a strong medical association have a slower increase in physician density than others, and a given increase has a lesser impact on relative medical incomes.*

13.3.3 Competition among Service Providers, Competition among Associations

At first glance, unfettered competition among individual service providers resulting in low prices and a high standard of care would seem to be beneficial to insured and patients. The uncertainty surrounding future health status, however, compounded by patients' inability to assess the performance of the physician in charge create an interest in fixing fees ex ante. The complementary agent of choice for such negotiations is the health insurer. But as soon as a health insurer, alone or in combination with others, begins to represent a large portion of a physician's patients, it becomes a threat to that physician who fears to have to lower the fees in order to be able to sign the contract. Given that competition among individual service providers is suppressed by professional associations, what are the chances for competition among professional associations, and what are the consequences of this type of competition? These questions will be examined from the point of view of the insured and patients on the one hand, and service providers on the other.

(1) *Insured and patients.* Competition among professional associations creates an opportunity for insurers to negotiate lower fees. More importantly, competition especially among medical associations facilitates the establishment of alternatives for the provision of health care, e.g., a Health Maintenance Organization (HMO). Only if physicians, either individually or in groups, are able to break away from an existing association that is determined to retain fee-for-service payment such an organization as described in Section 11.4 can be created. Physicians with such an interest in Managed Care can form a competing association, which negotiates the level of capitation payment on behalf of its members.

(2) *Physicians.* From their point of view, freedom of choice of professional association is a double-edged sword. On the one hand, medical associations form a collective monopoly for their members in negotiations with health insurers or the government, resulting in fees for their services that are higher than in the case of competition among associations. On the other hand, competition among associations forces them to closely heed the interests of their members.

Conclusion 13.8. *Competition among professional associations in health care may pave the way to new ways of providing health care, serving the interests of the insured and patients. For the majority of physician members, however, competition brings more disadvantages than advantages.*

13.4 Summary

(1) The theory of political economy or public choice seeks to explain the existence and functioning of political institutions. Applied to the financing of health care, it can be used to explain why many democracies have opted for the collective financing of their health care systems.

(2) In a democracy, the extent of public health care depends decisively on how the system is financed. Since income-related contributions induce redistribution not only from healthy to ill persons but also from rich to poor, public health care can receive support not only from the ill but also from individuals who are healthy but have low income.

(3) Behind a veil of ignorance about the risk type, a majority can vote for public health insurance with income-related contributions and reject public health insurance with uniform fees or a regime without public health insurance. This prediction receives a great measure of empirical support when tested against the experience of industrial countries.

(4) Professional associations are particularly prominent in health care. Again, public choice theory helps to explain the fact. The cost of creating and sustaining an association is comparatively low in the health care sector.

(5) Available empirical evidence suggests that the income interests of their members prevail since in countries with strong medical associations, physician density has increased at a comparably slow rate, and a given increase is associated with less pressure on relative physician incomes.

(6) Competition among professional associations in health care may pave the way to new ways of providing health care in the interest of the insured and patients. For the majority of physician members, this type of competition brings more disadvantages than advantages.

13.5 Further Reading

The literature on the public provision of private goods deals with similar problems as in section 13.2. The major contributions from a political economy perspective are BREYER (1995), EPPLE AND ROMANO (1996b), GOUVEIA (1997) and BLOMQUIST AND CHRISTIANSEN (1999). The model presented in section 13.2 is based on GOUVEIA (1997) and KIFMANN (2006a). EPPLE AND ROMANO (1996a) and GLOMM AND RAVIKUMAR (1998) examine the majority voting equilibrium when public services cannot be topped up and the alternative is to opt out of the public system. JACOB AND LUNDIN (2005) consider moral hazard and analyze how a uniform coinsurance rate is determined in the political process. BORCK (2007) reviews the literature on voting, inequality and redistribution. The politics of health legislation is analyzed in FELDSTEIN (2005, Chapter 18) and FELDSTEIN (2006).

13.E Exercises

13.1. Assume that the parameters of the model in Section 13.2 take the following values: $\pi_l = 0.2, \pi_h = 0.8, \lambda = 0.8, \bar{y} = 1,000$, and $\theta = 0.75$. The utility functions are

$$u(c) = -e^{-0.1c} \quad \text{and} \quad v(z) = e^{-0.1z}.$$

(a) Assume $y_p = 600$ and $y_r = 2,200$.

  (i) Determine the level of the public health insurance system under regimes UC und IR.

  (ii) How much private health insurance is bought by each type under regimes UC und IR?

  (iii) Compare expected utility for poor and rich individuals

$$EU_i = \lambda EU_{il} + (1 - \lambda)EU_{ih}, \quad i = r, p,$$

   for both methods of finance behind the veil of ignorance about the risk type. Discuss your result.

(b) Repeat your analysis for $y_p = 800$ and $y_r = 1,600$ and discuss how the results change.

(c) Repeat your analysis for $y_p = 400$ and $y_r = 2,800$ and discuss how the results change.

13.2. Explain why medical associations play an important role in the health care sector of all industrialized countries.

13.3. Discuss which groups are for and against a medical association with compulsory membership.

14

Future Challenges to Health Care Systems

14.1 Introduction

Actors on markets are under continuous pressure to adjust. Consumers' changes in taste lead to changes in demand, new technologies provide rivals with competitive advantage, and public authorities step in to regulate or even prohibit business. This pressure to adjust is transmitted by price signals indicating to firms the need to adapt their goods and services to new circumstances. In health care, however, fluctuating market prices for medical services are incompatible with the key principal-agent relationship between the patient and the service provider because they might violate both the participation and the incentive compatibility constraints (see Chapter 11, Appendix). One possibility of avoiding fluctuating prices is bargaining over fee schedules, which paves the way for the important role of professional associations and public authorities in health care. The inflexibility of fees and prices is further enhanced by the fact that purchases of health care goods and services such as pharmaceuticals abroad are often legally prohibited. This serves to insulate domestic markets from international shocks but also competition.

This departure from allocation through prices, however, has the adverse effect of reducing the system's *speed of adjustment*. For example, structural adjustment of a fee schedule usually takes years. On the one hand, this sluggishness prevents physicians, dentists, and hospitals from initiating and swiftly concluding contractual agreements with insurers because of temporary advantages, which would be to the detriment of many patients. On the other hand, it causes considerable delays in adjustment to exogenous shocks. The ensuing disequilibria are perceived as 'challenges to health care systems'. At the beginning of this century, such challenges have emerged in four areas.

P. Zweifel et al., *Health Economics*, 2nd ed., DOI 10.1007/978-3-540-68540-1_14,

(1) *The technological challenge.* The following citation gives a first impression of the speed of technological progress in medicine:

> "In 1980 alone the magazine Newsweek presented the following medical innovations: a new piece of equipment of a significance comparable to the CT scanner which makes brain-waves visible, revolutionary surgical methods for eliminating shortsightedness and infertility in women, new drugs for jaundice, sexually transmitted diseases and gout, various new cancer treatments, an operation for safe implantation of artificial breast following breast removal in females, new life-saving techniques in child heart surgery, and a new type of electric shock treatment to regenerate muscle and nerve tissue. Through this, one day even paraplegics will be able to walk."
>
> [KRÄMER (1982, p. 37)].

Almost all of these innovations are product innovations, i.e., they save lives or contribute to an improved quality of life, although at (much) higher cost: "When Christian Barnard transplanted the first human heart on 3rd December 1967, at that very moment the cost of such a treatment rose from zero to US$110,000" [KRÄMER (1982, p. 92)]. Conversely, process innovations which enable a particular service to be produced at lower cost are rare. There seem to be even fewer organizational innovations in health care, which promise cost savings through a rebundling of production processes resulting in economies of scope. Thus, technological change in medicine threatens to become the driving force of future 'cost explosions'.

(2) *The demographic challenge.* At first sight, this is simply to say that more and more people are getting older. In 1996, the share of aged individuals as percent of total population in the United States was 12 percent and is predicted to increase to 25 percent by the year 2050, a figure that will be even exceeded by Japan with a share of 30 percent [see FOUGÈRE AND MÉRETTE (1999)]. Old age is associated with an increased demand for medical and in particular nursing services, and the issue is how to meet this demand. On closer inspection, however, it is more the proximity to death than calendar age that seems to matter [ZWEIFEL ET AL. (1999b), ZWEIFEL ET AL. (2004b), WERBLOW ET AL. (2005)]. This would mean that the last, expensive year of life would simply occur at age 85 (say) instead of age 75 as at present. It is another demographic change that may turn out to be a more important driver of health care expenditure (HCE). Within just twenty years, the number of single person units has greatly increased, e.g., from 13 to 25 percent in the United States [see ROUSSEL (1986) and U.S. CENSUS BUREAU (2004)]. Persons living alone are much less able, in the case of illness, to fall back on support and care from relatives, causing them to demand more health care services.

(3) *The challenge of the 'Sisyphus Syndrome'.* The success of modern medicine reminds one of Sisyphus, the hero of Greek mythology who was condemned to roll a lump of rock up a mountain only to see it slip out of his grasp just before reach-

ing the summit, forcing him to start all over again. By prolonging human life, technological change in medicine may also increase the number of those who make more than average demands on the health care system. Because of their increased political clout, the elderly might exert their influence in public HCE. As a result of this process, the success of medicine may turn into a growing burden on the economy and on society.

(4) *The challenge of international competition.* This often neglected challenge to health care has its origin in the increasing economic integration of nations. With labor able to move about freely within the European Union (and some day within the North American Free Trade Area), workers will be attracted not only by attainable income but also by things such as the relative performance of a country's health care system. Physicians and medical staff will also be able to move about more freely, and finally, international direct investment into private health insurance and hospitals will become more prominent. Altogether, national health care systems will increasingly be subject to international competition.

These four challenges will be discussed in the following sections.

14.2 The Technological Challenge

14.2.1 Three Types of Innovation

In the economic literature, the following types of innovation are distinguished.

- *Process innovation.* Process innovation permits to produce a given good or service at lower cost. As an example in health care, twice as many parameters of a blood test can be examined in the same time by means of automated serological analysis.

- *Product innovation.* Product innovation provides a good or the recipient of a service with new qualities or with a new combination of existing qualities. It usually entails increased production costs compared to existing alternatives. New drugs and therapies for hitherto incurable diseases are examples of product innovations in health care.

- *Organizational innovation.* The cost of producing a good or service can also be lowered by reorganizing production processes, including the restructuring of entire firms. The separation of geriatric care from internal medicine in hospital care, the creation of Health Maintenance Organizations and of group practices exemplify organizational innovations in health care.

The objective of this section is to examine the optimal allocation of these three types of innovation in health care from an individual point of view. Through a sacrifice in terms of consumption during the current period, individuals have the opportunity to invest in innovations, whose pay-off will be in terms of improved health status during the following period.

To keep the analysis as simple as possible, the individual is assumed to evaluate innovations based on a utility function that averages over the different states of health. The utility function depends positively on consumption expenditures (X_1, X_2) and health states (H_1, H_2) in the two periods. For the sake of simplicity, utilities (u_1, u_2) will be additive and not discounted to present value [see LYTTKENS (1999) for an analogous macroeconomic formulation],

$$u = u_1(X_1, H_1) + u_2(X_2, H_2). \tag{14.1}$$

In the remainder of the section, the three types of innovation will be included into the health production function, proceeding step by step.

Process innovation only: the expenditure on process innovation occurs in the first period; for simplicity, it is symbolized by R^C without subscript for the period. In the second period, process innovation acts as if the quantity of medical services were augmented by a factor g^C, while all the other inputs (not detailed here) remain unchanged. This multiplier takes on the value of one without investment in process innovation $(g^C[0] = 1)$ and increases with R^C. Thus, the health production function is given by

$$H_2 = h_2(\tilde{m}_2), \quad \text{with} \quad \tilde{m}_2 = g^C(R^C)M_2, \ \frac{\partial h_2}{\partial \tilde{m}_2} > 0, \ g^C[0] = 1, \ \frac{\partial g^C}{\partial R^C} > 0. \tag{14.2}$$

Thanks to process innovation, M_2 units of medical services now have the effect of $\tilde{m}_2$ units, so M_2 itself can take on a lower value. This implies less expenditure on health, the price of M_2 being normalized to one [see the budget constraint (14.5) below]. A given health status can therefore be achieved at lower cost. An additional multiplier effect can be attained through organizational innovation R^O; if this is taken into account, $\tilde{m}_2$ is replaced by m_2 (see below).

Process and product innovation: a successful product innovation in health care should enable individuals to improve their health status beyond the value $h_2(\cdot)$, attained using existing medical technology. As in equation (14.2), this improvement is indicated by a multiplier whose value depends on the expenditure on product innovation R^D during the first period. Thus, the production function (14.3) is extended to

$$H_2 = g^D(R^D)h_2(\tilde{m}_2), \quad \text{with} \quad g^D[0] = 1, \ \frac{\partial g^D}{\partial R^D} > 0. \tag{14.3}$$

Process, product, and organizational innovation: economies of scope are typical for organizational innovations. In the present context, synergy effects are modeled to occur not among different production processes or firms but between different periods.[1] According to this definition, organizational innovation enhances the productivity of medical services in both periods rather than only in the second period.

---

[1] Thus, rather than having synergy result in an improved division of labor between 'plant No. 1' (ambulatory care) and 'plant No. 2' (hospital care), synergy increases effectiveness of 'period No. 1 medicine' as well as 'period No. 2 medicine'. This avoids supplementing the model by a spatial dimension, which would complicate the notation without providing additional insights.

Furthermore, organizational innovation is more important when resource input is large. Therefore, the production function can be written as

$$H_1 = h_1(m_1), \qquad \text{with } m_1 = g^O(R^O)M_1, \frac{\partial h_1}{\partial m_1} > 0,$$

$$H_2 = g^D(R^D)h_2(m_2), \text{ with } m_2 = g^O(R^O)\tilde{m}_2 = g^O(R^O)g^C(R^C)M_2, \qquad (14.4)$$

$$\text{and } g^O[0] = 1, \quad \frac{\partial g^O}{\partial R^O} > 0.$$

Let total income of both periods $\overline{Y}$ be spent on the purchase of consumer goods (X_1, X_2), medical services (M_1, M_2), and on three types of innovation (R^C, R^D, R^O). Then, the budget constraint reads

$$X_1 + M_1 + R^C + R^D + R^O + X_2 + M_2 = \overline{Y}. \qquad (14.5)$$

In period 1, individuals face the task of maximizing this function by their choice of X_1, M_1, and above all by optimizing R^C, R^D, and R^O. Using equations (14.1), (14.4), and (14.5), this optimization problem can be examined using the Lagrange function (see also Box 14.1),

$$\mathcal{L} = u_1\left(X_1, h_1[g^O(R^O)M_1]\right)$$
$$+ u_2\left(X_2, g^D(R^D)h_2[g^O(R^O)g^C(R^C)M_2]\right) \qquad (14.6)$$
$$- \lambda\{X_1 + M_1 + R^C + R^D + R^O + X_2 + M_2 - \overline{Y}\}.$$

14.2.2 Criteria for an Optimal Allocation of Innovative Effort

This subsection is devoted to the formulation of operational criteria for the optimal allocation of innovative effort from the point of view of an individual. These criteria amount to required marginal improvements of health status during the second period. First, by differentiating function (14.6) with respect to consumption expenditure X_1, the value of the Lagrange multiplier λ can be determined,

$$\frac{\partial \mathcal{L}}{\partial X_1} = \frac{\partial u_1}{\partial X_1} - \lambda - 0 \quad \Rightarrow \quad \lambda = \frac{\partial u_1}{\partial X_1}. \qquad (14.7)$$

Next, the optimal amount of expenditure on *process innovation* R^C has to satisfy the following condition,

$$\frac{\partial \mathcal{L}}{\partial R^C} = \frac{\partial u_2}{\partial H_2}\frac{\partial H_2}{\partial h_2}\frac{\partial h_2}{\partial m_2}\frac{\partial m_2}{\partial g^C}\frac{\partial g^C}{\partial R^C} - \lambda$$

$$= \frac{\partial u_2}{\partial H_2}g^D\frac{\partial h_2}{\partial m_2}g^O M_2\frac{\partial g^C}{\partial R^C} - \frac{\partial u_1}{\partial X_1} = 0 \quad [\text{see equation (14.4)}]. \qquad (14.8)$$

Obviously, the marginal health improvement that can be achieved in the second period has to balance the opportunity cost of process innovation. This opportunity cost in turn is determined by the utility which could be derived from additional consumption during the first period if no investment in innovation were made.

Based on the equations (14.6) and (14.7), the necessary optimality condition for product innovation R^D is given by

$$\frac{\partial \mathcal{L}}{\partial R^D} = \frac{\partial u_2}{\partial H_2} h_2 \frac{\partial g^D}{\partial R^D} - \frac{\partial u_1}{\partial X_1} = 0. \tag{14.9}$$

By spending more on product innovation, health status h_2 can be improved by the use of medical services and, possibly, process and organizational innovation. In an optimum, this benefit must equal the opportunity cost in terms of consumption sacrificed.

Finally, the following condition with respect to *organizational innovation* can be derived from function (14.6):

$$\frac{\partial \mathcal{L}}{\partial R^O} = \frac{\partial u_1}{\partial H_1} \frac{\partial H_1}{\partial h_1} \frac{\partial h_1}{\partial m_1} \frac{\partial m_1}{\partial g^O} \frac{\partial g^O}{\partial R^O} + \frac{\partial u_2}{\partial H_2} \frac{\partial H_2}{\partial h_2} \frac{\partial h_2}{\partial m_2} \frac{\partial m_2}{\partial g^O} \frac{\partial g^O}{\partial R^O} - \frac{\partial u_1}{\partial X_1}$$

$$= \frac{\partial u_1}{\partial H_1} \frac{\partial h_1}{\partial m_1} M_1 \frac{\partial g^O}{\partial R^O} + \frac{\partial u_2}{\partial H_2} g^D \frac{\partial h_2}{\partial m_2} g^C M_2 \frac{\partial g^O}{\partial R^O} - \frac{\partial u_1}{\partial X_1} = 0. \tag{14.10}$$

The conditions (14.8) to (14.10) may be compared by examining the required effectiveness of the respective expenditure on innovation, effectiveness being defined as the marginal contribution to health status in the second period. Rewriting equations (14.8) to (14.10), one obtains

$$\frac{\partial h_2}{\partial m_2} \frac{\partial g^C}{\partial R^C} g^D g^O M_2 = \frac{\partial u_1/\partial X_1}{\partial u_2/\partial H_2} \quad \text{(process innovation)} \tag{14.11a}$$

$$\frac{\partial g^D}{\partial R^D} h_2 = \frac{\partial u_1/\partial X_1}{\partial u_2/\partial H_2} \quad \text{(product innovation)} \tag{14.11b}$$

$$\frac{\partial h_2}{\partial m_2} \frac{\partial g^O}{\partial R^O} g^C g^D M_2 = \frac{\partial u_1/\partial X_1}{\partial u_2/\partial H_2} - \frac{\partial u_1/\partial H_1}{\partial u_2/\partial H_2} \frac{\partial h_1}{\partial m_1} \frac{\partial g^O}{\partial R^O} M_1 \tag{14.11c}$$

(organizational innovation).

The conditions (14.11a) to (14.11c) can be interpreted as follows.

- Regardless of the type of innovation, the required improvement of health in the second period has to be the higher the more important the *loss of utility* occasioned by the sacrifice in terms of consumption during the first period (large value of $\partial u_1/\partial X_1$). Conversely, the required improvement is relatively small in a situation where health is of overriding importance (large value of $\partial u_2/\partial H_2$).

- For every unit of money additionally spent, both process and product innovation should have the same effect on health status in the second period [LHS of (14.11a) equals LHS of (14.11b)].

Box 14.1. The Three Types of Innovation in a Two-Period Model

$u = u_1(X_1, H_1) + u_2(X_2, H_2).$	Utility function	(14.1)

$H_2 = h_2(\tilde{m}_2)$, with $\tilde{m}_2 = g^C(R^C)M_2$,

$\dfrac{\partial h_2}{\partial \tilde{m}_2} > 0,\ g^C[0] = 1,\ \dfrac{\partial g^C}{\partial R^C} > 0.$

Production of health with process innovation only   (14.2)

$H_2 = g^D(R^D)h_2(\tilde{m}_2),$

with $g^D[0] = 1,\quad \dfrac{\partial g^D}{\partial R^D} > 0.$

Production of health with process and product innovation only   (14.3)

$H_1 = h_1(m_1)$, with $m_1 = g^O(R^O)M_1, \dfrac{\partial h_2}{\partial \tilde{m}_2} > 0.$

$H_2 = g^D(R^D)h_2(m_2),$

with $m_2 = g^O(R^O)\tilde{m}_2 = g^O(R^O)g^C(R^C)M_2,$

$g^O[0] = 1,\quad \dfrac{\partial g^O}{\partial R^O} > 0.$

Production of health with process, product, and organizational innovation combined   (14.4)

$X_1 + M_1 + R^C + R^D + R^O + X_2 + M_2 = \overline{Y}.$ Budget constraint   (14.5)

$\mathcal{L} = u_1\{X_1; h_1[g^O(R^O)M_1]\}$ Lagrange function   (14.6)

$\quad + u_2\{X_2; g^D(R^D)h_2[g^O(R^O)g^C(R^C)M_2]\}$

$\quad - \lambda\{X_1 + M_1 + R^C + R^D + R^O + X_2 + M_2 - \overline{Y}\}.$

X_1: consumption in the first period (X_2: in the second period)
H_1: health status in the first period (H_2: in the second period)
λ: Lagrange multiplier pertaining to the budget constraint
M_1: expenditure on medical services in the first period (M_2: in the second period)
R^C: expenditure on process innovation, in first period only
R^D: expenditure on product innovation, in first period only
R^O: expenditure on organizational innovation, in first period only
$\overline{Y}$: total income of periods 1 and 2

- The marginal improvement of health status to be achieved in the second period is always *lower* for organizational innovation than for the other two types of innovation. This difference is the larger, the greater medical expenditure during the first period (M_1). Clearly, this argument hinges on organizational innovation having an effect already in the first period $[(\partial h_1)/(\partial m_1) \times (\partial g^O)/(\partial R^O) > 0$ in equation (14.11c)].

- The benchmark for process innovation in equation (14.11a) depends, inter alia, on the (optimal) extent of product innovation g^D. Since $\partial g^D/\partial R^D$ appears in equation (14.11b), the value of g^D is only known if h_2, the health status attained as a result of process and organizational innovation, is known. This highlights the *interdependence* of the three optimality criteria.

We summarize our results in

Conclusion 14.1. *The requirements for the three types of innovation in health care can be expressed as required improvements of health status. From the ex ante point of view of an individual, these requirements are always equal for both process and product innovation, but lower for organizational innovation.*

Note that Conclusion 14.1 does not contain statements about the values of R^C, R^D, and R^O. Indeed, it is not possible to infer from the marginal productivities, determined in the equations (14.11a) to (14.11c), the respective values of expenditures on innovation without additional assumptions. For instance, a high required value of the marginal product of product innovation does not necessarily mean that the individual wishes to reduce the amount of product innovation below the amount of process innovation. This would only be the case if the functional relationships between the expressions on the left-hand side of the equations (14.11a) to (14.11c) and R^C, R^D, and R^O were the same. However, the equations (14.2) to (14.4) imply no equality conditions of the kind $\partial g^C / \partial R^C = \partial g^D / \partial R^D = \partial g^O / \partial R^O$.

14.2.3 Distortions of Criteria at the Aggregate Level

In the previous subsection, benchmarks for innovation were derived that an 'average' individual would apply, e.g., as a potential purchaser of a patented innovative drug or a taxpayer who has to pay for innovation in public health; in this case, the excess burden of taxation would have to be taken into account. According to equations (14.11a) to (14.11c), such an individual would demand about the same improvement of health per additional unit of money.

This expectation does not seem to conform with experience, however, according to evidence from the United Kingdom. If health effects of innovation are measured in terms of quality adjusted life years (QALYs, see Section 2.3.2), estimates for the British National Health Service (NHS) range from £270 per QALY to £107,780 per QALY (see Table 14.1 which borrows from Table 2.1). The decisions taken by the NHS with regard to product innovation are based on a benchmark of only 0.009 QALYs per £1,000 (=1000/107,780) for a dialysis service in hospitals, but of as much as 3.70 QALYs per £1,000 (=1000/270) for a stop-smoking campaign (which, while not originating within the health service itself, nonetheless saves medical inputs and thus is entered as a process innovation in Table 14.1).

More generally, it seems that *process innovations* have to satisfy more stringent criteria than product innovations. Apparently, individuals' ex ante preferences concerning health care innovation are distorted at the aggregate level. There seem to be three possible reasons for such a distortion, viz. the influence of health insurance (moral hazard), a medical imperative at the level of objectives, and an imperative at the level of means.[2]

---

[2] The term 'technological imperative in medicine' was introduced by FUCHS (1968). It denotes the rapid diffusion of product innovation not only in U.S. health care but in all industrialized countries, apparently based on medical norms espoused by the rest of society.

Table 14.1. Costs per QALYs Gained in £ for Various Innovations

Therapy or Innovation	Type of Innovation	Cost / QALY (£ 1990)
GP advice to stop smoking	C	270
Anti-hyperintensive therapy to prevent stroke	C	940
Pacemaker implantation	C	1,100
Hip replacement	D	1,180
Coronary artery bypass graft (severe angina pectoris)	D	2,090
Kidney transplant	C	4,710
Breast cancer screen	C	5,780
Heart transplant	D	7,840
Coronary artery bypass graft (moderate angina pectoris)	D	18,830
Erythropoietin treatment for anaemia in dialysis	D	21,970
Neurosurgical intervention for Malignant intracranial tumors	D	107,780

C: process innovation.
D: product innovation including in particular life-saving therapies to which at the time of their introduction no alternative existed.

Source: MAYNARD (1991)

(1) *Effects of health insurance.* If covered by (social) health insurance, an individual does not have to pay separately for innovations in health care. A hospital stay usually costs just as much (frequently nothing at all), regardless of whether the hospital has a new operating room or not, or if use is made of a newly released drug that is twice as expensive as its conventional alternatives. As soon as individuals decide as patients, they therefore no longer have to pay the full opportunity cost of the innovation. Their sacrifice of consumer goods X_1 (and with it their loss of utility $\partial u_1/\partial X_1$ in exchange for improved health status) are reduced by health insurance.

According to equations (14.11a)–(14.11c), this serves to lower the benchmark for *all three types* of innovation because the common term $(\partial u_1/\partial X_1)/(\partial u_2/\partial H_2)$ on the right-hand side decreases. The effect of 'ex-post moral hazard' is therefore not limited to the boosting of demand for medical care in the current period (see Section 6.4.2), but also to speed up technological change in medicine.

In addition, health insurance distorts the balance between process innovation and product innovation by reducing the cost of medical services to the individual. For every single insured person, HCE at the time of utilization is lowered through insurance coverage. Accordingly, the value of M_2 (medical expenditure) decreases in equation (14.11a), resulting in a higher value of $\partial g^C/\partial R^C$ ceteris paribus.[3] Decreasing marginal returns to innovation then call for a lower value of R^C. In

---

[3] The ceteris paribus clause is violated as a rule because health insurance also causes a decrease of $\partial g^D/\partial R^D$ in equation (14.11b) and consequently an increase of g^D in equation (14.11a) – unless the health state prior to the product innovation h_2 is improved.

sum, health insurance does not foster process innovation to the same extent as it does *product innovation*.

(2) *Medical imperative at the level of objectives.* This imperative means that under the influence of physicians it becomes the norm in a society to fight disease as much as possible. Thus, everything must be done to ensure that the health of an individual in need of treatment attains a certain level.[4] If H_2 has to exceed some lower limit, then the medical imperative can be expressed by the condition

$$\partial u_2/\partial H_2 \leq \bar{u}'_2, \tag{14.12}$$

i.e., marginal utility of health must not exceed the value $\bar{u}'_2$. Judging from equations (14.11a) to (14.11c), this condition at first seems to push up standards of performance for all three types of innovation, since the denominator of the common term, $\partial u_2/\partial H_2$, is reduced. One must take into account, however, that a high value of H_2 should be achieved, which by equation (14.4) calls for increases in g^D, g^C, M_2, and also g^O. Therefore, the medical imperative at the level of objectives turns out to have an *accelerating* effect on the rate of innovation in health care.

(3) *Medical imperative at the level of means.* This imperative calls for availability of sufficient amounts of medical services. This means that medical expenditure must be pushed to a point where their marginal productivity is low. If this limit on marginal productivity is denoted by $\bar{H}'_2$, and considering period 2 for simplicity, then according to (14.4) this type of imperative can be expressed as

$$\partial H_2/\partial M_2 = (\partial h_2/\partial m_2)g^D g^C g^O \leq \bar{H}'_2. \tag{14.13}$$

The implications of such an imperative are disturbing. The more medical services M_2 are used, the lower the marginal productivity $\partial h_2/\partial m_2$, at a given value of g^C, and the higher the values of g^D, g^C, and g^O (and thus R^D, R^C, and R^O) that are compatible with the constraint (14.13). The medical imperative at the level of means thus encourages additional provision of medical services not only during the current period but also expenditure on all three types of innovation [whereas organizational innovation should be fostered relatively more, see equations (14.11a) to (14.11c)].

Conclusion 14.2. *In the transition from the individual to the social level, the required standards of performance for all three types innovation in health care are lowered. Insurance-induced moral hazard and medical imperatives at the level both of objectives and means constitute likely reasons for this, with health insurance facilitating product innovation in general, but process innovation and organizational innovation only to a limited extent.*

---

[4] Defining quantified health objectives (e.g., reduction of 50 percent of mortality caused by cardiovascular diseases by the year 2000), as is common in the Annual Health Reports of the U.S. government, may be interpreted as emanating from an imperative at the level of objectives.

14.3 The Demographic Challenge

14.3.1 Ageing of the Population

14.3.1.1 Improved Control over Health Thanks to Medicine?

As expounded in Chapter 4, life expectancy in industrialized countries is still increasing (see Table 4.1). On the longer run, there has been a certain slowdown that is often interpreted as evidence proving that modern medicine has to fight against *decreasing marginal returns*.

Marginal willingness to pay for a factor characterized by decreasing marginal productivity in the production of health should be decreasing. But in countries where individual willingness to pay for medical services tends to prevail over political considerations of cost control (for instance, the United States, the Netherlands, or Switzerland), the share of medical expenditure in the national product shows no tendency to fall. To resolve this puzzle, many observers resort to the hypothesis of supplier-induced demand (see Section 8.3).

An alternative explanation for medical services being consistently in high demand might be people's *aversion to risk in relation to their health*. For a risk-averse individual, the achievements of medicine possibly consist not so much in an increase in life expectancy or mean number of QALYs (see Section 2.3.2) as in a reduced volatility of these quantities. From this point of view, medicine has the advantage of directly lowering the risk associated with health status rather than lowering the wealth risk emanating from bad health, as does health insurance. This risk reduction is worth a premium to individuals who in the extreme may strive to attain complete control of their health status. Indeed, the ideal of western lifestyle seems to be to remain perfectly healthy far into old age and then to suddenly drop dead.

If a whole population were to successfully gain control over its health, then a 'rectangularization of the survival curve' would have to be observed at the aggregate level. This term conveys the notion that in the course of time, successive cohorts would lose fewer and fewer of their members through premature death. Rather, deaths would cluster around a biologically determined life span [see FRIES (1980)].

For a population as a whole, the point of the survival curve at age a is constructed by multiplying the age-specific survival rates of the present period between ages 0 and $a - 1$. Thus the survival curve is a synthetic product because it describes the fate of an artificial cohort which experiences the survival rates of the present period over the course of its lifetime. As age-specific mortality rates at younger ages shrink more and more and eventually tend to zero, this curve becomes more and more horizontal and then quickly drops to zero at the maximum achievable age.

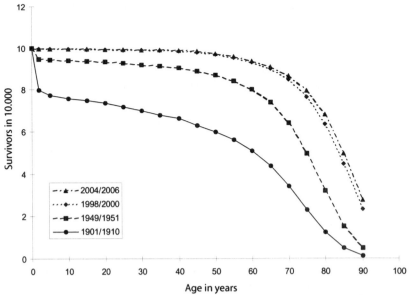

*Survivors among 100.000 persons of age X; German Reich 1901/10, Federal Republic of Germany 1949/51, Germany 1998/2000, Germany 2004/2006

Fig. 14.1. Rectangularization of Survival Curves of German Women*
Source: FEDERAL STATISTICAL OFFICE OF GERMANY (2003b, 2007)

In fact, since 1900 the survival curves for women in Germany have more and more approximated this ideal (see Figure 14.1; the survival curves for men show the same pattern). While in the early 20th century, a cohort would have lost 40 percent of its members by age 40, the cohort of 1998/2000 would have lost very few at this age. The rectangularization seems to be almost complete in the first 40 years of life, for women even more so than for men. Furthermore, there are signs that the same is happening for the age bracket 40 to 70. For example, the vertical distances between the survival curves for 1949/1951 and 2004/2006 in Figure 14.1 indicates that the largest gains in survival probabilities have been achieved for women around the age of 80 years (for men around 70 years). Thus control over health status seems to continually improve, extending into higher age groups. These observations (which are true for other countries as well) support

Conclusion 14.3. *The progressive rectangularization of the survival curve may be interpreted as the result of efforts to gain better control over health status. To the extent that this control is due to modern medicine, the unabated willingness to pay for medical services can be explained with reference to people's risk aversion.*

The question of whether modern medicine actually has contributed to the rectangularization of the survival curve is examined more closely in Section 14.4.2. At this point, however, a phenomenon related to Conclusion 14.3 merits mention-

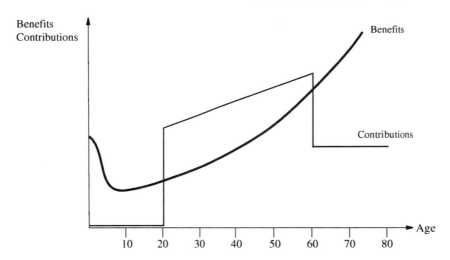

Fig. 14.2. Children, Workers, and Pensioners in Social Health Insurance
Source: SCHULENBURG (1989, p. 286)

ing. In fact, an important share of medical expenditure seems to benefit individuals whose remaining life expectancy amounts to one year or less. Analyzing data from the Medicare system in the United States, LUBITZ AND RILEY (1993) found that 27 to 30 percent of total HCE were spent on persons that were no longer alive 12 months later.[5] Apparently, a great many people are reaping the benefits of health care whose remaining life expectancy can be counted in months rather than years (see Section 14.4.2 for more details). If one were to measure the marginal productivity of these expenditures exclusively in terms of time spent in 'good' or 'better' health respectively (as suggested, e.g., in the simple model of Section 3.4), one would be tempted to speak of a *waste of resources*, benefiting at best hospital physicians but not patients themselves [see ZWEIFEL (1990)]. On the other hand, Conclusion 14.3 reminds us that even rather aged patients might display considerable willingness to pay for medical services which, while failing to improve their health status on average, serve to decrease its variance, thus enhancing their degree of control over it.

14.3.1.2 The Redistributive Effects of Ageing

Every health insurance system whose premiums are independent of age in spite of age-dependent health costs acquires features of a pay-as-you-go system of provision for old age and thereby 'inherits' its problems as well. As in provision for old age, the working generation pays contributions in excess of benefits received. This excess is used in social health insurance to balance the deficits resulting from the provision of care to children and pensioners (see Figure 14.2).

---

[5] This share may be larger than in the health care system as a whole because Medicare enrols retired people only. In this population group the share of people in their last year of life is much higher than in younger age groups.

Table 14.2. Average Net Lifetime Transfers to German Public Health Insurance, in constant US$ of 1980

Cohort	Variant I (purely demographic effect)	Variant II (demographic effect and effect of rising costs)
1900	−5,886	119
1920	−6,012	−707
1940	−3,180	−1,463
1960	−2,201	199
1980	8,088	8,082
2000	8,350	18,857
2020	10,673	54,200
2040	7,323	83,760
2060	2,965	76,653
2080	299	18,711
2100	0	0

Note: in variant I, constant HCE is assumed for the whole period of observation. In variant II it is assumed that HCE rises 1 percent p.a. until 1960, 10 percent p.a. from 1960 to 1990, 5 percent p.a. from 1990 on (due to increased efforts at cost control). Discounting to present value is 2 percent p.a. until 1960 and at the rate of cost increase from 1960 on. Net transfers on a life-cycle approach zero due to the assumption of constant fertility rates from the year 2030 on.

Source: SCHULENBURG (1989, p. 296)

As soon as the number of insured pensioners increases, the deficit multiplies. Therefore, contributions paid by workers must be increased in order to safeguard the financial equilibrium of the scheme, causing *intensified redistribution* from workers to pensioners.

Therefore, during a period of population ageing, membership in a social health insurance scheme may turn into an unprofitable investment for an entire generation of workers who must finance the high cost of treatment of several pensioners but in their turn can 'consume' the benefits of the scheme only once when in retirement age. The present value of their contributions exceeds the present value of the benefits which they stand to receive in the course of their lifetime. Such a cohort of workers pays a *net lifetime transfer to survivors of former cohorts* (positive entry in Table 14.2). If the effects of past and future cost inflation in health care is taken into account as well (variant II of Table 14.2), the cohort of 1960 is already about to pay a net lifetime transfer. These involuntary transfers will increase considerably in the future, reaching a point where acceptance of social health insurance in its present day form could be seriously undermined.

Conclusion 14.4. *The ageing of the population jeopardizes the financial equilibrium of social health insurance. The adjustment of contributions for safeguarding equilibrium may turn membership into an unprofitable investment for present and future generations of workers.*

Table 14.3. Share of Single-Person Households in Selected Industrialized Countries (in Percent)

	around 1960	around 1980	around 1990	around 2000
Germany	21	31	35	37
France	20	25	27	32
United Kingdom	15	22	26	30
Italy	11	18	22	23
Netherlands	12	22	29	34
Sweden	20	33	39	47
Switzerland	14	29	32	33
United States	13	23	25	25[a]

Source: 1960–90: HÖPFLINGER (1997), 2000: FEDERAL STATISTICAL OFFICE OF GERMANY (2003a), [a] U.S. CENSUS BUREAU (2004)

14.3.2 Changes in Household Composition

In industrialized countries, household composition has been changing rapidly as well. In the early 1960s, single-person units were the exception while at present they may make up one-third of all households today in some western countries. With a share of 25 percent, the United States is lagging behind in this development towards a 'singles society' (see Table 14.3). The growing share of single person units can be traced to two trends. On the one hand, marriage rates have tended to decrease, combined with an increase in the divorce rate that was not balanced by an increase in the rate of remarriage.

On the other hand, life expectancy in industrialized countries has been developing differently between the sexes. Around 1950, a German woman aged 60 years could expect to live another 17 years, her husband of the same age, another 16 years. Around 2004, however, remaining life expectancy at age 60 amounted to 24.25 years for a woman and 20.27 years for a man [see FEDERAL STATISTICAL OFFICE OF GERMANY (2007, p. 54)]. The probability of having to spend the last years of one's life alone has obviously increased considerably for women.

The relevance of single person units to the health care system may be illustrated by a simple probability argument. Let a person A fall ill with probability $\pi(A)$. If A lives alone, $\pi(A)$ also denotes his or her probability of demanding health care services. On the other hand, if A lives together with another person B, the healthy partner usually takes care of the sick one. In a two-person unit, claims on health care services are therefore only made if both members of the household are sick.

Using the formula for conditional probabilities, one may write the probability of a two-person unit exerting demand for health care services as

$$\pi(A,B) = \pi(A|B)\pi(B) = \pi(B|A)\pi(A). \tag{14.14}$$

$\pi(A,B)$:   probability of A and B being ill simultaneously (and hence demanding health care services).

$\pi(A|B)$:   probability of A being ill, given that B is ill.

From this equation it immediately follows that $\pi(A,B) \leq \pi(A)$ and $\pi(A,B) \leq \pi(B)$, because the conditional probabilities $\pi(A|B)$ and $\pi(B|A)$ can only be less or equal to one. The probability of both members of a two person household being ill at the same time therefore is less than the risk of illness of a single person in general. This means that living together in a family unit tends to relieve the health care system from some demands.

The extent of this relief effect is, according to equation (14.14), dependent on the conditional probabilities $\pi(A|B)$ and $\pi(B|A)$ respectively, which can be interpreted as the risk of infection. If these probabilities approach one, sickness of one partner inevitably leads to sickness of the other.

For countries afflicted by epidemics, living together in households is hardly an advantage. But communicable diseases no longer pose a threat in industrialized countries, causing multi-person households to demand less HCE, and conversely, single-person households, to demand more.

Conclusion 14.5. *The spreading of single-person units increases the likelihood of a health loss that translates into a demand for health care services ceteris paribus while its contribution to the control of epidemics is marginal in today's industrialized countries, in which communicable diseases are losing importance.*

14.4 Demographic Ageing, Medical Progress, and Health Care Expenditure

The challenges described in the two last Sections 14.2 and 14.3 not only contribute each by itself to an increase in HCE, but they can reinforce each other. In the following the so-called Sisyphus Syndrome is presented and its empirical relevance discussed. The section concludes with a discussion of a prominent proposal to solve the problem, viz. a transition from pay-as-you-go to capital funding as a method of financing future HCE.

14.4.1 The 'Sisyphus Syndrome' in Health Care

On the one hand, the rectangularization of the survival curve presented in Section 14.3 above means that gains in life expectancy are concentrated among the higher age groups. In Section 14.2, on the other hand, the predominance of product innovation in health care was noted, a type of innovation that usually goes along with increased cost of treatment. Taken together, these two facts may well result in a process reminiscent of a 'Sisyphus Syndrome in health care'.[6] Let technological progress in medicine in the guise of product innovation improve the chances of survival particularly at middle and advanced ages. Through their increased numbers, aged voters exert more influence on the political process, pushing through their preference in favor of public HCE and medical innovation. Thus, resources are channeled into health care, especially into product innovation. This in turn lays the basis for further successes of modern medicine, which serve to boost the ranks of the old and causing the spiral to go into its next turn. For a politician, investing in public health would amount to a ride on a tiger because of an ever-increasing health bill.

14.4.1.1 A Simple Dynamic Model of the Sisyphus Syndrome

The objective of this section is to give the Sisyphus Syndrome a simplified formal representation through a system of two dynamic equations. Let time t be measured in periods of approximately 30 years, corresponding both to the span of a generation and the maximum remaining life expectancy of a pensioner. The size of the aged population B_t^a at the middle of period t is given by the working population in the previous period B_{t-1}^e, times the rate of survival $(1 - \pi_t)$. In accordance with the hypothesis underlying the Sisyphus Syndrome, let the rate of mortality π_t depend (among other things) on the input of medical services during the previous period M_{t-1} (see also Box 14.2),

$$B_t^a = ([1 - \pi_t(M_{t-1},...)]B_{t-1}^e), \qquad \frac{\partial \pi_t}{\partial M_{t-1}} < 0. \qquad (14.15)$$

The second equation of the system serves to represent the argument that the quantity of medical services made available in a society depends on the population's age structure. Thus, let M_t depend positively on the age coefficient β_t, that is on the ratio of the aged to the working population in the same period. For one, this ratio mirrors the fact that the demand for medical care is likely to be strong in a relatively old (and hence less healthy) population. Second, however, β_t also reflects the proportion of aged voters and thus their power in the political process, tax money causing to flow into medical research and into HCE in general.

---

[6] According to Greek mythology, Sisyphus was condemned by the gods to roll a big rock uphill only to see it slip out of his hands just before reaching the top so he had to start all over again.

Neglecting other determinants, one has

$$M_t = M_t(\beta_t, ...), \quad \text{with} \quad \frac{\partial M_t}{\partial \beta_t} > 0 \quad \text{and} \quad \beta_t \equiv \frac{B_t^a}{B_t^e} : \text{age coefficient.} \quad (14.16)$$

To examine the *dynamic properties* of this interdependent model, consider its reaction to an exogenous shock. Let the quantity of medical services in the previous period increase by the amount $dM_{t-1} > 0$. By equation (14.15), this results in an increase of the aged population in period t,

$$dB_t^a = \left[\frac{-\partial \pi_t}{\partial M_{t-1}} \right] B_{t-1}^e dM_{t-1}. \quad (14.17)$$

According to equation (14.16), this increase in the number of the aged induces an increase of HCE. Because the working population is assumed to be exogenously given, differentiation of equation (14.16) yields

$$dM_t = \frac{\partial M_t}{\partial \beta_t} \frac{\partial \beta_t}{\partial B_t^a} dB_t^a = \frac{\partial M_t}{\partial \beta_t} \frac{1}{B_t^e} dB_t^a. \quad (14.18)$$

Now, expression (14.17) can be inserted into equation (14.18), which after slight rearrangement gives the following equation of motion for HCE,

$$dM_t = \underbrace{\left[-\frac{\partial \pi_t}{\partial M_{t-1}} \right]}_{(+)} \underbrace{\left[\frac{\partial M_t}{\partial \beta_t} \right]}_{(+)} \underbrace{\left[\frac{B_{t-1}^e}{B_t^e} \right]}_{(+)} dM_{t-1}. \quad (14.19)$$

Since all three expressions in parentheses have a positive sign, an exogenous increase of HCE in the past is predicted to entail increased HCE in the present, which in turn is transmitted into the future, as claimed by the Sisyphus Syndrome. Each term may be interpreted as one of three factors determining the dynamics of the spiral.

(1) *Success of medicine.* The more the rate of mortality π_t is reduced due to the additional HCE in the previous period dM_{t-1}, the more acute is the Sisyphus Syndrome, ceteris paribus.

(2) *Influence of the aged population on health care expenditure.* This is the second factor of equation (14.19). The more easily political institutions permit pensioners to bring their preferences for public HCE to bear, the greater $\partial M_t/\partial \beta_t$ and the more marked is the Sisyphus Syndrome.

(3) *Development of the working population.* The third factor of equation (14.19) represents the size of the working population in the previous period compared to the size of the active population in the current period. The less the working population grows (the more it diminishes, respectively), the higher is this factor and the more will an increase in HCE carry forward into the future, adding momentum to the Sisyphus Syndrome.

Box 14.2. Model of the Sisyphus Syndrome in the Health Care System

$$B_t^a = ([1 - \pi_t(M_{t-1})]B_{t-1}^e), \quad \frac{\partial \pi_t}{\partial M_{t-1}} < 0 \tag{14.15}$$

$$M_t = M_t(\beta_t), \quad \text{with} \quad \frac{\partial M_t}{\partial \beta_t} > 0 \quad \text{and} \quad \beta_t \equiv \frac{B_t^a}{B_t^e} \tag{14.16}$$

$$dB_t^a = \left[\frac{-\partial \pi_t}{\partial M_{t-1}}\right] B_{t-1}^e dM_{t-1} \tag{14.17}$$

$$dM_t = \frac{\partial M_t}{\partial \beta_t} \frac{\partial \beta_t}{\partial B_t^a} dB_t^a = \frac{\partial M_t}{\partial \beta_t} \frac{1}{B_t^e} dB_t^a \tag{14.18}$$

$$dM_t = \underbrace{\left[-\frac{\partial \pi_t}{\partial M_{t-1}}\right]}_{(+)} \underbrace{\left[\frac{\partial M_t}{\partial \beta_t}\right]}_{(+)} \underbrace{\left[\frac{B_{t-1}^e}{B_t^e}\right]}_{(+)} dM_{t-1} \tag{14.19}$$

B_t^a: aged population in the current period
B_t^e: working population in the current period, exogenously determined
β_t: ratio of pensioners to working population
M_t: expenditure on medical services
π_t: mortality rate

Conclusion 14.6. *In democratically organized countries, a Sisyphus Syndrome might exist, which means that present successes of medicine will burden the health care system with additional expenditure on medical care in the future. The acuteness of the alleged syndrome depends on the extent to which medical services contribute to longevity, the influence of the aged population on the public budget, and inversely on the growth of the working population.*

14.4.1.2 Empirical Evidence

The equation of motion (14.19) contains three factors, which must all have a positive sign for the Sisyphus Syndrome in health care to occur. The third factor, representing the development of the working population over time, can be set to one and hence be neglected. The reason is that at least in OECD countries, the workforce increases very slowly [see OECD (2006)]. This leaves the first two factors to be examined. In the light of the evidence presented in Chapter 4, it is doubtful whether $\partial \pi_t / \partial M_{t-1} < 0$ in fact holds, i.e., whether medical services are capable of significantly reducing the rate of mortality. Thus, this issue is to be settled first.

The model presented in Box 14.2 cannot be tested directly since a period of fixed length t does not quite fit the facts. In the model, t denotes the remaining life expectancy of those just retired. In fact, the remaining life expectancy at age 65 has been increasing during the past decades. This increase differs among countries, reflecting differences in the post-retirement mortality rate. A viable alternative is to use *remaining life expectancy instead of mortality* π_t as dependent variable [see OECD (1987)] in the first relationship, $\partial \pi_t / \partial M_{t-1} < 0$.

Considering the second factor in equation (14.19), it must be borne in mind that time to death rather than age seems to drive HCE [see ZWEIFEL ET AL. (1999b), ZWEIFEL ET AL. (2004b) and WERBLOW ET AL. (2005)]. This means that ageing of population may simply defer the costly last year of life, with no effect on HCE at all. However, an ageing population may still exert an influence on HCE at the macro-economic level. If the rectangularization of the survival curve discussed in Section 14.3.1.1 indeed reflects improved control over health status, ageing individuals may increasingly want to use HCE to achieve this control. Through their political clout, they could force politicians to increase public HCE in their interest.

A first attempt at assessing whether a Sisyphus Syndrome exists in health care was undertaken by ZWEIFEL AND FERRARI (1992). Their most noteworthy result was that remaining life expectancy seems to depend positively on HCE incurred about a decade earlier. In particular, a 10 percent increase in per capita HCE in 1970 is associated with a lengthening of remaining life expectancy by 1 percent (1.5 months for a 65 year old person) ten years later.

Thus, one of the conditions $(\partial \pi_t / \partial M_{t-1} < 0)$ for the existence of the Sisyphus Syndrome was satisfied. The other relevant factor states that an increased proportion of the aged population causes HCE to increase [see equation (14.16)]. To emphasize the feedback relation inherent in the Sisyphus Syndrome, remaining life expectancies of females and males at age 65 were used as explanatory variables rather than the age coefficient β_t. This may be justified by noting that these life expectancies determine the future size of the aged population and hence the value of β_t. Surprisingly, an impact of remaining life expectancy at age 65 on HCE *could not be established* by ZWEIFEL AND FERRARI (1992).

Later, ZWEIFEL ET AL. (2005) revisited the issue, using better data, theory, and econometric methods. Analyzing a panel of 30 OECD countries covering 30 years (1970-2000) [OECD (2001)], fixed versus random effects and several different lags were tested using HAUSMAN (1978) tests. An additional variable called $\widehat{SISYPH}$ (= Sisyphus) was created with the purpose of capturing the effect of additional survivors and their impact on HCE.

The tests revealed that the health production function should be estimated with a random effects model and lifestyle variables (calory intake and alcohol consumption) lagged 10 years. GDP enters contemporaneously, reflecting a budget constraint rather than a lifestyle variable in order to avoid extreme multicollinearity with HCE. To allow for possible nonlinearities, all explanatory variables enter in squared form as well. ZWEIFEL ET AL. (2005) first estimate the impact of these variables on remaining life expectancy of males and females (*RLEM* and *RLEF*) at age 65, the share of people over 65 (*POP65*), and mortality (*MORT*). Mortality is estimated in order to filter out the change in HCE due to proximity to death.

Table 14.4. Remaining Life Expectancy at Age 60, 1970–2000

RLE	Females			Males		
	Coefficient	z	$P > z$	Coefficient	z	$P > z$
GDP	0.122	5.43	0.000	0.077	4.90	0.000
GDP2	−0.002	−3.91	0.000	−0.001	−2.95	0.003
HCE_{-10}	2.045	4.82	0.000	2.022	4.49	0.000
$HCE2_{-10}$	−0.565	−3.60	0.000	−0.491	−2.95	0.003
ALC_{-10}	−0.043	−0.70	0.484	0.022	0.23	0.822
$ALC2_{-10}$	0.002	1.02	0.307	−0.001	−0.22	0.827
CAL_{-10}	0.786	0.65	0.515	−0.723	−1.08	0.281
$CAL2_{-10}$	−0.083	−0.50	0.614	−0.135	1.53	0.125
Constant	18.572	9.11	0.000	16.883	13.94	0.000
Wald $\chi^2(8)$:	210.640			338.330		
Prob $> \chi^2$:	0.000			0.000		
$1 - \dfrac{Var(\varepsilon_{it})}{Var(RLEF)}$:	0.601			0.559		
N	303			303		

Note: included in this equation are (frequency): Australia (21), Austria (29), Belgium (22), Canada (12), Denmark (18), Finland (17), Germany (13), Ireland (15), Japan (2), Luxembourg (4), New Zealand (19), Norway (29), Portugal (15), Spain (13), Sweden (16), Switzerland (25), United Kingdom (18), United States (15).

Source: ZWEIFEL ET AL. (2005, p. 137)

This amounts to a system of few equations,

$$
\begin{bmatrix} RLEF \\ RLEM \\ POP65 \\ MORT \end{bmatrix} = \begin{aligned} & \alpha + \beta_1 GDP + \beta_2 GDP2 + \beta_3 HCE_{-10} + \beta_4 HCE2_{-10} \\ & + \beta_5 ALC_{-10} + \beta_6 ALC2_{-10} + \beta_7 CAL_{-10} + \beta_8 CAL2_{-10} \\ & + \upsilon_i + \varepsilon_{it}. \end{aligned} \qquad (14.20)
$$

Estimation results are given in Table 14.4. Contemporaneous GDP (in US$) is associated with higher remaining life expectancy (*RLE*) in both sexes (with females possibly affected more strongly), confirming results found by ZWEIFEL AND FERRARI (1992) as well as FRECH AND MILLER (1999). A decreasing marginal effect of income cannot be excluded. The earlier study by ZWEIFEL AND FERRARI (1992) is also supported in that HCE_{-10} contributes to current *RLE* for both sexes. Since the squared explanatory variable proves highly significant too, a critical value can be calculated beyond which additional HCE is counter-productive ('flat-of-the-curve' medicine). Among women, this is approximately US$1,800, among men, US$2,060, compared to a mean value of US$1,375 in 2000. With regard to lifestyle, consumption of calories and alcohol do not seem to have an influence on remaining life expectancy.

The new variable $\widehat{SISYPH}$ consists of two components. The first reflects the average of estimated male and female remaining life expectancy ($\widehat{RLEM}$ and $\widehat{RLEF}$). However, if the share of individuals having a certain remaining life expectancy is small, $RLEM$ and $RLEF$ will have a small impact on the political process. Therefore they need to be weighted by the predicted share of the population at that age ($\widehat{POP}65$),

$$\widehat{SISYPH} = (\widehat{RLEF} + \widehat{RLEM})/2 \times \widehat{POP}65. \qquad (14.21)$$

The feedback relationship runs from $\widehat{SISYPH}$ and other variables back to the share of HCE in the Gross Domestic Product, HCE/GDP. Again a HAUSMAN (1978) test was carried out in order to determine whether a fixed or random effects specification should be favored. This time, the fixed effects proved to be better compatible with the data. This seems puzzling at first sight. However, HCE is importantly determined by institutional factors that are not represented well by an error component υ_i as in equation (14.20). The share of HCE in GDP rather than HCE is used as the dependent variable in order to control for a time trend,

$$HCE/GDP = \alpha' + \beta'_1 GDP + \beta'_2 RPH + \beta'_3 \widehat{MORT} \qquad (14.22)$$
$$+ \beta'_4 \widehat{SISYPH} + \beta'_5 D_i + \mu_{i,t}.$$

Here, D_i are dummy variables representing the 29 country fixed effects. The regression results pertaining to this equation are presented in Table 14.5.

Relative to the United States, most other OECD countries have a significantly lower health share in GDP, the difference amounting to 4 percentage points in the case of Luxembourg, Spain, and the United Kingdom. Interestingly, GDP does not have a significant coefficient. This result stands in a striking contrast with the political debate in major industrial countries, which has been revolving about the secular rise of the health share. It also implies that the income elasticity of HCE is one (apart from the Sisyphus effect, see below).[7] This is lower than most elasticities in GERDTHAM ET AL. (1992) but higher than the estimates presented in GERDTHAM ET AL. (1998). As to the role of relative price of health care RPH, the theoretical prediction is that both private and public decision makers tend to substitute health goods for other commodities (aggregated in the GDP) when RPH is high. The positive coefficient of RPH indicates that the implied price elasticity is slightly below

---

[7] The income elasticity of HCE can be calculated as follows. Using $HCE \equiv (HCE/GDP) \times GDP$, one obtains $\frac{\partial HCE}{\partial GDP} = \frac{\partial (HCE/GDP)}{\partial GDP} \times GDP + \frac{HCE}{GDP}$. The first derivative equals $\beta'_1 + \beta'_3 \frac{\partial \widehat{MORT}}{\partial GDP} + \beta'_4 \frac{\partial \widehat{SISYPH}}{\partial GDP}$ from equation (14.22); therefore, the elasticity is given by $e(HCE, GDP) = (\beta'_1 + \beta'_3 \frac{\partial \widehat{MORT}}{\partial GDP} + \beta'_4 \frac{\partial \widehat{SISYPH}}{\partial GDP}) \times (GDP)^2/HCE + 1 = 1.14$ evaluated at sample means [see ZWEIFEL ET AL. (2005) and Table 14.5].

Table 14.5. Health Share in GDP, 1970–2000, 30 OECD Countries in Percent

HCE/GDP	n	Coefficient	z	$P > z$
Dum_Australia	19	−3.057	−7.90	0.000
Dum_Austria	26	−3.167	−8.62	0.000
Dum_Canada	12	−2.179	−5.35	0.000
Dum_Denmark	16	−2.466	−6.26	0.000
Dum_Finland	15	−3.238	−8.21	0.000
Dum_Germany	11	−1.640	−3.89	0.000
Dum_Ireland	15	−2.706	−6.27	0.000
Dum_Luxembourg	4	−4.375	−8.45	0.000
Dum_NewZealand	16	−3.679	−9.29	0.000
Dum_Norway	28	−3.515	−9.64	0.000
Dum_Portugal	8	−2.890	−6.33	0.000
Dum_Spain	10	−4.001	−8.83	0.000
Dum_Switzerland	21	−3.081	−8.14	0.000
Dum_UnitedKingdom	17	−3.906	−9.89	0.000
GDP		−0.020	−1.13	0.260
RPH		0.012	2.03	0.042
$\widehat{MORT}$		0.010	1.72	0.085
$\widehat{SISYPH}$		0.069	2.98	0.003
constant		−18.092	−1.59	0.112
Wald $\chi^2(18)$:		524.260		
Prob $> \chi^2$:		0.000		
$1 - \dfrac{var(\varepsilon_{it})}{var(HCE/GDP)}$:		0.847		
N		232		

Note: n is the number of country-specific observations, with the benchmark United States being in the sample 14 times.

Source: ZWEIFEL ET AL. (2005, p. 141)

one.[8] Another prediction, already of relevance to the Sisyphus Syndrome, is not confirmed, viz. that a higher mortality rate in a given year (reflecting a greater number of individuals in their last year of life) cause *HCE* to be high ceteris paribus. The coefficient of $\widehat{MORT}$ is positive but insignificant.

Of course, the variable of crucial interest is $\widehat{SISYPH}$, the remaining life expectancy at age 60 weighted by the share of individuals close to retirement age. It has a highly significant coefficient, possibly raising the specter of an ageing population that keeps the Sisyphus spiral in motion indefinitely. This suspicion can be submitted to a test as follows.

---

[8] Since HCE/GDP is formed using nominal figures, it contains RPH. Noting that $RPH = PH/PGDP$ (the ratio of the health deflator to the GDP deflator), and using lower case symbols for real quantities, one has $(hce/gdp) \times RPH = \dots \beta_2' \times RPH + \dots$, or $hce \times RPH = \dots \beta_2' \times RPH \times gdp$. Differentiating with respect to RPH, one obtains, $hce \times (1+\eta) = \beta_2' \times gdp$, where η is the elasticity of demand for health care. Solving for η, one obtains $\eta = \beta_2' \times (hce/gdp)^{-1} - 1$. Evaluated at the sample means, this amounts to −0.90.

From the identity in equation (14.23),

$$HCE \equiv (HCE/GDP) \times GDP, \tag{14.23}$$

the effect of an increase in HCE ten years ago on current HCE is given by

$$
\begin{aligned}
\frac{\partial HCE}{\partial HCE_{-10}} &= \frac{\partial((HCE/GDP) \times GDP)}{\partial HCE_{-10}} \\
&= \frac{\partial(HCE/GDP)}{\partial HCE_{-10}} \times GDP + (HCE/GDP) \times \frac{\partial GDP}{\partial HCE_{-10}} \\
&= \frac{\partial(HCE/GDP)}{\partial HCE_{-10}} \times GDP, \tag{14.24}
\end{aligned}
$$

since $\partial GDP/\partial HCE_{-10}$ was assumed by ZWEIFEL ET AL. (2005) to be zero due to the long lag.[9] Now HCE_{-10} influences current HCE through $\widehat{SISYPH}$, which is designed to capture the impact of population-weighted RLE on the demand for health care and hence HCE. Implicit differentiation yields an expression for $\partial(HCE/GDP)/\partial HCE_{-10}$,

$$
\begin{aligned}
\frac{\partial(HCE/GDP)}{\partial HCE_{-10}} &= \frac{\partial(HCE/GDP)}{\partial SISYPH} \times \frac{\partial SISYPH}{\partial HCE_{-10}} \tag{14.25} \\
&= \frac{\partial(HCE/GDP)}{\partial SISYPH} \frac{1}{2} \left[\frac{\partial RLEF}{\partial HCE_{-10}} + \frac{\partial RLEM}{\partial HCE_{-10}} \right] POP65,
\end{aligned}
$$

since $\partial POP65/\partial HCE_{-10}$ may be set to zero according to estimation results (not shown). With HCE measured in thousands of US\$ contrary to GDP, equation (14.25) can be evaluated as follows.

$$\frac{\partial HCE}{\partial HCE_{-10}} = \tag{14.26}$$

$$= \underbrace{\frac{1}{2}}_{} \times \underbrace{\frac{\partial(HCE/GDP)}{\partial SISYPH}}_{} \times \underbrace{\left[\frac{\partial RLEF}{\partial HCE_{-10}} + \frac{\partial RLEM}{\partial HCE_{-10}} \right]}_{} \times \underbrace{POP65 \times GDP}_{} \times \frac{1}{1000}$$

$$= 0.5 \times \quad 0.069 \quad \times \quad [1.46 + 1.51] \quad \times \; 13.60 \times 15.76 \times 0.001 \approx 0.021.$$

The derivatives come from Tables 14.4 and 14.5 but have to be evaluated at specific values because the regressors of Table 14.4 appear not only in linear but also in quadratic form. Neglecting estimated coefficients that are insignificant and inserting overall sample means, one may conclude that US\$1 of HCE_{-10} induces some US\$0.02 of current HCE due to the dynamics of the Sisyphus Syndrome.

---

[9] There is research suggesting a significant influence of (contemporaneous) HCE on the GDP rate of growth [see, e.g., DEVARAJAN ET AL. (1996) or BERALDO ET AL. (2007)]. Estimating the elasticity of GDP with respect to HCE_{-10} at the sample means yields $e(GDP, HCE_{-10}) = 0.37$. This estimate is at the high end because it fails to control for increased inputs of labor and capital as well as technological change. In addition, replacing sample means by minimum and maximum values for the year 2000 yields $e(GDP, HCE_{-10})$ in the interval $(-0.681, 0.378)$, a range compatible with the assumption introduced.

Conclusion 14.7. *An empirical analysis using OECD country data suggests that additional health care expenditure may contribute to higher remaining life expectancy at higher ages, which serves to bias spending in favor of health care. Thus, the Sisyphus Syndrome is found to exist at the end of the last century. A one-time shock of US$1 carries over to US$0.02 ten years later. Therefore, the syndrome is not explosive.*

14.4.2 Ageing of Population and Health Care Expenditure

As mentioned in the preceding section, the relationship between ageing of the population and HCE is far from clear. First, as evidenced in Table 14.4, causality may well run from HCE to longevity. Even neglecting this complication, there are several pitfalls in relating the development of HCE over time to ageing. One of them of course is that medical technology has been changing at a rapid pace. But even when holding medical technology constant, there are three competing hypotheses with regard to the effect of ageing on HCE.

(1) The *status-quo hypothesis* assumes that age-specific per-capita HCE depends only on the state of medical technology and remains stable when the latter is controlled for. The impact of increasing life expectancy can thus be calculated by applying current age-expenditure profiles to the future age distribution of the population and simply scaling HCE up by a factor reflecting technological change in medicine.

(2) The *expansion-of-morbidity hypothesis* [see, e.g., OLHANSKY ET AL. (1991), KRÄMER (1982)] is based on the observed multimorbidity of many elderly patients and states that new possibilities of treating specific types of illness (e.g., heart disease) prolong life without perfectly restoring health. Little later, another disease sets in (e.g., cancer), which requires treatment again. According to this hypothesis, the main effect of technological change in medicine is to prolong the life of patients who would otherwise die, implying that average health status of the population deteriorates over time.

(3) The *time-to-death hypothesis* is based on the conjecture that the observed difference in HCE between young and old persons in cross-sectional data are not primarily due to calendar age. Rather, a larger share of old persons are in their last year of life, who – in a futile attempt to prevent death – consume a high amount of HCE [see FUCHS (1984b)]. An increase in life expectancy would therefore lower age-specific death rates hence the number of individuals in their last year of life in each age group. The strongest version of this hypothesis is the *compression of morbidity* first postulated by FRIES (1980), which states that as more people reach the natural limits of longevity, sickness is compressed in an ever shorter period before death.

While the expansion-of-morbidity hypothesis claims that a naive prediction of future HCE on the basis of present age-expenditure profiles underestimates the true growth in HCE (even with constant medical technology), the time-to-death hypothesis suggests the exact opposite. The compression-of-morbidity hypothesis, moreover, claims that an increase in life expectancy – through a drop in the total mortality rate – will even lower per-capita HCE.

While there is hardly any empirical evidence in favor of the expansion-of-morbidity hypothesis, the time-to-death hypothesis stands on a firm empirical basis. The increase of treatment costs in the years before death has been convincingly documented in numerous studies with data from various countries [e.g., LUBITZ AND RILEY (1993), ZWEIFEL ET AL. (1999b), ZWEIFEL ET AL. (2004b), STEARNS AND NORTON (2004), WERBLOW ET AL. (2005)].

An additional effect, supporting even the compression-of-morbidity hypothesis, is the reluctance of physicians to treat very old terminally ill patients as aggressively as they treat younger patients with similar symptoms, a behavior commonly interpreted as 'age-based rationing'. To the extent that this causes the costs of dying to decrease beyond a certain age, it accentuates the overestimation of future HCE based on the status-quo hypothesis.

Although it is no longer questionable that the status-quo hypothesis overestimates the impact of demographic ageing on per-capita health care expenditures, it is still of interest to assess the extent of the error. Such an attempt was made by BREYER AND FELDER (2006) using a data set from a Swiss sickness fund comprising over 91,000 persons of whom four percent died during the observation period of three and a half years.

The authors estimated age-expenditure profiles for men and women and survivors and decedents. These profiles are applied to the German population predicted by the German Statistical Office up to 2050, distinguishing several scenarios.

Scenario 1:   age-specific average HCE of the year 2002 are imputed to the predicted future age composition without adjustment, in keeping with the status-quo hypothesis.

Scenario 2:   the imputation distinguishes between persons in their last four years of life and persons who survived longer than that, as required by the time-to-death hypothesis.

Scenario 3:   HCE is shifted forward by as many years as remaining life expectancy is predicted to increase. For example, if the remaining life expectancy of a 65-year old is predicted to increase by 4 years by 2050, a 65-year old of 2050 is presumed to have the HCE of a 61-year old of 2002. This reflects the compression-of-morbidity variant of the time-to-death hypothesis.

Table 14.6. Predicted Future Per-Capita Health Care Expenditure in Germany

Year	Scenario 1 in €	Scenario 1 2002=100	Scenario 2 in €	Scenario 2 2002=100	Scenario 3 in €	Scenario 3 2002=100	Error of Sc. 1 in percent, compared to Sc. 2	Error of Sc. 1 in percent, compared to Sc. 3
2002	2,596	100.00	2,596	100.00	2,596	100.00	0	0
2010	2,691	103.66	2,674	103.00	2,642	101.77	18.0	51.7
2020	2,827	108.91	2,788	107.38	2,745	105.73	17.2	35.7
2030	2,961	114.05	2,894	111.45	2,798	107.78	18.5	44.7
2040	3,094	119.19	3,007	115.83	2,885	111.11	17.6	42.1
2050	3,217	123.92	3,102	119.49	2,959	113.96	18.5	41.6
2050[a]	5,688	219.08	5,485	211.25	5,232	201.51	6.6	14.7

[a]: Increase of 1 percent per annum assumed, reflecting technological change in medicine.

Source: BREYER AND FELDER (2006)

Table 14.6 shows the hypothetical development of per-capita HCE, holding medical technology and prices constant at their 2002 level. According to Scenario 1, annual per-capita HCE increases by 24 percent by 2050. In Scenario 2, this increase is predicted to be 19 percent only, and in Scenario 3, it even drops to 14 percent. Therefore, the status-quo hypothesis (Scenario 1) results in an overprediction of 18.5 percent [(24−19)/24] and of 41.6 percent [(24−14)/24], respectively.

When technological change in medicine is also accounted for in the form of an autonomous increase in age-specific HCE of 1 percent per annum, the values entered in the last row of Table 14.6 are obtained. The implicit assumption underlying this calculation is that future quality gains in medicine exceed future productivity gains in the economy by 1 percentage point p.a. This causes per capita HCE to more than double in real terms by 2050. One would still overpredict HCE under the status-quo hypothesis (Scenario 1), but the error shrinks to 6.6 percent (Scenario 2) and 14.7 percent (Scenario 3), respectively.

Similar effects are found by TELSER ET AL. (2007), who split up HCE into a regular and a cost-of-dying component and apply technological change in medicine to the latter component as well. These contributions permit to draw a number of conclusions regarding the likely effects of ageing versus technological change in medicine on future HCE.

- The effect of ageing on the future development of HCE is not dramatic as soon as medical technology is held constant.

- Accounting for the fact that HCE primarily is a function of proximity to death rather than calendar age (time-to-death hypothesis) does result in a downward adjustment of predicted future HCE growth due to ageing. However, the magnitude of this adjustment is only about one-fifth of the growth rate under the status-quo hypothesis. If the cost of dying is shifted to higher age (the compression-of-morbidity variant), the downward adjustment still is only two-fifths on the long run.

- Technological change in medicine is likely to have a larger impact on HCE than ageing, which serves to diminish the relative importance of errors in the demographic effects. This finding is in accordance with the historical evidence [see NEWHOUSE (1992)].

Conclusion 14.8. *Population ageing caused by increasing life expectancy has a positive but limited impact on per-capita health care expenditure. It is dwarfed by the influence of technological change in medicine.*

When drawing policy conclusions, it must be taken into account that the analysis presented is restricted to the expenditure side of health insurance, thus ignoring the impact of population ageing on labor income. However, such an impact is likely to exist, and it is of great relevance to systems that rely on contributions levied on labor income (in the guise of a payroll tax) to finance social health insurance (such as in Austria or Germany). Unless retirement age is adjusted, ageing typically causes the ratio of beneficiaries to contributors to increase, very much as in a pension scheme. This issue is addressed in the next section.

14.4.3 Funding of Health Insurance

In countries where social health insurance is financed through a levy on labor income, ageing of population implies a challenge reminiscent of that confronting a pension scheme of the pay-as-you-go type. While the number of contributors in the labor force remains constant or even shrinks, the number of beneficiaries (viz. the retired who do not contribute but have positive HCE) increases. A possible response to this challenge is to inject an element of capital funding into the financing of health insurance, in a way similar to ongoing reforms of social security for old age. By saving for their own future HCE, the young and middle-aged would become less dependent upon future generations for their health care than in a pure pay-as-you-go system.

Before examining the proposal to introduce capital funding to social health insurance, we want to discuss briefly its role in private health insurance. There, at least in principle, individuals cover their lifetime HCE by their lifetime premium payments. At first glance, it does not seem to matter whether insurers save up premium revenue for HCE when old (capital funding), or whether individuals simply pay a premium reflecting their age-specific HCE and save themselves. In Section 5.3.4.1, however, we found that capital funding can be useful to prevent ex-post low risks from opting out of the insurance. This applies to both guaranteed renewable contracts and premium insurance.

In Germany capital funding is imposed on private health insurers by law. Premiums must be calculated to remain constant over an individual's lifetime, at least in real terms. Since HCE rises with age, the premium paid by young individuals exceeds their expected HCE, permitting insurers to accumulate 'ageing provisions' designed to finance HCE in old age that are not covered by the premium. But ageing provisions are not portable, causing individuals hardly ever to switch insurers. In this way guaranteed renewability is imposed by regulation rather than the result of contracting for mutual benefit (as, e.g., in private health insurance of the United States or Switzerland [see, e.g., PATEL AND PAULY (2002)]).

Turning to social health insurance, mandatory membership implies that low risks cannot opt out. Therefore, capital funding could be used exclusively to alleviate the financial burden of future generations with fewer contributors. However, this aim could be reached through pay-as-you-go financing as well as long as every cohort of insured must cover their HCE in each period with their own contributions. As per-capita HCE rises with age, this would imply rising contributions over the life cycle as well. Individuals would need to accumulate private savings to be able to pay these contributions without having to reduce consumption in old age. In this case, capital accumulation would not occur within social health insurance but in private households.

From the point of view of political economy, the accumulation of capital by a public insurance agency is problematic. Politicians will have a strong incentive to keep the contribution rate low in order to gain popularity, especially around (re-)election time. The easiest way to achieve this is to run down any capital reserves that have been built up for future generations.

The political pressure on reserves is weaker if they are assigned to the individuals who generated the savings. This is the concept of *Medical Savings Accounts* (MSA, or, equivalently, *Health Savings Accounts*, HSA) that has been receiving much attention [PAULY AND GOODMAN (1995), HSIAO (1995)]. They typically work in the following way.

Many private health insurance contracts stipulate an annual deductible, making the insured pay the first units of money before coverage sets in. One way to administer these deductibles is to oblige the insured to pay units of money into an individual account at the beginning of each year and to use the accumulated funds to pay for their HCE until they are run down. On December 31, any balance in the account is paid back to the customer.

This provision can now be slightly changed by stipulating that a certain percentage of the balance has to remain in the account. This means that more HCE can be financed out of the account before it is run down. This amounts to an increase of the deductible, which allows the premium to be lowered (see Section 6.3). Provided HCE remain modest at first, the account balance grows over time. At old age, the insured need not to shoulder the burden of an increased premium.

Medical Savings Accounts have the important advantage over the traditional annual deductible of controlling moral hazard much better in the short run. Consumers have an incentive to accumulate MSA credit that is lacking in contracts with a constant annual deductible. Nevertheless, there are two important drawbacks. First, a single year with very high HCE can be enough to exhaust the MSA, forcing the insured to start all over again (unless the HCE is deemed catastrophic by authorities, in which case a separate scheme kicks in). Second, proximity to death is likely to become an even more crucial driver of HCE than in conventional health insurance. Unless the insured have the right to bequeath the MSA balance [which they have, e.g., in Singapore but not in the United States, see PHUA (1999)] they have every incentive to draw on accumulated funds to finance heroic attempts to stave off death. After all, these funds have no other use! In the United States, some plans permit the insured to offset conventional deductibles with MSA credits after a few years. Research by FELDMAN ET AL. (2007) suggests that this option of MSAs serves simply to defer moral hazard effects rather than alleviating them.

> **Conclusion 14.9.** *In private health insurance, capital funding can be useful to prevent ex-post low risks from leaving the plan. In a mandatory social health insurance scheme, capital funding is not necessary to alleviate the financial burden falling on future generations due to population ageing. Age-dependent contributions achieve the same objective; however, they call for capital accumulation in private households. Through Medical Savings Accounts, individuals can build up savings in years of low health care expenditure. However, moral hazard effects likely are merely deferred rather than reduced.*

14.5 International Challenges

14.5.1 Integration of Insurance Markets

Important challenges for European health insurers will originate from the integration of insurance markets within the European Union (EU); similar developments may become relevant for insurers in NAFTA countries in a more distant future. In 1987 the European Court of Justice decided that insurance is subject to the anti-cartel provisions of Art. 85 of the Treaty of Rome like any other branch of industry and that the EU has the authority to regulate insurance. Moreover, the Union Citizenship Directive 2004/38 establishes equal treatment with regard to social benefits of all EU citizens with permanent residence (to be granted after no longer than five years) [see HAILBRONNER (2005)]. At the same time the Court's decision accorded EU member states a long transition period for liberalizing social insurance. Thus, while social health insurers are exempt from the Court's decision in the foreseeable future, they will have to redefine their role – if only because they are increasingly becoming attractive partners for profit-seeking multinational insurance companies:

- Health insurance is characterized by *frequent, comparatively small losses*, occasioning frequent client contacts and hence opportunities for additional sales at low cost.

- Social health insurance covers the *majority of the population* in most countries, with the exception of the United States, its market share attaining 100 percent in many countries.

- Unless prohibited by law, social health insurers may provide the partner insurance company with information about enrollees. This constitutes a valuable input for risk rating in other products, such as life insurance or homeowner's insurance.

- The risk of ill health tends to be *negatively correlated* with risks covered under life insurance and automobile insurance. Costly medical treatment is concentrated among those aged 60 or over, when most life insurance policies have already expired. Likewise, someone who is sick in bed cannot cause a traffic accident. Negatively correlated losses serve to reduce the variance of total loss in a decisive way [see FAMA (1976)]. This means that a portfolio of insurance policies containing combinations of health and other lines of insurance requires less reserves per unit premium, conferring obvious cost advantage on the insurance company and the insured. In fact, the efficiency of entire insurance systems can be judged by its risk diversification effect, i.e., the degree to which payments below expected value in one line are neutralized by payments above expected value in some other line [see ZWEIFEL AND LEHMANN (2001), EUGSTER AND ZWEIFEL (2006)].

For these reasons, multiple-line insurers have considerable interest in cooperating with a social health insurer. They already have profited from this possibility, e.g., in the Netherlands (prior to the reform of 2006 that eliminated the distinction between social and private health insurance). Whereas only domestic insurance companies have been pursuing this strategy up to now [see SCHUT ET AL. (1991)], foreign insurers may well adopt it too in the future, appealing to national treatment provisions under EU and GATT rules. This also means that solidarity *within* a carrier of social health insurance can hardly be sustained.

A further challenge for social health insurance will come from increased mobility of workers in common NAFTA and EU labor markets. As to the EU, ordinance No. 1408/71 stipulates portability of health insurance coverage between member countries. Guest workers from Portugal are thus free to claim German health care services after a few years of residence in Germany, even if they have moved back to Portugal in the meantime [for more detail, see HAILBRONNER (2005)].

Evidently, the *problem of risk selection* (see Chapter 7) takes on a new dimension here. On a national scale it could be solved by getting (nearly) all inhabitants of the country to join social health insurance, either through subsidization or compulsory membership. However, compulsory EU-wide health insurance cannot be counted upon to come into force very soon for citizens of EU countries. In the meantime, national health insurance schemes offering high-quality treatment are running the danger of attracting high risks from other EU countries, causing them to lose their financial equilibrium [see ZWEIFEL AND EUGSTER (2008)].

14.5.2 Migration of Health Care Personnel

For some years now, national diploma of physicians and dentists have been mutually recognized within the EU. As shown in Figure 14.3, there is a definite incentive to migrate especially for physicians. At the end of the 1980s general practitioners in former West Germany earned approximately US$70,000 on average at prices and purchasing parities of 1990. Their colleagues in France had to put up with approximately US$45,000. Thus, by moving to the neighboring country, they would have been able to significantly increase their income. Yet language barriers in particular will continue to block large-scale migration among EU countries in the future. Even within a common language area, income differences of several US$10,000 may be insufficient for physicians to migrate, judging from Canadian experience. As may be gleaned from Figure 14.3, a general practitioner's income in the United States was 50 percent higher for many years without causing considerable migration of Canadian physicians to the United States [see EVANS (1984, p. 301)].

However, the decision to migrate will hardly be based on one year's income but rather on the income stream associated with an *entire career*. For example, general practitioners in the United Kingdom's National Health Service, according to Figure 14.3, earn a comparatively low annual income. In return, they start earning this income at a relatively young age. Evidently, the quantity of interest is not so much the annual income but the lifetime income of a cohort of fully educated physicians. Despite this qualification, Figure 14.3 suggests that Germany is an attractive country for French physicians.

In the case of *nursing staff*, the stakes associated with migration are smaller due to their generally lower income. This means that migration between countries of roughly comparable income levels is less likely for auxiliary health personnel, while the present value of the wage differential in comparison with most developing countries may be large enough to induce migration to industrialized countries [GRAY AND PHILLIPS (1993)].

14.5.3 Direct International Investment in Hospitals

A third international challenge in the future could come from multinational hospital chains. For example, such a chain may introduce new types of surgery not offered by public hospitals of a country. The potential for multinational operations exists, as can be seen in the United States, with the biggest U.S. hospital chain – the Hospital Corporation of America – having over 166 hospitals and 112 outpatient surgical centers at their disposal [see HOSPITAL CORPORATION OF AMERICA (2009)].

To assess the implications of this possible challenge, it is appropriate to recall the economic theory of the multinational enterprise. The existence of enterprises as such – which are founded on hierarchy rather than exchange relations between equals on a market – is explained with reference to the *role of transaction costs*. A multilateral

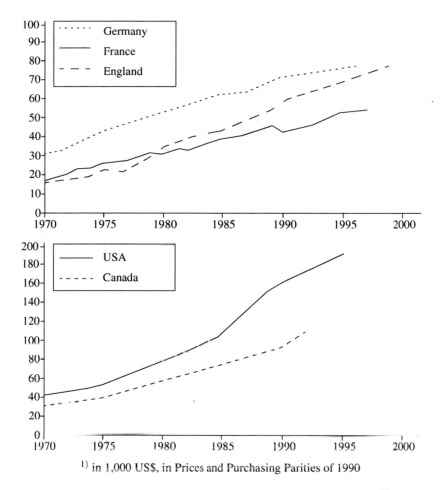

1) in 1,000 US$, in Prices and Purchasing Parities of 1990

Fig. 14.3. Average Physician Incomes, Selected Countries and Years[1)]
Source: OECD (2000)

network of contracts between members of a productive group can be very costly to implement and monitor. Thus, it is replaced by a set of bilateral contracts concluded between the manager and the respective subordinate. Multinational enterprises owe their existence and economic success to the fact that transaction costs loom particularly large in exchanges of goods and services between two countries, where great savings may be achieved by carrying out internal transactions using a standardized legal framework for contracts within the firm. International transfer of know-how in particular becomes less costly under a common set of norms. Indeed, multinational enterprises are specialized in introducing an innovation into many markets within a short period of time [see WILLIAMSON (1981) and MARKUSEN (2002)].

In the case of hospital treatment, transaction costs are considerable in view of the efforts that a patient and his physician must undertake for estimating a hospital's chance of success in a particular field of activity and its quality of treatment in general. A multinational enterprise may lower these costs by guaranteeing a certain *quality standard* worldwide (as do, e.g., Holiday Inn or Best Western in the case of hotel accommodation). Guaranteeing such a standard amounts to an organizational innovation in the sense of Subsection 14.2.1, serving to lower cost (not so much of production but rather of transaction) in several markets. This organizational innovation may be applied to hospitals.

In the long run, however, multinational enterprises should be able to extend their market share in national hospital sectors due to their ability to quickly transfer product innovations from one country to another. Even social health insurers may be willing to do business with these new suppliers, provided they offer a favorable price-performance ratio to their members. The challenge will consist in dropping the domestic purchasing clause in pertinent laws that has been prohibiting social health insurers from negotiating with foreign health care providers [ZWEIFEL (1999, p. 148)]. The advantages of a multinational for-profit enterprise in terms of efficiency will have to be weighed against the possible benefits of a professional ethics orientation.

Conclusion 14.10. *The integration of health insurance as well as the hospital sector in international markets will call for a rewriting of contracts in the health care sectors of countries participating in economic integration. In comparison, migration of physicians and nursing staff represents a less pressing challenge in the foreseeable future.*

14.6 Summary

In this chapter we have analyzed future challenges to health care systems. The focus was on technological and demographic change and on the increasing globalization of health care markets. The main results are the following:

(1) Innovation in health care, according to the medical imperative, must achieve a certain improvement of health status. From the ex ante point of view of an individual, the benchmark for acceptance is equal for process and product innovation but lower for organizational innovation.

(2) In the transition from the individual to the social level, the required standards of performance for all three types of innovation in health care are lowered. Insurance-induced moral hazard and medical imperatives at the level both of objectives and of means constitute likely reasons for this.

(3) The progressive rectangularization of the survival curve may be interpreted as the result of efforts to gain better control over health status. To the extent that this control is due to modern medicine, the unabated willingness to pay for 'flat-of-the-curve' medicine can be explained with reference to people's risk aversion.

(4) The ageing of the population jeopardizes the financial equilibrium of social health insurance. The adjustment of contributions for safeguarding equilibrium may turn membership into an unprofitable investment for present and future generations of workers.

(5) In democratic countries, there is evidence of a Sisyphus Syndrome, meaning that current successes of medicine will burden the health care system with additional expenditure on medical care in the future. The acuteness of the syndrome depends on the extent to which medical services contribute to longevity, the influence of the aged population on the public budget, and inversely on the growth of the working population.

(6) Empirical analysis using OECD country data suggests that additional health care expenditure does contribute to higher remaining life expectancy at higher ages and that higher life expectancy can be claimed to bias spending in favor of health care expenditure. The Sisyphus Syndrome is also found to be of some importance in that 68 percent of extra expenditure in the current year carries over to the following year.

(7) There are three hypotheses with regard to the impact of ageing on health care expenditures. According to the status-quo hypothesis, present age profiles can be extrapolated into the future. The expansion-of-morbidity hypothesis predicts increased survival of costly individuals that would have died. The time-to-death hypothesis claims that the expensive years prior to death will simply be shifted to higher ages.

(8) For the case of Germany and Switzerland at least, future per-capita health care expenditure as predicted by the status-quo hypothesis are 45 percent too high in 2030 if the time-to-death hypothesis is true and 19 percent, if the expansion-of-morbidity hypothesis is correct.

(9) In social health insurance, capital funding is not necessary to alleviate the financial burden falling on future generations. The same objective can be achieved through age-dependent contributions, which would necessitate capital accumulation in private households, where it is better protected from political pressure than in the hands of a social insurer. Medical Savings Accounts can serve this purpose only for those with sufficient income and consistently low health care expenditure.

(10) Economic integration will expose domestic social health insurers and health care providers to international competition, at least within the European Union. In comparison, international migration of physicians and nursing staff represents a less pressing challenge in the foreseeable future.

14.7 Further Reading

The forecasts of health care spending reported in Section 14.4 rely on empirical studies of health care demand. The methodology of individual demand estimation is discussed in DEB AND TRIVEDI (2006). A survey of cross-country comparisons of health care spending is found in GERDTHAM AND JÖNSSON (2000). SMITH (2006) provides an introduction to the issue of international trade in health services.

14.E Exercises

14.1. In the model of Section 14.2, the assumption was made that total income Y is exogenous. This appears restrictive.

(a) Which variables of the model could Y depend on, and how?

(b) Consider the possibility $Y = Y(R^D, ...), \partial Y / \partial R^D > 0$. How could such an assumption be justified, for instance in view of foreign trade?

(c) What are the consequences of b) for the optimal allocation of innovative effort? [Hint: modify equation (14.6) accordingly and start from there.]

14.2. The dynamic stability of the law of motion (14.19) is very important for health policy. Will a one-time increase of health care expenditure taper off as time goes on, or must an explosive process be expected?

(a) In order to clarify the problem, transform the terms of equation (14.19) into elasticities as far as possible. Divide by M_t and introduce the following elasticities,

$$e(\pi_t, M_{t-1}) \equiv -\frac{\partial \pi_t}{\partial M_{t-1}} \frac{M_{t-1}}{\pi_t} \quad \text{and} \quad e(M_t, \beta_t) \equiv \frac{\partial M_t}{\partial \beta_t} \frac{\beta_t}{M_t}.$$

(b) Interpret the resulting equation.

(c) The resulting equation can be written as

$$\dot{M}_t = c \dot{M}_{t-1}, \quad \text{with} \quad \dot{M}_t \equiv \frac{dM_t}{M_t}. \tag{14.19'}$$

   (i) What does c stand for?

   (ii) Use this formula to determine $M_{t+1}, M_{t+2}, \ldots, M_{t+k}$. Why is it important to know whether $c < 1$ or $c > 1$?

   (iii) Estimate the value of c using the evidence presented in Chapter 4 and the predicted age structure of the population. Is the case $c > 1$ a possibility?

References

ALLAIS, M. (1953). Le Comportement de l'Homme Rationelle devant le Risque. Critique de Postulats et Axiomes de l'École Ameéricaine, *Econometrica* 21: 503–546.

ALLEN, R. AND GERTLER, P. (1991). Regulation and the Provision of Quality to Heterogenous Consumers: The Case of Prospective Pricing of Medical Services, *Journal of Regulatory Economics* 3: 361–375.

ARROW, K. (1951). Alternative Approaches to the Theory of Choice in Risk-Taking Situations, *Econometrica* 19: 404–437.

ARROW, K. (1962). Economic Welfare and the Allocation of Resources for Invention, *in* K. ARROW (ed.), *The Rate and Direction of Inventive Activity*, Princeton University Press, Princeton, NJ, 609–625.

ARROW, K. (1963). Uncertainty and the Welfare Economics of Medical Care, *American Economic Review* 53: 941–973.

ARROW, K. (1970). *Essays in the Theory of Risk-Bearing*, North Holland, Amsterdam.

ARROW, K. (1974). Optimal Insurance and Generalized Deductibles, *Scandinavian Actuarial Journal* 57: 1–42.

ASH, A., ELLIS, R. AND YU, W. (1998). Risk Adjusted Payment Models for the Non-Elderly, *Final report*, Health Care Financing Administration, Washington, DC.

ATKINSON, A., RAINWATER, L. AND SMEEDING, T. (1995). *Income Distribution in OECD Countries*, OECD, Paris.

AUSTER, R., LEVESON, I. AND SARACHEK, D. (1969). The Production of Health, an Exploratory Study, *Journal of Human Resources* 4: 411–436.

AVERCH, H. AND JOHNSON, L. (1962). Behavior of the Firm Under Regulatory Constraint, *American Economic Review* 52: 1053–1069.

BAILY, M. (1972). Research and Development Costs and Returns: The U.S. Pharmaceutical Industry, *Journal of Political Economy* 80: 78–85.

BANKER, R. D., CHARNES, A. AND COOPER, W. (1984). Some Models for Estimating Technical and Scale Inefficiencies in Data Envelopment Analysis, *Management Science* 30: 1078–92.

BARR, N. (2004). *The Economics of the Welfare State*, 4th edition, Oxford University Press, Oxford.

BAUMOL, W. AND BRADFORD, D. (1970). Optimal Departures From Marginal Cost Pricing, *American Economic Review* 60: 265–283.

BAUMOL, W., PANZAR, J. AND WILLIG, R. (1982). *Contestable Markets and the Theory of Industrial Structure*, Harcourt Brace Jovanovich, New York.

P. Zweifel et al., *Health Economics*, 2nd ed., DOI 10.1007/978-3-540-68540-1_BM2,
© Springer-Verlag Berlin Heidelberg 2009

BECK, K. AND ZWEIFEL, P. (1998). Cream-Skimming in Deregulated Social Health Insurance: Evidence from Switzerland, *in* P. ZWEIFEL (ed.), *Health, the Medical Profession and Regulation*, Kluwer, Dordrecht, 211–227.

BECKER, G. (1965). A Theory of the Allocation of Time, *Economic Journal* 75: 493–517.

BEHREND, C., GRESS, S., HOLLE, R., REITMEIR, P., TOLKSDORFF, K. AND WASEM, J. (2004). Zur Erklärungskraft des heutigen soziodemografischen Risikostrukturausgleichsmodells – Ergebnisse empirischer Analysen an Prozessdaten einer ostdeutschen Regionalkasse, *Journal of Public Health – Zeitschrift für Gesundheitswissenschaften* 12: 20–31.

BENHAM, L. (1991). Licensure and Competition in Medical Markets, *in* H. FRECH, III (ed.), *Regulating Doctors' Fees: Competition, Benefits and Controls under Medicare*, AEI Press, Washington, DC, 75–90.

BENNETT, J. AND BLAMEY, R. (2001). *The Choice Modelling Approach to Environmental Valuation*, Edward Elgar, Cheltenham UK, Northampton MA.

BERALDO, S., MONTOLIO, D. AND TURATI, G. (2007). Healthy, Educated and Wealthy: Is the Welfare State Really Harmful for Growth?, *Department d'Hisenda Publica. Universitat de Barcelona* .

BHATTACHARYYA, G. AND JOHNSON, R. (1977). *Statistical Concepts and Methods*, J. Wiley & Sons, New York.

BIRCH, S. AND GAFNI, A. (1992). Cost Effectiveness/Utility Analyses: Do Current Decision Rules Lead Us Where We Want to Be?, *Journal of Health Economics* 11: 279–296.

BIRCH, S. AND GAFNI, A. (2006a). Decision Rules in Economic Evaluation, *in* A. JONES (ed.), *The Elgar Companion to Health Economics*, Edward Elgar, Cheltenham, 492–502.

BIRCH, S. AND GAFNI, A. (2006b). Information Created to Evade Reality (ICER), *PharmacoEconomics* 24: 1121–1131.

BLACKORBY, C. AND DONALDSON, D. (1990). The Case Against the Use of the Sum of Compensating Variations in Cost-Benefit Analysis, *Canadian Journal of Economics* 23: 471–494.

BLAMEY, R., BENNETT, J. AND MORRISON, M. (1999). Yea-Saying in Contingent Valuation Survey, *Land Economics* 75: 126–141.

BLEICHRODT, H. (2002). A New Explanation for the Difference Between Time-Tradeoff Utilities and Standard Gamble Utilities, *Health Economics* 11: 447–456.

BLEICHRODT, H. AND JOHANNESSON, M. (1997). An Experimental Test of the Theoretical Foundation of Rating-Scale Valuations, *Medical Decision Making* 17: 208–216.

BLEICHRODT, H. AND PINTO, J. (2005). The Volatility of QALYs Under Non-Expected Utility, *Economic Journal* 115: 533–550.

BLEICHRODT, H. AND QUIGGIN, J. (1997). Characterizing QALYs Under a General Rank Dependent Utility Model, *Journal of Risk and Uncertainty* 15: 151–165.

BLEICHRODT, H. AND QUIGGIN, J. (1999). Life-Cycle Preferences Over Consumption and Health: When Is Cost-Effectiveness Analysis Equivalent to Cost-Benefit Analysis?, *Journal of Health Economics* 18: 681–708.

BLEICHRODT, H., WAKKER, P. AND JOHANNESSON, M. (1997). Characterizing QALYs by Risk Neutrality, *Journal of Risk and Uncertainty* 15: 107–114.

BLOMQUIST, S. AND CHRISTIANSEN, V. (1999). The Political Economy of Publicly Provided Private Goods, *Journal of Public Economics* 73: 31–54.

BLOMQVIST, Å. (1997). Optimal Non-Linear Health Insurance, *Journal of Health Economics* 16: 303–321.

BOADWAY, R. AND BRUCE, N. (1984). *Welfare Economics*, Basil Blackwell, Oxford.

BOADWAY, R., LEITE-MONTEIRO, M., MARCHAND, M. AND PESTIEAU, P. (2003). Social Insurance and Redistribution, *in* S. CNOSSEN AND H.-W. SINN (eds.), *Public Finance and Public Policy in the New Millenium*, McMillan.

BORCK, R. (2007). Voting, Inequality, and Redistribution, *Journal of Economic Surveys* 21: 90–109.

BRENNER, H. (1979). Mortality and the National Economy: A Review and the Experience of England and Wales, 1936-76, *Lancet* 314: 568–573.

BRENNER, H. (1983). Mortality and Economic Instability: Detailed Analyses for Britain, *in* J. JOHN (ed.), *Influence of Economic Instability on Health*, Springer, Berlin, 28–84.

BREUER, M. (2006). Optimal Insurance Contracts without the Non-Negativity Constraint on Indemnities, Revisited, *Geneva Risk and Insurance Review* 31: 5–9.

BREYER, F. (1991). Distribution Effects of Coinsurance Options in Social Health Insurance Systems, *in* G. LÓPEZ-CASASNOVAS (ed.), *Incentives in Health Systems*, Springer, Berlin, 120–133.

BREYER, F. (1995). The Political Economy of Rationing in Social Health Insurance, *Journal of Population Economics* 8: 137–148.

BREYER, F. AND FELDER, S. (2005). Mortality Risk and the Value of a Statistical Life: The Dead-Anyway Effect Revis(it)ed, *Geneva Risk and Insurance Review* 30: 14–55.

BREYER, F. AND FELDER, S. (2006). Life Expectancy and Health Care Expenditures in the 21st Century: A New Forecast for Germany Using the Costs of Dying, *Health Policy* 75: 178–186.

BREYER, F., HEINECK, M. AND LORENZ, N. (2003). Determinants of Health Care Utilization by German Sickness Fund Members – With Application to Risk Adjustment, *Health Economics* 12: 367–376.

BREYER, F., KLIEMT, H. AND THIELE, F. (eds.) (2001). *Rationing in Medicine: Ethical, Legal and Practical Aspects*, Springer, Berlin.

BREYER, F. AND SCHULTHEISS, C. (2002). "Primary" Rationing of Health Services in Ageing Societies – A Normative Analysis, *International Journal of Health Care Finance and Economics* 2: 247–264.

BROOK, R., WARE, JR., J., ROGERS, W., KEELER, E., DAVIES, A., DONALD, C., GOLDBERG, G., LOHR, K., MASTHAY, P. AND NEWHOUSE, J. (1983). Does Free Care Improve Adults' Health? Results from a Randomized Controlled Trial, *New England Journal of Medicine* 309: 1426–1434.

BROOME, J. (1982a). Trying to Value a Life, *Journal of Public Economics* 9: 91–100.

BROOME, J. (1982b). Uncertainty in Welfare Economics and the Value of Life, *in* M. JONES-LEE (ed.), *The Value of Life and Safety*, North Holland, Amsterdam, 201–216.

BRYAN, S., BUXTON, M., SHELDON, R. AND GRANT, A. (1998). Magnetic Resonance Imaging for the Investigation of Knee Injuries: An Investigation of Preferences, *Health Economics* 7: 595–603.

BRYAN, S., GOLD, L., SHELDON, R. AND BUXTON, M. (2000). Preference Measurement Using Conjoint Methods: An Empirical Investigation of Reliability, *Health Economics* 9: 385–395.

BUNDESAMT FÜR STATISTIK (1973). *Statistisches Jahrbuch der Schweiz*, Verlag Neue Zürcher Zeitung, Zürich.

BUNDESMINISTERIUM FÜR GESUNDHEIT (2001). *Daten des Gesundheitswesens*, Schriftenreihe des Bundesministeriums für Gesundheit, Vol. 137, Stuttgart.

BUTLER, J. (1999). *The Ethics of Health Care Rationing*, Cassell, London et al.

BYRNE, M., O'MALLEY, K. AND SUAREZ-ALMAZOR, M. (2005). Willingness to Pay Per Quality-Adjusted Life Year in a Study of Knee Osteoarthritis, *Medical Decision Making* 25: 655–666.

CAMERON, A., TRIVEDI, P., MILNE, F. AND PIGGOTT, J. (1988). A Microeconometric Model of the Demand for Health Care and Health Insurance in Australia, *Review of Economic Studies* 55: 85–106.

CARLSEN, F. AND GRYTTEN, J. (1998). More Physicians: Improved Availability or Induced Demand?, *Health Economics* 7: 495–508.

CARLTON, D. AND PERLOFF, J. (2000). *Modern Industrial Organization*, 3rd edition, Addison-Wesley, Reading MA.

CHALKLEY, M. AND MALCOMSON, J. (1998a). Contracting for Health Services when Patient Demand Does Not Reflect Quality, *Journal of Health Economics* 17: 1–19.

CHALKLEY, M. AND MALCOMSON, J. (1998b). Contracting for Health Services with Unmonitored Quality, *Economic Journal* 108: 1093–1110.

CHALKLEY, M. AND MALCOMSON, J. (2000). Government Purchasing of Health Services, *in* A. CULYER AND J. NEWHOUSE (eds.), *Handbook of Health Economics*, Vol. Band 1A, Elsevier, Amsterdam, 847–890.

CHARNES, A., COOPER, W. AND RHODES, E. (1978). Measuring the Efficiency of Decision Making Units, *European Journal of Operational Research* 2: 429–444.

CHOLLET, D. AND LEWIS, M. (1997). Private Insurance: Principles and Practice, *in* G. J. SCHIEBER (ed.), *Innovations in Health Care Financing: Proceedings of a World Bank Conference*, Nr. 365 *in World Bank Discussion Paper*, World Bank, Washington, DC, 77–114.

CHRISTENSEN, L., JORGENSON, D. AND LAU, L. (1973). Transcendental Logarithmic Production Frontiers, *Review of Economics and Statistics* 55: 28–45.

CLARK, D., KORFF, M. V., SANDERS, K., BALUCH, W. AND SIMON, G. (1995). A Chronic Disease Score with Empirically Derived Weights, *Medical Care* 33: 783–795.

COATE, S. (1995). Altruism, the Samaritan's Dilemma and Government Transfer Policy, *American Economic Review* 85: 46–57.

COCHRANE, J. (1995). Time-Consistent Health Insurance, *Journal of Political Economy* 103: 445–473.

COELLI, T., RAO, D. AND BATTESE, G. (1998). *An Introduction to Efficiency and Productivity Analysis*, Kluwer, Dordrecht.

COMANOR, W. (1986). The Political Economy of the Pharmaceutical Industry, *Journal of Economic Literature* 24: 1178–1217.

COMANOR, W., FRECH, III, H. AND MILLER, JR., R. (2006). Is the United States an Outlier in Health Care and Health Outcomes? A Preliminary Analysis, *International Journal of Health Care Finance and Economics* 6: 3–23.

CONGLETON, R. (2003). The Median Voter Model, *in* C. ROWLEY AND F. SCHNEIDER (eds.), *The Encyclopedia of Public Choice*, Kluwer, 382–386.

CONGRESSIONAL BUDGET OFFICE (1998). *How Increased Competition from Generic Drugs has Affected Prices and Returns in the Pharmaceutical Industry*, Congressional Budget Office, Washington, DC. http://www.cbo.gov/doc.cfm?index=655.

COOK, P. AND GRAHAM, D. (1977). The Demand for Insurance Protection: The Case of Irreplaceable Commodities, *Quarterly Journal of Economics* 91: 143–156.

COOPER, W., SEIFORD, L. AND TONE, K. (2006). *Data Envelopment Analysis: A Comprehensive Text with Models, Applications, References and DEA-Solver Software*, 2nd edition, Springer, New York.

CREMER, H. AND PESTIEAU, P. (1996). Redistributive Taxation and Social Insurance, *International Tax and Public Finance* 3: 281–295.

CROCKER, K. AND SNOW, A. (1985a). The Efficiency of Competitive Equilibria in Insurance Markets with Asymmetric Information, *Journal of Public Economics* 26: 207–219.

CROCKER, K. AND SNOW, A. (1985b). A Simple Tax Structure for Competitive Equilibrium and Redistribution in Insurance Markets with Asymmetric Information, *Southern Economic Journal* 51: 1142–50.

CULYER, A. (1971). The Nature of the Commodity 'Health Care' and its Efficient Allocation, *Oxford Economic Papers* 23: 189–211.

CULYER, A. (1989). The Normative Economics of Health Care Finance and Provision, *Oxford Review of Economic Policy* 5: 34–58.

CULYER, A. (1990). Commodities, Characteristics of Commodities, Characteristics of People, Utilities, and Quality of Life, *in* S. BALDWIN, C. GODFREY AND C. PROPPER (eds.), *Quality of Life: Perspectives and Policies*, Routledge, London, 9–27.

CUMMINGS, R., BROOKSHIRE, D. AND SCHULZE, W. (1986). *Valuing Environment Goods: An Assessment of the Contingent Valuation Method*, Littlefield, Totowa, NJ.

CUTLER, D. AND REBER, S. (1998). Paying for Health Insurance: The Trade-Off Between Competition and Adverse Selection, *Quarterly Journal of Economics* 113: 433–466.

CUTLER, D. AND ZECKHAUSER, R. (2000). The Anatomy of Health Insurance, *in* A. CULYER AND J. NEWHOUSE (eds.), *Handbook of Health Economics*, Vol. 1A, Elsevier, Amsterdam, 563–643.

DAFNY, L. (2005). How Do Hospitals Respond to Price Changes?, *American Economic Review* 95: 1525–1547.

DAHLBY, B. (1981). Adverse Selection and Pareto Improvements Through Compulsory Insurance, *Public Choice* 37: 547–558.

DANZON, P. (1997a). *Pharmaceutical Price Regulation – National Policies versus Global Interests*, AEI Press, Washington, DC.

DANZON, P. (1997b). Price Discrimination for Pharmaceuticals: Welfare Effects in the US and the EU, *International Journal of the Economics of Business* 4: 301–321.

DANZON, P. (2000). Liability for Medical Malpractice, *in* A. CULYER AND J. NEWHOUSE (eds.), *Handbook of Health Economics*, Vol. 1B, Elsevier, Amsterdam, 1339–1404.

DANZON, P. AND CHAO, L.-W. (2000). Cross-National Price Differences for Pharmaceuticals: How Large, and Why?, *Journal of Health Economics* 19: 159–195.

DARBÀ, J. AND ROVIRA, J. (1998). Parallel Imports of Pharmaceuticals in the European Union, *PharmacoEconomics* 14 (Suppl.1): 129–136.

DARBY, M. AND KARNI, E. (1973). Free Competition and the Optimal Amount of Fraud, *Journal of Law & Economics* 16: 67–88.

DASGUPTA, P. AND MASKIN, E. (1986). The Existence of Equilibrium in Discontinuous Economic Games, *Review of Economic Studies* 46: 1–41.

DAVE, D. AND KAESTNER, R. (2006). Health Insurance and Ex Ante Moral Hazard: Evidence from Medicare, *NBER Working Paper 12764*.

DEB, P. AND TRIVEDI, P. (2006). Empirical Models of Health Care Use, *in* A. JONES (ed.), *The Elgar Companion to Health Economics*, Edward Elgar, Cheltenham, 147–155.

DEBREU, G. (1959). *Theory of Value: An Axiomatic Analysis of Economic Equilibrium*, Wiley, London.

DEBROCK, L. (1985). Market Structure, Innovation and Optimal Patent Life, *Journal of Law and Economics* 28: 223–44.

DEVARAJAN, S., SWAROOP, V. AND ZOU, H.-F. (1996). The Composition of Public Expenditure and Economic Growth, *Journal of Monetary Economics* 37: 313–344.

DIEWERT, W. (1974). Applications of Duality Theory, *in* M. INTRILIGATOR AND D. KENDRICK (eds.), *Frontiers of Quantitative Economics*, Vol. II, North-Holland, Amsterdam, 106–171.

DIMASI, J., HANSEN, R. AND GRABOWSKI, H. (2003). The Price of Innovation: New Estimates of Drug development Costs, *Journal of Health Economics* 22: 151–185.

DIMASI, J., HANSEN, R., GRABOWSKI, H. AND LASAGNA, L. (1991). Cost of Innovation in the Pharmaceutical Industry, *Journal of Health Economics* 10: 107–142.

DIONNE, G. (1992). *Contributions to Insurance Economics*, Kluwer, Dordrecht.

DIONNE, G. (2000). *Handbook of Insurance*, Kluwer, Dordrecht.

DIONNE, G. AND DOHERTY, N. (1992). Adverse Selection in Insurance Markets: A Selective Survey, *in* G. DIONNE (ed.), *Contributions to Insurance Economics*, Kluwer, Dordrecht, 97–140.

DOLAN, P. (2000). The Measurement of Health-Related Quality of Life for Use in Resource Allocation Decisions in Health Care, *in* A. CULYER AND J. NEWHOUSE (eds.), *Handbook of Health Economics*, Vol. 1B, Elsevier, Amsterdam, 1723–1760.

DRANOVE, D. (1987). Rate-Setting by Diagnosis Related Groups and Hospital Specialization, *Rand Journal of Economics* 18: 417–427.

DRANOVE, D. (1988). Pricing by Non-Profit Institutions: Cost Shifting, *Journal of Health Economics* 7: 47–57.

DRANOVE, D. AND SATTERTHWAITE, M. (2000). The Industrial Organization of Health Care Markets, *in* A. CULYER AND J. NEWHOUSE (eds.), *Handbook of Health Economics*, Vol. 1B, Elsevier, Amsterdam, 1093–1139.

DRANOVE, D. AND WEHNER, P. (1994). Physician-Induced Demand for Childbirths, *Journal of Health Economics* 13: 61–73.

DRÈZE, J. (1962). L'Utilité Sociale d'une Vie Humaine, *Revue Française de Recherche Opérationelle* 1: 93–118.

DRUMMOND, M., SCULPHER, M., TORRANCE, G., O'BRIEN, B. AND STODDART, G. (2005). *Methods for the Economic Evaluation of Health Care Programmes*, 3rd edition, Oxford University Press, Oxford.

DUAN, N. (1983). Smearing Estimate: A Nonparametric Retransformation Method, *Journal of the American Statistical Association* 78: 605–690.

DUAN, N., MANNING, W., MORRIS, C. AND NEWHOUSE, J. (1984). Choosing Between the Sample-Selection Model and the Multi-Part Model, *Journal of Business and Economic Statistics* 2: 283–289.

EECKHOUDT, L., GOLLIER, C. AND SCHLESINGER, H. (2005). *Economic and Financial Decisions Under Risk*, Princeton University Press, Princeton.

EISNER, R. AND STROTZ, R. (1961). Flight Insurance and the Theory of Choice, *Journal of Political Economy* 69: 355–368.

ELLIS, R. (1998). Creaming, Skimping and Dumping: Provider Competition on the Intensive and Extensive Margins, *Journal of Health Economics* 17: 537–555.

ELLIS, R. (2008). Risk Adjustment in Health Care Markets: Concepts and Applications, *in* M. LU AND E. JONSSON (eds.), *Financing Health Care: New Ideas for a Changing Society*, Wiley-VCH, Weinheim, 177–222.

ELLIS, R. AND MCGUIRE, T. (1986). Provider Behavior Under Prospective Reimbursement: Cost Sharing and Supply, *Journal of Health Economics* 5: 129–151.

EMONS, W. (1997). Credence Goods Monopolists, *International Journal of Industrial Organization* 19: 357–389.

ENTHOVEN, A. (1980). *Health Plan: The Only Practical Solution to the Soaring Cost of Medical Care*, Addison-Wesley, Reading, MA.

ENTHOVEN, A. (1988). *Theory and Practice of Managed Competition in Health Care Finance*, North Holland, Amsterdam.

EPPLE, D. AND ROMANO, R. (1996a). Ends Against the Middle: Determining Public Service Provision when There Are Private Alternatives, *Journal of Public Economics* 62: 297–325.

EPPLE, D. AND ROMANO, R. (1996b). Public Provision of Private Goods, *Journal of Political Economy* 104: 57–84.

EUGSTER, P. AND ZWEIFEL, P. (2006). Correlated Risks: A Conflict of Interest Between Insurers and Consumers and Its Resolution, *Working paper*, University of Zurich.

EVANS, R. (1974). Supplier-Induced Demand: Some Empirical Evidence and Implications, *in* M. PERLMAN (ed.), *The Economics of Health and Medical Care*, Macmillan, New York, 162–173.

EVANS, R. (1984). *Strained Mercy. The Economics of Canadian Health Care*, Butterworths, Toronto.

FAMA, E. (1976). *Foundations of Finance*, Basil Blackwell, New York.

FAYISSA, B. AND GUTEMA, P. (2005). Estimating a Health Production Function for Sub-Saharan Africa (SSA), *Applied Economics* 37: 155–164.

FEDERAL STATISTICAL OFFICE OF GERMANY (2001). *Statistical Yearbook (Statistisches Jahrbuch)*, Federal Statistical Office of Germany (Statistisches Bundesamt für Deutschland), Wiesbaden.

FEDERAL STATISTICAL OFFICE OF GERMANY (2003a). *International Statistical Yearbook (Statistische Jahrbuch für das Ausland)*, Federal Statistical Office of Germany (Statistisches Bundesamt für Deutschland), Wiesbaden.

FEDERAL STATISTICAL OFFICE OF GERMANY (2003b). *Statistical Yearbook (Statistisches Jahrbuch)*, Federal Statistical Office of Germany (Statistisches Bundesamt für Deutschland), Wiesbaden.

FEDERAL STATISTICAL OFFICE OF GERMANY (2007). *Statistical Yearbook (Statistisches Jahrbuch)*, Federal Statistical Office of Germany (Statistisches Bundesamt für Deutschland), Wiesbaden.

FELDMAN, R., PARENTE, S. AND CHRISTIANSON, J. (2007). Consumer Directed Health Plans: New Evidence on Spending and Utilization, *Inquiry* 44: 26–40.

FELDSTEIN, P. (2005). *Health Care Economics*, 6th edition, Delmar, Clifton Park, NY.

FELDSTEIN, P. (2006). *The Politics of Health Legislation: An Economic Perspective*, 3rd edition, Health Administration Press, Chicago.

FETTER, R., SHIN, Y., FREEMAN, J., AVERILL, R. AND THOMPSON, J. (1980). Case-Mix Definition by Diagnosis-Related Groups, *Medical Care* 18 (Suppl.): 1–53.

FOLLAND, S., GOODMAN, A. AND STANO, M. (2006). *The Economics of Health and Health Care*, 5th edition, Prentice-Hall, Upper Saddle River, NJ.

FOUGÈRE, M. AND MÉRETTE, M. (1999). Population Ageing and Economic Growth in Seven OECD Countries, *Economic Modelling* 16: 411–427.

FRANK, R., GLAZER, J. AND MCGUIRE, T. (2000). Measuring Adverse Selection in Managed Health Care, *Journal of Health Economics* 19: 829–854.

FRANKEL, M. (1979). Hazard, Opportunity and the Valuation of Life, *Preliminary report*, Department of Economics, University of Illinois, Urbana-Champaign IL.

FRECH, III, H. AND MILLER, JR., R. (1999). *The Productivity of Health Care and Pharmaceuticals: An International Analysis*, The AEI Press, Washington, DC.

FRICK, K. (1998). Consumer Capital Market Constraints and Guaranteed Renewable Insurance, *Journal of Risk and Uncertainty* 16: 271–278.

FRIES, J. (1980). Aging, Natural Death, and the Compression of Morbidity, *New England Journal of Medicine* 303: 130–135.

FUCHS, V. (1968). The Growing Demand for Medical Care, *New England Journal of Medicine* 179: 190–195.

FUCHS, V. (1974). Some Economic Aspects of Mortality in Developed Countries, *in* M. PERLMAN (ed.), *The Economics of Health and Medical Care*, Macmillan, London, 174–193.

FUCHS, V. (1978). The Supply of Surgeons and the Demand for Operations, *Journal of Human Resources* 13 (Suppl.): 35–56.

FUCHS, V. (1984a). The "Rationing" of Medical Care, *New England Journal of Medicine* 311: 1572–1573.

FUCHS, V. (1984b). Though Much Is Taken: Reflections on Aging, Health and Medical Care, *Milbank Memorial Fund Quarterly/Health and Society* 61: 143–166.

FUCHS, V. (1986). *The Health Economy*, Harvard University Press, Cambridge, MA.

GARBER, A. (2000). Advances in CE Analysis, *in* A. CULYER AND J. NEWHOUSE (eds.), *Handbook of Health Economics*, Vol. 1A, Elsevier, Amsterdam, 181–221.

GEGAX, D. AND STANLEY, L. (1997). Validating Conjoint and Hedonic Preference Measures: Evidence from Valuing Reductions in Risk, *Quarterly Journal of Business and Economics* 36: 31–54.

GERDTHAM, U.-G. AND JÖNSSON, B. (2000). International Comparisons of Health Expenditure, *in* A. CULYER AND J. NEWHOUSE (eds.), *Handbook of Health Economics*, Vol. Band 1A, Elsevier, Amsterdam, 11–53.

GERDTHAM, U.-G., JÖNSSON, B., MACFARLAN, M. AND OXLEY, H. (1998). The Determinants of Health Expenditure in the OECD Countries: A Pooled Data Analysis, *in* P. ZWEIFEL (ed.), *Health, the Medical Profession, and Regulation. Developments in Health Economics and Public Policy*, Kluwer Academic, Boston, 113–134.

GERDTHAM, U.-G. AND RUHM, C. (2006). Death Rise in Good Economic Times – Evidence from OECD, *Economics and Human Biology* 4: 298–316.

GERDTHAM, U.-G., SØGAARD, J., JÖNSSON, B. AND ANDERSSON, F. (1992). A Pooled Cross-Section Analysis of the Health Care Expenditures of the OECD Countries, *in* P. ZWEIFEL AND H. FRECH, III (eds.), *Health Economics Worldwide*, Kluwer Academic, Boston, 287–310.

GERFIN, M., SPYCHER, S. AND LEU, R. (1992). The Validity of the MIMIC Health Index – Some Empirical Evidence, *in* P. ZWEIFEL AND H. FRECH, III (eds.), *Health Economics Worldwide*, Kluwer, Dordrecht, 109–142.

GLAZER, J. AND MCGUIRE, T. (2000). Optimal Risk Adjustment in Markets with Adverse Selection: An Application to Managed Care, *American Economic Review* 90: 1055–1071.

GLAZER, J. AND MCGUIRE, T. (2002). Setting Health Plan Premiums to Ensure Efficient Quality in Health Care: Minimum Variance Optimal Risk Adjustment, *Journal of Public Economics* 84: 153–173.

GLAZER, J. AND MCGUIRE, T. (2006). Optimal Risk Adjustment, *in* A. JONES (ed.), *The Elgar Companion to Health Economics*, Edward Elgar, Cheltenham, 279–285.

GLIED, S. (2000). Managed Care, *in* A. CULYER AND J. NEWHOUSE (eds.), *Handbook of Health Economics*, Vol. 1A, Elsevier, Amsterdam, 707–753.

GLOMM, G. AND RAVIKUMAR, B. (1998). Opting Out of Publicly Provided Services: A Majority Voting Result, *Social Choice and Welfare* 15: 187–199.

GOLDBERGER, A. (1974). Unobservable Variables in Econometrics, *in* P. ZAREMBKA (ed.), *Frontiers in Econometrics*, Academic Press, New York, 193–213.

GOLLIER, C. (1987). The Design of Optimal Insurance Contracts without the Nonnegativity Constraint on Claims, *Journal of Risk and Insurance* 54: 314–324.

GOLLIER, C. (2000). Optimal Insurance Design: What Can We Do with and without Expected Utility?, *in* G. DIONNE (ed.), *Handbook of Insurance*, Kluwer, Dordrecht, 97–116.

GOTTSCHALK, P. AND SMEEDING, T. (1997). Cross-National Comparisons of Earnings and Income Inequality, *Journal of Economic Literature* 35: 633–687.

GOULD, J. (1969). The Expected Utility Hypothesis and the Selection of Optimal Deductibles for a Given Insurance Policy, *Journal of Business* 42: 143–151.

GOUVEIA, M. (1997). Majority Rule and the Public Provision of a Private Good, *Public Choice* 93: 221–244.

GRABOWSKI, H., HANSEN, R. AND DIMASI, J. (2002). Returns on Research and Development for 1990s New Drug Introductions, *PharmacoEconomics* 20 (Suppl.3): 11–29.

GRABOWSKI, H. AND VERNON, J. (1990). A New Look at the Returns and Risks to Pharmaceutical R&D, *Management Science* 36: 804–821.

GRABOWSKI, H. AND VERNON, J. (1994). Returns to R&D on New Drug Introductions in the 1980s, *Journal of Health Economics* 13: 383–406.

GRABOWSKI, H. AND VERNON, J. (2000). The Determinants of Pharmaceutical Research and Development Expenditures, *Journal of Evolutionary Economics* 10: 201–215.

GRAVELLE, H. (1984). Editorial: Time Series Analysis of Mortality and Unemployment, *Journal of Health Economics* 3: 297–306.

GRAVELLE, H. AND REES, R. (2004). *Microeconomics*, 3rd edition, Pearson Education, Harlow, England.

GRAY, A. AND PHILLIPS, V. (1993). Nursing in a European Labour Market: An Economic Perspective, *in* C. NORMAN AND J. VAUGHAN (eds.), *Europe Without Frontiers. The Implications for Health*, J. Wiley & Sons, Chichester, 91–110.

GREENE, W. (2008). *Econometric Analysis*, 6th edition, Prentice Hall, Upper Saddle River, NJ.

GREENWALD, L., ESPOSITO, A., INGBER, M. AND LEVY, J. (1998). Risk Adjustment for the Medicare Program: Lessons Learned from Research and Demonstrations, *Inquiry* 35: 193–209.

GROSSMAN, M. (1972a). *The Demand for Health: A Theoretical and Empirical Investigation*, Columbia University Press of the National Bureau of Economic Research, New York.

GROSSMAN, M. (1972b). On the Concept of Health Capital and the Demand for Health, *Journal of Political Economy* 80: 223–250.

GROSSMAN, M. (2000). The Human Capital Model, *in* A. CULYER AND J. NEWHOUSE (eds.), *Handbook of Health Economics*, Vol. 1A, Elsevier, Amsterdam, 347–408.

GRUBER, J. AND OWINGS, M. (1996). Physician Financial Incentives and Cesarean Section Delivery, *Rand Journal of Economics* 27: 99–123.

HADLEY, J. (ed.) (1982). *More Medical Care, Better Health?*, Urban Institute, Washington, DC.

HADLEY, J. AND ZUCKERMANN, S. (1994). The Role of Efficiency Measurement in Hospital Rate Setting, *Journal of Health Economics* 13: 335–340.

HAILBRONNER, K. (2005). Union Citizenship and Access to Social Benefits, *Common Market Law Review* 42: 1245–1267.

HAMMITT, J. AND GRAHAM, J. (1999). Willingness to Pay for Health Protection: Inadequate Sensitivity to Probability?, *Journal of Risk and Uncertainty* 18: 33–62.

HAMMITT, J. AND TREICH, N. (2007). Statistical vs. Identified Lives in Benefit-Cost Analysis, *Journal of Risk and Uncertainty* 35: 45–66.

HANSEN, R. (1979). The Pharmaceutical Development Process: Estimate of Current Development Cost and Times and the Effects of Regulatory Changes, *in* R. CHIEN (ed.), *Issues in Pharmaceutical Economics*, Lexington Books, Lexington MA, 151–187.

HARSANYI, J. (1955). Cardinal Welfare, Individualistic Ethics, and Interpersonal Comparisons of Utility, *Journal of Political Economy* 63: 309–321.

HAUSMAN, J. (1978). Specification Tests in Econometrics, *Econometrica* 52: 1219–1240.

HEALTH CARE FINANCING ADMINISTRATION (1983). *The New IDC-9-CM Diagnosis-Related Groups Classification Scheme*, Johns Hopkins University Press, Baltimore.

HELLWIG, M. (1987). Some Recent Developments in the Theory of Competition in Markets with Adverse Selection, *European Economic Review* 31: 319–325.

HENSHER, D. (1997). Stated Preference Analysis of Travel Choices: The State of Practice, *in* T. OUM, J. DODGSON AND D. HENSHER (eds.), *Transport Economics: Selected Readings*, Harwood Academic in cooperation with the Korea Research Foundation for the 21st Century, Amsterdam, 81–109.

HOFFMEYER, U. AND MCCARTHY, T. (1994). *Financing Health Care*, Vol. I, Kluwer, Dordrecht.

HOLLINGSWORTH, B. (2003). Non-Parametric and Parametric Applications Measuring Efficiency in Health Care, *Health Care Management Science* 6: 203–218.

HOLMSTRÖM, B. (1979). Moral Hazard and Observability, *Bell Journal of Economics* 10(1): 74–91.

HOLMSTRÖM, B. AND MILGROM, P. (1991). Multitask Principal-Agent Analyses: Incentive Contracts, Asset Ownership, and Job Design, *Journal of Law, Economics and Organisation* 7: 24–52.

HÖPFLINGER, F. (1997). Haushalts- und Familienstrukturen im intereuropäischen Vergleich (Structure of Households and Families Across Europe), *in* S. HRADIL AND S. IMMERFALL (eds.), *Die westeuropäischen Gesellschaften im Vergleich*, Leske und Budrich, Opladen.

HOSPITAL CORPORATION OF AMERICA (2009). HCA Fact Sheet, http://www.hcahealthcare.com/CPM/CurrentFactSheet1.pdf.

HOUSTON, M. (1989). New Insights and New Approaches for the Treatment of Essential Hypertension: Selection of Therapy Based on Coronary Heart Disease Risk Factor Analysis, Hemodynamic Profiles, Quality of Life, and Subsets of Hypertension, *American Heart Journal* 117: 911–951.

HOY, M., LIVERNOIS, J., MCKENNA, C., REES, R. AND STENGOS, T. (2001). *Mathematics for Economics*, 2nd edition, MIT Press, Cambridge, MA.

HSIAO, W. (1995). Peer Review: Medical Savings Accounts: Lessons From Singapore, *Health Affairs* 14 (2): 260–266.

HUBERMAN, G., MAYERS, D. AND SMITH, JR., C. W. (1983). Optimal Insurance Policy Indemnity Schedules, *Bell Journal of Economics* 14: 415–426.

HURLEY, J. (2000). An Overview of the Normative Economics of the Health Sector, *in* A. CULYER AND J. NEWHOUSE (eds.), *Handbook of Health Economics*, Vol. 1A, Elsevier, Amsterdam, 55–118.

JACK, W. (2006). Optimal Risk Adjustment with Adverse Selection and Spatial Competition, *Journal of Health Economics* 25: 908–926.

JACOB, J. AND LUNDIN, D. (2005). A Median Voter Model of Health Insurance with Ex Post Moral Hazard, *Journal of Health Economics* 24: 407–426.

JAYNES, G. (1978). Equilibria in Monopolistically Competitive Insurance Markets, *Journal of Economic Theory* 19: 394–422.

JOGLEKAR, P. AND PATERSON, M. (1986). A Closer Look at the Returns and Risks of Pharmaceutical R&D, *Journal of Health Economics* 5: 107–193.

JOHANNESSON, M. (1996). *Theory and Methods of Economic Evaluation of Health Care*, Kluwer, Dordrecht.

JOHANNESSON, M., PLISKIN, J. AND WEINSTEIN, M. (1994). A Note on QALYs, Time Tradeoff, and Discounting, *Medical Decision Making* 14: 188–193.

JOHANSSON, P. AND PALME, M. (2005). Moral Hazard and Sickness Insurance, *Journal of Public Economics* 89: 1879–1890.

JOHNSON, F. R., MANZHAF, M. AND DESVOUSGES, W. (2000). Willingness to Pay for Improved Respiratory and Cardiovascular Health: A Multiple-Format, Stated-Preference Approach, *Health Economics* 9: 295–317.

JONES, A. (2000). Health Econometrics, *in* A. CULYER AND J. NEWHOUSE (eds.), *Handbook of Health Economics*, Vol. 1A, Elsevier, Amsterdam, 265–344.

JONES-LEE, M. (1974). The Value of Changes in the Probability of Death or Injury, *Journal of Political Economy* 80: 623–648.

JONES-LEE, M., HAMMERTON, M. AND PHILLIPS, P. (1985). The Value of Safety: Results of a National Sample Survey, *Economic Journal* 95: 49–72.

JÖRESKOG, K. (1973). A General Method for Estimating a Linear Structural Equation System, *in* A. GOLDBERGER AND O. DUNCAN (eds.), *Structural Equation Models in the Social Sciences*, Seminar Press, New York, 85–112.

KAHNEMAN, D. AND TVERSKY, A. (1979). Prospect Theory: An Analysis of Decision Under Risk, *Econometrica* 47: 263–291.

KANNEL, W. AND THOM, T. (1984). Declining Cardiovascular Mortality, *Circulation* 70: 331–336.

KEELER, E. (1987). *The Demand for Episodes of Treatment*, Rand Corporation, Santa Monica.

KEELER, E. AND ROLPH, J. (1983). How Cost Sharing Reduced Medical Spending of Participants in the Health Insurance Experiment, *Journal of the American Medical Association* 249: 2220–2222.

KEENEY, R. AND RAIFFA, H. (1976). *Decisions with Multiple Objectives: Preferences and Tradeoffs*, Wiley, New York.

KESSEL, R. (1958). Price Discrimination in Medicine, *Journal of Law and Economics* 1: 20–53.

KIFMANN, M. (1999). Community Rating and Choice Between Traditional Health Insurance and Managed Care, *Health Economics* 8: 563–578.

KIFMANN, M. (2002). Community Rating in Health Insurance and Different Benefit Packages, *Journal of Health Economics* 21: 719 – 737.

KIFMANN, M. (2006a). Health Insurance in a Democracy: Why Is It Public and Why Are Premiums Income-Related?, *Public Choice* 124: 283–308.

KIFMANN, M. (2006b). Risk Selection and Complementary Health Insurance: The Swiss Approach, *International Journal of Health Care Finance and Economics* 6: 151–170.

KIFMANN, M. AND LORENZ, N. (2009). Optimal Cost Reimbursement of Health Insurers to Reduce Risk Selection, *Working paper*, Universität Konstanz.

KING, J., TSEVAT, J., LAVE, J. AND ROBERTS, M. (2005). Willingness to Pay for a Quality-Adjusted Life Year: Implications for Societal Health Care Resource Allocation, *Medical Decision Making* 25: 667–677.

KLARMAN, H., FRANCIS, J. AND ROSENTHAL, G. (1968). Cost-Effectiveness Analysis Applied to the Treatment of Chronic Renal Disease, *Medical Care* 6: 48–54.

KLOSE, T. (1999). The Contingent Valuation Method in Health Care, *Health Policy* 47: 97–123.

KRÄMER, W. (1982). *Wer leben will, muß zahlen. Die Kostenexplosion im Gesundheitswesen und ihre möglichen Auswirkungen (Who Wants to Live Must Pay. The Cost Explosion in the Health Care Sector and Its Possible Consquences)*, Econ, Düsseldorf.

KUMBHAKAR, S. AND LOVELL, C. (2000). *Stochastic Frontier Analysis*, Cambridge University Press, Cambridge.

LABELLE, R., STODDART, G. AND RICE, T. (1994). A Re-Examination of the Meaning and Importance of Supplier-Induced Demand, *Journal of Health Economics* 13: 347–368.

LAFFONT, J.-J. (1989). *The Economics of Uncertainty and Information*, MIT Press, Cambridge, MA.

LAFFONT, J.-J. AND TIROLE, J. (1993). *A Theory of Incentives in Procurement and Regulation*, MIT Press, Cambridge, MA.

494   References

LAMERS, L. (1999).   Risk Adjusted Capitation Based on the Diagnostic Group Model: An Empirical Evaluation with Health Survey in Formation, *Health Services Research* 33: 1727–1744.

LANCASTER, K. (1966). A New Approach to Consumer Theory, *Journal of Political Economy* 74: 132–57.

LANCASTER, K. (1971). *Consumer Demand: A New Approach*, Columbia University Press, New York.

LAUTERBACH, K. AND WILLE, E. (2000).   *Modell eines fairen Wettbewerbs durch den Risikostrukturausgleich*. Gutachten im Auftrag des Verbandes der Angestellten-Krankenkassen e.V., des AEV-Arbeiter-Ersatzkassen-Verbandes e.V., dem AOK-Bundesverband und dem IKK-Bundesverband.

LAVE, L. AND SESKIN, E. (1977). *Air Pollution and Human Health*, Johns Hopkins University Press, Baltimore.

LÉGER, P. (2008).   Physician Payment Mechanisms, *in* M. LU AND E. JONSSON (eds.), *Financing Health Care: New Ideas for a Changing Society*, Wiley-VCH, Weinheim, 149–176.

LEHMANN, H. AND ZWEIFEL, P. (2004).   Innovation and Risk Selection in Deregulated Social Health Insurance, *Journal of Health Economics* 23: 997–1012.

LEU, R. AND DOPPMANN, R. (1986a). Die Nachfrage nach Gesundheit und Gesundheitsleistungen (Demand for Health and Health Care Services), *in* G. GÄFGEN (ed.), *Ökonomie des Gesundheitswesens*, Duncker & Humblot, Berlin, 161–175.

LEU, R. AND DOPPMANN, R. (1986b). Gesundheitszustand und Nachfrage nach Gesundheitsleistungen, *in* E. WILLE (ed.), *Informations- und Planungsprobleme in öffentlichen Aufgabenbereichen*, P. Lang, Bern, 1–90.

LEU, R. AND GERFIN, M. (1992). Die Nachfrage nach Gesundheit – Ein empirischer Test des Grossman-Modells, *in* P. OBERENDER (ed.), *Steuerungsprobleme im Gesundheitswesen*, Nomos, Baden-Baden, 61–78.

LEVINTHAL, D. (1988). A Survey of Agency Models of Organizations, *Journal of Economic Behavior and Organization* 9: 153–185.

LICHTBLAU, K. (1999). Internationaler Vergleich der Umsatzrenditen in der Gewerblichen Wirtschaft (International Comparison of Rates of Return on Turnover), *IW-Trends* 26 (4): 28–38.

LICHTENBERG, F. (2005). The Impact of New Drug Launches on Longevity: Evidence from Longitudinal Disease-Level Data from 52 Countries, 1982-2001, *International Journal of Health Care Finance and Economics* 5: 47–73.

LOPEZ, E., PHILLIPS, L. AND SILOS, M. (1992). Deaths from Gastro-Intestinal Cancer in Mexico: Probable Cause for Water Sampling, *in* P. ZWEIFEL AND H. FRECH, III (eds.), *Health Economics Worldwide*, Kluwer, Dordrecht, 331–347.

LOUVIERE, J., HENSHER, D. AND SWAIT, J. (2000). *Stated Choice Methods – Analysis and Application*, Cambridge University Press, Cambridge.

LUBITZ, J. AND RILEY, G. (1993). Trends in Medicare Payments in the Last Year of Life, *New England Journal of Medicine* 328: 1092–1096.

LUCE, R. D. AND TUKEY, J. (1964). Simultaneous Conjoint Measurement – A New Type of Fundamental Measurement, *Journal of Mathematical Psychology* 1: 1–27.

LUFT, H. (1981). *Health Maintenance Organizations*, J. Wiley, New York.

LYTTKENS, C. (1999). Imperatives in Health Care. Implications for Social Welfare and Medical Technology, *Nordic Journal of Political Economy* 25: 95–114.

MA, C.-T. A. (1994). Health Care Payment Systems: Cost and Quality Incentives, *Journal of Economics and Management Strategy* 3: 93–112.

MAGNUS, J. (1979). Substitution Between Energy and Non-Energy Inputs in the Netherlands 1950-1976, *International Economic Review* 20: 465–483.

MALTHUS, T. (1798). *An Essay on the Principle of Population*. Reprint by Random House, New York (1960).

MANNING, W. (1998). The Logged Dependent Variable, Heteroskedasticity, and the Retransformation Problem, *Journal of Health Economics* 17: 283–295.

MANNING, W., LEIBOWITZ, A., GOLDBERG, G., ROGERS, W. AND NEWHOUSE, J. (1984). A Controlled Trial on the Effect of a Prepaid Group Practice on Use of Services, *New England Journal of Medicine* 310: 1505–1510.

MANNING, W., NEWHOUSE, J., DUAN, N., KEELER, E., LEIBOWITZ, A. AND MARQUIS, M. (1987). Health Insurance and the Demand for Medical Care: Evidence from a Randomized Experiment, *American Economic Review* 77: 251–277.

MARCHAND, M., SATO, M. AND SCHOKKAERT, E. (2003). Prior Health Expenditures and Risk Sharing with Insurers Competing on Quality, *RAND Journal of Economics* 34: 647–669.

MARKUSEN, J. (2002). *Multinational Firms and the Theory of International Trade*, MIT Press, Cambridge, MA.

MAS-COLELL, A., WHINSTON, M. AND GREEN, J. (1995). *Microeconomic Theory*, Oxford University Press, Oxford.

MAYNARD, A. (1991). Developing the Health Care Market, *Economic Journal* 101: 1277–1286.

MCCLELLAN, M. (1997). Hospital Reimbursement Incentives: An Empirical Analysis, *Journal of Economics and Management Strategy* 6: 91–128.

MCFADDEN, D. (1974). Conditional Logit Analysis of Qualitative Choice Behavior, *in* P. ZAREMBKA (ed.), *Frontiers in Econometrics*, Academic Press, New York, 105–142.

MCGUIRE, A., HENDERSON, J. AND MOONEY, G. (1988). *The Economics of Health Care: An Introductory Text*, J. Wiley, London/New York.

MCGUIRE, T. (2000). Physician Agency, *in* A. CULYER AND J. NEWHOUSE (eds.), *Handbook of Health Economics*, Vol. 1A, Elsevier, Amsterdam, 461–536.

MCGUIRE, T. AND PAULY, M. (1991). Physician Response to Fee Changes with Multiple Payers, *Journal of Health Economics* 10: 385–410.

MCKEOWN, T. (1976). *The Modern Rise of Population*, Edward Arnold, London.

MCKINLAY, J., MCKINLAY, S. AND BEAGLEHOLE, R. (1989). A Review of the Evidence Concerning the Impact of Medical Measures on Recent Mortality and Morbidity in the United States, *International Journal of Health Services* 19: 181–208.

MEHREZ, A. AND GAFNI, A. (1989). Quality-Adjusted Life Years, Utility Theory, and Healthy-Years-Equivalents, *Medical Decision Making* 9: 142–149.

MENZEL, P. (1990). *Strong Medicine. The Ethical Rationing of Health Care*, Oxford University Press, New York et al.

MEYER, J. (1987). Two Moment Decision Models and Expected Utility Maximization, *American Economic Review* 77: 421–430.

MILLER, JR., R. AND FRECH, III, H. (2000). Is There a Link Between Pharmaceutical Consumption and Improved Health in OECD Countries?, *PharmacoEconomics* 18: 33–45.

MILLER, JR., R. AND FRECH, III, H. (2004a). *Health Care Matters – Pharmaceuticals, Obesity, and the Quality of Life*, AEI Press, Washington, DC.

MILLER, JR., R. AND FRECH, III, H. (2004b). *Health Care Matters – Pharmaceuticals, Obesity, and the Quality of Life*, AEI Press, Washington, DC.

MIRRLEES, J. (1971). An Exploration in the Theory of Optimum Income Taxation, *Review of Economic Studies* 38: 175–208.

MITCHELL, R. AND CARSON, R. (1989). *Using Surveys to Value Public Goods: The Contingent Valuation Method*, Resources for the Future, Washington, DC.

MIYAMOTO, J. (1999). Quality-Adjusted Life Years (QALY) Utility Models under Expected Utility and Rank Dependent Utility Assumptions, *Journal of Mathematical Psychology* 43: 201–237.

MIYAMOTO, J. AND ERAKER, S. (1988). A Multiplicative Model of the Utility of Survival Duration and Health Quality, *Journal of Experimental Psychology: General* 117: 3–20.

MIYAMOTO, J., WAKKER, P., BLEICHRODT, H. AND PETERS, H. (1998). The Zero-Condition: A Simplifying Assumption in QALY Measurement and Multiattribute Utility, *Management Science* 44: 839–849.

MIYAZAKI, H. (1977). The Rat Race and Internal Labor Markets, *Bell Journal of Economics* 8: 394–418.

MOONEY, G. (2003). *Economics, Medicine and Health Care*, 3rd edition, Financial Times Prentice Hall, Harlow, England.

MOORE, S. (1979). Cost-Containment Through Risk Sharing by Primary Care Physicians, *New England Journal of Medicine* 300: 1359–1362.

MOSSIN, J. (1968). Aspects of Rational Insurance Purchasing, *Journal of Political Economy* 76: 553–568.

MULLAHY, J. (1998). Much Ado About Two: Reconsidering Retransformation and the Two-Part Model in Health Econometrics, *Journal of Health Economics* 17: 247–282.

MULLAHY, J. AND PORTNEY, P. (1990). Air Pollution, Cigarette Smoking, and the Production of Respiratory Health, *Journal of Health Economics* 9: 193–206.

MURRAY, C. (1994). Quantifying the Burden of Disease: The Technical Basis for Disability-Adjusted Life Years, *Bulletin of the World Health Organization* 72: 429–445.

MYLES, G. (1995). *Public Economics*, Cambridge University Press, Cambridge.

NATIONAL INSTITUTE FOR HEALTH AND CLINICAL EXCELLENCE (2008). *Guide to the Methods of Technology Appraisal*, National Institute for Health and Clinical Excellence, London.

NELSON, P. (1970). Information and Consumer Behavior, *Journal of Political Economy* 78(2).

NEWHOUSE, J. (1978). *The Economics of Medical Care*, Addison-Wesley, Cambridge, MA.

NEWHOUSE, J. (1994). Frontier Estimation: How Useful a Tool for Health Economics?, *Journal of Health Economics* 13: 317–322.

NEWHOUSE, J. (1996). Reimbursing Health Plans and Health Providers: Efficiency in Production versus Selection, *Journal of Economic Literature* 34: 1236–1263.

NEWHOUSE, J. AND FRIEDLANDER, L. (1980). The Relationship Between Medical Resources and Measures of Health: Some Additional Evidence, *Journal of Human Resources* 15: 201–217.

NEWHOUSE, J., MANNING, W., KEELING, E. AND SLOSS, E. (1989). Adjusting Capitation Rates using Objective Health Measures and Prior Utilization, *Health Care Financing Review* 10: 41–54.

NEWHOUSE, J. P. (1992). Medical Care Costs: How Much Welfare Loss?, *Journal of Economic Perspectives* 6: 3–21.

NEWHOUSE, J. AND PHELPS, C. (1976). New Estimates of Price and Income Elasticities of Medical Care Services, *in* R. ROSETT (ed.), *The Role of Health Insurance in the Health Services Sector*, National Bureau of Economic Reseach, New York, 261–312.

NEWHOUSE, J., PHELPS, C. AND MARQUIS, M. (1980). On Having Your Cake and Eating it Too: Econometric Problems in Estimating the Demand for Health Services, *Journal of Econometrics* 13: 365–390.

NOCERA, S., TELSER, H. AND BONATO, D. (2003). *The Contingent-Valuation Method in Health Care – An Economic Evaluation of Alzheimer's Disease*, Kluwer, Dordrecht.

NOCERA, S. AND ZWEIFEL, P. (1998). The Demand for Health: An Empirical Test of the Grossman Model Using Panel Data, *in* P. ZWEIFEL (ed.), *Health, the Medical Profession, and Regulation*, Kluwer Academic Publishers, Boston, MA., 35–49.

NORD, E. (1999). *Cost-Value Analysis in Health Care: Making Sense Out of QALYs*, Cambridge studies in philosophy and public policy, Cambridge University Press, Cambridge.

NORDHAUS, W. (1969). *Invention, Growth and Welfare*, MIT Press, Cambridge, MA.

NUSCHELER, R. AND KNAUS, T. (2005). Risk Selection in the German Public Health Insurance System, *Health Economics* 14: 1253–1271.

NYMAN, J. (1999a). The Economics of Moral Hazard Revisited, *Journal of Health Economics* 18: 811–824.

NYMAN, J. (1999b). The Value of Health Insurance: The Access Motive, *Journal of Health Economics* 18: 141–152.

NYMAN, J. (2001). The Income Transfer Effect, the Access Value of Insurance and the Rand Health Insurance Experiment, *Journal of Health Economics* 20: 295–298.

OECD (1987). *Financing and Delivering Health Care. A Comparative Analysis of OECD Countries*, OECD, Paris.

OECD (2000). *OECD Health Data*, OECD, Paris.

OECD (2001). *OECD Health Data*, OECD, Paris.

OECD (2006). Employment and Labour Force Statistics: 1960–2005.

OECD (2008). *OECD Health Data*, OECD, Paris.

OLHANSKY, S., RUDBERG, M., CASSEL, C. AND BRODY, J. (1991). Trading Off Longer Life for Worsening Health: The Expansion of Morbidity Hypothesis, *Journal of Aging and Health* 3: 194–216.

OLSON, M. (1965). *The Logic of Collective Action*, Harvard University Press, Cambridge, MA.

OSTRO, B. (1983). The Effects of Air Pollution on Work Loss and Morbidity, *Journal of Environmental Economics and Management* 10: 371–382.

PATEL, V. AND PAULY, M. (2002). Guaranteed Renewability and the Problem of Risk Variation in Individual Health Insurance Markets, *Health Affairs* 21: w280–w289. http://content.healthaffairs.org/cgi/reprint/hlthaff.w2.280v1.

PAULY, M. (1974). Overinsurance and Public Provision of Insurance: The Role of Moral Hazard and Adverse Selection, *Quarterly Journal of Economics* 88. 44–62.

PAULY, M. (1984). Is Cream-Skimming a Problem for the Competitive Medical Market?, *Journal of Health Economics* 3: 87–95.

PAULY, M. (1988). Is Medical Care Different? Old Questions, New Answers, *Journal of Health Politics, Policy and Law* 13: 227–237.

PAULY, M. (1994). Editorial: A Re-Examination of the Meaning and Importance of Supplier-Induced Demand, *Journal of Health Economics* 13: 369–372.

PAULY, M. (2000). Insurance Reimbursement, *in* A. CULYER AND J. NEWHOUSE (eds.), *Handbook of Health Economics*, Vol. 1A, Elsevier, Amsterdam, 537–560.

PAULY, M., DANZON, P., FELDSTEIN, P. AND HOFF, J. (1992). *Responsible National Health Insurance*, Washington, DC, AEI Press.

PAULY, M. AND GOODMAN, J. (1995). Tax Credits for Health Insurance and Medical Savings Accounts, *Health Affairs* 14 (1): 125–139.

PAULY, M., KUNREUTHER, H. AND HIRTH, R. (1995). Guaranteed Renewability in Insurance, *Journal of Risk and Uncertainty* 10: 143–156.

PECKELMAN, D. AND SEN, S. (1979). Measurement and Estimation of Conjoint Utility Functions, *Journal of Consumer Research* 5: 263–271.

PELTZMAN, S. (1973). An Evaluation of Consumer Protection Regulation: The 1962 Drug Amendment, *Journal of Political Economy* 81: 1049–1091.

PERSSON, T. AND TABELLINI, G. (2000). *Political Economics*, MIT Press, Cambridge, MA.

PHARMA INFORMATION (2001). *Pharma-Markt Schweiz*, Pharma Information, Basel.

PHELPS, C. (2003). *Health Economics*, 3rd edition, Harper Collins, New York.

PHELPS, C. AND NEWHOUSE, J. (1972). Effects of Coinsurance: A Multivariate Analysis, *Social Security Bulletin* 35: 20–28.

PHILIPSON, T. AND BECKER, G. (1998). Old-Age Longevity and Mortality-Contingent Claims, *Journal of Political Economy* 106: 551–573.

PHUA, K. (1999). Comparative Health Care Financing Systems with Special Reference to East Asian Countries, *Research in Healthcare Financial Management* 5: 111–131.

PLISKIN, J., SHEPARD, D. AND WEINSTEIN, M. (1980). Utility Functions for Life Years and Health Status, *Operations Research* 28: 206–224.

POMMEREHNE, W., SCHNEIDER, F. AND ZWEIFEL, P. (1982). Economic Theory of Choice and the Preference Reversal Phenomenon: A Reexamination, *American Economic Review* 72: 569–573.

POPE, G. (1989). Hospital Nonprice Competition and Medicare Reimbursement Policy, *Journal of Health Economics* 8: 147–172.

RAMSEY, F. (1927). A Contribution to the Theory of Taxation, *Economic Journal* 37: 47–61.

RATCLIFFE, J. AND BUXTON, M. (1999). Patient's Preferences Regarding the Process and Outcomes of Life-Saving Technology: An Application of Conjoint Analysis to Liver Transplantation, *International Journal of Technology Assessment in Health Care* 15: 340–51.

RAVIV, A. (1979). The Design of an Optimal Insurance Policy, *American Economic Review* 69: 84–96.

RAWLS, J. (1971). *A Theory of Justice*, Harvard University Press, Cambridge, MA.

REEKIE, W. (1996). *Medicine Prices and Innovations: An International Survey*, Institute of Economic Affairs (IEA), London.

REIS-ARNDT, E. (1993). Neue pharmazeutische Wirkstoffe 1961-1990, *Pharmazeutische Industrie* 55: 14–21.

RICE, T. (1983). The Impact of Changing Medicare Reimbursement Rates on Physician-Induced Demand, *Medical Care* 21: 803–815.

ROBINSON, J. (2001). Theory and Practice in the Design of Physician Payment Incentives, *Milbank Quarterly* 79: 149–177.

ROEMER, J. (1996). *Theories of Distributive Justice*, Harvard University Press, Cambridge, MA.

ROGERSON, W. (1985). The First-Order Approach to Principal-Agent Problems, *Econometrica* 53: 1357–1368.

ROOS, N., ROOS, L. AND HENTELEFF, P. (1977). Elective Surgical Rates – Do High Rates Mean Lower Standards? Tonsillectomy and Adenoidectomy in Manitoba, *New England Journal of Medicine* 297: 360–365.

ROSA, J. AND LAUNOIS, R. (1990). Comparative Health Systems: France, *Advances in Health Economics and Health Services Research* 1 (Suppl.): 179–195.

ROSEN, S. (1988). The Value of Changes in Life Expectancy, *Journal of Risk and Uncertainty* 1: 285–304.

ROSENZWEIG, M. AND SCHULTZ, P. (1983). Estimating a Household Production Function: Heterogeneity, the Demand for Health Imputs, and Their Effects on Birth Weight, *Journal of Political Economy* 91: 723–746.

ROTHSCHILD, M. AND STIGLITZ, J. (1976). Equilibrium in Competitive Insurance Markets: An Essay in the Economics of Incomplete Information, *Quarterly Journal of Economics* 90: 629–649.

ROUSSEL, L. (1986). Recent Trends in the Structure of Households in Several Industrialized Countries, *Population* 41: 913–934.

ROWLEY, C. AND SCHNEIDER, F. (eds.) (2003). *The Encyclopedia of Public Choice*, Kluwer, Dordrecht.

RYAN, M. (1995). *Economics and the Patient's Utility Function: An Application to Assisted Reproductive Techniques*, PhD thesis, University of Aberdeen, Aberdeen.

RYAN, M. AND GERARD, K. (2004). Using Choice Experiments to Value Health Care Programmes: Current Practice and Future Research Reflections, *Applied Health Economics and Health Policy* 2: 55–64.

RYAN, M. AND HUGHES, J. (1997). Using Conjoint Analysis to Assess Women's Preferences for Miscarriage Management, *Health Economics* 6: 261–73.

RYAN, M., MCINTOSH, E. AND SHACKLEY, P. (1998). Methodological Issues in the Application of Conjoint Analysis in Health Care, *Health Economics* 7: 373–78.

SALA-I-MARTIN, X. (2005). The Median Voter Model, *in* G. LOPEZ-CASASNOVAS, B. RIVERA AND L. CURRAIS (eds.), *Health and Economic Growth: Findings and Policy Implications*, MIT Press, Cambridge, MA, 95–114.

SALANIÉ, B. (2003). Testing Contract Theory, *CESifo Economic Studies* 49(3): 461–477.

SALKEVER, D. (2000). Regulation of Prices and Investment in Hospitals in the U.S., *in* A. CULYER AND J. NEWHOUSE (eds.), *Handbook of Health Economics*, Vol. 1B, Elsevier, Amsterdam, 1489–1535.

SAPPINGTON, D. AND LEWIS, T. (1999). Using Subjective Risk Adjusting to Prevent Patient Dumping in the Health Care Industry, *Journal of Economics and Management Strategy* 8: 351–382.

SCHERER, F. (2000). The Pharmaceutical Industry, *in* A. CULYER AND J. NEWHOUSE (eds.), *Handbook of Health Economics*, Vol. 1B, Elsevier, Amsterdam, 1297–1338.

SCHLANDER, M. (2007). *Health Technology Assessments by the National Institute for Health and Clinical Excellence: A Qualitative Study*, Innovation and Valuation in Health Care, Springer, New York.

SCHLESINGER, H. (2000). The Theory of Insurance Demand, *in* G. DIONNE (ed.), *Handbook of Insurance*, Kluwer, Dordrecht, 131–152.

SCHLESINGER, M., BLUMENTHAL, D. AND SCHLESINGER, E. (1986). Profits under Pressure. The Economic Performance of Investor-Owned and Nonprofit Health Maintenance Organizations, *Medical Care* 24: 615–627.

SCHOKKAERT, E. AND VAN DE VOORDE, C. (2004). Risk Selection and the Specification of the Conventional Risk Adjustment Formula, *Journal of Health Economics* 23: 1237–1259.

SCHULENBURG, J.-M. GRAF V.D. (1989). Gesundheitswesen (Krankenversicherung) und demographische Evolution (The Health Care System (Health Insurance) and Demographic Evolution), *in* H. RECKTENWALD (ed.), *Der Rückgang der Geburten-Folgen auf längere Sicht*, Verlag Wirtschaft und Finanzen, Düsseldorf, 279–297.

SCHUT, F., GREENBERG, W. AND VAN DE VEN, W. (1991). Antitrust Policy in the Dutch Health Care System and the Relevance of EEC Competition Policy and U.S. Antitrust Practice, *Health Policy* 17: 257–284.

SCHWABE, U. AND PAFFRATH, D. (2001). *Arzneiverordnungs-Report 2001*, Springer, Berlin.

SCITOVSKY, A. AND SNIDER, N. (1972). Effect of Coinsurance on Use of Physician Services, *Social Security Bulletin* 35: 3–19.

SEIFORD, L. AND THRALL, R. (1990). Recent Developments in DEA: The Mathematical Programming Approach to Frontier Analysis, *Journal of Econometrics* 46: 7–38.

SELDEN, T. (1998). Risk Adjustment for Health Insurance: Theory and Implications, *Journal of Risk and Uncertainty* 17: 167–180.

SELDER, A. (2006). Medical Associations, Medical Education and Training on the Job, *CESifo Economic Studies* 52: 548–564.

SHEN, Y. AND ELLIS, R. (2002). Cost-Minimizing Risk Adjustment, *Journal of Health Economics* 21: 515–530.

SHEPARD, D. AND ZECKHAUSER, R. (1982). Life-Cycle Consumption and Willingness To Pay for Increased Survival, *in* M. JONES-LEE (ed.), *Valuation of Life and Safety*, North-Holland, Amsterdam, 95–155.

SHEPARD, D. AND ZECKHAUSER, R. (1984). Survival Versus Consumption, *Management Science* 30: 423–439.

SILVER, M. (1972). An Econometric Analysis of Spatial Variations in Mortality Rates, *in* V. FUCHS (ed.), *Essays in the Economics of Health*, National Bureau of Economic Research, Washington, DC, 161–227.

SINN, H.-W. (1983). *Economic Decisions Under Uncertainty*, North-Holland, Amsterdam.

SLOAN, F. (2000). Non-For-Profit Ownership and Hospital Behavior, *in* A. CULYER AND J. NEWHOUSE (eds.), *Handbook of Health Economics*, Vol. 1B, Elsevier, Amsterdam, 1141–1174.

SMITH, R. (2006). Trade in Health Services: Current Challenges and Future Prospects of Globalization, *in* A. JONES (ed.), *The Elgar Companion to Health Economics*, Edward Elgar, Cheltenham, 164–175.

SMITH, V. (1968). Optimal Insurance Coverage, *Journal of Political Economy* 76: 68–77.

SMITH, V. AND DESVOUSGES, W. (1987). An Empirical Analysis of the Economic Value of Risk Changes, *Journal of Political Economy* 95: 89–114.

SPENCE, A. AND ZECKHAUSER, R. (1971). Insurance, Information, and Individual Action, *American Economic Review, Papers and Proceedings* 61: 380–387.

SPENCE, M. (1978). Product Differentiation and Performance in Insurance Markets, *Journal of Public Economics* 10: 427–447.

STAHL, I. (1990). Comparative Health Systems: Sweden, 1 (Suppl.): 197–210.

STEARNS, S. AND NORTON, E. (2004). Time to Include Time to Death? The Future of Health Care Expenditure Predictions, *Health Economics* 13: 315–327.

STEELE, H. (1962). Monopoly and Competition in the Ethical Drug Market, *Journal of Law and Economics* 5: 131–163.

STEINMANN, L. AND ZWEIFEL, P. (2003). On the (In)Efficiency of Swiss Hospitals, *Applied Economics* 35: 361–370.

STIGLER, G. AND BECKER, G. (1977). De Gustibus Non Est Disputandum, *American Economic Review* 67: 76–90.

STROMBOM, B., BUCHMUELLER, T. AND FELDSTEIN, P. (2002). Switching Costs, Price Sensitivity and Health Plan Choice, *Journal of Health Economics* 21: 89–116.

SYDSÆTER, K., STRØM, A. AND BERCK, P. (2005). *Economists' Mathematical Manual*, 4th edition, Springer, Heidelberg.

TELSER, H. (2002). *Nutzenmessung im Gesundheitswesen – Die Methode der Discrete-Choice-Experimente*, Verlag Dr. Kovač, Hamburg.

TELSER, H., STEINMANN, L. AND ZWEIFEL, P. (2007). The Impact of Ageing on Future Healthcare Expenditure, *Forum for Health Economics and Policy* 10(2): Article 1. http://www.bepress.com/fhep/10/2/1.

TELSER, H. AND ZWEIFEL, P. (2002). Measuring Willingness-to-Pay for Risk Reduction: An Application of Conjoint Analysis, *Health Economics* 11: 129–139.

TERPORTEN, M. (1999). *Wettbewerb in der Automobilindustrie: eine industrieökonomische Untersuchung des deutschen PKW-Marktes unter besonderer Berücksichtigung der nationalen Hersteller (Competition in the Automobile Industry: The Industrial Economics of the German Car Market, with a Focus on National Manufacturers)*, PhD thesis, Universität Duisburg.

THALER, R. AND ROSEN, S. (1975). The Value of Saving a Life: Evidence from the Labor Market, *in* N. TERLECKYJI (ed.), *Household Production and Consumption*, Columbia University Press, New York, 265–302.

THORNTON, J. (2002). Estimating a Health Production Function for the US: Some New Evidence, *Applied Economics* 34: 59–62.

TIKHOMIROV, V. (2001). Gâteaux Variation, *in* M. HAZEWINKEL (ed.), *Encyclopaedia of Mathematics*, Kluwer, Dordrecht.

TOBIN, J. (1970). On Limiting the Domain of Inequality, *Journal of Law and Economics* 13: 263–277.

TORRANCE, G. (1986). Measurement of Health State Utilities for Economic Appraisal, *Journal of Health Economics* 5: 1–30.

UBEL, P. (2000). *Pricing Life: Why It's Time for Health Care Rationing*, MIT Press, Cambridge, MA.

U.S. CENSUS BUREAU (2004). Living Alone: 1940-2000, *Report*, U.S. Census Bureau, Washington, DC.

VALLETTI, T. (2006). Differential Pricing, Parallel Trade, and the Incentive to Invest, *Journal of International Economics* 70: 314–324.

VAN BARNEVELD, E., LAMERS, L., VAN VLIET, R. AND VAN DE VEN, W. (2001). Risk Sharing as a Supplement to Imperfect Capitation: A Tradeoff Between Selection and Efficiency, *Journal of Health Economics* 20: 147–168.

VAN BARNEVELD, E., VAN VLIET, R. AND VAN DE VEN, W. (1996). Mandatory High-Risk Pooling: An Approach to Reducing Incentives for Cream Skimming, *Inquiry* 33: 133–143.

VAN BARNEVELD, E., VAN VLIET, R. AND VAN DE VEN, W. (1998). Mandatory Pooling as a Supplement to Risk-Adjusted Capitation Payments in a Competitive Health Insurance Market, *Social Science and Medicine* 47: 223–232.

VAN DE VEN, W. AND ELLIS, R. (2000). Risk Adjustment in Competitive Health Plan Markets, *in* A. CULYER AND J. NEWHOUSE (eds.), *Handbook of Health Economics*, Vol. 1A, Elsevier, Amsterdam, 755–845.

VAN DE VEN, W. AND VAN VLIET, R. (1992). How Can We Prevent Cream Skimming in a Competitive Health Insurance Market?, *in* P. ZWEIFEL AND H. FRECH, III (eds.), *Health Economics Worldwide*, Kluwer, Dordrecht, 23–46.

VAN DE VEN, W., VAN VLIET, R., SCHUT, F. AND VAN BARNEVELD, E. (2000). Access to Coverage for High-Risks in a Competitive Individual Health Insurance Market: Via Premium Rate Restrictions or Risk-Adjusted Premium Subsidies?, *Journal of Health Economics* 19: 311–339.

VAN VLIET, R. (1992a). Predictability of Individual Health Care Expenditures, *Journal of Risk and Insurance* 59: 443–460.

VAN VLIET, R. AND LAMERS, L. (1998). The High Costs of Death: Should Health Plans Get Higher Payments when Members Die?, *Medical Care* 36: 1451–1460.

VANE, J. (1964). A Plan for Evaluating Potential Drugs, *in* D. LAURENCE AND A. BACHARACH (eds.), *Evaluation of Drug Activities: Pharmacometrics*, Academic Press, London, 23–41.

VARIAN, H. (1992). *Microeconomic Analysis*, 3rd edition, W.W. Norton, New York.

VERBINDUNG DER SCHWEIZER ÄRZTINNEN UND ÄRZTE (2002). *Mitgliederstatistik*, Verbindung der Schweizer Ärztinnen und Ärzte (FMH). http://www.fmh.ch/ww/de/pub/homepage.htm.

VERBRUGGE, L. (1984). Longer Life But Worsening Health? Trends in Health and Mortality of Middle-Aged and Older Persons, *Milbank Memorial Fund Quarterly* 62: 475–519.

VICK, S. AND SCOTT, A. (1998). Agency in Health Care. Examining Patients' Preferences for Attributes of the Doctor-Patient Relationship, *Journal of Health Economics* 17: 587–605.

VIRTS, J. AND WESTON, J. (1981). Expectations and the Allocation of Research and Development Resources, *in* R. HELMS (ed.), *Drugs and Health*, Enterprise Institute, Washington, DC, 21–45.

VISCUSI, W. (1993). The Value of Risks to Life and Health, *Journal of Economic Literature* 31: 1912–1946.

VISCUSI, W. AND EVANS, W. (1990). Utility Functions that Depend on Health Status: Estimates and Economic Implications, *American Economic Review* 80: 353–374.

WAGSTAFF, A. (1986a). The Demand for Health: A Simplified Grossman Model, *Bulletin of Economic Research* 38: 93–95.

WAGSTAFF, A. (1986b). The Demand for Health: Some New Empirical Evidence, *Journal of Health Economics* 5: 195–233.

WAGSTAFF, A. (1991). QALYs and the Equity-Efficiency Trade-Off, *Journal of Health Economics* 10: 21–41.

WAGSTAFF, A. (1993). The Demand for Health: An Empirical Reformulation of the Grossman Model, *Health Economics* 2: 189–198.

WALKER, S. AND PARRISH, J. (1988). Innovation and New Drug Development, *in* B. WALKER AND S. WALKER (eds.), *Trends and Changes in Drug Research and Development*, Kluwer, Dordrecht, 1–28.

WALZER, M. (1983). *Spheres of Justice*, Basic Books, New York.

WARDELL, D., DiRADDO, J. AND TRIMBLE, A. (1980). Development of New Drugs Originated and Acquired by US-Owned Pharmaceutical Firms 1963–1976, *Clinical Pharmacology and Therapy* 28: 270–277.

WARE, JR., J., BROOK, R., ROGERS, W., KEELER, E., DAVIES, A., SHERBOURNE, C., GOLDBERG, G., CAMP, P. AND NEWHOUSE, J. (1986). Comparison of Health Outcomes at a Health Maintenance Organization with Those of Fee-For-Service Care, *Lancet* 326: 1017–1022.

WEINSTEIN, M. (1990). Principles of Cost-Effective Resource Allocation in Health Care Organizations, *International Journal of Technology Assessment in Health Care* 6: 93–103.

WEINSTEIN, M. (2006). Decision Rules for Incremental Cost-Effectiveness Analysis, *in* A. JONES (ed.), *The Elgar Companion to Health Economics*, Edward Elgar, Cheltenham, 469–478.

WEISBROD, B. (1968). Income Redistribution Effects and Benefit-Cost Analysis, *in* S. CHASE, JR. (ed.), *Problems in Public Expenditure Analysis*, The Brookings Institution, Washington, DC, 177–209.

WERBLOW, A., FELDER, S. AND ZWEIFEL, P. (2005). Population Ageing and Health Care Expenditure: A School of 'Red Herrings'?, *Health Economics* 16: 1109–1126.

WIGGINS, S. (1987). *The Cost of Developing a New Drug*, Pharmaceutical Manufacturers' Association, Washington, DC.

WILLIAMS, A. AND COOKSON, R. (2000). Equity in Health, *in* A. CULYER AND J. NEWHOUSE (eds.), *Handbook of Health Economics*, Vol. 1B, Elsevier, Amsterdam, 1863–1910.

WILLIAMS, B. (1962). The Idea of Equality, *in* P. LASLETT AND W. G. RUNCIMAN (eds.), *Philosophy, politics, and society, Series II*, Blackwell, Oxford, 110–131.

WILLIAMSON, O. (1981). The Modern Corporation: Origins, Evolution, Attributes, *Journal of Economic Literature* 19: 1537–1568.

WILSON, C. (1977). A Model of Insurance Markets with Incomplete Information, *Journal of Economic Theory* 12: 167–207.

WINTER, R. (2000). Optimal Insurance under Moral Hazard, *in* G. DIONNE (ed.), *Handbook of Insurance*, Kluwer, Dordrecht, 155–184.

WORLD BANK (1993). *World Development Report 1993, Investing in Health*, World Bank, Washington, DC.

WORLD BANK (2008). *World Development Indicators*, World Bank, Washington, DC.

WU, S. (1984). Social and Private Returns Derived from Pharmaceutical Innovations: Some Empirical Findings, *in* B. LINDGREN (ed.), *Pharmaceutical Economics*, Liber, Malmö, 217–254.

YIP, W. (1998). Physician Responses to Medical Fee Reductions: Changes in Volume and Intensity of Supply of Coronary Artery Bypass Graft (CABG) Surgeries in the Medicare and Private Sectors, *Journal of Health Economics* 17: 675–700.

YOUNG, W. (1991). Patient Management Categories, *in* G. NEUBAUER AND G. SIEBEN (eds.), *Alternative Entgeltverfahren in der Krankenhausversorgung, Beiträge zur Gesundheitsökonomie*, Vol. 24, Bleicher, Gerlingen, 405–426.

ZECKHAUSER, R. (1970). Medical Insurance: A Case Study of the Tradeoff Between Risk Spreading and Appropriate Incentives, *Journal of Economic Theory* 2: 10–26.

ZUCKERMANN, S., HADLEY, J. AND IEZZONI, L. (1994). Measuring Hospital Efficiency with Frontier Cost Functions, *Journal of Health Economics* 13: 255–280.

ZWEIFEL, P. (1981). Supplier Induced Demand in a Model of Physician Behaviour, *in* J. VAN DER GAAG AND M. PERLMAN (eds.), *Health, Economics and Health Economics*, North Holland, Amsterdam, 245–267.

ZWEIFEL, P. (1984). Technological Change in Health Care: Why Are Opinions So Divided?, *Managerial and Decision Economics* 5: 177–182.

ZWEIFEL, P. (1985). The Effect of Aging on the Demand and Utilization of Medical Care, *in* C. TILQUIN (ed.), *Systems Science in Health and Social Services for the Elderly and Disabled*, Pergamon Press, Toronto, 313–318.

ZWEIFEL, P. (1990). Ageing: The Great Challenge to Health Care Reform, *European Economic Review* 34: 646–658.

ZWEIFEL, P. (1999). Suggestions for Health Policy in the 21st Century: An Economist's Point of View, *in* H. LÖFFLER AND E. STREISSLER (eds.), *Sozialpolitik und Ökologieprobleme der Zukunft (Social Politics and Problems of Ecology in the Future)*, Österreichische Akademie der Wissenschaften, Wien.

ZWEIFEL, P. (2000). Reconsidering the Role of Competition in Health Care Markets – Switzerland, *Journal of Health Politics, Policy and Law* 25: 936–944.

ZWEIFEL, P. (2004). Multiple Payers in Health Care: A Framework for Assessment, *in* A. PREKER AND J. LANGENBRUNNER (eds.), *Buying Health Services for the Poor*, World Bank, New York, 319–38.

ZWEIFEL, P. AND BRAENDLE, A. (2008). What makes GPs Accept Changes?, *mimeo*, University of Zurich.

ZWEIFEL, P. AND BREUER, M. (2006). The Case for Risk-Based Premiums in Public Health Insurance, *Health Economics, Policy and Law* 1: 171–188.

ZWEIFEL, P. AND CRIVELLI, L. (1996). Price Regulation of Drugs: Lessons from Germany, *Journal of Regulatory Economics* 10: 257–274.

ZWEIFEL, P. AND EICHENBERGER, R. (1992). The Political Economy of Corporatism in Medicine: Self-Regulation or Cartel Management?, *Journal of Regulatory Economics* 4: 89–108.

504　　References

ZWEIFEL, P. AND EUGSTER, P. (2008). Life-Cycle Effects of Social Security in an Open Economy: A Theoretical and Empirical Survey, *Zeitschrift für die gesamte Versicherungswissenschaft – German Journal of Risk and Insurance* 97: 61–77.

ZWEIFEL, P., FELDER, S. AND MEIER, M. (1999a). Ageing of Population and Health Care Expenditure: A Red Herring?, *Health Economics* 8: 485–496.

ZWEIFEL, P., FELDER, S. AND MEIER, M. (1999b). Ageing of Population and Health Expenditure: A Red Herring?, *Health Economics* 8: 485–496.

ZWEIFEL, P., FELDER, S. AND WERBLOW, A. (2004a). Population Ageing and Health Care Expenditure: New Evidence on the 'Red Herring', *Geneva Papers on Risk and Insurance: Issues and Practice* 29: 652–66.

ZWEIFEL, P., FELDER, S. AND WERBLOW, A. (2004b). Population Ageing and Health Care Expenditure: New Evidence on the Red Herring, *The Geneva Papers on Risk and Insurance* 29: 652–666.

ZWEIFEL, P. AND FERRARI, M. (1992). Is There a Sisyphus Syndrome in Health Care?, *in* P. ZWEIFEL AND H. FRECH, III (eds.), *Health Economics Worldwide*, Kluwer Academic Publishers, Dordrecht, Boston, London, 311–330.

ZWEIFEL, P. AND GRANDCHAMP, C. (2002). Measuring the Effect of Cartelization in Medicine: An international Study, *in* D. SLOTTJE (ed.), *Measuring Market Power*, Nr. 255 in *Contributions to Economic Analysis*, Elsevier-North Holland, Amsterdam, 47–66.

ZWEIFEL, P., KREY, B. AND TAGLI, M. (2007). Supply of Private Voluntary Health Insurance in Low-Income Countries, *in* A. PREKER, R. SCHEFFLER AND M. BASSETT (eds.), *Private Voluntary Health Insurance in Development: Friend or Foe?*, World Bank, Washington, DC, 55–107.

ZWEIFEL, P. AND LEHMANN, H. (2001). Soziale Absicherung im Portfolio persönlicher Aktiva: Wie kann die Soziale Sicherung Teufelskreise verhindern? (Hedging the Portfolio of Personal Assets: How Can Social Insurance Avoid Vicious Cycles), *in* E. THEURL (ed.), *Der Sozialstaat an der Jahrtausendwende*, Physica Verlag, Heidelberg, 53–75.

ZWEIFEL, P., LYTTKENS, C. AND SÖDERSTRÖM, L. (eds.) (1998). *Regulation of Health: Case Studies of Sweden and Switzerland*, Nr. 7 in *Development in Health Economics and Public Policy*, Kluwer Academic Publishers, Boston.

ZWEIFEL, P. AND MANNING, W. (2000). Moral Hazard and Consumer Incentives in Health Care, *in* A. CULYER AND J. NEWHOUSE (eds.), *Handbook of Health Economics*, Vol. 1A, Elsevier, Amsterdam, 409–459.

ZWEIFEL, P. AND PEDRONI, G. (1985). *Innovation und Imitation – Eine wirtschaftspolitische Gratwanderung (Innovation and Imitation - A Knife-Edge Issue)*, Studien zur Gesundheitsökonomie 7, Pharma Information, Basel.

ZWEIFEL, P., STEINMANN, L. AND EUGSTER, P. (2005). The Sisyphus Syndrome in Health Revisited, *International Journal of Health Care Finance and Economics* 5: 127–145.

ZWEIFEL, P., TELSER, H. AND VATERLAUS, S. (2006). Consumer Resistance Against Regulation: The Case of Health Care, *Journal of Regulatory Economics* 29: 319–332.

ZWEIFEL, P. AND WASER, O. (1992). *Bonus Options in Health Insurance*, Kluwer, Dordrecht.

ZWEIFEL, P. AND ZAECH, R. (2003). Vertical Restraints: The Case of Multinationals, *The Antitrust Bulletin* 48: 271–298.

Author Index

Subject Index

CPSIA information can be obtained at www.ICGtesting.com
Printed in the USA
LVOW07*1652030813

346143LV00007B/157/P